THE COMPLETE
ENCYCLOPEDIA OF
PISTOLS
AND
REVOLVERS

A.E. Hartink

CHARTWELL
BOOKS, INC.

This edition published in 2002 by
Chartwell Books Inc.
A division of Book Sales, Inc.
114 Northfield Avenue
Edison, New Jersey 08837

© 2002 Rebo Productions b.v., Lisse

internet: www.rebo-publishers.com
e-mail: info@rebo-publishers.com

Text and photographs: A.E. Hartink
Production and editing: TextCase, Groningen
Cover design: Minkowsky, graphic design agency, Enkhuizen
Production: Studio Imago, Amersfoort

ISBN 0-7858-1519-8

Contents

Foreword

In this reference work, I would like to provide anyone who wants to know more about revolvers and pistols with the correct and most recent information about these handguns. The short introductory chapter on the development of firearms is followed by a description of the various makes and models, arranged alphabetically under each arms manufacturer. An outline of the development is given of each weapon, followed by all the relevant technical information. This is further clarified with color photographs and illustrations. The most common makes and models are included in this book, and the latest developments are also described in detail. For example, there is a description of the new Walther P22 model. This pistol was introduced in 2001 in two different versions. Other examples of recent developments include the Mauser M2 pistol made by Sig, and the latest series of models of Smith &Wesson in 2001. These models can also be found in this book. At the end of this encyclopedia you will find a very detailed and illustrated glossary of terms. This gives a clear definition of all the technical terms which are used in the book. I greatly enjoyed writing and compiling this book and I hope that the reader will enjoy it every bit as much.

Ton Hartink

The development of handguns

The development of firearms is related to the discovery of gunpowder as the propellant for projectiles. It is known that the Chinese were already using gunpowder for their fireworks in the eleventh century. Their knowledge of its composition probably came to Europe via Arab trading routes. Another view is that the well-known explorer Marco Polo brought gunpowder back from China. From 1271 to 1292, he traveled on a trading mission from Venice to China and back. A third theory is that gunpowder was developed in Europe itself. In this respect, one of the people credited with its discovery is the German monk, Berthold Schwarz, from Freiburg. In German, the gunpowder was therefore given the name Schwarzpulver (meaning 'black powder'). The usual composition is 75% saltpeter, 15% sulfur and 10% charcoal. The sulfur is responsible for the smell of the black powder when the weapon is fired. In the fourteenth century it was discovered that it could be used for other things than fireworks; it was also suitable as a propellant for projectiles. The first simple hand cannon were designed at the start of the fifteenth century. These were short iron or bronze tubes mounted on a long wooden post. The black powder was loaded through the muzzle. Then a stone or iron projectile was pushed into the primitive barrel through this muzzle. There was a small hole at the end of the tube, the so-called touch-hole. The powder was then ignited with a glowing chip of wood. When the charge was ignited, the pressure of the gas that was created propelled the projectile forward. It propelled the projectile in a fairly arbitrary way because the production process was not very precise in those days. In modern firearms, the precision is to a 100th of a millimeter, but in those days an inch more or less was not considered important. Up to the nineteenth century it was quite usual for only one in twenty shots to hit the target. Shooting was above all a matter of goodwill, combined with a big dose of luck.

Halfway through the fifteenth century the first real cannon and mortar appeared. They were mainly used for laying siege to cities, forts and castles.

Hand-colored etching of Medieval mortars

Copper engraving of a siege from 1500

The basic principle used in those days is still the same nowadays. The barrel is an iron tube which is closed at one end. The charge and the projectile are in the barrel. The powder is ignited, and then the pressure of the gas of the burning powder propels the projectile out. Originally, the powder was lit with a smoldering chip of wood. In about 1450, it was replaced by a real fuse.

In about 1470, the fuse was attached to a moving arm, which could be pushed to the touch-hole with a lever. This system is known as the fuse lock. It was a big step forward, but also had a number of disadvantages. The ignition was by no means always straightforward in a strong wind, and particularly in the rain. For military use, lighting the fuse was not very practical, especially in the dark. After all, a glowing fuse revealed the attacker's position.

The next development was the wheel lock. This consisted of a round metal disc with a coil spring. The spring was wound up with a key and blocked with a catch. The catch was in turn linked to a trigger. When the trigger was pulled, the catch was released, which in turn, removed the blocking coil spring. As a result, the metal disc rotated at a considerable speed, scraping along a flint. This resulted in a shower of sparks, which came down in a pan containing a small amount of fine powder which was ignited by the sparks. The powder pan was connected to the above-mentioned touch-hole, so that the flame of the powder was transferred to the main charge in the barrel.

The wheel lock was very complicated, and therefore expensive to make. These types of guns were also less suitable and too expensive to equip whole armies. Therefore there was a search for a cheaper alternative. This was the flintlock gun. In fact, the wheel and the spring mechanism were simply omitted.

The flint was held in the moving claws of a kind of hammer, as in the case of the fuse lock. The arm with the claws for the flint was known as the hammer. This hammer or cock could be drawn backwards against the pressure of a spring. A second type of hammer served as a sort of anvil. This was placed just above the flash pan. When the trigger was pulled, the hammer with the flint struck the anvil. This resulted in a spark falling in the flash pan and igniting the fine powder. This flame in the pan then ignited the main charge in the barrel through the touch-hole.

Example of a fuselock pistol

Detail of a wheel lock gun

The different systems were the subject of experimentation for more than two centuries. During the course of time, different types of locks were therefore designed. (These locks are described in detail and are shown in *The Illustrated Encyclopedia of Antique Firearms*, another publication of Rebo Productions).

Replica flintlock pistols by Pedersoli

There was a great breakthrough in the development of firearms in England. In 1799, the English chemist Howard invented fulminating mercury. In 1807, the English clergyman, Alexander Forsyth patented the percussion principle. A year later he developed fulminate, which was highly explosive and was accommodated in a small cup.

The problem of a naked flame for lighting the powder was now a thing of the past. A kind of little chimney, known as a piston or nipple, was placed in the touch-hole. The percussion cap or primer was then attached to this. The hammer of the flintlock was used to strike the percussion cap really hard. This hammer was pulled back and secured. By removing the obstacle with a lever, which developed to become a trigger, the hammer came forwards under the pressure of a spring.

Le Page percussion pistol by Pedersoli

Therefore the hammer struck the percussion cap forcefully so that the fulminate ignited with a flash. The flame then traveled to the main charge in the barrel through the hollow channel in the nipple.

The next important step was the development of a single cartridge. Initially this was a paper case containing the powder charge and the bullet packed together. Later, the primer was also added to this combination. In 1812, the Swiss gunsmith, Johann Samuel Pauly, was already experimenting with a brass cartridge with center-fire ignition. This type of cartridge could no longer be placed in the barrel through the muzzle. Therefore, solutions were looked for to open the closed end of the barrel so that the cartridge could be placed in the barrel from the back. However, after putting the cartridge in the barrel, it had to be securely closed again. This resulted in the development of a number of different locking systems.

The third important step in the development of firearms was the discovery of nitro-powder. The gas pressure could be increased much more effectively with this type of powder, and consequently the range of the bullet also greatly increased. However, some of this high gas pressure could also be used for an automatic locking system for the barrel. This development was the start of the autoloader.

In fact, handguns developed in the same way as shoulder arms. The first pistol was actually a shortened version of a fuse lock gun. The pistol was meant as a defense weapon for short distances and was used mainly by army officers. The fuse lock pistol was followed by the wheel lock pistol, and then by the flintlock pistol. In the course of time, this type of pistol also appeared on the civilian market, and was used in sport shooting, and particularly as the weapon for duels.

Until firearms were introduced, differences of opinion or disputes were usually settled with the sword or saber. From the sixteenth century, the trend was to use a pistol to settle these matters.

At the French court, duels were so frequent that King Louis XIV actually issued a decree in 1679 prohibiting them. In other countries, firearms were considered vulgar for defending one's honor up to the eighteenth century. In order to settle a quarrel as fairly as possible the two opponents had to have equal chances. For this reason, dueling pistols were often produced in a set with two identical weapons. Regulations were actually drawn up, such as the British Code of Duel dating from 1829. For example, this stipulated that the minimum distance between the two duelists should be set at twenty-five feet (7.6 meters). In addition, the shot had to be fired on the command of one or more seconds. According to the code of honor, only single shot weapons could be used in a duel.

One of the best-known victims of the dueling pistol was the Russian poet, Alexander Pushkin. He was shot dead in a duel in St. Petersburg in 1837 by Baron d'Anthãs, an adopted son of the Dutch ambassador, Baron Van Heeckeren.

There are many different sorts of dueling pistols: from very modest models to richly engraved pistols inlaid with gold, which reflected the owner's wealth. Fortunately, these weapons were not only used to shoot in duels, but also for target shooting, a greatly valued sport amongst the affluent.

Pistols with more than one barrel developed in about 1650. These were mainly used as weapons for defense against highwaymen, rabid dogs and predators. Initially, these were double or triple-barreled pistols, but in about 1650, flintlock revolvers were also developed in Germany, England and the Netherlands.

The percussion system became fashionable in about 1830, and the first so-called pepperbox revolver was designed. This has a series of barrels around a central axis and is the precursor of the cylinder revolver.

Four-barrel Trigg flintlock pistol of 1775

Modern revolvers for using cartridges have a single-action, double action or even double-action-only trigger action. However, this type of firing system is not particularly modern. For example, in 1830, the English gunsmith, Charles Lancaster from London, had already produced a double-action pepperbox. Eight years later, the American Ethan Allen even designed a pepperbox with a double-action-only trigger action. Colt, the well-known arms manufacturer, was able to manufacture a true double-action revolver only in 1877, followed by Smith & Wesson in 1880.

There were also many developments in the finish of handguns. Originally, firearms were made in polished metal. This required careful maintenance, because these weapons rusted all the time. In about 1650, more and more gunsmiths used an engraving, producing a gray or slightly bluish protective layer. For the rich elite, weapons could also be coated with a gilt or silver layer. In about 1700, firearms were produced which were 'cooked' in a bath of particular minerals, resulting in an attractive blue finish. Another method which was also often used, was the so-called flame-hardened finish. The metal of the frame was heated to a high temperature, and then rapidly cooled. The

Pair of dueling pistols

Coggswell pepperbox of 1850

nickel-coated finish only became fashionable in about 1820. When a layer of nickel had been applied, the weapon was sometimes polished to a shine.

The use of stainless steel only became common after the Second World War. This was a major breakthrough, because it resulted in a completely new trend. Nowadays, more stainless steel weapons are used for sports than 'blued' weapons. In about 1975, an intermediary finish appeared, the so-called duo finish, which was used particularly for pistols. The frame is made of blued steel or light metal, while the slide is made of stainless steel, or vice versa. This idea was later also used for revolvers, but never became very popular.

Fine stainless steel Taurus revolver

The use of synthetic materials for the manufacture of handguns was introduced in 1980. In that year, the Austrian arms manufacturer Glock produced the model 17 with a synthetic polymer frame. This not only caused a great stir, but also led to a real witchhunt against this pistol. In the American press there were articles about this 'terrorist special'. The so-called plastic pistol could not be easily detected, so it would be possible to transport it on airplanes undetected. Glock almost saw his important American market going up in smoke, and therefore hurriedly set out to prove that this was nonsense. Subsequently, more and more manufacturers started to use this material. In fact, synthetic materials are now very common in modern weapons.

Glock 26 with plastic casing

In 1998, a number of arms manufacturers started to use titanium. First, it was used as a protective layer, but later it was also used for entire components, and even for complete pistols and revolvers. In 2001, Smith & Wesson were the first to introduce a completely new material called scandium. In fact, this metal had been discovered in 1879 by the Swedish chemist Lars Nilson. As the mineral was mainly found in Scandinavia, he called it scandium. In 1971, large amounts of scandium were discovered in the

Beretta 3032 Tomcat with titanium coating

Ukraine. Russian scientists discovered that aluminum could be strengthened enormously by adding a small quantity of scandium.

Light metal alloys were made much more wear-resistant because of the scandium. In addition, the new alloy proved to be resistant to high pressures. The Russians used it in their new Mig fighter planes and in space travel. When the Iron Curtain came down, this material also became available in the west. In 1999, Smith & Wesson had just marketed a number of Airlite Titanium revolver models. When the designers heard about this new scandium, the firm introduced a whole new Scandium revolver series in 2001.

Smith & Wesson 340 AirLite Personal Defense with scandium alloy casing, introduced in 2001

The latest trend in the manufacture of weapons is the use of color. The above-mentioned synthetic frames are extremely suitable for this. For example, arms manufacturers try to tempt ladies to purchase pistols with a pink frame.

Weapons used in matches are also increasingly produced in different colors. Market surveys appear to have revealed that potential purchasers like to distinguish themselves in this way.

Furthermore, the use of color is no longer limited to the frame of the weapon. Nowadays, the sights are also produced with different colors. Formerly, this was the field of so-called custom gunsmiths, who would install these sorts of special accessories for an extremely reasonable price. Since 2001, Smith & Wesson have marketed a large number of pistols and revolvers with a brightly colored bead.

Colored plastic casings of Sarsilimaz

Smith & Wesson Model 22S of 2001 with Hi-Viz plastic bead

An A–Z of revolvers and pistols

AGNER

Agner M80 .22 caliber match pistol In 1983 the Danish firm Saxhoj Products introduced the competition Agner M80. This was designed by the Danish sport shooter, Bent Agner. The single-action weapon is made of Swedish stainless steel. It has a number of curious characteristics. The safety catch is actually a small key which has to be placed in a hole on the left of the weapon. The key can be pressed in, and then works as a magazine catch. In addition, the key can be turned from Safe to Fire. The trigger is completely adjustable and this not only applies for the trigger pressure, but also for the trigger pull, the trigger stop, and even the position of the trigger. The walnut grips of the weapon have an adjustable hand rest.

Obviously, it also has an accurately adjustable micrometer sight. The total length of this 10-shot match pistol is 257 mm (10 in), and the barrel length is 150 mm (6 in). The sight radius (the distance between the rear sight and the front of the bead is 220 mm (8¾ in). The pistol weighs 1120 g (39½ oz). The Agner M80 was produced up to approximately 1991.

AMT

AMT stands for Arcadia Machine & Tools Inc. The company has gone through a turbulent period. Initially, AMT was established in Covina, California. It became famous with the AutoMag pistol in .44 AutoMag and .357 AutoMag. In 1989, the factory moved and changed its name to IAI: Irwindale Arms Incorporated. New models were given the name IAI, though the old models continued to be called AMT. A few years ago, the company got into difficulties. After a new start, production continued under the name Galena Industries Inc. The company is still located in Irwindale, California. In the period 1965-1969, the American designer Harry W. Sanford designed a large heavy pistol. It had a completely new caliber: .44 AMP, the abbreviation for AutoMag Pistol. He marketed this pistol in 1969 under the name AutoMag. The auto loader has a rotating bolt with six locking cams. The locking system is similar to that of the Colt M16 Rifle. Sanford's small gun shop was extended to become the AutoMag Corporation (AMC). Special ammunition made for the AutoMag was manufactured by a Mexican subsidiary of Remington, the Cartouches Deportivos de

AMT logo

Mexico S.A., abbreviated as CDM. At that time, hand loaders often made their own cartridges by shortening .308 Winchester rifle cartridge cases. In 1971, a stainless steel version of the pistol was introduced, known as the Pasadena AutoMag. The production of various components was contracted out to suppliers, which often led to delays. This also affected the production rate of the pistol. The company finally went bankrupt in May 1976. The Thomas Oil Company bought the machinery and stocks of components, because it wished to assemble a number of complete pistols with the parts. The Trust Deed Estates Corporation (TDE) was established for this purpose. Therefore weapons dating from that period have the TDE stamp. Sanford was contracted in to manage the assembly.

TDE was initially established in North Hollywood, but the company subsequently moved to El Monte, also in California. The production of new pistols started there. Once the manufacture of the .44 AMP pistols was running well, a second type was produced in .357 AMP caliber, followed by two conversion sets for both calibers. In the meantime, a few special series were produced as well. These weapons are extremely valuable today as collectors' items. Lee Jurras, the director of the ammunition factory Super Vel Corp. at the time, had a hundred pistols made in .357 AMP caliber, with the serial numbers LEJ 001 to LEJ 100. The barrels of this series of pistols had compensator grooves by Mag-Na-Port. These are special grooves towards the muzzle which reduce the recoil. In addition, they had attractive grips and a gold-colored inscription: 'LEJ Custom Model 100'. As the demand far exceeded the number of pistols produced, another hundred LEJs were made in .44 AMP. Like Jurras, High Standard also bought a special series of two hundred pistols with serial numbers preceded by the letters H.S. Subsequently, several hundred AutoMags were made for High Standard, with the factory logo H.S. on the barrel and serial numbers

starting with the letters A.O. At that time, TDE was doing very well financially. Sanford was therefore able to repurchase the AutoMag company from the Thomas Oil Company. In 1974, he approached Lee Jurras of the Super Vel Corp. for the distribution and service of AutoMags. There were not yet any factory cartridges in the .357 AMP caliber, and Jurras was able to produce these in his own company. The .41 JMP caliber (.41 Jurras Magnum pistol) also dates from that time. In the following years, various types of AutoMags appeared on the market in relatively small series, such as the Jurras Custom Model 200 International with a 216 mm (8½ in) ventilated barrel, a Leupold pistol telescopic sight and an annex holster. In addition, they produced the Alaskan in .44 AMP caliber with a barrel 317 mm (12½ in) long and a carbine stock, as well as the Backpacker in .44 AMP caliber with a barrel 102 mm (4 in) long and a square trigger guard.

AutoMag I

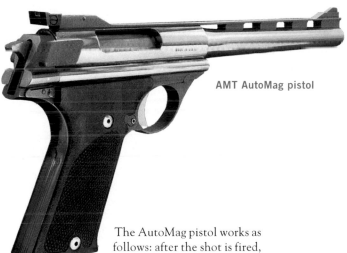

AMT AutoMag pistol

The AutoMag pistol works as follows: after the shot is fired, the barrel section is pushed back by the gas pressure. When the barrel has been pushed back about 8 mm (⁵⁄₁₆ in), the rotation pin in the spiraling head of the locking cam makes sure that the bolt is unlocked from the barrel. The bolt then moves back freely. The whole unlocking system only takes place when the gas pressure has fallen and the bullet has left the barrel. The barrel then goes a further 22 mm (⅞ in) back, until it comes up against the bolt housing. This is mounted on the back of the frame in the shape of a broad ring. The cartridge case that has been fired is then ejected to the right through the ejection port. The bolt is held back by the rotation pin and the heavy recoil springs mounted on either side of the frame. The two recoil springs, which are compressed, then relax, so that the bolt moves forward. The bolt takes a new cartridge from the magazine and presses it into the chamber of the

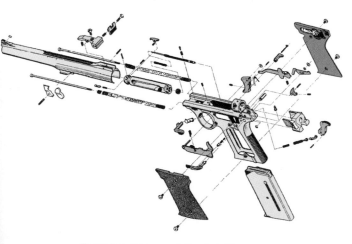

Exploded diagram of the AutoMag

barrel. At the same time, the barrel moves forward until it comes up against the takedown lever. The bolt is rotated and the locking cams of the bolt engage in the locked position. A safety catch at the front of the bolt ensures that the pistol cannot be fired until the bolt is completely locked. The trigger rod is disconnected from the sear until a complete lock has been achieved. The AutoMag has a safety system which works very well. In the 'safe' position, the trigger is disconnected from the rest of the firing mechanism. This means that the weapon is safe in the case of a fall, even with a cartridge in the chamber. The foot of the hammer also has a halfcock safety. The pistol has a slide catch so that the bolt remains in the last position after the last shot. Cocking the pistol by hand is extremely heavy, even with a pre-cocked hammer and requires quite a lot of strength. Experts advise fitting the weapon with a Mag-Na-Port barrel, because this reduces the recoil, particularly in .44 AMP caliber. In .357 AMP caliber, this effect is not as strong. Various types have been made during the production period of the AutoMag. The above-mentioned Custom and limited editions, including the International, Backpacker, Alaskan, LEJs, Grisley and Silhouette were included in the A-series. The more standard versions were inscribed with TDE/OMC, as well as being included in the B-Series. Great progress was made when later models were often delivered with interchangeable barrels. This was not only the length, but also in different 'custom-calibers', such as the .22 AMP, .25 AMP and .30 AMP. The last series, the C-Series, made by the newly established firm AMT (Arcadia Machine & Tool Inc.), in Covina, California, was not able to save the AutoMag I. Nowadays, AMT makes excellent autoloader AutoMag pistols.

In 2000, Galena Industries announced that a new Automag I would be produced in 2001 and that this model would be the Harry Sanford Commemorative in .44 AMP caliber with a 1.65 mm (6½ in) barrel. The planned introductory price was $2,750.

AutoMag II

In 1985, Harry W. Sanford and his company manager, Larry Grossman, designed the AutoMag II. This is a single-action pistol for rimfire caliber .22 WMR (Winchester Magnum Rimfire). AMT marketed this weapon in 1987. Following its introduction, various modifications were made in later models, such as a halfcock safety on the foot of the hammer.

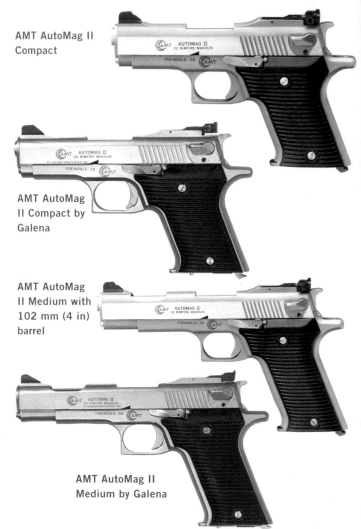

AMT AutoMag II Compact

AMT AutoMag II Compact by Galena

AMT AutoMag II Medium with 102 mm (4 in) barrel

AMT AutoMag II Medium by Galena

BALLISTIC INFORMATION:						
CALIBER/BARREL LENGTH	BULLET WEIGHT (GRAINS)	BULLET VELOCITY M/S			BULLET ENERGY IN JOULES	
		V0	V100	V200	E0	E100
.357 AMP/8½"	125	765	560	405	2370	1270
	158	670	540	435	2289	1487
.44 AMP/8½"	200	600	465	375	2340	1405
	240	535	430	360	2233	1442
	265	500	405	350	2150	1411

AMT AutoMag II
Medium with 152 mm
(6 in) barrel

The same gun by Galena
Industries

The pistol has a unique locking system which works as follows: immediately behind the chamber of the barrel, there are four gas pressure holes. There are also two circular groups of six holes, each in the block around the chamber. After the cartridge has been fired, the gas pressure presses straight on the outside of the cartridge case in the chamber. This means that the cartridge case is retained to remain in the chamber by force until the gas pressure has dropped to a safe level. As soon as the bullet leaves the barrel, the gas pressure can escape through the four gas pressure holes. Then the slide can move back in the normal way, as in any other autoloader. The safety catch on the left at the back of the slide blocks the firing pin the 'safe' position. A massive bar is rotated in front of the hammer so that it can never reach the firing pin. The pistol is made in three models. The 9-shot Standard has a total length of 235 mm (9¼ in) with a 152 mm (6 in) barrel and a weight of 910 g (32 oz). The 9-shot Modified model has a total length of 203 mm (8 in), a barrel length of 115 mm (4½ in) and a weight of 850 g (30 oz). The third model is the Compact. Its total length is 172 mm (6¾ in) with an 86 mm (3¼ in) barrel and a weight of 680 g (24 oz). The magazine capacity of the Compact is seven rounds, because of its shorter frame.

AUTOMAG III

The .30-M1 cartridge has always been popular, not only with American shooters, but also in the countries where stocks of .30-M1 carbines were left behind after the Second World War. Furthermore, the .30-M1 carbine continued to be part of the range of police weapons in a number of countries for a long time. Between 1980 and 1990, the police started to use more modern weapons, such as the Heckler &

Koch MP-5 carbine, the Beretta machine pistol, etc. For this reason, these carbines were rejected and became available for sport shooting. The fact that AMT made a handgun for this caliber is not really a new development. During the Second World War, Smith & Wesson were the first to make a revolver for this caliber. This project was not very successful. Later, in 1955 to be precise, the Kimball autoloader pistol was introduced on the market in .30-M1 caliber. This weapon worked on the basis of the principle of a delayed recoil action. The slide was extremely heavy, as were the recoil springs. Furthermore, the grooved chamber of the barrel had to hold the cartridge case for a fraction of a second after the shot by means of the high gas pressure, until the bullet had left the barrel. This adventure also came to an end, mainly for technical reasons. The pistol proved unable to cope with the relatively high gas pressure of the .30-M1 cartridge. In about 1965, the American arms manufacturer Ruger introduced the single-action Blackhawk revolver in .30-M1 caliber, and this is still manufactured today.

In addition, Thompson has made an interchangeable barrel in this caliber for its single-shot Contender series of pistols. Resolving the problem of the locking system was the biggest problem for the chief designer of IAI/AMT, Larry Grossman. Initially he used a special pressure chamber, like that in the AutoMag I and II. This system did not work very well with the .30-M1 cartridge. In fact, the gas pressure of the .30-M1 cartridge is much higher than that of the .22 WMR. In the end, he opted for the most widely tested Browning locking system. The barrel did not have a hinge on the side of the chamber, but a fixed chamber block. In addition, IAI/AMT used only one heavy locking cam on the barrel. This cam engages with a corresponding recess on the side of the slide when it is locked. The pistol is completely made of stainless steel. The single-action AutoMag III has the characteristic barrel bushing of Colt pistols. In

AMT AutoMag III by Galena

The old AMT
AutoMag III in
.30-M1 caliber

fact, it is disassembled in the same way as a Colt. The grips are made of the same synthetic material as those of the AutoMag II, also with horizontal recesses for a firm grip. The safety catch mounted on the left of the slide blocks the firing pin in a safe position and also rotates a steel bolt in front of the hammer. The magazine catch is on the left of the frame, behind the trigger guard. The total length of the 8-shot AutoMag III is 267 mm (10½ in), and it has a barrel length of 172 mm (6¾ in). The pistol is quite heavy, and the empty weight is about 1275 g (45 oz). This has the advantage that the recoil is largely absorbed by the weight of the weapon, and that is actually quite necessary. The .30-M1 cartridge was designed for a carbine with a much longer barrel than this pistol. At the moment the bullet leaves the barrel of the AutoMag, the total quantity of powder has not yet all been converted into gas pressure. This effect can be clearly seen from the significant flash produced from the muzzle, and the loud bang. The AutoMag III shoots normal carbine ammunition without any problem. The pistol is able to shoot bullets of 110 grains (standard cartridge) with a muzzle velocity of approximately 530 m/s. In 1992, the AutoMag III was available for a short time in the caliber 9 mm Winchester Magnum. However, this caliber never became popular.

AUTOMAG IV

The single-action AutoMag IV was originally designed for the 10 mm Auto caliber. In 1990, the pistol was introduced as the AMT 10 mm Auto Javelina Hunting pistol. The Javelina with a long slide was manufactured up to 1994. At the end of 1991, there was also a model in .45 Winchester Magnum caliber, followed in 1992 by the 10 mm Magnum caliber. The 10 mm Magnum cartridge has a cartridge case 31.8 mm (1¼ in) long. The length of the cartridge of the 10 mm Auto is 25.2 mm (1 in).

AMT AutoMag IV in
.45 Win.Magnum

The new AMT AutoMag IV
of Galena

The appearance and action of this pistol are the same as that of the AutoMag III. The model was meant for the market of silhouette shooters and hunters of small game. Shooting distances up to 200 meters are not a problem for this pistol and these calibers. Since 1997, the AutoMag IV has only been available in .45 Winchester Magnum caliber. The total length of the AutoMag IV is 276 mm (10⅞ in) with a barrel length of 165 mm (6½ in). The weight of this 7-shot pistol is approximately 1300 g (45½ oz). In addition, the weapon has a safety catch on the left side of the slide and a magazine catch on the left, behind the trigger guard.

AUTOMAG V

The large AutoMag V appeared on the market at the end of 1993. This pistol is the big brother of the AutoMag IV and shoots the heavy .50 AE (Action-Express) caliber. The barrel and slide have an integrated compensator, and considering the caliber, this is necessary. For reasons which are not entirely clear, this type was produced for only a few years,

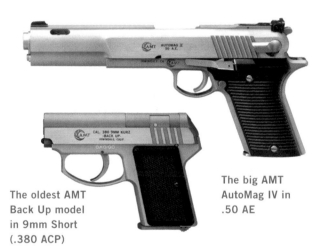

The oldest AMT
Back Up model
in 9mm Short
(.380 ACP)

The big AMT
AutoMag IV in
.50 AE

viz., up to 1996. The single-action AutoMag V has a total length of 273 mm (10¾ in). The barrel length is 165 mm (6½ in) and the pistol weighs 1305 g (46 oz). It has a magazine capacity of seven rounds.

AMT BACK UP

The first AMT Back Up pistol dates from 1976. The caliber was 9 mm Short (.380 ACP) and the weapon had a single-action trigger mechanism. This pistol had a magazine for five cartridges. The total length was 127 mm (5 in), and the barrel length was 64 mm (2½ in). The weapon was entirely made of stainless steel and weighed only 510 g (18 oz). The Back Up had no safety catch, but did have an automatic firing pin safety. The magazine catch was in the heel of the grip. Originally, the weapon was

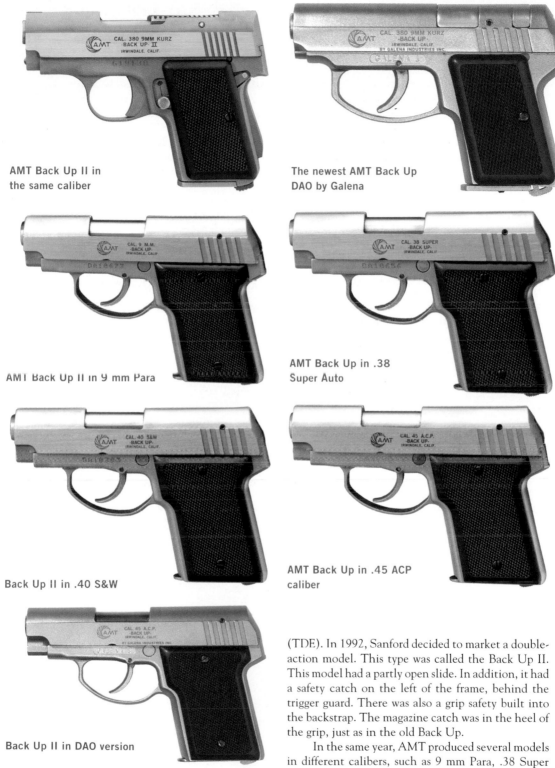

AMT Back Up II in
the same caliber

The newest AMT Back Up
DAO by Galena

AMT Back Up II in 9 mm Para

AMT Back Up in .38
Super Auto

Back Up II in .40 S&W

AMT Back Up in .45 ACP
caliber

Back Up II in DAO version

made by Ordnance Manufacturing Corporation
(OMC). Subsequently AMT (Arcadia Machine &
Tool) took over production. At that time, both firms
belonged to the Trust Deed Estates Corporation

(TDE). In 1992, Sanford decided to market a double-
action model. This type was called the Back Up II.
This model had a partly open slide. In addition, it had
a safety catch on the left of the frame, behind the
trigger guard. There was also a grip safety built into
the backstrap. The magazine catch was in the heel of
the grip, just as in the old Back Up.

In the same year, AMT produced several models
in different calibers, such as 9 mm Para, .38 Super
Auto, 40 S & W and .45 ACP.

In addition, the first double-action-only (DAO)
was introduced in the caliber 9 mm Short (.380 ACP)
in 1992. This 6-shot pistol has a larger trigger guard.
It only has automatic firing pin safety. The AMT
Back Up in the double-action-only (DAO) model

Dark gray Back Up
(III) Combat in .45
ACP by Galena

The old AMT Hardballer

Back Up in DAO in
the latest .357 Sig

The latest
Hardballer by
Galena

followed in 1994 in .45 ACP caliber. Models in other
calibers appeared on the market a year later.

The AMT Back Up DAO was produced in the
new .357 Sig caliber in 1998. In the USA, this type is
sold under the name Amt Texas 357 DAO.

AMT Government .45 ACP

OTHER AMT MODELS

AMT GOVERNMENT

In addition to the above-mentioned models, AMT
and IAI also made a number of other weapons.

The 7-shot Amt Government in .45 ACP
caliber is a Colt 1911-A1 clone, but made
completely in stainless steel. The total
length of the weapon is 220 mm (8¼ in)
with a barrel length of 127 mm (5 in).
The weight is actually 1770 g (62½ oz).
It is a single-action pistol with a safety
catch of the Colt 1911-A1 type on the left of
the frame. The magazine catch is also on the
left, behind the trigger guard. In addition, it
has a grip safety in the backstrap and
a halfcock safety on the foot of the
hammer. The pistol has fixed sights. This
model was developed for the American
Police Departments.

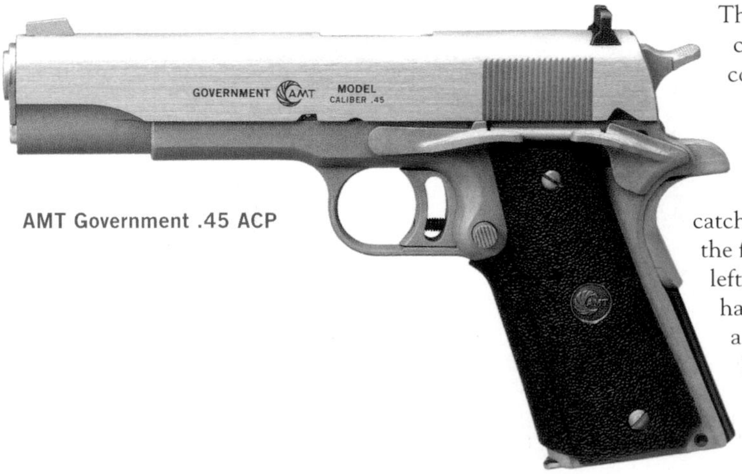

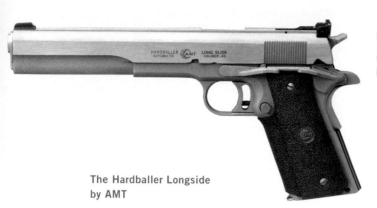

The Hardballer Longside
by AMT

The same pistol by Galena

AMT HARDBALLER/SKIPPER

The AMT Hardballer in .45 ACP caliber dates from 1977, and was developed as a sports pistol. It has adjustable sights, an extended combat safety catch and slide catch, a broad adjustable trigger, an enlarged magazine well and a cartridge indicator. The Hardballer has a total length of 220 mm (8¾ in) and a barrel length of 127 mm (5 in). The weight is the same as that of the Government, viz., 1770 g (62½oz). The same model, but with fixed sights, was marketed in 1978 as the Combat Government. Since 1985, this model has been called the Government and the term 'Combat' was omitted. A compact version of the Hardballer, which was 25.4mm (1 in) shorter, was introduced in 1980 as the AMT Skipper. By 1984, the Skipper had disappeared from the range again.

AMT HARDBALLER LONGSLIDE

The AMT Hardballer Longslide was introduced in 1980. It has the same qualities as the standard

Exploded diagram of the small caliber AMT Lightning pistol

Hardballer. In this pistol, the barrel and slide are lengthened. The weapon has a total length of 266 mm (10½ in) with a barrel length of 177 mm (7 in). The sight radius is also exceptional, viz., 220 mm (8¾ in); this is 50 mm (2 in) longer than the sight radius of the normal Hardballer. The weight of this enormous pistol is 1900 g (67 oz). The Longslide Hardballer has a longer safety catch and slide catch on the left of the frame. In addition, it also has the traditional grip safety.

AMT LIGHTNING

In 1984, AMT tried to enter the small caliber pistol market. The single-action Amt Lightning was introduced in that year in .22 LR caliber. The 10-shot pistol was available with barrel lengths of 127 mm (5 in), 165 mm (6½ in) and 216 mm (8½ in). The total lengths were respectively 235 mm (9¼ in), 273 mm (10¾ in) and 324 mm (12¾ in). The weight of the weapon with the 165 mm (6½ in) barrel was 1275 g (45 oz). The pistol had an adjustable trigger stop and a Millet micrometer sight. This stainless steel weapon looked very much like a Ruger MKII pistol. AMT produced it up to 1990.

AMT ON DUTY

The AMT 'On Duty' was designed in 1991. The pistol belonged to a new concept with a combined safety catch/uncocking lever, and was only available in double-action-only. The available calibers at that time were 9 mm Para (15-shot) and .40 S&W (11-shot). The weapon was mat black and had vertical ribs on the front and back of the slide. In 1994 a model was added in .45 ACP caliber (9 shot). The pistol had a total length of 197 mm (7¾ in) with a barrel length of 114 mm (4½ in). It weighed 900 g (32 oz). Production of the On Duty came to an end in 1996.

AMT-Galena Commando
introduced in 2000

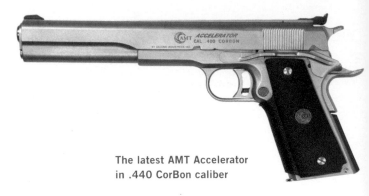

The latest AMT Accelerator
in .440 CorBon caliber

AMT COMMANDO

The AMT Commando in .40 S&W caliber, which
was introduced in 2000, is a new model made under
the Galena flag. It is a compact version of the
Government, but does have the frame of that model.
It has an adjustable rear sight and is made of stainless
steel. The single-action Commando has a magazine
capacity of 8 rounds. The total length is 195 mm
(7¼ in) with a barrel length of 102 mm (4 in). The
weapon weighs 1020 g (36 oz). In addition, it has
a longer safety and slide catch on the left of the frame.
The magazine catch is also on the left, behind the
trigger guard. The grip safety is also extended in a so-
called beavertail and the magazine well is enlarged.

AMT ACCELERATOR

In 1999, Galena introduced the single-action Amt
Accelerator in .400 CorBon caliber. This 7-shot
pistol is almost identical to the Hardballer Longslide.
The cartridge was originally a so-called wildcat,
designed by Bo Clerke of the American firm CorBon
in Sturgis, South Dakota. The cartridge has a .45
ACP cartridge case of which the mouth is compressed
to .41 in (10.4 mm). In the accelerator a bullet of 135
grains achieves a muzzle velocity of approximately
457 m/s (1500 fps). The muzzle energy is 920 Joules.
The weapon has a total length of 266 mm (10½ in)

The latest Supermodel of
2001 in .440 CorBon caliber

with a barrel that is 177 mm (7 in) long and it weighs
1300 g (46 oz).

This Accelerator is fitted with a beavertail grip
safety. In addition, the safety catch and slide catch are
extended. The magazine well is also enlarged, and has
an adjustable broad match trigger.

AMT AM440

One of the newest models in 2001 was the Galena
AMT AM 440 in the latest .440 CorBon Magnum
caliber. This single-action pistol can actually be seen
as a successor of the AMT AutoMag V. It also has the
same integrated compensator in the barrel and slide.
The cartridge case of the .50 AE is used for the .440
CorBon cartridge. The diameter of the mouth of the
cartridge case is reduced to .44 in. The weapon was
mainly designed for hunting and for silhouette
shooting. The total length is 266 mm (10½ in) with
a barrel length of 177 mm (7 in). This pistol weighs
1700 g (60 oz). The magazine capacity is seven
rounds. The AM (AutoMag) 440 has an
ambidextrous safety catch on the slide. A 240 grain
bullet has a muzzle velocity of 565 m/s. This means
that the projectile can achieve the dizzying muzzle
velocity of 2490 Joules. This is very high for
a handgun.

ARMINIUS

The German firm Weihrauch was established in
1899 by the master gunsmith Hermann
Weihrauch. Up to that time, he had worked for the
gun- making factory of Bartels in Zella St. Blasi.
In that year he took over the business and
started the Weihrauch firm with his three sons.
They mainly made hunting rifles. In the First World
War, the firm produced equipment for the war and
at that time it made the mounts for sights and parts
for the Mauser 98 rifle. In 1919, Weihrauch took
up making hunting and sport rifles once again.
At that time, the market was not very strong.

Arminius HW-75
revolver

Arminius logo of the Hermann Weihrauch firm

Weihrauch was forced to make other products as well, such as bicycles, doorstops and tools. In the Second World War, the firm was again used for the production of military equipment. Amongst other things, it made bicycles for the army and parts for weapons. In 1945, the firm was closed by the Allies. It was only in 1948 that Hermann Weihrauch was able to set up a new business with his sons in the Bavarian town of Mellrichstadt. As the manufacture of firearms was prohibited at that time, they made parts for bicycles and mopeds. In 1950, they expanded their production with air rifles.

When the prohibition on producing firearms was lifted, Weihrauch decided to start making revolvers as well in 1960, under the trade name Arminius. This was originally the name used by Friedrich Pickert, who made revolvers in Zella-Mehlis in the period 1920-1940. Weihrauch's current range consists of revolvers of the Arminius make. Air rifles and bullet rifles are made under the Weihrauch name. Weihrauch has not forgotten its other work, because the firm also produces bicycle parts. The business is still in the hands of the Weihrauch family. The first revolver model produced by Weihrauch in 1960 was the Arminius HW-3 in .22LR and .32 in S&W Long caliber. The .22 LR revolver had an 8-shot cylinder and the cylinder of the .32 had a capacity of seven rounds. The revolver was also sold in Europe under the name Gecado. This had been the trademark of the German firm Gustav Genschow up to 1959. That firm was taken over in that year by the Dynamit Nobel concern. In the USA, the HW-3 was marketed under the name Dickson Bulldog. The HW-4 was the next model in 1962. This revolver was made in several models. The length of the barrel varied from 64 mm (2½ in) to 102 mm (4 in) and 152 mm (6 in). These revolvers were made both in blued and in chrome finishes. The sport models usually had an anatomical wooden stock with a thumb rest. The HW-5, which came out in 1965 in .22 LR caliber, had an interchangeable cylinder in .22WMR. This revolver was available with various barrel lengths, such as 102 mm (4 in), 152 mm (6 in) and 305 mm (12 in). A model in .32 S&W Long caliber was also made specially for the American market. This had a 51 mm (2 in) or 102 mm (4 in) barrel, and was sold under the name Omega by L.A. distributors in Brooklyn, New York. In 1969, Weihrauch also started to manufacture single-action revolvers based on the Colt Peacemaker.

ARMINIUS HW-7

The double-action revolver model Arminius HW-7 was a sports model with an 8-shot cylinder in .22 LR caliber. The weapon had a 152 mm (6 in) barrel with a ventilated barrel rib and a total length of 265 mm (10½ in). The weight of this revolver was 865 g (30½ oz). The standard version with a fixed rear sight was marketed in the United States as the 'Herter's Guide Model' by the American company Herters, in Waseca, Minneapolis. After 1970, the American firm, Firearms Import & Export in Miami, Florida, took over sales. The sports model with an adjustable rear sight was called the Arminius HW-7S.

ARMINIUS HW-9

The 6-shot HW-9 in .22 LR caliber was a real sports revolver. The weapon was introduced in 1970. The double-action weapon had an adjustable trigger pressure of 1100 to 1550 g. In addition, it had an adjustable screw in the trigger guard as a trigger stop.

Arminius HW-9ST
with standard stock

Arminius HW-9 Sport with
barrel jacket

Arminius HW9-ST Silhouette
with 254 mm (10 in) barrel

Arminius HW-357 revolver

The Arminius HW-9ST, a model made completely in steel, was marketed in 1992. This revolver has a total length of 290 mm (11½ in) and a barrel length of 152 mm (6 in). The weight of the HW-9ST is 1020 g (36 oz). It has an adjustable rear sight.

In the course of time, this revolver has undergone a number of modifications. The first type had a ventilated barrel and a removable barrel shroud as extra weight for the barrel. The swing-out cylinder was operated by pulling the ejector rod forwards by hand. In the second type, the revolver was fitted with a thumb piece behind the recoil plate to unlock the cylinder so that it could swing out of the frame. The third type also has a separate barrel shroud as extra weight. In addition, the weapon has a trigger stop and a broad removable trigger shoe. The revolver has a special match stock with an adjustable hand rest.

The HW9-ST was also made with a 10 in barrel length, specially designed for silhouette shooting. Since 1993, this model, equipped with a hooded front and rear sight, has also been made in stainless steel. This model has a total length of 392 mm (15½ in) and a barrel length of 254 mm (10 in). It weighs 1650 g (58¼ oz).

ARMINIUS HW-357

In the following years, Weihrauch made a large number of different revolver models such as the HW-357 Hunter. The HW-357 revolver in .357 Magnum caliber was developed in 1977, and there are several

models, identified as HW-357 and HW-357T. The HW-357 revolver has barrels with lengths of 64 mm (2½ in), 102 mm (4 in) and 152 mm (6 in). The Target or sports model has a choice of barrel length between 76 mm (3 in), 102 mm (4 in) and 152 mm (6 in).

ARMINIUS WINDICATOR

Weihrauch developed the Arminius Windicator for the fast Practical Revolver Parcours. This revolver has an extra heavy, flattened barrel shroud, and is only available with a barrel length of 102 mm (4 in) in .38 Special and .357 Magnum calibers. The total length of this revolver is 240 mm (9½ in). Arminius revolvers are almost all equipped with a transfer rod safety and therefore have a so-called floating loose firing pin in the frame.

ARTAX

The Italian firm Artax in Cellatica in Brescia started in 1997 as an independent company manufacturing replicas of antique firearms. Since 1970, it has been engaged in the production of handmade replicas. It was necessary to invest in machinery in order to save costs. This resulted in the current company. Artax makes extremely high quality replicas of pistols and rifles. This is demonstrated by the results achieved in international competitions. The company specializes in special shooting disciplines in the field of black

Arminius Windicator

Artax logo

powder. These include Cominazzo, Lorenzoni, Tanegaschima, Vetterli and Withworth.

Cominazzo is a class in sports shooting which uses a front-loading pistol with a smooth barrel. In this respect, a smooth barrel means a barrel with no grooves and lands. The weapon should also have a flint or fuse lock. The maximum caliber permitted is 11 mm (.43 in) for round lead bullets.

Lorenzoni is a match class for every type of single and double-barrel front loading shotgun with a percussion lock. The gun must have one or two smooth barrels. The caliber of the shot is 11 or smaller. The prescribed charge is a maximum of 6.2 grains (0.40 g) of blackpowder with 35 g (1¼ oz) shot.

Tanegaschima is the name for any type of front-loading gun with a fuselock and a smooth barrel. The caliber is free. In this shooting discipline only round lead bullets are used.

Vetterli is a class for any type of front-loading gun with a fuselock, flintlock or percussion lock. The barrel may be smooth or grooved. The weapon is used for shooting from a standing position. The stock has a strong curve for this purpose. A trigger accelerator is permitted. Apart from this, a hand-rest is only permitted in matches if it is of the original model. The gun may have both a rear sight and a diopter sight. In addition, the front sight may be hooded. The caliber is free and lead round or pointed bullets are used.

Withworth is a shooting discipline for a front-loading gun with a rifled barrel and a percussion system. A Withworth rifle has a straight slender

Artax fuselock pistol

stock. The weapon can have a diopter sight and a hood for the front sight. The caliber for the lead, round or pointed bullets is free. This type of rifle is also used for the special Walkyrie section: 100 meter shots from a prone position for ladies.

ARTAX FUSELOCK PISTOL

The real fuselock was developed from the simple fuse ignition, dating from about 1400. The first examples of this date back to about 1470 and are found in manuscripts, drawings and paintings. The fuse lock consisted of a curved iron holder, which was attached to the gun. This holder, also known as a serpentine, was rotated and connected to an iron hook on the bottom of the wooden stock of the weapon. This hook was actually an ancestor of the trigger. The loading procedure was as follows: first, the shooter set his gun up vertically, and then he poured a quantity of gunpowder into the barrel via the muzzle. The powder was carefully tamped down with a ramrod. Then the projectile was put in through the muzzle, and again pressed down with the ramrod. The weapon was then ready to shoot. A burning fuse was held in the touch-hole so that the charge was lit. A later version of the fuse lock had a pan at the back of the barrel.

The shooter would scatter a small quantity of fine gunpowder into this. By pressing the hook against the stock, the serpentine was rotated around its axis so that the fuse was turned towards the pan. The gunpowder was ignited, and the flame went into the pan. The flame then moved through the channel, through a small hole into the main charge in the barrel. It then lit the charge at the back of the barrel. The main charge ignited and provided the gas pressure which propelled the projectile out of the barrel.

In later models the serpentine was fitted with a spring. As soon as the serpentine was tipped back, it was stopped by a firing catch. When the firing hook was pressed, the spring ensured that the serpentine moved forwards. In those days, the firing hook was sometimes replaced by a switch operating the firing catch, and in even later models the trigger was introduced.

The success of the reloading exercise depended to a large extent on the weather conditions. A hard wind could blow the fine powder out of the fire pan.

Musketeer with fuselock gun

Shooter with a fuselock gun

The Artax Boutet flintlock pistol is a typical dueling weapon. The history of dueling weapons goes back to the first centuries ad. Up to the introduction of firearms it was usual to settle disputes by sword, saber or rapier. From the sixteenth century, pistols were used increasingly. In fact, duels were so common, particularly at the French court of Louis XIV, that in 1679 the king even made them punishable by decree. In other countries, defending one's honor with firearms was considered vulgar up to approximately the eighteenth century. In order to settle these heated differences of opinion as honestly as possible, the two opponents had to have equal chances. Therefore the two pistols had to be identical. Rules were even drawn up, such as the British Code of Duel, dating from 1829. Amongst other things, this determined that the minimum distance between the two duelists must be at least 25 feet (7.6 meters) and it was determined that they should fire at the command of one or more seconds. According to the Code of Honor, only single-shot weapons could be used in duels.

One of the best-known victims of dueling pistols is the Russian poet, Alexander Pushkin. He was shot dead in St. Petersburg in 1837 by Baron d'Anthãs, the adopted son of the Dutch ambassador Baron Van Heeckeren.

There are all sorts of dueling pistols: from plain pistols to richly engraved pistols inlaid with gold, which reflected the owner's wealth. Some of the well-known manufacturers of dueling pistols included Clarke, Dickson, Henshall, Mills, Manton, Mortimer, Parker, Richards and Wogdon & Barton from England. In France, dueling pistols were made by Boutet, Gastinne & Renette, Moutier and Verney. Well-known German manufacturers in this field included Bramhoffer, Schenk and Ulbricht. Fortunately, these weapons were not only used in duels, but also in target shooting, a popular sport with the wealthy.

Rain obviously also had a bad effect on lighting the charge.

Later types of fuselocks dating from the seventeenth century had a flash pan with a lid. As long as it was not necessary to fire the gun, the powder was protected by a hinged lid. When the shooter had to fire, he turned or moved the lid from the flash pan so that the fuse could get to the powder. Military marksmen, the so-called musketeers, were already wearing bandoliers with cylinders in about 1600. These cylinders contained a measured quantity of gunpowder for every charge.

The use of larger powder horns or gunpowder flasks sometimes resulted in accidents. Experience had shown that a glowing piece of soot in the barrel could do a great deal of damage when the shooter started to pour some powder into the barrel from his powder horn for the next shot. The small quantities of gunpowder measured out in cylinders were much safer to use.

ARTAX BOUTET FLINTLOCK PISTOL

The French gunsmith and goldsmith, Nicolas Noel Boutet, lived from 1761 to 1833 and worked in a goldsmith's workplace in Versailles, near Paris. He was a protégé of Emperor Napoleon, for whom he made a number of specially decorated weapons. Craftsmen from the Belgian town of Liege worked in his atelier. In addition to beautiful dueling pistols and hunting weapons, Boutet also produced weapons for the army.

Pair of Boutet dueling pistols by Artax

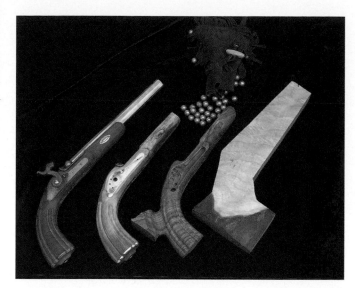

Moutier pistol by Artax with stocks at various stages of production

ARTAX MOUTIER PERCUSSION PISTOL

Moutier was a French gunsmith in the middle of the nineteenth century. He worked in Paris, and mainly produced hunting guns with a percussion system. In addition, he manufactured percussion pistols for target shooting.

ASTRA

Astra is the brand name of Esperanza y Unceta, later the Unceta Y Compañia (Unceta & Co) in Guernica, Spain. Nowadays, the company is called Astra-Unceta S.A. The firm was founded in 1908 by Pedro Unceta and Juan Esperanza, who both came from the town of Eibar in Northern Spain. In 1913, the firm moved to Guernica. The name of the company changed to Esperanza y Cia. The Astra brand name was registered in 1914. Other brand names at that time were: Brunswig, Firecat, Fortuna, Leston, Museum, Salso, Union, and Victoria. The new factory started the manufacture of the Campo

Astra's logo

Line illustration of the Astra 1911

Giro pistol for the Spanish army. This model was modified in 1918, after which it was called Model 1921. In 1921, Astra introduced a new pistol based on the Campo Giro model. This new type was called the Astra 400. In the period from 1921 to 1946, Esperanza y Cia produced a total of 106,000 pistols of the Astra 400 model for the Spanish army. Originally, this pistol was in 9mm Bergmann-Bayard caliber. However, it could also be used with other 9mm ammunition, such as the 9mm Largo and the 9mm Para. The Astra 400 was exported to many countries for the civilian market. In the course of the twentieth century, Astra designed and manufactured a large number of different handguns. The most important ones are shown below in chronological order:

1911: ASTRA MODEL 1911

The 1911 model is a copy of the Browning 1903 pistol, which Unceta marketed as the Victoria up to 1914. The single-action weapon had a total length of 145 mm (5¾ in) and a barrel length of 81 mm (3⅛ in). The caliber was 7.65 mm (.32 ACP). The magazine capacity was for seven rounds, and the pistol had an empty weight of 595 g (21 oz). The weapon was modified in 1916, when a grip safety was added. It was produced up to 1918.

1920: ASTRA MODEL 200 FIRECAT

This single-action pistol was based on the Browning 1906 and had a 6.35 mm (.25 ACP) caliber. The weapon was equipped with three safety: a grip safety devices, a magazine safety, and a safety catch above the trigger guard. The pistol was mainly exported to the USA, where it was sold as the Firecat. This weapon had a magazine capacity of 6 rounds. Its total length was 110 mm (4¼ in) and the barrel length was 56 mm (2¼ in). It weighed only 355 g (12½ oz). Astra produced this model up to 1968.

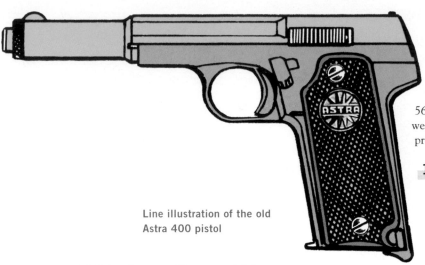

Line illustration of the old
Astra 400 pistol

1921: ASTRA MODEL 400

The Astra model 400 was introduced in 1921. In the same year, the weapon was chosen as the pistol for the Spanish army under the name Astra 1921 Militar in 9mm Largo caliber. The model can be recognized by its characteristic round barrel and slide. The single-action weapon was designed in such a way that it could shoot several calibers in 9mm, such as the 9mm Bergmann-Bayard and the 9mm Para cartridge. The total length of this pistol was 235 mm (9¼ in), the barrel length was 150 mm (6 in) and it weighed 880 g (31 oz). Astra ceased production in 1946, and had made more than 106,000 in 25 years.

1922: ASTRA MODEL 300

This is a compact version of the Astra 400 in 7.65 mm (.32 ACP) caliber or 9mm Short (.380 ACP) caliber, dating from 1922. In 1928, this pistol became the official weapon of the Spanish Navy in 9mm Short (.380 ACP) caliber. The weapon had a total length of 160 mm (6¼ in) and a barrel length of 98 mm (37/8 in). The empty weight was 630 g (22¼ oz). In 7.65 mm (.32 ACP) caliber, the weapon had a magazine capacity of 8 rounds. In 9 mm Short (.380 ACP) caliber, the capacity was for 7 cartridges. This model also had a single-action trigger action. In the Second World War the German army bought more than 85,000 pistols in each caliber. These weapons have the German stamp 'Wa A 57' with a stylized eagle above it. Astra stopped the production of this pistol in 1947. It had manufactured more than 171, 300 pistols of this model.

1924: ASTRA MODEL 1924

This model was also based on the Browning 1906. It was marketed under different names such as the Astra

Victoria and the Hope. The caliber was 6.35 mm (.25 ACP). From 1928, a safety grip was added to the weapon. The 6-shot single-action pistol had a total length of 110 mm (4¼ in), and the barrel length was 56 mm (2¼ in). The small pocket pistol weighed 340 g (12 oz) and remained in production up to approximately 1930.

1927: ASTRA MODEL 700

A 7.65 mm (.32 ACP) version of the Astra 400. In 1927, approximately 4000 were made for the civilian market. It was followed by the Astra 700 Special, which was introduced in 1928. This 12-shot single-action pistol had a total length of 160mm (6¼ in) and a barrel length of 95 mm (3¾ in). The empty weight was 725 g (25½ oz). Production of the 700 Special model ceased in 1946.

1927: ASTRA MODEL 900

This model is based on the Mauser C-96 pistol. The Astra looked very similar to the Mauser, but there were big differences internally. The caliber was 7.63 mm Mauser. Astra exported a batch of 8,000 of these pistols to China in 1928 in connection with the civil war between the communists and the nationalist Kuoh-Mintang. In addition, it was issued to the Spanish police. The total length was 308 mm (12 in) and the barrel was 160 mm (6¼ in) long. This large single-action pistol weighed 1275 g (45 oz). The weapon remained in production with various modifications up to 1933. Examples include the Astra 901 and 903, both with a firing selector for fully automatic fire.

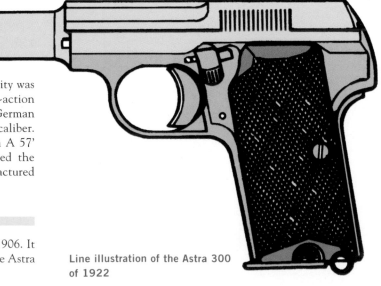

Line illustration of the Astra 300
of 1922

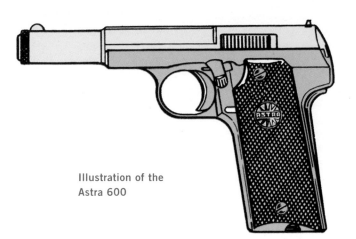

Illustration of the
Astra 600

Astra Club in 6.35 mm (.25 ACP)
caliber

1942: Astra Model 600

This is a compact version of the Astra 400 in 9 mm
Para caliber. Up to 1944, Astra made more than
10,000 of these for the German army. These
weapons have the German Wehrmacht stamp 'Wa
A 57' with a stylized eagle. Astra then continued
production up to the end of 1948. A small number
of pistols were issued to the West German Police
by the Allies after 1945. The 8-shot autoloader
had a total length of 205 mm (8 in). The barrel
length was 133 mm (5¼ in) and the weapon weighed
900 g (31¾ oz).

1946: Astra Model 1000

This is a single-action pistol in 7.65 mm (.32 ACP)
caliber, based on the Astra 200, dating from 1920.
The 11-shot weapon had a total length of 200 mm
(8 in), and the barrel was 130 mm (5 in)
long. The pistol had an empty weight of 1050 g
(37 oz). It was manufactured in small numbers up
to 1949.

1948: Astra Model 3000

This is a newer version of the Astra 300 model
dating from 1922. The single-action pistol
had a cartridge indicator at the back of
the slide. It was produced up to 1956.
In 7.65 mm (.32 ACP) caliber, this pistol
had a magazine capacity of 7 cartridges. In
9 mm Short caliber (.380 ACP), the
capacity was for 6 rounds. The weapon had
a total length of 160 mm (6¼ in) and a barrel
length of 98 mm (4 in). The empty weight was
624 g (22 oz). The first series up to about 1953
had a magazine catch in the heel of the grip. From
1953 to 1956, it was manufactured with a magazine
catch on the left of the frame, behind the trigger
guard. This model was succeeded in 1956 by the
model 4000.

1951: Astra Model 2000

This is a version of the Astra 1000 with an external
hammer, but without the grip safety of the model
1000. It was made in .22 Short caliber. The same
model in 6.35 mm (.25 ACP) caliber was called the
Cub. The pistol was also exported to the USA with
a 102 mm (4 in) barrel and an adjustable rear sight,
under the name Astra Camper. Up to 1968, Astra
produced the pistol in 6.35 (.25 ACP) caliber for
Colt, which marketed it in North America as the Colt
Junior. After the introduction of the 1968 Gun
Control Act, Astra exported this model to the USA
under its own name as the Astra Cub. The Astra 7000
was a version in .22 LR caliber. Moreover, it was 13
mm (½ in) longer than the Astra 2000 and had
a barrel 2 mm (¹⁄₁₆ in) longer.

1956: Astra Model 4000

This is a version of the Astra 3000 with an external
hammer. This model is still produced by Astra in
calibers .22 LR, 7.65 mm (.32 ACP) and 9 mm Short
(.380 ACP). Since its introduction it has been
widely sold in the USA, where it is marketed under
the name Astra Falcon, together with an
interchangeable set in .22 LR. The pistol has

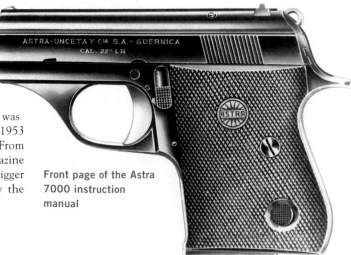

Front page of the Astra
7000 instruction
manual

a magazine catch at the bottom of the left grip plate. The total length of this single-action pistol is 163 mm (6½ in), with a barrel length of 100 mm (4 in). It weighs 624 g (22 oz). In .22 LR caliber the magazine has a capacity of 10 rounds. In 7.65 mm (.32 ACP) caliber, the magazine capacity is seven cartridges and in 9 mm Short (.380 ACP) caliber it has a capacity of six rounds.

1958: ASTRA MODEL 800

This model is based on the 600 model, in 9 mm Para caliber, and was also exported to the USA under the model name Condor. The pistol has an external hammer and a cartridge indicator. The safety catch is on the left at the back of the frame. In the 600 model, this catch is above the trigger guard. The single-action Astra 800 model has a magazine capacity of 8 rounds. The total length is 207 mm (8 in) with a barrel length of 135 mm (5¼ in). The pistol weighs approximately 1000 g (35¼ oz). It is curious that both the Astra 600 and this 800 model only have a recoil locking system. The recoil spring around the barrel is extra heavy. Astra produced approximately 11,000 pistols of this model between 1958 and the end of 1969.

1958: ASTRA MODEL CADIX

This model is based on the old Smith & Wesson revolvers. From 1958, the double-action weapon was produced in .22 LR caliber with a 9-shot cylinder in

barrel lengths of 51 mm (2 in), 102 mm (4 in) and 152 mm (6 in). In .22 LR caliber with a 51 mm (2 in) barrel, it was known as the Cadix 222. In 1962 Astra marketed a 5-shot version in .38 Special caliber with the same barrel lengths as the .22 LR Cadix. Up to 1968, the Cadix revolver had grips of which the width and length could be adapted with plates. From 1968, the model came with a large wooden grip. A second modification was a rotating ring in the grip with which the pressure of the hammer spring could be altered. Two other versions followed in 1969, a 6-shot revolver in .32 S&W Long caliber and a 9-shot version in .22 WMR caliber. One variation of this model is the Cadix 250. This revolver in .38 Special caliber and with a 51 mm (2 in) barrel was used as the service weapon by several units of the Guardia Civil (the Spanish state police) for a long time.

1965: ASTRA MODEL 5000/ CONSTABLE

This model is rather like the Walther PP. It is a double-action pistol in .22 LR, 7.65 mm (.32 ACP) or 9 mm Short (.380 ACP) caliber. The weapon has a combined safety catch/uncocking lever on the left of the slide. This catch blocks the firing pin and uncocks the hammer. The total length of this pistol is 165 mm (6½ in) and it has a barrel length of 85 mm (3½ in). The weapon weighs 735 g (26 oz). The magazine capacity in 9 mm Short (.380 ACP) caliber is 7 cartridges; in 7.65 mm (.32 ACP) caliber, it has a capacity of 8 cartridges and in .22 LR of 10 cartridges. The slide catch is on the left of the frame, at the top of the grips. The magazine catch is to the left behind the trigger guard. In the USA the pistol is sold under the name, Astra Constable. The version with a 152 mm (6 in) barrel, micrometer sights and exclusively made in .22 LR caliber is the Constable Sport.

Astra Falcon of 1956

Astra Cadix .22 LR revolver

Illustration from the original instruction manual of the Astra Constable

1972: ASTRA MODEL 357

This is the large version of the Cadix revolver in .357 Magnum caliber. This double-action weapon has a so-called transfer bar safety. The revolver was made with barrel lengths of 76 mm (3 in), 102 mm (4 in), 152 mm (6 in) and 216 mm (8½ in). Another version followed in 1976 with a barrel that was 216 mm (8½ in) long. There is also the Astra 357 Police with a barrel that is 102 mm (4 in) long and with an interchangeable cylinder for 9 mm Para, made in 1986. A stainless steel model, introduced in 1981 was the Astra 357 Inox. The Astra 357 Model 960 is a single-action match revolver in .38 Special caliber with a 152 mm (6 in) barrel and micrometer sights. All Astra 357 models have a coiled hammer spring around a hammer conductor rod. This spring is locked in the grips with a bar in a rotating ring. There are four different positions in this ring so that it is possible to change the pressure of the spring and therefore the trigger pressure.

1974: ASTRA MODEL 44

This is a variation of the Astra 357 in .44 Magnum caliber. This double-action revolver has an adjustable rear sight. The same models in different calibers are the following: Astra 41, for .41 Magnum and Astra 45 for the version in .45 Long Colt. Astra manufactured these revolvers until 1987.

1976: ASTRA MODEL TS-22

This single-action match pistol was only made in .22 LR caliber. The 10-shot weapon has a barrel that is 150 mm (6 in) and a total length of 235 mm (9¼ in). The weapon weighs 1000 g (35.3 oz). There is a high rib on the slide which also contains the micrometer sight. The magazine catch is on the left side of the frame, behind the trigger guard. The safety catch is mounted on the left side of the frame. The pistol has attractive walnut grip plates. The left plate has a protruding thumb rest.

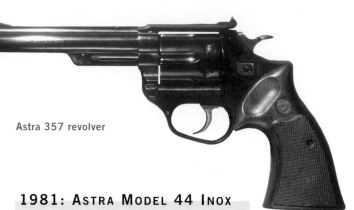

Astra 357 revolver

1981: ASTRA MODEL 44 INOX

This completely stainless steel revolver in .44 Magnum caliber was specially designed for the American market in 1981. The 6-shot cylinder has recessed chambers and the edges of the cartridge cases engage in these. The weapon has a transfer rod. The coiled hammer spring can be pre-cocked in four different positions by means of a rotating ring, so that the trigger pressure can be modified. The weapon has an adjustable rear sight. The Astra Inox is also made in .357 Magnum caliber (the 357 Inox) and .38 Special caliber (the Astra Inox 680).

1981: ASTRA MODEL A-80

The A-80 pistol is very similar to the Sig-Sauer pistol family in appearance. When it was introduced in the USA, an American armory magazine even suggested that the A-80 was a copy of the Sig P-220. However, there are great technical differences internally, such as the locking cam under the chamber block. The Astra A-80 pistol is made entirely of steel and is available in three calibers: 9 mm Para, .38 Super and .45 ACP. The double-action weapon does not have a safety catch. The trigger mechanism can be uncocked by the uncocking lever on the left above the grip plates. In addition, the pistol has an automatic firing pin safety. The magazine catch is at the bottom (the heel) of the grip. In the A-80 the extractor also serves as a cartridge indicator. If there is a cartridge in the chamber of the barrel, a red dot shows on the extractor.

The big Astra 44 revolver in .44 Magnum

Astra TS-22 match pistol

1982: ASTRA MODEL 44 TERMINATOR

This is an Astra 44 revolver with a 70 mm (2¼ in) or a 76 mm (3 in) barrel. This weapon has a coiled spring as a hammer spring which can be cocked in four positions to adjust the trigger pressure. In addition, it has an adjustable rear sight. The weapon is also available in .45 Long Colt caliber.

1985: ASTRA MODEL A-90

This is a modified version of the A-80 designed as an army pistol. For this model, the magazine catch is moved to the left of the frame, behind the trigger guard. The weapon has an improved double-action trigger mechanism. In addition, it has a firing pin in two parts. When the uncocking lever is used, the last part of the firing pin is pushed out of reach of the hammer. In addition, the front part of the firing pin is blocked by the automatic firing pin safety. The pistol is made in 9 mm Para, .38 Super and .45 ACP calibers.

The safety systems in the Astra A-90 are rather excessive. In addition to the uncocking lever, the two-part firing pin and the automatic firing pin safety, the A-90 also has a safety catch on either side of the slide. When this safety catch is pressed down, only the back part of the firing pin swivels out of reach of the hammer. The Astra A-90 has a total length of 180 mm (7 in), a barrel length of 97 mm (3¾ in) and a weight of 985 g (34¾ oz) in 9 mm Para or .38 Super calibers and 955 g (33¾ oz) in .45 ACP caliber. The magazine capacity is 15 cartridges in 9 mm Para or .38 Super caliber and 9 cartridges in .45 ACP caliber.

Astra A-90 pistol

1987: ASTRA MODEL A-60

This is a new version of the Model 5000 or Constable, exclusively made in 9 mm Short (.380 ACP) caliber. The pistol has an ambidextrous combined safety catch/uncocking lever on the slide. In addition, it has a double row magazine for 13 cartridges.

1990: ASTRA MODEL NEW POLICE 357

In 1990, Astra also introduced the new revolver model, Astra-Police. This is a modified version of the Astra Police, made in 1972 in .357 Magnum caliber. The weapon has a 76 mm (3 in) barrel and no adjustable sights. One interesting detail of this weapon is that it can also shoot 9 mm Para pistol cartridges in special clips. The old Astra Police had an interchangeable cylinder for 9 mm Para cartridges.

1991: ASTRA MODEL A-70

This is a compact 8-shot version of the pistol in single-action, exclusively available in 9 mm Para caliber. Astra developed this type for plain clothes government personnel. The pistol has a safety catch on the left of the frame. The locking system of the A-70 is of the Browning-Sig type. A guide lug is attached below the chamber block of the barrel. The top of the chamber block fits into the ejection port of the slide and is the actual locking system. The slide catch is on the left of the frame at the top of the grips. It looks like a uncocking lever, though it is not one. The magazine catch is to the left, behind the trigger guard. This short weapon never became very popular. The total length is 166 cm (6½ in) and it has a barrel length of 89 mm (3½ in). The weapon weighs 830 g (29¼ oz).

Astra A-70

Astra A-75

Astra A-75 with light
alloy casing

1992: ASTRA MODEL A-75 FIREFOX

Astra introduced the compact A-75 Firefox at the 1992 German IWA arms exhibition. It is actually an A-70 with a double-action trigger mechanism, also in the 9 mm Para caliber with a magazine capacity of 8 rounds. Apart from this, the measurements are identical to those of the A-70. However, the A-70 had a safety catch on the left side of the frame. The A-75 looks as though it has the same catch. However, this serves as a combined safety catch/uncocking lever. The Firefox is made entirely of steel and weighs 880 g (31 oz). A version in a light metal frame, the A-75 L(ight) Firefox was introduced in 1994. This weapon is identical to the A-75 in every other respect, only the weight is less, viz., 760 g (26¼ oz).

Apart from this, the pistol has an automatic firing pin safety, a halfcock safety on the hammer foot and black synthetic grips.

1993: ASTRA MODEL A-100

In 1993, the new Astra 100 pistol was introduced at the international arms fair in the German city of Nuremberg. Astra had already lost the battle for replacing army and police pistols in tests in a number of countries.

Astra A-100

This pistol was designed to increase the market share in the sector for commercial pistols. The Astra 100 was given the imaginative name 'Panther' in. The double-action pistol comes in 9 mm Para, .40 Smith & Wesson and .45 ACP calibers. The magazine capacity is 15 rounds in the 9 mm Para caliber, 12 rounds in the .40 S&W caliber and 9 rounds in the .45 ACP caliber. Astra has now managed to gain access to the domestic market with this pistol and sells the A-100 to the Spanish police. The pistol is fitted with a uncocking lever.

Because of the uncocking lever and the firing pin safety, the pistol can be carried with a cartridge in the chamber. Other versions of the model A-100 are the A-100 Duo Panther with a nickel-plated frame and a blued slide. In addition, there is the A-100 Panther Inox in stainless steel. The Astra A-100

Astra A-100
Light with light
alloy casing

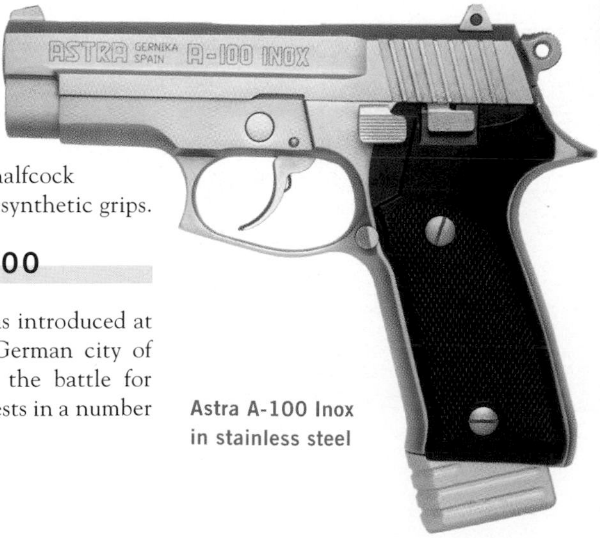

Astra A-100 Inox
in stainless steel

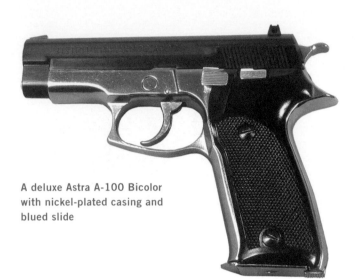

A deluxe Astra A-100 Bicolor with nickel-plated casing and blued slide

Thompson 1911-A1 DuoTone with mat nickel-plated casing and blued slide

models have a total length of 180 mm (7 in) and a barrel length of 97 mm (3¾ in). The weight depends on the model. The standard version of the A-100 and the A-100 Duo Panther weigh 985 g (34¾ oz), the A-100 Inox Panther weighs slightly more, viz., 995 g (35 oz). In addition, there is the A-100 L(ight) with a light metal frame, which weighs approximately 865 g (30½ oz).

AUTO-ORDNANCE CORPORATION

The original American firm, Auto-Ordnance Corporation, was established in 1919 for the production of the world famous submachine gun, the 'Tommy Gun'. Brigadier General John T. Thompson designed this weapon at the end of the First World War. The Auto-Ordnance Corporation introduced the weapon in 1919, as Model 1921. The submachine-gun became very well-known as the weapon used by gangsters during prohibition in America. In 1928, the American government bought a series of the modified model 1928 for the marines and the Coast Guard. There was a great demand for the Tommy Gun during the Second World War. Auto-Ordnance could not keep up

with the demand, and the Colt company took over the majority of production. At that time, Colt manufactured approximately 15,000 Thompson submachine-guns for the US army. In 1940, the British commissioned an enormous order for the modified model M1928-A1. Auto-Ordnance sought the help of Savage Arms for production. Later models, such as the M1 and the M1A1, also formed part of this British contract. Savage made more than 1.5 million of these weapons altogether. The first models of the Tommy Guns used the Blish locking system. This system consists of two steel bolts which slide alongside each other so that the return of the bolt is delayed.

The Blish system was rejected by the American government, and therefore Auto-Ordnance used the recoil locking system. The Tommy Gun was succeeded at the end of 1942 by the US-M3 submachine-gun known as the 'Grease Gun'. The M3 could be mass produced at a much lower cost. The current Auto-Ordnance Corporation is part of the Gun Parts Corporation and is established in West Hurley, New York. The Thompson machine pistol is still made in various different versions for the army and police. Auto-Ordnance manufactures the Thompson in a semi-automatic version for the civilian market. Various models of pistols based on the Colt M1911-A1 pistol are also produced under the Thompson brand name.

THOMPSON ZG-51 PIT BULL

In 1989, the corporation introduced a compact version of this as the ZG-51 or 'Pitbull'. This single-action pistol in .45 ACP caliber has a total length of 184 mm (7¼ in) and a barrel length of 89 mm (3½ in) instead of the standard 127mm (5 in). The magazine capacity is 7 rounds. The pistol has a safety catch and a slide catch on the left of the frame. In addition, it also has the typical grip safety of all Colt 1911-A1 models. The magazine catch is also on the left, behind the trigger guard.

TRADE MARK

Thompson.

REG. U.S. PAT. OFF.

Logo of Auto-Ordnance Corporation

Thompson ZG-51 'Pit Bull'
in .45 ACP caliber

Thompson Competition
with compensator

Thompson 'Pit Bull' viewed
from the other side

THOMPSON COMPETITION

The single-action Thompson Competition was introduced in 1993 at the international IWA arms fair in Nuremberg in Germany. The .45 ACP pistol has a 3-chamber compensator, a Commander hammer and enlarged operating catches. In addition, it has a special Videcki Speed trigger, a larger magazine well and an extended beavertail. The total length, including the compensator, is 256 mm (10 in). The barrel length is 130 mm (5 in). The weapon weighs 1255 g (44¼ oz) and has a magazine capacity of 7 rounds.

THOMPSON WORLD WAR II

The Thompson World War II is an exact copy of the old single-action Colt 1911-A1 dating from the Second World War, and therefore has a .45 ACP caliber. The pistol even has the characteristic dull anodized protective coat. The old name 'Model 1911A1 U.S. Army' is also engraved on the left of the slide. The weapon has a total length of 216 mm (8½ in) with

a barrel length of 127mm (5 in). The weight is 1110 g (39 oz) and the magazine capacity is 7 rounds.

THOMPSON GENERAL

The single-action Thompson General is the same size as the Colt Commander, i.e., it is a compact pistol. The weapon is available in .45 ACP or .38 Super Auto caliber. The total length is 197 mm (7¾ in), with a barrel length of 114 mm (4½ in), and it weighs 1050 g (37 oz). The General has a safety catch on the left of the frame. The magazine catch is standard on the left behind the trigger guard. The weapon has the characteristic grip safety, as well as a halfcock safety on the hammer foot.

In addition, Auto-Ordnance produces an extensive range of parts for pistols of the 1911-A1 model such as different types of beavertails, sights, compensators, longer magazine well, enlarged ejectors, safety and magazine catches, etc.

Thompson World War II
'GI' pistol

Thompson General

B

BAIKAL/IZHEVSKY MEKHANICHESKY ZAVOD

The Russian state arsenal of Izhevsk was founded in 1807 as an ammunition factory. The Izhevsky Mekhanichesky Zavod arms factory dates from 1885. The government at the time commissioned arms factories in Tula, Izhevsk and Sestroretsk to manufacture civilian weapons as well as military weapons. The Revolution in 1917 was a turbulent time for the arms manufacturers. The Red Army demanded the stocks of weapons from the Russian Tsarist army, but there was a great shortage of weapons and ammunition. During the period 1880 to 1920, the arms factories in Izhevsk produced altogether almost 1,300,000 rifles, 15,000 machine guns and 175,000 Nagant revolvers. In addition, they made millions of cartridges of different calibers for these weapons. During the Second World War the production capacity was devoted to military equipment. In 1949, the Izhevsky Mekhanichesky Zavod factory again started to make sports guns and shotguns. The double-barreled shotgun, Izh-49, was based on the Sauer Model 9. In 1954, Baikal introduced the Izh-54 double-barreled shotgun, designed by the engineers, Leonid Pugachyev and Anatoly Klimov. The most popular Baikal shotgun appeared on the market in 1973. This was the Izh-27 designed by Sergei Khuzyakhmetov. Baikal guns are also identified with the letter IJ. For example the IJ-27. Nowadays, the firm manufactures a series of shotguns and combination guns under the name Izh, better known in the West under the brand name Baikal. In fact, Baikal has produced the well-known Makarov pistol for more than 50 years. An entirely new series of pistols with a modified Browning locking system was developed on the basis of this old model .

NAGANT REVOLVER MODEL 1895

This revolver was designed by the Belgian designer, Nagant. The first batch of revolvers made for the Russian army was manufactured in Liege in 1895. Subsequently, production was taken over by different Russian state factories from 1896 to approximately 1933. The weapon has a special gas sealing system. When the hammer is cocked, the cylinder moves forwards against the back of the barrel. The cartridges are 1.7 mm (0.067 in) longer than the cylinder and protrude slightly at the front. This means that the front of the cartridge slides in the transitional cone of the barrel. This system results in a good gas seal, so that the space between the cylinder and the barrel is virtually entirely sealed. As the cylinder moves forwards before firing, the hammer has an extra long firing pin so that it can still easily reach the cartridges. Originally, soldiers were equipped with a Nagant revolver in single-action. The double-action version was issued to officers. This weapon was used until after the Second World War. The 7-shot Nagant revolver has a 7.62 mm Nagant caliber. The total length is 235 mm (9¼ in), the barrel length is 114 mm (4½ in) and the weapon weighs 770 g (27¼ oz). For safety, the hammer is blocked when the loading port is open.

The Russian Nagant service revolver model 1895

Logo of Russian Baikal

TOKAREV PISTOL

The Tokarev pistol was introduced by the Russian army as a service pistol in 1930. The weapon was designed by Feodor Tokarev. The model is rather similar to a Browning or Colt pistol. However, one of the big differences is that the firing mechanism is located in one block and can be removed from the weapon for maintenance. In addition, the magazine

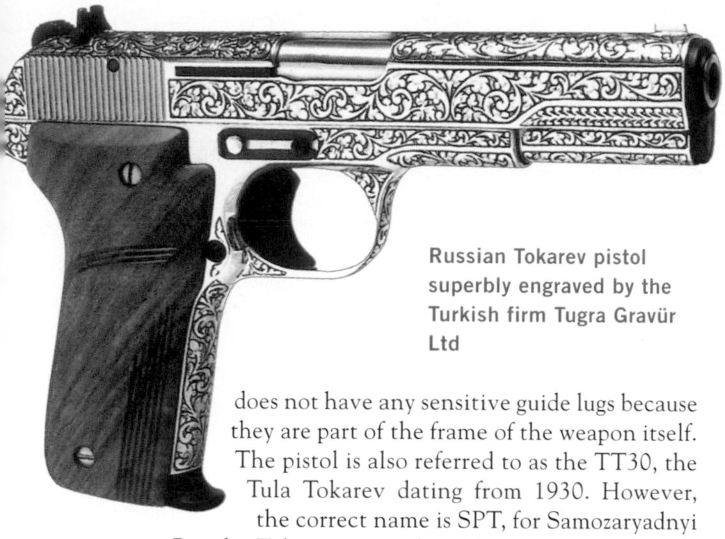

Russian Tokarev pistol superbly engraved by the Turkish firm Tugra Gravür Ltd

does not have any sensitive guide lugs because they are part of the frame of the weapon itself. The pistol is also referred to as the TT30, the Tula Tokarev dating from 1930. However, the correct name is SPT, for Samozaryadnyi Pistolet Tokareva, i.e., the Tokarev autoloader. The single-action weapon has a total length of 196 mm (7¾ in) and a barrel length of 116 mm (4½ in). The magazine capacity is 8 rounds in 7.63 Tokarev caliber. The weight is 830 g (29¼ oz). The TT33 is a version of the Tokarev. In the TT30, the bolt cams are fitted on the barrel. On the T33 they are replaced by bands which go right round. This modification was introduced partly to facilitate the manufacturing process. The pistol was used by the army until long after the Second World War. The Tokarev pistol illustrated here is beautifully engraved by the Turkish firm Tugra Gravur Ltd in Istanbul.

BAIKAL IZH-34M RAPID FIRE PISTOL

Baikal manufactured this autoloader in .22 Short caliber for the Olympic rapid shooting discipline. The total length of the single-action match weapon is 300 mm (11¾ in). It is 150 mm (6 in) high and the width is 50 mm (2 in). The sight radius, i.e., the distance between the rear sight and the front sight, is 235 mm (9¼ in). The weapon has a barrel length of 146 mm (5¾ in) and a large match stock with an adjustable hand rest. The pistol weighs 1260 g (44½ oz). The trigger is not only completely adjustable, but can also be moved or tipped depending on the shooter's requirements. In

addition, the pistol has a micrometer sight. According to international rules, the capacity of the magazine is 5 rounds.

BAIKAL IZH-35M MATCH PISTOL

Baikal match pistol IZH35M in .22 LR caliber

This single-action pistol in .22 LR caliber was specially designed for sports shooting. This weapon also has a completely adjustable trigger, like the model IZH-34M. The adjustable trigger pressure ranges from 1 to 25 Newton. Even the pressure point of the trigger can be adjusted between 1 and 2.5 mm (0.04 and 0.10 in). The pistol has a walnut match stock with an adjustable hand rest. It has a magazine capacity of 5 or 10 rounds. The measurements of the IZH-35M pistol is the same as that of the 34M weapon, viz., 300 x 150 x 50 mm (11¾ x 6 x 2 in). The IZH-35 weighs 1400 g (49½ oz). In addition, it has a 153 mm (6 in) barrel and a completely adjustable micrometer sight. One of the special features of this weapon is that it has a built-in automatic firing pin safety.

BAIKAL IZH-70 MAKAROV

This is a double-action pistol based on the original Makarov. The autoloader has a recoil locking system which is quite unusual for a pistol, for example, with a 9 mm Para caliber. The Makarov in the original 9 mm Makarov caliber (9 x 18 mm) was introduced as

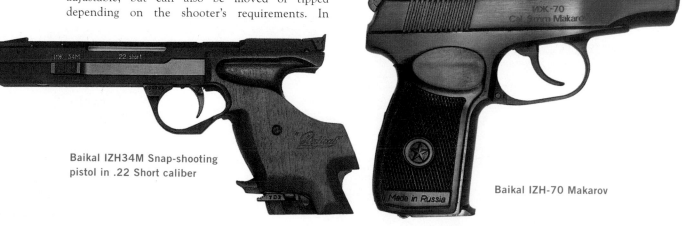

Baikal IZH34M Snap-shooting pistol in .22 Short caliber

Baikal IZH-70 Makarov

the service weapon for the Russian army in about 1961. In the following years, it was gradually used by the other Warsaw Pact countries. Baikal manufactures it in three different models and in 9 mm Para (8-shot) caliber, 9 mm Makarov caliber (12-shot) and 9 mm Short (.380 ACP) caliber (12-shot). All the models are available with fixed or adjustable sights. The safety catch is on the left of the frame. As in the real Makarov, the safety catch is in the heel of the grip. The 8-shot model in 9 mm Para caliber has a total length of 161 mm (6¼ in) with a barrel length of 93.5 mm (3¾ in). The height of the pistol is 127 mm (5 in) and it is 30.5 mm (1¼ in) wide. This model weighs 730 g (25¾ oz). The 12-shot model in 9 mm Makarov and 9 mm Short (.380 ACP) calibers has a total length of 165 mm (6½ in). It is also 127 mm (5 in) high, but it is 34 mm (1¼ in) wide. The 12-shot model is slightly heavier, viz., 760 g (26¾ oz). The barrel length is also the same as the 9 mm Para model.

BAIKAL PSM/IZH-75 COMPACT

This is a semi-automatic double-action pistol in the Russian pistol caliber 5.45 x 18 mm. The PSM pistol and the cartridge were designed in 1972. The abbreviation PSM stands for Pistolet Samozaryadniy Magolabaritniy. Freely translated this means: compact autoloader. The weapon was mainly used by the Russian security services. The pistol has a light metal frame and a steel slide. Furthermore, the frame has an enclosing synthetic grip. The original model had a magazine catch in the heel of the grip. In 1993, the PSM was modified and this ambidextrous magazine catch was placed behind the trigger guard. It has a magazine capacity of 8 cartridges. In addition, the weapon has an ambidextrous safety catch, which also serves as a uncocking lever for the hammer. The total length is 155 mm (6 in) and the height is 109 mm (4¼ in). In addition, it has a barrel length of 85 mm (3¼ in) and weighs only 460 g (16¼ oz). The 5.45 x 18 mm cartridge has a bottle-necked cartridge case. The initial velocity of the 40-grain bullet is 315 m/s (1035 fps). The kinetic energy (E0) is 130 Joules.

BAIKAL MCM MARGOLIN

The famous MCM Margolin pistol

This single-action training pistol is made in .22 LR caliber. The weapon has a steel frame and slide. The sights are the most special feature of this pistol. The large rear sight can only be adjusted on the side. The height of the front sight is adjustable. In addition, the weapon has a simple but extremely effective adjustable trigger stop at the bottom of the trigger guard. The synthetic grip plate on the left also has a thumb rest. The magazine catch is at the bottom of the grip. The total length of the Margolin is 245 mm (9½ in) with a barrel length of 152 mm (6 in). The pistol has a height of 140 mm (5½ in). The original magazine capacity was 7 rounds, but a 10-round magazine is also available. The weapon weighs 900 g (31¼ oz).

BAIKAL MCM-K MARGO

This is a single-action training pistol based on the MCM Margolin model. it has a total length of 190 mm (7½ in) and a barrel length of 98 mm (3⅞ in). The Margo weighs 800 g (28¼ oz). The original magazine capacity was 7 rounds, but a 10-round magazine is also available. In addition, it has a fixed rear sight. The left grip plate has a rib which serves as a thumb rest. The magazine catch is at the bottom of the grip. The pistol does not have a safety catch but it does have an automatic firing pin safety. Baikal also makes an MCM Margo type with an adjustable rear sight.

The compact PSM or IZH-75 pistol in Russian 5.45 mm caliber

Baikal MCM-K Margo pistol based on the Margolin

Baikal MP-442

The Baikal Model MP-442 is the export version of the Makarov pistol and succeeded the Baikal IZH-70. The double-action weapon is made in two different versions. The standard version has a 9 mm Makarov (9 x 18 mm) caliber, and an 8-round magazine. This pistol has a total length of 161 mm (6¼ in), a height of 127 mm (5 in) and a width of 30.5 mm (1¼ in). It weighs 730 g (25¼ oz). It has synthetic grip plates with a five-pointed star. The second version

Baikal MP-442 as successor to the IZH-70 pistol

has a magazine capacity of 10 rounds in the 9 mm Makarov caliber, or even a capacity of 12 rounds with an extended magazine. In addition, the pistol was also manufactured in 9 mm Para caliber with a content of 8 cartridges. The length and height of the weapon are the same as in the first version, but the width is 34 mm (1¼ in). This type weighs 780 g (27½ oz). The MP-442 is also available with a micrometer sight. All the versions have a combined safety catch/uncocking lever on the left of the slide. This catch uncocks the hammer and blocks the firing pin and the slide. The slide catch is also on the left of the frame. The older model has a magazine catch in the heel of the grip. Since 2000, this catch has been just under the slide catch.

Baikal MP-443 Grach

Baikal's designer Yarygin designed this pistol in 1999 at the request of the Russian army. The double-action weapon in 9 mm Para caliber has a steel frame and slide.

There is an ambidextrous safety catch on the frame. This blocks the sear, the trigger, the hammer and also the slide. The magazine catch behind the trigger guard can be moved for a left-handed shooter. For extra safety, the extractor also serves as a cartridge indicator. The pistol has a total length of 190 mm (7½ in) and a barrel which is 114 mm (4½ in) long. The height of the Grach is 140 mm (5½ in) and its width is 38 mm (1½ in). The double-action and single-action trigger pressure are respectively 58.9 and 24.5 Newton. The weapon has a capacity of 17 rounds and an empty weight of 1000 g (35¼ oz). In addition, it has a rear sight which can be adjusted for four fixed distances from 25 to 100 meters.

Baikal MP-444 Baghiira

MP 444 Baghira of 2000

This new model was introduced by Baikal in 2000. The weapon in 9 mm Para caliber has a polymer frame and a steel slide. It is a double-action pistol with an ambidextrous safety catch on the slide. This catch blocks the sear and also uncocks the hammer. The magazine catch can be moved for a left-handed shooter and the extractor also serves as a cartridge indicator. The locking system is of the Browning-Petter type. The barrel chamber block bolts in the ejector port in the slide. The Baghiira has a total length of 186 mm (7¼ in). The barrel length is 101 mm (4 in). The height of the weapon is 126 mm (5 in) and the width is 35 mm (1½ in). The empty weight is 760 g (26¾ oz) and the magazine capacity is 16 rounds. There is a triple aspect sight on the slide: two white dots on the fixed rear sight and one white dot on the back of the front sight. There

The new Russian MP-443 Grach service pistol

The left-hand side of the Baghira

is a rib at the front of the frame, in front of the trigger guard, for attaching extra equipment such as a light or a laser. Baikal also produces the pistol as the MP-444K in 9 mm Short (.380 ACP) and 9 mm Makarov (9 x 18 mm) calibers. Both models have a capacity of 15 rounds. The measurements of the MP-444K are the same as those of the Baghiira in 9 mm Para caliber.

MP446-Viking of 2000

BAIKAL MP-445 VARYAG

The modern MP-445 Varyag pistol introduced in 2000

Baikal marketed this new model in 2000. It has a polymer frame and a steel slide. This double-action pistol has an ambidextrous safety catch on the frame which also uncocks the hammer. In addition, the safety catch blocks the sear, the trigger and the slide. The small magazine catch behind the trigger guard is also ambidextrous. The MP-445 Varyag comes in .40 S&W (15 cartridges) and 9 mm Para (17 cartridges) caliber. The weapon has a total length of 210 mm (8¼ in) and the barrel length is 125 mm (5 in). The height and width are respectively 142 mm (5½ in) and 38 mm (1½ in). The weapon weighs 900 g (31¾ oz). The trigger pressure is 24.5 Newton in single-action and 57 Newton in double-action. Baikal also produces a compact type, the Varyag MP-445SWC in .40 S&W (13 cartridges) caliber and the MP-445 C in 9 mm Para caliber (15 cartridges). This compact version has a total length of 188 mm (7½ in), the height is 132 mm (5¼ in) and the width is 38 mm (1½ in). The compact version weighs 880 g (31 oz). The rear sight of the different Varyag versions is completely adjustable. There is a groove on either side of the front of the frame in front of the trigger guard to attach a light or laser equipment.

BAIKAL MP-446 VIKING

The third model introduced in 2000 is the MP-446 Viking. This double-action pistol also has a polymer frame and a steel slide. The safety catch on the frame is ambidextrous and blocks the sear, the trigger and the slide. The magazine catch on the left behind the trigger guard can be moved to the right. The extractor also serves as a cartridge indicator. The pistol has a 9 mm Para caliber and a capacity for 7 cartridges. This weapon has a total length of 190 mm (7½ in) with a barrel length of 114 mm (4½ in). The height is 140 mm (5½ in) and the width is 38 mm (1½ in). The Viking weighs 900 g (31¾ oz). The single and double-action trigger pressure are respectively 24.5 and 57 Newton. In addition, the weapon has a combat rear sight with an adjustable height and width.

BAIKAL MP-448 SKYPH MINI/MP-448C SKYPH MINI

The Baikal MP-448 Skyph dates from 2001. It is a 10-shot double action pistol in 9 mm Short (.380 ACP) caliber. The weapon is based on the Makarov, but has a frame made of synthetic material. The total length is 165 mm (6½ in). The height is 127 mm (5 in) and the width is 32 mm (1¼ in). The weapon weighs 640 g (22½ oz). It has a combined safety catch/uncocking lever on the left of the slide. The ambidextrous magazine catch is behind the trigger guard and the slide catch is on the left on the frame. There is a small switch just above the trigger. This is the

Baikal MP448 Skyph pistol with plastic casing

The compact MP-448C
Skyph Mini

takedown lever. Model MO-448 C Skyph Mini is a compact version of the Skyph. This pistol has the same characteristics as the larger model. The total length of the Skyph Mini is 145 mm (5¾ in). The height is 107 mm (4¼ in). The width is also 32 mm (1¼ in) and the weight is 590 g (20¾ oz). The magazine capacity of the Mini is 8 rounds in 9 mm Short (.380 ACP) caliber.

BENELLI

The Benelli firm is located in the Italian town of Urbino. Filippo and Giovanni Benelli established the company at the beginning the twentieth century. In the past, the factory was mainly known for its mopeds, but it also produced machines and tools. Since 1920, Benelli has made hunting weapons on a small scale. In 1967, the company started to focus on manufacturing firearms. The name of the company changed to Benelli Armi. It is mainly known for its extensive series of semi-automatic shotguns. From the technical point of view, the M-3 Super 90 is very interesting. This shotgun can be very simply converted from a semi-automatic to a pump-action firearm. To do this you merely turn an adjustment ring on the front of the stock through 180 degrees. In addition to shotguns for hunting and shooting, Benelli also produced a series of compact riot guns for government services. In 1975, a subsidiary company was established in Vitoria in Spain, where a significant proportion of the Spanish arms industry is concentrated. The barrels for the Benelli guns are produced by arms factories in France (St. Etienne) and in Italy itself (Brescia). In 1983, a proportion of the Benelli shares were taken over by Beretta.

MODEL B-76

In 1980, Benelli marketed a new 8-shot 9 mm Para double-action pistol. Benelli described this weapon in its publicity as a robust army and police pistol with the precision of a sports pistol. Nevertheless, the Benelli B-76 was not very popular with the government services in a number of countries because the pistol did not comply with the requirements imposed at the technical level. This was particularly because of the absence of a uncocking lever and an automatic firing pin safety, qualities which were already fashionable at the time. The most interesting feature of the weapon is the fact that the barrel is screwed into a sub-frame mounted on the frame. The locking system uses a bolt block connecting the slide and the sub-frame. One of the big advantages of this pistol is that parts which come into contact with powder gases are chrome-plated. Furthermore, the firing pin is made of stainless steel. The pistol was made in a number of calibers: 9 mm Para, 7.65 Luger (.32 Luger), 7.65 mm (.32 ACP), .32 S&W – Long and in 9 mm Ultra (9 x 18 mm). The total length of the B-76 is 205 mm (8 in) with a barrel length of 108 mm (4¼ in). The height of the weapon is 139 mm (5½ in) and it weighs 970 g (34¼ oz). In addition, it has attractive walnut grip plates. The magazine catch is on the left of the frame, behind the trigger guard. The safety catch which blocks the hammer, is also on the left on the frame. The pistol also has a halfcock safety on the foot of the hammer.

Benelli trade mark

Benelli B-76 of 1980

Benelli B-80 double action
pistol

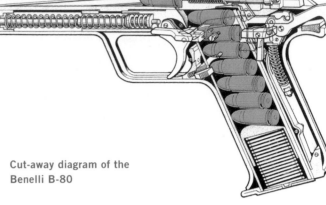

Cut-away diagram of the
Benelli B-80

Benelli B-80S sporting
pistol

MODEL B-80

The double-action model B-80 appeared in 1982 as an improved version of model B-76. The 8-shot B-80 was produced in 7.65 mm (.32 ACP) caliber or 7.65 mm Para caliber. Like the B-76, the barrel length of the standard model was 108 mm (4¼ in). The pistol never sold particularly well. This was mainly because of the calibers. As a pistol in 7.65 mm (.32 ACP), it was much too large compared with the compact models sold by competitors. In the special 7.65 Para caliber, it was only really used in Italy, where 9 mm Para pistols are prohibited for civilian use.

MODEL B-80S

This double-action sports model based on the B-80 was first made in 1983 in 9 mm Para, 9 x 18 mm (Ultra) and 7.65 mm Para caliber. The pistol has a total length of 205 mm (8 in) and a barrel length of 140 mm (5½ in). The weight is 930 g (32¾ oz). The slide is extended with a block where the front sight is attached. The weapon has an adjustable rear sight. The safety

catch is on the left of the frame. The magazine catch is also on the left, behind the trigger guard. The extractor also serves as a cartridge indicator, and the hammer has a halfcock safety. The attractive walnut grip plates have recessed finger grooves.

MODEL MP3-S

This pistol was introduced in 1984. It is a sports version of the Benelli B-76 and B-80. In this weapon the barrel is also screwed into a sub-frame, and this sub-frame is fixed to the frame. The unusual locking system uses a loose bolt, which ensures that the slide and the sub-frame are connected at the moment of firing. The MP3-S has a single-action trigger action and was available in 9 mm Para and .32 S&W Long calibers and has a magazine capacity of 6 rounds. In addition, there

Benelli MP3-S with
a standard match
stock

is an interchangeable set to convert the 9 mm Para into the .32 S&W- Long caliber. The special Target model has an elongated barrel with an extra barrel weight on which the front sight is mounted. In addition, it has a trigger stop which is adjustable with a bushing bolt at the back of the trigger guard. The total length of the MP3-S is 237 mm (9¼ in) and the barrel length is 143 mm (5½ in). The weapon is 142 mm (5½ in) high. It weighs 1175 g (41½ oz). It has a safety catch on the left of the frame, and the extractor also serves as a cartridge indicator. This pistol has not been made by Benelli since 1990.

MODEL MP90-S

Benelli tried to capture a market share in the sporting pistol market with this pistol. It was introduced at the IWA in 1990 and is available in .22 LR, .32 S&W Long calibers and as a rapid-fire pistol in .22 Short caliber. There are no conversion sets available to convert from one caliber to another. The magazine is in front of the trigger. The trigger mechanism can be removed as a unit and can then be easily adjusted. The length and the angle of the trigger are adjustable. Both the trigger pressure and the trigger creep are completely adjustable. In addition, a simple synthetic block can be placed in the pistol for dry training. This means that the firing pin is protected against excessive wear. An extra barrel weight of 65

g (2¼ oz) has been placed in the frame under the barrel and the shooter can add an extra lead weight to this. The pistol has anatomical walnut grip plates, with an adjustable hand rest. The barrel is made of chrome-nickel steel. The weapon is 300 mm (11¾ in) long. The barrel length is 110 mm (4¼ in) and the weight is 1110 g (39 oz). The MP-90S has an ambidextrous safety catch on the frame, above the grip. The magazine catch is on the front of the magazine housing.

MODEL MP-95E

Benelli introduced this match pistol in 1993. It is available in .22 LR or .32 S&W Wadcutter calibers. In both calibers, the pistol has a barrel length of 110 mm (4¼ in). The total length is 300 mm (11⅞ in) and the height is 132 mm (5¼ in). The empty weight is approximately 1000g (35¼ oz). The weapon has completely adjustable match sights. The trigger group can be removed from the weapon. For the 9-shot model in .22 LR caliber, the trigger pressure is adjusted to exactly 1000 g (2.2 lb). For the 5-shot model in .32 S&W, this is 1360 g (3 lb). Both adjustments are in accordance with international match rules. The weapon has an ambidextrous safety catch on the frame. The magazine catch is in the front of the magazine housing. The MP-95E is available in a blued finish as the 'Nera' or with a mat chrome finish as the 'Kromo'.

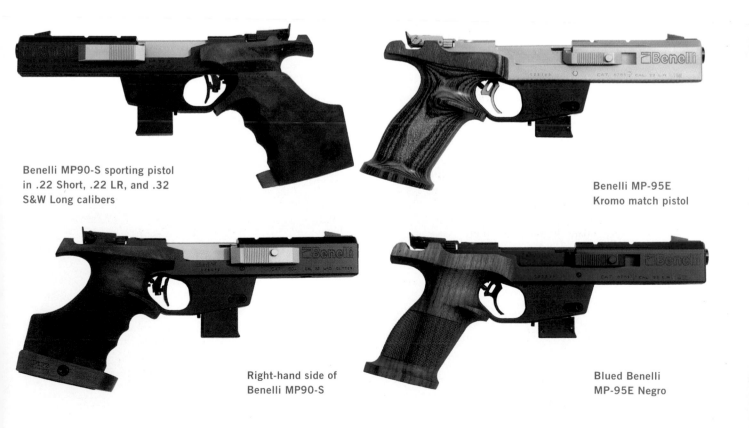

Benelli MP90-S sporting pistol in .22 Short, .22 LR, and .32 S&W Long calibers

Benelli MP-95E Kromo match pistol

Right-hand side of Benelli MP90-S

Blued Benelli MP-95E Negro

BERETTA

Weapons have been made in the region of Brescia in Northern Italy since Roman times. Up to the fourteenth century, swords, spears, daggers and knives were made there. Ancient documents reveal that iron cannon were already being made there in about 1350. In the fifteenth century, light weapons were made in Brescia such as the arquebus with a matchlock. In this context, the name Beretta first appears in 1526. In that year Bartolomeo Beretta delivered an order of barrels for arquebuses to the arsenal in Venice. The modern firm Pietro Beretta was officially established in 1680. In those days it manufactured hunting and military weapons, identified with the factory mark 'PB'. In the eighteenth and nineteenth centuries, Beretta made weapons for a number of European kingdoms and principalities. One example of this concerns the deliveries of weapons to the king of Naples in 1720. Beretta made large numbers of military guns during the Napoleonic era from 1750 to 1815.

The firm has always been a family business since it was established and every generation has made its own specific contribution. For example, Pietro Antonio Beretta (1791–1853) traveled throughout Italy to promote his weapons. His son Giuseppe (1840–1903) was mainly concerned with selling arms abroad. His son, Pietro (1870–1957), mechanized the whole production process of weapons. In the First World War, the Italian government commissioned Beretta to develop a pistol for the Italian army. This was the Beretta Model 1915. During the Second World War, the production was moved to a mountain close by for reasons of security. Large areas were excavated. These catacombs are now used as a shooting range. Both of Pietro's sons continued expanding the business. Giuseppe Beretta was the first Italian arms manufacturer to introduce computer-aided machines. The other son, Carlo Beretta turned the Italian business into a real multinational. In about 1970, Beretta established an arms factory in Brazil. This was later take over by the Brazilian firm Taurus. In addition, there are subsidiaries in France, Greece and the USA. Beretta also has large shops selling arms in New York, Dallas and Buenos Aires.

Beretta became best known for its prestigious contract with the USA. The Americans had been looking for a new army pistol since 1945 to replace the old Colt 1911-A1. Smith & Wesson had produced a prototype for this which was extensively tested. However, this plan was postponed in 1953. A second attempt was made in 1977. A detailed list of all the weapons being used revealed that actually about 25 different handguns of all sorts of models and calibers were in use. This meant that the American Ministry of Defense (the Pentagon) had to stock about 100 different sorts of ammunition. The army, Coast Guard and Navy mainly used the standard Colt 1911-A1 pistol. The air force had various models of .38 Special revolvers. Specialized units had introduced their own choices in the course of time. The JSSAP (Joint Service Small Arms Program) was set up to standardize these weapons. This was a research program in which all the army units were represented. The JSSAP soon became convinced that the caliber should coincide with the NATO standard, viz., 9 mm Parabellum. The USAF carried out a number of comparative tests in the period 1978–1980. In 1980, as a result of these tests, the JSSAP recommended opting for the Italian Beretta M92S-1 pistol in 9 mm Para caliber. However, the Ministry of Defense was not impressed. They thought that other army units had not had enough say in the matter. In addition they considered that the tests which had been carried out were not sufficiently scientific. The Pentagon wanted to carry out its own broadly based testing program to test as many 9 mm Para pistols as possible. A set of requirements was formulated for this purpose in June 1981, the JSOR (Joint Service Operational Requirement), in which the pistol to be selected was referred to as PDW-XM9 (PDW: Personal Defense Weapon). The list of technical requirements consisted of about 50 prescribed characteristics with which the pistols had to comply, the AQRs (Absolute Quantitative Requirements). The race for this weapon started at the end of 1981. The participants were Beretta, Heckler & Koch, Sig-Sauer and Smith & Wesson. The testing program was suddenly broken off

Beretta's trade mark

Beretta 92 FS Inox

Sig-Sauer P226, Beretta's
competitor in the US Army trials

The first to drop out was the Steyr GB pistol. FN withdrew its tender itself, followed by Colt. For technical reasons, the Walther P88, the HK P7-M13 and the S&W M459 also disappeared from the scene. This left two pistols, the Sig-Sauer P226 and the Beretta M92SB-F. Both firms submitted a tender for the delivery of 305,580 pistols, to be delivered over a period of five years. Sig-Suaer's offer was for US $ 176.33 per pistol, while Beretta's was for US$ 178.50. In the end, Beretta got the contract because the final total price, including spare parts, was about US$ 3 million lower than the Sig-Sauer price. The Beretta M92 SB-F was made the official service pistol for the joint US forces and was named the M9. Later on the contract was slightly increased to a total of 320,030 pistols. This had several consequences. The American arms manufacturers particularly could not tolerate the fact that a foreign pistol was being bought. In addition, Smith & Wesson, Heckler & Koch, and Sig-Sauer submitted a complaint, although this was rejected. Smith & Wesson went one step further and started a lawsuit against the US Defense Department. They claimed that incorrect test procedures had been used. This complaint was also rejected. However, Smith & Wesson did not leave it at that. After lengthy lobbying in the American Congress, they managed to arrange a new testing program. It was decided that this should be carried out in June 1988. The Beretta contract would be honored, but a new test project, known as XM-10, would be carried out. This was for an order of a second series of 142,292 pistols. The new contenders were Beretta, Sig-Sauer, Ruger (the P-85 pistol) and Smith & Wesson.

However, they did not achieve their aim. On 24 May 1989, the Pentagon declared that Beretta had again won the competition and also had the contract for the second series of pistols. Nevertheless, the US Congress still objected to a foreign pistol. In order to meet these objections, a separate firm, Beretta USA was established in Accokeek, Maryland. In 1995, the

in February 1982 because none of the tested pistols were able to comply with the formulated requirements (AQRs). A new list of specifications was issued in 1982, in which the technical requirements were less stringent. In November 1983, an official visit was made to all the arms manufacturers to make weapons available for testing. Interested manufacturers had to make 30 test pistols available to the research team free of charge.

- Eight firms presented test weapons, viz:
- Beretta with the M92SB-F pistol;
- Colt, with a new SSP pistol (Stainless Steel Pistol);
- FN with a newly developed double-action pistol;
- Heckler & Koch with their P7-M13 pistol;
- Sig-Sauer with the P226;
- Smith & Wesson with Model 459;
- Steyr with the GB pistol
- Walther with the P88.

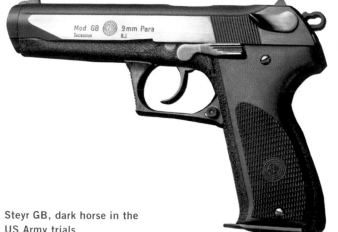

Steyr GB, dark horse in the
US Army trials

The Ruger P-85 pistol took part
in the re-examination trials in
1988

1931: Beretta Model 1931

The single-action Beretta 1931 was based on the 1915 model in 7.65 mm (.32 ACP) caliber with a magazine capacity of 8 rounds. It had an external hammer and the characteristic rotating safety catch of the 1915 model. It was mainly made for the Italian navy. These pistols were marked with an anchor with the letters RM: Regia Marina. However, the weapon was also sold to the civilian market. The length of the pistol was 150 mm (6 in) with a barrel length of 85 mm (3¼ in) and it weighed 560 g (19¼ oz).

Advertisement from an old Beretta catalogue of model 1931

1934: Beretta Model 1931/34

This was a version of model 1931 in 9 mm Short (.380 ACP) caliber with a magazine capacity of 7 rounds. Most pistols were made for the Italian armed forces. These single-action weapons have a number of different identifying marks: 'PS' for the police (Publica Sicurezza), 'RA' for the air force (Regia Aeronautica), 'RE' for the army (Regia Esercito) and 'RM' for the navy (Regia Marina). The total length was 150 mm (6 in) and the barrel length was 88 mm (3½ in). The weapon weighed 750 g (26.45 oz). The safety catch was on the

left of the frame as in previous models. The magazine catch is in the heel of the grip.

1935: Beretta Model 1935

This was a 7.65 mm (.32 ACP) version of the 1934 model. The weapon was produced in large numbers for the Italian Air Force (marked RA) and navy, (marked: RM). The measurements of this weapon are the same as those of the 1934 model, but it has a magazine capacity of 8 rounds. After the Second World War, this pistol was also made for the civilian market up to about 1948 as model 935.

1935: Beretta Model 318

Model 318 was an improved version of the 1919 model, also in 6.35 mm (.25 ACP) caliber. In fact, the only change was that the design of the frame was slightly streamlined. The pistol was made until 1946. It was mainly exported to the USA, where it was called the Panther.

1947: Beretta Model 418

This is a modified version of model 318 and was produced up to 1968. In the United States it was sold under the model names Puma or Bantam. A number of versions also had other model numbers. The chrome version was called Model 420, and a gilt 418 was called Model 421.

1948: Beretta Model 948

This pistol also became known as the Featherweight or Plinker. It was a 10-shot small caliber version of the 1934 model in .22 LR caliber with a barrel length of 152 mm (6 in). The total length was 214 mm (8½ in). The weapon weighed 820 g (29 oz).

Beretta model 1934

Old factory drawings of the Beretta Olimpico

Beretta Model 950
Jetfire Inox

1949: BERETTA MODEL 949 OR OLIMPICO

This weapon was based on the old 1915 model in .22 Short caliber with a magazine capacity of 6 rounds. The rapid-fire pistol had a barrel 220 mm (8¼ in) long with a compensator, interchangeable barrel weights and micrometer sights. The total length was 318 mm (12½ in) and the weapon weighed 1070 g (37¼ oz). The characteristic Beretta rotating safety catch was on the left of the frame above the trigger guard. The magazine was simply in the grip and not, as is to be expected, in the space in front of the trigger guard.

1950: BERETTA MODEL 950

In the USA, this model was sold under the model name Minx. It was made in .22 LR and .22 Short calibers (Model 950B) and in 6.35 mm (.25 ACP) caliber as Model 950 Jetfire. The single-action

model 950 is still made in 6.35 mm (.25 ACP) caliber in a blued finish, and since 1998 also in stainless steel. It has a magazine capacity of 8 rounds. It has a total length of 120 mm (4¾ in) and the barrel length is 60 mm (2½ in). The weapon weighs only 280 g (10 oz). The safety catch which blocks the hammer and the trigger is at the back on the left of the frame. The rotating takedown lever is above the trigger guard. When this is rotated forwards, the barrel can be hinged up for maintenance. The magazine catch is on the left in the bottom part of the grips.

1957: BERETTA MODEL M 1951 OR BRIGADIER

This model is very similar to the later Beretta 92 models. It has the familiar falling block lock-up. This single-action 9 mm Para pistol was designed at the request of the Italian army. It was produced by Beretta with a steel and a light metal frame. It has a magazine

Beretta Model 950
Jetfire

Workshop drawings of the
Beretta 951 Brigadier

capacity of 8 rounds. The total length is 203 mm (8 in) with a barrel length of 115 mm (4¼ in). The weapon weighs 875 g (30¾ oz) when it has a steel frame and 712 g (25 oz) when it has a light metal frame. The safety catch is in the form of a switch on both grips. It has to be moved from left to right for the weapon to be in the safe position. Obviously it must be moved the other way in order to fire. The magazine catch is at the bottom of the left grip. The weapon was also used by the Egyptian and Israeli armed forces. Some related models of the M 1951, also known as the 951, were produced in small numbers. Model 951R was a fully automatic pistol, while the 952 was made in 7.65 mm Para caliber.

1958: BERETTA MODEL 70

The Beretta 70 was intended to replace model 948. The single-action pistol was made in several different calibers. Model 70S existed in .22 LR (10-shot), 7.65 mm (.32 ACP) (7-shot), and 9 mm Short (.380 ACP) caliber with a magazine capacity of 6 rounds. This weapon had a total length of 160 mm (6¼ in) and a barrel length of 85 mm (3¼ in). The pistol had an empty weight of 660 g (23¼ oz). Model 70T was a match version in .22 LR caliber with a 152 mm (6 in) barrel and a total length of 225 mm (8¾ in). Another version was Model 71, which was only produced in .22 LR caliber. It had a light metal frame, a total length of 165 mm (6½ in) and a barrel length of 89 mm (3½ in). Model 72, also available in .22 LR caliber, was sold in the USA as the Beretta Jaguar. This weapon was delivered with a barrel 102 mm (4 in) or 152 mm (6 in) long. The Jaguar had the safety switch of the 951 Brigadier. Other versions, such as Models 73, 74 and 75 also had a .22 LR caliber, but had different barrel lengths.

Beretta Model 70 superbly engraved by Turkish firm Tugra Gravür Ltd

1975: BERETTA MODEL 76

This is a single-action match pistol with a closed slide which was intended to succeed model 70T. There was a barrel rib on the slide. The micrometer sight was attached to the back of this. This 10-shot pistol was only available in .22 LR caliber. The weapon had a total length of 241 mm (9½ in) and a barrel length of 152 mm (6 in). Model 76 weighed 990g (35 oz). The safety catch was on the left of the frame. The position of the magazine catch was based on the model 951 Brigadier and was on the left grip plate. Beretta produced this model until 1990, when it was succeeded by model 89.

Beretta 76 match pistol in .22 LR caliber

1976: BERETTA MODEL 83/84/85/86/87

Beretta introduced the Cheetah in 1976. With the exception of model 87 Cheetah, it has a double-action trigger action. The series consists of the following models:

• **Model 83 Cheetah** in 9 mm Short (.380 ACP) caliber with a 7-round magazine capacity, a total length of 177 mm (7 in) and a barrel length of 102 mm (4 in). The weapon weighs 640 g (22½ oz);

• **model 84 Cheetah** Model 84 Cheetah in 9 mm Short (.380 ACP) caliber, with a double-row 13-round magazine. The pistol has a total length of 172 mm (6¾ in), a barrel that is 97 mm (3¾ in) long and it weighs 660 g (23¼ oz);

Beretta 84

• **Model 85 Cheetah**, also in 9 mm Short (.380 ACP) caliber with an 8-round magazine capacity. The total length is 172 mm (6¾ in), the barrel is 97 mm (3¾ in) long and the weapon weighs 620 g (22 oz);

• **Model 86 Cheetah** in 9 mm Short (.380 ACP) caliber, with an 8-round magazine. The total length is 186 mm (7¼ in) with a barrel length of 111 mm (4½ in). The weapon weighs 660 g (23¼ oz). The 86 Cheetah is slightly different from the other Cheetahs because it has a tip-up barrel which hinges forwards;

• **Model 87 Cheetah** in .22 LR caliber with a magazine capacity of 8 rounds. This pistol is actually a small caliber version of the 84 or 85, but has a single-action trigger action. The total length is 172 mm (6¾ in) and it has a barrel length of 97 mm (3¾ in). It weighs 570 g (21 oz). The Cheetah models have a traditional safety catch on the left of the frame. Inn addition they have an automatic firing pin safety. The magazine catch behind the trigger guard can be moved for left handed shooters.

Beretta 84 FS Cheetah

1976: BERETTA MODEL 92

This pistol is an improved version of model 951 Brigadier and forms the basis for all the other 92 models which have been developed since then. It has a falling-block locking based on the well-known Walther P38 pistol. It is a double-action weapon, with an automatic firing pin safety. The extractor also serves as a cartridge indicator. The original double-action 92 dating from 1976 was introduced in 9 mm Para caliber with a magazine capacity of 15 rounds. The safety catch is on the left at the back of the frame. The weapon has a total length of 217 mm (8½ in), a barrel length of 125 mm (5 in) and a weight of 950 g (33½ oz). At the time, this pistol cost US $365.00.

1977: BERETTA MODEL 92 S

This is a version of model 92 with a combined safety catch/uncocking lever on the left of the slide. When it is used, this catch pushes the firing pin out of reach of the hammer, decocks the hammer and breaks the connection between the trigger and the sear. For the rest, the measurements are the same as those of the older model 92.

1979: BERETTA MODEL 92 SB

This model was developed in 1979 for the US Army tests, which took place from 1979 to 1980. At the request of the JSSAP (Joint Service Small Arms Program) this type has an ambidextrous combined safety catch/uncocking lever on the slide. Furthermore, the magazine catch is moved to the heel of the grips on the left of the frame, behind the trigger guard. The weapon also had a firing pin safety. The measurements are the same as those of the older model 92. Although the Beretta 92 SB won the competition set by the army, the Americans insisted on a number of modifications.

This modified version became model 92 F, and eventually model 92 FS in 1992.

1985: BERETTA 92 F

After concluding the weapon tests of the US Army, the JSSAP wished to carry out a few modifications on the Beretta 92 SB. These included an angular trigger guard and a slightly rounded front of the grip. In addition, they wanted a modification to the base plate of the magazine, a different grip and a different lanyard ring. The pistol has a combined ambidextrous safety catch/uncocking lever on the slide. It has a two-part firing pin of which the back half is pushed out of reach of the hammer. In addition, the inside of the barrel is chrome coated and the pistol was given a Teflon protective layer known as Bruniton. This new version of the pistol was called the Beretta 92 F and was used by the US Army in 1985 as Pistol 9 mm M9. In 1990, this model was succeeded by the 92FS.

Beretta 96

1986: BERETTA MODEL 98

This was originally a model 92 in 7.65 mm Para caliber with a 13-round magazine. The total length of the double-action pistol was 197 mm (7¾ in) with a barrel length of 109 mm (4¼ in). The weapon weighed 885 g (31¼ oz). At the time there was also a version with a smaller grip referred to as model 99. This had a single row magazine for 8 rounds in the same caliber. Both versions were made until 1989 after which the caliber was changed to 9 x 21 mm IMI. The name of the model remained the same. The present model 98 has a magazine capacity of 15 rounds. The total length is 217 mm (8½ in) with a barrel length of 125 mm (5 in) and a weight of 975 g (34½ oz).

1987: BERETTA MODEL 92 G

This model in 9 mm Para caliber was specially developed in 1987 for the French police, the Gendarmerie Nationale. The French Air Force introduced it as its service pistol in 1992. The catch on the slide serves only as a uncocking lever and therefore does not place the pistol on safe. The weapon does have an automatic firing pin safety. The measurements of this service pistol are the same as those of the other standard 92 models. In 1995, the 92G was given the reinforced slide of the Brigadier. The term 'Elite' was then added to the name of this model.

1988: BERETTA MODEL 21 OR BOBCAT

The Bobcat is based on model 950. The most characteristic differences are the shape of the trigger and the double-action trigger action. Model 21 is still made in .22 LR caliber with a 7-round magazine capacity and in 6.35 mm (.25 ACP) caliber for 8

Beretta 21 Bobcat in Deluxe EL version

Stainless steel Beretta 21 Bobcat Inox

rounds. Since 1999, the pistol has also been available in a stainless steel version as model 21 Bobcat Inox. The weapon has a total length of 125 mm (5 in) and a barrel length of 61 mm (2½ in). The weight of the .22 LR version is 335 g (11¾ oz) and in 6.35 mm (.25 ACP) caliber it weighs 325g (11½ oz). The Bobcat has a safety catch on the left of the frame. The takedown lever is above the trigger guard. This can hinge the barrel up at the front for maintenance. The magazine catch is in the left grip.

1990: BERETTA 92 FS

Model 92 FS was introduced in 1990 to succeed the 92F. In some American M9 army pistols, small tears had been discovered in the slide after a period of time. This meant that the slide could separate from the frame when the pistol was fired. A few minor modifications were made to improve this. The hammer axis and the guide rails in the slide were extended. In this way, the slide is blocked during the repeat action by the extended hammer axis, at the end of moving back. FS models also have an automatic firing pin safety, a divided firing pin and an ambidextrous safety catch/uncocking lever. The FS modification is available for models 92 and 92 Inox in 9 mm Para caliber, as 98 FS and 98FS Inox, in 9 x 21 mm caliber as 92 Brigadier FS and Brigadier FS Inox, 92 FS Centurion, and finally as model 98 Brigadier FS.

1990: BERETTA MODEL 89

In 1990, Beretta introduced this new match pistol in .22 LR caliber. The weapon has a light metal frame, a total length of 240 mm (9½ in) and a barrel length of 152 mm (6 in). The weight is 1160 g (41 oz). The sight radius is 185 mm (7¼ in). The steel slide has a special Bruniton coating. The single-action pistol

Beretta 89 match
pistol

Beretta Model 96 D in
DAO (double-action-only)

has a safety catch on the left of the frame. The magazine catch is also on the left, behind the trigger guard. It comes with a walnut target grip with a thumb rest and as the Gold Standard with a match stock with an adjustable hand-rest. This pistol was in production for almost ten years and was succeeded in 2000 by the model 87 Target.

1992: BERETTA 92 CENTURION

This is a compact double-action version. The total length is shortened by 20 mm (⅞ in) to 197 mm (7¾ in). The barrel length is shortened to 109 mm (4¼ in). The magazine capacity in 9 mm Para caliber is the same as that of larger models because it has the same frame. It weighs 940 g (33¼ oz). In .40 S&W caliber this weapon has the model name 96 Centurion.

1992: BERETTA 92 D

The letter 'D' in refers to a double-action-only (DAO) version. This type does not have any external safety mechanisms but does have an automatic firing pin safety. Since 1992, Beretta has

produced a DAO version of 92D in 9 mm Para caliber (15 cartridges) and the 96D in .40 S&W caliber (11 cartridges). The total length of this pistol is 217 mm (8½ in) and the barrel length is 125 mm (5 in). The height and width are respectively 137 mm (5½ in) and 36 mm (1½ in). In both calibers, it weighs 960 g (33¾ oz).

1994: BERETTA 92 BRIGADIER

The double-action model 92 Brigadier was introduced in 1994. The pistol has a reinforced slide and the rear sight and front sight are interchangeable. The total length is 217 mm (8½ in). The barrel length is 125 mm (5 in), and the height and width are respectively 140 mm (5½ in) and 38 mm (1½ in). The empty weight is 1000 g (35¼ oz). In 1999, Beretta made a small number of modifications to the Brigadier model. The 92 Brigadier has a magazine capacity of 15 rounds in 9 mm Para caliber. The same pistol in .40 S&W caliber is the model 96 Brigadier. In 9 x 21 mm (IMI) caliber it has the name model 98 Brigadier. It is also available in a blued finish, and since 2000 in stainless steel as model 92 or 96 Brigadier Inox.

Beretta Model 96
Centurion

Beretta Model 96
Brigadier

Beretta Model 96
Brigadier Inox

Beretta 96 Inox

1992: BERETTA MODEL 96

This is a model 92 pistol in .40 S&W (Smith & Wesson) caliber. This weapon in the Brigadier version with a reinforced slide was selected in 1994 as the service weapon for the US Immigration and Naturalization Service. Model 96 is available in a stainless steel version as the 96 Inox. In addition, there is a compact model, the 96 Compact with a barrel that is 109 mm (4¼ in) long. In stainless steel the weapon is model 96 Compact Inox. In addition, the 96 is also available in double-action-only as the Beretta 96 D.

1994: BERETTA 92 STOCK

In 1994 Beretta marketed the so-called Stock version for the basic models 92, 96 and 98. This double-action Stock version has a special barrel bushing for improved shooting precision, as well as the reinforced slide of the Brigadier. In addition, the weapon does not have a y lever, but does have a standard safety catch on the left of the frame. The hammer foot also has a halfcock safety. The measurements are the same as those of the large models.

Cut-away drawing of
Beretta Cougar

1994: BERETTA MODEL COUGAR 8000/8040/8045/8357

In this model 8000-Cougar Beretta moved away from the traditional falling block locking. The Cougar has a so-called rotation locking. Where the Colt All American failed miserably, Beretta was very successful with this compact model. The Cougar is available in many versions and calibers.

The Cougar D is produced in a double-action-only (DAO) version. The weapon does not have a safety catch or y lever, but does have an automatic firing pin safety. The extractor also serves as

Beretta Cougar type
D, without external
safety

Beretta 98 Stock

a cartridge indicator. The catch above the trigger guard is the slide catch. The rotating takedown lever is in front of this. The magazine catch to the left behind the trigger guard can be moved to the right for left-handed shooters. The pistol is available in 9 mm Para caliber as model 8000 Cougar D with a magazine capacity of 15 rounds. The measurements of this type are: total length, 180 mm (7 in), barrel length 92 mm (3½ in), weight 910 g (32 oz). In the .40 S&W caliber the model is known as the 8040 Cougar D. It has a magazine capacity of 11 rounds. This model has the measurements: total length, 180 mm (7 in), barrel length, 92 mm (3½ in), weight, 905 g (32 oz). The 8045 Cougar D has a .45 ACP caliber and a magazine capacity of 8 rounds. The pistol has a total length of 183 mm (7¼ in), the barrel length is 94 mm (3¾ in) and it has a weight of 905 g (32 oz).

Beretta Cougar
F Inox

Beretta Cougar F

The Cougar F is also a double-action model. The pistol has an ambidextrous combined safety catch/y lever on the slide, a two-part firing pin and a firing pin safety. In addition, a red dot appears on the extractor when there is a cartridge in the chamber. This model in 9 mm Para or 9 x 21 mm caliber is known as the 8000 Cougar F and has a magazine capacity of 15 rounds. The pistol has a total length of 180 mm (7 in), a barrel length of 92 mm (3½ in) and a weight of 925 g (32½ oz). The 8000 Cougar F is available in a blued and in a stainless steel version. In .357 SIG caliber (11 rounds), it is the 8357 Cougar F model. The measurements of the blued weapon in this caliber are the same as those of the 8000 Cougar F, except that it is slightly lighter, viz., 920 g (32½ oz).

The 11-round Cougar 8040 F has a .40 S&W caliber and is made in a blued or stainless steel version. This model has the following measurements:

total length 180 mm (7 in), barrel length 92 mm (3½ in) and a weight of 920 g (32½ oz). The same weapon in .45 ACP caliber is the model 8045 Cougar F and has a capacity of 8 rounds. It is only made in a blued version and has slightly different measurements from the other caliber models. The total length is 183 mm (7¼ in), the barrel length is 94 mm (3¾ in) and the weight is 905 g (32 oz).

Model 8000 Cougar L is only available in a blued version in 9 mm Para or 9 x 21 mm caliber. It does have the same slide as the other Cougars, but the frame has been reduced from the standard height of 140 mm (5½ in) to 126 mm (5 in). Therefore the magazine capacity is 13 rounds. In addition to the weight of 800 g (28¼ oz), it has the same measurements as the other Cougar models.

Beretta 8000
Cougar L

Beretta 3032 Tomcat
in blued finish

Beretta 3032
Tomcat Inox

1995: BERETTA MODEL 3032 TOMCAT

The 3032 Tomcat is based on model 950 and the later model 21. Compared to the older models, this double-action pistol has a modified trigger guard and a rear sight, which can be moved to the side. The weapon was initially made in .22 LR or 7.65 mm (.32 ACP) calibers. However, since 1999, it has only been available in 7.65 mm (.32 ACP) caliber with a magazine capacity of 7 rounds. The pistol has a safety catch on the left of the frame. This blocks both the hammer and the trigger. The takedown lever which hinges the barrel up is above the trigger guard. The magazine catch is in the left grip. In a stainless steel version, this model is known as the 3032 Tomcat Inox.

Since 2000, Beretta has also made the 3032 Tomcat Titanium. This model has a titanium frame and a stainless steel barrel and slide. The 3032 Tomcat has a total length of 125 mm (5 in) and a barrel length of 61 mm (2½ in). The weight of the blued and stainless steel version is 410 g (14½ oz). The titanium version is considerably heavier, viz., 480 g (17 oz).

1997: BERETTA 92 COMBAT COMBO

In 1997 Beretta introduced the Combat Combo version for IPSC shooting events. The pistol has a single-action trigger action and is available in 9 mm Para caliber (92 Combat), 9 x 21 mm caliber (98 Combat) and .40 S&W caliber (96 Combat). The magazine capacity is 15 rounds in 9 mm and 11 rounds in .40 S&W caliber. The total length is 242 mm (9½ in) with a barrel length of 150 mm (6 in). The weight is 1135 g (40 oz). The weapon comes with a shorter interchangeable barrel of 125 mm (5 in).

Beretta 3032 Tomcat with
titanium coating

Beretta Model 96 Combat
Combo with exchange barrel

Beretta Model 92 Short Combat
with special barrel tube, raised
bead, and micrometer sight

The Combat Combo has micrometer sights and
a special barrel bushing for extra shooting precision.
The pistol has an ambidextrous and extended safety
catch. The trigger action is factory tuned and has an
adjustable trigger stop.

1998: BERETTA MODEL MINI COUGAR 8000/8040/8045

The Mini Cougar has approximately the same length
as the large Cougars. However, the frame is
significantly shorter so that the weapon is even more
compact. The normal Cougar has a height of 140 mm
(5½ in) and in the Mini Cougar this is 115 mm (4½
in). Obviously, this also reduces the magazine capacity.

Like the large Cougar F, the Mini Cougar F model
has an ambidextrous combined safety catch/y lever on
the slide, a two-part firing pin and a firing pin safety. In
addition, the extractor also serves as a cartridge
indicator. Like the 8000 Mini Cougar F, this pistol is
available in 9 mm Para or 9 x 21 mm calibers. The
standard version has a magazine capacity of 10 rounds.
However, a longer magazine is also available with
a capacity of 15 rounds. This means that the height

of the weapon is the same as the large Cougar, viz.,
140 mm (5½ in). The 8000 Mini Cougar F has the
following measurements: total length 179 mm (7 in),
barrel length, 92 mm (3½ in), weight, 785 g (27½ oz).
This model is made both in a blued finish and in
stainless steel. The 8040 Mini Cougar F has a .40
S&W caliber with a magazine capacity of 8 rounds or
a longer magazine for 11 rounds. The measurements are
the same as those of the 8000 Mini Cougar F, except
that the weight is 780 g (27½ oz). In .45 ACP caliber,
the name of this model is 8045 Mini Cougar F. The
magazine capacity is 6 rounds, or with the extended
magazine, 8 rounds. The measurements of this model
are: total length, 182 mm (7 in), barrel length 94 mm
(3¾ in), weight 865 g (30½ oz).

Beretta Mini
Cougar Type D

Model Mini Cougar D has a double-action-only
(DAO) trigger action and no safety catch or
uncocking lever, but it does have an automatic firing
pin safety. The extractor also serves as a cartridge
indicator. This model has the same model names as
the other Mini Cougar pistols. The measurements are
also the same as those of the other Mini Cougars,
except that the weights are slightly different. The
8000 Mini Cougar D has a 9 mm Para caliber with
a 10-round or 15-round magazine and weighs 770
g (27 oz). The 8040 Mini Cougar D in .40
S&W caliber has a magazine capacity of 8 or
11 rounds. The weapon weighs 765 g (27 oz).
The 8045 Mini Cougar D in .45 ACP caliber
has a capacity of 6 or 8 rounds, depending on
the length of the magazine. The weight of this
version is 850 g (30 oz).

1998: BERETTA 92 COMPACT

This is the shortened version of models 92 and
96, which Beretta introduced on the market in
1998. The total length is 197 mm (7¾ in) and

Beretta Mini
Cougar F Inox

the barrel length is 109 mm (4¼ in) instead of the standard length of 125 mm (5 in). The magazine capacity is the same as that of the large models, viz., 15 rounds in 9 mm Para caliber and 11 rounds in .40 S&W caliber.

1998: BERETTA 92 COMPACT L

The Compact L is virtually the same as the compact version, but has a shorter frame. The height of the weapon is not 140 mm (5½ in), but 135 mm (5¼ in). This means that the magazine capacity is also reduced by two rounds to 13 rounds in 9 mm Para caliber. This model is not available in other calibers, though it is available in stainless steel as the Compact L Inox.

Beretta 92 CLTM-Inox

1998: BERETTA 92 COMPACT L, TYPE M

The Compact L type M is virtually the same as the compact L, but with a single row magazine. This means that the magazine capacity is reduced. For example, Model 92 (9 mm Para caliber) has a magazine capacity of 15 rounds. The Compact L has

Beretta 92 Compact L, type M

a capacity of 13 rounds and the compact L type M of only 8 rounds. The advantages are a thinner grip and smaller total weight. The total length is 197 mm (7¾ in), the barrel length is 109 mm (4¼ in), and the weapon weighs 875 g (31 oz). This type is only available in 9 mm Para caliber in a blued finish or as an Inox in stainless steel.

Beretta 87 Target

1999: BERETTA MODEL 87 TARGET

The Beretta 87 Target is the successor to model 89. This .22 LR match pistol is similar to the normal model 87 internally. However, the external appearance is more like the above-mentioned Beretta 89. The single-action 87 Target has a magazine capacity of 10 rounds. The total length of the weapon is 225 mm (8¾ in), the barrel length is 150 mm (6 in) and the weight is 835 g (29½ oz). The safety catch is on the left of the frame and blocks the external hammer and the trigger. The slide catch is above the trigger guard. The magazine catch is on the left behind the trigger guard. The barrel is enclosed in a light metal shroud, and the barrel and the barrel rib are also mounted on this. The barrel shroud has an extra sharp corner at the front. This means that the weapon can be placed vertically on a flat surface. In addition to a micrometer sight, the barrel shroud also has a Weaver rail for the sights.

2000: BERETTA 92 G ELITE

The original model 92 G was developed by Beretta in 1993 at the request of the French Gendarmerie, and later also for government services of other countries. The slide has the same design at that of the Brigadier and interchangeable telescopic sights. The barrel is made of stainless steel. In addition, the magazine well is angled for rapidly changing the magazine. The weapon only has an uncocking lever on the slide, but this does not operate as a safety catch. The firing pin does have an automatic safety. In 2000, Beretta marketed the G Elite. This is available in 9 mm Para caliber (92 G Elite) and in .40 S&W caliber (96 G Elite). The pistol has a total length of 211 mm (8¼ in) and a barrel length

**Beretta 87 match pistol
with Pro-Point**

Beretta 92 G Elite

of 119 mm (4¾ in). The magazine capacity is
15 rounds in 9 mm Para caliber and 11 rounds in
.40 S&W caliber. As the magazines have a rubber
protective cover, the height is greater, viz., 150 mm
(6 in). The weapon weighs 985 g (34¾ oz).

2000: BERETTA MODEL 9000 S

Beretta introduced this completely new design in
2000. The weapon has an ergonomically designed
high-tech polymer frame reinforced with fiberglass.
There are steel rails in this synthetic frame. Angular
lugs on either side of the chamber block of the barrel
engage in these. Therefore the locking system is not
that of the Browning-Petter type, in which the
barrel block engages in the ejection port.

In the Beretta 9000 it is actually the angular
base of the barrel block which engages in the frame.

**The new Beretta
9000 S**

After the shot, the barrel and the slide move back
together. The guide lug under the barrel block slides
down so that the barrel also comes down. The lugs
then disengage from the rails in the frame so that the
slide goes back on its own. The 9000 S is available
as a double-action pistol as model 9000 S type F and
with a double-action-only (DAO) trigger action as
model 9000 S type D. The measurements of these
two models are the same in different calibers. The
total length is 168 mm (6½ in) with a barrel length
of 88 mm (3½ in).

Model 9000 S, type F, with a double-action trigger
action, has an ambidextrous safety catch/uncocking
lever. This breaks the connection between the trigger
and the sear and also blocks the sear itself. In addition,
the extractor also serves as a cartridge indicator, as in
almost all Beretta pistols. The magazine catch is also
ambidextrous and is behind the trigger guard. There is
another catch above the trigger. This is the takedown
lever for taking the weapon apart. In addition, the
weapon has an automatic firing pin safety. Type F
is available in 9 mm Para or 9 x 21 mm calibers
with a magazine capacity of 12 rounds. This version
weighs 760 g (26¾ oz). It is also produced in
.40 S&W caliber with a capacity of 10 rounds
and a weight of 780 g (27½ oz). The width of type F
is 42 mm (1½ in).

**Right-hand side of
Beretta 9000 S**

Beretta 9000 S type D with external safety

Front of the Beretta 9000 S

Model 9000 S type D does not have any external safety mechanisms. It is a double-action-only (DAO) pistol and only has automatic firing pin safety. This weapon also has an ambidextrous magazine catch behind the trigger guard. The Beretta 9000 S type D is available in 9 mm Para, 9 x 21 IMI and .40 S&W calibers. In the 9 mm version, the magazine capacity is 12 rounds and the weapon weighs 730g (25¾ oz). The 10-round, .40 S&W version weighs 760 g (26¾ oz). Type D is narrower than type F, viz., 31 mm (1¼ in).

BERNARDELLI PISTOLS

Trade mark of Bernardelli

The Italian firm Bernardelli from Gardone Val Trompa in the Italian Alps dates back to 1721, when the firm was founded by the Bernardelli brothers. Following the unification of Italy in 1865, Vincenzo Bernardelli officially registered the company. Bernardelli is famous for its excellent shotguns, often with magnificent engraving and wonderful model names, such as Saturno, Hemingway and Holland. A significant proportion of the range consists of the traditional double-barreled side-by-side shotguns. Before the Second World War, the firm mainly made copies of so-called pocket pistols, e.g., of the Walther model 9. From the early 1960s, it also started manufacturing a series of small caliber pistols. During the course of its existence, Berndardelli produced the following pistols, amongst others.

BERNARDELLI MODEL 60

This model has been made since 1959 in .22 LR, 7.65 mm (.32 ACP) and 9 mm Short (.380 ACP) calibers with a magazine capacity of respectively 10, 8 and 7 rounds. The single-action weapon has a total length of 165 mm (6½ in) with a 90 mm (3½ in) barrel and a weight of 520 g (18¼ oz) or 530 g (18½ oz) in .22 LR. Model 60 has a blued finish and black synthetic grips. In addition it has fixed sights. The safety catch is on the left of the frame, behind the trigger guard. Imports were prohibited by the American Gun Control Act of 1968. Bernardelli therefore ceased the production of the model 60. The successor on the American market was the Model

Beretta 9000 S in repeat action

The old Bernardelli
model 60 of 1959

BERNARDELLI MODEL 69 SPORT

Bernardelli marketed this sports pistol in 1969.
The blued 10-round weapon in .22 LR caliber
has a total length of 228 mm (9 in) and
a barrel length of 150 mm (6 in). It weighs
1070 g (37¼ oz). In addition, it has
a micrometer rear sight. There is a broad rib on the
slide attached to a barrel weight. This barrel weight
also serves as a slide extension. The pistol has
walnut grip plates with a thumb rest. The safety
catch is behind the trigger guard. The
takedown lever is on the left of the frame
behind the grip. The model 69 Sport was
made up to 1989, and was succeeded by
model P100 and the P010 sports pistol.

USA, later renamed model P8. In Europe,
a modernized version of the old model was sold
under model name P6.

BERNARDELLI MODEL 60 SPORT

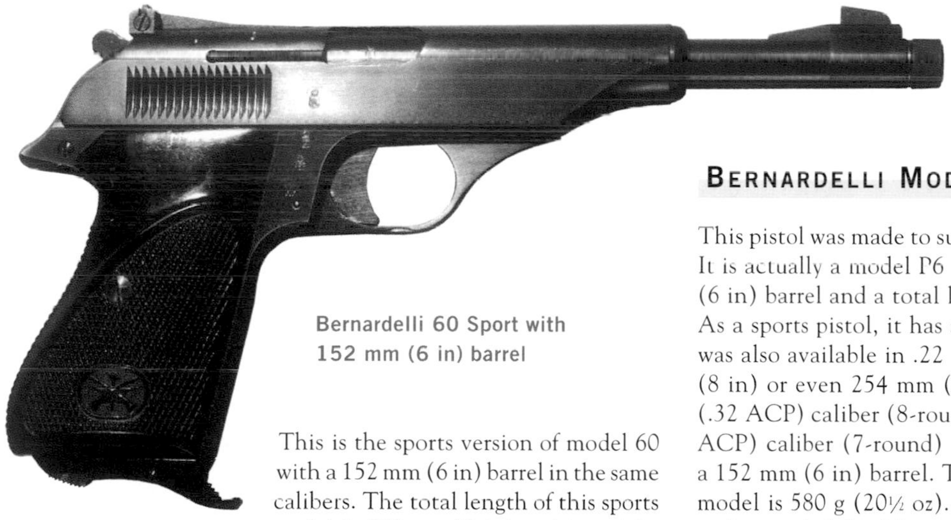

Bernardelli
Model 69
sporting pistol
of 1969

BERNARDELLI MODEL P90

This pistol was made to succeed the model 60 Sport.
It is actually a model P6 with an extended 152 mm
(6 in) barrel and a total length of 225 mm (8⅞ in).
As a sports pistol, it has an adjustable rear sight. It
was also available in .22 LR caliber with a 203 mm
(8 in) or even 254 mm (10 in) barrel. In 7.65 mm
(.32 ACP) caliber (8-round) and 9 mm Short (.380
ACP) caliber (7-round) it was only available with
a 152 mm (6 in) barrel. The weight of the standard
model is 580 g (20½ oz). It has a light metal frame
and a steel slide. There is a slide catch above the
safety catch behind the trigger guard as in the P6 and
the P8.

Bernardelli 60 Sport with
152 mm (6 in) barrel

This is the sports version of model 60
with a 152 mm (6 in) barrel in the same
calibers. The total length of this sports
model is 227mm (9 in) and it weighs
780 g (27½ oz). This type had an
adjustable rear sight, and was sold in the USA as the
Bernardelli AMR. The model 60
AMR-Silhouette was a special
version. This pistol was only
available in .22 LR caliber, had
a barrel length of 200 mm (8 in)
and a total length of 275 mm (11 in). It weighed
920 g (32½ oz).

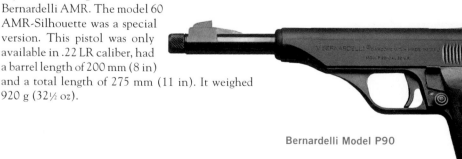

Bernardelli Model P90

Other models are the P One Sport with a micrometer sight and the P1 Compact with a barrel length of 102 mm (4 in) and a magazine capacity of 14 rounds in 9 mm, or 10 rounds in .40 S&W caliber. In addition, Bernardelli developed the P1 Police for government services. This is a compact pistol with a longer magazine for 20 cartridges in 9 mm Para caliber.

BERNARDELLI MODEL PRACTICAL VB

A new single-action sports pistol was introduced at the international IWA arms fair in 1992, the 'Practical VB' with a two or four-chamber compensator and an adjustable rear sight in calibers, 9 mm Para, .40 S&W and 9 x 21 mm IMI. This weapon has a steel frame and slide, and an enlarged safety catch on the left of the frame. In 9 mm caliber it has a magazine capacity of 16 rounds, in .40 S&W, of 12 rounds. The barrel length is 138 mm (5½ in). The Practical VB is available in various finishes: a blued or mat nickel finish, or in duotone with a nickel frame and polished slide, or vice versa. In addition, Bernardelli makes a target model and a stock model for IPSC, both without a compensator, and a so-called race model with a mount for the sight. The Practical VB Elite is a 'Formula 1' version

Bernardelli Practical VB Target version

for IPS shooting, which has a three-chamber compensator and an enlarged safety catch and magazine catch. The total length of the Practical VB is 2.65 mm (10½ in) or 2.28 mm (11 in) with a four-chamber compensator. The standard barrel length is 138 mm (5½ in). The weapon has a height of 160 mm (6¼ in), including the rubber protective cover under the magazine. The pistol weighs 1100 g (38¾ oz).

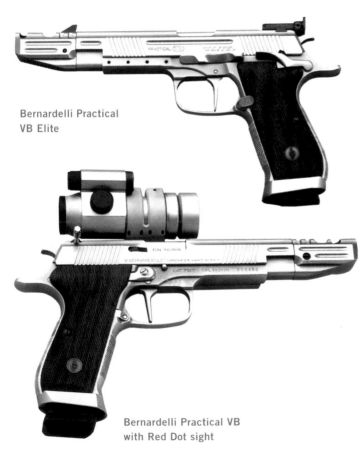

Bernardelli Practical
VB Elite

Bernardelli Practical VB
with Red Dot sight

Trade mark of
Bersa

BERSA

The Argentinean Fábrica de Armas Bersa in Ramos Mejía is not very well known in Europe, and that is the Europeans' loss. Since 1960, Bersa has concentrated mainly on the North and South American market. Bersa introduced two new pistols in 1984, model 223 in .22 LR caliber and model 383 in 9 mm Short caliber. In 1985 and 1986, Bersa introduced two more models of pistols on the market. These are models 85 and 86 in 9 mm Short caliber, which are based on the Walther PP and PPK pistols as regards their appearance. Both pistols have a magazine capacity of 13 rounds. All Bersa pistols have a double-action trigger system. Bersa presented an entirely new design at the American Shot Show in Houston, Texas in 1993. This appropriately named new pistol, the 'Thunder-9', is a modern pistol in 9 mm Para caliber. Bersa developed various new models between 1993 and 2000.

BERSA MODEL MINI THUNDER 9

Bersa introduced this 13-round double-action pistol at the American Shot Show in 1998. As the name of the model indicates, the weapon is made in 9 mm Para

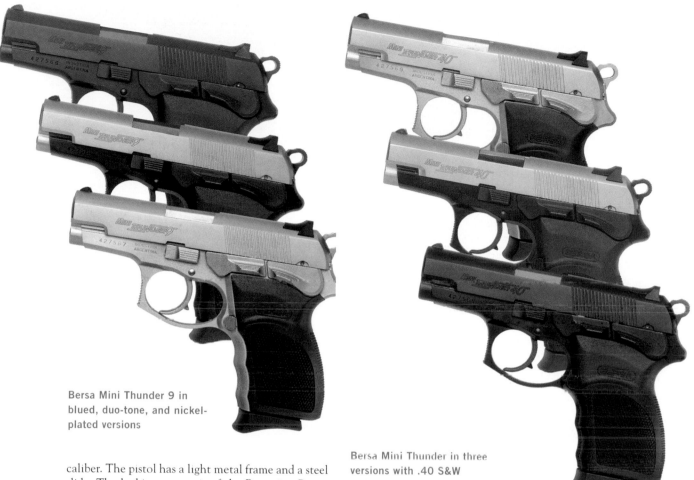

Bersa Mini Thunder 9 in
blued, duo-tone, and nickel-
plated versions

Bersa Mini Thunder in three
versions with .40 S&W
caliber

caliber. The pistol has a light metal frame and a steel slide. The locking system is of the Browning-Petter type in which the chamber block engages in the ejection port. There is a fixed locking cam under the chamber block. There is an ambidextrous safety catch on the frame which also serves as a takedown lever for the hammer. There is an enlarged slide catch on the left of the frame in front of the safety catch. In addition to the safety catch/takedown lever, this pistol also has an automatic firing pin safety. In addition, the weapon has a fixed combat sight. The magazine catch is on the left behind the trigger guard, but can be moved to the right for left-handed shooters. The total length is 165 mm (6½ in), the barrel is 83 mm (3¼ in) long and the weapon weighs 765 g (26 oz). The height of the Mini Thunder 9 is 130 mm (5 in) and the width is 37 mm (1½ in). This pistol is available in a blued, mat nickel or combination finish with a blued frame and a polished slide. The grips are made of black synthetic material.

BERSA MODEL MINI THUNDER 40

This model was also introduced at the 1998 Shot Show, at the same time as the Mini Thunder 9. The 10-shot pistol has a .40 S&W caliber. It has a combined ambidextrous safety catch/takedown

lever on the frame. In addition, it has a fixed combat sight and an automatic firing pin safety. The reversible magazine catch is on the left of the frame, behind the trigger guard. The weapon has a light metal frame and a steel slide. The total length is 165 mm (6½ in) with a barrel length of 83 mm (3¼ in). It weighs 765 g (26 oz). The height of the Mini Thunder 40 is 130 mm (5 in), and the width is 37 mm (1½ in). The weight is 765 g (26 oz). The locking system is the same as that of the Mini Thunder 9. The weapon is available in a blued, mat nickel or a combination finish with a blued frame and a polished slide, and it has black grips in synthetic material.

BERSA MODEL THUNDER 22

This 10-shot double-action pistol in .22 LR caliber, was introduced on the market in 1995. The weapon has a safety catch on the left of the slide. This catch blocks the firing pin and decocks the hammer. The rear sight is adjustable on the side. The magazine catch is on the left of the frame, above the trigger guard and just below the slide catch. The weapon has

Bersa Thunder 22 in
nickel-plated, blued, and
duo-tone versions

Bersa Thunder 32 in 7.65 mm
(.32 ACP) caliber

a total length of 168 mm (6½ in) with a barrel length of 90 mm (3½ in). The height is 120 mm (4¾ in) and the width is 33 mm (1¼ in). This pistol weighs only 535 g (18¾ oz). The Thunder 22 has a recoil locking system and is available in a blued, mat-nickel or combination finish with a blued frame and a polished slide with black grips in synthetic material.

BERSA MODEL THUNDER 22 SPORT

This model is actually a Thunder 22 with a barrel 152 mm (6 in) long. It was introduced in 1995 and is available only in a blued finish. The sight is only adjustable on the side, so that the pistol is not particularly suitable as a match weapon. However, it is an excellent 'plinker'. The weapon weighs 560 g (19¾ oz), and has black grips in synthetic material.

Bersa Thunder 22 Sport
with 152 mm (6 in) barrel

BERSA MODEL THUNDER 32

Bersa marketed this pistol in 1993 in 7.65 mm (.32 ACP) caliber. The magazine capacity of this double-action weapon is 10 rounds. It has a total length of 168 mm (6½ in) with a barrel length of 90 mm (3½ in). The pistol has a height of 120 mm (4¾ in) and a width of 33 mm (1¼ in). It weighs 560 g (19¾ oz). The safety systems include a safety catch on the left of the slide, which also decocks the hammer and blocks the firing pin. The rear sight is adjustable on the side. The magazine catch is on the left of the frame just below the slide catch. The Thunder 32 has a recoil locking system, and is available in a blued finish, a mat-nickel or a combination finish with a blued frame and a polished slide. The grips are made of black synthetic material.

BERSA MODEL THUNDER 380

This double-action 7-shot pistol is 9mm Short (.380 ACP) caliber was presented at the American Shot Show in 1995. In the United States it was sold until recently as model Series 95. The weapon has a rear sight that is adjustable on the side. In addition, it has a safety catch on the left of the slide, which decocks the hammer and blocks the firing pin. The magazine catch is in the usual place for a Bersa: on the left of the frame just below the slide catch. The pistol has a total length of 168 mm

Bersa Thunder 380

(6½ in) with a height of 120 mm (4¾ in), a width of 33 mm (1¼ in) and a barrel of 90 mm (3½ in). It weighs 560 g (19¼ oz). The Thunder 380 has a recoil locking system and is available in a blued finish, a mat-nickel or a combination finish with a blued frame and a polished slide. The grips are made of black synthetic material.

BERSA MODEL THUNDER 380 SUPER

This double-action pistol was introduced in 2000. It has a double row magazine for 15 cartridges in 9 mm Short (.380 ACP) caliber. The slide catch, which blocks the firing pin and decocks the hammer, is on the left of the slide. The magazine catch is on the

Bersa 15-shot Thunder
380 Super pistol of
2000

left of the frame above the trigger guard. In addition, the pistol has a total length of 168 mm (6½ in) and a barrel length of 90 mm (3½ in). The height is 125 mm (5 in), and the width is 34 mm (1¼ in). The weapon weighs 760 g (26¼ oz). The Thunder 380 Super has a recoil locking system and is available in a blued finish, a mat-nickel or a combination finish with a blued frame and a polished slide and black synthetic grips.

BERSA MODEL THUNDER 9

The double-action Thunder 9 dating from 1993, has a large capacity of 17 rounds in 9 mm Para caliber. There is an ambidextrous safety catch on the frame, which also serves as the takedown lever for the hammer. In addition the weapon has an automatic firing pin safety. The pistol has a light metal frame and a steel slide with a fixed combat sight. The magazine catch is on the left of the frame, behind the trigger guard and can be moved to the right for a left-handed shooter. The total length is 192 mm (7½ in) with a barrel length of 110 mm (4¼ in). The total height is 140 mm (5½ in) and the width is 37 mm (1½ in). It weighs 870 g (30¾ oz). The locking system is of the Browning-Petter type and the barrel block locks in the ejection port of the slide. The Thunder 9 is available in a blued, mat-nickel or a combination finish with a blued frame and a polished slide and black synthetic grips. It is also available with a factory laser.

Bersa Thunder 9 in 9mm Para
caliber, of which the bottom version
is equipped with a laser

BERSA MODEL THUNDER 40

This weapon was introduced in 1999 as a 13-shot double-action pistol in .40 S&W caliber. It has a large combined ambidextrous safety catch/takedown lever on the frame with a large slide catch in front of it. The magazine catch can be moved to the right and is behind the trigger guard. The pistol also has an automatic firing pin safety. The barrel length of the weapon is 102 mm (4 in) and the total length is 192 mm (7½ in). It weighs 870 g (30¾ oz). The total height is 140 mm (5½ in) with a width of 37 mm (1½ in). In addition, it has the same locking system as the Thunder 9. The pistol is available in a blued finish, a mat-nickel or a combination finish with a blued frame and a polished slide. In addition, there is a version available with a factory-mounted laser.

Bersa Thunder 40 with laser

BRILEY

In 1976 Jess Briley and his son-in-law, Cliff Moller, established the Briley firm to manufacture custom-made, special match weapons. The firm acquired a good reputation for the manufacture of excellent

Trade mark of Briley Pistol Division

interchangeable chokes and insert barrels for shotguns. In addition, it made all sorts of parts for tuning existing models of pistols. In 1990, Briley established its pistol division, under the management of Claudio Salassa. This manufactures special models of pistols based on the Colt 1911 and conversion sets. Briley also develops important parts and prototypes for other manufacturers such as Browning, Colt, Heckler & Koch, Krieghoff, Remington, Ruger and the US Repeating Arms Company (Winchester). The two-man firm has now expanded to become a company with more than 80 highly trained technicians. Briley's first pistols in 1990 had a skeleton trigger made by Strayer-Voigt. Later, the Videki or Chip McCormick trigger type was used. For models with a light metal frame, Briley uses a Caspian trigger. Steel frames were acquired in the past from Para-Ordnance, but since 1999 they are made by the firm itself. Modular pistols have a synthetic polymer frame made of STI. All Briley pistols have a so-called spherical bushing. This is a barrel bushing with a loose, moveable titanium inner jacket. Bushing bolts are used in all models for the screws for the grips. Briley uses the Bo-Mar micrometer sight for models with an adjustable sight. The company regularly produces new models, a few of which are described below.

BRILEY ADVANTAGE

This model is made in 9 mm Para, .40 S&W and .45 ACP calibers. The pistol has a Bo-Mar micrometer sight with a sight radius of 173 mm (6¾ in). The barrel with the special Briley barrel bushing has a length of 127 mm (5 in). The total length of the weapon is 221 mm (8¾ in) and it weighs 1077 g (38 oz). The slide has tension groves on both the front and the back. A special Briley recoil conductor rod is built into the weapon. The hammer, the trigger and the sear are those of a match model. The weapon has an enlarged ejection port and an enlarged safety catch on the left of the frame. There is an extended grip

Briley Advantage

safety, the so-called beavertail in the backstrap. The front and back of the grips are checkered for a better grip. The pistol has the safety catch and the slide catch on the left of the frame. The magazine catch is also on the left behind the trigger guard. The magazine capacity is 10 rounds in 9 mm Para and .40 S&W caliber and 8 rounds in .45 ACP caliber. In addition, it has completely tuned pistol walnut grips and a bluish purple finish.

BRILEY FANTOM

Briley Fantom F10 pistol

The Fantom is made in four different calibers:
Fantom F10 8-shot in .45 ACP caliber;
Fantom F13: 13-shot in .40 S&W caliber;
Fantom F15: 15-shot in 9 mm Para or .38 Super Auto caliber.

Briley also produces these versions with a single chamber compensator. The Fantom has a light metal frame made by Caspian and a steel slide. There are cocking grooves on both the front and the back of the slide. The slide also contains a light metal recoil conductor rod. The top of the slide is flattened and ribbed. The pistol has a fixed combat sight with a sight radius of 145 mm (5¾ in) and a Briley Match barrel of 91 mm (3½ in). The total length is 196 mm (7¾ in). The weight is 965 g (34 oz). The weapon has

Briley Fantom F10C with compensator

a special built-in Briley match trigger, match hammer and sear.

In addition, this weapon has an ambidextrous safety catch on the frame and an extended grip safety (beavertail). The magazine catch is on the left of the frame, behind the trigger guard. The ejection port in the slide is enlarged, as is the ejector. The front and back of the grips are checkered. The weapon is completely tuned and has a bluish purple finish.

BRILEY MODULAR

This is a version with a black or colored STI polymer frame. The steel slide has cocking grooves on the front and back. The micrometer sight is made by the Bo-Mar firm and has a sight radius of 173 mm (6¾ in). The pistol has a 127 mm (5 in) match barrel with the Briley barrel bushing. The total length of the weapon is 221 mm (8¾ in) and it weighs 1077 g (38 oz). The ejection port and the ejector itself are enlarged. There is an enlarged ambidextrous safety catch on the frame. The grip safety is extended (beavertail). The pistol is completely tuned and has a bluish purple finish. It is available in .40 S&W and .45 ACP calibers.

Briley Modular with red polymer casing

BRILEY PLATEMASTER

As the name of this model indicates, Briley makes this pistol for the 'falling plate' shooting discipline and similar shooting events. The weapon has both a steel frame and a steel slide. There are a series of cocking grooves on the front and back. The barrel length is 127 mm (5 in), including the double chamber TC II titanium compensator. The Briley sight is mounted on the slide. In addition, the weapon has an enlarged ejection port and ejector. The pistol also has the

Briley Platemaster

special Briley trigger, hammer and sear. There is an enlarged safety catch on the left of the frame and the grip safety is extended. The magazine well is enlarged and the front and back of the grip are checkered. The pistol has walnut grip plates, is completely tuned, and has a bluish purple finish. Briley produces this 15-shot weapon in 9 mm Para and 38 Super Auto calibers.

BRILEY EL PRESIDENTE

This pistol was introduced at the 1996 American Shot Show. It has a polymer frame and there is a special Briley sight mounted on the slide. The weapon has a Briley match barrel 127 mm (5 in) long, excluding the 4-chamber compensator and the special Briley barrel bushing. The front and back of the slide have cocking grooves. In addition, the pistol has an enlarged ejection port. The slide is partly open, to save weight. Other special features include the Briley recoil spring conductor rod, the enlarged Briley ejector and the special Briley trigger, hammer and sear. The enlarged ambidextrous safety catch is on the frame. The grip safety is also extended (beavertail). The total length of the

weapon is 221 mm (8¾ in) and it weighs 1077g (38 oz). The weapon is completely tuned, has a bluish purple finish and is available in 9 mm Para and .38 Super Auto calibers with a capacity of 10 cartridges.

BRILEY SIGNATURE

The Signature is built on a polymer STI frame. The pistol has a Bo-Mar micrometer sight with a sight radius of 173 mm (6¾ in). The 127 mm (5 in) match barrel has a special Briley barrel bushing. The total length of the weapon is 221 mm (8¾ in) and it weighs 1077 g (38 oz). This model also has cocking grooves on the front and back of the slide. It also has an enlarged ejection port and ejector, as well as the special Briley recoil spring conductor rod. The Briley match trigger, match hammer and sear are also built in. The enlarged safety catch is ambidextrous. Furthermore, the grip safety is extended (beavertail). The 10-shot pistol is available in .40 S&W caliber and is completely tuned, with a bluish purple finish.

Briley Signature

BRILEY VERSATILITY PLUS

This model comes in an STI polymer frame or a light metal frame made by Caspian. It has a steel slide with a 127 mm (5 in) Briley match barrel and the well-known Briley barrel bushing with a titanium inner bushing. The total length of the weapon is 221 mm (8¾ in) and it weighs 1077 g (38 oz). The ejection port is enlarged, like the ejector itself. In addition, the pistol has the Briley recoil spring conductor rod and a match

Briley El Presidente 'race gun'

Briley Versatility Plus pistol

trigger, hammer and sear. The weapon also has an enlarged ambidextrous safety catch on the frame. In this model the grip safety is also extended. Briley produces the completely tuned weapon in 9 mm Para, .38 Super Auto, .40 S&W and .45 ACVP calibers.

BROWNING/FABRIQUE NATIONALE

John Moses Browning lived from 1855 to 1926. As a designer, he had a decisive impact on the development of weapons in the nineteenth, twentieth, and even twenty-first centuries. The most modern pistols are still made today, on the basis of his patents in the nineteenth century. His father, Jonathan Browning already had his own workplace making weapons in Kentucky. In 1846, the family moved to Nauvoo in Illinois. Browning's father opened another shop selling arms there. Six years later, he moved again, to Ogden in the state of Utah, where he started another arms company. John Moses was born in 1855. He was brought up in the trade, and made his first gun at the age of 14. His father died in 1879. Together with his brother Matthew, John Moses took over the business. John Moses was responsible for production while his brother took care of sales. In 1880, the business was renamed the J.M. Browning & Brother Company. In the same year they started production of a series of the Browning Model 1878 single-shot rifle. Up to 1882, they made several hundred of these. The activities of the new company attracted the attention of competitors. In 1883, the stocks of M1878 rifles and the production rights were bought up by the Winchester Repeating Arms Company. Winchester marketed this rifle as the Winchester Model 1885 High Wall rifle. After this, Browning never produced any more weapons itself. John Moses designed more than 80 weapon systems and had 128 patents for weapons to his name. He sold many designs to Colt, Remington, Stevens and Winchester. Examples include the Colt 1900 and the

famous Colt 1911 pistols, the Winchester 1885 rifle, and the later lever-action rifles. The pump-action rifles of Remington and Winchester are also based on Browning's patents. In 1897, he designed a small model pistol with a recoil locking system in 7.65 mm (.32 ACP) caliber. He tried to sell this design to Colt, but Colt was not interested. A representative of the Belgian arms factory FN, traveling in the USA on business, was interested. He took a prototype back home with him. FN liked the design of this pistol and bought the production rights. The Fabrique Nationale in Herstal was founded in 1889 by a group of Belgian industrialists. They were licensed to make Mauser rifles for the Belgian army. They received support from Ludwig Loewe in Berlin to set up the necessary machinery. Later they also started manufacturing other firearms. The Fabrique Nationale bought up the American Browning Company in 1977. At that time, Browning was actually only a trading company. FN manufactured the pistols and the Browning shotguns were made by Mirouku in Japan.

The Belgian Herstal SA group consists of the subsidiaries Browning USA, (including Winchester and Browning Canada), Browning Europe, including the Japanese Miroku), FN-Herstal and the American branch FNMI (Fabrique Nationale Military Industries). FN and FNMI concentrate mainly on the manufacture of military firearms and ammunition. The other subsidiaries focus on the civilian market for sports and hunting weapons. In 1991, the French state-owned Giat bought up the whole Herstal concern. The French arms and airplane industries are combined in Giat. In the twentieth and twenty-first centuries, FN/Browning produced the following large caliber models of pistols:

BROWNING MODEL 1900

FN took over the production of the pistols designed by John Moses Browning in 1897. The single-action weapon in 7.65 mm (.32 ACP) caliber with a magazine capacity of 7 rounds was marketed as the Browning Model 1900. The name of this model is based on the fact that the Belgian army introduced

Browning Model 1900

this pistol as the service weapon in 1900. It had a recoil locking system and a recoil spring in the slide above the barrel. The total length of the pistol is 170 mm (6¾ in) with a barrel length of 102 mm (4 in). The weapon weighs 640 g (22½ oz). There is an adjustable rear sight on the slide. The safety catch is on the left of the frame. The magazine catch is in the heel of the grips. FN produced the pistol from 1900 to 1910.

BROWNING MODEL 1903

This single-action pistol in 9 mm Browning Long caliber was based on the Browning 1900. The weapon has a magazine capacity of 7 rounds. It has a recoil locking system with the recoil spring under the barrel. The grip safety is built into the backstrap. The weapon also has a safety catch on the left of the frame. The magazine catch is in the heel of the grip. The total length is 203 mm (8 in) and the barrel length is 128 mm (5 in). The weapon weighs 910 g (32 oz). It was brought for use by armies of a large number of powers such as Belgium, the Netherlands, Peru, Russia, Turkey and Sweden. In a period from 1903 to 1939, FN produced approximately 58,000 pistols of this model.

BROWNING MODEL 1906

In 1906, FN introduced a small single-action pocket pistol on the market as the Browning Model 1906. The 6-shot weapon in 6.35 mm (.25 ACP) caliber had a grip safety. The total length of the Model 1906 was 115 mm (4½ in). The barrel length was 54 mm (2 in) and the weight was 350 g (12¼ oz). From 1906 to 1959, FN manufactured more than 1,085,000 pistols of this model. In 1931, FN introduced a simpler version without a grip safety and called this the Baby Browning. FN made about 500,000 of these, up to 1969.

New type Browning Baby

No factory records were kept on the serial numbers of these pistols up to 1954. These records were kept for the newer Browning Baby from 1954. A new numbering system started for the series, starting with weapon number 0001. The production from 1954 to 1958 went from number 0001 to 181000. The serial numbers are shown by year below:

1959, weapon numbers: 181001 to 206439;
1960, weapon numbers: 206350 to 230999;
1961, weapon numbers: 231000 to 250999;
1962, weapon numbers: 251000 to 278999;
1963, weapon numbers: 279000 to 286099;
1964, weapon numbers: 286100 to 303499;
1965, weapon numbers: 303500 to 329999;
1966, weapon numbers: 330000 to 367443;
1967, weapon numbers: 367444 to 412999;
1968, weapon numbers: 413000 to 479000;
1969, weapon numbers: 479001 to 500000.

The Baby Browning was succeeded by model 1906 with slightly different measurements. The total length of this weapon is 104 mm (4 in) with a barrel length of 54 mm (2 in). The weight is 210 g (7½ oz).

Browning Model 1906 with grip safety, superbly engraved by the Turkish firm Tugra Gravür Ltd

Old type Browning Baby

BROWNING MODEL 1910

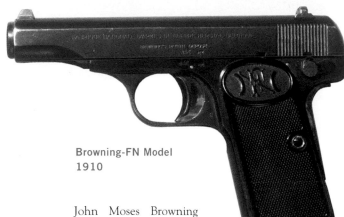

Browning-FN Model
1910

John Moses Browning
regularly went to Belgium.
In 1908, he designed a new
type of single-action pistol there. FN marketed this as
the Browning Model 1910 in 7.65 mm (.32 ACP) and
9 mm Short (.380 ACP) calibers, both with
a magazine capacity of 7 rounds. One of the special
features of this model is that the recoil spring is fitted
around the barrel. Up to that time, most pistols had
a recoil spring above or below the barrel. The weapon
has three safety mechanisms: the safety catch, a grip
safety and a magazine safety. The total length of the
1910 model is 152 mm (6 in). The barrel length is 88
mm (3½ in) and the weight is 600 g (21¼ oz). The pistol
was produced in large numbers for the commercial
market from 1910 to 1954. It was also used by the police
in many European countries for a long time.

BROWNING MODEL 1910/22

In 1922, a modified version of the Model 1910
appeared on the market, the Browning 1910/22. FN
had received a large order for the model 1910 from
the Serbian Army. However, the Serbs wanted
a longer barrel and a number of other minor
modifications. Because of the longer barrel, FN also
lengthened the slide. A separate retaining ring was
mounted at the front of the slide with a bayonet lug.
This pistol was used by the police in a number of
countries. In the Netherlands it was used by the
municipal police forces until approximately 1985, in

Browning-FN Model
1910/222

7.65 mm (.32 ACP) caliber. The Dutch National
Police Force used the same weapon in 9 mm Short
(.380 ACP) caliber. During the Second World War,
FN also manufactured Model 1910/22 for the German
occupying forces. In the period 1940 to 1944, FN
made approximately 20,000 in 7.65 mm (.32 ACP)
caliber, under the name 'Pistole Modell 626(b)'. The
same weapon in 9 mm Short (.380 ACP) caliber was
introduced by the German army as 'Pistole Modell
641(b)'. Both types had the German mark 'Ch', the
German production code for FN. In 1950, FN
resumed production of model 1910/22 and this was
made until 1959. The pistol has a total length of
178 mm (7 in). The barrel length is 114 mm (4½ in)
and the weapon weighs 730 g (25¾ oz). The magazine
capacity in both calibers is 9 rounds.

BROWNING MODEL 125

Browning 125

Model 1910/22 was succeeded by the
Browning Model 125. This pistol is very
similar to the older version, but has a short
retaining ring with a thread. In addition, the
pistol has an adjustable rear sight. The barrel
length is 113 mm (4½ in) and the total length
is 178 mm (7 in). The pistol weighs 720
g (25½ oz). It has a grip safety, a magazine
safety and a safety catch on the left of the frame. The
magazine catch is in the heel of the grip. It was made
up to 1980 in 7.65 mm (.32 ACP) and 9 mm Short
(.380 ACP) calibers.

BROWNING HIGH POWER MODEL 1935

In 1922, John Moses Browning started on the
development of a 13-shot military pistol in 9 mm Para
caliber. He died of a heart attack in his office at FN in
Liege in 1926. The design of the new single-action
pistol, the later HP-35 was completed by D.J. Saive,
a weapons engineer at FN. He later designed the famous
FN FAL rifle. The FN factory gambled that the new
model of this pistol would be bought by the Belgian
army. Because of the precarious economic situation, the
Belgian government did not decide on this until 1935.
This is why the weapon is still referred to as the HP-35
or P-35. Other names include the High Power (HP) or
Grand Puissance (GP). In his design, Browning had

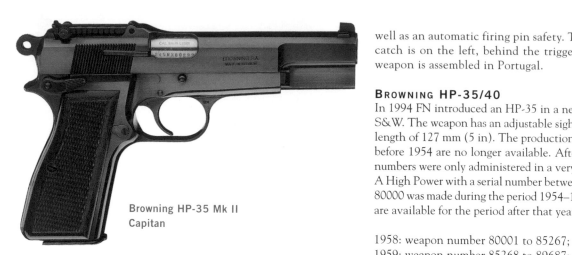

Browning HP-35 Mk II
Capitan

An annex holster could be clicked on to the backstrap, just as in the pre-war model. In 1993, a new version of the Browning HP-35 Capitan was introduced. This type also has the well-known ladder sight. It is assembled in Browning's subsidiary in Portugal.

BROWNING HIGH POWER PRACTICAL
FN introduced this new HP-35 MK III model on the market in 1993. The pistol has a light metal nickel frame and a stainless steel slide. The grip has a rubber Pachmayr Signature surround. The pistol is also available in a sports version with an adjustable rear sight. There is a third version with a chrome finish that was introduced in 1994. The pistol has a total length of 200 mm (7¾ in), a barrel length of 118 mm (4½ in) and a sight radius of 165 mm (6½ in). The Practical has a height of 132 mm (5¼ in) and a weight of 950 g (33½ oz). The pistol has an ambidextrous safety catch on the frame as

well as an automatic firing pin safety. The magazine catch is on the left, behind the trigger guard. The weapon is assembled in Portugal.

BROWNING HP-35/40
In 1994 FN introduced an HP-35 in a new caliber, .40 S&W. The weapon has an adjustable sight and a barrel length of 127 mm (5 in). The production records from before 1954 are no longer available. After 1954 serial numbers were only administered in a very general way. A High Power with a serial number between 70000 and 80000 was made during the period 1954–1957. Records are available for the period after that year.

1958: weapon number 80001 to 85267;
1959: weapon number 85268 to 89687;
1960: weapon number 89688 to 93027;
1961: weapon number 93028 to 109145;
1962: weapon number 109146 to 113548;
1963: weapon number 113549 to 115822;
Halfway through 1964, the letter 'T' was added to the serial number of the High Power:
1964: weapon number T115823 to T136568
1965: weapon number T136569 to T146372;
1966: weapon number T146373 to T173285;
1967: weapon number T173286 to T213999;
1968: weapon number T214000 to T258000.
 Halfway through 1969, the system of numbering was changed. Up to 1975, two figures were used to indicate the year of production, followed by the letter C for the High Power.
1969: weapon number T 258001.
1975: 75C 261000

In 1976, a new method of numbering was introduced, so that the letters in the serial number indicated the year of manufacture. The serial number also contained a code for the caliber. A High Power in 9 mm Para caliber was preceded by the figures 245. A High Power in .40 S&W caliber had the code 2W5. Every year started with number 01001. The codes used for the years were Z = 1; Y = 2; X = 3; W = 4; V = 5; T = 6; R = 7; P = 8; N = 9; M = 0. This method of numbering was used up to 1998. A High Power with the number 2W5NR01001 is therefore the first High Power in .40 S&W caliber to be made in the year 1997 (N = 9;R = 7). In 1998, Browning started a new method of numbering for the weapons. The weapon number of a High Power started with the figures 510, irrespective of the specific model. This was followed by the letter code of the year of manufacture, followed by the serial number of that year. Therefore a High Power with the serial number 510NN01002 was the second High Power pistol to be made in 1999 (NN = 1999).

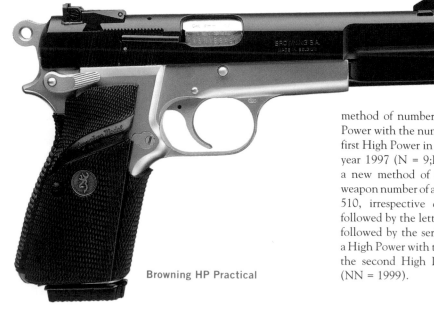

Browning HP Practical

A big Browning BDA

Browning BDA-380 pistol
made by Beretta

BROWNING BDA

In 1978 FN produced a special double-action pistol in 9 mm Para and .45 ACP calibers. Curiously, this pistol was initially only sold in the USA. The weapon was not mentioned in the European catalogues of FN until years later. The pistol had an ambidextrous, combined safety catch/uncocking lever on the frame.

Three different models were made of the BDA in 9 mm Para caliber: the 14-shot Browning BDA-9S with a barrel length of 118 mm (4½ in); the Browning BDA-9M, which had a shorter barrel, 96 mm (3¾ in) long and the Browning BDA-9C a compact 7-shot pistol, also with a barrel length of 96 mm (3¾ in). In 1995, FN introduced a double-action-only model in 9 mm Para caliber known as the Browning BDAO. This last model has a total length of 200 mm (7¾ in), a barrel length of 118.5 mm (4½ in) and a weight of 875 g (31 oz).

BROWNING BDA-380

This model was introduced in 1977 and was also known as the Browning 140-DA. It is a compact double-action pistol. A 13-shot model was available in 7.54 (.32 ACP) caliber. The second model was in 9 mm Short (.380 ACP) caliber with a magazine capacity of 12 rounds. The total length is 170 mm (6¼ in), the barrel length is 96 mm (3¾ in) and the weapon weighs 650 g (23 oz). The weapon was made in a blued and nickel-plated finish. It was produced for FN/Browning by Beretta in Italy. The logo 'PB' of Pietro Beretta is shown on the slide. This pistol was made up to 1977. The Browning BDA-380 pistols were numbered with various codes. The code for this model started with '425'. This was followed by two letters indicating the year of manufacture, followed by the actual serial number which started every new year with the figures 01001. The year codes for the BDA-380 are: Z = 1; Y = 2; X = 3; W = 4; V = 5; T = 6; R = 7; P = 8; N = 9; M = 0. Therefore the BDA-380 pistol with the weapon number 425NR01002 (N = 9; R = 7) is the second BDA-380 weapon to be made in 1997.

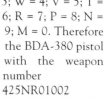

BROWNING BDM

This is a 15-shot double-action pistol in 9 mm Para caliber, which was introduced in 1991. With a separate rotating catch on the left of the slide, the shooter can choose for a double-action or a single-action trigger action. The BDM has a total length of 200 mm (7¾ in), a barrel length of 120 mm (4¾ in) and a weight of 850 g (30 oz). In 1997, FN introduced

The compact Browning
BDA-C pistol

Browning BDM pistol

The latest Browning Forty Nine pistol in 9 mm Para caliber

a model of the BDM with a chrome finish for the civilian market. Other models of the BDM were introduced shortly afterwards, such as the BDM Practical with a chrome frame, the BDM-D with only a uncocking lever and the BDM-DAO in double-action-only.

FN FIVE SEVEN

In 1996, FN introduced a completely new army pistol, the Five Seven, named after the newly developed caliber, 5.7 x 28 mm. This cartridge has a pointed bullet of 31 grains (2 g). The muzzle velocity (V0) is 649 m/s (2130 fps) and the muzzle energy (E0) is 421 Joules. The pistol has a steel barrel, and the frame, slide and magazine are made of synthetic material. It has a double-action-only trigger action. Apart from an automatic firing pin safety, it does not have a safety catch or other safety systems. The magazine capacity is 20 rounds and the weapon weighs only 618 g (21¾ oz). The total length of the Five Seven is 208 mm (8¼ in) and the barrel length is 122.5 mm (47/8 in). The pistol was introduced on the market together with the new P90 pistol in the same caliber.

FN FORTY-NINE

FN/Browning's latest pistol is the Forty-Nine, which was presented to the public at the special MILIPOL fair in Paris in November 1999. It is made by the FNMI (Fabrique Nationale Military Industries) in Columbia in the state of South Carolina. The pistol is available in 9 mm Para caliber (16 rounds) and .40 S&W caliber (14 rounds). The frame, including the trigger guard, is made of synthetic material. The slide, and obviously the barrel are made of stainless steel. There are slits in the bottom of the frame in front of the trigger guard. These can hold accessories such as a torch or laser. The weapon has a double-action-only trigger action and no safety mechanism at all. The new firing system Repeatable Secure Striker, was patented by FN. The firing pin is only cocked if the trigger is pulled. The total length of the pistol is 197 mm (7¾ in), the barrel length is 108 mm (4¼ in) and the weight is 737 g (26 oz). The trigger pressure is approximately 3600 g (8 lb). The pistol is mainly used by the army and police.

The small caliber pistol models produced by FN/Browning in the twentieth and twenty-first centuries are:

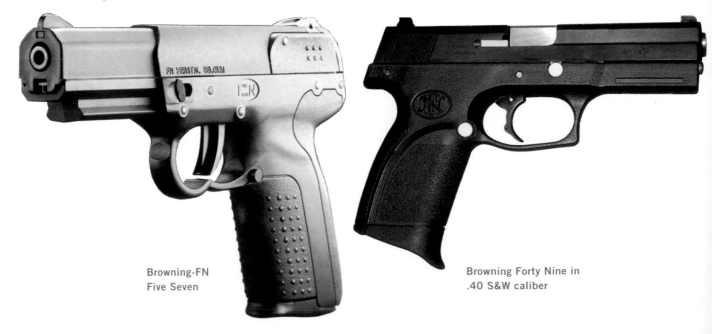

Browning-FN
Five Seven

Browning Forty Nine in
.40 S&W caliber

BROWNING NOMAD/DE TIRE

In 1962, FN introduced a 10-shot pistol with a recoil locking system in .22 LR caliber. In the USA this model was called the Nomad. In Europe it was marketed as the model 'de Tire'. The standard model had a total length of 283 mm (11¼ in) with a barrel length of 172 mm (6¾ in). In addition, there was a compact model with a total length of 225 mm (8⅞ in) with a barrel length of 114 mm (4½ in) and a weight of 737 g (26 oz). The pistol had a light metal frame. The safety catch was on the left of the frame. The magazine catch was in the heel of the grip. It was produced by FN from 1962 to 1974. The production year of the Nomad is shown in the weapon number. All Nomad pistols have the letter P, preceded up to 1969 by the last number of the year of manufacture. Therefore a Nomad or 'de Tire' with the serial number 3P5000 was made in 1963 and had the serial number 5000. The numbering system was changed in 1969. From that time up to 1974, FN used a serial number in which the first two numbers indicate the year of manufacture. For example, a Nomad with the serial number 71P6000 was made in 1971 and had the number 6000.

The old Browning 'de Tire' or 'Nomad' pistol

BROWNING CHALLENGER/CONCOURS

The Browning Challenger was a luxury version of the Nomad or de Tire. The pistol had a walnut stock and a gilt trigger. In addition, it had an adjustable rear sight. It was made by FN from 1962 to 1975. An extra luxury version of this model was known as the Medalist. This had a total length of 283 mm (11¼ in) and a barrel length of 172 mm (6¾ in) with a ventilated rib and different barrel weights.

The weapon also had a dry firing system. This meant that the shooter could practice without having to fire a cartridge. It was made by FN from 1963 to 1975. The pistol was made in different models, including two with a hand grip under the barrel. The serial numbers of the old Challenger started in the period 1962 to 1969 with the last number of the year, followed by the letter U. For example, a Challenger with the serial number 4U0001 was the first Challenger to be made in 1964. The Medalist was made from 1962 to the end of 1974. The serial number of the Medalist started with the last number of the year of manufacture followed by the letter T. For example: 2T0001 was the first Medalist pistol to be made. In 1969 this system was changed. From that year, the last two numbers of the year of manufacture were used. For example: 70T8000 was a Medalist pistol made in 1970 with the serial number 8000.

BROWNING CHALLENGER II

This was the successor of the Challenger originally made in 1962, which was made from 1976 to 1982 by the Browning factory in Salt Lake City in Utah. The 10-shot pistol had a barrel length of 172 mm (6¾ in) and a light metal frame. Browning produced its successor, the Challenger III, from 1983 up the introduction of the Buck Mark in 1985. Challengers had a serial number starting with the numbers 655. This was followed by a code for the year of manufacture and then the serial number of the specific year. The codes used for the years are: Z = 1; Y = 2; X = 3; W = 4; V = 5; T = 6; R = 7; P = 8; N = 9; M = 0. Every year started again with number 01001. For example, a Challenger with the serial number 655PX01001 (P = 8; X = 3) was a type III, and the first weapon to be made in 1983.

Browning Medalist

BROWNING INTERNATIONAL

Browning launched this new model match pistol in 1980 in .22 LR caliber. The fact that it was manufactured in the American city of Morgan in Utah or Montreal in Canada, and not by FN in Belgium, can be seen from the engraving on the slide of the weapon. It is a 10-shot pistol with a walnut stock and an adjustable hand-rest. The International has a safety catch on the left of the frame as well as a magazine safety. The total length of this pistol is 298 mm (11¾ in), the square barrel has a length of 150 mm (6 in) and the weapon weighs 1325 g (46¾ oz). In addition, it has a gilt trigger and an adjustable rear sight. A slightly simpler version of the International was marketed as the Browning Practice 150. This pistol did not have an adjustable hand-rest. Following the introduction of the Browning Buck Mark in 1985, both models disappeared from the scene.

BROWNING CHALLENGER III

This is a newer model of the older Challenger II match pistol, which was introduced on the market in 1982. The barrel was 140 mm (5½ in) thick, a so-called bull barrel. In addition, Browning made a model with a thinner tapering barrel 172 mm (6¾ in) long, known as the Challenger III Sporter. Both models were made in Salt Lake City from 1982 to 1986. The Challenger III was clearly identifiable as a precursor of the later Buck Mark.

BROWNING BUCK MARK

This successor of the Challenger and the International was presented at the 1985 Shot Show in Atlanta in the USA. The pistol in .22 LR caliber has a recoil locking system. The first model of the Buck Mark had a mat blue finish and synthetic grips. A nickel-plated finish appeared a few years later.

The serial numbers of all Buck Mark models consist of codes. The model code is 655. This is followed by letters indicating the year of manufacture. Each year starts with the numbers 01001. The letters for the year of manufacture of the Buck Mark are: Z = 1; Y = 2; X = 3; W = 4; V = 5; T = 6; R = 7; P = 8; N = 9; M = 0. Therefore a Buck Mark with the serial number 655PV01003 (P = 8; V = 5) is the third Buck Mark pistol to be made in 1985. In 1998, the serial numbering of the Buck Mark was changed. From that year, all the serial numbers of this model started with numbers 515. The codes for the year of manufacture remained the same. Therefore a Buck Mark with the serial number 515MM01001 (MM = 00) is the first Buck Mark pistol to be made in the year 2000. Browning made several models of the Buck Mark. Some of these are described below.

BROWNING BUCK MARK BULLSEYE

This Buck Mark match pistol was introduced in 1996. It has an adjustable trigger pressure from 1100 to 2300 g (2.4 to 5lbs) and an adjustable rear sight. The weapon has a total length of 287 mm (11¼ in) and it weighs 1000 g (35¼ oz). The barrel is 184 mm (7¼ in) long and is interchangeable with barrels in other lengths. The weapon was designed for small caliber silhouette shooting.

BROWNING BUCK MARK 5.5 SERIE

This is a Buck Mark with a 140 mm (5½ in) barrel, and an adjustable rear sight. The total length of the 5.5 pistol series is 245 mm (9½ in) and the weight is 1000 g (35¼ oz). The Buck Mark 5.5 has been made since 1990 in four different models.

BUCK MARK 5.5 BLUE TARGET

This pistol has a blued finish with walnut grips. The barrel has a raised rib for mounting a scope.

Browning International

Left-hand of the Browning International

Browning Buck Mark Bullseye with cooling ribs on barrel

Browning Buck Mark
Target 5.5

The micrometer sight and the bead are protected with
a hood.

BUCK MARK 5.5 FIELD
The 140 mm (5½ in) barrel and the frame have a blue
anodized finish. In a later model, the adjustable rear

Browning Buck
Mark Field 5.5

sight and bead are hooded. The pistol also has walnut
grips.

BUCK MARK 5.5 GOLD TARGET
A match model with a gold anodized frame and
a barrel rib. The slide is blued. The micrometer sight
and the bead are hooded.

Browning Buck Mark
Gold Target 5.5

BUCK MARK 5.5 NICKEL TARGET
The same model as the 5.5 Gold Target, but with
a nickel-plated finish.

Browning Buck Mark
Nickel Plus Target 5.5

BROWNING BUCK MARK GOLD
The Buck Mark Gold is a model with a barrel which
is 140 mm (5½ in) high. The frame and the sight rib
have an anodized layer of gold. The barrel is blued.
The total length of the Gold is 245 mm (9½ in) and
the weapon weighs 1000 g (35¼ oz).

Browning Buck Mark
Gold

BROWNING BUCK MARK MICRO PLUS
This is a luxury model of the Buck Mark
Micro with grips of laminated wood. The
Micro Plus has a barrel length of 102 mm
(4 in), a total length of 203 mm (8 in) and
a weight of 900 g (31¼ oz).

Browning Buck Mark
Micro Plus with 102 mm
(4 in) barrel

Browning Buck Mark
Standard with 102 mm
(4 in) barrel

BROWNING BUCK MARK MICRO STANDARD
This is a Buck Mark model dating from 1995 with a barrel 102 mm (4 in) high. A nickel-plated model, the Micro Nickel, and the extra luxury Micro Plus with wooden grips followed in 1996.

BROWNING BUCK MARK PLUS
This is a luxury version of the standard model with hardwood grips, dating from 1987. The weapon has a barrel length of 140 mm (5½ in), a total length of 241 mm (9½ in) and a weight of 1000 g (35¼ oz).

Browning Buck Mark
Plus with wooden hand
grip

BROWNING BUCK MARK PLUS NICKEL
This is a version of the Buck Mark Plus in a nickel-plated finish and with laminated grips, introduced in 1996.

Browning Buck Mark
Nickel Plus

BROWNING BUCK MARK SILHOUETTE
Since 1992, Browning USA has made a special model for small silhouette shooting with a barrel that is 251 mm (10 in) long. The total length is 350 mm (13¾ in) and the weapon weighs 1360 g (48 oz). It has a hardwood hand grip under the barrel and an adjustable rear sight. This sight and the bead are hooded so that the shooter is not bothered by light. A telescopic sight can also be mounted on the barrel rib.

Browning Buck Mark
Silhouette pistol

BROWNING BUCK MARK STANDARD

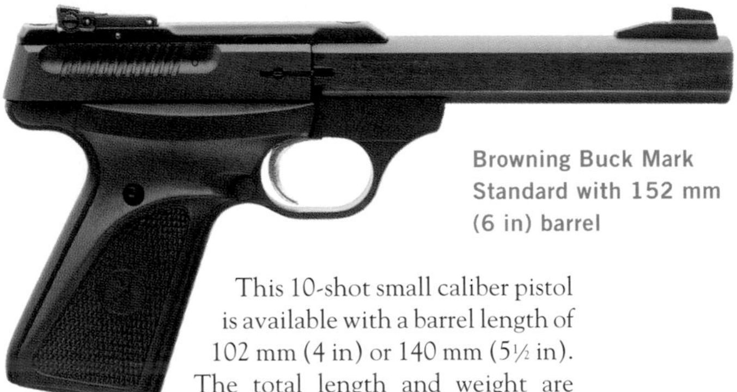

Browning Buck Mark
Standard with 152 mm
(6 in) barrel

This 10-shot small caliber pistol is available with a barrel length of 102 mm (4 in) or 140 mm (5½ in). The total length and weight are respectively 203 mm (8 in) and 900 g (31¾ oz) or 241 mm (9½ in) and 1000 g (35¼ oz). The pistol has a mat black finish and a gilt trigger. The safety catch is on the left of the frame. The magazine catch is also on the left, behind the trigger guard. There is an adjustable rear sight mounted at the back of the slide. In addition, the weapon has black synthetic grips. From 1992, the name of the Buck Mark Standard with a 102 mm (4 in) barrel was changed to the Micro Standard.

BROWNING BUCK MARK STANDARD NICKEL
The Standard Nickel has a black light metal frame, a nickel-plated slide and a standard barrel 140 mm (5½ in) long. The grips are made of a black synthetic material.

Browning Buck Mark

Browning Buck Mark Varmint
with telescopic sights

BROWNING BUCK MARK VARMINT

This Buck Mark model has a barrel 251 mm (10 in) long. The total length is 350 mm (13¾ in) and the weapon weighs 1360 g (48 oz). A special barrel rib is fitted on the barrel for a telescopic sight. The pistol does not have any scopes.

BUL TRANSMARK

Trade mark of Bul Transmark of Israel

Bull Transmark Ltd was established in Tel Aviv in Israel in 1990. In 2000, the firm employed about 25 employees including a large number of qualified gunsmiths. Bul's marketing manager is the young mechanical engineer, Saul Kirsch, who is also Israel's national IPSC champion. The technical manager is Miki Danzis, another national champion shooter in the standard class. In 1992, they decided to develop a design for a standard pistol which would be suitable as a military weapon and as a civilian weapon for defense, but could also serve as an IPSC pistol. The management opted for the 1911 style because this would give the individual shooter the greatest choice of accessories and special parts from any manufacturer. A large number of sports shooters were involved in the design. They contributed their own ideas of the 'ideal' pistol. The result was a lightweight, strong, hard-wearing but reliable weapon with a large magazine capacity. The first prototype was only presented in early 1993. Following extensive tests, the final product, the Bul M-5 was ready for the production of a series at the end of the year. The American arms factory Springfield was interested. They wished to market the pistol in North America under their own name, as the 13-shot Model XM4 in .45 ACP caliber. This is how the weapon was presented at the American Shot Show in Las Vegas in 1994. However, the cooperation foundered. Firstly, because the pistol infringed certain patent rights which the manufacturer Para-Ordnance had registered for North America, and secondly, because the magazine

capacity was too big. In the United States a law had been passed limiting the magazine capacity of handguns to a maximum of 10 rounds. This meant that the XM-4 would lose its marketing advantage in the face of heavy competition. Bul therefore decided to continue on its own and developed a series of models for different purposes, based on the M-5. The stainless steel auxiliary frame was made in the factory in Haifa, and this was later screwed into the synthetic frame and pressed. The frame is made of the special synthetic material, Xanex, which was originally developed in Israel for military purposes. The stainless steel slide is processed with computer-aided CNC machines. In 1998, Bul decided to design two other models. These were the double-action Bul Impact, intended for the services, and the Bul Storm, which is very similar to the famous CZ, and therefore also to the Jericho line of pistols. In 2000, Bul opened a special shooting range complex in Kfar Saba, north of Tel Aviv. The Bul training center is also situated there, and courses are given for bodyguards, combat training, ITSC training, shooting instruction for the police and special army units. Any type of interchangeable Bul set, consisting of a slide, barrel, spring and recoil spring conductor rod can be placed on the M-5 Xanex frame.

BUL IMPACT

The double-action Bul impact is a so-called Hi-Cap combat pistol. Hi-Cap refers to the large magazine capacity. In 9 mm Para caliber, a special magazine has a capacity of 18 rounds. In .40 S&W caliber the capacity is 17 rounds, and in the large .45 ACP caliber, the capacity is still 14 rounds. A normal, non-extended magazine has a capacity of respectively 13, 11 and 10 rounds. The standard model has a total length of 191 mm (7½ in) a barrel length of 98 mm (3⅞ in) and a weight of 735 g (26 oz). The weapon has a fixed combat rear sight with a sight radius of 145 mm (5¾ in). The Bul Impact Longslide has a barrel length of 121 mm (4¼ in). The slides of all three calibers fit on the synthetic Xanex frame. The safety catch is on the left of the frame. In addition, the pistol also has an automatic firing pin safety and obviously a lock-up safety. There is a built-in lock in the backstrap with which the weapon can be locked with a key that is provided. This locking system is comparable to that of the new Brazilian Taurus models.

Bul Impact of 2000

BUL M-5 IPSC

Bul M-5 ISPC
pistol

The single-action Bul M-5 IPSC was designed for the Limited and Standard IPSC class. The pistol has a frame of synthetic Xanex with a design very similar to the frames of STI, SPS and Stayer-Voigt. The weapon is available in the calibers, 9 mm Para (18 rounds), 9 x 21 mm (18), 9 x 23 (18), .38 Super (18), .40 S&W (17), and .45 ACP (14). The Bul M-5 IPSC has a barrel length of 127 mm (5 in), and a blued slide. The total length is 220 mm (8¾ in) and the weapon weighs 964 g (34 oz). The trigger pressure is between 1360 and 1600 g (3-3½ lb). The weapon has an adjustable rear sight. Both the front and the back of the slide have cocking grooves. There is an ambidextrous safety catch on the frame. In addition, the M-5 IPSC has an extended magazine catch on the left of the frame, behind the trigger guard and an enlarged aluminum magazine well. The pistol is delivered completely tuned, with three chrome magazines.

BUL M-5 MODIFIED

The Bul M-5 Modified is available in the calibers, 9 mm Para (18 rounds), 9 x 21 mm (18), 9 x 23 mm (18), .38 Super (14), .40 S&W (17), and .45 ACP (14). It has an Optima 2000 optical sight on the slide. There is a built-in compensator in the slide. This weapon also has an ambidextrous safety catch on the Xanex frame. The M-5 Modified also has an extended magazine catch on the left on the frame behind the trigger guard and an enlarged aluminum magazine well. The Bul M-5 Modified has a single-action trigger action with a trigger pressure between 1135 and 1360 g (2½-3 lb). The pistol has a total length of 191 mm (7½ in), a barrel length of 108 mm (4¼ in), and a weight of 850 g (30 oz).

Bul M-5
ISPC
Modified

BUL M-5 TARGET

The Target model has a barrel length of 152 mm (6 in) and a slide with a special barrel bushing for extra precision. This pistol also has a Xanex frame and a polished stainless steel slide. An Aristocrat micrometer sight is mounted on this. The weapon has a single safety catch on the left of the frame. This can easily be converted or altered into an ambidextrous catch. The single-action Bul M-5 Target is available in the calibers, 9 mm Para (18 rounds), 9 x 21 mm (18), 9 x 23 (18), .38 Super (18), .40 S&W (17) and .45 ACP (14). The total length is 244 mm (9½ in), and the weapon weighs 1080 g (38 oz). The trigger pressure is between 1135 and 1360 g (2½-3 lb).

Bul M-5
Target
match
pistol

BUL M-5 ULTIMATE RACER

Bul built the M-5 Ultimate Racer for the IPSC Open-Class. There is a large compensator at the front of the slide. In addition, the front of the slide is partly open to reduce the weight. Holes are bored in the Xanex frame for scope mounting. The weapon has an ambidextrous safety catch on the frame and an enlarged magazine catch on the left behind the trigger guard. At the bottom of the grips there is an enlarged aluminum magazine well. The total length, including the compensator is 265 mm (10½ in). The pistol has a barrel length of 152 mm (6 in). The Ultimate Racer is available in the calibers, 9 mm Para (18 rounds) 9 x 21 mm (18), 9 x 23 (18), .38 Super (18), .40 S&W (17) and .45 ACP (14). In addition, the weapon has a single-action trigger action with a trigger pressure between 1135 and 1360 g (2½-3 lb).

Bul M-5
Ultimate Racer

C

The renowned Colt
1846 Walker

COLT FIREARMS

Colt trade mark

Sam Colt and his firearms played an important role in American history. From the second half of the nineteenth century the Colt revolver was the most popular weapon on the North American continent. Colt's success started in 1836 when he registered his patent for a Colt firearm with a rotating cylinder for five or six bullets. The Colt revolver considerably increased the firepower of pistols compared with the single-shot flintlock pistols of the time. Some people believe that Colt thought of the design for a firearm

with a rotating cylinder during his trip on board the sailing ship, the Corvo. In his free time, Sam Colt carved a wooden model of this weapon. In 1836, he built his first factory in Paterson, New Jersey, one of the fastest growing industrial areas of America at the time. He manufactured the Colt Paterson 1836 revolver there. He had a wealthy uncle who was prepared to finance the business. At the age of 22, Colt became the manager of his own little weapon factory, the Patent Arms Manufacturing Company.

A short time later he developed and produced three different models of revolvers, the Colt Pocket, the Colt Belt Model and the Colt Holster revolver. In addition, he designed two different rifles, also with a rotating cylinder. However, the civilian sales were disappointing and he only sold a few hundred of these rifles to the American government. In 1842, the business went bankrupt. Sam Colt then tried to interest the American government in his other ideas, such as watertight ammunition and sea mines. In 1845, different US Cavalry units and the Texas Rangers were successful in their campaign against the Indians, and this was partly due to the use of Colt firearms. When the Mexican War broke out in 1846, Colt was visited by the US Army captain Samuel H. Walker. Together they developed a new and heavier revolver which Colt appropriately called the 'Walker'. Shortly afterwards, Colt received an order for 1000 of these new revolvers for the army.

This meant that Sam Colt could start manufacturing weapons again but he did not have a factory. However, his friend, Eli Whitney Jr., did have a factory in Connecticut, and allowed Colt to produce the revolvers for his order there. The year 1851 was very important for Colt. First, a factory was established in England to supply the European market; secondly, Colt bought large pieces of land cheaply in the water meadows on the banks of the Connecticut River in Hartford. When he had drained the land, he had a large industrial site to expand the factory which was completed in 1855. He equipped the new factory with the latest machinery. In this way, Colt was already producing about 5,000 firearms in the first year. In 1855, the firm was renamed the Colt's Patent Fire Arms Manufacturing Company. In 1856, production increased to 150 weapons per day. In gratitude for Colt's contribution to Hartford, the governor of Connecticut promoted Sam Colt to honorary Colonel.

Replica of 1836 Colt Paterson (Pietta)

The famous Colt
Peacemaker of 1873

Colt Model 1860 of the
American Civil War

Colt Match Target H-Bar rifle of
.223 Remington caliber

Colt had a very progressive way of doing business for those times. He soon realized that it was not only important to produce weapons, but above all, also to sell them. He established a whole network of agencies in the USA to sell to the local markets. In addition, he had sales offices in the cities of New York and London. By late 1860, when the Civil War was on the point of breaking out, he stopped delivering weapons to the Southern states.

At the end of 1861, the factory was running at full steam, and Colt employed more than 1,000 people. Sam Colt died on 10 January 1862 at the age of 47. In his short life, he made more than 400,000 firearms and earned about $ 15 million from this. This would now be worth about $ 300 million. The business remained in the Colt family. In 1864, the factory was burnt to the ground and the production capacity was reduced to almost zero. Sam Colt's widow rebuilt the factory, paying a great deal of attention to safety. The rebuilding was completed in 1867 and work started on the manufacture of the Gatling submachine gun, commissioned by the US Government. From 1869 to approximately 1871, Colt converted many thousands of percussion revolvers for use with metal cartridges which had to be loaded via the front of the cylinder. Loading this sort of conversion revolver was a lengthy process. Colt was bound by the patent of Rollin White, owned by Smith & Wesson. It was only in 1872 that Colt could start on the production of its first revolver with a completely bored cylinder for metal cartridges. This was the famous Colt Single Action Army, also known as the 'gun that won the West'. Up to 1940, Colt made more than 400,000 of these guns in different model

In about 1891, the management of Colt came into contact with John Moses Browning. They cooperated on the development of a water-cooled sub-machine-gun for the American navy. In addition, Browning designed the well-known BAR automatic rifle and the world-famous Colt 1911 and

the improved model, the 1911-A1 for Colt. In 1901, the Colt family sold the business to an investment group. During the First and Second World Wars, Colt had to switch to war production. In 1942, Colt employed more than 15,000 workers in three different factories. During the last year of the war, the war production stagnated and the company lost money. This was largely due to the age of the machinery which meant that the manufacture of the weapons for the war was inefficient.

After the Second World War, it was difficult for Colt to keep its head above water. The arms industry went into a sharp decline. Colt tried to survive by means of product differentiation and partly switched to the production of machinery, printing presses, synthetic materials and industrial washing machines. The war in Korea resulted in a financial recovery, but the company profits fell again when the armistice was signed in 1952. In 1955, the company was living off its financial reserves, and was even threatened with bankruptcy. The management decided to find a partner for a merger. In the end, Colt merged with the Penn-Texas Corporation, a large holding company of the Silberstein family. In 1959, the holding company was taken over by an investment group and the name changed to Fairbanks Whitney. Other subsidiaries in this holding company included the Pratt & Whitney airplane engine factory and the Fairbank Morse Company.

In 1960, Colt introduced its AR-15 semi-automatic rifle, followed by the fully automatic M16 army rifle. Business revived during the Vietnam War because there was a large demand for M16s. Tens of thousands of pages in hundreds of books have been written about the history of the AR-15 and its military counterpart, the M16. Some books are full of praise, while others are extremely critical in connection with experiences of the war in Vietnam. Despite this, the M16 is the most produced and copied gun apart from the AK-47.

There are many models of the M16. One of the standard works on this rifle is the book *The Black Rifle* by R.B. Stevens and E.C. Ezell. The history of the M16 is described in the course of 416 pages. Over the years, Colt made a number of civilian models of the extremely well-known Colt M16 Automatic army rifle under the brand name AR-15. Eugene Stoner designed the M16 in 1956 for the Armalite firm. At the time, this firm was part of the Fairchild Engine and Airplane concern, and Stoner was employed there as chief engineer. In 1959, Colt took over production. Altogether approximately 3,440,000 rifles were made of the M16 in various different models.

There were great changes in 1964 when the holding company was reorganized. The Colt Inc. Firearms Division became part of Colt Industries. In the 1970s, the company focused on the manufacture of the old Sharps rifle and black powder replicas of old Colt revolver models. This was so successful that it was decided to market these weapons as engraved models as well. The Colt gun shop was founded for this purpose in 1976. The famous Colt Walker and the 1860 Army model were made there, amongst other guns. In 1984, Colt introduced its Combat Government Model and the .380 ACP Government. Once again, the future looked bright for Colt, but in the same year the US Army decided to abolish the Colt 1911-A1. In addition, Colt soon dropped out of the race for a new army pistol. In 1986, the company celebrated its 150th anniversary and it was decided to produce a series of commemorative weapons, including a beautifully

Colt make many service rifles. The Colt M4 is shown with M203 grenade launcher

engraved Colt Single Action Army. However, a long period of industrial disputes and strikes started for Colt. Furthermore, in 1988, Colt lost the contract for the manufacture of M16 rifles for the US Army.

In 1989, Colt announced the sale of the company. The new owners were a large groups of investors, united in the Colt Firearms Holdings Corporation. The name of the production company changed to Colt's Manufacturing Company, Inc. As the American metal union was also part of the investment group, this bought an end to the wave of strikes. In 1990, three new Colt weapons were introduced, the Double Eagle pistol, the large Colt Anaconda and a new model of the AR-15: the Colt Sporter. Curiously, the Anaconda was the first Colt revolver in .44 Magnum caliber. Once again, Colt found itself in difficulties and threatened by bankruptcy. In 1994, the old factory in Hartford closed down and the company moved to new premises in West Hartford.

A government contract for 19,000 Colt M4 army rifles in 1994 saved the company financially. In the same year a new group of investors bought up the company. In 1995, Colt introduced a number of new models: the Colt 22 Target pistol, the .38 SF-VI revolver and the Match Target rifle based on the AR-15. Furthermore, there was an additional order for 16,000 M4 army carbines. In 1996, Colt started to develop a so-called Smart Gun in cooperation with the National Institute of Justice. The aim was to develop a digitally operated service pistol, which could only be used by a programmed user. Colt also joined the Professional Rodeo Cowboys Association. For these sorts of events, Colt introduced a number of models of the Single Action Army known as 'The Legend'. In 1997, Colt received another order from the army for 6000 M4 carbines. In the same year Colt again introduced a number of new models to the market. These were the Pony Double-Action pistol, the Defender Carry pistol and the DS II revolver. Colt's Custom Shop also produced the Python Elite and the Gold Cup Trophy pistol. 1998 was a good year for Colt. The US government decided to order weapons from the company again, and ordered 32,000 rifles of the M16-A2 model for the army. Shortly afterwards, there was an order to convert 88,000 M16-A1 rifles to M16-A2s for the US Air Force. In 1998, Colt merged with the American arms factory, Saco Defense. This company specializes in automatic weapons for the army. 1999 was another successful year. Colt received an exclusive army contract to produce M4 army carbines up to 2010. In addition, Colt bought up the company Ultra Light Arms, which specializes

Colt Z40 of the 'Smart Gun' project: 1. electronic lock 2.antenna 3. battery 4. microprocessor

Justice, they are focusing on the development of a service pistol with an electronic lock for the police. In fact, FBI statistics had shown that approximately 14% of American police officers who lost their lives while on duty had been shot with their own pistol. In many cases their weapon was taken or grabbed from their holster by criminals who used it to wreak death and destruction. A 'Smart Gun' could prevent this from happening. The technical design entails that the officer concerned should wear an electronic armband containing a transmitter. The grip of his service pistol contains an electronic locking system and a receiver. As long as the armband is near the pistol the weapon is on 'sharp'. When the armband is more than 20 cm removed from the pistol, the firing system is blocked. Colt used the Colt Z40 pistol manufactured by CZ for these tests.

in sports rifles. Colt introduced the Cowboy revolver and the compact Pocket Nine pistol. In 1999, Colt produced a double-action-only model of the Pocket Nine, the new Colt Tac Nine pistol and a new model of the Colt National Match pistol. This was followed by the multi-caliber Colt Survivor revolver at the beginning of 2000, This weapon can shoot a large number of different types of ammunition, from 9 mm Short to .357 Magnum. Because of a thorough reorganization, these new models had already disappeared from Colt's range by the end of 2000. In fact, Colt drastically reduced the whole production line of its firearms. There was a considerable reduction in the range of handguns, although the line of rifles was expanded. You can find a complete and up-to-date survey on the net at www.colt.com.

Since 1996, Colt's special research department has worked on a so-called Smart Gun project. Commissioned by the American National Institute of

COLT MODEL 1911

This military automatic was the first pistol in .45 ACP caliber (Automatic Colt Pistol) of the US Army. It was used in the army for more than 70 years. Following the official transfer of the first series of pistols in January 1912, a great number of major and minor modifications were made in the course of time. For example, there was a modification in 1913 when a different rear sight was used. In 1914, the hammer spur was extended and enlarged. In 1915, a small series was made for the Canadian army in a different caliber, .455, in connection with large surfeits of ammunition from the Webley & Scott ammunition for pistols. Several factories were licensed to manufacture the Colt 1911, because Colt was unable to deal with the large orders from the army on its own. These included Savage Ammunitions Co, North American Arms in Canada, Remington Arms, Union Switch & Signal

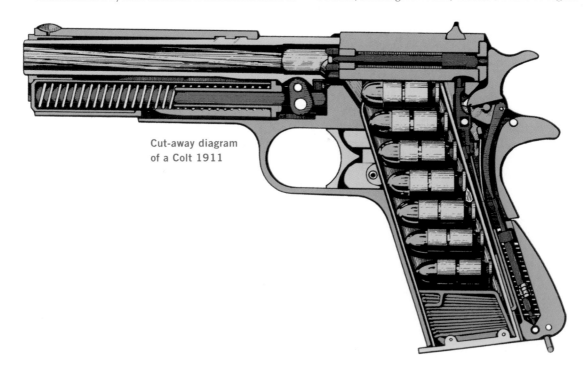

Cut-away diagram of a Colt 1911

Co , Singer Sewing Machines, Remington Rand (which also made typewriters), Caron Brothers in Canada, Springfield Armory (1914) and also Norway. They were licensed to manufacture this pistol model from 1917 to 1930. Altogether more than 700,000 Colt 1911 pistols were produced. In the pistols for the civilian market the serial number was preceded by a 'C'. The military models usually have an inscription on the slide such as 'United States Property', 'Colt Navy', 'USMC' (=United States Marine Corps), 'Model of 1911 US Navy', 'Model of 1911 US Army', 'Model of 1911/US Army Caliber .45', 'RAF', and the series made in 1915 for Russia was inscribed 'Anglo Zakazivat'.

The historic development which eventually resulted in the Colt 1911 actually started in 1892. In that year the old Colt Single-Action Army .45 was replaced by the .38 (.38 Long Colt) Double-Action New Army revolver. This represented great progress, because the revolver had a swing-out cylinder and could therefore be rapidly loaded or reloaded. In addition, the shooter could fire very quickly in double-action. However, in combat situations the cartridge appeared to be less ideal. This was demonstrated in a rather painful way during the Philippine rebellion of 1899. The stopping force of the new .38 Colt cartridge proved to be extremely unsatisfactory. Therefore the army was forced to dig up the rejected single-action .45 army revolvers. Subsequent tests also clearly showed that the army was only interested in a new weapon in the .45 caliber or larger. As the rest of the world was successively transferring to automatics, the American War Department considered that it should not fall behind. From 1907 to 1911, the army conducted extensive test series with all sorts of trial weapons. On the basis of these the arms commission unanimously agreed that the Colt 1911 should be the new army pistol. They also decided on the official cartridge, viz. the .45 Government Automatic Cartridge. This cartridge had a bullet of 233 grains and was developed by the American Frankford Arsenal based on an earlier Browning design. The 1911 was first used along the Mexican border. The US Army conducted a number of punitive expeditions there against the large Pancho Villa gangs. In the First World War, the Colt 1911 played an important role in the trenches in France and Belgium. The pistol proved to be very valuable there.

Since its introduction in 1911, various minor modifications have been made in the model, including a broader front sight, a larger grip safety, a shorter trigger and

finger grooves in the grip frame at the level of the trigger guard. The hammer spring housing in the backstrap was also made rounder so that the pistol was easier to use. These modifications were developed by the Springfield Armory. In 1926, the War Department approved all these modifications at the same time. The 'renovated' pistol was then given the name '1911-A1'. The year of manufacture can be deduced on the basis of the weapon number of the Colt 1911 pistols.

Serial numbers		Production year
from	to	
1	17.250	1912
17.251	60.400	1913
60.401	107.596	1914
107.597	133.186	1915
133.187	137.400	1916
137.401	216.986	1917
216.987	594.000	1918*
594.001	700.000	1919

*the serial numbers for 1918 include production of the 1911 Colt, Colt USN (Navy), Colt USMC (Marine Corps), and that of Springfield

Remington introduced its own numbering system in 1918-1919, being:

Serial numbers		Production year
from	to	
1	12.152	1918
12.153	21.676	1919

COLT 1911-A1

The Colt 1911 and 1911-A1 were used for more than 70 years before they were retired. They were succeeded by the Beretta pistol, model 92-F in 9 mm Para. In its time, the Colt 1911-A1 was used in quite a number of wars, including the First World War (model 1911), the Second World War (1911-A1) and the wars in Korea and Vietnam. In addition, US forces became embroiled in quite a number of other conflicts. The Colt 1911-A1 was always used in the most extreme circumstances: the heat of the desert

The renowned Colt 1911-A1 US Army pistol

in the Middle East, the humid tropical jungles of South America and the incomparable winters of Alaska. The pistol always worked reliably and could be used without any problems with most types of ammunition in a large variety of bullet weights, shapes and gas pressures.

As required for any good army pistol, the 1911-A1 can be dismantled without any tools, with exception of the grips, though these do not have to be removed for normal maintenance. The design of the hammer is adapted so that it can easily be cocked with the thumb of the shooting hand. The safety catch on the left of the frame is directly above the thumb of the shooting hand. The magazine catch is in a very logical, easily accessible place behind the trigger guard. The slide catch ensures that the slide remains in the open position after the last shot. The grip safety requires the use of both hands when the shooter wants to uncock the hammer. This is the most risky operation which can be carried out with a single-action pistol. 'Cocked and locked' is a particularly risky way of carrying the weapon which was often used by soldiers during the Second World War so that they could fire very quickly. The hammer is then fixed in the cocked (single-action) position, so that the safety catch is on 'safe'. As the standard weapon does not have a firing pin safety, it is certainly not safe if it falls. Colt did include an automatic firing pin safety in the 'Series 80' models. The locking mechanism of the Colt was taken over from the tried and tested Browning design. The fact that this system is so reliable is clear from the fact that many arms manufacturers have used it. Altogether many millions of this model were produced, for example, those by the Spanish Llama and Star factories, Ballester- Molina and Hispano Argentina in Argentina, the American firms AMT, Crown City, Safari Arms, Auto-Ordnance, Caspian, Falcon, Randall, Vega, Detonics, Springfield Armory and many others.

There is a large range of different models of the Colt 1911-A1, including the Colt Government, Model MKI to IV and the models described as 'Series 70' and 'Series 80'. The pistols in the 'Series 70' have a modified barrel bushing. All the models in the 'Series 80' have automatic firing pin safety.

In these 'main models' there are various different match models, such as the Gold Cup National Match in the models Mark IV, Series 70 in .45 ACP caliber and Series 80, including stainless steel models. Models based on the Colt 1911-A1 can be subdivided into three types: the large Government model, the smaller Commander model, and the practical Officers ACP pistols. The chief caliber used by Colt has always been the .45 ACP cartridge, although the weapon has been and is made in several other calibers, such as .455 caliber (during the Second World War, for example, for Canada),

9 mm Para, .38 Super, .41 Action Express, 10 mm Auto, .38 Special Wadcutter (with an extended slide) and in a number of less well-known calibers for export purposes such as .30 Luger, 9 mm Steyr, etc.

The Colt 1911-A1 also inspired many 'custom' gunsmiths, such as Randall with a stainless steel left-handed model. In addition, many gunsmiths have marketed their 'own' adapted models of the Colt in the past 40 years, sometimes for special shooting disciplines or adapted to the individual requirements of the purchaser. From 1924 to the end of the Second World War it was possible to base the year of manufacture of the Colt 1911-A1 from the weapon number:

Serial numbers		Production year
from 1	to 700.000	Serial numbers of the Colt 1911 from 1912–1919
700.001	710.000	1924
710.001	712.349	1937
712.350	713.645	1938
713.646	717.281	1939
717.282	721.977	1940
721.978	756.733	1941
756.734	801.000	1942
801.001	1.609.528	1943
1.609.529	2.075.103	1944
2.075.104	2.693.613	1945

The Colt 1911-A1 pistols of 1941–1945 mainly bear army inscriptions such as:
   -1   Model of 1911 US Army;
   -2   M1911 A1 US Army;
   -3   United States Property.
In the Second World War, Colt was unable to meet the demand and the pistol was also made by other manufacturers under license. These included, for example, Remington Rand Inc in Syracuse, New York, Remington Arms UMC Co Inc in Bridgeport, Connecticut, Ithaca Gun Inc in Ithaca, New York, Union Switch and Signal Co in Swissvale, Pennsylvania, North American Arms Co Ltd and Singer Sewing Machine Co. In the post-war period, the Colt 1911-A1 was more or less replaced by the more luxurious Government pistol is various different models. Nevertheless, the 'old workhorse' was occasionally revived and, under pressure from enthusiasts, Colt made a small series of this pistol. When Colt saw that other manufacturers (including Springfield Armory and Auto-Ordnance) were interested in this gap in the market, they decided to resume the production of the 1911-A1 after the sale of the Colt factories in 1991. The 'new old' Colt 1991-A1 was introduced at the beginning of 1991.

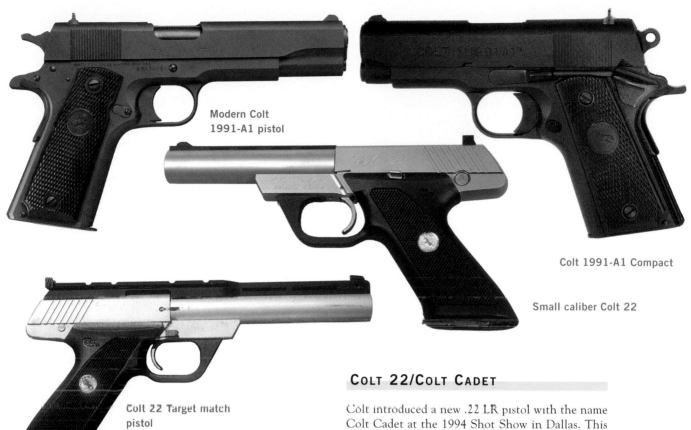

Modern Colt
1991-A1 pistol

Colt 1991-A1 Compact

Small caliber Colt 22

Colt 22 Target match
pistol

COLT 1991-A1

In 1991 Colt introduced a new model of the old army
pistol to the market as the Colt 1991-A1. This
single-action pistol is in .45 ACP caliber and has
a magazine for 7 cartridges. The total length is
216 mm (8½ in), the barrel length is 127 mm (5 in)
and the weight is 1077 g (38 oz). In addition, it has
an automatic firing pin safety. Colt introduced the
1991-A1 Compact in 1993. This shorter, 6-shot
pistol has a total length of 184 mm (7¼ in), a barrel
length of 89 mm (3½ in) and a weight of 964 g
(34 oz). In 1996, Colt also made the 1991-A1 in
9 x 23 mm caliber, specially for parcours shooting.
In addition, this pistol has been available in stainless
steel since 1996. In 1997, Colt made the Compact
model of the 1991-A1 in stainless steel for a short
time. Colt continued the existing serial numbering
of the 1911-A1 in the new model. In 2000, Colt
decided to reduce its range. Apart from the blued
standard 1991-A1, only the stainless steel model
and the shorter 1991-A1 Commander are still made.
This 7-shot model has a total length of 197 mm
(7¾ in) a barrel length of 114 mm (4½ in), and
a weight of 1021 g (36 oz).

COLT 22/COLT CADET

Colt introduced a new .22 LR pistol with the name
Colt Cadet at the 1994 Shot Show in Dallas. This
is a stainless steel, 10-shot pistol with a ventilated
barrel, 114 mm (4½ in) thick. The total length is
219 mm (8½ in) and the weight is 950 g (33½ oz).
The grip, with an integrated trigger guard, is made
by Pachmayr of hard rubber. The safety catch is at
the back of the frame. The switch has to be pressed
from right to left through the frame to set the
weapon on 'safe', and obviously from left to right,
remove the safe setting. In this pistol the magazine
catch is on the right of the frame, above the trigger
guard. In addition, the pistol has a slide catch.
Therefore the slide remains in the open position
after the last shot. The weapon is not a match pistol,
but is intended for use as a 'plinker' for recreational
shooting. This is apparent from the absence of an
adjustable rear sight. In 1995, Colt introduced
a match model on the market, the Colt 22 Target.
This weapon has a barrel 152 mm (6 in) long with
a ventilated barrel rib, a total length of 270 mm
(10½ in) and a weight of 1148 g (40½ oz). It does
have an adjustable micrometer sight. In 2000, Colt
decided to cease production of the Colt 22.

COLT 2000 ALL AMERICAN

With this new type of pistol, Colt entered
a completely new field of weapon design in 1992. The
system was totally different from what Colt had made
up until that time. The Colt 2000 is a double-action-
only pistol in 9 mm Para caliber and has a barrel

A failed concept: Colt 2000
All American with rotating
locking

length of 114 mm (4½ in). The total length is 191 mm (7½ in), and the weight is 935 g (33 oz). Colt also provided an interchangeable set with a short barrel, 95 mm (3¾ in) long, a shorter recoil spring with a recoil conductor bar and a shorter barrel bushing. The unusual aspect is the locking system: a rotating barrel. The 15-shot weapon was available with a light metal frame. The weight of this type, the AM 2800 is 935 g (33 oz). In addition, Colt also made a model with a polymer frame. This weighs only 822 g (29 oz). The 2000 All American did not prove to be a commercial success. In 1994, Colt ceased production. Altogether only a few of these pistols were made, and it is a popular collector's item.

COLT ACE

In the course of time special models have been introduced, based on the 1911-A1. For example, this applied to the Colt 'Ace'. This Colt pistol is a 1911-A1 in .22 LR caliber and first appeared on the market in 1931. In 1937 its name changed to the Colt Service Ace, and the weapon was also used as

Colt Ace conversion
in .22 LR caliber

a training pistol for US Army units. The unique aspect of the system used in the Ace is the 'floating chamber' principle. The cartridge chamber for the .22 LR cartridge is a separate block which ensures the acceleration and increase of the recoil, setting the repeat action of the pistol in motion. In 1938, Colt marketed a .22 LR conversion set for the Colt 1911-A1. Shooters who already had the 'large' weapon, could exchange the complete slide, the barrel and the 10-shot magazine. The small caliber interchangeable slide was marked 'Service Model Ace'. In 1942 production ceased because of the war. However, Colt resumed the manufacture in 1947. From 1978 to 1982, the complete Ace pistol reappeared in the range as the 'Colt Service Model Ace'. The total length of the Ace is 213 mm (8³⁄₈ in) with a barrel length of 127 mm (5 in). It weighs 1190 g (42 oz).

COLT ANACONDA

Colt Anaconda
revolver in .44
Magnum

Curiously, Colt only produced a large double-action revolver in .44 Magnum caliber in 1990. Up to that time, the market had been largely dominated by Smith & Wesson and Ruger. The Colt Anaconda is available with three different barrel lengths. The short model has a total length of 245 mm (9½ in), a barrel length of 102 mm (4 in), and a weight of 1333 g (47 oz). The second model has a total length of 295 mm (11½ in), a barrel of 152 mm (6 in), and a weight of 1503 g (53 oz). The third model has a barrel length of 203 mm (8 in), a total length of 346 mm (13½ in) and a weight of 1673 g (59 oz). All the barrels have a ventilated barrel rib like that of the Python. The ejector shroud extends right through to the muzzle, giving this revolver has a robust appearance. The 6-shot weapon is made entirely of stainless steel. In addition, there is a choice between an adjustable rear sight and a mounted scope. For users of heavy ammunition, it is interesting that the cylinder stop slits in the cylinder are between the cylinder chambers. This means that the cylinder chambers are less susceptible to high gas pressures. The

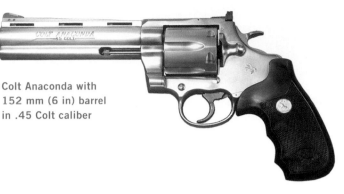

Colt Anaconda with
152 mm (6 in) barrel
in .45 Colt caliber

Anaconda came with a standard rubber grip. In 2000, Colt decided to cease the manufacture of the Anaconda.

COLT COMBAT COMMANDER

Colt has made the Commander model since 1949. The original Commander had a light metal frame. The weapon was at that time available in 9 mm Para, .38 Super and .45 ACP calibers. For some time, a small series was made in 7.65 Para caliber for exporting to countries where so-called government calibers are not permitted for private use. Since 1970, the weapon has been known as the Combat Commander. This pistol has a steel O-frame. The Combat Commander has a barrel length of 108 mm (4¼ in), a total length of 197 mm (7¾ in) and a normal 1911-A1 frame size with a height of 140 mm (5½ in). It weighs 1020 g (36 oz). Nowadays, the weapon is available in a blued or in a stainless steel model, but only in .45 ACP caliber. The Commander model with a light metal frame was renamed the 'Lightweight Commander'. The serial number of this Lightweight is preceded by the letters 'LW'. In 1972, Colt produced a new model of the Lightweight Commander. This has a grip made out of a strong light metal alloy. This Lightweight has a stainless steel slide and is available only in .45 ACP caliber with a magazine capacity of 8 rounds. It weighs 765 g (27 oz). The magazines are completely interchangeable with those of other Colt models. Other Commander models include the Commanding Officers, the Gold Cup Commander with an adjustable rear sight, the Stainless Commander, the Target Combat Commander and the double-action Double Eagle Combat Commander. In connection with the far-reaching reorganization in 1999 and 2000, Colt decided to drastically reduce production. Only the blued Colt 1991-A1 Commander with a barrel length of 108 mm (4¼ in) is still available.

Old model Colt
Commander

Modern version of
Colt Combat
Commander

Colt Combat Commander
MK IV with automatic
firing pin safety

Colt Combat
Commander MK IV
Series 80 in stainless
steel

COLT DEFENDER

Colt introduced the compact Defender in 1997. The barrel length was reduced to 76 mm (3 in) in a shorter slide. The total length of the Defender is 171.5 mm (6¾ in) and the weapon weighs 638 g (22½ oz). It is available in .40 S&W caliber (7 cartridges) and .45 ACP caliber (also 7 cartridges). The frame is the same size as that of the Officers ACP, so it was not necessary to make a new type of magazine. By using a new type of follower, the capacity was increased to 7 cartridges. The Defender has a light metal frame, a fixed combat rear sight and a triple aspect night sight. The grip safety is extended into a beavertail. In addition the pistol has a firing pin safety and an enlarged safety catch on the left of the frame. There is a rubber grip with finger grooves around the frame. The Colt Defender is still produced.

Colt Defender
of 1997

COLT DELTA ELITE

The 10 mm Auto cartridge was inherited from Jeff Cooper and Dornhaus & Dixon with their BrenTen pistol venture which ended in failure. In spite of this failure the cartridge was not lost altogether and since that time many manufacturers have produced pistols in this caliber or have marketed interchangeable sets for their existing pistols. In 1987, Colt also introduced an 8-shot 10 mm Auto pistol, based on the .45 ACP Government, which was known as the Colt Delta Elite. In comparison with the Government, the slide of the Delta Elite is heavier because of the higher gas pressure and the recoil of the 10 mm Auto cartridge. The recoil spring is also strengthened with a second spring in the normal recoil spring. In addition, there

Colt Delta Elite pistol in
10 mm Auto caliber

is a recoil spring guide made of special synthetic materials (Delrin) and a recoil buffer. It is actually the heavier weight of the Delta which makes it comfortable to shoot because the greater weight and mass absorbs part of the heavier recoil. The Delta Elite was produced up to 1998. Like the 1911-A1 and the Government, the Delta Elite has a barrel length of 127 mm (5 in). The magazine capacity is 8 rounds. The total length is 216 mm (8½ in) and the weapon weighs 1077 g (38 oz). The Delta Elite was also made in a stainless steel model for a short while. Colt made this single-action pistol up to 1997.

COLT DELTA ELITE GOLD CUP STAINLESS

The Delta Elite Gold Cup Stainless is the match model of the ordinary Delta Elite. Colt introduced this model in 1992. This pistol is actually a Gold Cup in 10 mm Auto caliber with a magazine capacity of 8 rounds. The total length of the weapon is 216 mm (8½ in), the barrel length is 127 mm (5 in) and it weighs 1106 g (39 oz). It has an adjustable Accro rear sight, a trigger with an adjustable trigger stop, and an enclosing rubber grip. The single safety catch is on the left of the frame. The magazine catch is also on the left, behind the trigger

Colt Delta Elite Gold
Cup in stainless steel

**Colt Double Eagle
(double action) pistol**

guard. In addition, it has a half-cock safety on the hammer foot and an automatic firing pin safety. Colt stopped making this model in 1998. The main reason was that the 10 mm Auto cartridge was replaced by the new .40 S&W caliber.

COLT DOUBLE EAGLE

Curiously, it was not until 1989 that Colt introduced its first double-action weapon on the market. Its main competitor, Smith & Wesson, had beaten Colt to it 34 years before with its model 39. However, better later than never, the engineer Don Khoury developed Colt's first double-action pistol in .45 ACP and 10 mm Auto in 1988 and it was introduced in 1989. Colt tried to obtain a larger market share with this model of the pistol. Small American 'custom' weapon firms were successful at cloning or converting Colt pistols in stainless steel and even with a double-action trigger system. At first sight, the Double Eagle looks like a Colt 1911-A1 pistol with a double-action

**Compact version of
Colt Double Eagle
Combat Commander**

trigger system. Nevertheless, the mechanism was thoroughly modified. The Double Eagle no longer has a grip safety and the characteristic triangular safety catch on the left of the frame has also gone. The pistol has an uncocking lever, also on the left of the frame, just below the slide catch. The cocked hammer is unocked by pressing this uncocking lever. In addition, the weapon has automatic firing pin safety. In 1991, an improved model appeared on the market, the Double Eagle MK II Series 90, in which the double-action trigger system was modified. Colt made four models of the Double Eagle design: the Double Eagle MK II/Series 90, the Double Eagle Combat Commander, the Double Eagle Officers ACP, and the Double Eagle Officers Lightweight. The first three models were made in stainless steel and the lightweight model was blued. The Double Eagle Combat Commander was also available in .40 S&W caliber from 1993. Because of the company's poor financial situation, Colt announced that the production of this pistol would cease at the end of 1992. This decision was revoked at the beginning of 1993, and the Double Eagle continued to be produced up to 1998.

COLT DOUBLE EAGLE COMBAT COMMANDER

The Double Eagle Combat Commander is a shorter model of the larger Double Eagle. The double-action pistol has a barrel length of 108 mm (4¼ in), 19 mm (¾ in) shorter than the standard Double Eagle. The total length is 197 mm (7¾ in), the height is 140 mm (5½ in) and the weapon weighs 1020 g (36 oz). The Double Eagle Combat Commander model appeared on the market in 1990 in .45 ACPO caliber. In 1992, this was followed by a model in .40 S&W caliber. The Double Eagle Combat Commander was only made in stainless steel, with a fixed rear sight. The magazine capacity was 8 rounds in both calibers. In 1991, an even shorter double-action pistol appeared on the market, the Double Eagle Officers Model. This weapon was only available in .45 ACP in a stainless steel or blued model. The Double Eagle Officers had a barrel length of 89 mm (3½ in), though it did have the same frame as the standard Double Eagle. Therefore the magazine capacity was also 8 rounds. Colt ceased the production of both models at the end of 1997.

Famous Gold Cup
National Match pistol in
.45 ACP caliber

The same pistol in
stainless steel

COLT GOLD CUP NATIONAL MATCH

Colt introduced the National Match .45 ACP pistol in 1932 during the American national matches in Camp Perry. In 1933, Colt introduced this match pistol based on the model 1911-A1 on the market as a series in .45 ACP caliber. The weapon was completely assembled by hand, using parts with the smallest possible tolerances. Initially, the pistol was fitted with a standard Stevens micrometer sight. In 1935, the weapon was also made in .38 Super caliber. However, in the Second World War the National Match became less important. It was relaunched in 1957 under the name Colt Gold Cup National Match. Special features of this Gold Cup National Match pistol are the broad match trigger with an adjustable trigger stop, a Colt-Elliason sports sight from 1965, an enlarged ejection port in the slide, and a flattened hammer spring housing. In addition, the pistol has very small tolerances and therefore a high degree of shooting precision. Initially the post-war weapon was only available in .45 ACP caliber. The different types of National Match model are referred to as Mark I, Mark II Mark III and Mark IV. The Mark

I was the 'old' National Match which was made from 1933 to 1942. Colt produced the National Match Mark II from 1957 to 1960. From 1960 to 1974 Colt also made the weapon in .38 Special Wadcutter Mid-Range caliber, and the model was called Gold Cup MK III National Match. Altogether, about 7,000 pistols were made in this caliber.

The Gold Cup National Match Mark IV/Series 70 was introduced on the market in 1970 with a caliber limited to .45 ACP. Colt modified the barrel-bushing for improved shooting precision. The Gold Cup was available in the blued Colt Blue or in a nickel-plated finish. Following the introduction of the Gold Cup National Match Mark IV/Series 80, the pistol is also available in stainless steel in a sandblasted or polished finish. Pistols in the Series 80 have automatic firing pin safety. Because of its increasing popularity, Colt also produced this model in 1989 in 10 mm Auto caliber under the name Gold Cup Elite and the Delta Gold Cup. The Gold Cup National Match has a total length of 216 mm (8½ in), a barrel length of 127 mm (5 in) and a weight of 1106 g (39 oz). In 2000, Colt had to scrap the manufacture of large number of models because of major reorganization. Only the Gold Cup Trophy model is still available.

COLT GOVERNMENT

In about 1970, Colt produced the Government MK IV Series 70 model. A number of improvements had been made to the original pistol, including a different barrel bushing. In addition, the pistol was made in .38 Super caliber (the Colt Super Commander) and 9 mm Parabellum caliber, as well as .45 ACP. A number of other disadvantages continued to apply, such as the rear sight which was too small and fixed, as well as a rather small safety catch. Many shooters actually wanted a special model of the Colt pistol. As Colt could not meet these wishes, it allowed a large number of small specialist weapon shops to make these sorts of modifications to Colt pistols. These

Gold Cup National Match in .38 Special Wadcutter
Mid-range caliber

Colt Government in special
'Classic .45' version

Colt Government MK IV Series
80 pistol

Colt Government with
nickel-plated casing and
blued slide

The same pistol with
compensator

Colt Government in
stainless steel

included Swenson, Wilson and Devel. In 1983, the next series of Colt pistols was introduced to the market, the MK IV Series 80, in which not only the rear sight was improved, but in addition, automatic firing pin safety was used, i.e., the firing pin is always blocked and no shot can be fired unless the trigger is completely pulled back. A new modification followed in 1991. In this model the top of the slide was flattened and the tension groove were diagonally cut into the back of the slide. In addition, Colt enlarged

the ejection port and lengthened the grips (beavertail). A shallow finger groove was also included in the frame under the trigger guard. The Government was available in .38 Super, .40 S&W and .45 ACP calibers, and from 1997 to 1998 also in 9 x 23 mm caliber. From 1999 Colt decided to only manufacture the Government in .45 ACP caliber in a blued and stainless stale model called the Colt 1991 Government Model. In 2000 Colt introduced the XS Government Model in stainless steel and only in .45 ACP. This is a slightly more luxurious model with mahogany grips, a triple aspect combat sight, a trigger with an adjustable trigger stop, and an ambidextrous safety catch. By using a modified follower the magazine capacity was increased to 8 rounds. Since 2000 Colt has only made one Government model, the Special Combat Government Competition. This single-action pistol in .45 ACP caliber has a barrel length of 127 mm (5 in), a Bo-Mar micrometer sight, an ambidextrous safety catch and a magazine capacity of 8 rounds.

COLT HUNTSMAN/CHALLENGER

Colt introduced the small caliber Challenger pistol in 1950. It was a simply made plinker with a fixed rear sight. The weapon was available in .22 LR caliber with a barrel length of 114 mm (4½ in) or 152 mm (6 in). The total length of the weapon was respectively 229 mm (9 in) or 267 mm (10½ in) and it weighed 850 g (30 oz) or 893 g (31½ oz). Furthermore, it had no slide catch and the magazine catch was in the heel of the grip. Colt produced approximately 77,000 of these pistols up to 1955. The Challenger was succeeded by the slightly more luxurious Huntsman. Up to 1960, the Huntsman had synthetic grips, and from 1960 to 1977 these grips were made of walnut. The measurements of the Huntsman were the same as those of the Challenger. Colt stopped making the Huntsman in 1977, when it had made approximately 100,000 of these pistols.

The old Colt
Huntsman pistol
of 1955

COLT KING COBRA

At the end of 1985, Colt announced the introduction of a new model, the Colt King Cobra. The production of this series was to start at the beginning of 1986, but Colt was affected by a strike, so that there were big delays in production. This was particularly unfortunate because Colt was celebrating its 150th anniversary in that year. The technology of this stainless steel revolver is similar to the Colt Trooper MK V, but it does have its own design. The heavy

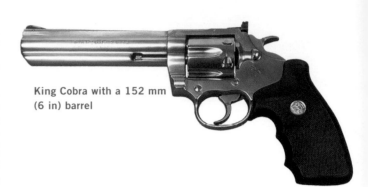

King Cobra with a 152 mm
(6 in) barrel

barrel has an extended ejector shroud which is beveled at the bottom of the muzzle. The double-action weapon has the special adjustable Colt-Accro rear sight. In addition, the revolver has the standard hard rubber Pachmayr 'Gripper' grips. The cylinder is bolted into the back of the frame. The revolver has a coiled hammer spring instead of the older leaf spring, such as that used in the Colt Python and the Trooper MK III. The King Cobra was initially available with four different barrel lengths. The model with the short barrel of 64 mm (2½ in) had a total barrel length of 191 mm (7½ in). The model with a barrel length of 102 mm (4 in) had a total length of 229 mm (9 in) and a weight of 1190 g (42 oz). The third model had a total length of 279 mm (11 in) and a barrel length of 152 mm (6 in). The fourth type had a barrel length of 203 mm (8 in) and a total length of 330 mm (13 in). Up to 1993, Colt also made a blued King Cobra. In 1994, Colt decided to manufacture only the 102 mm (4 in) and 152 mm (6 in) models. At the end of 1999, Colt ceased production of this revolver as a result of its far-reaching reorganization.

COLT MAGNUM CARRY

Colt introduced this small stainless steel pocket revolver in 1998. The 6-shot double-action weapon is only available in .357 Magnum caliber. It has a barrel length of 52 mm (2 in), a total length of 178 mm (7 in)

Colt King Cobra revolver in
.357 Magnum caliber

Colt Magnum Carry
back-up revolver

and weighs only 595 g (2 oz). In addition, it has enclosing rubber combat grips with one finger groove at the bottom and a fixed rear sight. Colt designed this revolver as a back-up weapon. Production ceased as a result of the reorganization in 2000.

COLT MUSTANG

The Colt Mustang was introduced in 1983 as a so-called mini-gun. This 6-shot single-action pistol in 9 mm Short (.380 ACP) caliber initially had a barrel length of 83 mm (3¼ in) a total length of 152 mm (6 in) and a weight of 595 g (21 oz). The stainless steel weapon had automatic firing pin safety and a traditional safety catch on the left of the frame. It had no grip safety. As in the large Colt pistols, the magazine catch is on the left of the frame, behind the trigger guard. In addition, it was only available with a fixed rear sight. The Mustang Pocket Lite followed in 1987 with a light metal frame. The barrel length was reduced to 70 mm (2¾ in). The total length was 140 mm (5½ in). The weapon weighed only 345 g (12½ oz). In 1988, Colt introduced the successor of the ordinary

Colt Mustang Pocket Lite pistol

Mustang Plus II

Colt Officer's ACP in .45 ACP caliber

Colt Officer's ACP in stainless steel

Mustang on the market as the Mustang Plus II. This pistol had a magazine capacity of 7 rounds. In 1999, the term 'Plus II' was dropped and only the standard Mustang with a weight of 420 g (14¾ oz) and the Mustang Pocket Lite 335 g (12½ oz) remained, both with a magazine capacity of 7 rounds. Colt ceased production of Mustangs in 2000.

COLT OFFICERS ACP

Colt introduced the Colt Officers ACP Mark IV 80, the official name of the pistol, in 1984. This is a compact model of the Colt 1911-A1 with a reduced length and height. It was not the first time that Colt decided to give this 'old workhorse' a new and compact design. In fact, the firm had already produced another compact pistol in 1949: the Colt Commander. The original Commander was only 20 mm Shorter than the 1911-A1, but it was a lot lighter. Colt had given the Commander a light metal frame so that its weight was reduced from 1105 g (39 oz) to 740 g (26 oz). In 1971, Colt introduced a completely stainless steel Commander called the Combat Commander. This pistol weighed slightly more than 900 g (31¾ oz). Colt became aware that many small weapon companies were concentrating on so-called custom-guns. The old 1911-

A1 was often shortened as a combat pistol. In addition, the firm was faced with quite a lot of competition from other makes, which either produced clones in stainless steel or sold compact factory versions for competitive prices. Colt decided to develop its own design, and this resulted in the Officers ACP. The Officers ACP has a total length of 184 mm (7¼ in), so that it is significantly smaller than the 1911-A1 or the Government 216 mm (8½ in) or Commander (203 mm/8 in). The height is particularly reduced. The Officers ACP has a height of 127 mm (5 in), approximately 13 mm (½ in) smaller than the Government or Commander. This did have an effect on the magazine capacity: 6 cartridges in .45 ACP caliber instead of the already fairly limited 7 rounds. The Officers ACP was initially available in two finishes: in mat black anodized or in an electrolytic nickel finish. The short barrel has a clear trumpet shape, which meant that the barrel centered well in the slide. In addition, a fixed rear sight was used with a triple aspect night sight. This is a good term for the two white dots on either side of the opening of the front sight and one white dot on the bead. To ensure that the locking system of the pistol works well, a double recoil spring was used. Furthermore, the housing of the main spring was flat and the grips were lengthened to a beavertail. In terms of safety systems, the Officers ACP had several systems, with grip safety, locking safety (the pistol cannot be fired when the slide is not completely shut), obviously a safety catch and automatic firing pin safety. In 1988, Colt made an Officers Match conversion set in stainless steel. This set consisted of a stainless steel slide, a barrel, recoil springs, and a recoil spring guide and an Officers cartridge ejector. If these parts were

interchanged with those of the Gold Cup, this produced an Officers ACP on a Gold Cup frame, so that it had a magazine capacity of 7 rounds. These sets are very popular collector's items nowadays. Colt also made several models of the Officers ACP, viz., in stainless steel. For the Lightweight, which weighed only 680 g (24 oz) a light metal frame was used. In 1990, Colt introduced a polished stainless steel Officers ACP as the 'Ultimate Stainless'. In 1991, the Colt Double Eagle Officers model .45 ACP was introduced. This was a compact Officers model of the Double Eagle introduced in 1990. The word 'double' stands for the double-action trigger system. This type does not have a traditional safety catch but has an uncocking lever on the left of the frame, just below the slide catch. In 1998 Colt scrapped the Officers ACP model and replaced it with the Concealed Carry Officer, abbreviated to the Colt CCO. This single-action pistol in .45 ACP had the stainless steel slide of the Combat Commander and the light metal frame of the 'old' Officers ACP. This type has a total length of 197 mm (7¾ in), a barrel length of 108 mm (4¼ in) and a weight of 737 g (26 oz). The CCO was no longer made after the reorganization in 2000.

COLT OFFICERS MODEL MATCH

Colt produced the Officers Model Special in .22 LR and .38 Special calibers from 1904 to 1952, with an interruption during the two World Wars. During these periods the production capacity had to be used for the war effort. The Officers Model Special was made in different models with barrel lengths from 102 mm (4 in), 114 mm (4½ in), 127 mm (5 in), 152 mm (6 in),and from 1908, even with a barrel length of 191 mm (7½ in). The model in .22 LR caliber was only made with a barrel length of 152 mm (6 in). Other names for the same revolver are: Officers Model or Officers Model Target. The successor of this model was the Officers Model Match made from 1953 to 1972. This was made in .22 LR and .38 Special calibers and with a barrel length of 152 mm (6 in), a total length of 286 mm (11¼ in) and a weight of 1075 G (38 oz). In 1960 Colt also made a small series in .22 WMR caliber. This match revolver is very precise particularly because of the special attention devoted to all the parts during the manufacturing process. The attractively blued revolver has a micrometer sight and walnut grips. The Colt Officers Model Match is very valuable to collectors as relatively few of these were made.

Colt Officer's Match model in .38 S&W Special caliber

The virtually unknown super match revolver: Colt Officer's Match in .22 LR caliber

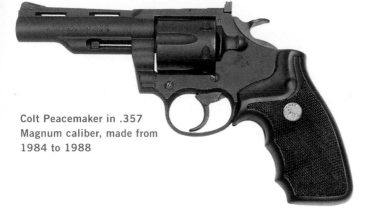

Colt Peacemaker in .357
Magnum caliber, made from
1984 to 1988

COLT PEACEKEEPER

At the end of 1984, Colt marketed the steel 6-shot
double-action Peacekeeper revolver in .357 Magnum
caliber. The weapon was similar to the Colt Python, but
had a short ejector shroud, and was made in a dull blued
finish with an adjustable sight and rubber combat grips.
The Peacekeeper was intended to oust the competition
in the sector of service weapons. It was available in two
barrel lengths. The short Peacekeeper had a barrel
length of 102 mm (4 in), a total length of 229 mm
(9 in) and a weight of 1077 g (38 oz). The longer model
had a barrel length of 152 mm (6 in), a total length of
279 mm (11 in) and a weight of 1190 g (42 oz). The
revolver was not a great success and disappeared from
the range by 1998.

COLT POCKET NINE

The Colt Pocket Nine pistol was introduced in 1999.
The weapon has a stainless steel slide and a light metal
frame with an enclosing rubber combat grip. It has
a magazine capacity of 8 rounds. The empty weight of
this double-action-only pistol in 9 mm Para caliber is
only 482 g (17 oz). The barrel length is 70 mm (2¾ in),
and the total length is only 140 mm (5½ in). Because
of its extremely short frame, the little finger of the
shooting hand cannot be used to hold this weapon.

Colt Pocket Nine
had a very short
life

Considering the relatively large 9 mm Para cartridge,
shooting this pistol does not appear to be very
comfortable. It is mainly meant as a back-up weapon.
As a result of the reorganization in 2000, Colt ceased
the manufacture of this pistol.

COLT PONY POCKETLITE

The Colt Pony was also developed as a 'mini-gun'
and was marketed in 1997 in 9 mm Short (.380
ACP) caliber. Like the Pocket Nine, this pistol also
has a capacity of 6 rounds. The Pony is also a double-
action-only pistol with a barrel length of 70 mm
(2¾ in), a total length of 140 mm (5½ in) and
a weight of only 389 g (13 oz). The weapon has
a stainless steel slide and a light metal frame. The
Pony does not have a safety catch but does have
automatic firing pin safety. The magazine catch is on
the left of the frame, behind the trigger guard. The
grips are made of black synthetic material.
Production ceased in 2000.

Colt Pony Pocket Lite
pistol in 9 mm Short (.380
ACP) caliber

COLT POLICE POSITIVE

The original of the double-action Colt Police Positive
dates from 1896 and was known as the New Model
Police. This revolver was made by Colt up to 1907 in .32
Colt New Police and .32 S&W calibers. Colt made the
weapon with barrel lengths of 64, 102, and 152 mm (2½,
4 and 6 in), and in a blued or nickel-plated finish. In

Colt Police Positive
Special Mark V

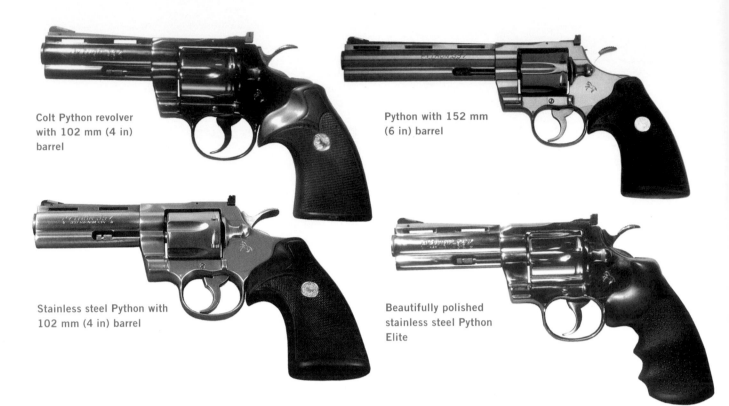

Colt Python revolver
with 102 mm (4 in)
barrel

Python with 152 mm
(6 in) barrel

Stainless steel Python with
102 mm (4 in) barrel

Beautifully polished
stainless steel Python
Elite

1905, the Police Positive appeared in .38 New
Police and .38 S&W calibers. Colt made this
model up to 1947. From 1907 to 1973, Colt
also made the Police Positive Special model.
This revolver has a slightly heavier frame for
the .38 Special caliber. In 1994 Colt
reintroduced a slightly modified model as the Police
Positive Special Mark V. This revolver has a heavy barrel
102 mm (4 in) long with a continuous ejector shroud.
The bottom of the grip is rounded. The weapon has
a rubber stock and fixed telescopic sights.

An old Python in nickel-
plated finish

COLT PYTHON

The Colt Python revolver has a special place in the
field of double-action revolvers. The Python is seen
as the BMW of double-action revolvers. Anyone
who has ever shot this revolver or driven a BMW
will understand this. In addition to its superior
trigger action, the finish of this revolver is
superlative. This is reflected in its price, which is
quite a lot above that of the competitors. Colt
introduced this weapon in 1955. It is the brainchild
of Bill Henry, a Colt representative. The prototype
was built by the Colt employee, Al De John, who
later became the head of the Colt Custom Shop. The
name of the revolver was completely in line with the
Colt trend at the time. The first 'Snake' revolver
dates back to 1951, the Cobra .38 Special. This
tradition has been continued since that time, as
revealed by later models of revolvers such as the
King Cobra and the Anaconda. At first, the Python

was only available in one barrel length: 152 mm
(6 in). A few years later, Colt introduced
a police model of the Python with a barrel
length of 102 mm (4 in) and a model with a short
barrel, 64 mm (2½ in) long. The Python Hunter,
with a barrel length of 203 mm (8 in) was introduced
in 1980. The Colt Python with a barrel length of
64 mm (2½ in) has a total length of 203 mm (8 in)
and weighs 935 g (33 oz). The total length of the
model with a barrel length of 102 mm (4 in) is 241
mm (9½ in), and the weapon weighs 1077 g (38 oz).
The model with a barrel length of 152 mm (6 in)
has a total length of 292 mm (11½ in) and weighs
1233 g (43½ oz). The largest model with a barrel
length of 203 mm (8 in) has an impressive total
length of 343 mm (13½ in) and actually weighs 1361
g (48 oz). During the period of production from 1955
to 2000, there were several caliber experiments
which were abandoned after a while owing to a lack
of success. For example, this resulted in a Python in
the .38 Special caliber, as well as a model in .22 LR
caliber. Other changes mainly concern the finish of

Python in stainless steel with 152 mm (6 in) barrel

The same weapon in polished Elite version

the exterior. The standard Python came in a highly polished royal blue, but there is also a nickel-plated and a stainless steel model. The Colt Python Ultimate is a polished stainless steel model. In 1999, Colt decided to produce only the stainless steel model with a barrel length of 102 mm (4 in), called the Python Elite. This revolver had a walnut Hogue Finger Grip stock. Unfortunately, Colt decided to cease production of the Python in 2000.

COLT SINGLE ACTION ARMY 1873 (PEACEMAKER)

The Colt Single Action Army dates from 1873, the days of the Wild West. Other names for the same weapon are the Colt 1873 and the Colt Peacemaker. The production of firearms in America was already dominated by Colt and Smith & Wesson. The latter concentrated mainly on military orders from other countries, and Colt focused more on the domestic market. The Peacemaker was initially developed for the US Army, particularly for the cavalry. Hence the name Single Action Army. However, the revolver was also popular with the American public. This was because of its great reliability. Occasionally something might break but even then the shooter was still able to fire the revolver. The single-action trigger was not even really necessary. By pushing the hammer back manually and letting it go again, it was possible to fire several shots very quickly. This is known as fanning. The Colt Single Action Army has been made in a large number of models and finishes, with barrel

lengths from 76 mm (3 in), to 254 mm (10 in) and in calibers from .22 LR to .476 Eley. Well-known models include the so-called Buntline, the Frontier Six-shooter, Sheriffs Model, Frontier Scout, Storekeepers model, Bisley model and many others. The basic model can be divided into four different periods of manufacture or generations:

The first generation was produced from 1873 to 1940, and divides into two models. The first was the black powder model which Colt made from 1873 to 1900. This can be identified by the centerpin locking plunger, at the front of the frame. The second model, suitable for nitro powder, starts at serial number 192000 and has a plunger for the centerpin in the side of the frame. The most common calibers were .32-20 Win., .38-40 Win., .40 Long Colt, .44-40 Win. and .45 Colt. Altogether, Colt made more than 357,000 of these revolvers. During the Second World War, Colt had to switch over to the production of arms for the war effort, and the manufacture of the Single Action Army had to be interrupted.

The second generation was made from 1956 to 1974. Approximately 74,000 were made in this period in a large number of different calibers. Colt started with a new serial numbering from 00001. The introduction of the weapon was mainly a result of the competition. In 1955 the American Sturm, Ruger & Co. introduced a similar model on the market, the Blackhawk single-action revolver. This model was so successful that Colt saw an opportunity to share in the success and started making the Peacemaker again. Since then Colt has produced 250,000 Peacemakers. The Single Action Army was not produced between 1974 and the end of 1976. The third generation started at the end of 1976 with serial number 80000 SA. In 1978 this numbering was used up at 99999SA. Colt changed the numbering to SA 0001, etc. Initially the weapon was only available in .45 Colt caliber. Shortly afterwards the .357 Magnum was added. In 1982 the Colt was also made in the old caliber, .44-40 Win. Colt ceased production in mid-1983. The Single Action Army was only available through a special order from the Colt Custom Shop.

The best-known Colt revolver: the Single Action Army 1873 or Peacemaker

The fourth generation started when Colt reintroduced the model in 1992 because of a new trend in American sports shooting: Cowboy Action Shooting. In 1993, Colt had got to the end of the serial numbers available with number SA 99999, and a new series was introduced starting with S00001A. The models of the Colt Single Action Army from 2000 are:

Colt Cowboy in .45 Colt caliber with a 140 mm (5½ in) barrel in a blued finish with a flame-hardened frame;

The Colt Single Action Army in .45 Colt or .44-40 Win. caliber with a barrel length of 121 mm (4½ in) or 140 mm (5¾ in) with a blued, flame hardened or nickel-plated finish. The Peacemaker still appeals to the imagination. No cowboy film is complete without this faithful six-shooter. This weapon has been copied by many manufacturers, with or without a license.

COLT TAC NINE

Colt introduced the Tac Nine in 1999. It is a 6-shot double-action-only in 9 mm Para caliber. It is actually a Pocket Nine, but the model is mat black with a triple aspect tritium sight. The stainless steel slide has a mat black coating, as does the light metal frame. The Tac Nine has a total length of 140 mm (5½ in), and a barrel length of only 70 mm (2¾ in). The pistol weighs 482 g (17 oz). Colt stopped production of this model in 2000.

Colt Tac Nine, made from 1999–2000

COLT TROOPER MARK III/MARK V

After the Second World War, Colt had to convert many of its factories for the production of civilian weapons. One of the new models was the Trooper revolver which was manufactured from 1953 to 1967. In the 1960s, Colt decided to develop a new revolver design. This was the Colt Trooper Mark III which was

A old Colt Trooper Mark III

introduced on the market in 1969. The Trooper Mark III was first made in .357 Magnum caliber, but later also in other calibers, such as .22 LR, .22 WMR and .38 Special. Models based on this included the Lawman Mark III with a fixed rear sight, the Official Police and the Officers Model Mark III, both in .38 Special caliber, as well as the Metropolitan revolver. The trigger mechanism was based on that of the Python. However, Colt used a coiled spring, rather than the Python leaf spring as the hammer spring. The revolvers were available in different finishes, such as a blued finish a nickel-plated finish and a special luxury model known as the Colt-Guard, a highly polished nickel-plated model. The chambers in the cylinder of the small caliber model were recessed, so that the protruding rim of the cartridge case engaged in this. This system was not used in the large caliber model. This used a raised outer rim on the back of the cylinder, so that the bottom of the cartridge case engaged in the chambers. Approximately 300,000 revolvers of this model were manufactured. They were made with barrel length of 102 mm (4 in) and 152 mm (6 in). The Colt Trooper Mark V was introduced in 1982 to replace the Mark III. Colt retained the Trooper design, but introduced a number of cosmetic modifications. The most striking of these is the ventilated barrel rib. In addition, the angle of the main spring was changed so that angle at which the hammer strikes the firing pin is also changed, viz., from 54 to 46 degrees. This has a positive effect on the trigger pressure for the double-action firing of this revolver. The hammer spring itself was also much longer. With the introduction of the Colt King Cobra in 1986, the production of the Trooper came to an end.

COLT WOODSMAN

The Colt Woodsman was a small caliber pistol designed by John Moses Browning. The 10-shot pistol was introduced in 1915 when it had a barrel length of 165 mm (6½ in). Colt made approximately 54,000 pistols of this model up to 1927. Its successor appeared in 1927, also called the Woodsman. Up to 1932, the

Colt's first small caliber
pistol: the Woodsman

only pistol in .40 S&W caliber
with a barrel length of 111 mm
(4¼ in) and a total length of
205 mm (8 in). The weight is
905 g (32 oz). In addition the
weapon has a fixed combat rear
sight. The blued weapon has a light
metal frame and a steel slide. It is
mainly intended for use as a service
weapon by the army and police. It
is strange to see that the left of
the frame is entirely a Colt
design and shows the Colt name
and inscription, Colt Mfg Co,
Hartford CT, USA while the right
hand of the pistol shows where the
weapon is made: Made in Czech Republic. Colt
sold this weapon on the American market for a short
while, but the cooperation soon foundered. In 1999,
Colt removed it from its range, though it did integrate
the Z40 in the Smart Gun project.

pistol was only suitable for standard ammunition.
However, from serial number 83790 it could also
shoot high velocity cartridges. This new Woodsman
was available with barrel lengths of 114 mm (4½ in)
or 165 mm (6½ in). Both models had walnut grips. In
the period from 1938 to 1944, Colt also made two
match models with a heavy barrel 165 mm (6½ in)
long, the Bull's Eye and the Match Target. As only
16,000 pistols of these models were made, they are
valuable collector's items. Colt made more than
112,000 pistols of the standard Woodsman model up
to 1937. In 1948 a revised model was introduced,
again called the Woodsman. In contrast with
previous models, this had a slide catch and a magazine
catch on the left of the frame, behind the trigger
guard. There were also several models of the new
Woodsman, such as the Woodsman Sport, with
a barrel length of 114 mm (4½ in), the Woodsman
Target with a barrel length of 152 mm (6 in), and the
Match Target with a heavy bull barrel 114 mm (4½
in) or 152 mm (6 in) long. In 1955, Colt produced
yet another new model of the Woodsman. Curiously,
the magazine catch of this new model was moved back
from behind the trigger guard to the heel of the frame.
Up to 1960 the weapon had synthetic grips, which
were then replaced up to 1977 by walnut grips. The
third generation of the Woodsman was also available
in the Sport model (barrel length of 114 mm/4½ in),
Target (barrel length of 152 mm/6 in) and the Match
target with a heavy barrel 114 mm (4½ in) or 152 mm
(6 in) long. Colt stopped manufacturing the
Woodsman in 1977.

COONAN

COONAN .357 MAGNUM PISTOL

The Coonan .357 Magnum pistol was the first
automatic on the market in this caliber. It was
introduced at the end of 1983 by the American firm
Coonan Arms in St. Paul in Minnesota. The
exterior of the weapon clearly shows the type of
pistol it was based on, viz., the Colt Government.
The most obvious difference is that from the very
beginning the Coonan was made in stainless steel
while the Colt was not ready for this at the time. The
first model, subsequently called model A, uses
a locking system of the familiar Browning/Colt type.
This has only one locking lug on top of the barrel
just before the chamber. Underneath the chamber
of the barrel a movable hinge point is attached
which enables the barrel to drop after the shot, when

COLT Z40

The story of the Colt Z40 is rather curious.
As the sales of the Colt Double Eagles were
not very successful Colt decided to have
another try with a double-action pistol.
However, it had never really mastered the double-
action technology. Colt thought it could solve this by
contracting out the development and manufacture of
this sort of weapon to another manufacturer.
Obviously Colt could not ask Smith & Wesson, its
chief competitor for assistance. It therefore opted for
the Czech firm, CZ. In 1998, this resulted in the
introduction of the Z40, a 12-shot double-action-

A failed project: the
double-action Colt-CZ Z40,
made by CZ for Colt

**Coonan .357
Magnum pistol**

it travels backwards a little, together with the slide, so that the locking is reversed. Model B, which was introduced in 1986, was considered an improved model by Coonan itself. This used the FN/ Browning system (as in the FN Hi-Power: which involves a fixed barrel shank under the barrel with only one lug on top of the barrel, which locks inside the corresponding grooves inside the slide). The pistol is adapted to the high gas pressure of the .357 Magnum cartridge. This can be seen, amongst other things, from a pin at the back of the top of the chamber, which engages in an extra recess in the hole in the outside of the slide. This prevents the barrel from rotating as a result of the spin of the bullet. Coonan also thought of the shooter's comfort. The short round hammer is small, while the back of the grip safety (the so-called beavertail) is deepened so that the hammer engages neatly into the recess when it is cocked.

The 7-shot Coonan has a total length of 226 mm (9 in), a barrel length of 125 mm (5 in) and a weight of 1190 g (42 oz). The height of this model is 150 mm (6 in). The safety catch is on the left of the frame. In addition, the weapon has a grip safety and a half-cock safety on the hammer foot. The magazine catch is also on the left, behind the trigger guard. The grips are made of walnut. In 1992, a shortened model of this pistol was introduced, the Coonan Cadet, also in .357 Magnum. This stainless steel weapon has a total length of 198 mm (7¼ in) and weighs 1120 g (39½ oz). For legal reasons, the name Cadet was changed to Coonan .357 Baby shortly after it was introduced.

CZ PISTOLS

CZ is an abbreviation for Ceska Zbrojovka or Ceskoslovenska Zbrojovka. The precursor of this firm Jihoceska Zbrojovka was founded in Pilsen in 1919. Amongst other things, this company produced

**Trade mark
of CZ**

the Czech Fox pistol in 6.35 mm (.25 ACP caliber). In 1921, the company moved to Strakonice. From 1923, CZ had the contract to supply the Czech army with weapons such as pistols and rifles, as well as bicycles, motorcycles and artillery. One example of this is the famous ZB-26 submachine gun, designed by Vaclav Holek in 1924. This weapon was produced by the factory Zbrojovka Brno. In 1936, the design was sold to the British. They developed their famous Bren gun on the basis of the ZB-26. In fact, Bren is a combination of Brno and Enfield. In the same year, CZ moved to a new factory in Uhersky Brod. In the Second World War, Czechoslovakia was annexed by Germany. Up to 1945, CZ made machine guns, amongst other things, for the German army, under the factory name Böhmische Waffen Werke. From 1947, Czechoslovakia was in the Russian zone and the company was nationalized. In 1958, the communist regime reorganized the company, and CZ became part of the state-run company, October Revolution. During that period CZ mainly produced rifles for the army, such as model 58, the Czech model of the AK-47 (Kalishnikov), and CZ motorcycles. There was another reorganization in 1965, resulting in the VHJ Zbrojovka Brno, also called Precision Machine-Tooling Company. The CZ-75 was introduced to the market in 1975 and was to some extent based on the Hi-Power design of FN-Browning. The CZ designers turned this design into a modern double-action pistol. During the period of the Cold War and the Iron Curtain, this pistol contributed to the reserves of currency although the weapon could not be exported to the USA at the time. As an army pistol, it did not play a major role, because the Warsaw Pact concentrated on 9 mm Makarov 7.62 mm Tokarev and 5.45 Russian calibers for handguns. In 1983, the name of the company changed to the Agrozet Brno Group, followed by another reorganization in 1988, resulting in the Ceska Zbrojovka Uhersky Brod. The CZ concern in its current form dates from 1992 when the Iron Curtain was raised. The modern company is one of the biggest producers of weapons in the world. It has a huge range of sports and hunting rifles and a large number of models of pistols. In 1996, CZ introduced the model CZ-100 in 9 mm Para and .40 S&W calibers with a double-action-only (DAO) trigger action. The model CZ-101 followed in 2000 in double-action.

CZ-27 pistol in
7.65 mm (.32
ACP) caliber

Exploded diagram
of the CZ-50

CZ-27

The CZ-27 pistol is based on an earlier model, the CZ-24. This weapon was developed for Mauser in 1923 by Josef Nickl, and CZ had the license for its production. The CZ-24 had a locking system based on a rotating barrel. As indicated above, the CZ-27 was based on this but has an ordinary recoil locking system. These models are often confused because they look identical. The CZ-27 was the model used by the Czech army and police for a long time. During the Second World War, the Nazis ordered the production of this pistol for the German army. Pistols dating from this period are marked with the code of the Wehrmacht FNH. At the end of 1945 CZ resumed the manufacture of this model. Pistols from that time have the inscription, 'Ceska Zbrojovka Narodni Podnik – Strakonice'. CZ made approximately 500,000 pistols of the CZ-27 model up to 1950. The CZ-27 is an automatic with a single-action trigger action. The total length is 165 mm (6½ in), the barrel length is 97 mm (3⅞ in) and the weapon weighs 710 g (25 oz). The 78.65 mm (.32 ACP) caliber has a magazine capacity of 8 rounds. The magazine catch is the heel of the grip. The pistol has a safety catch on the left of the frame, behind the trigger guard. The slide catch is just above this. The square lever above the trigger guard is the takedown lever.

CZ-50

Following the nationalization of CZ in 1948, the company introduced the double-action the CZ-50 pistol. It was developed by the Kratochvil Brothers. The weapon was used by the Czech police, among others. It has a recoil locking system and repeats using the recoil energy of the 7.65 mm (.32 ACP) cartridge. The CZ-50 is very similar in appearance to the well-known Walther PP pistol. The safety catch is on the

left at the back of the frame. When it is pressed right down, the cocked hammer uncocks and the firing pin is blocked at the same time. There is a cartridge indicator on the left of the slide. This slightly protrudes when there is a cartridge in the chamber. The total length of the CZ-50 is 167 mm (6½ in). The barrel length is 96 mm (3¼ in) and the weapon weighs 700 g (24¼ oz). The magazine catch for the 8-shot magazine is on the left of the frame. The takedown lever is on the right, in front of the trigger guard. After the last shot, the slide remains in its furthest position. The CZ-50 was succeeded in 1983 by the model CZ-83.

CZ-75

The CZ-75 is one of the most widely copied models of pistols. The double-action pistol was developed in 1975 by the Koucky brothers. It has a Browning locking system. Many different models have developed from the standard design in the course of time. The standard model has a large magazine capacity, viz., 16 rounds in the calibers, 9 mm Para and 9 x 21 mm, and 11 rounds

The famous CZ-75 (B-type shown) with integral firing pin safety in .40 S&W caliber. The standard CZ-75 models have a barrel length of 1120 mm (7 in), a total length of 206 mm (8 in) and they weigh approximately 1000 g (35¼ oz). The height of the standard weapon is 138 mm (5½ in). The ordinary CZ-75 has a safety catch on the left of the frame and a half-cock safety on the foot of the hammer. The magazine catch is also on the left, behind the trigger guard.

CZ-75B

The CZ-75B succeeded the previous model and was introduced in 1993. The main differences in comparison with the CZ-75B are a square trigger guard and a round hammer. In addition to the normal CZ-75 safety mechanisms, this weapon has an automatic firing pin safety, which is indicated by the letter B. The measurements of the CZ-75B are identical to those of the standard model.

CZ-75BD

The model CZ-75BD followed in 1997. The letter D stands for 'Decocker'. This weapon does not have a safety catch, but has a decocking or uncocking lever on the left of the frame. The measurements and the weight are the same as the standard CZ-75. Like the 75B, the 75BD also has a half-cock safety on the foot of the hammer, as well as a built-in automatic firing pin safety. The CZ-75BD was specially developed for government services such as the army and police.

CZ-75 Compact with
nickel-plated casing and
blued slide

on the left of the frame, a half-cock safety on the foot of the hammer and automatic firing pin safety. The pistol shown here has a blued slide and a mat nickel coated frame.

CZ-75 in semi-compact
version

CZ-75 BD with uncocking lever
instead of a safety catch

CZ-75 COMPACT

The double-action CZ-75 Compact dates from 1992 and is a smaller model of the standard CZ-75B. The 75 Compact has a total length of 186 mm (7¼ in) and a barrel length of 100 mm (4 in). The total height of the CZ-75 compact is 128 mm (5 in), and it weighs 920 g (32½ oz). The weapon is only available in 9 mm Para caliber and has a magazine capacity of 13 cartridges. In addition, this pistol has a safety catch

CZ-75 SEMI-COMPACT

The CZ-75 Semi-Compact was introduced in 1994 as a model halfway between the Compact and the standard model. The Semi-Compact has the slide and the barrel of the Compact and the large frame of the standard CZ-75. Therefore the Semi-Compact is 20 mm (¾ in) shorter, but it has a magazine capacity of 16 rounds in 9 mm Para caliber. Like the Compact, its total length is 186 mm (7¼ in) and the barrel length is 100 mm (4 in). The Semi-Compact weighs 960 g (34 oz). The height of the weapon is the same as that of the standard model: 138 mm (5½ in). The safety catch and slide catch are on the left of the frame. In addition, this model also has a half-cock safety on the foot of the hammer and an automatic firing pin safety.

CZ-75 police
pistol

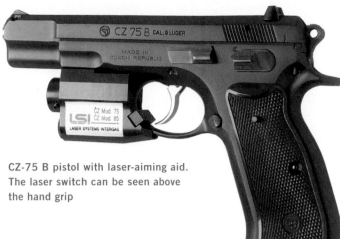

CZ-75 B pistol with laser-aiming aid.
The laser switch can be seen above
the hand grip

CZ-75 POLICE/CZ-75BD POLICE

The CZ-75 Police was developed in 1978 as a service model for the government. The first model was part of the 75 B series, although this was not indicated on the slide. The most obvious characteristic at that time was the uncocking lever, instead of the ordinary safety catch on the left of the frame. In addition, there was a lanyard ring under the grip.

Modernized version:
CZ-75 BD Police

In 1997, this model was succeeded by the CZ-75 BD Police. In addition to an uncocking lever, this weapon also has a cartridge indicator. Furthermore, it has a magazine catch behind the trigger guard which can be moved to the right side and a lanyard ring at the bottom of the grips. The slide catch is ambidextrous and the bead and the rear sight have a tritium night sight marking. This pistol is available in 9 mm Para and 9 x 21 mm calibers (both 16 cartridges) or .40 S&W caliber (11 cartridges). It has the same measurements as the standard CZ-75. The CZ is also available with a laser telescopic sight for police

purposes. This laser is clearly shown in the photograph. It is mounted on the front of the square trigger guard. The switch for this sighting device is not so easy to see. It is concealed as a peg in the left grip plate on the frame.

CZ-75 DAO

Model CZ-75 DAO was also designed as a pistol for the services and was introduced to the market in 1999. It does not have an external safety catch or uncocking lever. There is no hammer spur or hammer ring either. The trigger can only be operated in double-action-only. The weapon only has an automatic firing safety. It is always carried with a cartridge in the chamber and can therefore be fired immediately. In 9 mm Para or 9 x 21 mm caliber the 75 DAO has a capacity for 16 cartridges. In .40 S&W caliber the capacity is for 11 rounds. The CZ-75 DAO also has the same measurements as the standard model. There are also a number of sports models of the standard CZ-75.

CZ-75 DAQ double-
action-only

CZ-75 Champion with three-chamber compensator

CZ-75 sporting version with Aimpoint red dot sights

sight mounted on this. The advantage of this is that the rear sight can be left on the rear of the slide. There is an ambidextrous cocking grip on the slide of the 75CH, because the ordinary cocking grooves are difficult to reach with the thumb and index finger. In addition, the pistol has a three-chamber compensator. The photograph shows that the CZ-75CH has an ambidextrous safety catch.

CZ-75 AIM

The CZ-75 AIM has a special scope mounted on the left of the frame. Various different bridges can be placed on this. The scope produced by CZ itself is shown here. This is just above the slide, so that the balance of this pistol remains intact as far as possible. To do this it is necessary to remove the rear sight. The total length of this model is 206 mm (8 in). The barrel length is 120 mm (4¼ in) and the height, including the telescopic sight is 192 mm (7½ in). The total weight is approximately 1125 g (39½ oz).

CZ-75 CH

The CZ-75 CH has a mounted scope which is attached to the front of the frame on the right with three bushed bolts. There is a C-More reflection

CZ-75 Champion

The model CZ-75 Champion was designed for sporting use. The single-action pistol has a three-chamber compensator as well as an LPA micrometer sight. The safety catch and slide catch are ambidextrous. The specially lengthened magazine catch can be moved to the right. This sports model has an adjustable synthetic match trigger. The 12-shot 75 Champion in .40 S&W caliber was specially designed for IPSC events. The same weapon in 9 mm Para or 9 x 21 mm caliber for 16 cartridges has a two-chamber compensator and is specially designed for target shooting. The CZ-75 Champion has a total length of 240 mm (9½ in) and a barrel length of 114 mm (4½ in). It weighs 1010 g (35½ oz).

CZ-75 Kadet

The CZ-75 Kadet is a complete CZ-75 pistol in .22 LR caliber. This model was introduced in 1997. A Kadet model had already been marketed by CZ before, but this was as an interchangeable set for the

CZ-75 CH Sport with three-chamber compensator and C-More optical sight

CZ-75 Kadet small caliber training pistol

CZ-75M IPSC

CZ-75 OPTE with
extended hand grip as
sights

large caliber model of the CZ-75 and
CZ-85. The 10-shot small caliber
weapon has a square bead and an
adjustable micrometer sight. The
barrel of the Kadet is fixed on a sort
of upper bridge to which the sight is also attached.
The actual slide slides underneath this when the
weapon repeats. The advantage of this is that the
sight does not move and remains fixed. The total
length of the Kadet is 187 mm (7.4 in) and the barrel
length is 124 mm (5 in). The pistol has a double-
action trigger action.

CZ-75 M-IPSC
The CZ-75 M-IPSC was specially made for the IPSC
Open Class shooting discipline. The pistol has
a two chamber compensator. There is a reflection
sight on the front of the slide of the pistol. This is
protected from the gas pressure by a vertical flame
shield. The weapon does not have any other
ordinary sights. The safety catch and the slide catch
are ambidextrous and the magazine catch can easily
be moved to the right of the frame. In addition, this
model has a specially adjustable synthetic trigger.
The front and back of the frame
are ribbed for a firmer grip.

CZ-75 ST IPSC
The CZ-75 ST IPSC is
a model for the standard
class in the IPSC shooting
discipline. The weapon has an
ambidextrous safety catch and slide catch,
a synthetic match trigger and a micrometer rear
sight on the slide. The backstrap and the front of the
framer are finely ribbed with the so-called checkered
design.

CZ-75 OPTE
The CZ-75 OPTE model has a special mount for the
scope. This consists of a continuous grip plate on the
right, which ends in a bracket over the slide. A sight
or other scope can be attached to this bracket. The

illustration shows the SG3-OPTE red dot sight.
From the back of this optical sight a red dot is
projected onto the glass at the front. This red dot
can be adjusted for height, width and light. The peg
of the cartridge indicator can be clearly seen in the
recess of this mount.

CZ-83

This double-action pistol was introduced in 1983.
The automatic has a recoil locking system and
repeats using the recoil energy of the cartridge that
is fired. The barrel of the CZ-83 is fixed on the
frame. The pistol is available in 7.65 mm (.32 ACP)
caliber with a magazine capacity of 15 rounds, and
in 9 mm Short (.380 ACP) or 9 mm Makarov, both
for 12 rounds. The model in 9 mm Makarov has

CZ-75 ST ISPC pistol for
the standard class

CZ-83 pistol

CZ-85

a polygonal barrel, while the barrels of other models have standard grooves and lands. The total length of the CZ-83 is 172 mm (6¾ in), the barrel length is 97 mm (3¼ in) and the height is 127 mm (5 in). The weapon weighs 800 g (28¼ oz). It has a slide catch on the left of the frame. This catch ensures that after the last shot the slide remains in the open position. There is an ambidextrous safety catch on each side of the frame. In order to disassemble the weapon, the trigger guard must be pulled down slightly at the front. The trigger guard is blocked with an extra safety mechanism when there is a magazine in the weapon. This also works the other way round; if the trigger guard is not properly secured in the frame, the magazine does not fit into the weapon. It also has a fixed rear sight.

In 1996, CZ developed a modern version of this model. The main difference is the square trigger guard. Apart from this, the sight has a triple aspect tritium night sight.

CZ-85

The double-action CZ-85 pistol is a modernized model of the CZ-75 and was introduced in 1985. The CZ-85 has an ambidextrous slide catch and safety catch. In addition, the hammer has an additional half-cock safety. The slide catch ensures that after the last shot the slide remains in the last position. In addition, the standard model has a fixed rear sight. The sight can optionally be provided with a triple aspect tritium night sight. The pistol is only available in 9 mm Para caliber with a capacity of 16 cartridges. The CZ-85 has the same measurements as the CZ-75. The total length is 206 mm (8 in), the barrel length is 120 mm (4¾ in) and the weapon weighs approximately 1000 g (35¼ oz). In 1986 CZ introduced the CZ-85B model. Apart from the standard safety mechanisms, this model also has an automatic firing pin safety. It is also available in 9 x 21 mm caliber with a capacity of 16 cartridges.

Latest model CZ-83 with angular trigger guard

CZ-85 B pistol

Combat version of CZ-85 with adjustable folding sight

The CZ-85 Combat was introduced in 1996. This is the standard model with an adjustable micrometer sight. In the Combat, both the slide catch and the safety catch are also ambidextrous. The magazine catch, on the left behind the trigger guard, is enlarged and can easily be moved to the right. The CZ-85 Combat does not have an automatic firing pin safety.

CZ-92

CZ has made this pocket automatic since 1992. It was developed for personal security at short range. The weapon is only available in 6.35 mm (.25 ACP) caliber and has a magazine capacity of 8 rounds. The total length of the CZ-92 is 128 mm (5 in) and the barrel length is 63.5 mm (2½ in). The height of the weapon is 88 mm (3½ in), the width is

only 21 mm ($^{13}/_{16}$ in) and the weight is 430 g (15¼ oz). Apart from this, this pistol has a recoil locking system and repeats using the recoil energy of the cartridge that is fired. The trigger action is double-action-only. The CZ-92 does not have a safety catch but does have a half-cock safety on the foot of the hammer. The hammer can only reach the firing pin when the trigger is pulled completely back. This pistol does have a magazine safety. If the magazine is not placed in the weapon, the trigger mechanism is blocked. The CZ-92 has an optional magazine catch on the left of the frame, behind the trigger guard, or a magazine hook in the heel of the grip. It does not have a rear sight or bead, but a groove along the length above the slide, which is used to aim.

CZ-97

The double-action CZ-97 pistol dates from 1997. The weapon has a locking system based on the Browning-Petter type. The chamber block of the

The latest CZ-97 B pistol in .45 ACP caliber

The small CZ-92 DAQ (double-action-only)

barrel locks into the ejection port of the slide. The CZ-97 has many safety mechanisms. First the weapon has a safety catch on the left of the frame which blocks the hammer and the trigger. In addition, it has an automatic firing pin safety as well as a cartridge indicator. There is a half-cock safety on the foot of the hammer. The slide catch is on the left of the frame. The magazine catch is on the left, behind the trigger guard. The barrel is enclosed in the slide with the barrel bushing. The CZ-97 has a triple aspect sight. It is possible to opt for either a tritium night sight or a micrometer sight. This pistol is only made for CZ in .45 ACP caliber and has a magazine capacity of 10 rounds. The total length is 212 mm (8¼ in), the barrel length is 123 mm (4¾ in) and the steel weapon weighs approximately 1150 g (40½ oz).

CZ-100

The CZ-100 pistol was introduced in 1995. It has a double-action-only trigger mechanism. This means it can only be fired in double-action. The firing pin returns to the starting position after every shot and is then blocked. When the trigger is pulled, the firing pin (spring) is cocked. The CZ-100 locks with a chamber block in the barrel in the ejection port of the slide.

CZ-100
with laser

The latest CZ-100
pistol

The pistol has a slide catch on the left of the frame, at the top of the grip. The catch above the trigger guard is used to disassemble the weapon. The magazine catch is also on the left, behind the trigger guard. This trigger guard is extra large so that it is also possible to shoot with a gloved hand. The peg on the slide behind the ejection port is a characteristic feature. This serves to cock the weapon with one hand. The shooter can press it against a fixed object so that the pistol is recocked. The CZ-100 is available in 9 mm Para and 9 x 21 mm calibers with a magazine capacity of 13 rounds. A third model in .40 S&W caliber for 10 cartridges has compensator holes in the barrel and the slide. The total length of the CZ-100 is 177 mm (7 in). The barrel length is 95 mm (3¾ in) and the weapon weighs only 645 g (22½ oz). The height is 130 mm (5 in) and the weapon is 32 mm (1¼ in) wide. Apart from the automatic firing pin safety, this pistol does not have any other safety systems. The frame is made of synthetic material and the weapon has a steel slide. There is a rail at the front at the bottom of the frame. Various devices can be secured in this, such as a torch or a laser. In 2000, CZ introduced the model CZ-101. This is the double-action model of the CZ-100. The CZ-101 has a cartridge indicator, an automatic firing pin safety and a combined slide catch/uncocking lever on the left of the frame. This latest model has a magazine for 7 cartridges.

Left side of CZ-100

CZ-122 match pistol in
.22 LR caliber

CZ-122 Sport

For a long time CZ did not really make a true sports pistol in .22 LR caliber. The Kadet had existed for some time, but this was more of a small caliber training weapon than a match pistol. The CZ-122 was introduced in 1997. This single-action pistol has a fixed barrel with a raised rib for the sight and an adjustable LPA micrometer sight. During the repeat action, the slide moves under this rib. The slide catch is on the left of the frame. The switch behind this is the safety catch, which can only be used when the hammer is cocked. On request, the weapon can be provided with a magazine hook in the heel of the grip, or with a magazine catch on the left, behind the trigger guard. The CZ-122 has a total length of 238 mm (9½ in) and a barrel length of 152 mm (6 in). This pistol is in .22 LR caliber, with a magazine capacity of 10 rounds. It weighs 875 g (31 oz).

CZ-Colt Z40

The CZ-Colt Z40 dates from 1998. The pistol was developed by CZ, together with Colt. Colt wanted to make a good double-action pistol, but had never managed to master the double-action technology. Colt thought it could solve this by having another manufacturer develop and make this weapon. Colt could obviously not ask Smith & Wesson, its main competitor, for help. Therefore it opted for the Czech company CZ. In 1998 this resulted in the introduction of the Z40. It is a 12-shot double-action-only pistol in .40 S&W caliber with a barrel length

of 111m (4.3 in) and a fixed combat rear sight. The blued weapon has a light metal frame and a steel slide. It is mainly meant as a service weapon for the army and police. It is curious to see that the left of the frame is entirely made by Colt, i.e., with the Colt name and the inscription Colt Mfg Co., Hartford CT USA, while the words 'Made in The Czech Republic' on the right of the pistol show where the pistol was made. Colt sold the weapon on the American market for a short time, but the cooperation with CZ soon foundered. In 1999, Colt removed it from its range. In the same year CZ decided to start selling the weapon itself. This was obviously not without problems either, because CZ ceased production of this model in 2000.

CZ-Colt Z40 made by
CZ for Colt

D

Daewoo DP-51

Daewoo

Daewoo is an extremely large Asian concern. The consortium includes the car industry, shipping, mining, electronics and machine building. The Korean factory, Daewoo Precision Industries Ltd. in Seoul has made a number of models of pistols since 1990. The DP-51 13-shot pistol in 9 mm Para caliber has a slightly different trigger mechanism which is described by the manufacturer Tri-Action. This means that the pistol can be fired in three ways. The first method is the normal double-action technique. The weapon is not cocked, but there is a cartridge in the chamber of the barrel. The hammer is first cocked by means of the trigger and then released so that the shot is fired. The double-action trigger pressure is approximately 5.4 kg (12 lb). The second method is the usual single-action for repeat shots. After the first shot, the pistol is automatically reloaded and the hammer remains in the last, cocked position. The single-action trigger pressure is 2.7 kg (6 lb). This pistol also allows for a third method in which the weapon is first loaded and therefore cocked. Then the hammer can be pressed forwards into the rest position with the thumb. The hammer is uncocked, but the hammer or hammer spring remains cocked. To fire a shot, only a slight trigger pressure is needed to tip the hammer back again and fire the pistol. In this Tri-Action, the trigger pressure is about 2.2 kg (5 lb). Other manufacturers of similar systems also call this the Fast-Action or Selective-Action system. The barrel is clearly thicker at the muzzle, so that it fits tightly in the slide. This benefits the precision of shooting. The pistol comes standard with an extra magazine and a device for filling the

magazine quickly. A compact 13-shot model of the DP-51, the DP-51 Compact was introduced to the market in 1993. In the same year, the pistol was also introduced in the new caliber, .40 S&W, with the name DH-40.

Daewoo DP-51

The Daewoo DP-51 is only available in 9 mm Para caliber, and has a magazine capacity of 13 rounds. The weapon has a total length of 191 mm (7½ in), a barrel length of 104 mm (4 in) and a height of 122 mm (4¾ in). The width of the pistol is 34 mm (1¼ in) and it weighs 794 g (28 oz). The weapon has an ambidextrous safety catch on the frame. This safety catch disconnects the trigger rod, i.e. the connection between the trigger notch and the sear. The slide catch is on the left of the frame, above the trigger guard. The magazine catch is also on the left of the frame, behind the trigger guard. For left-handed shooters it can be moved to the right. The DP-51 has a light metal frame and a steel slide. The weapon has a fixed rear sight which can only be moved to the side. There is a lanyard ring in the heel of the grip. In addition, the weapon has a grip made of black synthetic material.

Daewoo DP-51C

The Daewoo DP-5C is a compact model of the larger DP-51 and was introduced in 1995. Apart from the fact that the pistol is slightly shorter, the Daewoo has also straightened the backstrap. The total length of the Compact is 178 mm (7 in), the barrel length is 91 mm

Daewoo's trade mark

Daewoo DP-51C pistol

Intermediate form: Daewoo DP-51S with compact slide and standard casing

(3½ in) and the height is 114 mm (4½ in). The width is 32.5 mm (1½ in) and the weight is 737 g (26 oz). The Compact is available in 9 mm Para caliber with a magazine capacity of 10 rounds. The weapon has the same sights as the DP-51.

DAEWOO DP-51S

The DP-51 S dating from 1995 has approximately the same measurements as the compact model. This pistol has the shorter slide and barrel of the DP-51 Compact but the frame of the larger DP-51. This means that the magazine capacity in 9 mm Para caliber is 13 rounds, as in the DP-51. The total length is 178 mm (7 in), the barrel length is 91 mm (3½ in) and the height is 122 mm (4¾ in). The width is 34 mm (1¼ in) and the weight is 765 g (27 oz).

DAEWOO DH-40

The Daewoo DH-40 is actually a DP-51 in .40 S&W caliber. The weapon is identical to the 9 mm Para model. The magazine capacity is 10 rounds. The total length is 191 mm (7½ in), the barrel length is 104 mm

Daewoo DH-40 in .40 S&W caliber

(4 in) and the height is 122 mm (4¾ in). The width of the pistol is 35 mm (1¼ in) and it weighs 907 g (32 oz).

DAEWOO DP-52

In 1995, Daewoo introduced the double-action model DP-52 in .22 LR caliber. The same pistol in 9 mm Short (.380 ACP) caliber was the model DH-380. The weapon is an almost exact copy of the Walther PP. It is only available in a mat blue finish. Both the slide and the frame are made of steel. The safety catch on the slide is ambidextrous. It blocks the firing pin and uncocks the hammer. The magazine catch is on the left of the frame, behind the trigger guard. In the DH-380 the slide catch is above the magazine catch. The DP-52 model does not have a slide catch. There is a lanyard ring in the heel of the grip. The DP-52 has a magazine capacity of 10 rounds in .22 LR caliber. The model DH-380 has a capacity of 8 rounds in 9 mm Short (.380 ACP) caliber. Both pistols have a total length of 170 mm (6¼ in), a barrel length of 96.5 mm (3¾ in) and

Daewoo DP-52 pistol in .22 LR caliber

a height of 104 mm (4 in). The weapon weighs 652 g (23 oz) in .22 LR and 680 g (24 oz) in 9 mm Short (.380 ACP). They both have grips of black synthetic material with a thumb rest in the left grip.

DALY

Charles Daly started an arms shop in New York City in 1865, together with his partner Schoverling. In addition to their retail outlet, they also engaged in importing firearms. In 1873, the business was reorganized and a third partner joined the business. They changed the name of the company to Schoverling, Daly & Gales. In 1875, they made firearms with the name Daly. They considered this short name to be attractive, and hoped to increase their turnover with it. The company acquired a good reputation because it only sold high quality firearms. It had its shotguns made in Prussia (Germany) by factories such as Heym, Lindner, Sauer and Schiller. It imported guns by Jolley from England and

Trade mark
of KBI and
Daly

The big Daly 1911-A1
Field FS

by Neumann from Belgium. In 1919, the company
was bought up by Henry Modell. He sold the
company on to the Walzer family in 1928. This
family also owned Sloan's Sporting Goods in
Ridgefield, Connecticut. The name of the company
in New York changed to the Charles Daly &
Company. From that time, Daly also imported
shotguns from Beretta and Bernardelli in Italy, from
Miroku in Japan and Garbi in Spain. In 1976, the
wholesale company, Outdoor Sports Inc., in Dayton,
Ohio, took over the Daly division. The new owner
kept on the Daly brand name and extended the
range further with blackpowder replicas, telescopic
sights, ammunition, hunting clothes and knives. In
about 1985, the Daly range consisted of firearms and
hunting accessories. From 1976 to 1985, the imports
of Daly brand name articles were mainly carried out
by Kassnar Import Inc. In 1996, the business was sold
to the wholesale company Jerry's Sports Center Inc.
in Forest City, Pennsylvania. Only a few months
later, KBI of Harrisburg, Pennsylvania bought the
Daly brand name. This was good for KBI. In fact the
managing director of KBI, Michael Kassnar, was also
the owner of Kassnar Imports Inc. In 1997, he
revised the whole range of Daly shotguns. In 1998,
this was expanded with small caliber guns and
pistols with the Daly brand name. The first double-
action pistol, the Daly DDA, followed in 2000.

DALY 1911-A1 EMPIRE CS

The Daly 1911-A1 Empire CS, introduced in 2000,
is a compact single-action pistol in .45 ACP caliber
with a magazine capacity of 6 rounds. The weapon
has a mat stainless steel frame and slide. The total
length is 184 mm (7¼ in), the barrel length is 89 mm

(3½ in) and the weapon weighs 1006 g (35½ oz). The
bead and the fixed rear sight are secured in the slide
with a dovetail joint. The rear sight can also be
adjusted at the side. The safety catch is on the left
of the frame. The weapon also has a grip safety,
which is lengthened in a beavertail. Apart from this
the pistol also has an enlarged magazine well. The
grips are made of attractive hardwood.

DALY 1911-A1 FIELD FS

The Daly Field FS model dating from 1998 is a large
pistol in .45 ACP caliber with a magazine capacity
of 8 rounds. It has a mat steel frame and slide. The
total length of the Field FS is 222 mm (8¾ in), the
barrel length is 127 mm (5 in) and the weight is
1106 g (39 oz). There are cocking grooves in both
the front and back of the slide. The weapon has an
ambidextrous safety catch on the frame and an
extended slide catch on the left of the frame. The
grip safety is lengthened in a beavertail. In addition,
it has the enlarged Daly magazine well. The grips are
made of black synthetic material.

DALY 1911-A1 FIELD MS

The Daly Field MS in a medium-sized model. The
pistol has the frame of the large FS, and the shorter
barrel and slide of the CS models. The total length
is 197 mm (7¾ in) and the barrel length is the same
as that of the CF, i.e., 89 mm (3½ in). The weapon

Compact Daly 1911-A1
Empire CS of 2000

The medium-sized Daly
1911-A1 Field MS pistol

weighs 1035 g (36½ oz). The Field MS has a mat steel frame and slide and an ambidextrous safety catch. It also has an extended beavertail grip safety and an enlarged magazine well in the grip. The grip plates are made of black synthetic material. The pistol is available only in .45 ACP caliber, with a magazine capacity of 8 rounds.

DALY 1911-A1 FIELD PC

The Daly Field PC, dating from 2000, has a polymer frame of the so-called 'wide body' type. Because of this extra wide frame, the weapon in .45 ACP caliber has a capacity of 10 rounds, although it is relatively light, weighing 935g (33 oz). The slide is made of steel. The total length is equal to that of the MS, i.e. 197 mm (7¾ in). The barrel length is 102 mm (4 in). In addition, it has an ambidextrous safety catch, a beavertail grip safety and an enlarged magazine well.

Daly 1911-A1 Field PC
with polymer casing

DALY 1911-A1 SUPERIOR MS

The Superior model was introduced to the market in 2000. The pistol has a lengthened beavertail grip safety, a special combat trigger and an enlarged magazine well. In addition, the ejection port at the back is enlarged and lowered. The Superior MS has

Daly Superior MS pistol
with stainless steel
casing and blued slide

a total length of 197 mm (7¾ in), a barrel length of 89 mm (3½ in), and a weight of 953 g (37½ oz). The weapon is only available in .45 ACP caliber and has a magazine capacity of 8 rounds. In addition, it has a mat stainless steel frame and a mat blue carbon steel slide. The single safety catch is on the left of the frame, as are the slide catch and magazine catch. The grips are made of black synthetic material.

DALY 1911-A1 SUPERIOR PC

In the Superior PC, the colors are exactly the other way round. The weapon has a frame made of black synthetic material with integrated grips and a mat stainless steel slide. This wide body PC frame has a capacity of 10 rounds in .45 ACP caliber. The total length is 197 mm (7¼ in) with a barrel length of 102 mm (4 in). The weapon weighs 36 g (33 oz). In addition, it has an ambidextrous safety catch, a beavertail grip safety and an enlarged magazine well.

DALY DDA-CS

The Daly double-action DDA was introduced in 2000. The weapon has a polymer frame and comes in .45 ACP and .40 S&W calibers. It has a magazine capacity of 10 rounds. The pistol in .40 S&W caliber should actually be able to hold at least 12 cartridges but this is not permitted by American law. The total

Superior PC with black
polymer casing and
stainless steel slide

Compact Daly DDA-CS
of 2000

Left side of Daly
DDA-CS

DAN WESSON REVOLVERS

Trade mark of Dan Wesson

length of the weapon is 187 mm (7⅜ in) and the barrel length is 92 mm (3⅝ in). The pistol weighs 737 g (26 oz). The slide is in mat carbon steel. The ergonomically designed DDA-CS has a safety catch on the left side of the frame, and automatic firing pin safety. The enlarged magazine catch behind the trigger guard can be moved to the right. In addition, it has an enlarged magazine well.

DALY DDA-FS

The Daly DDA-FS is a larger model of the DDA-CS. The double-action pistol has a total length of 210 mm (8¼ in), a barrel length of 111.5 mm (4⅜ in) and weighs 808 g (28½ oz). It is available in .45 ACP and .40 S&W calibers, both with a magazine capacity of 10 rounds. The DDA-FS also has a safety catch, slide catch and magazine catch on the left of the frame. Only the grips are longer, with a rubber block on the magazine.

The history of the American Dan Wesson weapons factory is related to that of Smith & Wesson. Originally, Daniel B. Wesson worked in the Smith & Wesson company of his distant ancestor, but he broke away when the company was taken over in the 1960s by the huge Bangor Punta concern. In 1968, Wesson started his own company called Dan Wesson Arms in Monson in Massachusetts. When the founder, Dan Wesson died in 1978, the company went downhill. In 1979 it fell into other hands and as a result of a recession in the arms industry, times were difficult. The founder's son, Seth Wesson, stayed in the company until 1983. In 1990, Dan Wesson Arms was involved in a suspension of payments. Seth Wesson decided to take over the reins himself together with a few of the employees. In January 1991, the company reverted to the Wesson family under the name Wesson Firearms Company and was established in Palmer, Massachusetts. Initially it produced .38 Special and .357 Magnum revolvers, but the range of revolvers was expanded on the basis of experience, from light to very heavy revolvers. The most important characteristic of Wesson revolvers is that the barrels can be interchanged. For each caliber there is a choice of barrel from 2½ to 15 in. The barrel can be unscrewed very simply from the frame and replaced by a barrel of another length. Consequently, the Dan Wesson revolver is the only revolver available in a Pistol-Pac design. This is a case containing a Wesson revolver with one, two or more interchangeable barrels of different lengths. Barrel shrouds are also available in different types, such as solid barrel shrouds with an integrated barrel weight,

The big Daly DDA-FS pistol with extended grip

shrouds without a barrel weight, with or without a ventilated rib on the barrel, in stainless steel or a dark blue color. In addition, the front sight on the barrel can easily be exchanged for one in another color. As the barrel of a Dan Wesson revolver is screwed into the back (in the frame) as well as the front (into the barrel shroud with a barrel bolt), it has a high level of precision in shooting. This is particularly noticeable over long distances. This is the reason why many silhouette shooters who shoot at distances from 50 to 200 meters have a preference for Dan Wesson revolvers. In international classes, 60 to 80% of the top twenty silhouette shooters use Dan Wesson revolvers. Another characteristic is the tapered choke-boring of the barrel. This becomes a few hundredth of a millimeter narrower towards the muzzle, and means that the contact between the bullet, and the grooves and lands in the barrel remains intact, despite the high bullet velocity. Another characteristic feature is the type of locking system in the cylinder. In the Dan Wesson revolver the locking system is on the cylinder yoke. Most other revolvers lock at the back of the cylinder via the cylinder axis and the extractor star. In a Dan Wesson, the cylinder is completely enclosed by a locking lug at the front and a cylinder aligning ball at the back. The current range includes revolvers in .22 LR, .22 WMR, .32 H&R Magnum, .38 Special, .357 Magnum, .357 SuperMag (Maximum), .41 Magnum, .44 Magnum, .45 Long Colt and .445 SuperMag. The types of barrel shroud are:

- Standard (without a barrel weight);
- Ventilated (without a barrel weight, with a ventilated rib on the barrel shroud);
- Vent-Heavy (with a barrel weight and with a ventilated rib).

DAN WESSON MODEL 15-VH6/ 715-VH6

The Model 15 is a Dan Wesson revolver in .357 Magnum caliber with a blued finish. 'VH6' stands for Ventilated Heavy barrel, a heavy barrel with a barrel weight and a ventilated barrel rib which is 162 mm (6 in) long. The total length of this 6 shot weapon is

Stainless steel version of model 715-VH6

Model 715-VH6 with red dot sights

285 mm (11¼ in) and the weight with this barrel length is 1190 g (42 oz). The same revolver model is shown below, in stainless steel. This is the Model 715-VH6. The measurements of the Model 15 and 715 are the same. Dan Wesson makes a number of different interchangeable barrels for this model:

- a 673.5 mm (2½ in) barrel with a total length of 196 mm (7¾ in) and a weight of 907 G (32 oz);
- a barrel length of 102 mm (4 in) and a total length of 234 mm (9¼ in) and a weight of 1050 g (37 oz);
- a barrel length of 203 mm (8 in) with a total length of 335 mm (13¼ in) and a weight of 133 g (47 oz);
- a barrel length of 254 mm (10 in), with a total length of 386 mm (15¼ in) and a weight of 1560 g (55 oz).

Dan Wesson revolvers all have a transfer rod which serves as a safety system. In addition the cylinder locking system is on the cylinder yoke.

DAN WESSON MODEL 22-VH6/ MODEL 722-VH6

Dan Wesson Model 22 is in .22 LR caliber. This weapon is also only available in a blued finish. The revolver illustrated below has a VH barrel with a barrel length of 152 mm (6 in), i.e. with an extended ejector shroud as extra barrel weight and a ventilated barrel rib. All the stainless steel models have a model number starting with the figure 7. The same model is illustrated below, this time in stainless

Blued Dan Wesson Model 15-VH6

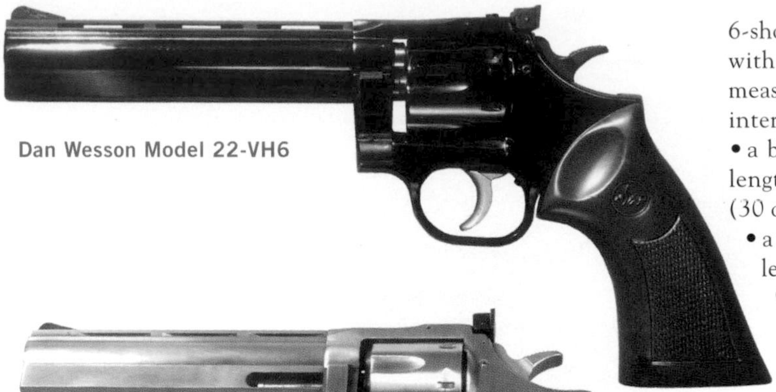

Dan Wesson Model 22-VH6

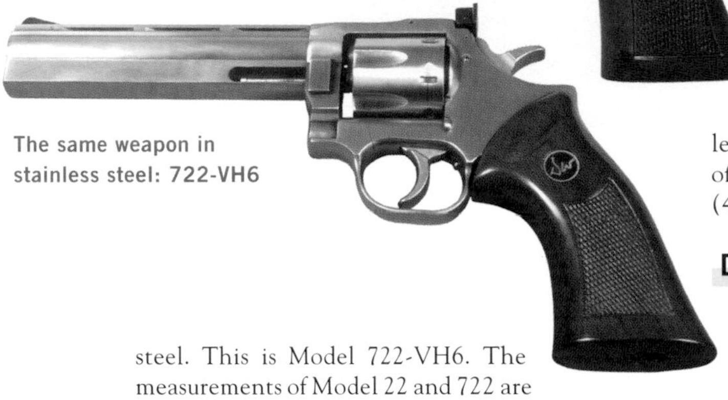

The same weapon in
stainless steel: 722-VH6

6-shot weapon is 285 mm (11¼ in) and the weight
with this barrel length is 1020 g (36 oz). The
measurements of this revolver with different
interchangeable barrels are:
• a barrel length of 63.5 mm (2½ in), with a total
length of 196 mm (1 in) and a weight of 850 g
(30 oz);
• a barrel length of 102 mm (4 in), with a total
length of 234 mm (9¼ in) and a weight of
935 g (33 oz);
• a barrel length of 203 mm (8 in), with a total
length of 335 mm (3¼ in) and a weight of
1105 g (39 oz).
• Since 1999 there has also been a barrel
length of 254 mm (10 in), with a total length
of 386 mm (15¼ mm) and a weight of 1275 g
(45 oz).

DAN WESSON MODEL 22-V4/722 V4

This is the small caliber Dan Wesson revolver
in .22 LR caliber, with a ventilated barrel rib,
but without the barrel weight of the extended
ejector shroud. The stainless steel weapon
illustrated here has a barrel length of 102 mm (4 in).
The total length of this revolver is 234 mm (9¼ in)
and the weight is 1050 g (37 oz). The measurements
of this revolver with different interchangeable
barrels are:
• a barrel length of 63.5 mm (2½ in), with a total
length of 196 mm (7¾ in) and a weight of 950 g
(33½ oz);
• a barrel length of 152 mm (6 in), with a total
length of 285 mm (11¼ in) and a weight of 1162
g (41 oz);
• a barrel length of 203 mm (8 in) with a total length
of 335 mm (13¼ in) and a weight of 1305 g (46 oz).
• Since 1999 there has also been a barrel length of
254 mm (10 in), with a total length of 386 mm
(15¼ in), and a weight of 1360 g (48 oz).

steel. This is Model 722-VH6. The
measurements of Model 22 and 722 are
the same. The total length of this weapon is 285 mm
(11¼ in) and the weight in this barrel length is
1333 g (47 oz). The measurements of this revolver
with different interchangeable barrels are:
• a barrel length of 63.5 mm (2½ in); the total length
is 196 mm (7¾ in) and the weight is 1020 g (36 oz);
• a barrel length of 102 mm (4 in); the total length
is 934 mm (9¼ in) and the weight is 1160 g (41 oz);
• a barrel length of 203 mm (8 in); the total length
is 335 mm (13¼ in) and the weight is 1530 g (54 oz).
• Since 1999 there has also been a barrel 254 mm
(10 in) long; the total length is 386 mm (15¼ in)
and the weight is 1644 g (58 oz). This small caliber
revolver also has a transfer rod safety.

DAN WESSON MODEL 15-V6/715-V6

Model 715-V6 indicates that this Dan Wesson
revolver is made of stainless steel (number 7) and is
available in .357 Magnum caliber (number
15). This 'V6' reveals that it has
a ventilated barrel, without a barrel
weight, and that the barrel length is
152 mm (6 in). The total length of this

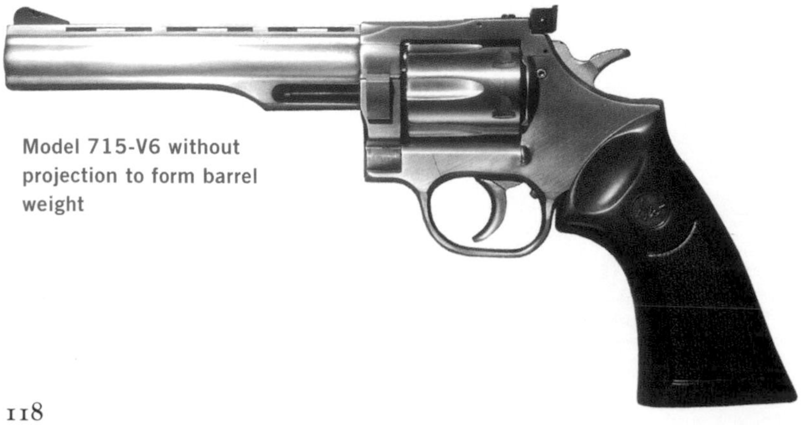

Model 715-V6 without
projection to form barrel
weight

Model 722-V4 without
projection to form barrel
weight with 102 mm (4 in)
barrel

The heavy Dan Wesson 744-VH6 in .44 Magnum caliber

DAN WESSON MODEL 44-VH6/744 VH6

This Dan Wesson revolver has a .44 Magnum caliber. The weapon illustrated here is made of stainless steel and has a ventilated barrel rib and an extended ejector shroud as a barrel weight. The 6-shot weapon has a total length of 185 mm (11¼ in) and the weight in this barrel length is 1588 g (56 oz). The measurements of this revolver with different barrel lengths are:
• a barrel length of 102 mm (4 in), with a total length of 243 mm (9¼ in) and a weight of 139 g (49 oz);
• a barrel length of 203 mm (8 in) with a total length of 335 mm (13¼ in) and a weight of 1814 g (64 oz);
• since 1999, there has also been a barrel length of 254 mm (10 in), with a total length of 386 mm (15¼ in) and a very high weight of 1956 g (69 oz).

DOMINO/FAS

Domino's trade mark

In the course of time, the Italian firm Fabrico Armi Sportivi, abbreviated FAS, has introduced several different sports pistols on the market. Initially these had the name FAS, later they were made with the brand name Igi Domino. Since 1986 Fas has produced model 602 in .22 LR caliber and the same pistol in .32 S&W Long caliber as model 603. A new model, the 607 was introduced in .22 LR caliber at the end of 1993. FAS weapons are typical small caliber sports pistols and belong in the same category as the Walther, GSPs, the Uniques, etc. These models have an extremely low sight line which means that the weapon hardly comes above the shooting hand. Any

recoil that occurs when it is fired is not vertical, but only back in a straight line. The most striking detail of FAS pistols is the fact that the magazine has to be loaded into the pistol from above.

Domino-FAS SP602 match pistol in .22 LR caliber

DOMINO-FAS SP602

The Domino match pistol SP602 is made in .22LR caliber and has a magazine capacity of 5 cartridges. The weapon has a total length of 285 mm (11¼ in), a barrel length of 145 mm (5¾ in) and a sight length of 220 mm (8¾ in). It weighs 1100 g (38¾ oz). The trigger pressure of this pistol can be adjusted at 1000 or 1360 g (2¼ or 3 lb) with a click mechanism. The match stock has an adjustable hand rest. In 1999, a few modifications were made to the SP 602. Since then, the trigger has been made of light metal and the weapon has a new type of match barrel. In addition, the trigger group can be removed from the weapon as a whole. The carefully adjustable micrometer sight has a rear sight leaf with an opening of 3.7 mm (.15 in). This can optionally be exchanged for a rear sight leaf with an opening of 3.5 mm (.15 in). For the bead, the shooter can choose between a width of 3.5 or 4.0 mm (0.14 and 0.16 in).

DOMINO-FAS SP603

The Domino-FAS 603 pistol has a .32 S&W Long Wadcutter caliber with a capacity of 5 cartridges. This centerfire sports cartridge has a lead bullet of 100 grains (6.5 g) with a flat point or rather without a point. The bullet has a muzzle velocity (V0) of 225 m/s and a muzzle energy (E0) of 170 Joules. The

Domino-FAS SP603 in .32 S&W Long Wadcutter caliber

total length of the weapon is 275 mm (10¼ in) and the barrel length is 135 mm (5¼ in). The weapon has a sight radius of 220 mm (8¾ in) and weighs 1130 g (39¼ oz). The trigger pressure is 1360 g (3 lb) in accordance with the international competition rules. The rear sight leaf of the micrometer sight has an opening of 3.5 mm (0.14 in), but can be exchanged for a rear sight leaf with an opening of 3.7 mm (0.15 in). For the width of the front sight, the shooter can choose between 3.5 or 4.0 mm (0.14 and 0.16 in). In addition, the laminated stock has an adjustable hand-rest.

DRULOV

Logo of the Czech company DruLov

The Czech arms company Drulov has existed since the early twentieth century. The original name was Lidové Druzstvo Puskaru Lov. The company was nationalized in 1948 following the Communist takeover. When the Iron Curtain came down, the company returned to private ownership in 1992. The current name of the company, DruLov, is a combination of the old factory name. DruLov specializes in simple single-shot small caliber pistols with a bolt action. The original design dates from 1963, and was developed by the weapon designer Pavlicek. In addition, the company makes stun guns, small caliber carbines, and a number of CO_2 air pistols.

DRULOV MODEL 70

Model 70 was designed as a single-shot pistol for target shooting in .22 LR caliber for shooting distances between 25 and 50 meters. The weapon has a bolt action locking system. The bolt behind the barrel has to be turned through 90 degrees. Then it can be pulled back and the chamber of the barrel can be loaded. The bolt is replaced and the firing pin is cocked. The pistol can now be fired. DruLov also makes the same weapon with a trigger accelerator and a firing button instead of a trigger. There is a safety switch above the trigger which blocks the trigger. The total length of this model is 370 mm (14½ in), the barrel length is 250 mm (9¾ in) and the sight radius is 300 mm (11¼ in). It has a height of 150 mm (6 in) and a width of 60 mm (2½ in), including the stock with a thumb rest. Model 70 is also available with a left-handed stock. The pistol weighs 1250 g (44.1 oz). The width of the simple rear sight is adjustable. A mount for a scope is available on request.

DRULOV MODEL 75

Model 75 was also developed as a single-shot target pistol in .22 LR caliber for shooting distances between 25 and 50 meters. The weapon has the same bolt action locking system as model 70. Drulov also produces model 75 with a trigger accelerator and a firing button instead of a trigger. There is a safety switch above the trigger which blocks the trigger. The total length of this model is 370 mm (14½ in), the barrel length is 250 mm (9¾ in) and the sight radius is 300 mm (11¼ in). The height is 150 mm (6 in) and the width is 60 mm (2½ in), including the stock with a thumb rest. The model is also available with a left-handed stock. The pistol weighs 1250 g (44 oz). The height and width of the rear sight are adjustable. A mount for the scope is available or can be ordered with this model.

DruLov Model 75 with adjustable notched sight

DruLov Model 70 single shot pistol

DruLov Model 97 MSP
for IMSSU standard class
silhouette shooting

DruLov Model 97 MSP standard Class

Model 97 MSP was specially made for small caliber silhouette shooting for ranges of 25, 50, 75 and 100 meters in accordance with the international competition rules for standard pistols of the IMSSU. The weapon has a bolt-action locking system which is opened with a bolt. There is a safety catch just in front of this bolt to block the firing pin. The total length of this model is 356 mm (14½ in), the barrel length is 250 mm (9¾ in) and the sight radius is 322 mm (12¾ in). It has a height of 160 mm (6¼ in), and a width of 45 mm (1¼ in), excluding the bolt. It is also available with a stock for left-handed shooters. The pistol weighs 1450 g (51 oz). The height and width of the rear sight are adjustable, and there is a rail on the barrel to mount a scope.

DruLov Model 97 MSU unlimited Class

Model 97 MSP was specially made for small caliber silhouette shooting for shooting distances of 25, 50, 75 and 100 meters, in accordance with the international competition rules for the unlimited class of the IMSSU. The weapon has a bolt-action locking system which is opened with a bolt. There is a safety catch just in front of the bolt to block the firing pin. The total length of this model is 495 mm (19½ in), the barrel length is 379 mm (15 in) and the sight radius is 365 mm (14½ in). The height is 160 mm (6¼ in) and the width is 45 mm (1¼ in) without the bolt, and the pistol is also available with a stock for left-handed shooters. It weighs 1650 g (58¼ oz). The height and width of the rear sight are adjustable. There is a rail on the barrel where the scope can be mounted.

DruLov 97 MSU pistol for free
class

E

a trigger pressure between 1 and 25 Newton. Even the pressure point of the trigger can be adjusted between 1 and 2.5 mm (0.04 and 0.1 in). The pistol has a walnut match stock with an adjustable hand rest. The magazine capacity is 5 or 10 rounds. One of the special features of the weapon is that it has a built-in automatic firing pin safety. The total length of IZH-35M pistol is 300 mm (11¾ in). The height is 150 mm (6 in) and the width is 50 mm (2 in). The barrel length is 153 mm (6 in) and the weapon weighs 1400 g (49½ oz). In addition, it has a completely adjustable micrometer sight. At EAA's request, Baikal has placed a special mounting rail on the barrel. A telescopic sight can be secured to this.

EUROPEAN AMERICAN ARMORY

Logo of European American Armory Corporation

The European American Armory Corporation in Sharpes, Florida has specialized in the import and sales of European weapons on the American continent since 1990. Several European manufacturers of weapons produce special models of their guns at the EAA's request. The American firm does business with Baikal in Russia, Tanfoglio in Italy and Weihrauch-Arminius in Germany. It has an interesting website on the Internet. This not only has illustrations and provides technical specifications, but you can also download complete manuals and exploded drawings.
The Internet address is: www.eaacorp.com.

EAA – BAIKAL EZH-35

This single-action pistol in .22 LR caliber was specially developed for the shooting sport. The weapon has a completely adjustable trigger with

Baikal IZH-35M match pistol in America EAA version

EAA-ARMINIUS BOUNTY HUNTER

Arminius Bounty revolver in .22 LR caliber

EAA has imported the Bounty Hunter since 1992. The German company Weihrauch makes this revolver and sells it under the name Arminius Western Single-Action. The EAA Bounty Hunter is available in .22 LR caliber with an interchangeable cylinder in .22 WMR caliber. There are several models of this 6-shot single-action revolver. The short model has a barrel length of 120 mm (4¾ in), a total length of 264 mm (10½ in) and weighs 1100 g (38¾ oz). The barrel length of the second model is 171 mm (6¾ in). It has a total length of 315 mm (12½ in) and weighs 1240 g (43¾ oz). EAA can also provide the same models with an 8-shot cylinder. In addition, all the models are available with a blued or nickel-plated finish. The standard models have walnut grips. In the luxury models, these grips are made of ivory colored polymer. The revolver has fixed telescopic sights. The loading port is on the right. The Bounty Hunter has a firing pin mounted in the frame and a transfer bar safety.

EAA-ARMINIUS BIG BORE BOUNTY HUNTER

EAA has made this large caliber model in the calibers, .357 Magnum, .44 Magnum and .45 Long Colt since 1992. Up to 1995 this model was also available in .41 Magnum and .44-40 Win. calibers. The Big Bore Bounty Hunter has a 6-shot cylinder and a single-

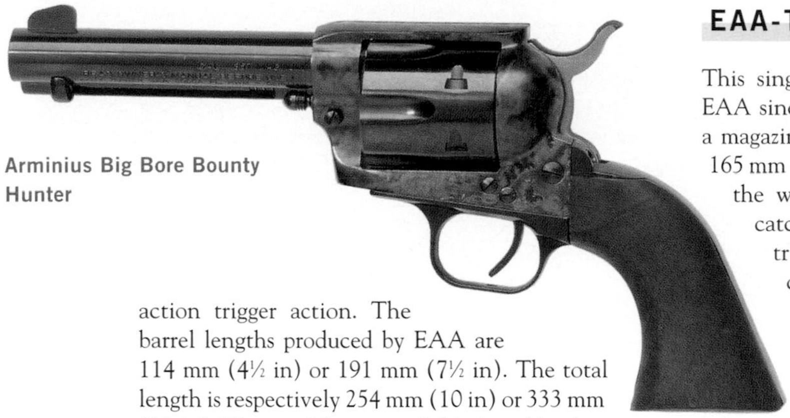

Arminius Big Bore Bounty
Hunter

action trigger action. The
barrel lengths produced by EAA are
114 mm (4½ in) or 191 mm (7½ in). The total
length is respectively 254 mm (10 in) or 333 mm
(13 in). The models are available in a blued or
hard chrome-plated finish. Like the small caliber
model, the Big Bore has transfer bar safety.

Nickel-plated Arminius
Big Bore Bounty Hunter

EAA-ARMINIUS WINDICATOR

The Windicator revolver has a double-action trigger
and EAA imported this 6-shot weapon from 1991 to
2001 in .38 Special and .357 Magnum calibers. The
revolver was available in two models. The snub-nose
model has a barrel length of 51 mm (2 in), a total
length of 170 mm (7 in) and a weight of 750
g (26½ oz). The second model has a barrel length of
102 mm (4 in), a total length of 220 mm (8¾ in) and
a weight of 900 g (31¼ oz). The cylinder of the
weapon bolts at the front with a spring catch in the
ejector rod. There is a spring-powered plunger in the
extractor star at the back. The Windicator has
a transfer bar safety.

EAA-TANFOGLIO GT-32 NICKEL

This single-action pocket pistol has been made by
EAA since 1991 in 7.65 mm (.32 ACP) caliber with
a magazine capacity of 7 rounds. The total length is
165 mm (6½ in), the barrel length is 80 mm (3 in) and
the weapon weighs 700 g (24¾ oz). The safety
catch is on the left of the slide and blocks the
trigger bar and the firing pin. The magazine
catch is on the heel of the grip. There is
a hook-shaped extension at the bottom of
the magazine which can be removed, so
that the weapon can be gripped firmly.
The pistol has a mat nickel-plated layer
and wooden or black synthetic grips. The
rear sight is secured on the slide with a dovetail joint,
and can be adjusted on the side.

The EAA GT-32 Nickel
pistol made by Tanfoglio

EAA-TANFOGLIO GT-380

The EAA GT-380 pistol also has a single-action
trigger action. EAA has made this 7-shot weapon
since 1992 in 9 mm Short (.380 ACP) caliber. The
GT-380 has a total length of 165 mm (6½ in) a barrel
length of 80 mm (3 in) and a weight of 700
g (24¾ oz). As in the GT-32, the safety catch is on
the left of the slide. This catch blocks the trigger bar
and the firing pin. The magazine catch is in the heel

Snub nose Arminius
Windicator of EAA

Blued EAA GT-380 in
9 mm Short (.380 ACP)
caliber

The EAA Witness pistol
with polymer casing

Compact version of EAA
Witness with plastic
casing

of the grip. The takedown lever is just above the trigger. When it is turned through 180 degrees to the front, the slide can be taken off the frame. The pistol has black synthetic grips. The left grip plate has a thumb rest.

EAA-TANFOGLIO WITNESS-P

The Witness was specially produced by Tanfoglio for EAA. This American name is printed at the bottom of the grip. Tanfoglio sells this model as Force '99. The Witness has a double-action trigger and is available in the calibers, 9 mm Para., .38 Super, .40 S&W, and .45 ACP. Because of US gun laws, the magazine capacity in all calibers is limited to 10 rounds. The actual magazine capacity is respectively 16 rounds (9 mm Para., .38 Super), 12 rounds (.40 S&W) and 10 rounds (.45 ACP). The frame is made of polymer, with a steel inset rail to guide the slide. The safety catch is on the left of the frame and this can also be used to cock the hammer. The pistol is also available with an ambidextrous safety catch/uncocking lever. In addition the Witness has automatic firing pin safety. The magazine catch is also on the left, behind the trigger guard. The pistol has a total length of 216 mm (8½ in), a barrel length of 114 mm (4½ in) and a weight of 880 g (31 oz). The height of the weapon is 142 mm (5½ in) and the width is 32 mm (1¼ in). The rear sight can only be adjusted on the side.

EAA-TANFOGLIO WITNESS COMPACT-P

The Witness Compact also has a polymer frame and is available in the same calibers as the large Witness. In fact, the Compact also has the same limited magazine capacity: 10 rounds in all calibers. The total length of the pistol is 191 mm (7½ in), the barrel length is 89 mm (3½ in) and the height is 114 mm (4½ in). The weapon weighs 737 g (26 oz). This compact model has cocking grooves in the slide, both

at the front and at the back. The rear sight can only be adjusted at the side. There is a combined safety catch/uncocking lever on the left of the frame. The pistol is also available with an ambidextrous safety catch/uncocking lever on request.

EAA-TANFOGLIO WITNESS STEEL CARRY COMP

The Witness Steel Carry Comp has a steel frame and slide. EAA has produced this pistol since 1992 in 10 mm Auto and .45 ACP caliber, both with a magazine capacity of 10 rounds. The slide of the Carry Comp is extended with a single chamber compensator. The total length is 206 mm (8 in), the barrel length is 108 mm (4¼ in) and the height is 140 mm (5½ in). The weapon weighs 935 g (33 oz). This Witness model has a double-action trigger action. The rear sight is adjustable on the side and has a white dot on either side. There is also a white dot on the front sight. When these three are aligned, the pistol is correctly aimed. The Carry Comp has cocking grooves in the slide, both at the front and at the back. The grips are made of black rubber. The weapon is available in a mat blue, or nickel-plated finish, the so-called wonder finish.

Witness Carry Comp
pistol with single
chamber compensator

EAA-TANFOGLIO WITNESS STANDARD STEEL COMPACT

The Witness Steel Compact also has a steel frame and slide. EAA produces this double-action pistol in the calibers, 9 mm Para., 10 mm Auto, .40 S&W and .45 ACP. In .45 ACP caliber, it has a magazine capacity of 8 rounds. The capacity in the other calibers is limited to 10 rounds for the American market. The total length of the Compact is 184 mm (7 ¼ in), the barrel length is 91.5 mm (3 ½ in), the height is 114 mm (4 ½ in), and the width is 35 mm (1 ¼ in). The weapon weighs 850 g (30 oz). This pistol has tension grooves both in the front and the back of the slide. The grips are made of black rubber. In addition, it has a triple aspect sight and the rear sight is adjustable on the side. The weapon illustrated here has the so-called wonder finish, but is also available in a mat blue finish.

Witness Standard Steel Compact

EAA-TANFOGLIO WITNESS STEEL FULLSIZE

Tanfoglio sells this model as the 95-F Combat. It is made in the calibers, 9 mm Para (16 rounds), 9 x 21 mm (16 rounds), .38 Super Auto (16 rounds), 10 mm Auto (14 rounds), .40 S&W (12 rounds) and .45 ACP (10 rounds). EAA makes the same model as the Witness Steel Fullsize, but in this model the

magazine capacity is limited to 10 rounds. The total length of this pistol is 206 mm (8 in), the barrel length is 114 mm (4 ½ in) and the height is 140 mm (5 ½ in). The weapon weighs 935 g (33 oz). This double-action Witness model has a combined safety catch/uncocking lever on the left of the frame. This blocks the trigger bar and uncocks the hammer. In addition, it has automatic firing pin safety. The magazine catch to the left of the trigger guard can be moved to the right for left-handed shooters. The triple aspect sight system is on the front sight and the rear sight, which is adjustable at the side. The pistol is available in a mat blue or nickel-plated wonder finish.

EAA-TANFOGLIO WITNESS STEEL LIMITED CLASS

The Witness Limited Class is specially made by the Tanfoglio Custom Center for the Practical Shooting discipline. The single-action pistol is available in the calibers, 9 mm Para (16 rounds), 9 x 21 mm (16), .38 Super Auto (16), 10 mm Auto (14), .40 S&W (12) and .45 ACP (10). For the North American market the magazine capacity is limited to 10 rounds. The total length of this competition weapon is 266 mm (10½ in), the barrel length is 121 mm (4¾ in), the height 137 mm (5¼ in) and the weight is 1050 g (37 oz). It has a completely adjustable micrometer sight and an adjustable trigger stop. The trigger guard has a square shape for two-handed shooting. The front and back of the grips are ribbed. There is an extended beavertail on the backstrap. There are screw holes in both the left and the right of the frame for mounting a scope. This pistol has cocking grooves in the slide both in the front and at the back. In addition, the enlarged magazine catch to the left, behind the trigger guard, can be moved to the right, and the frame has an enlarged magazine well. The weapon is available in a mat blue, nickel-coated or duotone finish.

Witness Full-size pistol

Witness Limited Class

**Witness Silver Team
pistol of EAA**

EAA-Tanfoglio Witness Silver Team

The Witness Silver Team is made by the Tanfoglio Custom Center for the open class of the Practical Shooting discipline. It is made by EAA in the calibers 9 mm Para, 9 x 21 mm, .38 Super Auto, .40 S&W and .45 ACP. The magazine capacity of all calibers is limited to 10 rounds. The model made by Tanfoglio itself does have a larger magazine capacity. The total length of the Silver Team is 248 mm (9¾ in), the barrel length is 133 m (5¼ in), and the height is 137 mm (5¼ in). The weapon weighs 1200 g (42 oz). There is a two-chamber compensator at the front of the slide. The trigger guard has a square shape and there is an extended beavertail on the backstrap. This pistol has cocking grooves in the slide, both at the front and the back. It has a completely adjustable micrometer sight. The enlarged magazine catch to the left, behind the trigger guard can be moved to the right.

ERMA

The German firm ERMA, an abbreviation of the 'Erfurter Maschinenfabrik' in Dachau was founded in 1949. Initially, Erma owed its commercial success mainly to the manufacture of copies of famous pistols. For example, the firm made small caliber models of the Luger P08 pistol in different models and also of the Walther P38, PP, and PPK pistols. In addition, ERMA has an excellent small caliber interchangeable set for the Luger/Mauser P08 pistol. The firm has also been successful in the field of carbines, e.g., with a .22 LR model of the Winchester

.30-M1 carbine (model EM-1) and different models of Winchester lever-action 'Wild West' carbines (Models EG-712). Furthermore, in the course of its existence, Erma has introduced a large number of revolvers to the market in blued and stainless steel models and in .22 LR to .357 Magnum calibers. The special series of sports revolvers in .22 LR, .32 S&W Long and .357 Magnum calibers, with an anatomical stock and an adjustable hand rest, models ER-773 Match and ER 772 Match, are all famous. At the beginning of 1980, a match pistol was developed which was finally introduced to the market in 1985. This pistol, the ESP-85A, could be provided with an interchangeable set for .32 S&W Long caliber. In 1989, a second shorter model followed as a so-called hunting pistol. Meanwhile, a number of minor modifications were made to the pistol in response to recommendations by shooters. In the first place, this concerned the possibility of adjusting the trigger. The appearance of the weapon was also modified, from a highly polished to a more mat finish. In addition, the grip was made slightly broader. A longer diagonal plate was added to the bottom of the magazine and the design of the trigger was also modified. The ESP-85 Junior was introduced in 1994. This pistol is a simple model of the match pistol. The end of the barrel is round. Therefore the barrel weights available as extra accessories cannot be mounted on the Junior.

ERMA MODEL EP-882

Erma introduced this model of the Walther P38 in 1968. The weapon has a double-action trigger. As in the real Walther, the safety catch on the left of the slide ensured that the hammer is cocked. The firing pin is also blocked at the same time. The magazine capacity of the pistol in .22 LR caliber is 8 rounds. The magazine catch is in heel of the grip. The total length of this model is 202 mm (8 in), the barrel

Trade mark of German company Erma

Erma EP-882: a small version of the Walther P38

Erma ER-77
revolver

Erma ESP-85A match
pistol

length is 127 mm (5in), and the
height is 120 mm (4¾ in). The
weight is 760 g (26¾ oz). Erma also
makes model EP-882S. This model
has a barrel length of 152 mm (6 in) and an
adjustable rear sight, but otherwise, it is the same as
the weapon illustrated .

ERMA MODEL ER-77

Erma makes this double-action sports revolver in the
calibers, 4 mm-M20, .22LR, .32 S&W Long, and .357
Magnum. The 4 mm M20 (.16 in) rimfire cartridge is
made especially for Germany because it can be freely
sold there to anyone over the age of 18. The revolver
has a swing-out 6-shot cylinder in every caliber. The
model with a barrel length of 102 mm (4 in) like the
weapon shown has a total length of 244 mm (9½ in),
a height of 148 mm (5¾ in) and a sight radius of
160 mm (6¼ in). Depending on the caliber, the
weight is between 1120 and 1200 g (39½ to 42¼ oz).
Model ER-77 is also available with a barrel length
of 140 mm (5½ in) or 152 mm (6 in). The revolver
has a raised barrel rib which runs over the bridge of
the cylinder. The adjustable rear sight is secured in
this. The cylinder has a locking system at the front
and back. At the front, the ejector rod fits into
a spring catch in the ejector shroud. There is a spring
pin which engages in a recess of the extractor star at
the back.

ERMA MODEL ESP-85A

Erma has made this match pistol since 1985 in .22 LR
and .32 S&W-Long Wadcutter calibers, both with
a magazine capacity of 5 rounds. The magazine catch
is in the heel of the grip which is enclosed in a walnut
stock with an adjustable hand-rest. The weapon has
a completely adjustable micrometer sight. In addition,
the trigger pressure can be adjusted for 1000 or
1360 g (2¼ or 3 lb), and the trigger has an adjustable
trigger stop. The safety catch which blocks the firing
pin is on the left of the slide. The total length is
255 mm (10 in), the barrel length is 153 mm (6 in),
the height of the weapon is 130 mm (5 in) and the
sight radius is 200 mm (7¼ in). The weight in both
calibers is 1140 g (40¼ oz). Furthermore, the weapon
can be made heavier with an extra barrel weight of

110 or 180 g (4 or 6¼ oz). In the
pistol illustrated above, a barrel
weight has been placed over the
front of the barrel. The pistol is available in various
models like the weapon shown below in a duotone
finish. Erma also produces interchangeable sets for the
ESP-85A in a blued or chrome-plated finish in .22 LR
and .32 S&W Long Wadcutter calibers.

ESP-85AHV with
nickel-plated slide

ERMA MODEL ESP-85A JUNIOR

The ESP-85A Junior is a simpler model of the ESP-
85 A with a magazine capacity of 8 rounds. The
weapon has a completely adjustable micrometer sight.
The safety catch, which blocks the firing pin, is on the
left of the slide. The magazine catch is in the heel of
the grip which has walnut grip plates. The total length
of the weapon is 254 mm (10 in), the barrel length is
153 mm (6 in), the height is 138 mm (5½ in) and the
sight radius is 200 mm (7¾ in). The weapon weighs
1060 g (37½ oz). The trigger has an adjustable trigger
stop and the trigger pressure can be adjusted from 800
to 2500 g (1¾ to 5½ lb). The Junior does not have
a separate barrel weight.

ESP-85A Junior match
pistol of Erma

F

FEG (FEG ARMY)

Feg trade mark

The Hungarian company, Feg Army, was founded in 1881 when it was called the Arms and Machine Factory Company. In Hungarian its name was Femaru Fegyver es Gepguar Kft. In addition to the firearms themselves, it also manufactured the machines for their production at that time. At the beginning of the twentieth century, Feg introduced the well-known Frommer pistol. After the Second World War, when Hungary joined the Warsaw Pact, it was licensed to make Kalashnikov rifles for the army, amongst other things. Since democracy has been restored, the FEG company has produced a number of interesting models of pistols for some years. The Feg model FP9 pistol is very similar to the FN Hi-Power HP35. The FP9 has a ventilated rib above the slide which contains the telescopic sights. Another Feg pistol, Model P9R looks like a combination of the FN High-Power and the Smith & Wesson Model 59 pistol. In the P9R, the safety catch/uncocking lever is on the left of the slide. The pistol was designed and produced for the Hungarian army in 9 mm Para caliber, an unusual caliber for a former Warsaw Pact army unit. In the USA, the weapon was marketed as an MBK-9HP. The pistol has a combined safety catch/uncocking lever which blocks the firing pin and uncocks the hammer. The P9R went into production in 1985 and has been marketed for some years by Mauser in Western Europe as the model Mauser 90 DA. At the end of 1993 Feg introduced a similar double-action pistol in .45 ACP caliber specially for the North and South American market, first with the model name GKK45, but later as model AC-45.

FEG MODEL AC-45

Feg introduced this double-action pistol in 1997. It looks like the FN-Browning Hi-Power with a Smith &Wesson safety catch on the slide. This safety catch rotates a block in front of the firing pin so that the hammer cannot touch it. In addition, the hammer has a half-cock safety in the foot. The locking system is of the FN-Browning type. This weapon is also made in a compact model as the ACK. The large AC-45 pistol has a magazine capacity of 8 rounds in .45 ACP caliber. The total length is 210 mm (8¼ in), the barrel length is 118.5 mm (4¾ in), the height is 147 mm (5¾ in), and the width is 33 mm (1¼ in). The empty weapon weighs 1120 g (39½ oz), and when the magazine is full it weighs 1290 g (45½ oz). The compact ACK-45 has a shorter barrel and slide. The total length of this model is 197 mm (7¾ in) with a barrel length of 105.6 mm (4⅛ in). The empty weight is 1080 g (38 oz), and with a full magazine it weighs 1250 g (44 oz). Both models have a steel frame and slide and a fixed rear sight. The magazine catch is on the left of the frame behind the trigger guard. The weapon is only available in a blued finish.

Feg AC-45 pistol in .45 ACP

FEG MODEL AP-9

Feg developed this model back in 1951. At the time it was called Model 48 or Walalm. Initially this pistol was made for the Egyptian army but these plans did not materialize. Therefore it was mainly sold to the commercial market. In addition, an unknown number of Walams were used by the Hungarian police. It is a double-action pistol in 9 mm Short (.380 ACP) caliber. The safety catch is on the left of the slide. This blocks the hammer. In addition, the weapon has automatic firing pin safety. The magazine catch is also on the left of the frame, some way above the trigger

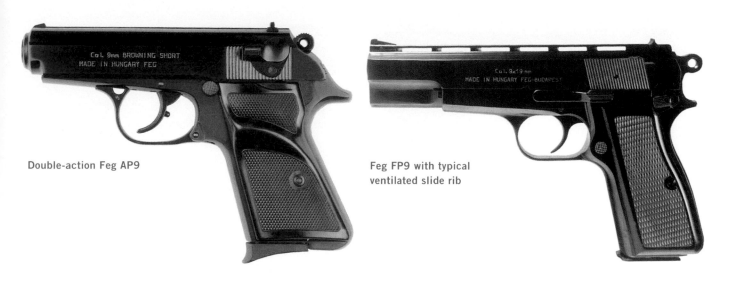

Double-action Feg AP9

Feg FP9 with typical
ventilated slide rib

guard. To disassemble the weapon, the trigger guard has to be pulled down at the front. The same system is used for the Walther PP and PPK. The Feg AP-9 is made in two models. The large AP-9 has a total length of 179 mm (7 in), a barrel length of 100 mm (4 in), a height of 113 mm (4½ in), and a width of 34 mm (1 ¼ in). The empty weight of the pistol is 770 g (27¼ oz), and with a full magazine of 7 rounds it weighs 840 g (29½ oz). In addition, Feg also produces a compact model, the APK-9. The total length of this model is 165 mm (6½ in) and the barrel length is 86 mm (3½ in). The empty weight is 730 g (25 ¾ oz) and with a full magazine it weighs 800 g (28¼ oz). The other measurements are the same for both models. They both have a steel frame and slide and are only available in a blued finish with black synthetic grips.

FEG MODEL B9R

This double-action pistol was introduced by Feg in 1993. The weapon has a light metal frame and a steel slide. The safety catch on the left of the slide rotates a safety block between the hammer and the firing pin. There is also half-cock safety in the foot of the

hammer. The pistol is made in 9 mm Short (.380 ACP) caliber and has a standard magazine capacity of 15 rounds. For countries where this number of cartridges is prohibited, Feg produces a blocked magazine for a maximum of 10 rounds. Despite this large magazine capacity and the hardwood grips, the weapon is only 35 mm (1¼ in) wide. The total length is 174 mm (6⅛ in), the barrel length is 101 mm (4 in) and the height is 133 mm (5¼ in). The empty weight of the pistol is 700 g (24½ oz) and with a full 15-round magazine it weighs 840 g (29 ½ oz). The magazine catch is on the left of the frame, behind the square trigger guard. In addition, the weapon has fixed telescopic sights.

FEG MODEL FP9

Feg's FP9 pistol dates from 1990. It is a single-action weapon in 9 mm Para caliber with a magazine capacity of 13 rounds. It is very similar to the Browning Hi-Power. The safety catch is on the left of the frame. It blocks the hammer, which also has half-cock safety. The magazine catch is on the left, behind the trigger guard. The pistol has a steel frame and slide. There is a ventilated rib on the slide, where the fixed rear sight and front sight are secured. The total length is 198 mm (7¾ in), the barrel length is 118 mm (4½ in), the height is 130 mm (5 in) and the width of the weapon is 35 mm (1¼ in). The weight of the empty weapon is 950 g (33½ oz), and with a full magazine it weighs 1110 g (39 oz).

15-shot Feg
B9R pistol

Feg P9L
sporting pistol

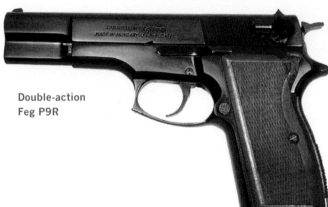

Double-action
Feg P9R

Feg Model P9L Sport

The Feg P9L sports pistol is actually a longer model of the P9M model. The single-action weapon has an extended slide at the front of the barrel with the front sight on it. There is a completely adjustable micrometer sight at the back of the slide. The safety catch on the left of the frame is extended. The magazine catch, also on the left of the frame, behind the trigger guard, is enlarged. In addition, the weapon has a steel frame and slide. The frame is enclosed by a rubber grip with finger grooves. The pistol is made in 9mm Para caliber and has a magazine capacity of 13 rounds. The total length is 234 mm (9¼ in), the barrel length is 150 mm (6 in) and the height is 130 mm (5 in). The empty weight is 1008 g (35½ oz) and with a full magazine it weighs 1168 g (41¼ oz). The P9L Sport is only available in a blued finish.

Feg Model P9M

Feg introduced the P9M pistol in 1981 in 9 mm Para caliber. The single-action weapon is virtually a copy of the Browning Hi-Power. It has a magazine capacity of 13 rounds. The pistol has a steel frame and slide with fixed telescopic sights. In 1991, Feg introduced a new modified model to the market. This has a longer safety catch on the left of the frame and a larger slide catch. There is half-cock safety on the foot of the hammer.

The weapon illustrated here is this newer model. The total length of the P9M is 198 mm (7¾ in). The barrel length is 118 mm (4½ in), the height is 126 mm (5 in) and the width is 35 mm (1¼ in). The weapon weighs 910 g (32 oz) empty, and when it the magazine is fully loaded it weighs 1070 g (37¾ oz). It is only available in a blued finish with black synthetic grips.

Feg Model P9R (DA)

The double-action Feg P9R pistol is very similar to the Feg AC-45 described above. However, the P9R is in 9 mm Para caliber and has a magazine capacity of 14 rounds. The safety catch is on the left of the slide and turns a safety block between the hammer and the firing pin. There is also half-cock safety in the foot of the hammer. Feg manufactures this model in large and compact models. The P9R model has a total length of 203 mm (9 in), a barrel length of 118.5 mm (4¾ in), a height of 134 mm (5¼ in) and a width of 35 mm (1¼ in). The empty weight of this steel pistol is 1000 g (35¼ oz) and loaded with a full magazine it weighs 1170 g (41¼ oz).

The compact model, P9RK has a total length of 190 mm (7½ in), a barrel length of 105.5 mm (4 in) and a weight of respectively 970 g (34¼ oz) or 1140 g (40¼ oz). There are finger grooves cut in the front of the grip, and the backstrap is ribbed. In addition, both models have fixed telescopic sights.

Single-action Feg P9M,
a faithful copy of
the Browning Hi-Power

Compact P9RK

Compact double-action
only Feg P9RZ pistol

FEG MODEL P9RZ

In 1998 Feg decided to join the trend for
small double-action-only pistols and
introduced the Feg P9RZ. The caliber of
this model is 9 mm Para and it has
a magazine capacity of 10 rounds. Despite its
small height of 116 mm (4½ in) and double
row magazine, the pistol is only 31.6 mm (1¼ in)
wide. The total length is 178 mm (7 in) and the
barrel length is 92.3 mm (3½ in). When it is empty
the weapon weighs 830 g (29¼ oz) and with a full
magazine it weighs 910 g (32 oz). On the left of the
slide there is a combined safety catch/uncocking
lever. In addition, it has automatic firing pin safety.
This model is also available as a double-action pistol
with an ambidextrous safety catch on the slide. The
double-action trigger pressure is 15 Newton (11 lb)
and in single-action the trigger pressure is 20 Newton

Feg P40RZ: the .40
S&W caliber version
of the P9RZ

(4½ lb). Both models have a steel frame and slide and
dark gray synthetic grip plates.

Virtually the same weapon with the model name
P40 RZ is available in .40 S&W caliber with
a magazine capacity of 8 rounds.

FEG MODEL RL-61

The double-action RL-61 model was introduced by
Feg in 1991. It is in .22 LR caliber with a magazine
capacity of 8 rounds. It is very similar to a Walther
PPK, and also has the same takedown system with
a trigger guard which flips down. The safety catch is
on the left of the slide. This catch rotates the safety
block between the hammer and the firing pin. In
addition, there is half-cock safety on the foot of the
hammer and the same magazine catch high up, as in
the larger model AP9. The frame and slide are made
of steel and there is a rear sight adjustable on the side.

Feg RL-61 pistol
for .22 LR caliber

The total length is 157 mm (6 in), the
barrel length is 86 mm (3½ in) and
the height of the weapon is 110 mm
(4¼ in). The empty weight is
650 g (23 oz) and with a full 8 round
magazine the weight is 680 g (24 oz).

FEINWERKBAU

Feinwerkbau is actually a
contraction of the name of the
German arms factory Feinwerkbau
Westinger & Altenburger KG. The firm
is established in Oberndorf on the Neckar.
It has produced precision instruments
since it was established in 1949. It has
focused on the manufacture of air rifles
and pistols only since 1961. They have
an extensive range in this field.
Feinwerkbau sells a range from light
air rifles to the highest precision
arms. It became famous in the field of
match air pistols. First it introduced

Feinwerkbau
trade mark

can be adjusted from 1000 to 1360 g (2 ¼ to 3 lb). In addition, the so-called pre-pressure of the trigger action can be adjusted from 600 to 1050 g (1 ¼ to 2 ¼ lb). The weight of the pressure point varies from 0 to 600 g (0 to 1 ¼ lb) and finally, the trigger shoe can be moved a distance of 14 mm (⁹⁄₁₆ in). The total length of the AW93 is 217 mm (8 ½ in). The barrel length is 152 mm (6 in). The height of the weapon is 145 mm (5 ¾ in), and the total width of the anatomical stock is 50 mm (2 in). Without the magazine, the weapon weighs 1135 g (40 oz).

the Model 65 air gun, followed by models 80 and 90, the last of which even has an electronic trigger. In addition, Feinwerkbau was one of the first manufacturers to introduce a CO_2 air gun to the market, its Model 2. In 1992, it developed new air guns, viz., models 102 and C25. In 1990, Feinwerkbau started a production program for rifles in .22 LR small caliber. The firm introduced a prototype of its first small caliber sports pistol at the 1994 IWA International Arms Fair.

FEINWERKBAU MODEL AW93

This pistol was designed in 1993 by Edwin Wohrstein and Bernhard Knaeble. They were both employed at Feinwerkbau. In the development of this pistol, great attention was devoted to its balance. The point of balance is exactly at the trigger guard. This is particularly anusual since the magazine is in the grip of the weapon, and not as in many match pistols, in front of the trigger group. In addition, the pistol sits low down on the anatomical stock so that the line of sight is very low above the shooting hand. The weapon has a special adjustable trigger which can be set at different levels. The single-action pistol has a magazine capacity of 5 rounds. The magazine catch is on the left at the bottom of the grip. This grip is made of walnut and has an adjustable hand rest. The safety catch is at the top, just in front of the adjustable micrometer sight. In addition, there is a slide catch above the right of the grip or stock, which can be adjusted per shot. The trigger pressure

Left side of
Feinwerkbau AW93

FREEDOM ARMS

The fine trade mark of Freedom Arms

Feinwerkbau
AW93 pistol

Up to 1956, the .44 Magnum revolver was the heaviest handgun in the world. In about 1956, the young American gunsmith, Dick Casull, from Utah, experimented with Colt Single-Action and Bisley revolvers. He developed a number of new calibers, such as the .454 Casull on the basis of these weapons. Initially he mainly used Ruger Super Blackhawks and converted these to 5-shot revolvers in this heavy caliber. Later, he produced complete revolvers in stainless steel himself. After a series of business problems, he started the firm Freedom Arms in

The mini-revolver of Freedom Arms, incorporated into a belt buckle

Freedom, Wyoming in 1978 together with a colleague. Initially, they also made small single-action mini-revolvers with a 5 shot cylinder in .22 Short, .22 LR and from 1980, also in .22 WMR calibers. These were made in a number of models by Freedom Arms up to 1990, including a holster containing a removable mini-revolver.

In addition to the mini-revolvers, Freedom Arms also produced the large Casull revolvers. These are used in the USA, both for hunting and for silhouette shooting. Since then, Freedom Arms has made several types and models, including a .22 LR revolver in 1990, the 252 Casull model, and a .357 Magnum, the 353 Casull, which was introduced in 1991. For the .454 Casull revolver there is an interchangeable cylinder in the calibers, .45 Long Colt, .45 ACP and .45 WM (Winchester Magnum). Casull also makes revolvers in .44 Magnum caliber, particularly in the silhouette model with a barrel length of 254 mm (10 in). In 1993, the Casull 555 model was introduced for the special pistol caliber .50 AE (Action-Express). The names of the models were changed in 1999. Since then Freedom Arms has made the model 83 in Field, Premier and Silhouette Grade with a large frame and model 97 with a smaller frame. The Casull revolvers have transfer bar safety and half-cock safety on the foot of the hammer.

FREEDOM ARMS CASULL MODEL 83 FIELD GRADE

The Freedom Arms range comprises a number of different models. One of these is Model 83 Field Grade. This revolver is available in the calibers, .50 Action Express, .475 Linebaugh, .454 Casull, .44 Magnum, .41 Magnum, .357 Magnum and .22 LR. The magazine capacity is 5 rounds in every caliber. The available barrel lengths in these calibers are

121 mm (4¾ in), 152 mm (6 in), 191 mm (7½ in) and 254 mm (10 in). The total length of the revolvers is respectively 286 mm (11¼ in), 318 mm (12½ in), 356 mm (14 in) and 419 mm (16½ in). The weight of the weapon with a barrel length of 191 mm (7½ in) is 1418 g (50 oz). The Field Grade has an adjustable rear sight and the black rubber Pachmayr grip is standard. The .475 Linebaugh caliber was designed in 1988 by John Linebaugh from Maryville, Montana. He tried to develop the most powerful revolver cartridge and was very successful in this. He shortened the cartridge case of a .45-70 rifle cartridge to a length of 38.1 mm (1½ in). He used bullets with a diameter of 12.07 mm (.475 in) and with weights of 370 or 440 grains. The Linebaugh cartridges with bullets of 370 grains (24 g) have a muzzle velocity between 305 and 455 m/s (1000 to 1495 fps), and a muzzle energy of 1116 to 2484 Joules. The muzzle velocity of cartridges with a bullet of 400 grains (25.9 g) is between 390 and 411 m/s (1280 and 1350 fps). The muzzle energy is between 1970 and 2188 Joules.

The heavy Casull Model 83 Field Grade revolver

FREEDOM ARMS CASULL MODEL 83 PREMIER GRADE

The Casull Premier Grade is also available in a special model with an octagonal barrel 191 mm (7½ in) long. The total length is 356 mm (14 in) and the weapon weighs 1474 g (52 oz). The same barrel type is also

An special Casull Model 83 Premier Grade with octagonal body

Special version in 1999 of
Model 83 Premier Grade
revolver with fixed sights

available with a barrel length of 140 mm (5 ½ in).
These models are available in the same caliber as the
Field Grade. The weapon shown here is in .454 Casull
caliber. This cartridge was developed in 1957 by Dick
Casull and Jack Fulmer. The cartridge case is based on
the .45 Colt, but is 2.54 mm (0.1 in) longer. In this
way, they wanted to prevent this cartridge from being
fired in a standard .45 Colt revolver. The .454 Casull
cartridge is available with a bullet of 260 or 300 grains
(16.8 or 19.4 g). The muzzle velocity of the 260 grain
bullet is 525 m/s (1723 fps), and the muzzle energy is
2315 Joules. The cartridge with a 300 grain bullet has
a muzzle velocity of 412 m/s (1353 fps), and a muzzle
energy of 1647 Joules. A special model is shown
below. This is a model 83 Premier Grade with
a 121 mm (4 ¾ in) barrel and fixed sight. The grips are
made of tropical hardwood.

FREEDOM ARMS CASULL MODEL 97 PREMIER GRADE

The model 97 Casull revolver has a medium-sized
frame and a cylinder for 5 cartridges. It is available in
the calibers, .45 Colt, .41 Magnum and .357
Magnum. It has a barrel length of 140 m (5 ½ in), or
191 mm (7½ in). The total length is 273 or 324 mm
(10¾ in or 12¾ in). The weight of the 140 mm
(5½ in) model is 1134 g (40 oz). Interestingly, the
revolver is also available with an interchangeable
cylinder in other calibers. For the model in .45 Colt,
there is an interchangeable cylinder for the caliber
.45 ACP. An interchangeable cylinder in .38 Special
is available for the model in caliber .357 Magnum.
The 97 Premier Grade is made with hardwood or
Micarta grip plates.

Medium-sized Freedom
Arms Casull Model 97
Premier Grade

G

GAMBA

Trade mark of Renato Gamba

Ancient documents show that the Gamba family has been established in Gardone, in the region of Val Trompia in Italy since the beginning of the eighteenth century. Originally they came from Bergamasco where they were well-known gunsmiths. Val Trompia was already a center of the arms industry in those days. The Gamba family soon settled in Gardone. Their influence increased with the marriage of Giuseppe Gamba and Maddalena Belleri. At the time, Belleri family was one of the leading families in the field of the manufacture of weapons in the area. Later, the family was linked with another famous family in this field, the Bernardellis, through marriage. The present firm, Renato Gamba, is famous above all for its extensive series of shotguns decorated with extremely beautiful engraving.

The well-known master engraver Angelo Galeazzi heads the Gamba department. This creates unique works of art on the weapons. Some of the well-known models of Gamba hunting weapons include the Ambassador, Concord, Daytona, London, Maxim, Mustang, Oxford, Prince and Zanotti. The parts of the weapons are mainly produced with computer-aided CNC machines. In addition to hunting guns, Gamba has also produced a small series of handguns since 1970, mainly as weapons for defense while hunting. In many countries it is permitted to use a revolver or pistol to finish an animal off humanely when it has been shot. In addition, it is important for a hunter to be able to defend himself, for example, from boar that have been shot, as these can be extremely dangerous. In 1984, the firm encountered financial problems. In 1988, it continued under the new name, Societa Army Bresciane Linea Renato Gamba.

GAMBA HSC SUPER G15

Gamba has been licensed by Mauser to make this double-action pistol since 1970. At the time, this 8-shot weapon was an exact replica of the Mauser HSC in 7.65 mm (.32 ACP) caliber. Since 1979 Gamba has marketed a new model. This pistol has a square trigger guard. In addition, the grip is broader so that the magazine capacity is greater. The new model is available in 7.65 mm (.32 ACP) caliber with a content of 12 cartridges and in 9 x 18 mm (9 mm Ultra) caliber with a capacity of 9 cartridges. This model has a total length of 152 mm (6 in), a barrel length of 85 mm (3¼ in) and a weight of 700 g (24¾ oz). In 1980, Gamba also introduced the

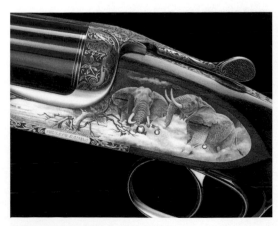

Example of engraving on a Gamba gun

A cut-away model of the Gamba HSc-80

model HSC Super G15. This pistol is a larger model and has a magazine capacity of 15 rounds in 9 mm Short (.380 ACP) caliber. The total length of this weapon is 173 mm (6¾ in). The barrel length is 90 mm (3½ in) and the weapon weighs 800 g (28¼ oz). In the old HSC the magazine catch was in the heel of the grip. In the Super G15, this catch is on the left of the frame, behind the trigger guard. The safety catch is on both sides of the slide, which also serves as the uncocking lever of the hammer.

Match version of the Gamba G90 with compensator and micrometer sights

GAMBA SAB G90

The Gamba SAB G90 pistol was introduced in 1989. It is a 15- shot double-action pistol. Gamba produces this weapon in 9 x 21 mm caliber and in 9 mm Para caliber for export. The last caliber may not be used for the civilian market in Italy. The SAB G90 has a steel frame and slide. The total length of the weapon is 202 mm (8 in), the barrel length is 120 mm (4 ¼ in) and it weighs 1000 g (35 ¼ oz). The safety catch is on the left of the slide. This blocks the hammer and the firing pin. The magazine catch is also on the left, behind the trigger guard. The pistol is available in a blued or mat nickel-plated finish. In addition, it has fixed sights. The model SAB G90 Service Competition is actually the same pistol but has an adjustable micrometer sight and a single-action trigger action. In addition, Gamba produces an interchangeable set for the caliber .40 S&W.

in .40 S&W. The total length, including the compensator is 260 mm (10¼ in). The barrel length is 140 mm (5½ in), and the weapon weighs 1120 g (39½ oz). Gamba makes this model in a blued or mat nickel-plated finish, both with an adjustable micrometer sight. The ambidextrous safety catch is on the left of the frame and blocks the hammer. This sports model also has an enlarged magazine catch on the left of the frame, behind the trigger guard.

Compact SAB G91

Gamba SAB G90 pistol

GAMBA SAB G90 COMPETITION

The SAB G90 Competition is a single-action sports model of the SAB G90. This weapon has a choice of a two or three-chamber compensator on the front of the barrel. Gamba produces this 10-shot pistol in 9 x 21 mm caliber and also has an interchangeable set

GAMBA SAB G91 COMPACT

Gamba introduced this compact model in 1990. It is a double-action pistol in the calibers, 9 mm Para., 9 x 21 mm or 7.65 mm Para., with a magazine capacity of 12 rounds. The total length of the weapon in 175 mm (7 in), the barrel length is 90 mm (3½ in) and the weight is 850 g (30 oz). Gamba produces this pistol in a blued or mat nickel-plated finish. It has an ambidextrous combined safety catch/uncocking lever on the slide and fixed sights.

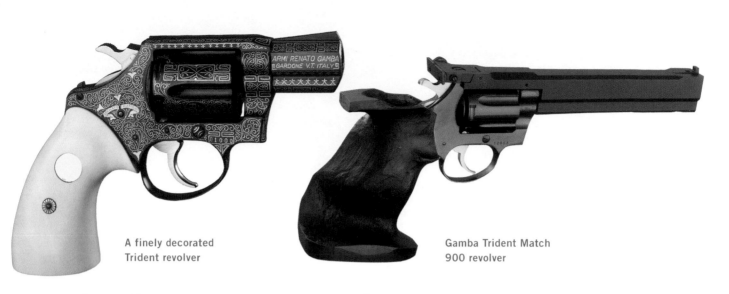

A finely decorated
Trident revolver

Gamba Trident Match
900 revolver

GAMBA TRIDENT

The Gamba Trident double-action revolver dates
from 1980. Up to 1999 Gamba made it with different
barrel lengths. The standard Trident had a barrel
length of 63.5 or 76 mm (2 ½ or 3 in) and fixed sights.
The Trident Vigilante had a barrel length of 102 mm
(4 in) and a micrometer sight. The Trident Super was
a simple match model with a barrel length of 152 mm
(6 in) and a micrometer sight. All the models
had a 6-shot cylinder in the .38 Special or .32
S&W caliber. At the moment, Gamba only provides
the Trident 25 with a barrel length of 63.5 mm
(2½ in). This revolver has a total length of 174 mm
(6¼ in) and a weight of 650 g (23 oz). It has a transfer
bar system as the safety system. The weapon is also
available in a mat nickel finish.

GAMBA TRIDENT MATCH 900

In 1982, Gamba introduced a real match revolver on
the market. This 6-shot double-action weapon has
a heavy angular barrel with a barrel length of 152 mm
(6 in) and an unbroken ejector shroud. The total
length is 300 mm (11¾ in) and it weighs approximately 1000 g (35¼ oz). In .38 Special caliber, it is
called the Match 900 and in .32 S&W, the name of
the model is Match 901. It is available with a rubber
Pachmayr combat grip or with an anatomical walnut
grip, which extends behind the hammer in a sort of
beavertail. Both models have a micrometer sight and
are made only in a blued finish.

GAUCHER ARMES

In 1834 Antoine Gaucher established the arms
factory, Gaucher Armes. He established his firm
in the ultimate city of
weapons: Saint Etienne.
Up to the First World
War, Gaucher mainly
produced heavy doubled-
barreled express rifles for
hunting heavy game. After
the Second World War the firm also
made guns in lighter calibers. The current range

Trident in stainless look

Trade mark of
French arms
company Gaucher
Armes

of weapons consists of double-barreled express guns, shotguns, and small caliber guns. Gaucher also makes two different single-shot pistols for silhouette shooting or hunting. The weapons have a good price/quality ratio and are extremely suitable for daily use.

GAUCHER GN 1 SILHOUETTE

This single-shot bolt-action pistol was especially made for silhouette shooting. It is only available in .22 LR caliber. The total length is 395 mm (15 ½ in), the barrel length is 254 mm (10 in) and the weight is 1100 g (38 ¾ oz). The steel receiver and the barrel have a mat chrome-plated finish. It has an anatomical wooden stock with finger grooves. The trigger pressure can be adjusted between 300 and 1000 g (10 ½ oz to 2 ¼ lb). The height and width of the rear sight can be adjusted. The bead in the hooded front sight is screwed down, and can be exchanged with other types of bead.

Gaucher Phantom GP pistol with integrated sound damper

European countries, this sort of weapons is prohibited by law. The total length of this pistol is 440 mm (17¼ in), the barrel length is 254 mm (10 in) and the weapon weighs 1300 g (46 oz). It has an adjustable rear sight and a hooded front sight. The bead can also be adjusted in terms of height. There is a dovetail rib on the tail end for mounting a sight. The trigger pressure can be adjusted from 300 to 1000 g (½ to 2¼ lb). The bolt-action pistol does not have a safety, but this is not really necessary for a single-shot weapon.

GLOCK

The Austrian engineer Gaston Glock designed the Glock pistol in 1980. It became known all over the world as the plastic pistol. This name was given to the pistol because many parts were made of a special impact-resistant synthetic material. Glock was the first make of weapons to use this new material. In the USA its introduction to the civilian market resulted in media hysteria. It was thought that the 'plastic pistol' would not be detected at airports and it was soon described as a 'terrorist special'. However, tests have very clearly shown that this is nonsense. Furthermore, most manufacturers have now followed Glock in the past twenty years with one or more models with a synthetic frame. The Glock construction is simple and modern. There are no manually operated safety systems on the outside of the weapon, and there is no hammer. The built-in safety systems operate automatically on the basis of

Gaucher silhouette pistol

GAUCHER PHANTOM GP

In 1970, Gaucher introduced this single-shot bolt-action pistol in .22 LR caliber. It was mainly intended for hunting small game. One of the special features of this weapon is the silencer integrated in the barrel. A standard .22 LR cartridge usually produces approximately 80 dB (decibel). Using the device, the sound level of a .22 LR subsonic bullet from the Phantom GP is no more than 53 DB. The Winchester T-22, a typical standard cartridge produces about 55 dB. This is permitted in France, but in many other

Trade mark of Austrian firm of Glock

Cut-away diagram of
a Glock pistol that
shows the locking
clearly at the front

the trigger action. All Glock
models have a so-called
safe-action trigger. This is
actually a double-action-only
(DAO) system with three built-in
safety systems. There is a hinged lip in the trigger
itself. This is the trigger safety. If this lip is not
depressed, the trigger is blocked. In addition, the
weapon has automatic firing pin safety. Finally every
Glock has falling block safety. The small catch above
the trigger is the takedown lever. The ambidextrous
magazine catch is behind the trigger guard and this is
found in every Glock model. The locking system of
all Glock models is based on the Browning-Petter
type. The block around the chamber barrel bolts in
the ejection port of the steel slide. There is a double
guide lug for unlocking this, under the chamber
block. Since 1998 all the larger Glock models have
had a rail in the part of the frame in front of the
trigger guard. This rail is for mounting laser systems
or other sights. In addition, most Glock
models since 1999 have had a grip
with integrated finger grooves. The
Glock 17 was introduced to the
Austrian army and police in 1982, as
the P-80. The weapon was also
introduced for the armed forces in
Norway, Sweden and the Netherlands.
Meanwhile, many countries have adopted this pistol
for their army, police or security forces. In 1984 the
Glock 17 was approved as the army pistol for NATO
units. As an extra accessory, Glock provides specially
extended magazines for all models so that the
magazine capacity is increased by two extra
cartridges. Glock has developed its Model 17 over
more than twenty years into a complete series of
pistols. This series actually consists of the large
model, several semi-compact models and truly
compact models.

GLOCK MODEL 17

The Glock 17, or G17, as the pistol is also known,
was developed in 1980 by the Austrian engineer,
Gaston Glock. In 1982, the Austrian army chose the
Glock 17 as its service pistol. The weapon only
became popular in the USA in 1985. When the
Miami Police Department introduced Model 17 as its
weapon in 1987, many other American police
departments followed their example, such as the
NYPD in New York in 1989. As indicated in the
introduction, the Glock 17 has a double-action-only
trigger. This is described by Glock as a safe-action
system. The model number 17 is related to the
magazine capacity, viz., 17 rounds in 9 mm Para
caliber. With a special magazine, this capacity can
even be increased to 19 rounds. In North America,
the magazine capacity is restricted by law to 10
rounds. The total length of the Glock 17 is 186 mm
(7¼ in), the barrel length is 114 mm (4½ in) and
it has a hexagonal profile with a right-hand twist
of 250 mm (9¾ in). The height of the weapon is
138 mm (5½ in), and its width is only 30 mm (1 in).
The empty weight of the pistol is 625 g (22 oz). The
standard trigger pressure is 2500 g (5½ lb). However,
some American police departments wanted a heavier
trigger pressure. Glock therefore developed an
interchangeable set of 3600 g (8 lb). In 1990, the
New York Police Department (NYPD) requested
a modified trigger action which was to be like that of
a double-action revolver. Glock responded promptly
and designed the New York trigger spring. It seems
that the New Yorkers still considered this too light
because it was followed one year later by the New
Yorker Two trigger action with a trigger pressure of
5440 g (12 lb).

Glock has two different models for training
purposes. Model 17 T in 9 mm FX caliber shoots
9 mm rounds filled with paint, or 9 mm cartridges
with a rubber round. The frame of this

Glock Model 17 pistol

Glock G17TFX
training pistol

Full-automatic Glock 18
with firing regulator on left
of slide

model is bright blue. In addition, there is the 17T
7.8 x 21 AC pistol which works with replaceable air
pressure cartridges, which can also shoot rubber or
paint rounds. This weapon has a bright red frame.

GLOCK MODEL 17L

Glock introduced the 9 mm Para model 17 L in 1988.
It has the frame of the Model 17 with a longer slide
and barrel. The total length is 225 mm (8¼ in). The
barrel has a length of 153 mm (6 in) and a hexagonal
profile with a twist of 250 mm (10 in). The sight
radius is 205 mm (8 in). The magazine capacity,
height and width of the weapon are the same at that
of the standard Model 17. It weighs 670 g (23½ oz)
without the magazine. The standard trigger pressure
is 2000 g (4½ lb).

GLOCK MODEL 18/MODEL 18C

At the request of the Austrian army, Glock designed
the fully automatic pistol Model 18 in 1984. The
selector with which the weapon can be adjusted for

Glock 18C with integrated
compensator

Glock 17L with longer
slide and barrel

semi-automatic or fully automatic firing is on the left
of the slide. This Glock has a total length of 183 mm
(7¼ in), a barrel length of 114 mm (4½ in) and
a weight of 620 g (22 oz). Glock Model
18 C has a built-in compensator. There
is an oblong slit in the top of the slide
for this. In the barrel there are slits at
various intervals for the pressure of the
gas to escape as the bullet passes
through the barrel. The recoil of the weapon
is reduced in this way.

GLOCK MODEL 19

There were already signs of a compact
model of the Glock 17 in 1988. At
the time, it was referred to as the
G-17 Compact. In 1990 Glock
introduced this as Model 19.

It comes in 9 mm Para caliber with a standard magazine capacity of 15 rounds. With a special magazine, this capacity can be increased by two rounds. The pistol has a total length of 174 mm (6 ¼ in). The hexagonal barrel is 102 mm (4 in) long and has a right-hand twist of 250 mm (10 in). The height of the weapon is 127 mm (5 in), and the sight radius is 152 mm (6 in). Without a magazine the pistol weighs 595 g (21 oz). The standard trigger pressure is 2500 g (5 ½ lb). The same type with a built-in compensator is the model 19C.

GLOCK MODEL 20

In 1990, Glock decided to join the 10 mm trend at the time and introduced Model 20 in 10 mm Auto caliber. As this is rather a large cartridge, the model

Glock Model 19 pistol

was also introduced to the market with a built-in compensator as Model 20C. The total length of Model 20 is 193 mm (7 ½ in). The barrel has a length of 117 mm (4 ½ in) and a hexagonal profile with a right-hand twist of 25 mm (1 in). The magazine capacity is 15 rounds. The height of the pistol is 139 mm (5 ½ in) and the width is 32.5 mm (1 ¼ in). The empty weight of the weapon is 785 g (27 ¾ oz). The standard trigger pressure is 2500 g (5 ½ lb).

Glock Model 21 pistol in .45 ACP caliber

GLOCK MODEL 21

In 1990, Glock decided to market a pistol in .45 ACP caliber as well. This was actually a Model 20 in a different caliber. The measurements of this weapon are the same as those of Model 20. Because of the .45 ACP caliber the profile of the barrel was changed. The 117 mm (4 ½ in) barrel has an octagonal profile with a right-hand twist of 400 mm (15 ¼ in). The weight is 745 g (26 ¼ oz).

GLOCK MODEL 22

A third new model dating from 1990 came with the introduction of the Glock Model 22 in .40 S&W caliber. A more compact model followed in the same year: Model 23 in the same caliber. The FBI adopted both these models as the weapon for its officers in 1997. In these models the FBI uses special ammunition developed by Federal. This is a Hydra-Shok cartridge with a Jacketed Hollow-Point bullet of 165 grains (10.69 g). This achieves a muzzle velocity of approximately 290 m/s (950 fps). The muzzle energy is 450 Joules. Model 22 has a total length of 186 mm (7 ¼ in). The barrel length is 114 mm (4 ½ in) and it has a hexagonal profile with a right-hand twist of 250 mm (10 in). The empty weapon weighs 650 g (23 oz). Glock also makes this model with a built-in compensator as Model 22C. Because of the openings in the top of the slide, the empty weight of the 22C is slightly less,

Glock 20 in 10 mm
Auto caliber

Glock 22 in .40
S&W caliber

639g (22 ½ oz). The standard magazine capacity is 15 rounds. With a special magazine it is 17 rounds. For the American civilian market, the magazine capacity is restricted to 10 rounds.

GLOCK MODEL 23

Model 23 is the compact model of the large Model 22. Glock introduced both models to the market in 1990. In 1997, the FBI chose Model 22 and Model 23 as their service weapons. The larger Model 22 is

Semi-compact
Glock 23

used by the 'duty officers', while the smaller Model 23 is used by lesser agents. The total length of Model 23 is 174 mm (7 in). The profile of the barrel and the twist are the same as that of Model 22. The standard magazine capacity is 13 rounds. There is also a model with a compensator with the model name 23 C.

GLOCK MODEL 24/MODEL 24C

Models 24 and 24C with a built-in compensator date from 1994. They are both in .40 S&W caliber. They are based on Model 17 L with a long slide, but have a larger caliber. The standard magazine capacity is 15 rounds. The total length of both models is 225 mm (9 in). The barrel length is 153 mm (6 in), and it has a hexagonal profile with a right-hand twist of 250 mm (10 in). The height of the weapon is 138 mm (5 ½ in) and without the magazine it weighs 757 g (26¾ oz). The standard trigger pressure is

The large Glock 24

Glock Model 24C with
integral compensator

2000 g (4½ lb). The photograph shows Model 24 C with a built-in compensator.

GLOCK MODEL 25

Model 25 was introduced at the IWA, the International Arms Fair, in Nuremberg, Germany, in 1995. This Glock pistol is in 9 mm Short (.380 ACP) caliber. The market had indicated that Glock should add a model in this caliber to its range. The weapon has a standard magazine capacity of 15 rounds and with a special magazine, even of 17 rounds. Nevertheless it is only 30 mm (1 in) wide. The American Crime Bill prohibits a magazine capacity of more than 10 rounds for civilian use. Because of this restriction on the magazine capacity and heavy competition, this model is not for sale in the USA. The pistol has a total length of 174 mm (7 in). The barrel has a length of 102 mm (4 in) and a hexagonal profile with a right-hand twist of 250 mm (10 in). The height of the weapon is 127 mm (5 in) and the weight is 570 g (20 oz) without the magazine. The trigger pressure is about 2500 g (5 ½ lb).

Compact Glock 25 in
9 mm Short (.380 ACP)

Compact Glock 26
in 9 mm Para

GLOCK MODEL 26

In 1996, Glock introduced the compact Model 26 to the market. This small pistol is available in 9 mm Para caliber and in .40 S&W caliber as Model 27. The magazine capacity of Model 26 is 12 rounds. The total length of this weapon is 160 mm (6 ¼ in). The barrel has a length of 88 mm (3 ½ in) and an hexagonal profile with a right-hand twist of 250 mm (10 in). The height of the pistol is only 106 mm (4 in) and the width is 30 mm (1 in). The empty weight is 560 g (19 ¾ oz). It is an ideal weapon for police detective departments.

GLOCK MODEL 27

Glock also introduced the compact model in .40 S&W caliber in 1996 as Model 27. This pistol has exactly the same measurements as Model 26 in 9 mm Para. Only the magazine capacity is different, i.e., 11 rounds, because of the slightly thicker .40 S&W cartridge.

GLOCK MODEL 28

A compact model of model 25 appeared on the market in 1997, known as Model 28. In the USA this model

Glock 27, a compact
version of Model 22

is only issued to the police departments as a back up pistol. The total length of Model 28 is 160 mm (6 ¼ in), the barrel length is 99 mm (3 ½ in), the height is 106 mm (4 in) and the weapon weighs 529 g (18 ½ oz). It has a magazine capacity of 10 rounds in 9 mm Short (.380 ACP) caliber.

GLOCK MODEL 29

Glock developed this compact model of Model 20 in 10 mm Auto caliber in 1997 and introduced it on the market as Model 29. The slide is 21 mm (⅞ in) shorter and the height is only 113 mm (4 ½ in). In order to retain the reasonable magazine capacity of

Compact Glock
Model 29 pistol

10 rounds, the width remained the same as in the large model, viz., 32.5 mm (1 ¼ in). The total length of this compact pistol is 172 mm (6 ¾ in). The barrel length is 96 mm (3 ¼ in). The barrel has a hexagonal profile with a right-hand twist of 250 mm (10 in). The empty weight is 700 g (24 ½ oz).

GLOCK MODEL 30

A compact model of Model 21 in .45 ACP caliber was introduced in 1997 as Model 30. This pistol has a standard magazine capacity of 10 rounds. A magazine for 9 rounds is also available. The total length is 172 mm (6¾ in). The barrel is 96 mm (3¾ in) long, and has an octagonal profile with a right-hand twist of 400 mm (15¾ in). The height

Mini-version Glock 30
in .45 ACP caliber

of the weapon with a 9-shot magazine is 113 mm (4½ in), and with a 10-shot magazine it is 121 mm (4¾ in). The width is 32.5 mm (1¼ in). The empty weight is 680 g (24 oz).

GLOCK MODEL 31/31C

In 1998, Glock introduced a number of models in the new .357 Sig caliber. This cartridge was developed by the Swiss SIG arms factory. The caliber is based on

The big Glock 31 in the
new .357 SIG caliber

a .40 S&W cartridge case with a compressed shoulder for a 9 mm bullet. Several other ammunition factories are now also making cartridges in this caliber. A bullet of 125 grains (8.1 g) achieves a muzzle velocity of 412 m/s (1350 fps) and a muzzle energy of 688 Joules. The Czech ammunition manufacturer Sellier & Bellot even makes this caliber with a full mantle jacket bullet of 149 grains (9.1 g). This also has a muzzle velocity of 412 m/s (1350 fps) and a muzzle energy of 764 Joules. The total length of Model 31 is 186 mm (7 ¼ in). The barrel has a length of 114 mm (4 ½ in) and a hexagonal profile with a right-hand twist of 406 mm (16 in). The height of the weapon is 138 mm (5 ½ in), and the empty weight is 660 g (32 ¼ oz). The standard magazine

capacity is 15 rounds and with a special magazine can even be increased to 17 rounds. Glock also provided this pistol with a built-in compensator as Model 31C, as illustrated below.

GLOCK MODEL 32/32C

Glock also introduced the semi-compact model of Model 31 on the market in 1998 as Model 32 and Model 32C with a built-in compensator. The total

Semi-compact Glock 32
in .357 SIG

length of this pistol is 174 mm (7 in) and it differs very little from that of the larger model: only 12 mm (½ in). The height of the weapon is 127 mm (5 in). The standard magazine capacity in .357 SIG caliber is 13 rounds. The barrel has a length of 102 mm (4 in) and the barrel profile and twist are the same as those of the slightly larger Model 31. The weight is 610 g (21 ½ oz). Model 32C is slightly lighter because of the gas slits in the slide and weighs 605 g (21 ¼ oz).

Glock 31C with integral
compensator

Glock 32 C with
compensator

The newer model has integrated finger grooves in the grip, a rear sight that is adjustable on the side and an ambidextrous enlarged magazine catch. Model 34, in 9 mm Para caliber has a magazine capacity of 17 or 19 rounds depending on the magazine that is used. The total length is 207 mm (8 in). The barrel has a length of 135 mm (5 ¼ in), and a hexagonal profile with a right-hand twist of 250 mm (10 in). The sight radius is 192 mm (7 ½ in). The weapon weighs 650 g (23 oz) without the magazine. The standard trigger pressure is 2000 g (4 ½ lb). Model 34 comes standard with a compensator integrated in the barrel.

Mini-version Glock
33 in .357 SIG

GLOCK MODEL 33

Model 33 is a truly compact pistol in .357 SIG caliber which was introduced in 1998. This weapon has approximately the same measurements as the other compact models. The total length of Model 33 is 160 mm (6 ¼ in). The barrel has a length of 88 mm (3½ in) and a hexagonal profile with a right-hand twist of 406 mm (16 in). The pistol has a standard magazine capacity of 9 rounds. With a special magazine, this capacity can be increased to 11 rounds. The weapon is only 106 mm (4 in) high and it weighs 560 g (19 ¾ oz).

GLOCK MODEL 34

The large Model 34 appeared on the market in 1998. It was specially developed as the match pistol for the so-called Practical/Tactical shooting discipline of the International Defense Pistol Association (IDPA). In addition, it is used by various Tactical Response teams of the American Police. The first model had a flat grip and a fixed rear sight but this was modified in 1999.

IDPA Glock 35 in
.40 S&W caliber

GLOCK MODEL 35

This model was also introduced in 1998, together with Model 34. The latter is in .40 S&W caliber and was also developed as a match pistol for the so-called Practical/Tactical shooting discipline of the International Defense Pistol Association (IDPA). The weapon was modified in 1999 with integrated finger grooves in the grip, as well as being fitted with a rear sight adjustable on the side, and an ambidextrous enlarged, magazine catch.

The pistol has a magazine capacity of 15 or 17 rounds. The measurements are the same as those of Model 34. However, it is slightly heavier, viz., 695 g (24½ oz). Model 35 comes standard with a compensator integrated in the barrel.

GLOCK MODEL 36

The semi-compact model 36 in .45 ACP caliber dates from 1999. The pistol has a single row magazine for only 6 rounds. This does make it extra narrow, viz. 28.5 mm (1 in). The total length is 172 mm (6¾ in). The barrel has a length of 96 mm (3¾ in) with an octagonal profile and a right-hand twist of

IDPA match model 34
in 9 mm Para caliber

The 6-shot mini Glock
Model 36

Blued version
of the Grizzly

400 mm (15¾ in). The height of the weapon is
121 mm (4¾ in) and it weighs 570 g (20 oz). The
standard trigger pressure is 2500 g (5½ lb).

GRIZZLY

Logo of LAR
Grizzly

Up to 1979, the 'Dirty Harry' Smith & Wesson .44
Magnum was considered to be the heaviest handgun
caliber, but in that year, this caliber was surpassed by
the .45 Winchester Magnum cartridge, originally
intended for the Wildey Automatic. At the same
time, a second special cartridge was introduced on the
market: the 9 mm Winchester magnum. As the
production of the Wildey was fraught with problems,
the single-shot Thompson Center Contender was the
only pistol series at that time which could shoot the
.45 Win. Magnum cartridge. This new type of
cartridge led a rather obscure existence because there
was hardly any choice in the type of handguns for
these 'giant calibers'. In 1983, the manufacturer of
ammunition even considered ceasing production. The
Grizzly Winchester Magnum in .45 Win Magnum was
introduced to the market at the end of 1983, made by
LAR Manufacturing in West Jordan in the State
of Utah. This company, which was established in
1968, mainly manufactured components of weapons
for other manufacturers. For example, they made
mountings for different types of submachine guns for
the US Army, and parts for M16 rifles. The Grizzly
looks like an enlarged Colt-1911 A1, and in fact, that
is what it is. Thirty-nine of the forty-nine parts can be
exchanged with a normal Colt Government. The
other ten parts, such as the hand grips, magazine,
slide, barrel, barrel bushing, firing pin, recoil spring
and extractor cannot be exchanged because these are
linked to the caliber. The Grizzly locking system is
that of the Browning-Colt type. In comparison with
other locking systems, it is most remarkable for its

simplicity. The system is not
very sensitive to dust and dirt,
the manufacturing costs are
reasonable, and its reliability has been proven
countless times. The first models had a barrel with two
gas outlets cut out at the muzzle as a compensator. The
Grizzly has three safety systems. The ambidextrous
extra large safety catch locks both the hammer and
the sear. In addition, the pistol has a grip safety at the
back of the frame and lastly it has a bolt safety. The
magazine well in the grip is beveled on the inside in
the so-called combat style. This means that it is easier
to exchange magazines. The feature which makes the
Grizzly particularly interesting is the possibility of
using conversion kits. For example, the pistol can be
converted in no time at all from .357 Magnum to .45
ACP or .45 Win. Magnum. Originally, conversion kits
were also made for the 9 mm Winchester Magnum,
but production of this cartridge has now ceased. The
latest model of the Grizzly is in .50 AE caliber, also
known as .50 Magnum. Unfortunately LAR decided
to cease production of its pistols in 1999.

LAR GRIZZLY

LAR introduced the single-action Grizzly pistol in
1983, initially in .45 Win. Magnum caliber. This was
later followed by the calibers, 9 mm Win. Magnum, .45
ACP, .357 Magnum, the 10 mm Auto and .357/45
Win. Magnum, a cartridge with a bottleneck. The
most recent caliber was the .50 Action Express. The
total length of the Grizzly is 267 mm (10½ in). The
length of the barrel was either 137 or 165 mm (5½ or
6½ in). The magazine capacity in most calibers is
7 rounds, and only in .50 AE is it 6 rounds. Depending
on the caliber, the empty weight of the weapon is
between 1360 and 1590 g (48 and 56 oz). All Grizzlys
have an adjustable micrometer sight, an ambidextrous
safety catch and an adjustable trigger stop. Up to 1999,
the Grizzly was available in a blued, mat blue or mat
chrome-plated finish.

Mat-chrome version
of Grizzly with extended
barrel

H

HÄMMERLI SPORT PISTOLS

**A subsidiary of
SIG Swiss Industrial
Company**

Logo of
Hämmerli

The Swiss firm Hämmerli was founded in 1863. Up to 1900 the firm mainly produced barrels for rifles for various Swiss army rifles. In 1897, the name Hämmerli became very well known in sports shooting. In fact, the world championships were won in that year with Martini rifles converted by Hämmerli. Up to 1914, the Swiss Hämmerli/Martini team won seventeen of the nineteen world championships. Hämmerli then started to specialize in sports weapons. In 1933, the firm introduced the free pistol model 33 MP in .22 Extra Long caliber. This weapon secured the success of the Swiss Hämmerli team for years afterwards. During the Second World War, the production capacity served to defend the territory of the neutral state of Switzerland. In 1952, Hämmerli introduced its first rapid-fire pistol in .22 Short caliber. The firm started a subsidiary company in Waldshut-Tiengen in Germany in 1956. This produces mainly high quality air guns, and from 1961 also large caliber match rifles under the name Hämmerli-Tanner. These rifles won the world championships in the 300 meter Match Rifle discipline in Cairo in 1962. In 1971, the Swiss SIG concern bought a majority interest in the Hämmerli firm. SIG is an abbreviation for the Schweizerische Industrie Gesellschaft. This company, together with numerous subsidiaries, is engaged in the production of trains, electronics, industrial robots, mining, the timber industry and packaging systems. In the weapons sector, the concern makes pistols under the Sig-Sauer name, match pistols under the Hämmerli

name, hunting guns under the Sauer name, and sports, army and police rifles under the SIG name. Hämmerli has a wide range of pistols, including both single-shot, so-called free pistols and automatics in .22 LR caliber. Both sorts have been widely used by top shooters during the Olympic Games and world championships. In the course of time, Hämmerli pistols have undergone various modifications. For example, the single-shot pistols of the models 150, dating from 1972, and 152-Electronic, dating from 1980, were replaced in 1992 by the Hämmerli 160 and 162-Electronic. In the field of automatics, the models 211, 212 and 215 were discontinued. In addition, from 1972 Hämmerli produced a special large caliber match pistol for a number of years, the Hämmerli P240 in calibers, .32 S&W-Long and .38 Special Wadcutter. In 1987, Hämmerli introduced the P280 pistol in .22 LR and .32 S&W Long caliber. This weapon is mainly made of synthetic materials. In 1998, Hämmerli introduced the SP20 on the market in .22 LR and .32 S&W Long calibers. The latest model dating from 1999 is the X esse in .22 LR caliber. This weapon is sold in the USA as the Trailside PL 22.

HÄMMERLI MODEL 160

In 1992, Hämmerli introduced the single-shot models 160 and 162-E (Electronic) to replace the older models 150 dating from 1972 and 152-Electronic dating from 1980. Both Model 160 and Model 160-E have a walnut match stock with an adjustable hand rest. In addition, the weapon has a free barrel. There is a synthetic pawl under the barrel to hold balanced weights. In Model 160-E, part of the room is taken up by the batteries for the electronic trigger system. Model 160 has a mechanical trigger. The trigger itself is completely adjustable in both models. The micrometer sight is a long way up the tailpiece, which extends over the stock. The total length of the weapon is 445 mm (17½in). The barrel length is 287 mm (11¼ in). The height of the pistol is 145 mm (5¾ in), and the width is approximately 80 mm (3 in) because of the large wide stock. The sight radius is 370 mm (14½ in), and the weapon weighs 1330g (47 oz). The trigger weight of Model 160 can be adjusted from 10 to 100 g (¼ to 3½ oz) and that of Model 160-E from 5 to 80 g (less than ¼ oz to 2¾ oz). With regard to the width of the interchangeable bead, the shooter can choose

Hämmerli Model 160

Hämmerli 208
International

Simpler Model 215

between 6 different widths from 3.0 to 5.5 mm (.118 to .217 in). For the rear sight leaf, there are three different widths available: 3.2 mm, 3.6 mm and 4.0 mm (.126 in, .142 in, and .157 in).

HÄMMERLI MODEL 208/MODEL 208S

The Hämmerli Model 208 was introduced in 1966. This is a specific sports pistol in .22 LR caliber. The weapon has a steel frame and slide and a magazine capacity of 8 rounds. The older model, the Hämmerli 208 International, has a trigger guard around the frame. The newer model, Model 208S is illustrated below and has a square trigger guard. Both models have a walnut stock with an adjustable hand rest. In addition, they have an interchangeable bead and a micrometer sight with an interchangeable rear sight leaf. The trigger is adjustable with regard to the trigger pressure, the trigger crawl, and the trigger stop. The total length of the pistol is 255 mm (10 in). The barrel length, as well as the height, are 150 mm (6 in), and the width is 50 mm (2 in). The sight radius is 208 mm (8 in) and the weapon weighs 985 g (34¼ oz). A removable barrel weight is attached under the square barrel. The model which has a rear sight that can be simply adjusted on the side is Model 212. This model does not have a match stock but has flat walnut grips.

HÄMMERLI MODEL 215/MODEL 215S

The Hämmerli Model 215 pistol is a less luxurious model of the Hämmerli 208 described above. The finish was made more economically, but the whole of the internal mechanism, including the trigger mechanism, is identical to that of the more expensive model 208. The older model with the round trigger guard is illustrated above. The newer Model 215S with the square trigger guard is shown below. The measurements of Model 215 are the same as those of Model 218.

Newer version,
Model 215S

HÄMMERLI MODEL 280

The Hämmerli Model 280 was introduced to the market in 1987 as Hämmerli's new match pistol. The weapon is mainly made of synthetic materials. In Model 280, the housing of the magazine is in front of the trigger guard. There is an ambidextrous magazine catch under the trigger guard. The slide catch is on the right of the frame, above the trigger. The weapon is available in .22 LR caliber with a magazine capacity of 6 rounds and in .32 S&W Long caliber with a capacity of 5 rounds. In addition, Hämmerli provides conversion kits for both calibers. The total length is 300 mm (12 in). The barrel is 116.4 mm (4½ in). The height of the weapon is 150 mm (6 in) and the width is 50 mm (2 in). The sight radius is 220 mm (8½ in) and the weight is 120 g (42¼ oz), excluding the extra barrel

The new
model 108S

Hämmerli Model 280
match pistol

Hämmerli SP20 is
available in various colors

weights. In addition, the trigger can be adjusted from 1000 to 1360 g (2¼ to 3 lb). In 1992, the pistol was partly modified. Before that time two screws had to be removed in the front under the barrel to disassemble the pistol. After the modification it was only necessary to loosen a single screw with a single take down key.

The illustration below shows the left of the pistol and clearly reveals the three individual barrel weights.

Left side of
Hämmerli 280

HÄMMERLI MODEL SP20

The Hämmerli Model SP20 match
pistol dates from 1998. The weapon is based on Model 280, but has a number of special adjustment possibilities. The synthetic frame has an integrated grip, trigger guard and magazine shroud. The grip is available in five different sizes, from Narrow to XXL. The weapon has an adjustable buffer system. This serves to adjust the recoil for a particular sort of ammunition or to the needs of the individual

shooter. In addition, the pistol has a bolt housing. During the repeat action only the loose bolt moves. In order to load the weapon there is a cocking handle on the right of the bolt housing. This is available in the colors blue, gold, purple, red or black. The bolt catch is also on the right, above the trigger. The weapon is available in .22 LR caliber (6-shot) or .32 S&W Long caliber (5-shot). In addition, Hämmerli has conversion kits in both calibers. The total length of the pistol is 300 mm (12 in). The length of the barrel is 122 mm (4¾ in). The height is 140 mm (5½ in). The sight radius is 220 mm (8½ in). The weapon weighs 1150 g (40½ oz) in .22 LR caliber and 1250 g (44 oz) in the .32 S&W Long model. The square bead of the SP20 can be rotated resulting in different bead widths. The rear sight leaf of the micrometer sight can also be adjusted, not only sideways and in height, but the width of the rear sight can also be adjusted gradually between 2.5 and 4.5 mm (.10 in and .177 in). For the trigger pressure, the shooter can switch from 1000 to 1360 g (2¼ to 3 lb). When Model SP20 was introduced, the production of the older models 208 and 215 came to an end.

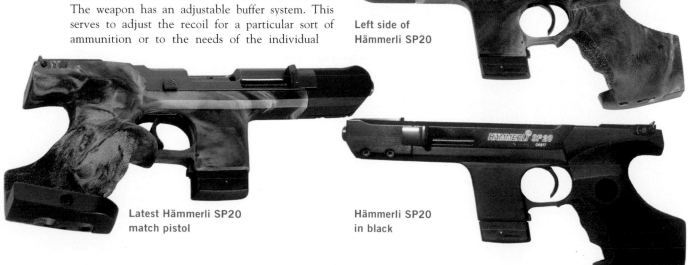

Left side of
Hämmerli SP20

Latest Hämmerli SP20
match pistol

Hämmerli SP20
in black

Hämmerli X-esse
pistol of 1999

X-esse in macho black

HÄMMERLI MODEL X-ESSE/MODEL TRAILSIDE PL22

The latest Hämmerli is the X-ESSE sports pistol in .22 LR caliber with a magazine capacity of 10 rounds. The weapon has a synthetic frame which is available in several different colors such as black, blue, red and yellow. Model X-ESSE has a safety catch on the left of the slide. The slide catch is above the left grip. The magazine catch is also on the left, behind the trigger guard. The X-ESSE is available in two main models. The short model has a barrel length of 115 mm (4½ in), a total length of 197 mm (7¾ in), a height of 127 mm (5 in) and a weight of 800 g (28¼ oz). The longer Model X-ESSE pistol has a barrel length of 152 mm (6 in), and a total length is 235 mm (9¼ in). The height of the weapon is the same as that of the short model. The weight is 950 g (33½ oz). The bead is integrated in the square barrel. At the back of the slide there is an adjustable micrometer sight. The pistol is disassembled in more or less the same way as the Walther PP. First, the slide has to be secured in

the final position. Then the trigger guard can be pulled down from the frame at the front. The block under the barrel has to be unscrewed and taken off. Finally, the slide can be pulled up slightly at the back and slid forwards off the frame.

HARRINGTON & RICHARDSON/ NEW ENGLAND FIREARMS

Trade mark of
Harrington &
Richardson

The American arms factory, Harrington & Richardson, was founded in 1871 by Gilbert Henderson Harrington and Franklin Wesson. Before that, Harrington was employed by a small revolver factory, Ballard & Fairbanks in Worcester, Massachusetts. At the age of 26, he had already designed the first self-ejecting revolver. Franklin Wesson owned a small workshop where he manufactured guns. In 1871, Ballard & Fairbanks decided to stop the production of revolvers. In the same year, Wesson and his nephew Harrington established their new firm aiming to start producing firearms themselves. They appointed a former colleague, from Ballard & Fairbanks, William Augustus Richardson as their technical manager. A single-shot Wesson & Harrington Model 1871 rifle dates from that period, amongst other firearms. Uncle Franklin Wesson left the company in 1874, and it was taken over by Harrington and Richardson. At that time, production concentrated mainly on revolvers,

Right side of
Hämmerli X-esse

Trade mark of New England Firearms Company, subsidiary of H&R

usually sold under the name Aetna. Because of the great demand for double-barreled shotguns, it was decided to start making these. A licensing contract was concluded with the English firm Anson & Deely for this purpose. As there was a great increase in the demand for Harrington & Richardson revolvers and production was unable to keep up with this, the cooperation came to an end in 1886. In 1888 the firm was thoroughly reorganized and renamed the Harrington & Richardson Arms Company. The two directors died shortly one after the other in 1897. The company continued trading with three managers: Mr. Brooks, the former administrator, Edwin C. Harrington, the 20-year-old son of the founder, and the daughter Mary A. Richardson. After a long period in Worcester, the factory finally moved to Gardner in Massachusetts. The current range of H&R includes a series of single-barreled shotguns and rifles. In addition, a series of single-barreled shotguns and rifles are also produced under the name of the subsidiary, New England Firearms. The products of H&R are extremely simple and reliable. In 2000, the company decided to stop manufacturing revolvers.

H&R MODEL 929 SIDEKICK

The old model 929 Sidekick dates from 1956 and was produced up to 1985. It is a double-action revolver with a 9-shot swing-out cylinder in .22 LR caliber. It has a blued finish and black synthetic grips. Model 929 was available at that time with barrel lengths of

H&R Model 929 Sidekick revolver

64, 102 or 152 mm (2½, 4 or 6 in). The last two models also had an adjustable rear sight. Model 929 sidekick was introduced on the market in 1996. This 9-shot model was only available with a heavy 102 mm (4 in) barrel in .22 LR caliber. The total length is 228 mm (9 in) and the weapon weighs 850 g (30 oz). The revolver has a fixed sight groove in the top of the cylinder bridge. The cylinder can be tipped out of the frame by pulling the ejector rod forwards. The safety is a transfer bar system. The model is made with hardwood grips and a blued finish.

H&R MODEL 939 PREMIER

Model 939 Premier model

Harrington & Richardson introduced this 9-shot double-action revolver model in 1958. It was produced up to 1982 in two different models. Model 939 Ultra Sidekick had a barrel length of 152 mm (6 in) and an adjustable sight. It is interesting that this revolver could be locked with the key that came with it. This meant that the weapon could not be fired. The second, slightly more luxurious model was the 939 Premier. This weapon had a polished blued finish and a barrel length of 152 mm (6 in) with a raised barrel rib and an adjustable rear sight. Both models were made up to 1982. In 1995, Harrington & Richardson decided to give the weapon a new lease of life and introduced the new 9-shot Model 939 Premier on the market. This revolver has a heavy barrel 152 mm (6 in) long, with a raised barrel rib just like the old model. In addition, it has an adjustable rear sight. The total length is 279 mm (11 in) and the weight is 1020 g (36 oz). The grips are made of hardwood. This weapon also has a transfer bar as a safety system.

H&R MODEL 949 WESTERN/FORTY NINER

The old Model 949 dates from 1960 and was made up to 1985. The original name of the model was 949 Forty-Niner. It was a 9-shot revolver with a fixed cylinder in .22 LR caliber. The loading port was on the right of the frame. This is a characteristic feature of a single-action revolver. Curiously, this weapon had a double-action trigger action. Model 949 had a blued finish, and as Model 950 it was

H&R Model 949
Western/Forty-Niner

NEF Standard revolver

nickel-plated. The weapon was reintroduced in 1994 in exactly the same model as the old model dating from 1960. The new 9-shot Model 949 Western was available in .22 LR caliber with a barrel length of 140 or 191 mm (5½ or 7½ in). The total length is respectively 267 or 318 mm (10½ or 12½ in). Depending on the barrel length, the revolver weighs 1020 or 1077 g (36 or 38 oz). The frame is flame hardened. The cylinder and the barrel are blued, and the grips are made of hardwood. The shroud for the typical western ejector rod is on the right of the barrel. The new Model 949 has a transfer bar safety.

H&R Model 999 Sportsman

The old Model 999 Sportsman also dates from 1960 and was made up to 1986. At the time it was available in a blued finish and as an engraved model, with barrel length of 102 or 152 mm (4 or 6 in). In 1992, Harrington & Richardson introduced a new Model 999 Sportsman on the market, in exactly the same finish as the old model. This is a top-break revolver. There is a switch in the upper bridge above the cylinder which operates the bolt. When the weapon is hinged open, the barrel hinges forwards with the

fixed cylinder. At the same time, the empty cartridge cases are automatically ejected by means of a spring extractor star. This new 9-shot double-action revolver in .22LR caliber was available with a barrel length of 102 or 152 mm (4 or 6 in) with a ventilated barrel rib. The total length is 216 or 267 mm (8½ or 10½ in) and the weight is 850 or 964 g (30 or 34 oz). The rear sight can be adjusted on the side, and the bead can be adjusted in height.

NEF Standard Revolver

The Standard revolver series of New England Firearms (NEF) dates from 1988. This double-action weapon was available in a blued or nickel-plated finish and in calibers, .22 LR (9-shot) or .32 H&R Magnum (5-shot). It has a barrel length of 64 or 102 mm (2½ or 4 in). The total length of the standard is respectively 178 or 216 mm (7 or 8½ in) with a weight of 650 or 795 g (23 or 28 oz). The revolver has a transfer bar safety. The .32 H&R Magnum cartridge was developed by Harrington & Richardson in 1984 in collaboration with the Federal Cartridge Company. For this cartridge, the cartridge case of the .32 S&W Long was extended by 4 mm (.155 in) to 27.6 mm (1.085 in). The result is that the NEF revolver can shoot .32 S&W ammunition. However, a .32 S&W Long revolver cannot be loaded with .32 H&R Magnum cartridges. The .32 H&R Magnum has almost 70% more bullet energy than the .32 S&W Long and this is even more than an ordinary .38 Special cartridge. The ballistic properties are shown below. Lead semi-wadcutter bullets are used for the comparison.

Model 999 Sportsman

caliber bullet grain/gram (V0)	muzzle velocity (E0)	muzzle energy	
.32 S&W-Long	98/6.4	238	181
.32 H&R Magn.	95/6.2	314	306
.38 Special	158/10.2	230	270

NEF ULTRA REVOLVER

The NEF Ultra revolver dates from 1989 and is available in three different models. These all have a double-action trigger action, an adjustable rear sight, a heavy barrel with a raised barrel rib and a transfer bar safety system. The .22 LR Ultra has a 9-shot cylinder. The weapon has a heavy 152 mm (6 in) barrel, a total length of 270 mm (10⅝ in) and weighs 1020 g (36 oz). The UltraMag Model has a 6-shot cylinder in .22 WRM caliber. The barrel is also 152 mm (6 in) long. The total length is 270 mm (10⅝ in) and the weight is 1020 g (36 oz). The third model is the Lady Ultra, a 5-shot revolver in .32 H&R Magnum caliber. This has a barrel length of 76 mm (3 in), a total length of 184 mm (7¼ in) and weighs 880 g (31oz).

NEF Ultra revolver

HECKLER & KOCH

The German firm Heckler & Koch was founded in 1949 by Edmund Heckler and Theodor Koch. The company was established in the old Mauser arms factory in Oberndorf. This had been emptied by the French after the Second World War as provisional compensation for war damage they had suffered. As the German army was being built up in the early 1950s, the company received a contract to manufacture the G3 automatic army rifle in .308 Winchester caliber. The Heckler & Koch is based on the Spanish CETME rifle which was in turn based on a Mauser design. The CETME design was then modified to German requirements with the help of

HECKLER & KOCH

Logotype of Heckler & Koch

the development department of Rheinmetall, resulting in the G3 army rifle. This rifle has the famous roller locking system. Heckler & Koch was also one of the first arms manufacturers to use a polygonal barrel profile. This type of barrel does not have any grooves and lands, but a polygonal inside which allows for a certain rotation (twist) ensuring that the bullet rotates. Many of the technical designs of the army weapons can also be found in the Heckler & Koch sports and hunting weapons, such as the above-mentioned roller locking system, the military rotating diopter sight for particular distances and the polygonal barrel. In addition to the well-known HK MP5 submachine-gun in several different models, Heckler and Koch also make a small series of specialized rifles for sharpshooting. In the mid-1980s, Heckler & Koch developed a special army rifle, the G-11, for ammunition without cartridge cases. In the late 1990s the concern was in financial difficulties because of the loss of certain government orders. The choice of the American armed forces for the Beretta M-92 pistol, rather than the Heckler & Koch P7-M13 pistol was a particularly severe blow. In addition, there was not enough interest in the G-11 rifle project, In 1990 the French Giat arms concern announced that it would take over Heckler & Koch but it pulled out of the merger in January 1991. In March 1991, the company was bought up by the British Royal Ordnance, a subsidiary of Aerospace. In 1995, the firm was taken over by the German Wischo concern. The USP pistol proved to be extremely successful. This army pistol was chosen under the name SOCOM, amongst others, by the US Navy Seals and other special units of the American armed forces. On the basis of this weapon, Heckler & Koch designed a number of different models as sports and service pistols. In 1997, Heckler & Koch introduced a completely new rifle design, the HK G36E. This new family of rifles consists of an attack rifle, a light sub-machine-gun and a carbine. It is very surprising that Heckler & Koch abandoned the roller locking system for this new type of rifle. In fact, the HK 36E has a rotation locking system.

HECKLER & KOCH MODEL HK4

The HK4 pistol was the first weapon produced by Heckler & Koch. It was based on the Mauser HSC. The weapon was introduced in 1952 and was made up

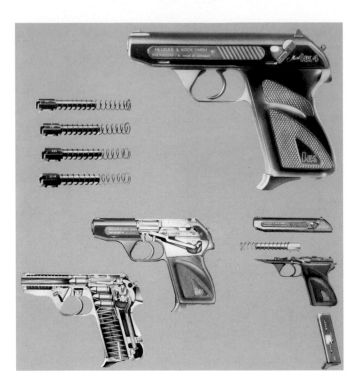

The all-round HK4 pistol

to 1984. The interesting aspect of this pistol is the possibility of changing calibers. Interchangeable barrels were available for the HK4 in complete sets, or separately in the calibers, 9 mm Short (.380 ACP), 7.65 mm (.32 ACP), 6.35 mm (.25 ACP) and .22 LR. The set for the last caliber also contains a separate extractor. In addition, the angle of the firing pin has to be modified for the rimfire cartridge. From 1968 to 1973, the pistol was sold by Harrington & Richardson in the USA under its own name in 9 mm Short (.380 ACP) caliber, and with an interchangeable set in .22 LR. The safety catch is on the left of the slide and blocks the firing pin. In addition, the weapon has magazine safety and half-cock safety on the foot of the hammer. The HK 4 has a total length of 157 mm (6 in), a barrel length of 85 mm (3¼ in), and a height of 120 mm (4¾ in). The pistol has a fixed rear sight and a sight radius of 121 mm (4¾ in). When it is empty, the weapon weighs 480 g (17 oz).

HECKLER & KOCH MODEL VP-70

Keckler & Koch introduced Model VP-70 in 1970. It was a revolutionary design for that time. The frame with the integrated trigger guard was made completely of synthetic material. The pistol was in 9 mm Para caliber and had a magazine capacity of 18 rounds. At that time it was also unusual that the VP-70 had a double-

action-only trigger. The weapon had a recoil locking system and a fixed barrel. A synthetic extended stock, annex holster could be clicked onto the back of the backstrap. This stock had a pin which slid into the back of the pistol to change the trigger action so that the pistol could also fire 3-shot rounds. On the stock there was also a firing selector with which the weapon could be switched to semi-automatic fire. In 1971, the original VP-70 was renamed the VB-70M (Military). Subsequently, Heckler & Koch also introduced a civilian model to the market as the VP-70Z (Zivil), exclusively as an autoloader. The VP-70 has a total length of 204 mm (8 in), a barrel length of 116 mm (4½ in), a height of 142 mm (5½ in) and a width of 32 mm (1¼ in). The sight radius is 175 mm (7 in). The barrel did not have a polygonal profile but ordinary grooves and lands. Without the magazine, the weapon weighed 820 g (29 oz) and when it was loaded with 18 rounds, it weighed 1135 g (40 oz). This progressive design was obviously ahead of its time because the pistol was never a big success. Occasionally Heckler & Koch would sell a few to South African countries in the context of development aid. In addition, a small number of pistols of the Model VP-70Z were issued to some of the German police forces. Because of this disappointing interest, Heckler & Koch decided to cease production in 1984.

HECKLER & KOCH MODEL P9S

Heckler & Koch introduced the P9 pistol to the market in 1970 in 7.65 mm (.32 ACP) caliber and in 9 mm Para caliber. It was a single-action weapon with a magazine capacity of 9 rounds. In 1973, Heckler & Koch introduced a double-action model, the P9S in 9 mm Para and .45 ACP calibers (7-shot). The additional S stands for Spannabzug (double-action). In 1973, a third model was introduced, the P9S-Sport, with an extended barrel with a barrel weight mounted on the front together with a front sight. This sports model also has a completely adjustable rear sight. In 1979, the trigger guard was enlarged and from 1981, it was given a squarer shape.

HK VP-70 civil version

Double-action HK
P9S double action

Cut-away drawing of old
Model P7 with cartridge
holder in heel of the hand
grip

Old model HK P7

Heckler & Koch ceased production of the P9 and
P9S and P9S-Sport in 1984. The pistol has a very
striking technique, particularly because of the
polygonal barrel and the special roller locking
system. Another special feature is the cocking lever
on the left of the frame, behind the trigger guard.
This means that the lever could easily be mistaken
for a magazine catch. However, the magazine catch is
in the heel of the grip in the form of a hook. The
cocking lever serves to cock the firing mechanism.
The pistol can shoot with a double-action
mechanism, but when the cocking lever is cocked, it
can also be fired in single-action for the first shot.
The extractor also serves as a cartridge indicator if
there is a cartridge in the chamber. When the trigger
mechanism is cocked, a pin protrudes from the back
of the frame. The total length of the PNS is 192 mm
(7.6 in). The barrel has a polygonal profile and
a length of 102 mm (4 in). The P9S has a fixed rear
sight with a sight radius of 147 mm (5¾ in). The
height of the weapon is 141 mm (5½ in), and the
weight when it is empty is 875 g (31 oz). In .45 ACP
caliber it is slightly lighter, viz., 790 g (28 oz). The
P9S-Sport has a total length of 230 mm (9 in),
a barrel length of 140 mm (5½ in) and a sight radius
of 190 mm (7½ in). The empty weight of the sports
model is 910 g (32 oz).

HECKLER & KOCH MODEL P7/MODEL P7-M8/MODEL P7-M13

Following the terrorist acts during the Olympic
Games in Munich in 1972, the German government
decided to completely revise the arms used by the
German police. Various technical requirements were
specified for the different weapons for this purpose,
and several manufacturers were asked to design new
police weapons. As a result, Heckler & Koch started
to develop the P7 pistol at the end of 1974. By the
end of 1976, Heckler & Koch had completed the first
prototype. Following a large number of tests of these

weapons, by different users, the
first series was issued in 1979 under
the name PSP, an abbreviation of
Polizei Selbstlade Pistole. The other
name: P7 stands for Pistole 7, i.e., the
seventh type of pistol used by the
German police. In 1981, Heckler & Koch introduced
the weapon for the civilian market as the PSP P7.
This new weapon combined a large number of
revolutionary techniques for that time. In the first
place, the pistol has a polygonal barrel. Instead of
having lands and grooves, the inside of the barrel is
polygonal with a particular rotation so that the bullet
also has this rotating movement. In addition, the
weapon has a squeeze-action instead of the more
usual double or single-action trigger mechanism. The
pistol is always uncocked until the squeeze action is
pressed at the front of the frame. Only then is the
firing pin cocked and is it possible to fire. In addition,
the pistol has a gas pressure locking system. There is
a hole for the gas to escape at the bottom of the barrel
just behind the barrel chamber. When the pistol is
fired, there is a great deal of pressure in the barrel
until the bullet has left the barrel through the muzzle.
Part of the gas pressure escapes through the hole into
a cylinder below the barrel. There is a piston in the
cylinder to inhibit the recoil of the slide. As soon as
the bullet leaves the barrel, this pressure from the

a height of 128 mm (5 in) and a width of 29 mm (1 in). The polygonal barrel is 105 mm (4 in) long. The weapon weighs 785 g (27¾ oz) without a magazine, and 845 g (30 oz) with an empty magazine. The P7-M13 has a total length of 175 mm (7 in), a height of 135 mm (5¼ in) and a width of 33 mm (1¼ in) because of the double row magazine. The barrel length is also 105 mm (4 in). The weight of the weapon is 850 g (30 oz) and including an empty magazine it is 975 g (34½ oz).

P7 made under license by EBO, subsidiary of Hellenic arms works of Greece

cylinder flows back out through the barrel via the hole. This means that the gas pressure in the cylinder disappears so that there is no longer a break on the slide and it can slide back. The weapon does not have a slide catch, but after the last shot the slide does move back in an open position. For the slide to move forwards again, the squeeze action has to be pressed.

The P7 pistol is made under license in Greece by EBO, a subsidiary of the Hellenic arms factory. The original PSP P7 pistol was made up to 1984. The most characteristic difference with its successor was that the magazine catch was in the back of the heel of the grip. In addition, the weapon had a magazine capacity of 8 rounds. Heckler & Koch introduced two successors to this pistol in 1984. These are the 8-shot P7-M8 and the P7-M13 with a magazine capacity of 13 rounds. Both models have an ambidextrous magazine catch behind the trigger guard, just above the squeeze action. The P7-M8 has a total length of 171 mm (6¾ in),

HK P7-M13 pistol

In 1987, the P7 pistol was introduced to the US market as a converted P7-M8 in .45 ACP caliber, with the model name P7-M45. This weapon had a magazine capacity of 7 rounds. The P7-K3 was another model of the R7 special sports model, for which conversion kits are available in the calibers, .22 LR, 6.35 mm (.25 ACP), 7.65 mm (.32 ACP) and 9 mm Short (.380 ACP). This model was introduced in 1988. It did not have a gas-retarded locking system, but a buffer filled with hydraulic oil. The 6.35 mm (.25 ACP) caliber was no longer made after 1990.

HK P7-M8 in 9 mm Para caliber

HK P7-M13 with extended barrel and compensator

The P7-M13 was not chosen as the US Army pistol so that Heckler & Koch had to concentrate on the civilian market. That is why the factory also introduced a 10-shot P7 model of this pistol in .40 Smith & Wesson caliber as the P7-M10. Because of the heavier cartridge, the M10 pistol is also a heavier model. Curiously the M10 does not have a polygonal barrel but a barrel with conventional grooves and lands. The P7-M10 has a total length of 175 mm (7 in) and a weight of 1220 g (43 oz).

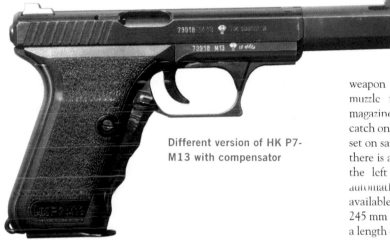

Different version of HK P7-M13 with compensator

HECKLER & KOCH MODEL USP

In order to tackle the competition, Heckler & Koch wished to develop a modern pistol design, but did not have sufficient financial means. In the summer of 1999, the company received a commission for a study from the Pentagon. The Pentagon wanted to have a special .45 ACP pistol designed for the Socom (Special Operations Command) for special units of the army, navy and air force. This Socom modular pistol had to be fitted optionally with laser, infra red, white light sights, and/or silencers. In 1992, Heckler & Koch completed a prototype which was accepted by the Pentagon. The weapon has a synthetic frame with an integrated trigger guard. In the frame in front of the trigger guard there is a groove on either side to mount various devices. Because of the American funding of the development, the pistol is also known as the United States Pistol, and another name introduced in 1998 was the USP 45 Tactical Pistol.

The original Socom model was called the HK Mark 23 Special Operations Pistol. This double-action weapon has an extended barrel with a thread at the muzzle for a silencer. There is an ambidextrous magazine catch behind the trigger guard, and a safety catch on either side of the frame. The pistol can only be set on safe when the hammer is cocked. In front of this there is also an uncocking lever, though this is only on the left of the frame. In addition, the pistol has automatic firing pin safety. The HK Mark 23 is available only in .45 ACP caliber. The total length is 245 mm (9½ in). The barrel has a polygonal profile and a length of 149 mm (6 in) including the protruding part with the thread. The height is 150 mm (6 in) and the width is 38.8 mm (1½ in). In addition, the weapon has a special combat rear sight and a sight radius of 197 mm (7¾ in). When it is empty the weapon weighs 1100 g (39 oz) and with the magazine and 12 rounds it weighs 1465 g (51½ oz). The double-action trigger action is 15 Newton (N). For the subsequent single-action shots the trigger pressure is 20 N.

Cut-away drawing of HK USP

HK Mark 23 Special Operations pistol

HK USP

In 1993, the civilian model based on this Socom pistol was introduced to the market, the USP: Universal Selbstlade Pistole. The standard USP pistol is available in 10 different models, each in the calibers 9 mm Para (15-shot), .40 S&W (13-shot) and .45 ACP (12-shot). The 9 mm Para and .40 S&W models of the USP have a total length of 194 mm (7½ in), a polygonal barrel with a length of 108 mm (4¼ in), a height of 136 mm (5¼ in) and a width of 32 mm (1¼ in). The empty weight in 9 mm Para is 720 g (25½ oz) and in .40 S&W it weighs 780 g (27½ oz). The model in .45 ACP caliber has a total length of 200 mm (8 in), a barrel length of 112 mm (4½ in), a height of 141 mm (5½ in) and a width of 32 mm (1¼ in). The weight of this weapon without the magazine is 783 g (27½ oz).

There is an ambidextrous magazine catch behind the trigger guard. The slide catch is on the left of the frame. The different models of the standard USP pistol are:

MODEL 1: a double-action trigger and a combined safety catch/uncocking lever on the left of the frame;

MODEL 2: a double-action trigger and a combined safety catch/uncocking lever on the right of the frame;

MODEL 3: a double-action trigger and only an uncocking lever on the left of the frame;

MODEL 4: a double-action trigger and only an uncocking lever on the right of the frame;

MODEL 5: a double-action only (DAO) trigger and a safety catch on the left of the frame.

MODEL 6: a double-action-only (DAO) trigger and a safety catch on the right of the frame;

MODEL 7 & 8: only a double-action-only (DAO) trigger;

MODEL 9: a double-action trigger and only a safety catch on the left of the frame;

MODEL 10: a double-action trigger and only a safety catch on the right of the frame.

All these models are available with a mat black steel slide, or with a stainless steel slide.

HK USP pistol with stainless steel slide

HK P8 service pistol of the German army

In 1996, the German army chose the USP as its official service pistol in 9 mm Para caliber, as model P8. This weapon has the same measurements as the standard USP pistol. Only the indications Fire and Safe are shown on the front of the safety catch in the P8. The USP compact pistol was introduced in 1996 in the calibers, 9 mm Para (13-shot), .40 S&W (10-shot) and .45 ACP (8-shot). The total length of this compact in 9 mm Para and .40 S&W is 173 mm (7 in). The polygonal barrel is 91 mm (3½ in) long. The twist of the polygonal barrel in 9 mm Para is 240 mm (10 in) and in .40 S&W it is 380 mm (15 in). The height of both models is 127 mm (5 in). The empty weight is 645 g (22¾ oz) in 9 mm Para and 695 g (25½ oz) in .40 S&W. The model in .45 ACP has a total length of 180 mm (7 in), a barrel length of 96 mm (3¾ in) and a thread of 406 mm (16 in). The height is 128.5 mm (5 in) and the empty weight is 708 G (25 oz). The USP Compact is available in the same 10 models as the standard models and also with a stainless steel slide. One of the models of the USP

HK USP Match

Compact is Model USP P10. This is a double-action pistol in 9 mm Para caliber. Heckler & Koch developed this weapon specially as a police pistol, and introduced it to the market in 2000.

In 1997 Heckler & Koch introduced the USP match pistol. This weapon has an extended barrel with a barrel weight at the front of the slide. There is a special buffer in the recoil spring guide to absorb the force of the recoil. Other special characteristics are the adjustable micrometer sights, a trigger stop, and a stainless steel slide. There is a combined safety catch/uncocking lever on the left of the frame. The pistol is available in the calibers 9 mm Para (15-shot), .40 S&W (13-shot) and .45 ACP (12-shot). The total length in all the calibers is 240 mm (9½ in). The polygonal barrel has a length of 153 mm (6 in). The sight radius is 167 mm (6½ in) for 9 mm Para/.40 S&W and 171 mm (6¾ in) for the model in .45 ACP. The height is 145 mm (5¾ in) or 150 mm (6 in) for the .45 ACP. The empty weight of the 9 mm Para model is 1120 g (39½ oz) and for both other calibers it is 1180 g (41½ oz).

The USP Expert, introduced in 1999, is very similar to the USP Match but has a standard barrel length. The Expert does have an adjustable micrometer sight and a trigger stop. The USP pistol of Heckler & Koch has developed as a complete series of weapons with many different models. One of the latest models dating from 2000 is the double-action USP Elite pistol in the calibers, 9 mm Para and .45 ACP with a barrel length of 152 mm (6 in) and an adjustable micrometer sight. This weapon was specially designed for sports shooting. The model in 9 mm Para caliber has a magazine capacity of 18 rounds. In .45 ACP the capacity is 12 rounds. The total length is 212 mm (8¼ in) and the pistol weighs respectively 920 g or 860 g (32½ or 30¼ oz) in 9 mm Para and .45 ACP.

HECKLER & KOCH MODEL P2000

The latest HK P2000 pistol

Heckler & Koch are planning a new pistol which will probably be introduced in 2002 or 2003. This is Model P2000 which will provisionally only be available in 9 mm Para caliber with a magazine capacity of 13 rounds. The pistol has a double-action trigger action. There is an ambidextrous magazine catch behind the trigger guard, and an uncocking lever on the left of the frame. Apart from this, the weapon has only an automatic firing pin safety and a half-cock safety on the foot of the hammer. The total length of the weapon is 171 mm (6¾ in) and the polygonal barrel is 92 mm (3½ in) long. The height is 127 mm (5 in) and the width is 34 mm (1¼ in). Without the cartridges, the pistol weighs approximately 690 g. The construction of the backstrap is cleverly designed. The backstrap is mounted as a separate element in the frame and can be changed for a different size. This means that the pistol can be adapted for use by someone with small hands, or someone with enormous hands.

HK USP Elite match pistol

Trade mark
of High
Standard

HIGH STANDARD

The High Standard Manufacturing Company was established in Hamden, Connecticut in 1926. At that time the company made special drills and machines for a number of arms factories. In 1932 it took over the Hardford Arms and Equipment Company and started to manufacture small caliber pistols. The first pistols made by High Standard were made in the period between 1932 and 1942 and were known as Model A and Model B. Model A was a match pistol with barrel lengths of 114 and 171 mm (4½ and 6¾ in) and had an adjustable rear sight. Model B was actually more of a so-called plinker pistol with affixed rear sight. From 1942 to 1945, the Model HD was issued to the American armed forces. This series is marked with the inscription, 'Property of the US'. During the Second World War the pistol was used as the training weapon for the army. In addition to these pistols, High Standard also made hundreds of thousands of submachine-guns in .50 caliber during the war. In 1951 it started production of the Duramatic model with a tapering barrel 6½ in long, a fixed sight and an internal hammer. A new series of models was also introduced in that year: the Supermatic, the Field King, the Sport King, and the Military trophy. These new pistols were the first to be fitted with a bolt locking catch in front of the trigger guard. At that time, High Standard was using two basic models for the frame. First, there was the slim match model with an extra beveled grip. The second type was the military model with the straighter frame. In 1968 the company was purchased by the Leisure Group investment company. This was followed by difficult times because of the introduction of the Gun Control Act in 1968. Turnover declined dramatically as a result of this act. In the period up to 1975, there were a number of reorganizations. The factory and the museum of weapons in Hamden were sold and the business moved to a new location in East Hartford in 1976. In 1978, the director at that time, Clem Confessore bought the company, together with a group of

investors. From 1982, High Standard again experienced a serious decline of sales, and in 1984 the company went bankrupt. During a public auction, the parts that were in stock and the brand name were sold. A new company was established in Houston Texas in the spring of 1983. The line of pistols and the brand name were also repurchased. The new High Standard Manufacturing Company restarted production and the first line of pistols was delivered in March 1994. Since then, the company has prospered, and many of the original models have been restored.

HIGH STANDARD OLYMPIC

The Olympic pistol was introduced by High Standard in 1950. The 10-shot single-action weapon was only available in .22 Short caliber. It was designed for the Olympic rapid-fire shooting discipline. The Olympic could be purchased as a set with one or more interchangeable barrels. The first model was made up to 1951 with a barrel length of 114 or 171 mm (4½ or 6¾ in), and a light metal slide. The total length is 235 or 292 mm (9¼ or 11½ in). This weapon already had a catch at the front of the frame to dismantle the pistol. In addition, there is a simple adjustable rear sight on the slide. The second model of the Olympic was made from 1951 to 1958, also exclusively in .22 Short caliber, with a barrel length of 114 or 171 mm (4½ or 6¾ in). The third type was made by High Standard from 1963 to 1966. This was made with the so-called bull barrel with a barrel length of 171 mm (6¾ in). It weighed 1134g (40 oz). In all three models the magazine catch is in the heel of the grip. The safety catch is on the left of the frame, above the grip plate. The slide catch is in the same place, but on the right of the frame.

High Standard Olympic
pistol with exchangeable
barrels

HIGH STANDARD OLYMPIC ISU

The old model Olympic ISU was a 10-shot match model in .22 Short caliber. High Standard introduced this model in 1958. It was available with a tapering barrel 171 or 203 mm (6¾ or 8 in) long and with movable barrel weights which could be removed. The model with a barrel length of 203 mm (8 in) was made up to 1964. The total length of this weapon is 279 or 311 mm (11 or 12¼ in), depending on the barrel length. In the old model, the magazine catch is in the heel of the grip. The safety catch is on the left of the frame and the slide catch is on the right. In 1995, High Standard reintroduced the Olympic model. In the ISU model the new pistol only has a 171 mm (6¾ in) barrel with an integrated compensator. The military model of the Olympic has a bull barrel of 140 mm (5½ in).

High Standard
Olympic ISU

Old High Standard
Sharpshooter

HIGH STANDARD SHARPSHOOTER

The 10-shot model Sharpshooter in .22 LR caliber dates from 1971 and was made by High Standard up to 1983. Up to 1979 the pistol had a magazine catch in the heel of the grip. In the later model this catch was moved to the front of the bottom of the grip. The weapon has a heavy barrel 140 mm (5½ in) long and an adjustable rear sight. The total length is 254 mm (10 in) and the weight is approximately 1360 g (48 oz). In addition, the pistol has walnut grips with a thumb rest on the left grip plate. The weapon also had another interesting feature. As it was a cheap model of the Citation series, the barrel of the Sharpshooter could be interchanged with barrels of the Citations,

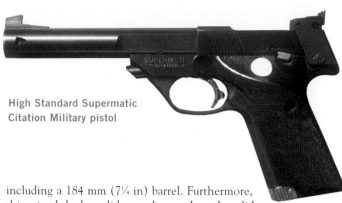

High Standard Supermatic
Citation Military pistol

including a 184 mm (7¼ in) barrel. Furthermore, this pistol had a slide catch, so that the slide remained in the last position after the last shot. In 1974 it cost $ 109.95.

HIGH STANDARD SUPERMATIC CITATION MILITARY

The single-action Supermatic Citation Military was made from 1965 to 1984 and was reintroduced in 1995. The military model has a squarish grip in the style of the Colt 1911-A1. Originally this Supermatic had an adjustable rear sight mounted on the slide. In about 1970 these models were made with a sight mounted on the grip over the slide. During the repeat action, the slide moves under this sight mount. In addition, the 10-shot pistol in .22 LR caliber has an adjustable trigger stop. This weapon has a heavy barrel 140 mm (5½ in) long. The total length is 214 mm (9½ in) and the weapon weighs 1250 g (44 oz). This Supermatic Citation also has an adjustable trigger stop. Furthermore, the trigger pressure can be adapted.

HIGH STANDARD MODEL SUPERMATIC CITATION MS

In 1997, High Standard introduced a new model based on the Supermatic Citation. This is a 10-shot pistol in .22 LR caliber designed for small caliber Metallic silhouette shooting. The weapon has a barrel length of 54 mm (10 in), a total length of 356 mm (14 in) and weighs 1530 g (54 oz). There is a rail on the barrel to mount a telescopic sight. There is a short rail by the muzzle. The model illustrated here has a micrometer sight and a hooded front sight, but the pistol comes standard without telescopic sights.

High Standard Model
Supermatic Citation MS

High Standard Supermatic
Trophy pistol with slanting grip

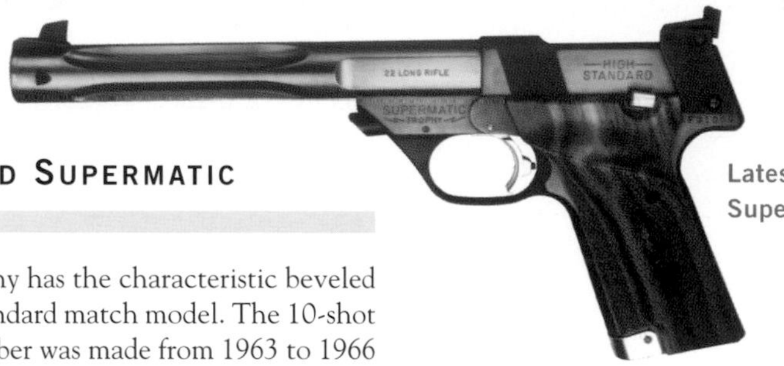

Latest version of
Supermatic Trophy

Left side of
Supermatic
Trophy Military

HIGH STANDARD SUPERMATIC TROPHY

The Supermatic Trophy has the characteristic beveled frame of the High Standard match model. The 10-shot weapon in .22 LR caliber was made from 1963 to 1966 with a heavy barrel 140 mm (5½ in) long or with a barrel length of 184 mm (7¼ in) with lengthwise slits. The illustration here shows the old model with an adjustable rear sight on the slide. The total length is 241 mm (9½ in) or 186 mm (11¼ in) with the longer barrel. The weapon weighs respectively 1250 or 1304 g (44 or 46 oz). In this old model the magazine catch is still in the heel of the grip. The various elements are not gilded, as in later models. In 1995, High Standard started producing this weapon again, though only with a military grip.

HIGH STANDARD SUPERMATIC TROPHY MILITARY

High Standard produced the Supermatic Trophy Military from 1963 to 1966 in .22 LR caliber. The pistol illustrated here has a heavy barrel 140 mm (5½ in) long. However, this model was also available with a longer barrel of 184 mm (7¼ in) with lengthwise slits to save weight. The total length of the model with a short barrel is 241 mm (9½ in) and it weighs 1250 g (44 oz). The Supermatic Trophy Military with the longer barrel has a total length of 186 mm (11¼ in) and weighs 1300 g (46 oz). This pistol also has a sight mount over the slide to mount the micrometer sight. Production of this pistol started again in 1995. The new model has gilt elements such as the trigger, the slide catch and safety catch, and the magazine catch at the front of the bottom of the grip. For the new model there is an interchangeable set available for .22 Short.

HIGH STANDARD MODEL 10-X

The original Model 10-X in .22 LR caliber dates from 1981 and was produced up to 1984. The weapon resembles the Trophy and has a heavy barrel, 140 mm (5½ in) long. The whole weapon, including the trigger and catches, is in a mat black finish. This has the advantage that it does not reflect any light, which is a positive feature at outside ranges. Model 10-X was High Standard's pride and joy. This match pistol has been made again since 1995 in limited editions of approximately 150 pistols per year. This model is very carefully assembled with parts specially selected for the lowest tolerances. The assembly is carried out under the management of the chief gunsmith Bob Shea who was also employed by the original company from 1943 to 1984 The new 10-X is available in the Citation model with a heavy barrel, 140 mm (5½ in) long, a total length of 241 mm (9½ in) and a weight of 1250 g (40 oz). The weapon has a anodized finish and the sight mount of the Citation. The same pistol is also available in a 10-X Shea Citation model. Bob Shea tuned this model himself. Another model is the Shea 10-X Victor with a barrel length of 114 or 140 mm (4½ or 5½ in).

HIGH STANDARD VICTOR

The High Standard Victor model was produced in .22 LR caliber from 1965 to 1984. Originally the 10-shot weapon had a barrel length of 114 mm (4½ in) with a solid barrel rib which included the micrometer sight. An extra barrel weight can be secured under the barrel with bushing bolts. From 1974 the model was also available with a ventilated barrel rib in the same length, or with a barrel length of 140 mm (5½ in), also with a ventilated barrel rib. The total length of the weapon with the short barrel is 216 mm (8½ in) and it weighs 1275 g (45 oz). The model with the longer barrel has a total length of 241 mm (9½ in) and a weight of 1304 g (46 oz). Production of this model was resumed in 1995.

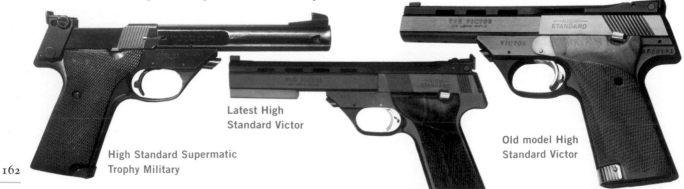

Latest High
Standard Victor

High Standard Supermatic
Trophy Military

Old model High
Standard Victor

I

of a 1911 pistol. The weapon has a larger, polished feed ramp by the chamber, and an enlarged magazine well. The grip safety in the back strap is extended with a beavertail. In addition, the slide catch and the safety catch, both on the left of the frame, are enlarged. The weapon also has a so-called combat hammer, a combat trigger and a fixed combat rear sight. It is available in a model completely made of stainless steel, or with a stainless steel frame and a blued steel slide. The frame is enclosed by a rubber grip with finger grooves. The total length is 152 mm (6 in) and the barrel is 108 mm (4½ in) long. The height of the weapon is 127 mm (5 in) and it weighs 1020 g (36 oz).

IAI M-999

The IAI M-999 pistol dates from 1999. This is also an 8-shot single-action pistol in .45 ACP caliber, with an enlarged magazine well and a polished ramp, known as the feed ramp. The grip safety has a beavertail and the slide catch and safety catch are enlarged. In addition, the weapon has a combat hammer and trigger and a fixed combat rear sight. The total length of this pistol is 216 mm (8½ in), the barrel length is 127 mm (5 in) and the height is 133 mm (5¼ in). The weapon weighs 1077 g (38 oz). The M-999 is available in a stainless steel model, or with a stainless steel frame and a blued steel slide. There are extra cocking grooves in the front of the slide. In addition, it is enclosed by a rubber grip with finger grooves.

IAI M-999 in
.45 ACP caliber

ISRAEL ARMS INTERNATIONAL (IAI)

Logo of Israel Arms International (IAI)

The American firm, Israel Arms International (IAI) in Houston, Texas, has gone through some turbulent times. The company was established in 1995 with the name, J.O. Arms. In 1997, this name was changed to Israel Arms International. In 1999, the management decided to change the name to Firearms International, and since 2000, the weapons have again been made under the name, Israel Arms International. The reason for these curious decisions remains obscure. The company makes very good pistols based on the model 1911. In addition to pistols, IAI also makes the M-333, a remake of the M1 Garand rifle in caliber .30-06. In addition, it makes the M-888 US Carbine caliber .30-M1 in the original, and in a new caliber, the .22 Carbine Wildcat.

IAI M-777 COMPACT

The 8-shot, single-action M-777 pistol in .45 ACP caliber was introduced in 1998. It is a compact model

IAI M-777
Compact pistol

IAI M-2000

The M-2000 pistol in .45 ACP caliber is a traditional version of the Colt 1911-A1 and was introduced on the market in 2000. It looks like an exact copy of the famous old GI pistol, but it does have the technical specification of the other IAI weapons. The grip safety is slightly extended in a beavertail. The pistol has the original GI hammer and trigger. It has a magazine

IAI M-2000, introduced
in 2000

IAI M-6000

The model M-6000 is a simple version of
the large model M-999. The single-action
pistol has a magazine capacity of 8 rounds
and is only available in .45 ACP caliber.
The slide and the frame are made of steel with
a blued finish. The magazine has a rubber buffer and
the grip plates are also made of rubber. The catches
and the grip safety have been further developed. The
hammer and the trigger are made in combat style. The
total length is 216 mm (8½ in), the barrel length is
127 mm (5 in). The height of the weapon is 133 mm
(5½ in) and it weighs 1077 g (38 oz).

Simpler IAI M-6000
version of M-999

capacity of 7 rounds. Apart from this, the weapon has
a steel frame and slide, both with a mat black anodized
finish. The grip plates are made of hardwood. The fixed
rear sight is also the same as in the original GI model.
The total length is 216 mm (8½ in), the barrel length is
127 mm (5 in). The weapon weighs 1077 g (38 oz).

IAI M-5000

This pistol is a simpler version of the model M-777. It
is also an 8-shot single-action pistol in .45 ACP
caliber. The weapon has an enlarged feed ramp and
a larger magazine well. In addition, the slide catch
and the safety are also larger, and the grip safety also
has a beavertail. The frame and slide are made of steel
and completely blued. The hammer and trigger are in
combat style, but the fixed rear sight is that of the
original GI model. There is a large rubber buffer at
the bottom of the magazine. The grip plates are made
of hard rubber. The total length of the M-5000 pistol
is 152 mm (6 in) and the barrel length is 108 mm
(4¼ in). The height of the weapon is 133 mm
(54¼ in) and the weapon weighs 1050 g (37 oz).

ISRAEL MILITARY
INDUSTRIES (IMI)

Following the creation of the state of Israel, the
country was confronted with enormous problems. It
not only had hostile neighbors, but it also became
politically isolated. As the state was also short of
currency, the brand new army was largely dependent
on its own resources for its weapons. In 1949, the
Israeli colonel, Uziel Gal, a famous weapon
designer, designed the Uzi submachine gun,
based on the Czech submachine gun, the CZ-
23. There were many advantages in Israel having
its own arms industry, and the Uzi was
specially designed to keep production
costs low. The Israeli-Arab War of 1948
broke out as soon as the independent state of
Israel was proclaimed on 14 May 1948. Israel did
not have nearly enough submachine guns, and
the ones it did have were old English Sten guns.
In 1951, the Israeli army was equipped with
Uzis on a large scale. It became the most
reliable submachine gun in the world. It was
produced in enormous numbers, and for

IAI M-5000 pistol

Trade mark of Israel Military Industries (IMI)

Desert Eagle in
.41 Magnum

The same weapon
in .44 Magnum

a long time the FN factories had a license to manufacture them at Herstal-Liege (Belgium). Many West-European countries, including the Netherlands, Belgium and other NATO countries used, or still use Uzis. In addition, the Uzi is, or was, the weapon used in Iran, South Africa, Venezuela and Surinam. At a later date, the Mini Uzi and the Micro Uzi were added to the Uzi family. The latter is a fully automatic model of the Uzi, and was specially designed for the security services. The Uzi pistol is an automatic and is eminently suitable for fans of the 'Military Look'. It is a useful weapon because of its large magazine capacity (20 rounds), although it is not particularly suitable for wearing in a holster. IMI also concentrated on the civilian market, for weapons in the sports fields. A number of excellent sports pistols were developed in collaboration with the American firm, Magnum Research in Minneapolis. The Israeli drive for efficiency is revealed here as well, because the standard models of these pistols were also eminently suitable as police and army weapons. The Desert Eagle pistol was introduced to the market in 1984. This pistol has a rotating bolt locking system. Initially the Desert Eagle was only available in .357 Magnum caliber, but it later became available in .41 and .44 Magnum calibers, and recently also in .50 AE (Action Express) and .50 Magnum calibers. A smaller version, the Baby Eagle, followed in 1990. This is also known as the Jericho 941.

IMI DESERT EAGLE

The Desert Eagle was designed by the American firm, Magnum Research Inc. in Minneapolis, and has been produced by Israel Military Industries, abbreviated as IMI since 1984. The standard model of this enormous

Desert Eagle in .357
Magnum caliber

pistol is available in the calibers, .357 Magnum, .41 Magnum, .44 Magnum and .50 AE (Action Express), and since 1998 also in .440 Cor-Bon. The weapon has a gas-operated repeating system, which was originally developed for army rifles. There is a hole for releasing the gas in the bottom of the barrel, just after the chamber. This hole opens into a gas channel, which runs parallel to the weapon up to the muzzle. The channel curves away there, and enters a cylinder via a gas block. There is a piston in this area. The pistol locks with a rotating head with three lugs. These lugs engage in corresponding recesses around the chamber of the barrel. The first model in 1984 still had six bolt lugs. When a cartridge is fired in the chamber, the bullet takes a few milli-seconds to shoot through the barrel. For this brief period, there is an enormous pressure in the barrel. Some of this gas pressure enters the cylinder through the gas release hole. This causes a sharp blow against the piston in the cylinder area, and it is struck back against the bottom of the barrel block. This produces the backward movement of the slide. As a result of this movement, the bolt rotates so that the bolt lugs are disengaged. The slide containing the bolt can then move back. At the same time, the empty cartridge case is extracted from the magazine and ejected. As a result of the movement of the slide, the hammer is cocked again. The two recoil springs are now almost entirely compressed, stopping the

Desert Eagle in mat nickel finish with Aimpoint sights on top and laser in front of trigger guard

several finishes for this weapon: a mat black epoxy layer, a mat or polished nickel-plated finish, and a chrome or blued finish. Up to 1998, the Desert Eagle was also available with a stainless steel or light metal frame. The pistol comes standard with an enclosing rubber grip, but there is also a walnut stock available sold by Herrett's. The technical specifications of the Desert Eagle depend on the caliber. The Desert Eagle in .357 Magnum caliber has a magazine capacity of 9 rounds. The total length is 269, 371 or 472 mm (10.6, 14.6 or 18.6 in). The barrel length is 152, 254 or 356 mm (6, 10 or 14 in), the height is 142 mm (5½ in) and the width is 32 mm (1¼ in). The polygonal barrel has a thread of 355 mm (14 in). Depending on the material of the frame, the .357 Desert Eagle with a 152 mm (6 in) barrel has the following weight: with a light metal frame, 1355 g (47¾ oz) and with a steel or stainless steel frame, 1653 g (58¼ oz). In .41 Magnum or .44 Magnum caliber, the pistol has a capacity of 8 rounds. The total length is 269, 371 or 472 mm (10½ , 14½ or 18½ in). The barrel length is 152, 254 or 356 mm (6, 10 or 14 in). The polygonal barrel has a twist of 457 mm (18 in). The height of the weapon is 145 mm (5¼ in). The weight of the .41/.44 Magnum pistol with a 152 mm (6 in) barrel is 1483 g (52¼ oz) with a light metal frame, and 1780 g (62¾ oz) with a steel or stainless steel frame. The Desert Eagle in .50 AE has a magazine capacity of 7 rounds. The weapon is only available with a 152 mm (6 in) polygonal barrel with a twist of 483 mm (19 in). The total length is 267 mm (10½ in). The height is 149 mm (6 in) and the pistol weighs 2053 g (72½ oz).

backward movement of the slide and bolt. As the recoil springs now start to go back to their original position, the slide and the bolt are pushed forward, taking a new cartridge from the magazine. As soon as this is pushed into the chamber, the angled locking lugs come into contact with the recesses in the chamber. The head of the bolt then turns through about one eighth of a rotation so that the slide and barrel are locked. The gun is now ready to fire a second shot. One disadvantage of the gas release hole is that it is not possible to use lead bullets. This material is too soft, and lead particles could block up the hole. The Desert Eagle comes standard with a fixed combat rear sight, but Millett makes a special micrometer sight for this pistol. In addition, Trijicon makes a three-dot tritium sight set. There is an ambidextrous safety catch at the back of the slide. This blocks the firing pin and disconnects the trigger bar. The trigger bar is the connection between the trigger and the sear. The Desert Eagle has a polygonal barrel profile. There are several interchangeable barrels available for this weapon, with lengths of 152 or 254 mm (6 or 10 in). Up to 1999, IMI also made an extra-long barrel, 356 mm (14 in) long. For all the barrel lengths there is a rail to secure telescopic sights or other systems. There are

The big Desert Eagle in .50 AE (Action Express) caliber

IMI Jericho 941

The Jericho 941 pistol was introduced in 1992. In the USA it was sold by Magnum Research as the Baby Eagle up to 1998. Since 1999, the Uzi America company has imported the weapon with the name Uzi Eagle. Uzi America is a joint venture between IMI and Mossberg. However, from the technical point of view the weapon is not related to the Desert Eagle in any way. The repeat action is activated by the recoil energy of the cartridge that has been fired. In addition, the pistol has a Browning locking system with locking lugs on the upper side of the barrel, just after the chamber. The Jericho is available in the calibers, 9 mm Para, 9 x 21 mm IMI, .40 S&W, and .41 AE (Action Express). The double-action pistol has a magazine capacity of 16 rounds in 9 mm, 12 rounds in .40 S&W, and 11 rounds in .41 AE. The compact Jericho 941 FB holds three cartridges less for each caliber. The standard Jericho has a total length of 207 mm (8 in), a height of 140 mm (5½ in), and a width of 35 mm (1¼ in). The barrel length is 1.2 mm (4½ in) and the weight is 1000 g (35¼ oz). Model 941 has a combined safety catch/uncocking lever on the left of the slide. In the 941F the safety catch is on the left of the frame, and does not serve as a uncocking lever. This also applies for model 941 FS. However, the slide and the barrel of this model are shorter. The total length of the weapon is 184 mm (7¼ in), and the barrel length is 90 mm (3½ in). The height and the width are the same as those of the standard model. The 941FS weighs 900 g (31¼ oz). The compact 941 FB is actually a 941 FS, though with a shorter frame. The total length and the barrel length are the same as those of the 941FS, but the height is 125 mm (5 in). The weight is 870 g (30¼ oz).

Standard Jericho 941 pistol

Jericho 941FS

Jericho 941FB pistol in stainless steel

J

JANZ

Trade mark of German firm Janz Technik

The Janz Technik & Labor company, abbreviated to JTL, was established in Kiel in North Germany in 1935. The company specializes in precision mechanical engineering, computer-operated CNC processing machines and equipment for the dairy industry. In 1999, it decided to build a double-action super revolver, based on the Korth revolver, as a hobby. It was also a topical thing to do, because the German Korth factory was in danger of going bankrupt in 1998. The JTL-E revolver is not an ordinary weapon, but a precision instrument. All the parts are made of special sorts of steel, chosen for their high degree of hardness. The weapon has minimum tolerances. The frame is cut from a solid piece of chrome manganese steel by a CNC machine. When it has been processed and polished, it is hardened even further. The cylinder is made of chrome steel and is also hardened after the finish. The chambers are then cut with a CNC machine. The weapon has a micrometer sight. In addition, both the front sight and the rear sight leaf are interchangeable. The trigger has a system, with which the pressure point can be adjusted as required. The trigger pressure can also be adjusted progressively. In single-action, this is between 1000 to 2000 g (2¼ to 4½ lb) and in double-action between 4000 to 6000 g (8¾ to 13¼ lb). The trigger itself has an adjustable trigger stop. The JTL-E revolver has a blocking bar system as a safety system. The hammer has a wide spur and can easily be placed in the single-action position with the thumb of the shooting hand. The hammer is activated with a coiled spring, in a hard steel case. The spring pressure is adjusted at 5.00 Newton. Next to the hammer there is a gilt bearing, with which the cylinder locking system can be canceled. There is a chrome catch on the right of the frame to release the yoke. In this way the cylinder can be removed from the frame very quickly. The revolver is available in .357 Magnum / .38 Special calibers, when it has a cylinder with 7 chambers. The second model has a capacity of 6 cartridges in .44 Magnum caliber. The third 6-shot model has a .454 Casull/.45 Colt caliber. The available barrel lengths are 102, 127, 152, 178 and 203 mm (4, 5, 6, 7 and 8 in). The total length of the weapon with a 152 mm (6 in) barrel is 285 mm (11¼ in). The weight of the JTL-E with a 152 mm (6 in) barrel is approximately 1500 g (53 oz). The weapon is available highly polished and blued, but other finishes are also possible. The beautiful walnut stock is made by the Nill company.

Janz JTL in .44 Magnum caliber

Janz TL revolver

K

Kahr K9 pistol in
9 mm Para caliber

KAHR ARMS

Kahr Arms logo

Kahr Inc. is a large company in the metalwork industry, and a supplier of parts for the airplane, automobile and weapons industry. In 1986, it was decided to establish a separate division for the production of handguns. This became the Kahr Arms Company, established in Worcester, Massachusetts. The Kahr K9 pistol was designed under the direction of Justin Moon, head of the R&D (Research & Development) division. The pistol was largely designed on a computer screen, using CAD-CAM systems. Production is carried out by computer-aided CNC machines. The slides and barrels are cut from solid steel. In 2000, Kahr bought the American Auto-Ordnance Corp. from Numrich Arms. Kahr pistols combine six new patents, one of which is the guide lug under the chamber of the barrel. This lug is not perpendicular to the chamber in the usual way, but to the side. This seems to reduce the force of the recoil. In addition, it creates space, so that the trigger mechanism is partly next to this guide lug. One result of this is that the total height of the weapon can be reduced. Another patent concerns the self-cleaning extractor. When powder residue accumulates, the extractor sometimes fails to work. The Kahr magazine is designed in such a way that it cleans itself.

KAHR K9/K40

The ultra compact K9 pistol was first shown as a prototype at the 1994 Shot Show. The first models were ready for production in the following year. The Kahr K9 in 9 mm Para caliber has a double-action-only (DAO) trigger action. The magazine has a capacity of 7 rounds. Apart from the automatic firing pin safety, the weapon does not have any external safety catches. The slide catch is above the trigger on the left of the frame. The magazine catch is also on the left, behind the trigger guard. The Kahr is made completely of steel or stainless steel. Consequently, the weapon is strong enough to shoot 9 mm Para +P cartridges. The pistol has a modified Browning locking system with a guide lug under the chamber of the barrel, which is positioned off-center. In 1996, Kahr introduced the 6-shot K40 pistol in .40 S&W caliber. Apart from the caliber, this is actually the same weapon as the K9 and also has the same measurements. The total length of both models is 152 mm (6 in). The barrel length is 89 mm (3½ in) and the weight is 709 g (25 oz). Since 1997, both models have also been available in stainless steel in a mat finish. The Kahr K9 and the K40 have a fixed combat rear sight. There is also a three-dot tritium sight system available.

Kahr P9 pistol in
stainless steel

Compact Kahr
MK40 in .40 S&W

a synthetic polymer frame and a stainless steel slide. The P9 has a magazine capacity of 7 rounds, a total length of 152 mm (6 in), a height of 114 mm (4½ in) and an empty weight of 502 g (17¾ oz). The barrel is 89 mm (3½ in) long, and has a polygonal profile with a right-hand twist of 254 mm (10 in). The Kahr P40 is slightly longer, with a length of 155 mm (6 in). It has a capacity of 6 rounds in .40 S&W caliber. The height is also 114 mm (4½ in). The barrel length is 89 mm (3½ in), and it has a polygonal profile with a right-hand twist of 406 mm (16 in). The weight, with an empty magazine, is 530 g (18¾ oz).

KAHR MK9/MK40

In 1998, Kahr introduced the MK9 micro pistol in 9 mm Para caliber and the MK40 pistol in .40 S&W. Both double-action-only models are very similar to the K9/K40, although they are shorter. The 6-shot MK9 has a stainless steel slide and frame, a total length of 135 mm (5¼ in) and an empty weight of 737 g (26 oz). The barrel has a polygonal profile with a right-hand twist of 254 mm (10 in) and a length of 76 mm (3 in). The height is 102 mm (4 in). The MK40 is slightly longer, viz., 136 mm (5¼ in). The barrel length is 78.2 mm (3 in) and it has a polygonal profile with a right-hand twist of 406 mm (16 in). The height is also 102 mm (4 in) and the weight, with an empty magazine is 709 g (25 oz). The magazine capacity is 5 rounds.

KAHR P9/P40

In 2000, Kahr introduced the P9, and in 2001 it introduced the P40 pistol in 9 mm Para and .40 S&W calibers. Both double-action-only models are virtually identical to the K9, but they have

The Kel-Tec logo

KEL-TEC

The American company, Kel-Tec CNC Industries Inc., in Cocoa, Florida is a relative newcomer to the arms business. In 1995 it introduced the 10-shot P-11 pistol in 9 mm Para with a trigger system which only fires in double-action. The weapon is the lightest and smallest 9 mm Para pistol ever designed. It weighs only 400 g (14 oz) and has a total length of only 140 mm (5½ in). The weapon was completely computer-designed for government services, or as a second, back-up weapon for use by the police and

Kahr P40 pistol with
polymer casing and
stainless steel slide

Kel-Tec P11 pistol with
11 9 mm Para cartridges

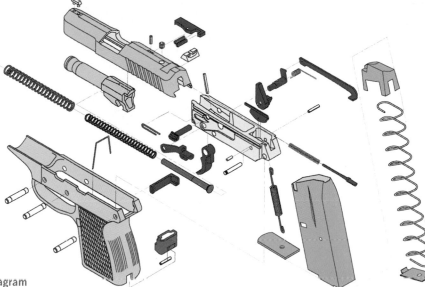

Exploded diagram of the Kel-Tec P11

the army. It is a good quality pistol because of the materials used in its manufacture. The barrel is made of SAE-4140 steel hardened to 50 Rockwell. The slide, as well as the firing pin and extractor, are made of the same sort of steel.

The separate bolt housing is machined from a solid block of 7075-T6 aluminum. The frame is made of the high impact synthetic material, DuPont ST-800. The magazine and trigger guard are also integrated in the frame. Because of the special construction and position of the firing pin, the weapon does not need an automatic firing pin safety. The firing pin is always completely uncocked, until it is struck by the hammer. The pistol can also be operated with double row Smith & Wesson magazines. The total length of the P-11 is 142 mm (5½ in). The barrel length is 79 mm (3 in). The height is 109 mm (4¼ in), and the weapon has a width of only 25.4 mm (1 in). The weight of an empty P11 is 397 g (14 oz). The P11 pistol is also available with a hard chrome-plated slide.

Kel-Tec P11 with stainless steel slide

KEL-TEC P32

In 2000, Kel-Tec introduced a double-action-only pistol in 7.65 mm (.32 ACP) caliber, with a magazine capacity of 7 rounds. This Kel-Tec P32 pistol also has a synthetic frame with an integrated trigger guard. It has an internal slide catch, so that the slide remains in the furthest position after the last shot. When a new, full magazine is introduced, the slide has to be pulled back slightly by hand to remove the blocking. The flat catch on the right above the trigger is the takedown lever. The magazine catch is on the left of the frame, behind the trigger guard. The total length of the P32 is 129 mm (5 in). The barrel length is 68 mm (2¾ in) and the empty weapon is extremely light, viz., 187 g (6½ oz), when it is not loaded.

Compact Kel-Tec P32 pistol in 7.65 mm (.32 ACP)

KEL-TEC P40

The Kel-Tec P40 pistol was introduced to the market in 2001. This is a .40 S&W model of the compact P11. The P40 pistol has a magazine capacity of 9 rounds. It also has a synthetic frame with an integrated trigger guard and a double-action-only trigger. The synthetic frame comprises a separate 7075-T6 aluminum housing for the whole firing mechanism. The rails for the steel slide are also attached to this. The total length of the P40 is 150 mm (6 in). The barrel length is 84 mm (3¼ in). The height of the weapon is the same as that of the P11, viz., 109 mm (4¼ in) and the weight is 401 g (15¾ oz). The sights, consisting of a fixed rear sight and bead, have tritium night sight as standard.

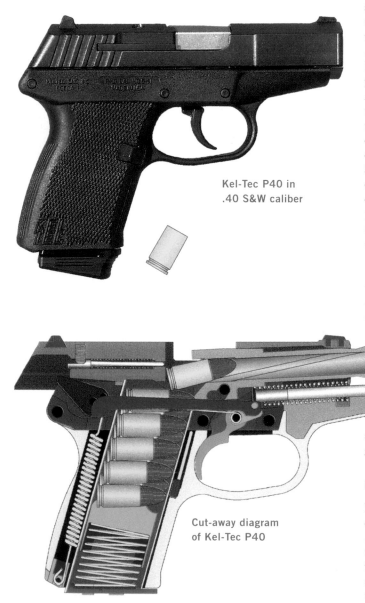

Kel-Tec P40 in
.40 S&W caliber

Cut-away diagram
of Kel-Tec P40

KIMBER

Kimber trade mark

In 1979, the American company Kimber became famous with the introduction of its small caliber, bolt action carbine, Model 82. It had a Mauser bolt, and the wing safety catch of the Winchester Model 70 rifle. In 1995, Kimber introduced a pistol, the Classic .45 ACP. This was the start of the Classic Pistol Project. This quality program was aimed at the production of a series of the best 1911-A1 pistol. A new factory was established for this purpose, with the latest technology in the field of computer-aided machines. This policy resulted in the measurements of all the parts having a maximum degree of precision of 0.0025 mm (.0001 in). In addition, more than $ 500,000 was invested in molds and measurement equipment. Even the CNC cutting machines were computer operated and replaced in good time. The pistols were designed with CAD-CAM computer systems, under the direction of the well-known pistol shooter, Chip McCormick. The light metal frames of the Kimber models were machined from blocks of 7075-T7 aluminum with CNC machines. Kimber made all the steel frames, slides and barrels, using only high quality steel. All Kimber pistols have a special match trigger group, a special beavertail grip safety and an enlarged magazine well. In addition, the ejector port is lowered and enlarged, and a tactical extractor is used. Sharp corners are rounded, and the pistols have low combat sights. A Kimber pistol with a light metal frame has been thoroughly tested by firing 20,000 cartridges. This is followed by a precision test, in which the diameter of the trigger group is below 50 mm (2 in).

KIMBER GOLD COMBAT STAINLESS

Kimber introduced the stainless steel Gold Combat on the market in 1999. It is a single-action pistol in .45 ACP caliber with a magazine capacity of 8 rounds. There are additional cocking grooves at the front of the stainless steel slide. The pistol has a combat sight with a tritium night sight. The sight radius is 173 mm (6¾ in). The total length is 221 mm

Kimber Gold Medal Combat Stainless in .45 ACP

specially selected for each pistol. Throughout the manufacturing process it is subjected to more than 200 inspections. There are extra cocking grooves at the front of the slide. The total length is 221 mm (8¾ in). The stainless steel barrel is 127 mm (5 in) long and has a left-hand twist of 406 mm (16 in). The Gold Match is 32.5 mm (1¼ in) wide. It has a Kimber micrometer sight with a sight radius of 173 mm (6¾ in). The empty weight is 1077 g (38 oz). There is an enlarged magazine well in the grip, so that magazines can be changed rapidly. The grip is made of mahogany. There is an extended safety catch on each side of the frame and an extended slide catch on the left of the frame. The aluminum Premium trigger has a trigger pressure of 1587 to 1814 g (3½ to 4 lb).

KIMBER SUPER MATCH

The Kimber Super Match dates from 1999. It is a single-action match pistol in .45 ACP caliber with

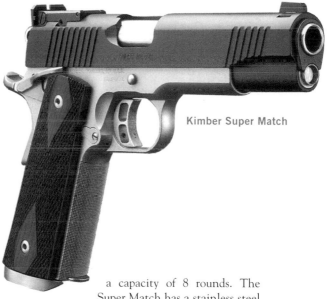

Kimber Super Match

(8¾ in), including the grip safety extended in a beavertail. The barrel is 127 mm (5 in) long, and has a left-hand twist of 406 mm (16 in). In addition, the pistol has an extended, ambidextrous safety catch on the frame, an extended slide catch and an enlarged magazine well. This model is 32.5 mm (1¼ in) wide and weighs 1077 g (38 oz). The grips are made of mahogany. The pistol has a built-in aluminum Kimber Premium trigger with a trigger pressure of 1587 tot 1814 g (3½ to 4 lb). The special recoil spring has a recoil pressure of 7.3 kg (16 lb).

Kimber Gold Match pistol

KIMBER GOLD MATCH

The Kimber Gold Match was specially developed for the Limited Class shooting competitions. The 8-shot single-action pistol is in .45 ACP caliber. It is available in a polished and blued finish or in stainless steel. The stainless steel barrel is fitted into the slide by hand. At the start of production the parts are

a capacity of 8 rounds. The Super Match has a stainless steel frame. The slide is also made of stainless steel and has a hard thermally applied protective layer, known as the KimPro finish. Extra cocking grooves are cut into the front of the slide. A special magazine enlarger is placed under the grip to increase the size of the well. The front and back of the grip are ribbed, and the grip safety has a beavertail. The pistol has a Kimber micrometer sight with a sight radius of 173 mm (6¾ in). The total length is 221 mm (8¾ in). The barrel is 127 mm (5 in) long, and has a left-hand twist of 406 mm (16 in). The pistol has mahogany grips. It is 32.5 mm (1¼ in) wide and weighs 1077 g (38 oz). In addition, it has an ambidextrous extended safety catch, and an extended slide catch on the left of the frame. The aluminum Premium trigger has a trigger pressure of between 1587 to 1814 g (3½ to 4 lb).

KORA

Trade mark of Czech Kora weapon maker

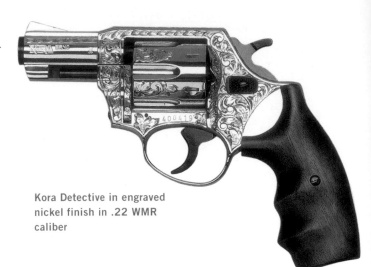

Kora Detective in engraved
nickel finish in .22 WMR
caliber

The Czech Republic has a special place amongst the countries of the former East Bloc. Because of a tradition of gun making going back centuries, the country was able to emerge from its long period of isolation very quickly. For connoisseurs, 'Czech made' is a guarantee of quality at an attractive price. The Kora Brno company has made revolvers for the internal market since 1990, and the export of arms has also grown since that time. Kora has therefore been keen to cooperate with other European arms manufacturers. Kora's revolvers are a combination of lasting qualities and a light weight. The frames are made of light metal, while the barrel and cylinder are made of hardened steel. The revolvers are made in three standard models and there is a choice of six different grips. Before they are delivered, the revolvers are tested at the test range in Prague.

KORA DETECTIVE

Kora Detective is a double-action revolver with a cylinder for 8 cartridges in .22 LR caliber. The frame is made of a light metal zinc alloy, while the barrel and the cylinder are made of hardened steel. The total length is 190 mm (7½ in), and the barrel length is 63.5 mm (2½ in). The weapon weighs 750 g (26½ oz). There are five different

types of grips available for the Kora Detective, as well as an interchangeable cylinder for .22 WMR caliber. The safety consists of a transfer bar. The Detective is made in a blued and nickel-coated finish, which is sometimes engraved. Kora also produces the revolver in .22 WMR caliber with an interchangeable cylinder for .22 LR. The measurements and the weight are the same as those for the .22 LR model. The Kora Detective has a fixed rear sight.

KORA FLOBERT

Kora Detective in
.22 LR

Kora Flobert Nickel
in 6 mm Flobert caliber

In several countries, handguns in the rimfire caliber 6 mm Flobert are freely on sale for people of eighteen years and older. For this market, Kora produces a double-action revolver series in a blued, nickel-plated or nickel-plated and engraved finish. This weapon is available with a barrel length of 102 mm (4 in) and an adjustable rear sight, or with a barrel of 63.5 mm (2½ in) and a fixed rear sight. The frame is made of light metal and the 8-shot cylinder and

Kora Flobert revolver with short 53.5 mm (2¹/₂ in) barrel

Kora Prima in .38 Special caliber with 102 mm (4 in) barrel

barrel are made of steel. The total length of the model with the 102 mm (4 in) barrel is 228 mm (9 in). The weight is 800 g (28¼ oz). The short snub-nose with a barrel length of 63.5 mm (2½ in) has a total length of 190 mm (7½ in) and a weight of 760 g (26¼ oz).

KORA PANDA

The double-action Kora Panda revolver is made in .38 Special caliber. The cylinder has a capacity of 6 rounds. The weapon has a barrel length of 63.5 mm (2½ in), a total length of 190 mm (7½ in) and a weight of 750 g (26½ oz). The Panda is available in a blued finish, a nickel-plated finish, or in a nickel-coated and engraved finish. In addition, the revolver has a transfer bar safety. There is a choice of five different types of grips.

Kora Prima in engraved nickel finish

KORA PRIMA

Kora also makes a parcours revolver with a barrel length of 102 mm (4 in) barrel and an adjustable rear sight, based on the Panda frame. This double-action weapon has a cylinder for 6 cartridges in .38 Special caliber. The total length is 228 mm (9 in) and the weapon weighs 800 g (28 ¼ oz). The Prima is available in a blued or nickel-plated finish or in an engraved and nickel-plated finish. The Prima has a transfer bar as a safety.

KORA RIVAL

The double-action Rival revolver is available in .22 LR caliber with an 8-shot cylinder or as a 6-shot revolver in .38 Special caliber. The two models have the same measurements. The total length is 280 mm (11 in) and the barrel length is 152 mm (6 in). The weapon weighs 850 g (30 oz). The Rival is made in a blued or nickel-plated finish, or in

Kora Panda in .38 Special caliber

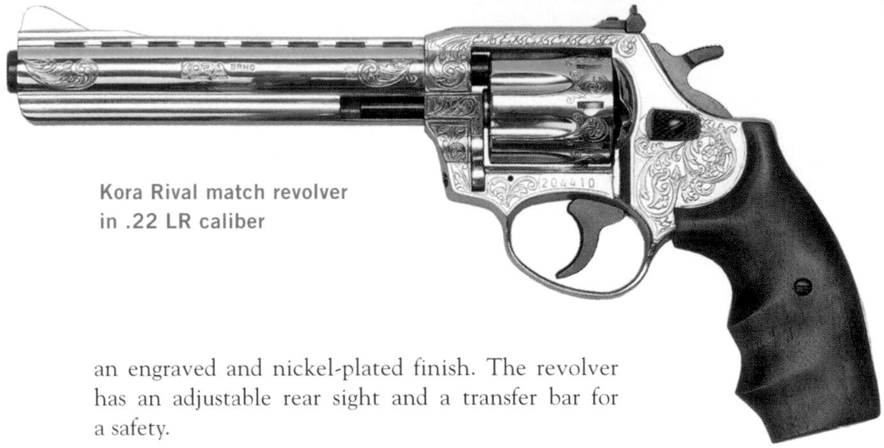

Kora Rival match revolver
in .22 LR caliber

Kora Rival in .38
Special caliber

an engraved and nickel-plated finish. The revolver
has an adjustable rear sight and a transfer bar for
a safety.

KORA SPORT

The Kora Sport revolver has a double-action trigger.
The weapon is made in .22 LR of .22 WMR caliber,
and has an interchangeable cylinder in .22 LR. This
small caliber model has an 8-shot cylinder. The
available models are blued, nickel-plated, or nickel-
plated and engraved. This sports model has a barrel
length of 102 mm (4 in). The total length is 228 mm
(9 in) and the weight is 800 g (28¼ oz). The width
and height of the rear sight are adjustable.

KORA SPORT SPECIAL

Kora has a special match revolver in the calibers .22
LR and .22 WMR. This double-action weapon has
a barrel length of 152 mm (6 in) and an extended
ejector shroud as an extra barrel weight. In addition,
the barrel has a ventilated barrel rib. The Sport
Special is available with a smooth wooden stock with
finger grooves, or with a special match stock with an
adjustable hand rest. The cylinder of both models has
8 chambers and an adjustable rear sight. The revolver
is only made in a blued finish. The total length is
280 mm (11 in) and the weight is 850 g (30 oz). In
addition, the revolver has a transfer bar safety.

Kora Sport in .22
WMR

Kora Sport Special with
152 mm (6 in) barrel in
.22 WMR

Kora Sport in .38
Special caliber

The same revolver
in .22 LR

KORRIPHILA

Trade mark of Korriphila

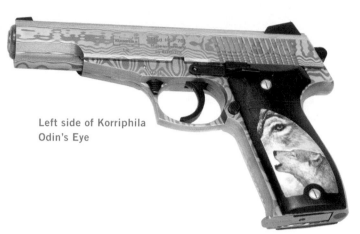

Left side of Korriphila
Odin's Eye

The Korriphila HSP-701 pistol was designed by the Czech designer, Edgar Budichowsky from Heidelberg, Germany. For the production of this pistol, priority is given to quality, and costs are a subsidiary consideration. The Korriphila has a special roller locking system developed by Budichowsky. He used a single roller-locking bolt across the frame. It is constructed in such a way that the weapon can be entirely adapted to the specific requirements of the client, in three basic models.

DEFENSE: A double-action pistol with a barrel length of 102 mm (4 in) with a uncocking lever. The pistol has an automatic firing pin safety.

COMPACT: A double-action pistol with a barrel length of 127 mm (5 in), a safety catch, a uncocking lever and an automatic firing pin safety.

COMPETITION: A single-action pistol with a choice of either a 102 mm (4 in) or 127 mm (5 in) barrel, an ambidextrous safety catch and an automatic firing pin safety.

The pistol is cut from solid blocks of steel. The manufacturing process does not involve any casting of metal or synthetic materials. In 1998 the patent right and the name was taken over by the German firm, Intertex Maschinenbau GmbH in Eislingen. They produce a small number of weapons per year, usually made to order.

Intertex made the unique model HSP-701 'Odin's eye' for the IWA-2000 Fair in Nuremberg,

Germany. This pistol is entirely made of single block of damask stainless steel. This means that Intertex was the first to make a firearm in this material. The grips are made of walnut, inlaid with a mammoth's ivory, and decorated with a scrimshaw design. Scrimshaw is a technique for scratching designs into ivory with fine steel pens. The artist often colors in the design, creating a beautiful effect. The best scrimshaw is scratched by hand. There are also computer techniques for producing machine-drawn scrimshaw designs. Reverse scrimshaw works the other way round. The background is black and the scratched lines of the design appear in white and gray. Intertex makes the Korriphila in 9 mm Para (9-shot) and .45 ACP (7-shot) calibers. The barrel length is 102 of 127 mm (4 or 5 in). The total length is respectively 182 or 207 mm (7¼ or 8 in). The height of the pistol is 136 mm (5¼ in) and the width is 34 mm (1¼ in). The model with the 102 mm (4 in) barrel weighs 1000 g (35¼ oz). The longer model weighs 1200 g (42¼ oz). The single-action trigger pressure is 1800 g (4 lb) and in double-action, it is 4800 g (10½ lb). The height of the combat rear sight can be adjusted on the side. Other features of the Korriphila include a fixed barrel, a trigger stop, an automatic firing pin safety and an extractor which also serves as a cartridge indicator, The takedown lever is on either side of the front of the trigger guard.

Damask steel Korriphila
Odin's Eye pistol

Standard Korriphila pistol

KORTH

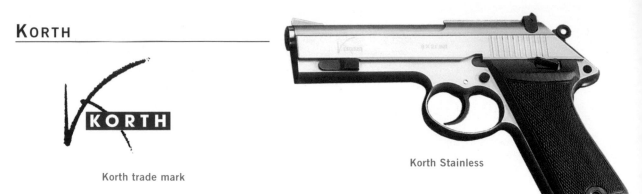

Korth trade mark

The German firm, Korth, in Ratzeburg, was established in 1956, and has manufactured pistols and revolvers since that time. At the start of 1999 the firm almost went bankrupt, but Korth has been completely operational since the end of that year. The firm is known above all for the high quality of its firearms. Korth revolvers are made of a special sort of hardened steel. The barrels are hammered cold, resulting in a very dense steel structure. The internal mechanism of Korth revolvers includes a small wheel in the trigger arm instead of the usual catch found in other makes. It is possible to modify the pressure point of the trigger action by changing this wheel. Furthermore, the trigger pressure of the revolvers can be adjusted between approximately 1000 and 2500 g, by means of an adjustment screw. The Korth pistol was introduced in 1987 in 9 mm Para caliber. It was designed by Willi Korth. The Korth 10-shot double-action pistol has an interesting falling block locking system. This falling block is at the front of a block around the muzzle, and bolts the barrel and the slide. The unusual position of this bolt has a moderating effect on the recoil of the weapon when a shot is fired. The pistol does not have a safety catch. Korth considers that this sort of safety is not necessary for a defensive pistol, and only results in mistakes in stressful situations. In terms of technology, craftsmanship and finish, this weapon is top of the range, which is reflected in its price. All the parts are cut from solid steel.

KORTH PISTOL

The Korth pistol was introduced in 1987 in 9 mm Para caliber with a magazine capacity of 10 rounds. This was followed by the calibers 9 x 21 mm IMI

Korth Stainless

(10-shot) and .40 S&W (9-shot). Since 1998 the weapon has also been available in .357 SIG caliber (9-shot). The double-action pistol does not have an external safety catch. The slide catch is on the left of the frame above the grip plates. The takedown lever is also on the left of the frame, close to the muzzle. The magazine catch is on the left above the trigger. The safety system is a half-cock safety at the foot of the hammer. For the American market the weapon has automatic firing pin safety. The Korth pistol is made with a polished or mat blue finish. In addition, it is also available in a mat or polished chrome-plated finish, or with a protective titanium coating. For the barrel length there is a choice of a 102 or 127 mm (4 of 5 in) barrel. The total length is 206 or 231 mm (8 or 9 in). The empty weight is 1240 g (43¾ oz). The single-action trigger pressure is 1500 g (3¼ lb) and in double-action, it is 5000 g (11 lb). In addition, the weapon has an adjustable rear sight. The grip plates are made of walnut.

KORTH COMBAT

Korth has produced the 6-shot double-action Combat revolver since 1966. The first model to be introduced on the market was Model 66. This did not have an ejector shroud. The ejector rod was under the barrel, without any cover. The cylinder could be tipped out of the frame by pulling the ejector rod forwards. The improved Model 71 appeared on the market in 1971. This had the characteristic cylinder bolt next to the hammer. In addition, the revolver

Korth Deluxe pistol

Korth Combat revolver

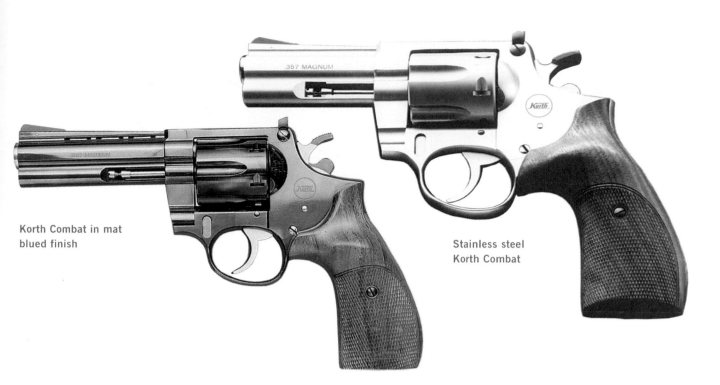

Korth Combat in mat
blued finish

Stainless steel
Korth Combat

had a short ejector shroud. In the summer of 1972, Korth designed the current Combat model with an ejector shroud which continued up to the muzzle. This ejector shroud also serves as a barrel weight. This revolver has a built-in blocking bar system as a safety. The Combat is available, with interchangeable cylinders, in the following calibers:
– .22 WMR with an interchangeable cylinder for .22 LR;
– .32 S&W-Long;
– .357 Magnum with an interchangeable cylinder for .38 Special and/or 9 mm Para en/of 9 x 21 mm IMI.
In addition, there is a choice of different types of barrels:

– a 76.2 mm (3 in) barrel without a ventilated barrel rib;
– a 102 mm (4 in) barrel with a ventilated barrel rib;
– a 133 mm (5¼ in) barrel with a ventilated barrel rib;
– a 152 mm (6 in) barrel with a ventilated barrel rib.
Depending on the barrel length, the total length of the Combat revolver varies from 203 to 279 mm (8 to 11 in). The weight of the weapon is 935 to 1160 g (33 to 41 oz). The Combat has a simple rear sight, though the height can be adjusted on the side. On request, this revolver can be decorated with engraving. The Combat is available in a blued, polished or mat finish, or in a polished or mat, silver-colored plasma finish. The grips are made of walnut, with a recess in the left grip plate for the use of a speed loader.

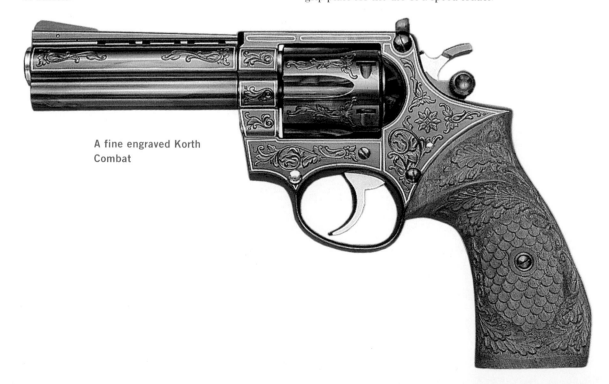

A fine engraved Korth
Combat

Korth Match revolver

Korth Sport with
102 mm (4 in) barrel

Korth Sport Stainless

KORTH MATCH

The Korth Match revolver is only made with barrel lengths of 133 or 152 mm (5¼ or 6 in), both with a ventilated barrel rib. In addition to the usual features of the sports model, this weapon has a few other special features. At the shooter's choice, the trigger crawl can be entirely adjusted by hand. In addition, the pressure point of the trigger, the trigger pressure and the trigger stop are also adjustable. The micrometer sight has an interchangeable rear sight leaf, with a choice of a rear sight of 3.4, 3.5 of 3.6 mm (.134, .138 of .142 in). The bead has a width of 3.8 mm (.15 in). The match stock has an adjustable hand rest.

KORTH SPORT

The Korth Sport Revolver is also based on the older Model 71. In terms of design and finish, it is almost the same as the Combat. However, this sports model has a completely adjustable micrometer sight. The available barrel lengths are 102 mm (4 in), 133 mm (5¼ in) and 152 mm (6 in), all with a ventilated barrel rib. The available calibers of the sports model are .22 LR, .38 Special, .32 S&W Long and .357 Magnum, but there are also interchangeable cylinders available.

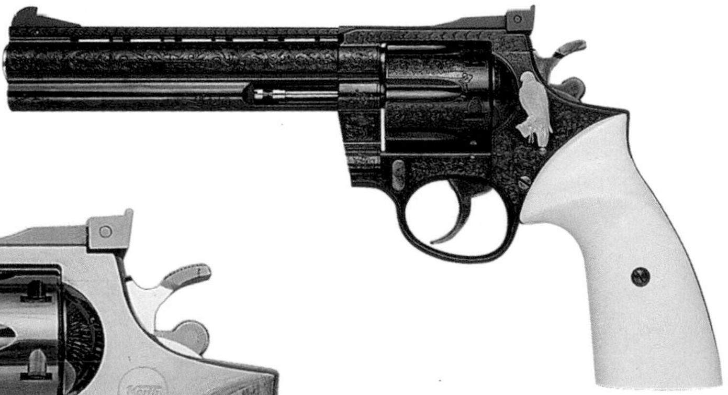

Korth Sport revolver with
152 mm (6 in) barrel
and micrometer sights

Korth revolver as
a work of art

L

LLAMA

Llama trade mark of Spanish Gabilondo company

The Spanish Basque firm was established in Guernica in 1904, as Gabilondo y Urresti. After the First World War it moved to Elgoibar, and the name of the firm changed to Gabilondo Y Compañia. After the Second World War the factory moved to the Basque town of Vitoria. Gabilondo manufactured Ruby revolvers and Llama and Star pistols. The name Llama (pronounced: 'liama') means 'flame'. After the reorganization in 1995, the name of the firm changed to Fabrinor. A number of Llama pistols have been made under the names of Tauler and Mugica, particularly for the South American market. Many models were inspired by the familiar Colt 1911 pistol or smaller models of this, such as the XI-B model. The calibers vary from .22 LR to .45 ACP Special, and a model was also made in the .38 Super caliber for the American market. Like the original Colt, a number of Llama pistols have a grip safety in the back of the frame. Llama was already using automatic firing pin safety long before Colt introduced this in the Series 80 models. Llama also produced a number of revolvers with some imaginative names, such as the Comanche, Super Comanche, Crusader and Martial in calibers from .22 LR to .44 Magnum. As a result of pressure from competitors, Llama regularly modified its range. For example, in 1991 it introduced a stainless steel Super Comanche silhouette revolver in .357 Magnum caliber, with an 8½ in barrel, but this disappeared from the range again two years later. Llama produced its 'Martial

series' of revolvers up to approximately 1976. In 1978, this was again known as the Comanche series with a slightly modified construction and a new type of rear sight. In addition, the Comanche .44 Magnum was introduced in 1978 with barrel lengths of 6½ in and 8⅜ in. However, production of this .44 Comanche ceased again in 1993. The new Llama range comprises a small series of double-action revolvers with a unique safety system. The hammer axis is in an ex-centric position, and in the rest position, the hammer cannot reach the firing pin in the frame. When the trigger is completely pulled back, the hammer drops slightly, so that it can touch the firing pin. As soon as the shooter releases the trigger, the hammer moves up again.

LLAMA COMANCHE

The double-action Llama Comanche I revolver was produced from 1977 to 1983. It succeeded the Martial model, which was made from 1969 to 1977. The weapon has a 6-shot cylinder in .22 LR caliber. The 6-shot Llama Comanche II is in 38 Special caliber and was made from 1977 to 1983. The third model, the Comanche III, is in .357 Magnum caliber. This is also a 6-shot revolver, made from 1978. Initially this model was also called Comanche II, but in 1979 this was changed to 'III'. This model is still in production in a blued or a mat chrome-plated finish. The Comanche III is available with barrel lengths of 102 or 152 mm (4 or 6 in). The total length is 235 or 285 mm (9¼ or 11¼ in). The height of the weapon is 130 mm (5 in) and the width is 40 mm (1½ in). The sight radius is 150 or 200 mm (6 or 8 in). The weapon weighs 1035 or 1135 g (36½ or 40 oz). It has walnut grips. The Comanche III has two safety mechanisms. The hammer is blocked as soon as the cylinder is tipped out of the weapon. In addition, the weapon has an ex-centric hammer axis. This means that the hammer moves up when the trigger is pulled so that it can touch the firing pin. When

Llama Comanche III revolver in .357 Magnum caliber

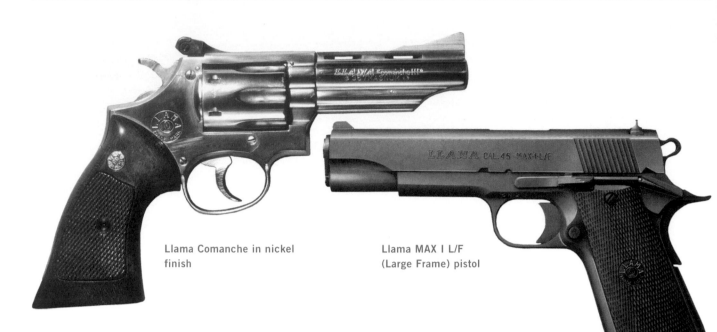

Llama Comanche in nickel
finish

Llama MAX I L/F
(Large Frame) pistol

the trigger is released, the hammer moves down, so
that the firing pin is out of reach of the nose of the
chamber.

LLAMA MARTIAL

The Llama Martial revolver was made from 1969 to
1977 in the calibers, .22 LR and .38 Special. This is
a double-action weapon with a 6-shot cylinder. In
both calibers the Martial was available with a barrel
length of 152 mm (6 in). The model with a 102 mm
(4 in) barrel was only available in .38 Special caliber.
From 1976 to 1977, there was also a Martial available
in .357 Magnum caliber, but only with a barrel length
of 102 mm (4 in). After 1977, the Martial was
succeeded by the Comanche revolver. Depending on
the barrel length, the total length is 235 or 285 mm
(9¼ of 11¼ in). The weight is 950 or 1020 g (33½ or

36 oz). The weapon has an adjustable rear
sight, walnut grip plates, and is only made
in a blued finish.

LLAMA MAX I LARGE FRAME/
COMPACT FRAME

The Llama Max I dates from 1995 and is still in
production. It is a single-action pistol, based on the
Colt 1911. The Max I is available in two different
models: the Large Frame (LF) and the Compact
Frame (CF). Both models are available in the
calibers, 9 mm Para (9-shot), .40 S&W (8-shot) or
.45 ACP (7-shot). The pistol has synthetic neoprene
grip plates. The Max I is available in a polished or
mat blue model, in a satin chrome or in a duotone
finish. The Max I LF has a fixed rear sight with
a three-dot system. Apart from this, the slide
catch and the safety catch
are extended. The grip
safety has a beavertail, and
the pistol has a combat
hammer. The Large Frame
has a total length of
216 mm (8½ in) and
a barrel length of 127 mm (5 in). The
height of the pistol is 137 mm (5½ in) and
the width is 34 mm (1.34 in). The sight radius is
150 mm (6 in). The weapon weighs 1150
g (40½ oz). The compact version of the Max I has
a total length of 200 mm (8 in) and a barrel length
of 108 mm (4¼ in). The height and width are the
same as the large Max I. The sight radius is
143 mm (5½ in) and weight is 1050 g (37 oz).

Llama Martial in
.38 Special caliber

LLAMA MAX II LARGE FRAME/MODEL VIII-C

The first model of the single-action Llama Max II Large Frame pistol in .38 Super Auto caliber was made from 1968 to 1975. This weapon has a magazine capacity of 9 rounds. The model was slightly adapted in 1975. The next modification was made in 1991, when a combat hammer was incorporated, amongst other things. In 1993 Llama introduced a new model with an extra-wide frame, increasing the magazine capacity to 18 rounds. This new model was made up to 1996. The total length of the Max II is 216 mm (8½ in) and the barrel length is 127 mm (5 in). The height is the same as that of the Max I, viz., 137 mm (5½ in). The width is 40 mm (1½ in) and the weight is 1200 g (42¼ oz). The pistol has a fixed rear sight and a sight radius of 150 mm (6 in). The weapon is only made in a blued finish with black rubber grips. In addition, the slide catch and the safety catch are extended and the grip safety has an extra long beavertail. There is also automatic firing pin safety.

Llama Max X-C in .45 ACP caliber

Llama Model VIII-C pistol in .38 Super Auto

LLAMA MAX I GOVERNMENT/MAX II LARGE FRAME/MODEL IX-C

This is the original model IX-C, dating from the period 1936 to 1954. The single-action pistol was made in the calibers, 7.65 mm Para, 9 mm Largo and .45 ACP. Grip safety was added to a newer model in 1954. In 1960, the calibers 7.65 mm Para and 9 mm Largo disappeared from the range. Since 1988, the weapon has had an extended beavertail, an extended slide catch and a safety catch. Since 1990, the model has also had a combat hammer. The pistol was marketed as the Max II Large Frame .45 up to 1995. The model was then renamed the Max-I Government and available in a polished or mat blue

finish, or in a satin chrome or duotone finish. This model is still being produced in .45 ACP caliber with a magazine capacity of 13 rounds. The total length of the weapon is 216 mm (8½ in) and the barrel length is 127 mm (5 in). The height and width are respectively 137 and 40 mm (5½ and 1½ in). The weapon has a fixed rear sight with a three-dot system and a sight radius of 150 mm (6 in). It weighs 1200 g (42¼ oz). The pistol has rubber grips and a grip safety with a beavertail and an automatic firing pin safety. Both the slide catch and the safety catch are extended. The safety catch blocks the hammer, the trigger and the slide.

LLAMA MAX II COMPACT FRAME/MODEL XI-D

The first Llama Model XI was produced in the period, 1936 to 1954. This single-action pistol has a magazine capacity of 9 rounds in 9 mm Para caliber. In 1995, Llama introduced a new compact model XI-D with an extra wide frame for 18 cartridges. This model is still manufactured now. However, it is not

Compact Llama Model XI-D pistol

exported to the USA, because a magazine capacity of more than 10 rounds is prohibited there by law. The total length of Model XI-D is 200 mm (8 in) and the weapon has a barrel length of 108 mm (4¼ in). The height is 137 mm (5½ in) and the width is 40 mm (1½ in). The weapon has a fixed rear sight and a sight radius of 143 mm (5½ in). The weight is 1100 g (38¼ oz). The pistol has rubber grips and is only available in a blued finish. There is an extended slide catch and an extended safety catch on the left of the frame. This safety catch blocks the combat hammer, the trigger and the slide. In addition, Model XI-D has a grip safety with an extended beavertail and an automatic firing pin safety.

Micromax pistol in
7.65 mm (.32 ACP) caliber

LLAMA MICROMAX .380/MODEL III-A

The Micromax was originally introduced as the Model II in 1933. The single-action pistol in 9 mm Short (.380 ACP) caliber has a magazine capacity of 7 rounds. In 1936, it was succeeded by Model III. This new model was actually the same as Model II with a few minor modifications to the trigger mechanism. The production of Model III ceased in 1954, and it was succeeded by Model III-A in 1955. In 1997, Llama renamed this pistol the Micromax. It is available in a blued and in a mat chrome finish. The Micromax has an automatic firing pin safety, a grip safety and a safety catch on the left of the frame. Both the slide catch and the safety catch are extended. There is a raised sight rib on the slide for the bead and the fixed rear sight. The new Micromax is in 9 mm Short (.380 ACP) caliber and has a magazine capacity of 7 rounds. The total length is 160 mm (6¼ in) and the barrel length is 94 mm (3¹¹⁄₁₆ in). The height of the weapon is 110 mm

(4¼ in) and the width is 30 mm (1 in). The sight radius is 110 mm (4¼ in). The empty weight of the Micromax is 625 g (22 oz). The grips are made of synthetic material.

LLAMA MICROMAX .32/MODEL X-A

The history of the Llama Micromax .32 began in 1935, when it was marketed as Model X. Llama manufactured it up to 1954, when a grip safety was added. In 1997 the name of the model changed to Micromax .32. This single-action pistol in 7.65 mm (.32 ACP) caliber has a magazine capacity of 8 rounds. The total length of the weapon is 160 mm (6¼ in). The barrel length is 94 mm (3¹¹⁄₁₆ in). The width of the grip is 30 mm (1 in) and the height is 110 mm (4¼ in). The pistol has a raised sight rib above the slide containing a fixed rear sight. The sight radius is 110 mm (4¼ in). The Micromax .32 weighs 625 g (22 oz) when it is empty. It is only available in a blued finish with black synthetic grips. The extended slide catch and extended safety catch are on the left of the frame. In addition, the pistol has an automatic firing pin safety.

LLAMA MINIMAX SUBCOMPACT

Llama introduced the Minimax Subcompact in 1996. This weapon was specially developed to be carried unobtrusively and as a back-up pistol for police services. It is a single-action pistol available in the calibers, 9 mm Para (8-shot), .40 S&W (7-shot) and .45 ACP (6-shot). A special 10-shot magazine is available for each caliber. The weapon has a steel frame and slide. The hammer is of the combat type and the extractor also serves as a cartridge indicator. The slide catch and safety

Llama Micromax .380

Minimax Subcompact

Llama 82 has a falling block locking system, based on the tried and tested Walther P38 or Beretta 92 system. The pistol does not have an automatic firing pin safety, but does have a magazine safety. The extractor also serves as a cartridge indicator. A red dot shows on the extractor when there is a cartridge in the chamber. There is a combined, ambidextrous safety catch/ uncocking lever on the slide. This safely uncocks the hammer when there is a cartridge in the chamber. The magazine catch is on the left of the frame, behind the trigger guard. This catch can be moved for left-handed shooters. The guide for the slide runs the whole length of the frame, which benefits the precision of the weapon. It is a robust weapon, designed as a service pistol for the army or police. In 1985, the Llama 82 was introduced for service by the Spanish army. The Llama 82 has a double-action trigger action a magazine capacity of 15 rounds. The total length is 210 mm (8¼ in). The barrel length is 114 mm (4½ in). The height of the weapon is 135 mm (5⁵⁄₁₆ in) and the width is 35 mm (1⅛ in). The grips are made of black synthetic material. Model 82 was available only in a blued finish. Production of this model ceased in 1995.

catch are extended, as is the beavertail grip safety. Furthermore, the ejector port in the slide is enlarged and lowered. The weapon has a three-dot sight with a fixed rear sight and a sight radius of 108 mm (4¼ in). The grips are made of synthetic black polymer. The 10-shot magazine has a rubber extension on the front for extra grip. The total length is 165 mm (6½ in) and the barrel length is 80 mm (3 in). The height is 114 mm (4½ in). The pistol is available in a mat blue, mat chrome or duotone finish.

LLAMA MODEL 82

The Llama Model 82 was introduced in 1985. The pistol is in 9 mm Para caliber and has a steel frame and slide. This is reflected in its weight: 1110 g (39 oz). Llama also introduced a lighter model to the market, the 82-LM, which weighs 875 g (31 oz). The

LLAMA MODEL 87

In 1987 Llama introduced a sports model of the military Llama M82 pistol. The Llama Model 87 Shooting Competition in 9 mm Para caliber was made specially for large caliber matches, such as the practical pistol competition (PPC), the falling-plate and bowling pin competitions. The 15-shot pistol has a double-action trigger mechanism and an external hammer. It has an adjustable rear sight. In addition, the magazine catch is on the left of the frame, behind the trigger guard. There is a combined ambidextrous safety catch/ uncocking lever on the side. The weapon has an enlarged magazine well and a trigger stop. The butt plate of the magazine has a rubber buffer plate. The pistol has a two-chamber compensator on the front of the slide. The total length of the pistol, including the two-chamber compensator, is 245 mm (9¾ in). The barrel length is 133 mm (5¼ in) and the height is 143 mm (5½ in). The width is 35 mm (1½ in) and the weapon weighs 1235 g (43½ oz). Two newer sports models were introduced

Llama Model 82 pistol

Llama 87 in 9 mm
Para caliber

to the market at the end of 1992. These are the standard model M87 and the compensator model M87 with a three-chamber compensator. Both models have a blued slide and a mat nickel-plated frame. Llama ceased production of this type of pistol in 1993.

LLAMA MODEL XXVI

Model XXVI was preceded by the double-action Martial revolver in .22 LR caliber. This 6-shot weapon was produced as the Martial from 1969 to 1977. The revolver had a barrel length of 152 mm (6 in), a simple adjustable sight, and a short catch under the barrel to bolt the ejector rod. The weapon was also available in .22 WMR caliber, with an interchangeable cylinder in .22 LR. In 1978, the revolver was given a facelift and renamed Model

XXVI, the Roman numerals for the number 26. This model is almost identical to the later Comanche, with an attractive adjustable rear sight and a half-length ejector shroud under the barrel. This revolver was made as Model XXVI from 1978 to 1989. It was available with a barrel length of 102 or a 152 mm (4 or 6 in). In 1989 the weapon was renamed the Comanche I. This was also available with a barrel length of 102 or 152 mm (4 or 6 in). The total length is 235 or 285 mm (9¼ or 11¼ in). The width of the revolver is 39 mm (1½ in) and the weapon weighs 1115 or 1240 g (39¼ or 43¾ oz). It has a completely adjustable rear sight and a sight radius of 150 or 200 mm (6 or 8 in). It was made only in a blued finish with walnut grips. The weapon has a hammer locking system with a folded-out cylinder and an ex-centric hammer axis as a falling block locking. Llama stopped manufacturing this model in 1995.

LLAMA SCORPIO

The Llama Scorpio is also based on the Martial. This 6-shot double-action model with a 51 mm (2 in) barrel was made from 1968 to 1985 in .38 Special caliber. It was then made as the Piccolo up to 1988. The Piccolo has a continuous ejector shroud and a large diagonal front sight. In 1988, the Llama renamed this model the Scorpio. It had a short ejector rod catch under the barrel and a smaller front sight than the Piccolo. The Scorpio remained in production up to 1997. The total length of the revolver is 180 mm (7 in) and

Llama Model XXVI in
.22 LR caliber

The small Llama Scorpio

the barrel length is 51 mm (2 in). The height is 126 mm (5 in) and the width is 38 mm (1½ in). The revolver has fixed sights and walnut grips. It was made only in a blued finish.

LLAMA SUPER COMANCHE

The 6-shot double-action Llama Super Comanche revolver was introduced in 1978 in .44 Magnum caliber and is still produced. At that time the weapon was available with barrel lengths of 165 or 213 mm (6½ or 8⅜ in). Llama stopped manufacturing the model with the 213 mm (8½ in) barrel in 1995. The total length of the weapon is 311 or 362 mm (12¼ or 14¼ in). The weight of the weapon with the 165 mm (6½ in) barrel is 1418 g (50 oz). In 1979, Llama also introduced the Super Comanche on the market in .357 Magnum caliber. This model differed from the ordinary Comanche because of the extra large frame of the .44 Magnum. The .357 Super Comanche was

Llama Super Comanche
in .44 Magnum caliber

made up to 1995 in barrel lengths of 102, 152 or 216 mm (4, 6 and 8½ in). The total length of this model was 235, 285 or 348 mm (9¼, 11¼ or 13¾ in). The weapon weighed 1035, 1135 or 1285 g (36½, 40 or 45¼ oz), depending on the barrel length. From 1991 to 1994, Llama also manufactured a stainless steel model with a barrel length of 216 mm (8½ in).

LES BAER

Les Baer trade mark

In 1992, Les Baer, who was the head the Springfield Custom Shop at the time, decided to start his own business. He established the firm, Les Baer Custom Inc., in Hillsdale, Illinois. Initially he specialized in the conversion of all sorts of types of pistols to meet the specific requirements of his customers. This service has now been extended to a considerable range of parts based on the Colt 1911-A1 pistol. The Les Baer range comprises special pistol frames, slides, barrels, compensators, scope mounts, recoil buffers, firing pins, extractors, ejectors, magazine extensions and triggers. In addition, Les Baer developed an extensive line of pistols, also based on the Colt 1911-A1. Furthermore, it is interesting to note that Les Baer was commissioned to developed a special pistol by the FBI, the Les Baer SRP (Swift Response Pistol) intended for use by special police departments. This pistol was subjected to a demanding series of tests, together with pistols made by other firms, and it won the test. Les Baer pistols use a frame developed by the firm itself, or those of Para-Ordnance. Les Baer pistols are available in a blued finish, in stainless steel, or in a combination.

LES BAER MONOLITH

Les Baer introduced the Monolith pistol in 1999. It is a single-action weapon in the .45 ACP caliber with a magazine capacity of 7 rounds. The pistol has a 127 mm (5 in) match barrel, a special match barrel bushing and a Les Baer slide with cocking grooves at the front and the back. The front of the grip is finely ribbed with 30 LPI (lines per inch). In addition, the ejector port is enlarged, and the weapon has a combat hammer. The aluminum match trigger has an adjustable trigger stop and a trigger pressure of 1814 g (4 lb). The grip safety is extended with a special Baer beavertail. The Monolith pistol has a special Bo-Mar micrometer sight and wooden grips. It has an ambidextrous, extended safety catch. The total length of the Monolith is 221 mm (8¾ in). The height is 149 mm (6 in) and the width is 34 mm (1¼ in). The weapon weighs 1160 g (41 oz).

Les Baer Monolith

Les Baer Swift Response
Pistol (SRP), developed
for the FBI

LES BAER SRP

In 1995, Les Baer was commissioned to design
a special pistol for special units of the FBI. It was to be
a tactical weapon, designed for the most extreme
conditions. In 1997 it was decided to produce the
pistol for the civilian market as well. The single-
action Swift Response Pistol has a large, wide frame
by Para-Ordnance, with a capacity of 14 rounds in .45
ACP caliber. A 10-shot magazine is made
for the USA. The slide is made of
a special sort of steel, and is of the
Les Baer National Match type. It
also has a match barrel with
a stainless steel barrel
bushing. The combat
rear sight is designed by
the firm itself, with
a three-dot tritium night
sight. The firing pin, the
automatic firing pin safety and
the sear are all of a special match
type. The ejector port is enlarged
and lowered. The slide catch
and the ambidextrous safety
catch are extended. The
special Baer speed trigger has
an adjustable trigger stop.
The grip safety has a long
beavertail. In addition,
the magazine well is
enlarged. The whole

weapon is accurately tuned, using special Wolff
springs. It has a special, mat black Baer Mag-na-flux
protective layer. It is guaranteed to shoot 76 mm
(3 in) at 50 meters. The total length is 220 mm
(8½ in) and the barrel length is 127 mm (5 in). The
height of the weapon is 158 mm (6¼ in) and the
width is 36 mm (1½ in). The pistol weighs 1170
g (41¼ oz) when it is empty. It has black rubber grips.

LES BAER STINGER

The Les Baer Stinger was introduced to the market
in 1999. It is a compact model with a match barrel
108 mm (4¼ in) and a special Baer barrel bushing.
The weapon has a special Baer Comanche steel slide
with an adjustable Baer combat rear sight. The
aluminum match trigger has an adjustable trigger
stop. In addition, the Stinger has an ambidextrous
safety catch, an enlarged ejector port, a Commander
hammer and a Baer beavertail. The pistol is only
made in .45 ACP caliber and has a magazine capacity
of 7 rounds.

Les Baer Stinger

M

MANURHIN

The name Manurhin is a combination of the words manufacture, Mulhouse, a location in France, and Rhin (the river Rhine). The company was originally active in engineering with the manufacture of ammunition. The firearms history of this factory goes back to just after the Second World War. The American allied forces had taken the region of Thuringia, where a branch of the weapons manufacturer Walther had been set up in the town of Zella-Melis. This 'sector' had been handed to Russia, under the Treaty of Yalta. A political agreement had been reached between the American President Roosevelt, the English Prime Minister Churchill, and the Russian President Stalin. This agreement determined how Europe should be divided between the various super powers, and forced Walther to leave their factory complex and move to the western sector. After the surrender of Nazi Germany, the allies banned Germany from manufacturing firearms.

However, because of the continuing demand for Walther pistols, an agreement was made with Manhurin allowing them to produce Walther pistols under license. In 1955, Germany regained their sovereignty enabling Walther to resume their own production. Manhurin then concentrated their firearms manufacturing on revolvers, and in the last few years on special weapons for various governments. This applied especially to the MR 35 Punch, a cross between a pistol and a carbine, capable of firing rubber balls with a diameter of 35 mm. The revolver range of Manhurin includes a series of police revolvers known as the Defense and Gendarmerie, and a series of sport revolvers. The present company name is Manhurin Equipment. In the year 2000, Manurhin was taken over by the French company Chapius Armes, a manufacturer of luxury shot and bullet firearms used in hunting based in Saint-Bonnet-le-Chateau.

MANURHIN 22 SPORT

Just after the Second World War the German Walther factory signed a contract with the French firearms manufacturer Manhurin, and because Germany was banned from firearm production, Manhurin manufactured Walther pistols for export under license. In 1955 Walther were once again allowed to manufacture their own pistols. However, Manhurin did continue to manufacture the PP, PPK and PPK/S models until 1985. The French sent unblued weapons to Ulm, where Walther added their brand name to the slide, and completed the finishing of the weapons. The double-action Manhurin 22 Sport, although a Manhurin design, is based on the Walther PP, except that Manhurin had designed a longer barrel. This pistol was then available with a barrel length of 152 mm from 194 mm (6 or 7½ in). The total lengths of this weapon are 224 mm and 266 mm (8¾ and 10½ in) respectively, and it weighs 640 and 670 g (22½ and 23½ oz) The magazine capacity is eight rounds. The safety catch, located on the left-hand side of the slide, places a safety block between the firing pin and the hammer while at the same time uncocking the hammer.

French Manurin trade mark

Manurin 22 Sport

Exploded diagram of a Manurin

MR73 revolver

Manurin MR73 Sport with a 152 mm (6 in) barrel

MANURHIN MR73

The Manhurin MR 73 revolver was introduced in 1973. It is a double action weapon with a cylinder for six, Magnum .357 caliber cartridges (also in .38 Special), with an interchangeable cylinder for caliber Para 9 mm. A special match version with a 152 mm (6 in) barrel is also available in S&W Long .32 caliber. This model of revolver has a number of special built-in features. A trigger bar connects the trigger to the hammer. This trigger bar hooks into a guide piece, the same as with the Smith and Wesson revolvers. The guide mechanism does not run along the frame of the Manhurin revolver, but over it with the aid of four guide wheels. A fifth wheel is located in the guide mechanism for the trigger spring guidance. This results in a particularly good trigger action that literally runs on wheels. In addition, the trigger spring pressure can be adjusted by means of an adjusting screw at the front of the grip. The MR73 has also a fixed firing pin point on the hammer. A blocking bar is built in for added safety. The firing pin point can not reach the cartridge cap until the trigger travel in single or double action has been completed. Another special feature is the extremely hard and robust type of steel used for the barrel. This means that it is almost impossible to blow up the barrel, by for example, using the wrong powder charge in reloaded cartridge. The cylinder is capable of resisting the double gas pressure of a Magnum .357 cartridge, and is guaranteed to 6.300 bar, although to test this would not be advisable. The MR 73 model is still being produced in the following versions:

MANURHIN MR73 G.-3 GENDARMERIE
This 6 shot double action revolver is available in a Magnum .357 caliber with an optional interchangeable cylinder for Para 9 mm. This weapon has a barrel length of 76 mm (3 in). The total length is 205 mm (8 in). It has an adjustable rear sight and

an interchangeable front sight. The sight radius is 117 mm (4½ in). This revolver weighs 910 g (32 oz) when empty, and is only available in a blued finish, with a hardwood or rubber grip.

MANURHIN MR73 G-4 GENDARMERIE
This version is almost identical to the MR73 G.-3, apart from the dimensions. The G-4 has a total length of 233 mm (9¼ in). The barrel length is 102 mm (4 in) and the sight radius is 142 mm (5½ in). The G.-4 weighs 970 g (34¼ oz).

MANURHIN MR73 S-6 SPORT
This is the sport version of the MR73 and is also a caliber Magnum .357 with an optional cylinder for 9 mm Para. This revolver has a barrel length of 152 mm (6 in). The total length is 283 mm (11¼ in) and the sight radius is 193 mm (7½ in). This weapon weighs 1070 g (37¾ oz). The rear sight is adjustable. The MR73 Sport is only available with a blued finish and walnut grips with or without finger grooves. The model illustrated is the luxury version with gold livery. Another sport version is the MR73-M6 S&W-Long .32 caliber. The remaining specifications of this revolver are the same as that of the S-6.

Manurhin MR88

The MR88 model was introduced on to the civilian market in 1988. This weapon is based on the French F1 Special Police revolver of 1986. The MR88 is manufactured in the Magnum .357 caliber with an optional interchangeable cylinder for 9mm Para. There are two different versions. The MR88 Defense has fixed sights and is available with 76 or 102 mm (3 or 4 in) barrels with a stainless steel or blued finish. The MR88 Sport is only available in stainless steel, with a micrometer sight and a barrel length of 102, 133 or 152 mm (4, 5¼, or 6 in). The trigger action of the MR88 is different to that of the MR73. The spring pressure for the MR88 trigger is supplied by a spiral shaped hammer spring. This weapon is still in production.

Manurhin MR88 Defense DX-4
This revolver has a total length of 231 mm (9 in), a barrel length of 102 mm (4 in), a sight radius of 150 mm (6 in) and it weighs 1005 g (35½ oz). This weapon has a sight slot in the upper bridge of the frame. It is supplied with a rubber grip with finger grooves.

Manurhin MR88 Sport SX-4
This revolver is identical to the Defense model, with the exception of the adjustable micrometer sight. The weapon illustrated has a barrel length of 102 mm

(4 in). The total length is 231 mm (9 in) and the sight radius is 150 mm (6 in). This weapon weighs 1005 g (35½ oz) and has a walnut grip with finger grooves. The other barrel lengths are 133 or 152 mm (5¼ or 6 in).

Manurhin MR93

The MR93 was launched in 1993. Manurhin only manufactured this model for a short time as it was soon followed in 1996 by the MR96. However, the MR93 is an extremely interesting weapon. It offers the possibility to change the length of the barrels, as was the case with the Wesson revolvers of that day. The MR93 offered a choice of 76, 102, 133 or 152 mm (3, 4, 5¼ or 6 in) barrel lengths, complete with separate matching barrel shrouds. Another interesting feature is the catch for the cylinder release, which is located on the right-hand side at the front of the frame. The double-action MR93 has the same trigger system as the MR88, with the hammer spring also supplying spring pressure for the trigger. The safety is supplied via a transfer bar. This weapon is only available in the caliber Magnum .357 with the sport version having a micrometer sight.

Manurhin MR93 Sport S-3
The Manurhin MR93 Sport S-3 has a total length of 222 mm (8¼ in). The barrel length is 76 mm (3 in). This weapon has an adjustable rear sight with a sight

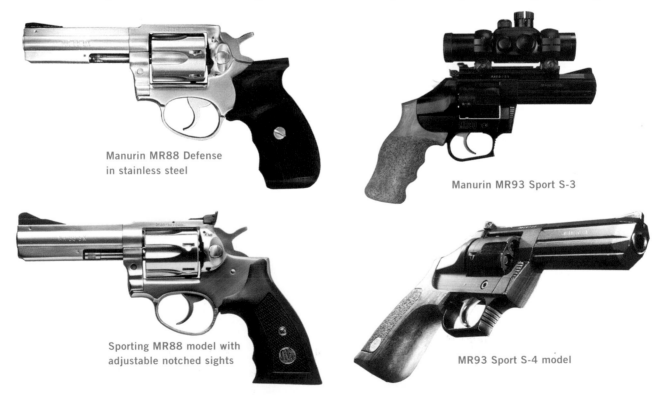

Manurin MR88 Defense in stainless steel

Manurin MR93 Sport S-3

Sporting MR88 model with adjustable notched sights

MR93 Sport S-4 model

radius of 125 mm (5 in). This revolver weighs 1080 g
(38½ oz). It has a wooden stock with finger grooves
and has a mat blued finish.

MANURHIN MR93 SPORT S-4

The Sport S-4 version of the MR93 has a 102 mm
(4 in) barrel. The total length of this weapon is
245 mm (9¾ in). The sight radius between the front
sight and the adjustable rear sight is 150 mm (6 in)
and this weapon weighs 1160 g (41 oz). The grip of
the weapon illustrated does not have finger grooves,
however a version with a stock with finger grooves is
available, as with the Sport S-3. The special button
for releasing the cylinder can be clearly seen in the
illustration of this weapon.

MANURHIN MR93 SPORT S-5/S-6

There are two remaining variations of the sport
version of the MR93. The Sport S-5 has a total
length of 280 mm (11 in) a barrel length of 133 mm
(5¼ in) and it weighs 1226 g (43¼ oz). The MR93
S-6 has a total length of 299 mm (11¾ in), a barrel
length of 152 mm (6 in) and it weighs 1330 g (47 oz).

MANURHIN MR96

The 1996 Manurhin MR96 revolver is the successor
to the MR93 model. The design was the result of
collaboration between Manurhin engineers and
a number of prominent French sport shooters.
A number of its predecessor's features have been
incorporated in this MR96 model. The cylinder
release is on the right hand side at the front of the
frame. The barrel is enclosed in a separate outer
shroud. This allows the space between the cylinder
and barrel cone to be easily adjusted, while still
retaining the correct sight alignment. This separate
outer shroud has a raised ventilated barrel rib. The
continuous ejector shroud has resulted in extra barrel
weight. Unlike the MR93, the barrel complete with
barrel shroud is not easily changed. A removable
sideplate carrying the trigger mechanism complete
with transfer bar safety is located on the right hand
side of the frame.

    The stock of this revolver consists of a large
rubber grip with shallow finger grooves and an
opening that allows the use of speedloaders. This
weapon is only available in the Magnum .357 caliber,
but obviously still leaving the option to fire .38
Special cartridges. An interchangeable cylinder for
Para 9 mm is not available. The MR96 is only
manufactured in a polished or a blued finish. There is
a choice of barrel lengths from 76, 102, 133 or 152
mm (3, 4, 5¼ or 6 in). The total lengths are 226, 252,
284 or 303 mm (9, 10, 11, or 12 in), respectively. The
weights of this weapon depending on the barrel
lengths are 1090, 1150, 1217 or 1860 g (38½, 40½, 43
or 65½ oz).

Manurin MR96

Mauser trade mark

MAUSER

The founder of the famous Mauser firearms factory,
Peter Paul Mauser, was born in 1838 in Oberndorf an
de Neckar in the province of Württenberg in Germany.
Peter's father, Franz Andreas Mauser was employed
as a Master Gunsmith for the Royal Württemberg
Firearms Factory (Königliche Württembergischen
Waffenfabrik). In 1859 Peter Paul Mauser was
conscripted for military service and was assigned to the
artillery. His first invention was a rear loading cannon,
which attracted very little interest from the military. In
1865, he developed his first bolt action rifle. The bolt of
this weapon had a spring-loaded firing pin. This proved
to have a great advantage over older designs that
had a protruding fire pin, which occasionally resulted
in a loaded cartridge being fired accidentally before
the rifle could be closed. Paul Mauser received
a development grant for the purchase of machines and
materials on the basis of his prototype. The Mauser
company was born. Brother Wilhelm was brought in to
take care of the commercial activities, but was faced
with the lack of demand for a new army rifle in
the surrounding countries. In 1866 the Mauser
brothers came in contact with Samuel Norris,
a representative of the American Remington Arms
Company, who recognized the commercial potential of
the Mauser design. These rifles were manufactured at
a firearms factory in Liege, Belgium and in the USA.
This resulted in the Mauser Norris rifle, which was
introduced in 1867. Norris had hoped to sell this
weapon to the French army, who were looking to
replace the Chassepot rifle. This plan hit a snag
however, when France decided to choose a home
produced weapon, resulting in the directors of
Remington withdrawing their support, a decision that
they surely must have regretted the future. In 1871, the
rifle was the preferred choice of the Prussian army, and

was issued to their soldiers as the M71. The rifle was an 11 mm (½ in) caliber with a black powder cartridge 11.15 x 60R. In 1871, Mauser took over the state arsenal in Oberndorf, and under the company name of Mauser & Cie, Paul and Wilhelm Mauser were given the use of a production facility. This rifle was also being manufactured in Amberg, Danzig, Erfurt, Spandau and at Steyr in Austria. Wilhelm Mauser died in 1882, when the company was transformed into the Mauser Firearms Factory AG (Waffenfabrik Mauser AG.) In the same year, a new M71 type was developed with a tubular magazine for eight rounds, followed by the M71/84, and then in 1887, the M87 model with a 9.5 mm (½ in) caliber for the Turkish army. The German army leaders were not happy with the M71 rifle with the tubular magazine, which led to the Rifle 88 (Gewehr 88) or the Commissions Rifle (Kommissions Gewehr) with a 7.92 mm (8 x 57 mm) caliber being produced for the German army in 1888. In 1889, the Belgian army decided to change in favor of the Mauser rifle with a caliber of 7.65 Mauser, manufactured under license by the FN factories. The Spanish army also wanted this weapon, but with a caliber of 7 mm (7x57 mm). This proved to be such an exceptional weapon for its day that the Americans found it to quite a handful during the Spanish-American War in 1898. The US Army commissioned the Springfield Armory to develop a similar type of rifle which resulted in the Springfield M1903. This weapon was so identical to the Mauser design that the American Government were forced to pay Mauser $200.000 in patent compensation. In 1898, the German army decided to introduce the rifle developed by Mauser as the Rifle-98 (Gewehr-98) with a caliber of 7.92 Mauser. Shorter versions of which were later given the names, Kar-98a in 1904, Kar-98b (after the First World War) and Kar-98l in 1935. In 1890, Mauser decided to get involved in a variety of contracts to supply a new army pistol, and so he designed a new Autoloader. This weapon was introduced in 1896 with the model name C-96. At the turn of the century a large number of firearms manufacturers were engaged in a fierce competition battle trying to secure large orders from the military. George Luger, a German engineer, collaborated with Borchardt in the development of a new army pistol. In 1898, this pistol was tested during Swiss army trials. At the request of the Swiss, the caliber was changed from Borchardt 7.65 to Parabellum 7.65 mm. In 1900, the Swiss army introduced this weapon as a service pistol giving it the name Ordinance Pistol 1900 (Ordonnanz Pistole 1900) This type is provided with a grip safety. In 1908, the German army placed a large order for this weapon, and introduced it into service as the P08 Model. The initial caliber of Para 7.65 mm, was later supplemented with the Para 9 mm. Paul Mauser died in 1914 and in 1922

the name of the company was changed to Mauser-Werke AG. After the Second World War and after the ban on firearms production imposed by the allied forces had been lifted, the company resumed production under the name of Mauser Works Oberndorf Firearms Systems GmbH (Mauser-Werke Oberndorf Waffensysteme GmbH). In 1979, the company became part of the industrial group Diehl. In 1999, the Swiss SIG concern, to which Sig-Sauer and Hämmerli also belong, purchased the rights to use the Mauser name. The most recent Mauser M2 pistol is in fact manufactured by the American Sig factory in Exeter, New Hampshire.

MAUSER ZIG-ZAG REVOLVER MODEL 1878

Peter Paul Mauser designed this classic revolver in 1878. The system works as follows. As the trigger is tightened a locking lug slides under the cylinder by means of the zigzag grooves. This rotates the cylinder so that the next cylinder chamber is positioned in front of the barrel. After the cartridge is fired the locking lug slides back for the next round. The hammer spring is situated in an unusual place, in the frame between the cylinder and the trigger. After pulling the ring shaped bolt in front of the trigger this weapon swings open. The model illustrated is a civilian model without a lanyard ring at the bottom of the grip. Mauser has also manufactured the Zig-Zag Model 2 revolver with a closed frame. This weapon is not hinged, but is loaded through a loading port on the right hand side, behind the cylinder. A distinguishing feature of the second model is that the round barrel has crowning around the muzzle. The 6 shot double-action 1878 Model is manufactured with the caliber 7.6, 9 or 10.6 mm. The length of this weapon is 298 mm (11¾ in) and the barrel length is 80 mm (3¼ in). This revolver weighs 1150 g (40½ oz). It has a fixed sight and a hard rubber grip.

Mauser Zig-Zag revolver of 1878

Mauser C-96 engraved by Turkish
company Tugra Gravür

Mauser C-96 Flatside pistol

MAUSER C96 PISTOL

Mauser decided to try for the contract to supply a new army pistol. A department manager named Federle made a concept design for an automatic, for which Mauser developed the ammunition. The cartridge was based on the Borchardt 7.65, and was a tremendous success for Mauser.

This pistol was named the C-96 because it was introduced in 1896. Mauser continued to improve the design and made 22 modifications between 1896 and 1934. In addition, there are known to be a number of different versions:

– grip: small and large grip types with a wooden or hard rubber grip;
  magazine: fixed magazine with a capacity for 6, 10 and 20 rounds;
– removable magazine with 6, 10, 20 or even 40 rounds;
– semi or fully automatic firing (model 1932);
– calibers: 7.63 Mauser, 7.65 Para, 8.15 mm, 9 mm Mauser, 9 mm Para, 9 mm Largo (Spanish) and .45 ACP (Chinese model);
– sights: fixed or adjustable.

Between 1912 and 1918 Mauser produced large quantities of this pistol, particularly for export with the caliber 9 mm Mauser. This version was known as the Mauser Military M12 or the Mauser Bolo. In 1916 the C96 was also manufactured with the caliber of 9 mm Para. The number '9' was clearly milled into the grip and colored in red lacquer. During the total production period a considerable number of C-96 pistols were exported to other countries including: Italy, Finland, France, Norway, Austria, Iran, Thailand and Turkey. A few Mauser C-96 versions were equipped with a combat grip for long distance shooting. These models have a special ladder sight for distances up to 450 or even 700 meters. Apart from the name Mauser, other company names can be found on these pistols such as Westley Richards & Co , Stoeger Inc , Jeffery & Co and Lengerke & Detmold. The Mauser C96 was reproduced by a number or companies, including the Spanish firearms factory Astra and by a variety of Chinese firearms factories with the caliber .45 ACP. Winston Churchill favored the Mauser C-96 as his own personal pistol. The entire production came to a halt after the surrender of the Germany army in 1945. This single-action Mauser pistol is manufactured in the calibers of 7.63 Mauser, 7.65 Para, 8.15 mm, 9 mm Para, 9 mm Mauser, 9 mm Largo and .45 ACP. The standard magazine capacity is 10 rounds. The total length is 298 mm (11¼ in) and the standard barrel length is 162 mm (6½ in). The safety catch is located at the rear or the frame next to the hammer. The Turkish company Tugra Gravur Ltd based in Istanbul has beautifully engraved the C-96 pistol illustrated above.

MAUSER P08 PISTOL

In the period between 1890 and 1900 a number of firearms manufacturers were fighting to secure large army orders. In Germany it was Mauser, Bergmann and the American combination Borchardt-Bayard.

The first automatic were susceptible to jamming, and there was a lack of good ammunition, and so the expected orders were not realized. George Luger, a German engineer, collaborated with Borchardt to develop a new army pistol. In 1898, this pistol was tested during Swiss army trials. At the request of the Swiss, the caliber was changed from Borchardt 7.65 to

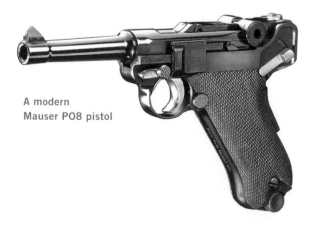

A modern
Mauser P08 pistol

Parabellum 7.65 mm. In 1900 the Swiss army introduced this weapon as their service pistol giving it the name Ordinance Pistol 1900 (Ordonnanz Pistole 1900) This type is provided with a grip safety. In 1908, the German army placed a large order for a pistol that was introduced into German army service and was known as the Model P08 (Pistole '08) initially with a caliber of 7.65 mm Para, but later also in the caliber 9 mm Para. This weapon has a unique toggle locking, which swings the weapon open when released. Originally, DWM, the German Firearms and Munitions Factory (Deutsche Waffen- und Munitionsfabrik) manufactured this pistol in Berlin, however in 1930, the production was taken over by Mauser. This pistol was manufactured until 1942, when Mauser were ordered by the Wehrmacht to transfer their production to the Walther P38 pistol. There is a large variety of Luger P08 pistols, the basic models of which are:

- Model P08 with the caliber of 7.65 mm Para and 9 mm Para;
- Model P08/20 with a caliber of 7.65 mm Para and with a maximum barrel length of 102 mm (4 in);
- Model 1917 with a 190 mm (7½ in) barrel, a combat grip and a 32-cartridge magazine.

The P08 is sold to many countries, including Bulgaria, Morocco, The Netherlands, Iran, Portugal, Russia and Sweden. Furthermore, it is manufactured under license by the British firearms factory Vickers. This pistol was even tested during the US Army trials in 1900 and 1907, but was rejected in favor of the Colt 1911 pistol. Various manufacturers, including Mauser, still produce small quantities of Lugers in a blued finish and even in stainless steel versions in different calibers from .22 LR up to .45 ACP. Mauser also manufactured special versions, to commemorate a number of special occasions including, the IWE, the International Firearms Exhibition in Nuremberg, Germany. The standard length of the Luger P08 is 230 mm (9 in). The standard barrel lengths are 100 and 150 mm (4 and 6 in). The height of this weapon is 135 mm (5¼ in) and the standard weight is 835 g (29½ oz). The standard P08 is manufactured in the calibers of 7.65 mm Para and 9 mm Para with a magazine capacity of 8 rounds. Other caliber versions followed later. Some of the early models had a grip safety, but normally the safety catch was located on the left-hand side of the frame.

MAUSER MODEL 1914

In 1910 Mauser brought a small single-action pocket pistol onto the market with a caliber of 6.35 mm (.25 ACP) and known as the Model 1910. In 1914 Mauser increased the size of this weapon and introduced it as the new Model 1914. This pistol is in the caliber 7.65 mm (.32 ACP) and has a magazine capacity of 8 rounds. The retaining catch for the recoil spring is fixed at the front of the frame by means of a bayonet fitting.

Dutch army Mauser P08. The upper pistol is made by DWM of Germany, the lower M11 by Vickers of UK

A fine engraved Mauser P08

Jubilee issue Mauser P08

Mauser P08 with long barrel and adjustable ladder sights

Mauser Model
1914 pistol

The total length of Model 1914 is 153 mm (6 in). The barrel has a length of 87 mm (3½ in) and this weapon weighs 600 g (21¼ oz). The stock has a wrap-around wooden or a hard rubber grip. The safety system of Model 1914 is quite remarkable, by pushing down a lever on the left-hand side of the frame, both the slide and the trigger can blocked. When the round button is depressed, this blocking is released. This button, although similar, should not be mistaken for the magazine release, which is in fact located in the grip heel. One other special feature is the half-open slide. Model 1914 was manufactured until 1938.

MAUSER MODEL 1934

In 1934, the Mauser Model 1914 was slightly modernized. Mauser reintroduced the new version onto the market as Model 1934. The biggest modification was the change in the manufacturing technique. Instead of milling the components, a large number were machine stamped. The shape of the frame grip was also slightly more rounded. The noteworthy safety catch, together with the release button was retained, as was the magazine release in the grip heel. The caliber of Model 1934 is also 7.65 mm (.32 ACP) and this pistol has a magazine capacity of 8 rounds. When this weapon is cocked, the back of the firing pin protrudes slightly from the slide. The total length of this weapon is 159 mm (6¼ in). The barrel has a length of 87 mm (3½ in) and this pistol weighs 610 g (21½ oz).

Mauser M1934

MAUSER MODEL HSC

The development of the Mauser HSc pistol did not proceed without the occasional hitch. The first prototype, the HSa appeared in 1937. However, Mauser had infringed the patent rights of Walther with the production of certain components. The design was therefore revised into the Hsb prototype. During testing, it became apparent that further modifications were needed. In 1940, Mauser finally started with the production of this pistol and gave it the name Model HSc. The repeating action of this weapon utilized the recoil. An unusual feature, is the deep groove at the rear of the slide from which the hammer protrudes. The standard caliber is 7.65 mm (.32 ACP), but small numbers were manufactured .22 LR and 9 mm Short (.380 ACP). The double-action pistol has a beautiful styling, mainly thanks to the broad sloping trigger guard. The safety catch is located on the left-hand side of the slide. This catch pushes the firing pin upwards out of the hammer's reach.

Mauser Model
HSc pistol

In 1940, Mauser took part in a variety of tests for the German army. Eventually preference for the army pistol was given to the Walther P38, however the German air force, the navy and the police did use this weapon. Approximately 250.000 of these weapons were manufactured up to 1945. The wartime versions can be recognized by the Wehrmacht codes on the slide: 'byf' or 'svw'. After the Second World War, Mauser resumed production until about 1981. As of 1970, the Italian Renato Gamba also manufactured this weapon under license. The total length is 162 mm (6½ in). The barrel length is 86 mm (3½ in) and it weighs 640 g (22½ oz). The magazine capacity is 8 rounds.

MAUSER MODEL 80 SA

In 1991, Mauser introduced the single-action pistol Model 80 SA. This weapon was manufactured for Mauser by the Hungarian firearms factory Feg and is almost identical to the Feg P9R. Model 80 SA was only manufactured in the caliber 9 mm Para, with a magazine capacity of 13 rounds. This weapon was available up until 1996 in a blued version with

Single-action Mauser 80 made by Hungarian FEG factory

a hardwood grip. The safety catch of this weapon is located on the left-hand side of the slide. This catch blocks the hammer and disconnects the trigger bar: the connection between the trigger and the tumbler. The total length is 203 mm (8 in), the barrel length is 120.7 mm (4¾ in) and this pistol weighs 890 g (31½ oz). The Mauser commercial emblem is added to the left-hand side of the slide together with the text 'Mauser-Werke Oberndorf GmbH'.

MAUSER MODEL 90 DA/90 DAC

The Mauser Model 90 DA was also introduced in 1991 and was launched at the same time as the Model 80 SA. The Mauser 90 DA did not however have a double-action trigger. The Hungarian Feg also manufactured this pistol for Mauser. This weapon is manufactured with a caliber of 9 mm Para with a magazine capacity of 14 rounds. The safety catch works in the same manner as by the Model 80 SA. This pistol is only manufactured in a blued version, with hardwood grips and with a fixed rear sight. The total length is 203 mm (8 in). The barrel has a length of 121 mm (4¾ in) and this weapon weighs 992 g (35 oz). From 1992 up until 1996 a semi-compact version was available with the model name 90 DAC. This pistol also has a capacity of 14 rounds. The barrel length is 105 mm (4¼ in) and the total length is 188 mm (7½ in). The weight is 940 g (33¼ oz).

MAUSER MODEL HUNTER

In 1998 Mauser introduced a 6-shot double-action .38 Special revolver, the Mauser Hunter, especially for the European hunter. The Czechoslovakian firearms factory Alfa Proj manufactured this revolver for Mauser. In several countries, including West Germany, it was usual for the hunters to have a back-up handgun for personal protection. This weapon would also be used for any mercy killing of wild animals, the so-called Coup de Grace. The use of a handgun for hunting is forbidden in a few European countries. The Hunter has a total length of 220 mm (8¾ in) and a barrel length of 102 mm (4 in). The weight is 800 g (28¼ oz). This weapon has a micrometer rear sight. This weapon has a mat black plastic protective coating with a hardwood grip with finger grooves.

MAUSER MODEL M2

Sig introduced the latest Mauser M2 pistols in 2001. This weapon is available in different calibers: .357 Sig (10-shot), .40 S&W (10-shot) and in .45 ACP (8 shot). This pistol has a so-called lockup. As the barrel rotates, a lug locates with the slide. A guide lug, that starts the rotation after firing, is accommodated in an opening in the frame. This barrel rotation lockup is similar to that of the Beretta Cougar pistol. The Mauser M2 does not have a hammer. When loading this weapon the firing pin is partially cocked. The double-action-only trigger applies further pressure to the firing pin, which is then subsequently released. The Mauser pistol does not have a safety catch, but does have automatic firing pin safety. The slide catch lever located on the left-hand side of the frame is directly above the trigger guard, in front of a lever that resembles a safety catch, but is in fact a takedown lever. The M2 also has a magazine safety. This weapon can not be fired if the magazine has been taken out. The grips are made of unbreakable polymer composite. The total length of the Mauser M2 is 184 mm (7¼ in) and the barrel length is 95 mm (3¾ in). The empty weight is 936 g (33 oz) and the trigger pressure is 3.6 kg (8 lb). This pistol has fixed sights and a mat black finish.

Double-action Mauser Model 90, also by FEG

Mauser Hunter revolver, reproduced by Alfa Proj

New Mauser M2 pistol of 2001,
made by Swiss SIG in the USA

Moravia CZ-G2000
in 9 mm Para
caliber

Moravia CZ-G2000 with
nickel finish slide

MORAVIA ARMS

The Czech Moravia Arms Ltd. was founded in 1992 for the export, import and production of weapons and ammunition. This company deals in both sport weapons and military weapons and is based in Ostrava. Moravia Arms has its own shooting range complex on a former army base in Prerov, where they carry out official inspection of firearms for import and export. A branch of the Prague proof house also uses this complex. In 1997, Moravia received a state license for international weapon trading.

Apart from being a wholesaler for a variety of affiliated Czech firearms factories, Moravia also produce their own firearms. An example of this is the CZ-G2000 pistol with a caliber of 9 mm Para and .40 S&W that was introduced in 1999. Moravia also manufacture new pistols from an older design, such as the VZ-50/70 from 1950, the VZ-52 with a caliber of 7.62 Tokarev and the VZ-82 from the Czech firearms factory CZ. In addition, they exported the VZ-61 Scorpion, the VZ-24 and the VZ-26 machine pistols. Another interesting weapon is the Falcon sniper's rifle: In the version OP96 this sniper is in the caliber 12.7 x 107 mm. The model Falcon-OP97 is in the caliber .50 BMG.

Works
logo of
Moravia
Arms

MORAVIA CZ-G2000

Moravia brought this futuristic pistol onto the market in 1999. This is a double-action pistol with a composite frame and the caliber 9 mm Para (15 shot) and .40 S&W (12-shot). This weapon has a modified Browning-Petter locking, which locks the chamber block of the barrel via the ejection port in the slide. The CZ-G2000 has only an automatic firing pin safety with a release button on the left-hand side of the slide. The extractor also functions as a cartridge indicator. The release lever is on the left-hand side of the frame. At the front of the frame, in front of the trigger guard, there is a horizontal groove on both sides, intended for the mounting of sight lighting or a laser sight. The fixed combat sight has a white triple dot. At the front and rear of the slide, pressure grooves have been added on both sides. The magazine lever is located on the left-hand side of the frame, behind the trigger guard. The total length of the CZ-G2000 is 185 mm (7¼ in). The barrel length is 102 mm (4 in). The height of this pistol is 134 mm (5¼ in) and the width is 31 mm (1¼ in). The empty weight is 780 g (27½ oz). This pistol is available in a mat black version or in a two-tone version with a mat nickel-plated slide.

N

M-54, a Chinese
Tokarev

The Chinese
M59 Makarov
pistol

NORINCO

The company name Norinco is derived from the name China North Industries Corporation. This company is an export cooperative, founded in 1985, and based in Beijing (Peking) in China. Norinco has brought a surprisingly large assortment of weapons onto the market in an amazingly short time. The objective is clearly financial: to manufacture anything that can possibly be sold in order to out do the West. The Norinco company was first heard of in 1986 when it introduced a number of cloned versions of the Russian army rifles AK-47, AK-74, SKS and the sniper's rifle NDM-86, based on the Russian Dragunov. The company also launched a cloned Makarov pistol, with the name Model 59. In 1988, 1989 and 1990 the American and European firearms trade exhibitions were surprised by the enormous expansion of models and types. A sales organization has been set up in the USA under the name of Norinco China Sports Inc. Norinco also manufactures and exports ammunition, such as Jialing shot cartridges for trap and skeet, Norinco .22 LR small caliber ammunition in Standard and Match, .223 Remington cartridges and the Russian calibers 7.62 x 39mm. The latest models are based on the Sig-Sauer pistols, and are extremely accurate copies. The Model 93 is especially nice, a replica of the famous Colt Woodsman and Model TT-Olympia, based on the old Walther Olympia small caliber sport pistol. Norinco also manufactures the Tokarev, a copy of the CZ-75, a variety of Colt 1911-A1 pistols, a copy of

Trade mark of Chinese Norinco
organization

the Walther PPK and the Browning High Power. As well as pistols, Norinco also manufactures a large quantity of shotguns and bullet rifles. There are also a series of riot guns that no police officer would be ashamed of. The Chinese copy of the semi-automatic Browning Auto-5 shot rifle also looks very authentic. There is hardly any difference between their copies and the real Remington and Winchester bullet rifle model series. The models JW-101 with the calibers of 7.62 x 39 mm and JW-25 in .22 LR, are very attractive, and appear to be identical to the Mauser K98.

NORINCO MODEL M54 (TOKAREV)

The Norinco M54 pistol is a copy of the Tokarev pistol. The frame and the slide are made of steel. This weapon has a slide catch on the left-hand side of the frame. The magazine release is a small round button, on the left-hand side behind the trigger guard. The hammer has a halfcocked safety. Model M54-1 is also available with a safety catch on the left-hand side of the frame. This pistol is mat blued and has black composite grips. A lanyard ring is at the bottom of the grip, on the left-hand side. This single-action pistol has a magazine capacity of 8 rounds in the caliber 7.62 x 25 mm Tokarev. The barrel has a length of 116 mm (4½ in) and the total length is 196 mm (7¾ in). This weapon weighs 850 g (30 oz).

NORINCO MODEL M59 (MAKAROV)

Since 1990 Norinco has manufactured their own version of the well-known Makarov pistol with a double-action trigger. This weapon also has the Makarov caliber of 9 x 18 mm and a magazine capacity of 8 rounds. This pistol is made totally of steel, and has a mat blued finish with dark brown composite grips with a thumb support. The safety catch is at the left-hand side of the slide, as is the slide catch above the trigger guard. The magazine release is located in the original place, in the grip heel. A ring for a lanyard is at the bottom of the grip heel, on the left. The total length of this weapon is 161 mm (6.3) and the barrel length is 93.5 mm (3¾ in). The empty weight is 730 g (25¼ oz). As Model NP19 this weapon is available in the caliber 9 mm Short (.380 ACP) and as Model NP39 with a caliber of 7.65 mm (.32 ACP).

NORINCO MODEL M77B (M77)

Model M77B from 1989 is a sort of sporting version of the Chinese M77 army pistol. This weapon is made totally of steel and has an adjustable rear sight. The safety catch is on the left-hand side of the frame, just behind the slide catch. The magazine release is on the left-hand side, behind the trigger guard. This weapon has a single-action trigger. An interesting point is that the thin front of the trigger guard acts as cocking lever for the firing pin. This pistol can be carried uncocked with a cartridge in the chamber. It is then possible to take the first shot by pushing in the front of the trigger guard and pulling the trigger. The grips are made of black composite. A ring for a lanyard is at the bottom of the grip heel. The M77B is available in the caliber 9 mm Para and has a capacity of 9 rounds. The total length is 190 mm (7½ in) and the barrel length is 127 mm (5 in). This weapon weighs approximately 1000 g (35¼ oz).

NORINCO MODEL M93 (WOODSMAN)

An extremely beautiful piece is the replica of the nostalgic Colt Woodsman pistol. The Colt Woodsman is a small caliber pistol designed by John Moses Browning. Colt introduced this 10-shot pistol in 1915. This weapon then had a 165 mm (6½ in) barrel. Its successor followed in 1927, and was also known as the Woodsman. The new Woodsman was available with an 114 mm (4½ in) or a 165 mm (6½ in) barrel. Both versions had walnut grips. In 1948 Colt introduced a Revised Version, once again known as the Woodsman. This type differed from its predecessors in that the slide catch and the magazine release were on the left-hand side of the frame, behind the trigger guard. In 1955 Colt introduced yet another new version of the Woodsman. Strangely enough, the magazine release on this new model was once again behind the trigger guard at the heel of the frame. Up to 1960 it had composite grips, after which the grips were made of walnut until 1977. Colt stopped manufacturing the Woodsman in 1977. The Chinese Woodsman of 1992 has automatic firing pin safety, a magazine safety and a safety catch on the left-hand side of the frame. This weapon is totally of steel and is mat blued. The slide catch is on the left-hand side of the frame and the magazine release is at bottom of the grip heel. The grips are made of black composite. This single-action pistol has a magazine capacity of 10 rounds in the .22 LR caliber. The total length is 213 mm (8½ in) and the barrel has a length of 118 mm (4½ in). This weapon weighs 700 g (24¼ oz). An original prewar Colt Woodsman has a market value of approximately $ 725. The versions from after the Second World War are worth around $ 500. The Norinco M93 is considerably cheaper.

NORINCO MODEL M201C (TOKAREV)

This Chinese version Tokarev strongly resembles the already previewed Model M54. The single-action M201C has a safety catch however on the left-hand side of the frame. The magazine also has an extra support at the bottom. This type of Tokarev also has a half-cock lever on the hammer spur. The slide catch and the magazine release are located on the left-hand side of the frame behind the trigger guard. This weapon does not have a lanyard ring. The total length of this weapon is 196 mm (7¼ in) and the barrel length is 116 mm (4½ in). The

M77B, a sporting version of the Chinese army pistol

Model M93, a fine copy of the Colt Woodsman

M201C pistol,
an improved Tokarev

M1911-A1,
a Chines
Colt

weight is 940 g (33 oz). The 8-shot pistol in the caliber 9 mm Para has a Browning bolt-action.

NORINCO MODEL M213 (TOKAREV)

Model M213 is also based on the Tokarev pistol. This 8-shot weapon is available in the caliber 9 mm Para. The model M213A has a thicker grip, allowing a double rowed magazine that can hold 14 rounds. The safety catch is on the left-hand side of the frame. The slide catch, the magazine release and the lanyard ring are on the left-hand side of the frame. This pistol has also a half-cock lever on the hammer spur. This weapon is mat blued and has black composite grips. The total length is 196 mm (7¾ in), the barrel length is 116 mm (4½ in) and it weighs 880 g (31 oz).

NORINCO MODEL M1911-A1

This Norinco pistol is an exact copy of the military version of the Colt 1911-A1. This weapon has the slide catch, the safety catch and the magazine release on the left-hand side of the frame. The grips are made of brown composite. This single-action pistol has a capacity of 7 rounds in the caliber .45 ACP. The total length is 218 mm (8½ in) and the barrel length

is 127 mm (5 in). This weapon weighs 1130 g (40 oz). Norinco can also supply the Model M1911-P10/NP30 with a magazine capacity of 10 rounds and an ambidextrous safety catch.

NORINCO MODEL M1911-A1C

This compact model is based on the Colt Commander. This single-action pistol is also in the caliber .45 ACP and has a capacity of 7 rounds with a caliber of .45 ACP. This is a steel weapon with a round combat hammer and a wrap-around black rubber grip. The sight has white triple dot aspect marking. The total length is 200 mm (8 in) and the barrel length is 109 mm (4¼ in). This weapon weighs 1090 g (38½ oz).

M213, another version
Tokarev from China

The Chinese Colt
Commander

NORINCO MODEL M1911 P9/ MODEL NP29 P15/MODEL NP28

This is a sort of sporting version of the M1911-A1. This single-action pistol can hold 9 rounds in the caliber 9 mm Para. The grip safety has been developed into an extended beavertail. This weapon also has a round combat hammer and a wrap-around black rubber grip with wide finger grooves. The sight has a white three-dot marking. The total length is 218 mm (8½ in) and the barrel length is 128 mm (5 in). The steel weapon weighs 1150 g (40½ oz). This pistol is also available with a wide frame for a double rowed magazine for 15 rounds in the caliber 9 mm Para. This type has the model name M1911 P15/NP28. This version is slightly longer at 221 mm (8¾ in). The barrel length is 128 mm (5 in) and it weighs 1240 g (43¾ oz).

M1911 P9 sporting pistol

NP28 15-shot in 9 mm Para caliber

NORINCO MODEL NP10 (TOKAREV)

Norinco launched this model as an improved version of the Tokarev pistol. This weapon is more or less the same as the M201C, but has a couple of interesting features. This single-action pistol has a magazine capacity of 8 rounds in the caliber 7.62 x 25 mm Tokarev. There are also adapter sets available for the caliber 9 mm Para and .38 Super, of great benefit to shooters in countries where a maximum number of sport weapons are allowed. The accessories available include a matching pocket knife and a combat grip. The latter also serves as a holster. This steel weapon has the safety catch and the slide catch on the left-hand side of the frame. The magazine release is

behind the trigger guard also on the left-hand side. This pistol also has an openwork speed trigger. The total length of this weapon is 203 mm (8 in). The barrel length is 116 mm (4½ in) and it weighs 880 g (31 oz).

NORINCO MODEL NP11

Norinco themselves have described this single-action weapon as an improved version of the Tokarev pistol. Personally, I find it a bit of a hotchpotch. The safety catch mounted on the slide is ambidextrous and resembles that of the Walther or Smith & Wesson weapons. The protrusion at the back of the frame resembles a strangely shaped beavertail, but without the grip safety. Noticeable is that the hammer spur is curved upwards. This steel pistol is in the caliber 9 mm Para with a capacity of 8 rounds. The total length is 196 mm (7¾ in), the barrel length is 102 mm (4 in) and the empty weight is 910 g (32 oz).

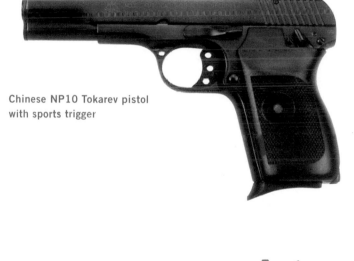

Chinese NP10 Tokarev pistol with sports trigger

The unusually turned out NP11

NORINCO MODEL NP15

Norinco also describes this weapon as an improved version of the Tokarev. This single-action pistol is in the caliber 9 mm Para and has a magazine capacity of 8 rounds. However, It can best be described as a Colt clone, with the typical Colt safety catch on the left-hand side of the frame. This weapon is nickel-plated and has black rubber grips. The total length of the NP15 is 195 mm (7¾ in) and the barrel length is 109 mm (4¼ in). The empty weight is approximately 1000 g (35¼ oz).

NP15 pistol as Colt clone

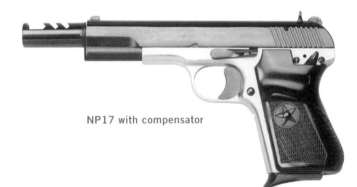

NP17 with compensator

NP18 pistol copies Browning High-Power with Walther safety catch on slide

NORINCO MODEL NP17 (TOKAREV)

Model NP17 is a typical of a Tokarev. The single-action pistol is in the caliber 9 mm Para and the magazine capacity is 8 rounds. A special feature is the three chamber compensator on the barrel. The steel frame is nickel-plated and the slide is blued. It has a wrap-around grip made of black composite. The total length of this weapon is 203 mm (8 in), including the compensator. The barrel length is 116 mm (4½ in) and it weighs 940 g (33 oz).

NORINCO MODEL NP18

At first glance, the Norinco NP18 resembles the Browning High Power. However, the safety catch, which also serves as a uncocking lever is on the left-hand side of the slide. This weapon has a double-action trigger action. The magazine capacity of this weapon is 14 rounds in the caliber 9 mm Para. This weapon is totally made of steel and has black composite grips. The total length of this pistol is 204 mm (8 in) and the barrel length is 118.5 mm (4¾ in). The weight is approximately 1000 g (35¼ oz).

NP20 civil version of the Chinese army pistol

NORINCO MODEL NP20

This single-action pistol is almost identical to the Chinese army pistol M77. The only differences with the army weapon are the built-in automatic firing pin

safety and adjustable rear sight. The safety catch is located on the left-hand side of the frame, with the slide catch just in front. The magazine release is also at the left-hand, behind the trigger guard. As well as the firing pin safety and the safety catch this pistol also has magazine safety. Furthermore, the extractor also serves as a cartridge indicator. The grips are made of black composite. This weapon has a magazine capacity of 9 rounds in the caliber 9 mm Para. The NP24 model has a capacity of 15 rounds. The total length is 190 mm (7½ in), the barrel length is 127 mm (5 in) and it weighs 1100 g (38¾ oz).

NP22 copy of Sig-Sauer
P226

NP34 pistol copy
of Sig-Sauer P228

NORINCO MODEL NP22
(SIG-SAUER P226)

Model NP22 is an exact copy of the Sig-Sauer P226, complete with the uncocking lever on the left-hand side of the frame. This pistol has an alloy frame and a steel slide, and automatic firing pin safety. The sight has a white triple dot aspect marking. The double-action pistol is available in the caliber 9 mm Para and has a capacity of 15 rounds. The total length of this pistol is 196 mm (7¾ in) and the barrel length is 112 mm (4½ in). The empty weight is 890 g (31½ oz). The grips are made of black composite.

NORINCO MODEL NP34
(SIG-SAUER P228)

With the NP34 Norinco has manufactured a copy of the Sig-Sauer P228 pistol. This weapon also has a uncocking lever on the left-hand side of the frame, just as the German-Swiss original. This double-action weapon has in the caliber 9 mm Para a capacity of 13 rounds. The frame is made of alloy and the slide is made of steel. The total length is 180 mm (7 in) and the barrel length is 98 mm (3¾ in). The weight is 740 g (26 oz).

NORINCO MODEL NP38
(BROWNING HI-POWER)

The Norinco NP38 is a copy of the Browning Hi-Power. The safety catch on the left-hand side of the frame has the distinctive shape of the Browning type MKIII. Interesting, is the fact that this Norinco version has a double-action trigger action. This pistol has also automatic firing pin safety. The NP38 is available in the caliber 9 mm Para and has a capacity of 8 rounds. The total length is 200 mm (8 in) and the barrel length is 118.5 mm (4¼ in). This weapon weighs 900 g (31¾ oz).

NP38 resembles
a modern Browning

NORINCO MODEL NZ75 (CZ-75)

Appropriately this Norinco model is known as the NZ75, because this is a copy of the Czech CZ-75 pistol. The NZ75 is in the caliber 9 mm Para and has a capacity of 15 rounds. This double-action weapon has a safety catch on the left-hand side of the slide. The slide catch and the magazine release are on the left-hand side of the frame. The sight has a white triple dot aspect marking. There is also a version available with a white stripe rear and front sight. This weapon is available with grips made of black composite or hardwood according to choice. The total length is 208 mm (8¼ in) and the barrel length is 113.8 mm (4½ in). The weight is approximately 1000 g (35¼ oz).

NZ75 pistol, copy of the CZ-75

Chinese
Walther PPK

NORINCO MODEL PPN (WALTHER PPK)

The Norinco PPN is a copy of the Walther PPK pistol. This double-action weapon has an alloy frame and a steel slide. The safety catch on the left-hand side of the slide also serves as a uncocking lever for the hammer. This weapon is available in the caliber 9 mm Short (.380 ACP) with a capacity of 8 rounds. The fixed sight has a white triple dot aspect marking. This weapon has black composite grips. The total length of the PPN is 196 mm (7¾ in) and the barrel length is 100 mm (4 in). The empty weight is 600 g (21¼ oz).

NORINCO MODEL TT-OLYMPIA (WALTHER OLYMPIA)

The Norinco TT-Olympia is a copy of the 10-shot Walther Olympia pistol of 1934. This Walther pistol was used by the German shooting team at the 1936 Olympic Games. The Norinco pistol is derived from the Walther Jäger model used in the German national championships. This Chinese weapon is in the caliber .22 LR and the magazine capacity is, strangely enough, 8 rounds. The total length is 196 mm (7¾ in) and the barrel length is 120 mm (4¾ in). The balance weight is 800 g (28.2). This pistol is available with walnut grips, but their unusual shape has made the weapon heavier. The safety catch is located on the left-hand side of the frame, just under the magazine release. The trigger guard also serves as a takedown lever. As with the Walther PP/PPK the trigger guard can be pulled downwards, releasing the slide on the frame.

NORTH AMERICAN ARMS

The American company, North American Arms in Provo, Utah, have produced weapons since 1980. In 1984, the company introduced the well-known mini revolvers with the calibers of .22 LR and .22 WMR. These single-action mini revolvers were manufactured up until 1985 by

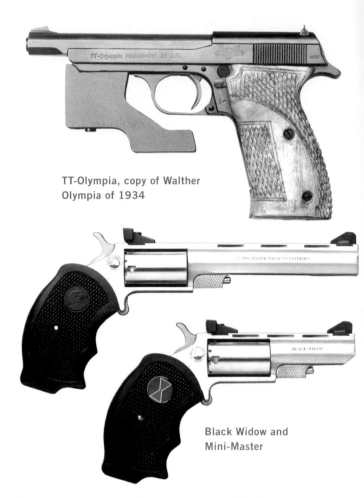

TT-Olympia, copy of Walther
Olympia of 1934

Black Widow and
Mini-Master

the American company Freedom Arms. In 1998, they introduced a small pocket pistol, the Guardian, with a caliber of 7.65 mm (.32 ACP).

NAA BLACK WIDOW/MINI-MASTER

The Black Widow is derived from the mini revolver of North American Arms. This is a single-action weapon made of stainless steel with a 5-shot cylinder in the calibers .22 LR or .22 WMR. A replacement cylinder in .22 LR can be ordered for the .22 WMR revolver. The total length is 149 mm (6 in) and the barrel length is 51 mm (2 in). The height and width are 92 and 22 mm (3½ and 1 in) respectively. The weight of this small weapon is 250 g (8¾ oz). The Black Widow has a fixed rear sight and an interchangeable front sight. The barrel has a raised and ventilated barrel rib. This weapon has a rubber grip.

A variant of the Black Widow is the Mini-Master. This is almost the same weapon, but with a longer 102 mm (4 in) barrel

Trade mark of North American Arms

Guardian promotional photograph

Both revolvers with changeable cylinder shown are .22 LR caliber

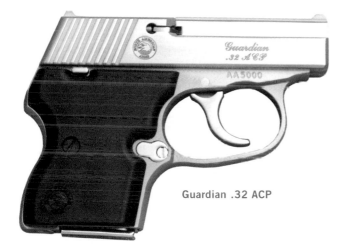

Guardian .32 ACP

and an adjustable rear sight. The total length of the Mini-Master is 200 mm (8 in) and it weighs 303 g (10¾ oz). The height and width are the same as that of the Black Widow. The Mini-Master is also available in the calibers .22 LR or .22 WMR, and with an optional replacement cylinder in .22 LR.

NAA GUARDIAN

In 1998, North American Arms brought the small Guardian back-up pistol with a caliber of 7.65 m (.32 ACP) onto the market. This double-action-only weapon is manufactured totally from stainless steel. The total length of the Guardian is exceedingly small at 110.7 mm (4¼ in). The barrel length is only 55.5 mm (2¼ in). The height of this weapon is 82 mm (3¼ in) and the width is 22 mm (¾ in). The magazine capacity is 6 rounds. The Guardian weighs 387 g (13½ oz) unloaded and it weighs 420 g (14¾ oz) when loaded with 6 rounds. This is one of the smallest pocket pistols

ever manufactured, certainly in this caliber. The Guardian does not have safeties and has only two operating elements. These are the magazine release on the left-hand side of the frame, behind the trigger guard and the takedown lever on the right-hand side of the frame. The trigger pressure, being very high, approximately 5.5 kg (12 lb), is in fact the only form of safety. The Guardian .32 has a fixed rear sight.

In 2001, North American Arms announced a new version of the Guardian .380 in the caliber 9 mm Short (.380 ACP). This 6-shot pistol is only a fraction larger then the .32 Guardian and also has a double-action-only trigger action. The total length of the Guardian .380 is 120.7 mm (4¾ in) and the barrel length is 63 mm (2½ in). The height and width are 89.7 and 23.6 mm (3½ and 1 in) respectively. This weapon weighs 590 g (20¾ oz) when loaded and 530 g (18¾ oz) when empty. The trigger pressure is approximately 4.6 kg (10 lb). Below is an illustration of the prototype that was exhibited at the German IWA in 2001.

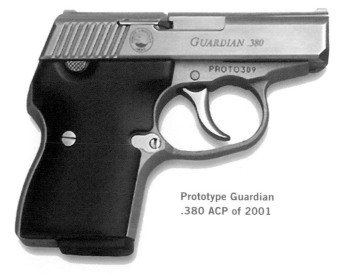

Prototype Guardian
.380 ACP of 2001

Mini revolver in
.22 LR

NAA Mini 22

This mini revolver from North American Arms can be supplied with the calibers of .22 Short, .22 LR and in .22 WMR, with a replacement cylinder for .22 LR. This 5-shot single-action stainless steel weapon has a barrel length of 28.6 or 41.3 mm (1¼ or 1¾ in). The total length of the .22 WMR Mini-Magnum version is 120.7 or 133.4 mm (4¾ or 5¼ in) and it weighs 167 or 158 g (6 or 6¼ oz). The width and height dimensions are 22.2 and 73 mm (1 and 3 in). The Mini-Long Rifle version has a total length of 102 or 114 mm (4 or 4½ in). The weight is 127.6 or 130.4 g (4.5 or 4½ oz). The height is 60.3 mm (2½ in) and the width is 20.6 mm (¾ in). The Mini-22 Short barrel is only a 28.6 mm (1¼ in), has a total length of 92 mm (3½ in) and it weighs 113.4 g (4 oz).

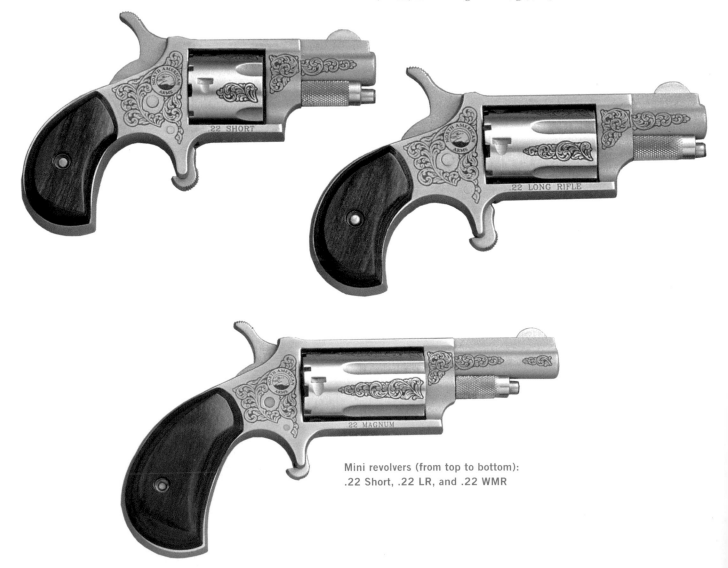

Mini revolvers (from top to bottom):
.22 Short, .22 LR, and .22 WMR

P

Trade mark of Para-Ordnance of Canada

Small P6.45 LDA double-action pistol

The 6-shot double-action P6.45 LLDA as ideal back-up pistol

PARA-ORDNANCE

Para-Ordnance from Ontario, Canada has manufactured special versions of the Colt model 1911-A1 pistol since 1988. In 1988, this company introduced a 12-shot 1911-A1 pistol with a caliber of .45 ACP and in 1990, a 1911-A1 pistol with a magazine capacity of 14 rounds. In addition, all manner of technical novelties were built-in into these pistols, such as automatic firing pin safety, a triple dot aspect sight and a 'combat style' trigger guard and hammer. The Para-Ordnance has also developed a special feed ramp on the barrel that ensures reliable loading even of lead bullets. The company has developed special grips that have made this weapon narrower, even when a double rowed magazine is used. The guidance of the slide over the frame is via two long guide rails, unlike the original Colt 1911-A1 design. There are five basic types of the Para-Ordnance. The very compact P10 has a capacity of 10 rounds with a caliber of .45 ACP and the P12, a semi-compact pistol for 12 rounds. The P13, is a slightly longer version with a 13-shot magazine and the P14 can take 14 rounds in this caliber. Finally, Para-Ordnance manufactures the P16, a 16-shot 1911-A1 pistol in the caliber .40 S&W and 18 rounds in the caliber 9 mm Para. In 1989, Para-Ordnance developed a special conversion set for the Colt model 1911 and related pistols. This set consists of a steel frame with matching magazine, allowing the magazine capacity of a .45 ACP Colt pistol to be increased to 15 rounds. The Para-Ordnance a good choice for pistol shooters that prefer a Model 1911-A1 pistol with a large magazine capacity and would like to develop such a weapon in to a concourse pistol. The finish of these weapons is of a high standard, especially considering the price. In 2001, Para-Ordnance introduced a variety of double-action versions of the existing models, the compact 6-shot 6.45 LDA pistol and the 6.45 LLDA with a double-action trigger action. Para-Ordnance used exclusively match barrels for this new series. These barrels have a polished feed ramp for a trouble free loading of cartridges with all manner of bullets. In addition, the ejection port is in the slide, and is lowered and beveled. The grip safety has a beavertail, with the Limited models even having an extended beavertail. Both the slide catch and the safety catch are extended. All models are equipped with an automatic firing pin safety. The LDA Limited, P-series Limited and the new P series of 2001 have a long recoil spring locking bar.

PARA-ORDNANCE P6.45 LDA/LLDA

In the year 2000 Para-Ordnance introduced the new compact model 6.45 LDA Undercover Lightning. This small pistol has a single row magazine for

6 rounds in the caliber .45 ACP. This weapon has a double-action LDA trigger action. LDA stands for Lightning Double-Action. In 2001, this weapon was given the new low rear combat sight. In addition, the safety catch of the new 2001 model is ambidextrous. This weapon also has automatic firing pin safety and beavertail grip safety. The grips are made of palisander. The ejector port is in the slide and is lowered and beveled. The total length of this stainless steel pistol is 165 mm (6½ in). The match barrel has a length of 76 mm (3 in) and the height of this weapon is 127 mm (5 in). The weight is 907 g (32 oz). In 2001 a second type, Model 6.45 LLDA, also appeared on the market. This double-action pistol also has the new combat rear sight and an ambidextrous safety catch. This weapon also has automatic firing pin safety. In order to keep this weapon as short as possible the grip safety does not have a beavertail. The magazine capacity is 6 rounds in the caliber .45 ACP. The dimensions of the 6.45 LLDA are the same as that of the 6.45 LDA. This pistol is only available in stainless steel.

PARA-ORDNANCE P7.45 LDA/LDA LIMITED

The Model 7.45 LDA originates from 2000 and is a large 1911-A1 pistol with a single-stack, or a single row magazine for 7 rounds in .45 ACP. The LDA model has a double-action trigger. This weapon has a safety catch on the left-hand side of the frame. The grip safety has been developed into an extra long beavertail. This weapon also has automatic firing pin safety. The ejector port in the slide is lowered and beveled. The total length is 216 mm (8½ in) and the barrel length is 127 mm (5 in). The height of this pistol is 146 mm (5¾ in) and this weapon weighs 1106 g (39 oz). This weapon is available in steel or stainless steel. The 7.45 LDA Limited of 2001 is almost the same pistol, however this weapon has adjustable micrometer sights and an ambidextrous safety catch. The dimensions are the same as the normal model, but the weight is 1134 g (40 oz).

PARA-ORDNANCE P10.9

The new P10.9 pistol, was introduced in 2001, and is a particularly compact weapon with a magazine capacity of 10 rounds with a caliber of 9 mm Para. This weapon has a single-action trigger and is only available with an alloy frame and a steel slide. It has an extended safety catch on the left-hand side of the frame, a beavertail grip safety and automatic firing pin safety. The new Para-Ordnance combat rear sight is located on the slide. In addition, the ejector port is lowered and beveled. The total length is 165 mm (6½ in), the barrel length is 76 mm (3 in) and it weighs 680 g (24 oz).

PARA-ORDNANCE P10.40

The new Para-Ordnance P10.40 pistol with a caliber of .40 S&W also originated in 2001. The single-action weapon has a magazine capacity of 10 rounds. This compact weapon with the new combat rear sight comes from the same series as the Model P10.9. This weapon has an extended safety catch on the left-hand side of the frame. The grip safety is developed in to a beavertail. This pistol also has automatic firing pin safety.

Slim double-action P7.45 LDA pistol

P7.45 LDA Limited with micrometer sights

The 10-shot mini pistol P10.9

P10.40 in .40 S&W caliber

The ejector port in the slide is lowered and beveled. The length of the match barrel with a polished feed ramp is 76 mm (3 in). The total length is 165 mm (6½ in) and the height is 114 mm (4½ in). This pistol has an alloy frame, a steel slide and it weighs 680 g (24 oz).

PARA-ORDNANCE P10.45/ P10.45 LIMITED

Model P10.45 is a compact pistol and was introduced In the year 2000. This 10-shot single-action weapon with a caliber of .45 ACP is available in stainless steel, blued carbon steel or with an alloy frame. A slightly modified model followed in 2001 with a low combat rear sight and grip safety with an extended beavertail. Both models are illustrated. This weapon also has an extended safety catch and an extended slide catch on the left-hand side of the frame. The magazine release is also on the left-hand side, behind the trigger guard. This pistol has a total length of 165 mm (6½ in), a barrel length of 76 mm (3 in) and a height of 114 mm (4½ in). The weight of this pistol in steel or stainless steel is 879 g (31 oz). A two-tone version with a stainless steel frame and a blued steel slide is also available. The version with an alloy frame weighs 680 g (24 oz).

The P10.45 Limited single-action pistol was also launched in 2001. The 10-shot weapon is available in the .45 ACP caliber. The Limited is totally factory tuned. This pistol has an ambidextrous extended safety catch on the frame. The slide catch is also extended. In addition, the trigger has an adjustable trigger stop. The grip safety is extended into a beavertail. This pistol has a blued steel version, stainless steel versions, and a model with an alloy frame. The total length of this weapon is 165 mm (6½ in). The length of the special match barrel is 76 mm (3 in). The height is 114 mm (4½ in). The steel or stainless steel model weighs 880 g (31 oz) and the version with the alloy frame weighs 680 g (24 oz).

P10.45 pistol in .45 ACP caliber

New 2001 version of P10.45 pistol

P10.45 pistol duo-tone

P10.45 pistol in stainless steel

New stainless steel P10.45 pistol of 2001

P10.45 Limited with double-side safety catch of 2001

P10.45 Limited in stainless steel

PARA-ORDNANCE P12.45/LIMITED

The semi-compact Para-Ordnance P12.45 pistol has been around since 1990, but was provided with a number of new features in 2001. The most distinctive is the renewed rear combat sight. The front sight is no longer built-in to the slide, as was the case with older models, but is now contained within a swallowtail seating. In addition, the safety catch has been enlarged, and the recoil spring locking bar extended. The 2001-model of the P12.45 pistol also has a combat hammer, and a match barrel with a polished feed ramp. As well as the safety catch, this pistol has an extended grip safety and an automatic firing pin safety. In addition, the ejector port in the slide is lowered and beveled. The P12.45 single-action pistol is in the caliber .45 ACP and has a magazine capacity of 12 rounds. A choice can be made from blued steel, stainless steel or an alloy frame. A two-tone version with a stainless steel frame and a blued steel slide is also available. The total length is 181 mm (7¼ in) and the barrel length is 89 mm (3½ in). Both steel versions weigh 964 g (34 oz) and the alloy version weighs 737 g (26 oz). The height of this pistol is 127 mm (5 in).

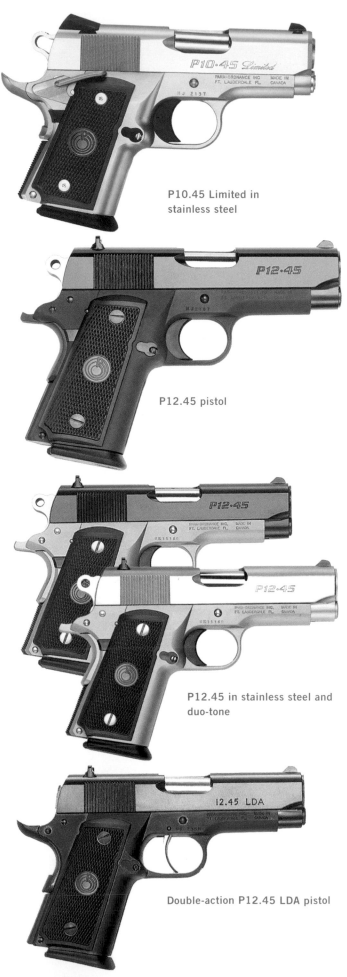

P12.45 pistol

P12.45 in stainless steel and duo-tone

Double-action P12.45 LDA pistol

P12.45 Limited of 2001

The P12.45 Limited pistol has, as well as the distinguishing features of the standard P12.45, a number of extra features. This weapon has an extended beavertail, an ambidextrous safety catch and an adjustable trigger stop. The dimensions and weights are identical to that of the standard P12.45 model.

PARA-ORDNANCE P12.45 LDA

Model P12.45 LDA is a double-action version of the standard P12.45 pistol. This medium-sized weapon also has a magazine capacity of 12 rounds in .45 ACP caliber. This weapon is available in steel and stainless steel versions, with an extended safety catch on the left-hand side of the frame. The grip safety is developed into an extra long beavertail. The ejector port in the slide is lowered and beveled. The hammer does not have a hammer spur. The total length of the P12.45 LDA is 181 mm (7¼ in). The match barrel has a length of 89 mm (3½ in) and the height of this pistol is 127 mm (5 in). The weight is 964 g (34 oz).

PARA-ORDNANCE P13.45/LIMITED

Model P13.45 is a medium-sized single-action pistol with a magazine capacity of 13 rounds in .45 ACP caliber. The old model of 1991 has retained the typical Colt rear sight. The new series of 2001 has a special low rear combat sight. The total length of this weapon is 197 mm (7¾ in) and the match barrel has a length of 108 mm (4¼ in). This pistol is available in blued steel, in stainless steel or with an alloy frame. The weight of both steel versions is 1021 g (36 oz) and the alloy version weighs 794 g (28 oz). The height of this weapon is 133 mm (5¼ in).

P12.45 LDA in stainless steel

P13.45 13-shot pistol for .45 ACP caliber in blued and duo-tone finishes

The P13.45 also has extended grip safety, an extended safety catch and built-in automatic firing pin safety. The P13.45-2001 has a long recoil spring locking bar. The ejector port is also lowered and beveled.

The P13.45 Limited is the match version of the standard model. This pistol has adjustable micrometer sights and a grip safety with an extended beavertail. In addition, the front flanks of the slide have been provided with extra pressure grooves. This pistol has an extended safety catch on

P13.45 Limited pistol with micrometer sights

P13.45 Limited in stainless steel

Double-action P14.40 LDA

P14.40 LDA in
stainless steel

P14.45 14-shot
pistol in .45 ACP
caliber

P14.45 in stainless steel

both sides of the frame, and a built-in automatic firing pin safety. The trigger has an adjustable trigger stop. This model has the familiar match barrel and the ejector port in the slide is lowered and beveled. This model is equipped with a competition hammer. The dimensions of this Limited pistol are the same as that of the standard model, and are also available in a steel or stainless steel version with an alloy frame.

PARA-ORDNANCE P14.40 LDA

Para-Ordnance introduced the P14.40 LDA pistol in 1999. This is a medium-sized double-action weapon without a hammer spur on the hammer. This weapon has a magazine capacity of 14 rounds in the caliber .40 S&W. The extended safety catch is located on the left-hand side of the frame. The grip safety has an extended beavertail, and, as with all recent Para-Ordnance pistols, automatic firing pin safety. The P14.40 LDA is available in a blued steel or in a stainless steel version. The total length of this pistol is 181 mm (7¼ in). The barrel has a length of 89 mm (3½ in) and the height is 127 mm (5 in). This weapon weighs 964 g (34 oz).

PARA-ORDNANCE P14.45/LIMITED

The P14.45 is a large single-action pistol. This weapon is only available in the .45 ACP caliber and has a magazine capacity of 14 rounds. The older model, shown in the illustration, has a rear sight in Colt-style. The new model that was introduced in 2001, has a low, rounded rear combat sight. The P14.45 has a total length of 216 mm (8½ in) and a barrel length of 127 mm (5 in). This weapon also has versions in steel, stainless steel or with an alloy frame. The weight of the steel versions is 1134 g (40 oz) and the alloy version weighs 879 g (31 oz). The height of the P14.45 is 146 mm (5¾ in). The new 2001 type has the extras, the beavertail extended grip safety, an extended safety catch and the enlarged and beveled ejector port. This pistol of course also has automatic firing pin safety and an extended recoil spring locking bar.

Just as with the P13.45 Limited this pistol also has a match version. This weapon has an adjustable micrometer sight, an ambidextrous extended safety catch and an extended beavertail. This pistol also has a special competition hammer and a trigger stop. The front of the slide flanks are provided with extra pressure grooves. In addition, this weapon has all the distinguishing features and the same dimensions as the standard P14.45. This pistol is available in blued steel and in stainless steel.

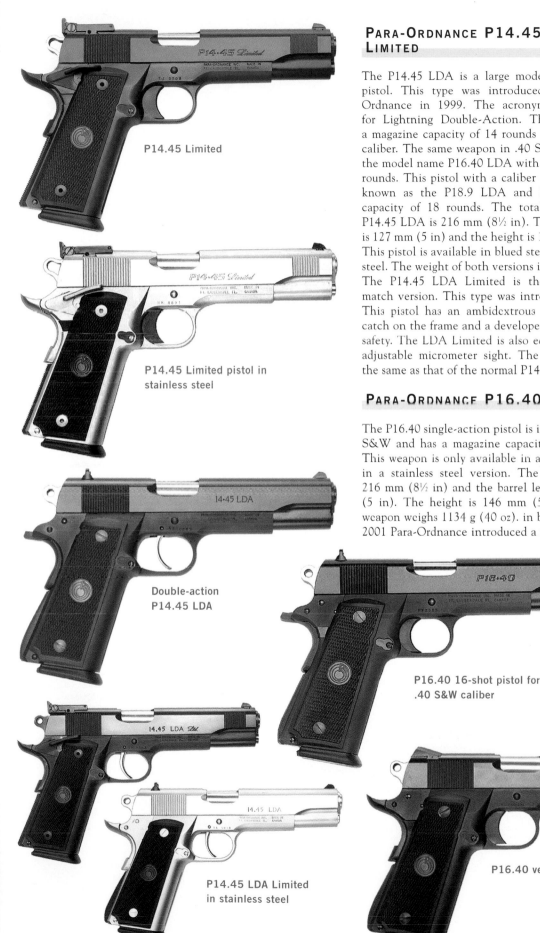

P14.45 Limited

P14.45 Limited pistol in
stainless steel

Double-action
P14.45 LDA

P14.45 LDA Limited
in stainless steel

P16.40 16-shot pistol for
.40 S&W caliber

P16.40 version of 2001

PARA-ORDNANCE P14.45 LDA/LDA LIMITED

The P14.45 LDA is a large model double-action pistol. This type was introduced by the Para-Ordnance in 1999. The acronym 'LDA' stands for Lightning Double-Action. This weapon has a magazine capacity of 14 rounds in the .45 ACP caliber. The same weapon in .40 S&W caliber has the model name P16.40 LDA with a capacity of 16 rounds. This pistol with a caliber of 9 mm Para is known as the P18.9 LDA and has a magazine capacity of 18 rounds. The total length of the P14.45 LDA is 216 mm (8½ in). The barrel length is 127 mm (5 in) and the height is 146 mm (5¾ in). This pistol is available in blued steel or in stainless steel. The weight of both versions is 1134 g (40 oz). The P14.45 LDA Limited is the double-action match version. This type was introduced in 2001. This pistol has an ambidextrous extended safety catch on the frame and a developed beavertail grip safety. The LDA Limited is also equipped with an adjustable micrometer sight. The dimensions are the same as that of the normal P14.45 LDA.

PARA-ORDNANCE P16.40/LIMITED

The P16.40 single-action pistol is in the caliber .40 S&W and has a magazine capacity of 16 rounds. This weapon is only available in a blued steel and in a stainless steel version. The total length is 216 mm (8½ in) and the barrel length is 127 mm (5 in). The height is 146 mm (5¾ in) and this weapon weighs 1134 g (40 oz). in both versions. In 2001 Para-Ordnance introduced a renewed version with a low rear combat sight and an extended beavertail. The P16.40 Limited came onto the market in 1998. This weapon has an ambidextrous extended safety catch and a micrometer sight.

P16.40 Limited

PARA-ORDNANCE P16.40 LDA/LIMITED

The double-action P16.40 pistol is a large format pistol with a capacity of 16 rounds with a caliber of .40 S&W. In addition, this pistol has an extended safety catch on the left-hand side of the frame and an extended grip safety. The total length of this weapon is 216 mm (8½ in), the barrel length is 127 mm (5 in) and the height is 146 mm (5¾ in). This pistol is available in steel or stainless steel versions and it weighs 1134 g (40 oz). Model P16.40 LDA Limited is the luxury version with the ambidextrous safety catch and the micrometer sight. The dimensions and the weight are the same as that of the P16.40 Limited.

Double-action P16.40 LDA pistol

P16.40 LDA Limited

P18.9 18-shot pistol in 9 mm Para caliber

Stainless steel P18.9 Limited

PARA-ORDNANCE P18.9

The single-action P18.9 pistol is a special match version in the caliber 9 mm Para with a magazine capacity of 18 rounds. This large weapon model was launched in 1994, and only available in stainless steel. This pistol has an adjustable micrometer sight as standard. The total length is 216 mm (8½ in), the barrel length is 127 mm (5 in), the height is 146 mm (5¾ in) and this weapon weighs 1134 g (40 oz).

PARA-ORDNANCE P18.9 LDA/LDA LIMITED

Para-Ordnance introduced a renewed model of the P18.9 LDA in 2001. This is a double-action pistol with a capacity of 18 rounds in 9 mm Para caliber. This weapon is available in a blued or stainless steel version. This weapon has an extended safety catch on the left-hand side of the frame and a beavertail grip safety. In addition, it has built-in automatic firing pin safety. The P18.9 LDA Limited has an ambidextrous safety catch and a micrometer sight. The front of the slide on both flanks is also provided with extra pressure grooves. The total length of both LDA versions is 216 mm (8½ in). The match barrel has a length of 127 mm (5 in) and the height is 146 mm (5¾ in). The weight of the P18.9 LDA and LDA Limited is the same at 1134 g (40 oz).

Double-action P18.9 LDA and P18.9 LDA Limited

PARDINI

Trade mark of Pardini Armi

The Pardini sport pistols originated in 1978. The brand name is connected with the Italian sport shooter Giamiero Pardini. As well as being a match shooter, Pardini is also a gunsmith. This brand was part of the Italguns International group until 1984. Since 1984, Pardini became part of Fiocchi, who were mainly known as a manufacturer of ammunition. In 1992, Pardini decided to found his own company known as Pardini Armi, based in Lido di Camaiore.

PARDINI K22 FREE PISTOL

The single shot Pardini K22 pistol is in the caliber .22 LR and is used for the Free Pistol 50 meters shooting discipline. This weapon is derived from the older

Model K50 of 1980. The K22 has a rotating bolt. In order to load this weapon the unlocking button in front of the rotating bolt must first be depressed. The striking bolt can then be pulled upwards, applying the pressure to the firing pin. After the introduction of the cartridge the half cock lever, a sort of trigger, on the left-hand side of the frame is depressed. The pistol is then ready for firing. Every conceivable adjustment can be made to the trigger mechanism, allowing it to be moved and rotated horizontally. The trigger pressure and the trigger pull can also be set separately. A bar has been attached above the barrel for balance weights. This pistol has a walnut grip with a special cut-out for the shooting hand. The total length of the K22 is 460 mm (18 in) and the barrel length is 300 mm (11¼ in) with a right-hand twist of 450 mm (17¼ in). The height of this weapon is 145 mm (5¼ in) and the maximum width is 80 mm (3¼ in). This pistol has a micrometer sight with a sight radius of 420 mm (16½ in). The weight is 1100 g (38¼ oz).

PARDINI PC

Giampiero Pardini and his colleague Carlo Cechri developed the single-action Pardini PC pistol in 1993. They make three types of pistol based on this model for a variety of shooting disciplines. The basic PC model can be used for both the 'military pistol' class (defense pistol) and for the 'Stock' class. This weapon was used successfully by a number of match teams in the Police World Games. Model PCS Open has a three chamber compensator and has as standard a number of holes tapped in the frame for the

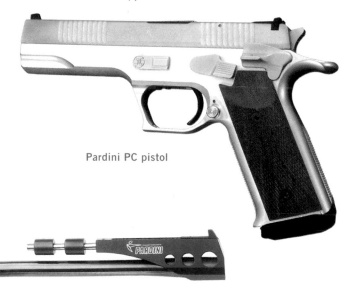

Pardini PC pistol

Pardini K22 Free Pistol

type in two calibers. The .36 caliber has a barrel with grooves and lands and a rifling twist of 380 mm (15 in). The barrel of this weapon with a caliber of .45 has twelve grooves and lands with a rifling twist of 450 mm (17¼ in). Both versions have a total length of 420 mm (16½ in), a barrel length of 280 mm (11 in) and it weighs 1200 g (42¼ oz).

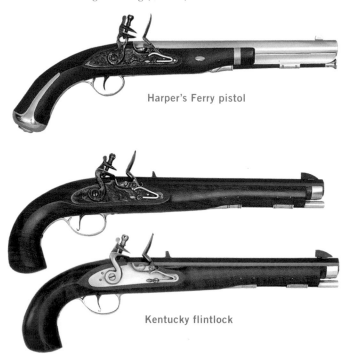

Harper's Ferry pistol

Kentucky flintlock

HARPER'S FERRY

The Harper's Ferry flintlock-action pistol was the first weapon to be purchased by the US government for their navy. The name of this weapon is derived from the place where this firearms factory was based at. This arsenal was destroyed during the Civil War. This pistol is .58 caliber. The barrel has seven grooves and lands with a rifling twist of 1200 mm (47¼ in). The barrel length is 255 mm (10 in). The total length is 410 mm (16 in) and it weighs 1100 g (38¼ oz).

KENTUCKY PISTOOL

The Kentucky pistols date from the end of the eighteenth century. They played a part in both the colonization of America, and the War of Independence. The flintlock-action pistol manufactured by Pedersoli is based on the original model of 1780. This pistol is available with the calibers of .45 and .50. Both have barrels with 12 grooves and lands with a rifling twist of 450 mm (17¼ in). The barrel length is 262 mm (10½ in) and the total length is 390 mm (15¼ in). The weight is approximately 1000 g (35¾ oz).

Engraved percussion locking Kentucky
and Kentucky Bounty Hunter

The percussion-version dates from 1850. The dimensions are the same as that of the flintlock-action pistol. The Kentucky Bounty has a longer barrel for shooting over greate distances. According to tradition, this pistol was much loved by the Bounty Hunters. In those days, if a criminal was convicted in his absence, a price was put on his head: 'Wanted dead of alive'. A bounty hunter hunted down such criminals, in order to claim the reward. The Pedersoli Bounty Hunter is in .45 caliber. The barrel has 12 grooves and lands with a rifling twist of 450 mm (17¼ in). The barrel length is 420 mm (16½ in) and the total length is 540 mm (21¼ in). The weight is 1350 g (47½ oz).

KUCHENREUTER

Bartholomeus Joseph Kuchenreuter, a gunsmith, lived from 1782 to 1864 in Steinweg, a small village in the Regensburg area of Germany. He was the son of Joseph II Kuchenreuter. The whole family were known as excellent weapon manufacturers and good shooters. In that time the Kuchenreiter was a popular pistol because of both its high quality and accuracy. The original Kuchenreuter pistol originates from 1854. Pedersoli manufactures an accurate replica of this model. The browned barrel carries the original silver inscription 'Barth. Jos. Kuchenreuter'. In 1998, at Warwick in England, a Kuchenreuter replica pistol won a gold medal in the world championships in the 'Kuchenreuter-class'. This pistol is available in three calibers. The Large-caliber .38 with a barrel with seven grooves and lands and a rifling twist of 380 mm (15 in). In

Kuckenreuter pistols

.40 caliber the barrel has 8 grooves and lands with a rifling twist of 406 mm (16 in). The .44 caliber has a barrel with 7 grooves and lands and a rifling twist of 450 mm (17¾ in). The barrel length in this caliber is 285 mm (11¼ in). The total length is 430 mm (16 in) and it weighs approximately 1200 g (42¼ oz). The jubilee model shown below, is a year 2000 limited edition. It is inlaid with gold and engraved by the Italian master engraver Sanzogni Renato.

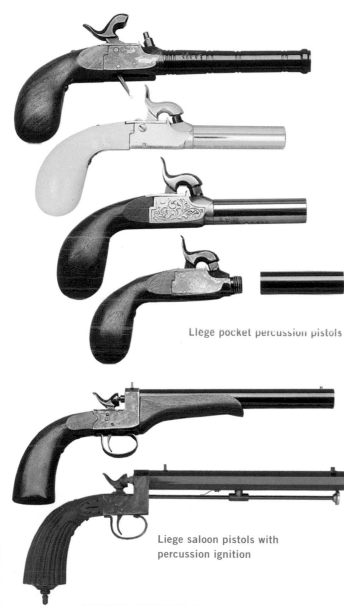

Liege pocket percussion pistols

Liege saloon pistols with percussion ignition

LIEGE PISTOLS

These Belgian pocket pistols were manufactured in and around the city of Liege throughout the whole of the eighteenth century. Liege was then a famous center of the weapon industry and still is. Many gunsmiths from that period manufactured small pocket pistols. Famous names included Boutet and Le

Page. This weapon was intended as a pocket or small traveling pistol for personal protection. An interesting feature is the detachable barrel that can be unscrewed and loaded from the rear. This sort of small pistol is often engraved. After cocking the hammer a retractable trigger is released from the underside of the frame. The Liege replica of Pedersoli is in the caliber .44. The barrel has 8 grooves and lands with a rifling twist of 450 mm (17¾ in). The barrel length is 60 mm (2¼ in) and the total length is 165 mm (6½ in). The weight is approximately 200 g (7 oz).

LIEGE SALON PISTOLS

Liege was also known in the eighteenth century for their salon pistols. Society gentlemen took great pleasure in informal after-dinner shooting matches. A variety of Liege gunsmiths manufactured simple black powder percussion pistols just for this purpose. The barrel of both Pedersoli replicas is in the caliber .36 with 7 grooves and lands and a rifling twist of 380 mm (15 in). The barrel length is 205 mm (8 in) and the total length is 320 mm (12½ in). The weight is approximately 800 g (28¼ oz).

MANG

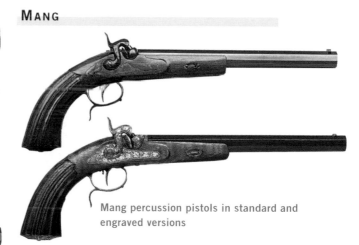

Mang percussion pistols in standard and engraved versions

The Austrian gunsmith Martin Mang manufactured this type of percussion pistol between 1850-1855. In that time he manufactured both disk pistols and dueling weapons. This engraved replica is an accurate copy of the original Mang pistol. On the top of the barrel is the original master's mark of Mang, together with his name in a gold inscription. The Pedersoli replica is available in two calibers. The .38 caliber has a barrel with 7 grooves and lands with a rifling twist of 380 mm (15 in). The barrel in .44 caliber also has 7 grooves and lands, but with a rifling twist of 450 mm (17¾ in). The barrel length is 290 mm (11 in) and the total length is 430 mm (17 in). The weight is 1160 g (41 oz).

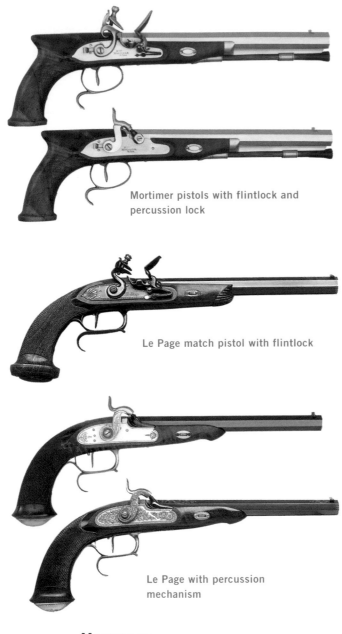

Mortimer pistols with flintlock and
percussion lock

Le Page match pistol with flintlock

Le Page with percussion
mechanism

MORTIMER

The weapon production of the Mortimer family of London spanned the period from 1753 until 1923. This English firearms dynasty manufactured amongst other things, army rifles and a large variety of dueling and hunting weapons. The most famous gunsmith in this family was H.W. Mortimer. Mortimer pistols have the typically shaped saw-grip. The Pedersoli replicas of this model are especially suitable for the black powder shooting disciplines Cominazzo and Kuchenreuter. The model is available in three different calibers. The pistol with the flintlock with a caliber of .44 has a smooth barrel. The percussion pistol in .36 caliber has a barrel with 7 grooves and lands with a rifling twist of 380 mm (15 in). The

barrel in .45 caliber has 12 grooves and lands with a rifling twist of 450 mm (17¾ in). The barrel length in all versions is 255 mm (10 in). The total length is 390 mm (15¼ in) and it weighs 930 g (32¼ oz).

LE PAGE

Le Page was a well known name in the field of firearms in the eighteenth and nineteenth century. The family had firearms work shops in Paris and Liege in Belgium. Bastin Le Page was even the royal gunsmith for the French king Louis XVI. In 1832, he received the patent for the pin fire cartridge that he had developed and in 1837 on a rimfire cartridge. The Pedersoli replica of the Le Page flintlock pistol has had great success in international competitions, winning the. Gold and silver medals in the Cominazzo shooting discipline during the world championships in 1996 and 1998. The flintlock-action pistol has a smooth barrel in .45 caliber or an extended barrel with a caliber of .44 with a rifling twist of 450 mm (17¾ in). The barrel length is 260 mm (10¼ in) and the total length is 435 mm (17 in). The weight is 1100 g (38¼ oz). The percussion model is an accurate replica of the Le Page pistol of 1840. This type is available in a four calibers. The barrels with the calibers of .31 and .38 have 7 grooves and lands with a rifling twist of 380 mm (15 in). With calibers of .36 and .44 the barrels have 7 grooves and lands, but the rifling twist is 450 mm (17¾ in). This weapon with a caliber of .31 has a barrel length of 250 mm (10 in), a total length of 425 mm (16¼ in) and it weighs 1100 g (38¾ oz). The other calibers have a barrel length of 260 mm (10¼ in), a total length of 435 mm (17 in) and it weighs approximately 1150 g (40½ oz).

Replica Queen Anne flintlock
pistols

QUEEN ANNE PISTOLS

The Queen Anne flintlock-action pistol from Pedersoli is an exact replica of the well-known English pistol, and dates from the end of the 1600s up to the start of the 1700s. During the reign of Queen Anne it was issued as an army and navy pistol. The models illustrated brass barrels, but this weapon is also available with a silver plated or plain steel barrel. This weapon has a smooth barrel in .50 caliber. The barrel length is 192 mm (7½ in) and the total length is 335 mm (13¼ in). This weapon weighs 1000 g (35¼ oz).

REMINGTON ARMY 1858

Pedersoli replica of
Remington Army 1858

Remington produced approximately 132.000 weapons of the Model 1858 Army between 1863 and 1873. This revolver has an octagonal barrel. The Model 1858 Navy is manufactured in .36 caliber. This weapon was highly valued by soldiers in the Civil War because of its strong closed frame. The replica of the Pedersoli has the original .44 army caliber and is highly suitable for the Mariette shooting discipline. The barrel of the Remington has 7 grooves and lands with a rifling twist of 450 mm (17¾ in). The barrel length is 200 mm (8 in) and the total length is 350 mm (13¼ in). This revolver weighs 1200 g (42¼ oz).

RODGERS & SPENCER ARMY 1865

Rodgers & Spencer of Utica, New York manufactured this Army revolver between 1863 and 1865. The model name of this weapon is derived from an army order of 1865 for 5000 weapons. In total approximately 5800 of these revolvers were produced. Pedersoli manufactures a replica, all parts

Rodgers & Spencer
Army 1865 replica

of which are manufactured by CNC computerized machines. The barrel in .22 caliber has 6 grooves and lands with a rifling twist of 450 mm (17¾ in). The barrel length is 190 mm (7½ in) and the total length is 340 mm (13¼ in). This revolver weighs approximately 1400 g (49½ oz).

PETERS STAHL

Peters Stahl logo

Franz Josef Peters was born and raised in Paderborn, German. Peters learned the trade with the German air force, and after finishing his term of service, returned to Paderborn and founded the Peters Stahl company. Until the start of 1982 the factory specialized in heavy machine parts and therefore had nothing at all to do with weapons. Peters' hobby was responsible for the about-turn to the weapon industry. His wanted a .22 Long Rifle conversion set for his own Browning High Power 9 mm Para pistol, and because there was not one available, he decided to develop one himself. This was such a success that these sets were soon in demand by other shooters. This meant that production was on a modest scale at first, but because the idea had caught on, he decided to develop a similar small caliber system for a number of large caliber pistols, and quickly manufactured such conversion sets for a variety of pistol types. By the end of 1982 Peters had reached the stage where he could switch entirely to firearms production. The sets that were then being manufactured were:
– PSW I, for the Sig-Hämmerli P240 pistol;
– PSW II, for the Sig P210 pistol;
– PSW III, for the FN (Browning) High Power;
– PSW IV, for the Smith & Wesson M39 and M59 pistols;
– PSW V, for the CZ (Brünner) 75.
At the start of 1985 he had the idea to develop and manufacture a conversion set for the .45 ACP Colt pistols in 9 mm Para caliber. This led to further sets also being developed for other calibers. In 1986 a version of the 9 mm Para system was manufactured suitable for the .38 Special Wadcutter match caliber and a short time later for .38 Super caliber which was then popular in America. As then was usually the case, an extractor was fitted. Subsequently, he looked for solutions that would enable the shooting of several different calibers with

one weapon. Because of the variation in cartridge cases in the different calibers, Peters developed with the American company Springfield Armory, a slide with two extractors together. The collaboration agreement included a clause that allowed Peters Stahl to be the European representative for Springfield Armory. Springfield in turn masketed the Peters Stahl pistols in the USA. Many special models were developed during this collaboration. One of which is the Multical pistol, based on the design of the Colt Model 1911-A1 with two extractors in the slide. It is quite easy to change the caliber of this pistol. The adapter sets available have the calibers of: 9 mm Para, 9 mm Steyr, .38 Special Wadcutter, .38 Super, .45 ACP and 10 mm Auto. Peters based the frame of this pistol on a Springfield Armory weapon. This weapon was later to be renamed the 'PSP-07 Multical' pistol which was available in a variety of versions, such as a blued and stainless steel version with a 127 mm (5 in) or 152 mm (6 in) barrel, the PSP-87 pistol and the PSP-07 Combat-Sport. The Peters pistol types have a polygonal barrel and a specially patented locking system, based on the Browning-Petter/Sig system. The more recent types have tension grooves on the flanks at the front and back of the slide.

Other models manufactured by Peters are:
- Model PLS, a 1911-A1 with an extended barrel and a compensator;
- Model PSP Combat Compensator, also a 1911-A1 with a separate compensator screwed to the muzzle. This pistol can be converted with caliber adapter sets;
- Omega Match, an Omega pistol from the German stable with a 152 mm (6 in) barrel with the calibers of .45 ACP, 10 mm Auto, .38 Super and 9 mm Para;
- Omega Match II, a renewed version of the KPS-Omega with the calibers of .45 ACP, .45 HP (High Power), 10 mm Auto, .40 S&W, .38 Super, 9 mm Para and 9x21 mm;
- Omega Match .22 LR, a small caliber match pistol based on a 1911-A1.

The 1992 versions of the PSP-07 Multical pistol were fitted with American Wichita rear sights. All types of complications were then to follow within the Peters Stahl company. This resulted in Peters leaving his own business and starting a new company named Peters Präzisionstechnik, or KPS Präzisionstechnik for short. Shortly after this he set up another company by the name of Joe Peters. During his time at KPS Präzisionstechnik Peters developed his own model of pistol. This is the KPS Ultimate Match Stainless, based on the Omega pistol that had been jointly developed with Springfield Armory. The current Omega adapter sets cover a large number of caliber

Peters Stahl Hi-Cap with compensator and mounting for sights

varieties. These are .45 ACP, the bottle neck cartridge .38-.45 ACP, .400 Corbon, .40 S&W, 10 mm Auto, .38 Super Auto, 9 x 24 KC, 9 x 22 MJR, .357 Sig, 9 mm Para, 7.65 Para and 7.63 Mauser. Peters Stahl also manufactures polygonal match barrels for the Colt, Sig (P210), CZ-75, and the Beretta F92 models. In addition, he also produced polygonal match barrels for the Smith & Wesson 586/686 and the Ruger GP100 revolvers.

PETERS STAHL HC PISTOL

The single-action Peters Stahl Hi-Cap pistols have an extra wide frame for a double rowed magazine. This pistol with a caliber of .45 ACP has a capacity of 14 rounds and in 9 mm Para even 19 rounds. This model has an extended ambidextrous safety catch on the frame. Both the slide catch and the magazine release are enlarged. The grip safety is developed into an extended beavertail. The Champion version has a stainless steel frame with an enlarged magazine well and a stainless steel slide. Both the front and back flanks of the slide have pressure grooves. The polygonal barrel is manufactured from forged Krupp steel. In addition, this weapon has a long recoil spring locking bar and a special National Match barrel bushing. The adjustable micrometer sights and the interchangeable front sight are provided with white sighting points. In addition, the aluminum speed trigger has an adjustable trigger stop. This pistol has a total length of 246 mm (9¼ in) and a barrel length of 150 mm (6 in). The height is 140 mm (5½ in) and

Peters Stahl Hi-Cap Millennium pistol of 2000

Peters Hi-Cap
'Out of the Box'

Hi-Cap Champion
Titanium pistol of 2001

the sight radius is 195 mm (7¾ in). The weight of this weapon is approximately 1220 g (43 oz) and the trigger pressure is approximately 1360 g (3 lb). This weapon can also be supplied with a variety of compensators and telescopic sights as required. In 1998 Peters Stahl introduced the Hi-Cap 'Out of the Box' model, a blued version with a classic Colt bolt-action. In the year 2000, Peters Stahl introduced the Hi-Cap Millennium Titanium model with a 152 mm (6 in) barrel.

PETERS STAHL PSP 07 MULTICALIBER

The Peters Stahl PSP 07 Multicaliber pistol has been manufactured to take adapter sets in all popular calibers. To this end, this weapon has an extractor on both sides of the slide. This weapon is available in three versions: a stainless steel frame with a blued slide, a blued version and a totally stainless steel model. Unlike the later models, the older PSP 07 model does not have extra pressure grooves in the front flanks of the slide. This pistol has an extended ambidextrous safety catch, an extended slide catch and a magazine release on the left-hand side of the frame. The alloy speed trigger has an adjustable trigger stop. The grip safety is extended into a beavertail and this weapon has also a special

Blued Peters PSP 07
Sport pistol

combat hammer. This model also has micrometer sights with an interchangeable front sight in a dovetail seating in the slide. The magazine capacity of this single-action pistol is 7 rounds with a caliber of .45 ACP and 8 rounds in 9 mm Para. The total length of this weapon is 246 mm (9¾ in) and the polygonal barrel has a length of 150 mm (6 in). The height is 145 mm (5¾ in) and the sight radius is 195 mm (7¾ in). The empty weight is 1280 g (45¼ oz) and the trigger pressure is approximately 1360 g (3 lb). As of April 2001 this pistol is also manufactured in the special match caliber .38 Special WC (Wad Cutter).

Peters Stahl PSP 07
Multicaliber in duo-tone

Peters PSP 07 Sport
in stainless steel

Peters PSP 92
Multicaliber Sport

PETERS STAHL PSP 92 SPORT

The single-action PSP 92 Sport pistol is also designed as multi-caliber pistol. This weapon has an extended and ambidextrous safety catch on the frame. The slide catch and the magazine release are also extended and enlarged. The grip safety has been further extended into a beavertail. this model also has a speed trigger, an adjustable trigger stop, and special combat hammer. A beautiful finger groove has been milled in the front of the frame. Both the front and back flanks of the slide have pressure grooves. The trigger guard is square with an extra finger support for two-handed concourse shooting. The micrometer sight and the interchangeable front sight have a white triple dot aspect marking. This pistol and the adapter sets are available in all popular calibers. As of April 2001, this pistol has also been manufactured in the special match caliber .38 Special WC (Wad Cutter). The dimensions of the PSP 92 are the same as that of the PSP 07 pistol.

PETERS STAHL TROPHY MASTER

The Trophy Master was especially built as a large caliber match pistol. The single-action weapon is available as blued, stainless steel or in a combined two-tone version. As of 2001, the stainless steel Trophy Master is also available with a titanium coating. This pistol has an extended slide catch and an enlarged

magazine release on the left-hand side of the frame. An extended safety catch is on both sides of the frame. The grip safety is extended into a beavertail. The front and back flanks of the slide have pressure grooves. In addition, this weapon has a micrometer sight, a speed trigger with trigger stop and a combat hammer. The magazine capacity is 7 rounds with a caliber of .45 ACP and 8 rounds in 9 mm Para. This pistol is also available with one milled-out finger grip or with a rubber Pachmayr grip with finger grooves. The total length of this pistol is 245 mm (9½ in). The length of the polygonal barrel is 150 mm (6 in). The total height is 145 mm (5¾ in) and the sight radius is approximately 200 mm (8 in). This weapon weighs 1280 g (45¼ oz).

PETERS STAHL TWENTY-TWO

Peters Stahl introduced the .22 LR match pistol at the 2001 IWA, German firearms trade exhibition. The firing system of this special match pistol can be removed as a complete unit. The standard trigger pressure is 1000 g (2.2 lb). Incidentally, the trigger can be set in every conceivable manner. The frame and the slide are made of alloy, reducing the weight of this weapon to 1080 g (38 oz). A version with a steel

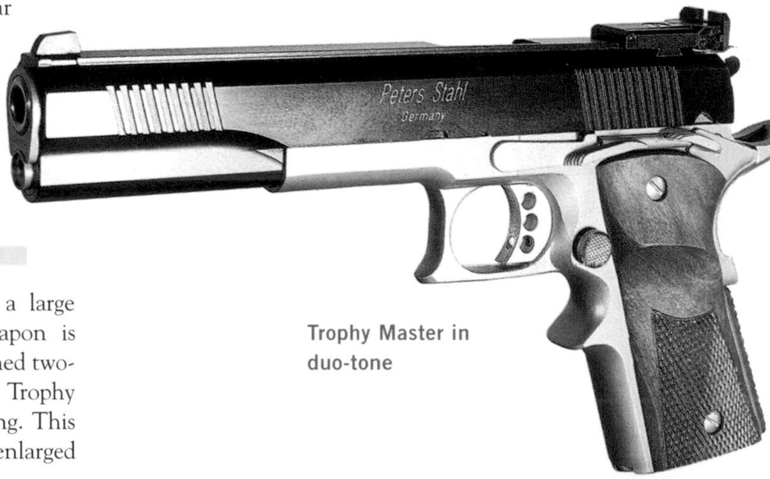

Trophy Master in
duo-tone

Trophy Master
pistol

Stainless steel Trophy
Master Titanium

New Peters Stahl .22 LR
match pistol of 2001

slide is also available and weighs 1335 g (47 oz). The micrometer sight is supplied by the Italian company Pardini. This sight can be slid along a rail to increase the sight radius. The smallest sight radius is 215 mm (8½ in). The walnut grip is manufactured for Peters Stahl by the Italian company Morini. The magazine can hold 5 rounds in the caliber .22 LR. The total length of this pistol is 275 mm (10¾ in). The total height is 149 mm (6 in). The barrel length is 140 mm (5½ in). In the near future, this weapon will also be available in other calibers and with other barrel lengths. The .22 Short and .32 S&W-Long to mention just two.

PIETTA/NAVY ARMS

Trade mark of Pietta of Italy

Italy is the foremost country for production of historic firearm replicas. The Italian companies Pietta and Uberti are market leaders in this field. Pietta was founded in 1960 and initially primarily manufactured hunting shotguns. In 1964, there was a large demand for American Civil War replicas. Pietta saw the great commercial potential, and started a production line for percussion revolvers. The first model was a replica of the Colt 1851 Navy. They then introduced the Colt 1860 Army, the Remington New Model Army 1858, the Spiller & Burr revolver and a series of Le Mat revolvers. Nowadays, Pietta has extremely modern machinery, still managing to preserve traditional working practices. The assembly, polishing and the final inspection is still carried out manually by highly skilled gunsmiths. One of the latest developments is

a comprehensive series of Colt Single-Action Army revolver models. In the North American market place, Pietta mainly deals with the American company Navy Arms Co based in Ridgefield, New Jersey. In 1957, the owner of the company, Val Forgett, founded the Service Armament Company, that specialized in the sale and distribution of superfluous weapon stocks from all over the world. This company skillfully restored old rifles from the First and Second World War for collectors and sport shooters. In his spare time, Val Forgett was an ardent black powder shooter. This led to his involvement with the North-South Skirmish Association, that studies and re-enacts battles of the American Civil War. This association uses uniforms and antique weapons for historical shooting matches. Firearms from that period were somewhat expensive. Forgett decided to have replicas made, and so he traveled to Europe and visited several Italian firearms manufacturers. In 1960, he finally made a selection of Italian firearms manufactures that wanted to manufacture his weapons. Forgett set up a separate enterprise for the import and sale of this sort of black powder replica. The first commercial success was a replica of the Colt 1851 Navy. This revolver was also responsible for the company name: Navy Arms. Navy Arms has now sold more Civil War replicas than were actually available to both armies throughout the entire Civil War.

PIETTA COLT 1836 PATERSON

This is a replica of the first cylinder revolver that was designed and manufactured by Colt. The Patent Arms Manufacturing Company in Paterson, New Jersey manufactured the Colt Paterson both with and without a loading lever between 1837 and 1838. The first model of this revolver is known as the Pocket of Baby Paterson Model 1. This weapon is manufactured

Paterson replica Colt 1836

with different barrel lengths that can vary from 44.5 up to 120.7 mm (1¾ up to 4¾ in). The standard model does not have a loading lever under the octagonal barrel. The Pocket Paterson is a 5-shot single-action percussion revolver and has a standard caliber of .28. This weapon is manufactured in a blued version. Approximately 500 of the Model 1 were manufactured. The second model Paterson, known as the Colt Belt Model Paterson No. 2 was manufactured from 1837 until 1840. There were probably no more than 850 weapons produced. This revolver in .31 caliber, has a 5-shot cylinder and does not have a loading lever. The barrel length varies from 63.5 up to 139.7 mm (2½ up to 5½ in). The Belt Model Paterson No. 3 is also in .31 caliber and was manufactured in the same period as the No. 2. This type has barrel lengths of 88.9 up to 139.7 mm (3½ up to 5½ in). The majority of these weapons are provided with a continuous bottom grip, and do not have a loading lever. In total there were about 2500 weapons manufactured from the Paterson series range, until the company went bankrupt in 1843. Related models are the Texas Paterson with a caliber of .36 and the Holster model with a caliber of .36 manufactured between 1836 and 1841. All Paterson models are without a trigger guard, but have a retractable trigger. As soon as the hammer is cocked with the thumb, the cylinder rotates and the trigger drops out of the frame. The barrel length of the Colt Paterson revolver models range from 44.5 up to 304.8 mm (1¾ up to 12 in). The total lengths therefore vary considerably, from 144.5 up to 406 mm (5¾ up to 16 in). The weight varies dependent on the barrel length, from 255–1700 g (9–60 oz). The Pietta Colt Paterson has the original caliber of .36. The octagonal barrel has a length of 229 mm (9 in) and the total length is 349 mm (13¾ in). This weapon weighs 1220 g (43 oz).

PIETTA COLT 1851 NAVY

This Pietta percussion revolver is a replica of the Colt 1851 Navy. Approximately 215,000 of the

Colt Model 1851 Navy revolver by Pietta

Colt Model 1851 Old Model Navy

original model were produced between 1850 and 1873. The London Colt factory also manufactured a further 42,000 weapons. This is a 6-shot single-action percussion revolver in the caliber .36. The octagonal barrel has a length of 190.5 mm (7½ in). A loading lever is located under the barrel. The total length is 330 mm (13 in) and this weapon weighs 1200 g (42¼ oz). The cylinder is engraved with the Mexico and Texas sea battle of 1843. This would suggest that this revolver was used by the US Navy as a service weapon, however, Colt supplied most of these weapons to the army. This revolver has an octagonal barrel and a brass grip, and is manufactured in blued and blank versions. During the Civil War this model was copied by a variety of manufacturers in the Southern States: Dance Brothers, Griswold & Grier, Rigdon & Ansley and Spiller & Burr. Many copies of the Model 1851 Navy were manufactured by the Belgian gunsmiths of Liege. These revolvers have a Liege proof mark and the inscription 'Colt Breveté'. Some models carry the inscription: 'Col. Colt London' and are worth much less. The models reviewed below are a series of Navy 1851 revolver versions manufactured by Pietta:

PIETTA NAVY 1851 WITH A CALIBER OF .36:
This type is available with an octagonal barrel length of 127 or 191 mm (5 or 7½ in). The total length is 271 and 335 mm (10½ and 13¼ in) respectively. The frame is made of tempered steel and the trigger guard and the grip are made of brass. The weight is 1100 or 1200 g (38¾ or 42¼ oz).

PIETTA NAVY 1851 WITH A CALIBER OF .44:
This revolver has an octagonal barrel with a length of 127 or 188 mm (5 or 7½ in). The total length is 271 or 335 mm (10¾ or 13¼ in). The weight of this revolver is 1100 or 1200 g (38¼ or 42¼ oz). Pietta gave this weapon with the 127 mm (5 in) barrel the name Model 1851 Navy Yank Sheriff. This revolver with the longer 191 mm (7½ in) barrel is known as the Model 1851 Navy Yank.

Pietta replica Colt 1860 Navy

PIETTA-COLT 1860 NAVY/1860 ARMY

The Colt 1860 was the revolver most wideln used by the Union Army during the American Civil War. Colt supplied approximately 127,000 weapons throughout this period. More than 200,000 weapons of this model were produced between 1860 and 1873. This revolver has a steel grip and a brass trigger guard. There are two known types of the Army version, one of which has an opening in the grip frame for a adapter piece. The 1860 Army is in the caliber .44. the Colt Model 1851 Navy is in the caliber .36. Both models have a round barrel and a creeping style loading lever. The cylinder of the Navy has an engraving of a sea battle. Pietta manufactures several versions in the Colt 1860 series:

MODEL 1860 ARMY .44: This 6-shot single-action percussion revolver with a caliber of .44 has a round barrel with a length of 203 mm (8 in). The total length of this weapon is 349 mm (13¾ in) and it weighs 1200 g (42¼ oz). It has a steel grip and a brass trigger guard.

MODEL 1861 NAVY .36: This is also a 6-shot percussion revolver with a round barrel and a barrel length of 222 mm (8¾ in), a total length of 349 mm (13¾ in) and it weighs 1200 g (42¼ oz). The grip and the trigger guard are made of steel.

MODEL 1860 ARMY SHERIFFS .44: This is the 1860 Army with a round 133 mm (5¼ in) barrel, a total length of 285 mm (11¼ in) and it weighs 1100 g (35¾ oz).

MODEL 1862 POLICE .36/.44: This weapon in the calibers .36 or .44 has a 140 mm (5½ in) round barrel, a total length of 285 mm (11¼ in) and it weighs 1100 g (35¾ oz). The cylinder is half fluted, and the grip and trigger guard are made of brass. Other Pietta models include the 1862 Police Pony Express and the 1862 New York Metropolitan Police, in both .36 and .44.

PIETTA-LE MAT 1856 ARMY/NAVY

Jean Alexandre Francois Le Mat studied medicine in Paris. In 1843 he moved to New Orleans in Louisiana, where he married the niece of General Piere G.T.

Pietta replica Colt 1860 Army

Le Mat revolver by Pietta

Replica Le Mat Army revolver

Replica Le Mat Navy revolver

Beauregard of the Confederate Army. Together with Beauregard in 1856 he designed a new type of officers, revolver for the Confederate army and navy, including the well-known 18th regiment of Georgia. In October 1856, he received a patent for his invention: a revolver with 9 cartridge chambers and a barrel axis that can also be used as a shotgun barrel. The governor of Louisiana even promoted Le Mat to the rank of Colonel as reward for his efforts. The first Le Mat revolvers were manufactured in Philadelphia. The Civil War resulted in the production being moved to France, where this revolver is now produced by Girard & Fils of Paris and by several other manufacturers in Belgium, the UK and the USA. These weapons were shipped to Britain where they were tested and given a proof house mark, they were then shipped to Bermuda, and from there were smuggled throught the sea blockade to the Southern States of America. This weapon has two barrels. The upper barrel is rifled with grooves and lands. The lower barrel, which also serves as the cylinder axis, is a shotgun barrel. The most popular calibers are .36 bullet with .50 shot, .41 bullet with .66 shot or .44 bullet with .72 shot. For the firing of the shotgun barrel the firing pin point on the hammer has to be changed using the

lever at the top of the hammer. This revolver was also later converted for the use of .44 pin fire and .38 centerfire cartridges. The bullet compositor of the first model was fitted on the right-hand side of the barrels. In addition, the trigger guard was provided with of a finger hook. The second model has the bullet compositor on the left-hand side and has a rounded trigger guard. The Italian factory Pietta manufactures a series of excellent replicas of historical examples of the Le Mat revolver. This weapon is a single-action percussion revolver with a 9-shot cylinder plus a shotgun barrel. The total length is 340 mm (13½ in). The octagonal barrel with a caliber of .44 has a length of 171 mm (6¾ in). The round shotgun barrel with a caliber of .65 is shorter at 127 mm (5 in). This weapon weighs 1600 g (56½ oz). This revolver has half-cock safety on the hammer and a walnut stock. Pietta manufactures the models Cavalry, Navy and Army, all three having the same dimensions.

PIETTA-REMINGTON MODEL 1858

Remington manufactured approximately 132,000 weapons of this model in the period from 1863 until

Pietta-Remington Model 1858

Remington 1858 New Model Army by Pietta

Replica Remington 1858 New Model Navy

1873. This weapon has an octagonal barrel with a length of 169 or 203 mm (6⅔ or 8 in). The same revolver with a caliber of .36 was known as the Model 1858 New Model Navy. The original weapons have the barrel inscription: 'Patented Sept. 14, 1858 E. Remington & Sons, Illinois, New York, USA New Model'. This weapon was highly valued by the soldiers in the American Civil War because of its strong closed frame. Pietta manufactures different percussion replicas of historical examples in .36 and .44 calibers.

PIETTA REMINGTON 1858 NEW MODEL ARMY .44:
This revolver has an octagonal barrel with a length of 203 mm (8 in), a total length of 371 mm (14½ in) and it weighs 1250 g (44 oz).

PIETTA REMINGTON 1858 NEW MODEL NAVY .36:
Has an octagonal barrel of 169 mm (6¼ in), a total length of 339 mm (13¼ in) and it weighs 1250 g (44 oz).

PIETTA REMINGTON 1858 NEW MODEL ARMY TARGET:
This revolver is available with a 169 (.36) or 203 (.44) mm (6¼ or 8 in) barrel and a total length of 339 or 371 mm (13¼ or 14¼ in). The weight is 1250 g (44 oz). The Target has an adjustable rear sight. This weapon is also available in a nickel-plated version.

PIETTA 1858 BUFFALO .44:
Has an octagonal barrel with a length of 305 mm (12 in) and a total length of 472 mm (18¼ in). The weight is 1400 g (49½ oz).

PIETTA REMINGTON 1858 TEXAS:
Is in the calibers of .36 or .44 with a 169 or 203 mm (6¼ or 8 in) barrel, a total length of 339 or 371 mm (13¼ or 14¼ in) and it weighs 1250 g (44 oz).

PIETTA STARR MODEL 1858

The double-action Model 1858 Navy percussion revolver was designed by Ebenezer Townsend Starr.

Pietta replica Remington 1858 Texas

Replica double-action Starr 1858

His family owned the Starr Arms Company in New York. This weapon was based on his patent of 1856. The frame consists of two parts, held together by a large round knob on the right-hand side behind the cylinder. Starr produced approximately 3,000 weapons of this model between 1859 and 1860. The American Ordnance Department purchased approximately 1,400 of these revolvers in 1861, but because of its relatively small caliber the army hierarchy did not consider the .36 to be suitable as a weapon. Starr decided make a larger model, the .44 double-action Model 1858 Army. The army accepted this weapon and 20,000 were ordered, however Starr was not able to compete commercially within the civilian market because of the strong competition of Colt, Remington and Smith & Wesson. He therefore decided to manufacture a percussion revolver with a single-action trigger, which was not so complicated and therefore cheaper to produce. He named this model the Starr Model 1863 Army .44. In 1864, re contracted with the US Army for 25,000 weapons, and by the end of the Civil War had sold them in total more than 47,000 revolvers. This weapon, apart from being manufactured by Starr, was also produced by Savage Revolving Fire Arms from Middletown in Connecticut. After the war, weapon sales fell so sharply that Starr decided to stop the production of firearms in 1867. The original Starr Model 1858 with a caliber of .36 has a 6-shot cylinder. The total length is 305 mm (12 in). The barrel length is 152 mm (6 in) and this weapon weighs 1450 g (51 oz). The original double-action Starr 1858 Army .44 has a total length of 296 mm (11¼ in), a barrel length of 152 mm (6 in)

and it weighs 1250 g (44 oz). The original single-action model 1863 Army .44 has a total length of 347 mm (13¼ in), a barrel length of 203 mm (8 in) and it weighs 1350 g (47½ oz). The Italian firearms factory Pietta manufactures a fine replica of all three versions.

PIETTA STARR DA MODEL 1858 NAVY:
A double-action percussion replica with a caliber of .36. This weapon has a round barrel with a length of 152 mm (6 in), a total length of 296 mm (11¼ in) and it weighs 1250 g (44 oz).

PIETTA STARR DA MODEL 1858 ARMY:
This revolver is in .44 caliber. The dimensions are the same as that of the Navy model.

PIETTA STARR S.A. MODEL 1863 ARMY .44:
The single-action version with a caliber of .44. This weapon has a round barrel or 203 mm (8 in), a total length of 347 mm (13¼ in) and it weighs 1350 g (47½ oz).

PIETTA DANCE MODEL 1862

The Colt Dragoon and the Colt Navy inspired J.H. Dance to start producing revolvers in the winter of 1861-1862 in the town of Columbia, Texas. He designed the Dance revolver with a caliber of .36 and had the prototype ready by April 1862. However the production, which was divided between the Army model with a caliber of .44 and the Navy in a .36 never exceeded more than 350 weapons. The army showed no interested in this revolver, and so Dance sold them to the civilian market. This weapon became reasonably well known due to some famous owners,

Pietta replica Dance 1862 revolver

Griswold & Gunnison 1862 Nord Navy

including the Apache Chief Geronimo and the outlaw Bill Longley. Pietta manufactures a replica of the Navy in .36 caliber. This single-action revolver has a round barrel with a length of 191 mm (7½ in). The total length is 335 mm (13¼ in) and it weighs 1100 g (38¾ oz). The Dance revolver has a brass grip, frame and trigger guard. Distinctive, is the lack of a recoil shield on the frame behind the cylinder.

PIETTA GRISWOLD & GUNNISON CONFEDERATE MODEL 1862

In 1862, the Southern states were searching desperately for firearms for the Civil War. Samuel Griswold was the owner of a cotton factory and decided to restructure his company for the manufacture of arms. Together with A. Gunnison he founded the Griswold & Gunnison Company. The production of revolvers started at the end of 1862. The new company had secured an army contract even before it manufactured a single weapon, however the company found steel hard to come by. After a plea by the government, the firearms industry received a large donation of church bells, allowing production to continue. Pietta manufactures a variety of replica models of this type, such as the Confederate .36/.44, the Nord Navy with a caliber of .36 or .44,

the Confederate Sheriff and the Nord Sheriff. These single-action revolvers from Pietta have a round or octagonal barrel with a length of 127, 188, 191 or 305 mm (5, 7¼, 7½, or 12 in). The total length varies from 271, 335 up to 451 mm (10¼, 13¼ up to 17¼ in). The weights of these models are 1100, 1200 or 1350 g (38¾ , 42¼ or 47½ oz).

PIETTA SPILLER & BURR MODEL 1862

In the autumn of 1861 Eduard Spiller and David Burr founded the Spiller & Burr Company in Richmond, Virginia. Spiller was the nephew of James Henry Burton, a Lieutenant-Colonel in the Southern army. Thanks to Burton, the company secured an army order for 15,000 revolvers that had to be supplied within 2½ years. The company then moved to factory premises in Atlanta. The company started with the manufacturing output of approximately 1,000 single-action revolvers per month. After the outbreak of the Civil War firearms were in great demand. Spiller & Burr could not satisfy this demand because of the steel shortage. When the company was nationalized, due to them not fulfilling their contractual obligations, it was relocated from Atlanta to Macon, where production was resumed. Pietta has a fine

Pietta replica of Griswold & Gunnison Confederate revolver

Replica Spiller & Burr Model 1862

Pietta Colt Peacemaker

replica of this model with a caliber of .36. The octagonal barrel has a length of 178 mm (7 in) and the total length is 310 mm (12¼ in). The weight is 1100 g (38¾ oz). The frame is made totally of brass.

PIETTA COLT MODEL 1873 SINGLE ACTION ARMY

The Colt Model 1873 Single Action Army was produced between 1873 and 1941 (approximately 360,000 weapons) and from 1955 up to the present day in a large number of calibers, including: .22 Long, .22 LR, .32 WRF, .32 Colt, .32 S&W, .32-20 WCF, .38 S&W, .38 Special, .357 Magnum, .41 S&W, .44 S&W Special, .44 Magnum, .44-40 WCF, .45 ACP and .455 Eley. There are many variations of this weapon some of which have their own name. The barrel lengths can vary from 76 mm (3 in) up to

Various replica Colt Peacemakers

457 mm (18 in). The most well known versions are the Storekeeper (without ejector bar), Sheriffs Model, Frontier (with a caliber of .44-40 Win.), Bisley Model and Buntline (from 305 mm/12 in barrel length). One or the first series 1873 Army Models that Colt manufactured was for General George Armstrong Custer's 7th Cavalry regiment. These weapons carry the proof mark of the Ordnance inspector Orville W. Ainsworth. The frame is marked with 'U.S.' and the name of the 7th Cavalry regiment is engraved on the butt. The series numbers run to approximately 25,000. In 1996 one specimen in good condition sold for $ 20,700 at an auction at the Rock Island Auction Company. The Single Action Army revolver is the most well known and celebrated Colt model, and has been manufactured with or without license by an infinite number of manufacturers. Since 1873, Colt has produced this model 1873 during a number of different periods, from 1899 until 1940, 1956 until 1975 and from 1977 to the present day. Pietta manufacture replicas in different barrel lengths and calibers:

– with a barrel length of 89 mm (3½ in) with the calibers of .357 Magnum, .44-40 Win. and .45 Colt;
– with a barrel length of 121 mm (4¾ in) with the calibers of .22 LR, .32-20 Win., .38-40 Win., .357 Magnum, .44 Special, .44-40 Win. and .45 Colt;
– with a barrel length of 140 mm (5½ in) with the calibers of .22 LR, .32-20 Win., .38-40 Win., .357 Magnum, .44-40 Win. and .45 Colt;
– with the barrel length of 152 mm (6 in) only in the caliber .22 LR;
– with a barrel length of 191 mm (7½ in) in the calibers .22 LR, .32-20 Win., .38-40 Win., .357 Magnum, .44-40 Win. and .45 Colt;

Buntline Peacemaker with stock extension

- with the barrel length of 254 mm (10 in) only in the caliber .357 Magnum;
- with a barrel length of 298 mm (11¼ in) with the calibers of .22 LR, .38-40 Win., .357 Magnum, .44-40 Win. and .45 Colt;
- with a barrel length of 419 mm (16½ in) with the calibers of .22 LR, .357 Magnum, .44-40 Win. and .45 Colt;
- with a barrel length of 500 mm (19¾ in) with the calibers of .22 LR, .38-40 Win., .357 Magnum, .44-40 Win., and .45 Colt.

PIETTA COLT MODEL 1894 BISLEY

Colt produced the original model between 1896 and 1912. The name Bisley is derived from the English shooting center where international matches are held. The Bisley revolver has the frame, the barrel and the ejector bar of the 1873 model. The only differences being the trigger, the hammer and the high butt. Pietta manufactures a replica model of this weapon in different barrel lengths and calibers:

- with a barrel length of 121 mm (4¾ in) with the calibers of .22 LR, .38-40 Win., .357 Magnum, .44-40 Win. and .45 Colt;
- with a barrel length of 140 mm (5½ in) with the calibers of .22 LR, .38-40 Win., .357 Magnum, .44-40 Win. and .45 Colt;
- with a barrel length of 191 mm (7½ in) in the calibers .22 LR, .32-20 Win., .38-40 Win., .357 Magnum, .44-40 Win. and .45 Colt;
- with a barrel length of 500 mm (19¾ in) in de calibers .22 LR, .38-40 Win., .357 Magnum, .44-40 Win., and .45 Colt.

Replica Colt 1894 Bisley

R

REMINGTON XP-100

Remington logo

The American company E. Remington was founded in 1825 by Eliphalet ('Lite') Remington (1793-1861). His son Philo joined the company in 1844. They mainly manufactured firearms for the Civil War. After the war, this father and son company switched to the production of hunting and sporting weapons. This proved to be quite an effort, and the company went bankrupt in 1886. Two years later a couple of businessmen bought up the inventory, and changed the name to the Remington Arms Company.

This was followed in 1912 by a merger with the Union Cartridge Company, an ammunition factory. During the First World War, mainly Enfield rifles were manufactured. The ammunition factory, Petersen Cartridge Company was added in 1936. In the Second World War, Remington had to revert temporarily to the war effort. Remington has been part of the Du-Pont concern since 1980.

THE REMINGTON XP-100

This single shot bolt-action pistol originates from the start of 1963 and is derived from the Remington Model 600 rifle. This pistol was designed by Wayne Leek and Mike Walker, who were both employed as designers by Remington. In those days, the use of small arms for hunting varmint was very popular in the United States. Silhouette shooting, the so-called Metallic Silhouette, was introduced from countries like Mexico. In actual fact, there was not much new about this weapon. The bolt housing, the bolt and the barrel originated from the standard bolt-action rifle, together with the adjustable rear sight. Remington manufactured the stock, including the hand grip from a Du Pont Zytel composite. What was new in this concept was the short stock, the short barrel, and the variety of rifle calibers. The first version of the XP-100 was in the caliber .221 Fire Ball. This cartridge was made up of a shortened .222 Remington rifle cartridge. A 50 grains (3,2 g) bullet, fired with an XP-100, achieved a velocity of approximately 880 m/s and was extremely accurate up to 200 meters. Long-distance pistol shooters bought this weapon, but generally it did not fulfill the original expectations. However Remington did continue producing this pistol, but mostly to special order. Sports shooting started to take off around 1975 when silhouette shooting became more well known, due to regular articles in weapon magazines, together

Remington XP-100R

with the founding of the IMSHA (International Metallic Silhouette Handgun Association), which certainly played an important role in establishing this pursuit. After José Porras won the international silhouette match using an XP-100 in 1976, Remington could hardly keep up with demand. Since the .221 Fire Ball caliber was found to be too weak to topple the 22 kilo steel animal figures from 200 meters, other calibers of the XP-100 were introduced, resulting in the 7 mm BR (Bench Rest) version in 1980. This caliber was accurate even up to distances of 300 meters and also had the required bullet energy. The calibers available run from the old .221 Fire Ball up to and including the .35 Remington. In addition, Remington brought an XP-100R bolt-action pistol onto the market in 1990. This had 5-shot magazine and was based on the Remington Model Seven bolt-action rifle. The stock of the XP-100R is produced in Kevlar. Remington stopped production of the XP-100 in 1996, but reintroduced it to their range in 1998. The calibers available were .22-250 Rem , .223 Rem , .260 Rem and .35 Rem. The standard barrel length is 368 mm (14½ in). Sadly, Remington once again withdrew the XP-100R in 2001.

Rossi trade marks

ROSSI REVOLVERS

Rossi, the Brazilian firearms factory was founded in 1881 by an Italian immigrant gunsmith and was based in Caxias do Sul. In 1937 the company moved to Sao Leopoldo. The official name of the company is Amadeo Rossi SA. Until the middle of the last century, Rossi concentrated mainly on the South-American market. In about 1957, they started exporting inexpensive revolvers and carbines to the USA, which at that time were being imported by the Garcia Corp. of Teaneck, New Jersey. This importing was later taken over by Interarms of Alexandria, Virginia. BrazTech, an American subsidiary of Taurus, has represented the Rossi brand in North America since 1994. Rossi manufactures quality weapons equal to those of any other manufacturers in the world, and exports to more then seventy countries. Their range includes approximately twenty revolver models and a range of 25 shotguns and carbines. Rossi is one of the largest weapon manufacturers in South-America and is among the ten largest weapon producers in the world. Many Rossi revolvers fall within the category of defense weapons that is to say a 5-shot revolver with a 51 mm (2 in) or 76 mm (3 in) barrel and fixed sights. Rossi also has a series of sporting revolvers with micrometer sights, with or without a heavy barrel (Bull barrel), some with a ventilated barrel and in blued or stainless steel versions. In the middle of the last century the Rossi revolvers had fine model names, a couple of examples being the Ranger revolver, introduced in 1964, and the 5-shot Pioneer revolver in the caliber .38 Special of 1966. The sporting revolver of the day in 1969 was known as the Champion. The sporting revolver with a caliber of .22 LR had the model name Sportsman. Rossi started to give their revolvers model numbers from 1988 onwards. In 1995, Rossi had a range of 44 different revolver models, which led to a drastic restructuring In the year 2000. This resulted in the company retaining just two basic models, the stainless steel version and the blued version.

ROSSI MODEL 87

Rossi introduced the Model 87 in 1983, a so-called snub-nose revolver with a 51 mm (2 in) barrel. This weapon is a 5-shot double-action revolver in the caliber .38 Special, and has a rubber grip with finger grooves. This grip has a high back that conceals most of the hammer, giving this revolver a 'double-action' character. This weapon is made totally of stainless steel. A sight slot has been added to the bridge above the cylinder. The cylinder locks in to the recoil shield at the back. The cylinder axis and ejector bar locate with a locking slot at the front. This revolver has a fixed firing pin point and blocking bar safety. The total length is 174 mm (6¾ in) and the barrel length is 51 mm (2 in). The height of this weapon is 124 mm (5 in) and it weighs 630 g (22¼ oz).

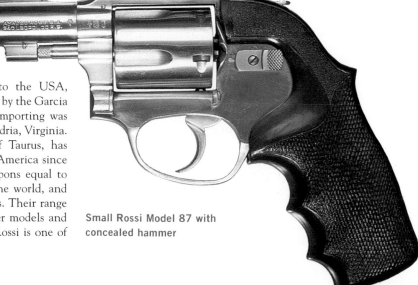

Small Rossi Model 87 with concealed hammer

Rossi 712 revolver with
64 mm (2½ in) barrel

Rossi Model 845 in
.38 Special caliber

ROSSI MODEL 712

The Rossi 712 revolver originates from 1992.
This weapon strongly resembles a Smith & Wesson.
The Rossi has a continuous ejector shroud that runs
through to the muzzle. This houses the combination of
the cylinder axis front locking and the ejector bar. This
weapon has an adjustable rear sight and a high front
sight. The 6-shot double-action revolver is in the
caliber .357 Magnum and is made totally of stainless
steel. This weapon has a fixed firing pin point on the
hammer and a blocking bar safety. The total length is
187 mm (7½ in) and the barrel length is 64 mm
(2½ in). The height is 130 mm (5 in) and it weighs
800 g (28¼ oz). This weapon also has a wrap-around
rubber grip with finger grooves.

ROSSI MODEL 763

The Model 763 first appeared on the market in 1989.
This is a 6-shot double-action revolver in the caliber
.357 Magnum. This weapon is mainly intended as
sporting revolver. It has a 152 mm (6 in) barrel with
a ventilated barrel rib and a continuous ejector shroud.
The rear sight is adjustable and the sight radius is
195 mm (7¾ in). The total length of this stainless steel
weapon is 280 mm (11 in) and the height is 138 mm
(5½ in). The empty weight is 1125 g (39¼ oz). This
revolver has a hammer with a fixed firing pin point and
a blocking bar safety. In addition this weapon has
a wrap-around rubber grip with finger grooves.

ROSSI MODEL 845

The 6-shot double-action Rossi Model 845 with
a caliber of .38 Special was introduced in 1991. This
weapon is also is made totally of stainless steel. It has
a barrel length of 102 mm (4 in) and a fixed rear
sight with a sight radius of 140 mm (5½ in). This
weapon is mainly intended as a service revolver
for police forces. The total length of this revolver is
230 mm (9 in) and the height is 138 mm (5½ in).
The weight is 850 g (30 oz). The hammer has a fixed
firing pin point and a blocking bar safety. In
addition, this weapon has a wrap-around rubber
combat grip with finger grooves.

ROSSI MODEL 873 LADY ROSSI

The Lady Rossi 873 is a 5-shot double-action revolver
that came on the market in .38 Special caliber in
1995. This stainless steel weapon is available with
palisander or smooth polished grips. The total length
is 174 mm (6¼ in), the barrel length is 51 mm (2 in)
and the height is 123 mm (4¾ in). This weapon has
a fixed rear sight with a sight radius of 92 mm (3½ in).
The empty weight is 600 g (21¼ oz). The hammer has
a fixed firing pin point and a blocking bar safety.

Rossi 763 Sport
revolver of 1989

873 Lady Rossi

New 5-shot Rossi R351
and R352 of 2000

Blued 6-shot Rossi R461
and stainless steel Model
R462

Rossi Model R351/R352

In the year 2000, Rossi stopped the production of all former revolver models and introduced two new types in four different versions. Model R351 is a 5-shot double-action revolver in .38 Special caliber P. This weapon has a 51 mm (2 in) barrel, a total length of 165 mm (6½ in) and it weighs 680 g (24 oz). The hammer has a fixed firing pin point and a blocking bar safety. A special feature of this new model is the exterior built-in hammer spur lock. This patented Taurus lock is operated with a small separate key. This revolver in blued steel has the model number R351. The version in stainless steel is known as the R352. Both versions have a rubber grip with finger grooves and a fixed rear sight.

Rossi Model R461/R462

The Rossi R461 revolver is available in blued and stainless steel versions. Model R462 is a 6-shot double-action weapon in the caliber .357 Magnum P. Rossi brought both types onto the market in the year 2000. As with the other models, the models 351/352 have the Taurus hammer lock. The total length of both versions is 165 mm (6½ in). The barrel has a length of 51 mm (2 in) and this weapon weighs 737 g (26 oz). It has a soft rubber grip with finger grooves. The R461/462 also has a fixed firing pin point on the hammer and a blocking bar safety.

Model R352 with cylinder swung out. The cocking lock is clearly visible

Rossi R462 with 6-shot cylinder and hammer locking

RUGER (STURM, RUGER & COMPANY)

Ruger trade mark

William (Bill) B. Ruger was the son of a lawyer, born on 21 June 1916 in Brooklyn, New York. He became interested in firearms technology at a very early age. While in Connecticut, Ruger worked on the design of a semi-automatic version of the Savage lever-action carbine, however the Savage concern showed no interest in this concept. Bill presented this concept to Colt without success. Finally, the US Army showed interest in the Savage-design. Bill was offered a job by the then nationalized Springfield Armory, where he never even completed the first year. Bill found that a nationalized company offered too few prospects to progress quickly. He moved to North Carolina and continued to work on a design for a light machine gun. This aroused the interest of another firearms factory, Auto-Ordnance. This company produced the world famous Thompson machine pistol, also known as the Tommy-gun. In 1940, Bill Ruger started working in the Auto-Ordnance design department in Bridgeport, Connecticut. The Sturm, Ruger & Company history began in 1948, when William B. Ruger and Alexander M. Sturm rented a shed in Southport, Connecticut. With a starting capital of $ 50.000 the young entrepreneurs produced their first weapon in 1949, a semi-automatic small caliber pistol. When Alexander Sturm died in a tragic aircraft accident in 1951, William (Bill) Ruger continued the business alone. Showing piety for his deceased business partner, Bill changed the trademark color to black. In 1953 Ruger brought a small caliber revolver to the market, the Single Six, a single-action revolver based on the Colt Peacemaker. Ruger had a strong feeling that there was a market for this type of weapon. He tackled the production in the typical Ruger manner: maximize the simplicity of the manufacturing, maximize the profit margin. This Single-Six formed the basis for a whole range of single-action revolvers. This weapon remained in the collection until 1973. In 1956 Ruger introduced an alloy model, with the same model being made available in 1959 in .22 WMR (Winchester

Magnum Rimfire). The range was further extended in 1964 with the addition of the Super Single Six with an adjustable sight. The first Blackhawk single-action revolver was launched in 1955 with a caliber of .357 Magnum. This was followed in 1956 by the Blackhawk with a caliber of .44 Magnum and in 1967 with a caliber of .30-M1, the famous carbine caliber. In 1971, Ruger brought a Blackhawk version onto the market with a caliber of .45 Colt with a replacement cylinder in .45 ACP. In 1958, the Bearcat single-action revolver was introduced in .22 L.R. This weapon was manufactured up until 1973 being slightly modified in 1971, with a totally steel frame, and becoming known as the Super Bearcat. The Super Blackhawk revolver appeared in 1963. This single-action revolver was a strengthened and further embellished Blackhawk with a caliber of .44 Magnum and an adjustable sight. The revolver range of Ruger was further extended in 1971 with the addition of the Security Six, the Speed Six and the Police Service Six, double-action revolvers with a caliber of .357 Magnum and .38 Special. It was quickly apparent that this basic model was a box-office success. Other versions, including the stainless steel version were launched in 1975. The New Model Single Six, the New Model Blackhawk and the Super Blackhawk with a new firing pin safety system known as the transfer bar were introduced in 1973. All old models of the single-action revolvers, that were manufactured and sold up until 1973 could be adapted free of charge. Stainless steel versions of the New Model Single Six and New Model Blackhawk were launched in 1974. The Ruger Redhawk revolver with a caliber of .44 Magnum was launched in 1979. This revolver, originally only available in stainless steel, had a number of unique technical improvements. As of 1985, the Redhawk was also available in a blued version. In 1982, Ruger found that the time was ripe for a new model of small caliber pistol and introduced the Mark II Standard Automatic Pistol with a caliber of .22 LR. This pistol is in fact the old Mark I with a 'facelift'. In 1985, the New Model Super Single-Six revolver in the new caliber .of 32 H&R Magnum was launched. In 1986, the single-action range was extended with the introduction of the Ruger Bisley Single-Action revolvers in blued versions and with the calibers of .22 LR., .32 H&R Magnum, .357 Magnum, .41 Magnum, .44 Magnum and .45 Long Colt. Ruger again introduced a number of new versions in 1987, such as the Super Redhawk with a caliber of .44 Magnum and the Ruger GP-100 as successor to the famous Security Six. In 1987 Ruger also launched his first 9 mm Para pistol, the Ruger P-85, a 15-shot army pistol. Certain parts that Ruger considered unnecessary for the functioning of a pistol, such as a various small levers, pins and springs, were simply left-hand out of the P-85. The grip is manufactured from a lightweight aluminum alloy known as T-6. This pistol range was then extended with the models P89, P90, P91, P93, P94,

P95 and P97 pistols with the calibers of 9 mm Para, .40 S&W and .45 ACP. In 2001 Ruger introduced the Super Redhawk revolver in the caliber .480 Ruger, a caliber that he had developed himself. This was the year Vaquero also extended their model range. As well as manufacturing a number of revolvers and pistols, Ruger also produced several different versions of the Ruger Mini-14 carbine, together with a variety of double-barreled shotguns and single shot bullet rifles.

RUGER .22 MARK I (MODEL T678)

At the start of 1949, Ruger introduced this original semi-automatic small caliber pistol as the Mark I. The standard weapon then had a fixed rear sight with a barrel length of 121 or 152 mm (4¾ or 6 in). The grip resembles that of the Luger P08. In 1950, Ruger launched the target version, known as the Mark I Target. This model has an adjustable rear sight and was sold in the barrel lengths 140 or 174 mm (5½ or 7 in). Both versions have tapered barrels. Between the series numbers 2600 and 2800, modifications were made to the gun lock and the firing pin. A target model was launched in 1964 with a bull barrel with a length of 140 mm (5½ in). The construction of this pistol was especially aimed at producing it as simply and as cheaply as possible. This pistol is made up of a number of machine stamped parts. The frame for example, consists or two pressed steel shells that are welded together. The gun lock housing consists of a steel pipe, in which the barrel is screwed. The repeating action of this weapon utilizes the recoil force of the cartridge when fired. The Mark I has a magazine capacity of 9 rounds. The magazine release is in the grip heel and the safety catch is on the left-hand side of the frame. This weapon does not have a slide catch. The grips of the first series are made of hard rubber. In later versions wooden grips were also available. In 1982 Ruger introduced the successor to this pistol, the Mark II. This more recent model has a slide catch, a 10-shot magazine, a modified trigger and a modified safety catch.

Small caliber pistols by Ruger

RUGER .22 MARK II

Ruger launched the Mark II in 1982. This single-action pistol with a caliber of .22 LR was then only available in a blued version with black Delrin grips. This weapon has a tapered barrel with a length of 174 mm (7 in) and an adjustable rear sight. A Target model with a thick 140 mm (5½ in) barrel appeared in 1983. As of 1984 both models were also manufactured in stainless steel. In the same year Ruger also introduced a special silhouette model with a heavy barrel with a length of 254 mm (10 in). The Government Model followed in 1987. Ruger then also introduced model numbers. Model MK-512 has a thick barrel or 140 mm (5½ in). Model MK-678-G. is the Mark II Government with the 174 mm (6 in) barrel and the MK-10 is the silhouette-version with a barrel length of 254 mm (10 in). Ruger decided to add the letter K to model numbers to indicate the stainless steel versions. The Government Model is specially developed in accordance with military specifications. At the time, this weapon was used as a US Army-training weapon. Ruger decided this type could also be manufactured for the civilian market. The only difference between both series is that the series numbers of the military pistols begin with 'US'. Ruger manufactured the two millionth specimen of the Mark I and Mark II pistol models in 1990. Over the years, most versions have remained unchanged.

Old Ruger Mark I pistol of 1949

Ruger Mark II of 1952

Ruger KMK-678
Government Competition

RUGER MARK II STANDARD

The standard Mark II pistol MK-4 in a blued steel version has a barrel length of 120.7 mm (4¾ in) and a total length of 228 mm (9 in). This weapon has a fixed rear sight and it weighs 992 g (35 oz). The same pistol in stainless steel has the model number KMK-4. Model MK-6 or KMK-6 has a barrel length of 152 mm (6 in), and a total length of 262 mm (11 in) and it weighs 1049 g (37 oz). This pistol also has a fixed rear sight.

RUGER MARK II TARGET

The Mark II Target pistol has an adjustable rear sight. The MK-678 has a tapered barrel with a length of 174 mm (7 in) and a total length of 283 mm (11 in). The weight is 1191 g (42 oz). In the stainless steel model, this pistol has the model number KMK-678. A notable version, which does not appear in the Ruger-catalogue, is the KMK-4 Target. This pistol has a tapered barrel of 120.7 mm (4¾ in), an adjustable

KP-4 pistol with
plastic casing

rear sight and a special match grip with an adjustable hand palm support. In 1992 Ruger brought a new model onto the market. This stainless steel weapon has the model number KMK-678GC and is known as the Mark II Government Competition. This pistol has a thick barrel with flattened sides and a length of 174 mm (7 in). An adjustable rear sight is on the top

Ruger Mark II MK-678 pistol
and KMK-678 in stainless steel
with 174 mm (7 in) barrel

The strange KMK-4
Target pistol

of the gun lock housing, complete with a rail for mounting telescopic sights. This weapon has an empty weight of 1276 g (45 oz). In 1993 Ruger introduced the Model 22/45. This new type has a black Zytel composite frame with the same grip angle as the Colt 1911 pistol. The magazine release is on the left-hand side of the frame, behind the trigger guard. The KP-4 model has a tapered stainless steel barrel length of 120.7 mm (4¾ in). The total length is 223 mm (8¾ in). The height of this pistol is 140 mm (5½ in) and the width is 30.5 mm (1¼ in). The weight of the KP-4 is 794 g (28 oz).

RUGER MARK II BULL BARREL

P4 of 1993 with 102 mm
(4 in) bull barrel and
plastic casing

Model P-4 originates from 1993. This pistol has a black Zytel composite frame and a thick 102 mm (4 in) barrel. The magazine release is on the left-hand side of the frame behind the trigger guard. The knob above is the slide catch. The safety catch is at the rear of the frame. The total length of this model is 203 mm (8 in) and it weighs 879 g (31 oz). This

MK-512 Bull Barrel Target
and stainless steel KMK-512

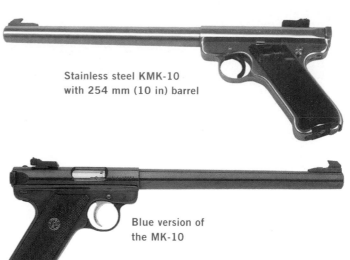

Stainless steel KMK-10
with 254 mm (10 in) barrel

Blue version of
the MK-10

weapon has an adjustable rear sight. The same type is also available as the blued P-512 or the stainless steel KP-512 with a thick 140 mm (5½ in) barrel. The total length of this version 241 mm (9½ in) and it weighs 992 g (35 oz).

The Bull Barrel Target version with an adjustable rear sight has the model number MK-512 in the blued version and KMK-512 in a stainless steel version. The heavy barrel has a length of 140 mm (5½ in) and the total length is 248 mm (9¾ in). This weapon weighs in both versions 1190 g (42 oz). A special version, is the silhouette model with a thick 254 mm (10 in) barrel. This pistol is available in a blued version as the MK-10 and in stainless steel with the model name KMK-10. The total length of this weapon is 364 mm (14¼ in) and it weighs 1446 g (51 oz). This weapon has an adjustable rear sight.

RUGER P-85

In 1986 Ruger introduced a completely new weapon. They manufactured a double-action pistol for the first time in the history of the company. It was known as the Model P-85 and was in the caliber 9 mm Para. Ruger did not incur the high development costs just for the sake of the civilian market, but was then ogling army orders. In the meantime, Beretta had secured the largest weapon order of the century: Replacing the Colt 1911-A1 with their Model 92F. After pressure from the American congress, the Pentagon announced new army trials for future orders. It therefore came as no surprise when the new P-85 pistol satisfied the newly formulated military standard requirements. These included a magazine capacity of at least 10 rounds (Ruger P-85:

Ruger P-85 of 1986

The magazine release is also ambidextrous. Instead of a button, as is the case with most weapons, a slide release has been installed that when pushed forward releases the magazine for removal from the weapon. This system resembles the magazine release of the Glock 17 pistol. The magazine is provided with an applicator made of unbreakable composite. This has the advantages of both preventing the entrance of debris and reducing friction in the magazine housing. The hammer has a ring shaped spur. The extractor of the P-85 is manufactured from 4140 chrome-molybdenum steel and is furthermore tempered into a type of spring steel. The claw of this extractor is robustly made, and exerts more then enough grip on the cartridge case.

The Ruger P-85 has Xenoy grips. Instead of the usual diamond design, preference has been given to 16 horizontal grooves, giving this pistol a more comfortable grip. The stainless steel barrel has a drawn diameter of 9.04 mm (1½2 in) and a rifling twist of 1:10. The locking of the barrel and slide is derived from the Browning-Sig principal. The barrel or the P-85 is contained within a sort of chamber block, which Ruger has named the monoblock. Its sharp angular profile allows this block to be locked into the ejector port in the slide. Totally loaded the P-85 1077 g weighs (38 oz). The total length is 199 mm (7¾ in), the height is 143 mm (5½ in) and the grip width is 32.5 mm (1¼ in), surprisingly narrow for a pistol with such a large magazine capacity. The sight radius is 155 mm (6 in). The length of the barrel is 114 mm (4½ in). The front sight has a white point and there are two white dots on either side of the rear sight. This is an excellent aspect marking, which allows this weapon to be brought swiftly and accurately on target, especially when light is poor. Without graceful styling, the Ruger P-85 is not an attractive pistol. This is a pistol for military use. In 1990 Ruger also introduced a stainless steel version with the model name KP-85. In 1990, Ruger also introduced the P-85 onto the market with only an uncocking lever. This type was given the model name P-85DC and in stainless steel the KP-85DC.

15 rounds), one hand operation, (the P-85 has an ambidextrous magazine- and safety catch), the standard caliber 9 mm Para, a double-action trigger action, combined safeties- with a uncocking lever and a firing pin safety. In addition, it had to be possible to dismantle a test pistol without the use of extra tools. The Ruger P-85 met all of these requirements easily. One of the army tests carried out was a durability test with the firing of 6,500 cartridges. During the development phase the P-85 prototype successfully withstood a shooting test of 10,000 cartridges. The Ruger P-85 has an alloy frame, however almost all of the internal parts are made of stainless steel, not only because of its anti-rusting properties, but also for durability. A variety of tests showed that the P-85 could carry all possible types of 9 mm Para cartridges. This was to do with the angle of the feed ramp in relation to the height of the first cartridge in the magazine. It is clear from the exterior that the Ruger P-85 is designed specifically for use as a service pistol. Sadly, this does not make this weapon look anymore graceful. Ruger are known for the high quality of their cast-steel parts, that because of special techniques, hardly needs additional working. Any milling required is only carried out with computerized equipment. The grip is manufactured from a lightweight alloy, known as T-6. In addition, it has a special coating with the same surface hardness as that of chrome-molybdenum steel, from which the slide is manufactured. This type of steel is also used for all blued Ruger revolvers. The slide of the P-85 has a large ejector port. At the back of the slide is an ambidextrous safety catch that also functions as a uncocking lever. The safety catch blocks the firing pin, breaks the connection between the trigger and tumbler, and releases the hammer.

Side-view of solid Ruger P-85

RUGER P-89

The Ruger P-89 pistol did not originate in 1989 as the name suggests, but in 1991. The double-action pistol is a continuation of the P-85 design. This weapon also has the combined ambidextrous safety/ uncocking lever on the slide. The frame is also made of alloy and the slide is manufactured from 4140 chrome-molybdenum steel. The magazine release located behind the trigger guard is also ambidextrous. In 1992, Ruger introduced the stainless steel KP-89. In the same year the Model 89 with only an uncocking lever was launched. This was the P-89DC in mat black and the KP-89DC with a stainless steel slide. A third version of the KP-89DAO was released in 1992, a stainless steel model in double-action-only. This pistol is still available with a caliber of 9 mm Para and a magazine capacity of 15 rounds. The total length of all versions is 200 mm (7¾ in). The barrel length is 114 mm (4½ in) and the height is 145 mm (5¾ in). This pistol has a fixed rear sight that can only be adjusted laterally. The sight radius is 144 mm (5¾ in). This weapon weighs 907 g (32 oz). It has black Xenoy grips with horizontal grooves. The locking is identical to that of the P-85 pistol.

Ruger KP-90 with light alloy casing and stainless steel slide

RUGER P-90

The double-action Ruger P-90 pistol was introduced in 1991 and is still in production. This model is available in three versions. The P90 has an alloy frame and a mat black steel slide. This weapon has a capacity of 7 rounds in .45 ACP caliber. It has a combined ambidextrous safety/uncocking lever on the slide. The same weapon in stainless steel is the KP-90. In addition, Ruger also produces the KP-90D, with only an ambidextrous uncocking lever. This pistol has a barrel length of 114 mm (4½ in) and a total length of 197 mm (7¾ in). The weight for all versions is 950 g (33½ oz). This weapon also has black Xenoy grips with horizontal grooves. The action and the locking are the same as that of the Ruger P-85 pistol.

RUGER P-91

From 1992 until 1995 Ruger manufactured the double-action P-91 pistol with a caliber of .40 S&W. This 11-shot weapon was then only available in stainless steel in two different versions. The KP-91DC has an ambidextrous uncocking lever on the slide, which does not function as a safety catch. The second version is the KP-91DAO with a double-action-only trigger action. The total length of this weapon is 200 mm (8 in), the barrel length is 114 mm (4½ in) and this weapon weighs 935 g (33 oz).

Ruger P-90 pistol of 1991 in .45 ACP caliber

Ruger KP-91DC pistol in .40 S&W, manufactured from 1992 till 1995

Compact 15-shot Ruger
P-93DC in 9 mm Para

RUGER P-93

The Ruger P-93 pistol originates from 1993. This is a compact double-action weapon in 9 mm Para caliber with a magazine capacity of 15 rounds. The P-93 has a barrel length of 99 mm (4 in) and a total length of 185 mm (7¼ in). The weight is 879 g (31 oz). As with the P-93DC, this pistol is available in mat black molybdenum steel with only an ambidextrous uncocking lever on the slide. The stainless steel version also only has a uncocking lever and has the model name KP-93DC. The third version, also in stainless steel, has a double-action-only trigger action and is known as the P-93DAO.

RUGER P-94

The Ruger P-94 pistol came on the market in 1994. This is a double-action pistol with a caliber of 9 mm Para or .40 S&W and has a whole series of different versions all with the same dimensions. The barrel length is 108 mm (4¼ in) and the total length is 191 mm (7½ in). The weight of the 9 mm Para versions is 936 g (33 oz) and this pistol with .40 S&W caliber weighs 964 g (34 oz). The magazine

Ruger KP-94 pistol in
9 mm Para or .40 S&W

capacity for both calibers is 10 rounds. The P94 models have Xenoy grips with a checkered motif. The standard P-94 is a mat black model in the caliber 9 mm Para. It has an ambidextrous safety/uncocking lever on the slide. The KP-94 is the same pistol, but with a stainless steel slide. The KP-94DC pistol does not have a safety catch, but an ambidextrous uncocking lever. The KP-94DAO is also made of stainless steel with a double-action-only trigger action. This weapon does not have a catch mounted on the slide. The P-944 is in fact the same weapon as the P-94, but with a caliber of .40 S&W. The stainless steel version has the model name KP-944. The stainless steel weapon with only an ambidextrous uncocking lever is known as the KP-944DC and in double-action-only trigger action it has the model name KP-944DAO.

RUGER P-95

Ruger KP-95DAO,
double-action only, in
9 mm Para with a Xenoy
plastic casing

Model P-95 appeared in 1997. This is a 9 mm Para pistol with a composite Xenoy frame and a built-in trigger guard. This weapon has a magazine capacity of 10 rounds, in accordance with American firearms legislation. This pistol is available in six different versions, but all with the same dimensions. The total length of this weapon is 185 mm (7¼ in) and the barrel length is 99 mm (4 in). The use of composite has reduced the weight to 765 g (27 oz). Model P-95 has a mat black molybdenum steel slide. The combined ambidextrous safety/uncocking lever is located on the slide. The P-95D has only an ambidextrous uncocking lever that does not function as a safety catch. The P-95DAO has a double-action-only trigger. In stainless steel the models names are KP-95, KP-95D and KP-95DAO respectively.

Compact Ruger KP-97DC
in .45 ACP caliber

RUGER P-97

The Model P-97 was launched in 1997. This is an 8-shot pistol in the .45 ACP caliber. This weapon is only available with a mat black composite Xenoy frame and a stainless steel slide. The total length of this weapon is 184 mm (7¼ in) and the barrel length is 105 mm (4 in). This weapon weighs 865 g (30½ oz). There are two versions of this weapon in production. The KP-97DC has an ambidextrous uncocking lever on the slide that does not function as a safety catch. The second version is known as the P-97DAO and has a double-action-only trigger action.

RUGER OLD ARMY REVOLVER

The Ruger Old Army percussion revolver was launched in 1972. Two years later this was followed by a stainless steel version. This weapon is based on the Remington Army of 1858, but with modern gadgetry. Ruger uses spiral springs instead of the old traditional flat springs of the past. This applies not only to the hammer or percussion spring, but also to

the trigger spring. The blued version is manufactured in chrome-molybdenum steel. The 6-shot cylinder of the same material has stainless steel pistons. An interesting point is the locking of the loading lever at the muzzle. The original Remington model has a spring-loaded catch that is sometimes difficult to release. Ruger designed an easily operated, spring-loaded case that slides over the far end of the loading lever. The total length of this revolver is 340 mm (13½ in) and the barrel has a length of 190 mm (7½ in). This weapon has an adjustable rear sight with a sight radius of 250 mm (9¾ in). This weapon is also available with a fixed rear sight as Model BP-7F and in the blued version in stainless steel as the KBP-7F. The height of the Old Army is 135 mm (5¼ in) and it weighs 1290 g (45½ oz). The trigger pressure of the single-action weapon is 740 g (24 oz). The caliber of this revolver is .45. The diameter between the 6 right-hand twisting grooves in the barrel is 11.46 mm (½ in) and the distance between the lands is 11.25 mm (½ in). The rifling twist is 406 mm (16 in). This weapon has been designed for round or conical bullets with a diameter of 11.61 mm (½ in). The grips are made of palisander.

RUGER BEARCAT

Ruger produced the old model of the 6-shot Ruger Bearcat single-action revolver with a caliber of .22 LR between 1953 and 1972. This weapon has an alloy frame. The solid steel cylinder has engravings of a bear, a puma and the Ruger Bearcat model name. The Bearcat revolvers manufactured until 1972 do not have a transfer bar safety. It is therefore advisable not to load the cylinder chamber in front of the hammer. In 1993, Ruger introduced a new Bearcat model that did have this built-in safety feature. The owners of an old model with a series number, lower than 93-XXXXX can still have these weapons converted free of charge. Both the old and the new Bearcat revolver have the same dimensions. The total length is (9 in) and the barrel has a length of 102 mm (4 in). This weapon has a fixed sight slot in the bridge above the cylinder. The weight is

Ruger Old Army
percussion revolver
in blued steel and
stainless steel

The old Ruger
Bearcat of 1953

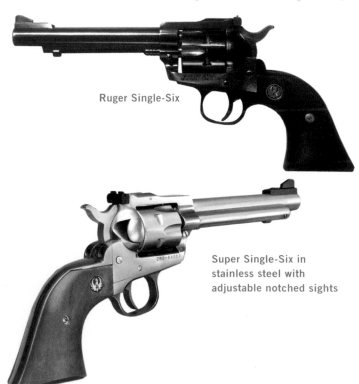

The new Bearcat
of 1993

680 g (24 oz). The old Bearcat had impregnated wooden grips until 1963. After 1963 the grips of these models were replaced by walnut. The new Bearcat models have palisander grips. A second difference between the old and new model is the trigger guard. The old Bearcat trigger guard was made of alloy with an anodized brass coating. The new Bearcat has a blued alloy trigger guard. Between 1971 and 1974 Ruger produced a totally steel version of the Bearcat with the model name Super Bearcat. This type had a solid brass trigger guard until 1973, which was later followed by one made of steel.

RUGER SINGLE-SIX

The 6-shot single-action Ruger Single-Six originates from 1953. Until 1957, this revolver had a flat loading gate safety. This weapon had hard rubber grips until 1962, which were later replaced by walnut grips. Then followed the black Ruger emblem, later replaced by

Ruger Single-Six

Super Single-Six in
stainless steel with
adjustable notched sights

the silver colored emblem in 1971. The first model has a fixed rear sight and a barrel length of 140 mm (5½ in). In 1959 Ruger also introduced other barrel lengths, such as the 118, 165 and 241 mm (4½, 6½ and 9½ in). This revolver is based on the Colt Single-Action Army. The biggest difference is the use of spiral springs instead of the old flat springs, together with the independently spring-loaded firing pin. The Ruger Single-Six revolvers before 1973 do not have a transfer bar. Ruger converts the old Single-Six revolvers free of charge. In between 1956 and 1958, Ruger also manufactured a lightweight Single-Six. This type has an alloy frame with an 118 mm (4½ in) barrel. The first 6,500 weapons even had an alloy cylinder with inserted steel cylinder chambers. Ruger manufactured the Single-Six Magnum model between 1960 and 1962. This weapon is in the caliber .22 WMR with a replacement cylinder for .22 LR. Ruger later changed this to the Single-Six Convertible model. This type has the standard caliber of .22 LR with a replacement cylinder for .22 WMR. The Super Single-Six dates from 1964. This revolver was then manufactured with an adjustable rear sight and in the barrel lengths 140 and 165 mm (5½ and 6½ in). The current Single-Six series has three basic models: the blued steel New Model Single-Six with a fixed rear sight and with the barrel lengths or 140 and 165 mm (5½ and 6½ in). The Super Single-Six has an adjustable rear sight. In a blued version this type is available with the barrel lengths of 118, 140, 165 or 241 mm (4½, 5½, 6½ and 9½ in). The stainless steel version is only manufactured with a 140 or 165 mm (5.5 or 6½ in) barrel. In 1985 Ruger introduced the model Single-Six also in the new .32 H&R Magnum caliber developed by Harrington & Richardson. This single-action revolver was then available in the same barrel lengths as the Super Single-Six and with an adjustable rear sight. In 1997 Ruger ceased to produce this model, but re-introduced this revolver in 2001 in blued and stainless steel versions with an 118 mm (4½ in) barrel and a fixed rear sight.

RUGER BLACKHAWK

The Single-Six model proved to be so popular that Ruger decided to start making a larger model. In 1955, the company introduced the 6-shot single-action Blackhawk with a caliber of .357 Magnum. An adjustable rear sight had been added to the flat bridge top above the cylinder, giving this model the nickname 'flat top'. This weapon was only available in a blued steel with black hard rubber grips. In the period up until 1962 there were approximately 42,600 weapons manufactured in the barrel lengths 118, 165 and 254 mm (4½, 6½ and 10 in). In 1956 the newly developed .44 Remington Magnum caliber was

Old Blackhawk model of
1955 and New Blackhawk
with 9 mm Para exchange
cylinder

Blackhawk in stainless steel
for .45 Long Colt caliber

KBN-34 Blackhawk
in stainless steel
for .357 Magnum

launched. Ruger reacted swiftly with a Blackhawk for this new cartridge. This is a slightly larger and heavier version of the flattop Blackhawk in .357 Magnum. The .44 Magnum Blackhawk was available in the barrel lengths 165, 191 and 254 mm (6½, 7½ and 10 in). Ruger manufactured more then 28,000 of this model up until 1963. In 1962 a successor to the flat top came on the market. This weapon is practically identical to the previous model, with only a slight modification of the cylinder bridge. Ruger manufactured this revolver up until 1972 in a variety of calibers, such as .30-M1, .357 Magnum, .41 Magnum, .44 Magnum and .45 Colt. This weapon in the carbine caliber .30-M1 has a different barrel length with 188 mm (7½ in). The barrel lengths of the other calibers are standard at 118, 165 and 191 mm (4½, 6½ and 7½ in). In that period, this model could also be purchased with a replacement cylinder. For .357 Magnum caliber there was a replacement cylinder in 9 mm Para and for the .45 Colt a replacement cylinder for .45 ACP. In 1973, Ruger brought a new Blackhawk model onto the market. This new type had a transfer bar safety, and was also available in stainless steel versions, and also with the calibers of .357 Magnum, .44 Magnum and .45 Colt. The New Model Blackhawk Convertible was supplied with a replacement cylinder in 9 mm Para for the .357 Magnum revolver and with a replacement cylinder for .45 ACP for the .45 Colt. Production of the Convertible was stopped in 1985. This decision was poorly received by the consumer, so much so that Ruger reintroduced the Convertible in 1988. The current range of the Blackhawk includes the calibers .30-M1, .357 Magnum, .41 Magnum and .45 Long Colt. A replacement cylinder for the caliber .357 Magnum is still available in the caliber of 9 mm

Para. This revolver in the caliber .30-M1 is only available in a blued steel version, with a barrel length of 191 mm (7½ in), a total length of 340 mm (13½ in) and it weighs 1247 g (44 oz). This weapon in .357 Magnum was manufactured in blued or stainless steel. The available barrel lengths are 118 and 165 mm (4½ and 6½ in). The total lengths are 264 and 318 mm (10½ and 12½ in) respectively and it weighs 1134 or 1190 g (40 or 42 oz). The blued or stainless steel Blackhawk with a caliber of .41 Magnum has a barrel length of 118 or 165 mm (4½ or 6½ in), a total length of 260 or 308 mm (10¼ or 12 in) and it weighs 1077 or 1134 g (38 or 40 oz). The available barrel lengths in .45 Long Colt caliber are 118, 140 from 191 mm (4½, 5½ or 7½ in). The total length is 264, 283 or 333 mm (10½, 11 or 13 in). The weight is 1106, 1134 or 1162 g (39, 40 or 41 oz).

RUGER SUPER BLACKHAWK

The single-action Super Blackhawk was developed as early as 1959. The vicious recoil of the powerful .44 Magnum cartridge proved too much for the light frame of the normal Blackhawk. Furthermore the grip of the Blackhawk was too narrow to be comfortable enough when shooting a .44 Magnum revolver. Ruger therefore decided to build a larger type with a heavier frame and a larger grip. The Super Blackhawk was manufactured until 1972 with a 191 mm (7½ in) barrel. The successor of this weapon was the New

Ruger Super Blackhawk
in .44 Magnum

Super Blackhawk with 267 mm (10¹⁄₂ in) barrel

Two stainless steel Super Blackhawks

Model Super Blackhawk in 1973. This type was given the new transfer bar safety. The New Model Super Blackhawk is still available in a blued or stainless steel version. Ruger manufactures this revolver in the barrel lengths 118, 140, 191 and 267 mm (4½, 5½, 7½ and 10½ in). The total lengths are 267, 289, 340 and 416 mm (10½, 11½, 13½ and 16½ in) respectively. The weight is 1276, 1304, 1361 or 1446 g (45, 46, 48 or 51 oz). Most versions have a solid round cylinder. Only the blued S45N and the stainless steel KS45N have a fluted cylinder. The blued models S47N, S411N and the stainless steel KS47N and the KS411N have an angular trigger guard.

RUGER BISLEY

Ruger launched the Bisley in 1986. The single-action revolver is based on the well-known Colt Bisley, which was used by match shooters on the shooting range complex in Bisley, England. The Bisley varies with the Blackhawk with a slightly modified grip angle and a raised grip back. This revolver model was then available with the calibers of .22 LR, .32 H&R Magnum, .357 Magnum, .41 Magnum, .44 Magnum and .45 Long Colt. From .22 LR up to and including .32 H&R Magnum the barrel lengths are 165 mm (6½ in), The total length is 292 mm (11½ in) and the weight 1162 g (41 oz). These weapons in the larger calibers have a barrel length of 191 mm (7½ in), a total length of 330 mm (13 in) and weigh 1361 g (48 oz). The Bisley model was then only manufactured in a blued steel version. In 1997, Ruger stopped manufacturing the Bisley with the calibers of .32 H&R Magnum and .41 Magnum.

RUGER VAQUERO

In 1995, Ruger decided to take advantage of the Western Style Shooting craze that was growing increasingly popular in North America. The new model Vaquero is manufactured in the style of the classic Colt Single-Action Army with a fixed rear sight on the bridge above the cylinder. Ruger designed a blued version with a tempered frame for the real classic connoisseurs, together with a highly polished version. When it was introduced this revolver was available in the calibers of .44-40 Win., .44 Magnum and .45 Long Colt. The barrel lengths were 118, 140 and 191 mm (4½, 5½ and 7½ in). The total lengths were 260, 292 and 333 mm (10¼, 11.5 and 13⅛ in). This weapon weighed 1106, 1134 and 1162 g (39, 40 and 41 oz) respectively. In 1997, the caliber .357

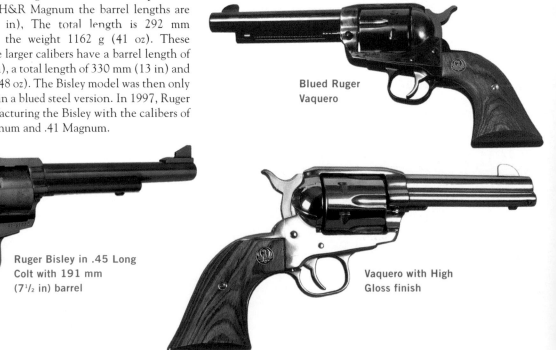

Ruger Bisley in .45 Long Colt with 191 mm (7¹⁄₂ in) barrel

Blued Ruger Vaquero

Vaquero with High Gloss finish

Ruger SP-101 in the KSP-240
version in .22 LR caliber and
KSP-831 in .38 Special +P caliber

Left side of KSP-831
and KSP-931

Magnum was added to the Vaquero series. The
available barrel lengths in this caliber were 118 and
140 mm (4½ and 5½ in). In addition, Ruger also
introduced the Bisley-Vaquero: a Vaquero revolver
model with a Bisley grip. This new type is available
with the calibers of .357 Magnum, .44 Magnum and .45
Long Colt with the barrel lengths of 118 and 140 mm
(4½ and 5½ in), in a blued finish with a tempered frame
and in a polished stainless steel version.

RUGER SP-101

In 1991 Ruger introduced a new double-action
revolver based on the GP-100 revolver, with a small
frame and in different calibers. The 6-shot SP-101 in
.32 H&R Magnum and a 6-shot version with the
calibers of 9 mm Para and .357 Magnum. In 1992,
Ruger brought the SP-101 version onto the market in
.22 LR caliber with the barrel lengths of 57 and
102 mm (2¼ and 4 in). Double-action-only versions
followed in 1993 with a caliber of .357 Magnum and
a separate revolver in a .38 Special P. These DAO
models do not have a hammer spur. All models
are made of stainless steel. These revolvers in .32

H&R Magnum and .22 LR have an
adjustable rear sight, with the other
versions only having a sighting slot in the
upper bridge of the frame. The model in .32
H&R Magnum was then available with the barrel
lengths 78 and 102 mm (3 and 4 in). The 9 mm Para,
.38 Special and .357 Magnum versions had the barrel
lengths 57 and 78 mm (2¼ and 3 in). The SP-101 is
a powerful revolver. Ruger also introduced new
cylinder locking. Most revolvers lock the cylinder at
the back in the recoil shield, with the ejector bar
locating with a spring-loaded pin under the barrel.
Ruger decided to do away with the frontal locking of
the Ruger SP-101, and to lock the cylinder arm
directly into the frame. In addition, this revolver was
given the tried and tested transfer bar safety and
closed safety. The hammer remains blocked unless
the cylinder is in its exact position within the frame.
The grip of all versions is made of Xenoy with
horizontal grooves. In 1999, the short barrel 57 mm
(2¼ in) version of this revolver with a caliber of .22
LR was discontinued, as were the double-action-only
model with a caliber of .38 Special and the double-
action SP-101 in 9 mm Para caliber in 2001.

KSP-931 revolver
in 9 mm Para

Double-action only KSP-321XL
in .357 Magnum

Blued Security-Six of
1970 with 152 mm (6 in)
barrel

RUGER SECURITY SIX

I personally think that the Security Six is the most beautiful revolver ever manufactured by Ruger. This model was launched in 1970 and remained in production until 1986. The design was far ahead of its time. The trigger group is especially ingenious, as the entire mechanism and trigger guard all can be removed from this weapon. The Security Six was available in a blued version with an adjustable rear sight. Until 1975, the 6-shot double-action Security-Six was manufactured with a fixed rear sight in .38 Special caliber as the model 108 and as model 107 with a of .357 Magnum caliber. The same weapon with an adjustable rear sight had the model number 117. The model in .38 Special was withdrawn in 1976. In the same year, Ruger brought the model 717 onto the market, the Security-Six-Stainless with a caliber of .357 Magnum. Both the blued and the stainless steel versions were available in the barrel lengths 70, 102 and 152 mm (2¾ and 6 in). The barrel has five grooves and lands with a right-hand twist of 476 mm (18¾ in). The total lengths of this weapon are 203, 235 and 286 mm (8, 9¼ and 11¼ in) respectively. This weapon was available with wooden Goncalo Alves grips up until 1984, but also later with rubber grips. The Security Six was provided with a transfer bar safety as of 1973. In 1976 the Security-Six with the fixed rear sight was re-christened the Police Service-Six. This revolver retained the old model numbers with the calibers of .357 Magnum (model 107) and .38 Special (model 108). The stainless steel versions had the model numbers 707

and 708. The Police Service-Six was available in both versions with a 70 or 102 mm (2¾ or 4 in) barrel. The police force were able to order these models with a lanyard ring at the underside of the grip. The Speed-Six was introduced in 1973. The Speed-Six is actually a Service-Six with a shorter and rounded grip. This blued steel model versions with a caliber of .38 Special had the model number 208 and with a caliber of .357 Magnum it was known as the Model 207. Both versions were then available with a 70 or 102 mm (2¾ and 4 in) barrel. The stainless steel versions of the Speed-Six were given the model numbers 737 (.357) and 738 (.38). As of 1974, the Speed-Six could be specially ordered without a hammer spur and with a double-action-only trigger action. Ruger stopped manufacturing the Security-Six, Service-Six and Speed-Six revolvers in 1986, the Ruger GP-100 followed these in the same year. Ruger continued supplying the Service-Six and Speed-Six up until the end of 1987.

RUGER GP-100

In 1986, the 6-shot double-action Ruger GP-100 was introduced as the successor to the Security-Six revolver. Ruger designed an extra strong frame for the most powerful .357 Magnum cartridges. The grip is made of black rubber inlaid with wood. The cylinder is also reinforced with the cylinder stop grooves being in the thicker sections between the cylinder chambers. A new system was also developed for locking the cylinder. The traditional cylinder locking at the back was retained. The front of the cylinder is locked in to the frame by a locking cam in the cylinder arm. The ejection system was borrowed from the Ruger Redhawk revolver. The removable trigger group of the Security-Six models was also applied to the GP-100. This weapon is manufactured from 4140 chrome-molybdenum steel or special stainless steel. The first models of 1986 were only available with a heavy barrel with a continuous ejector shroud. The barrel lengths were 102 and 152 mm (4 and 6 in). In 1987, there followed a stainless steel version. In 1988, Ruger extended the model series with a number of different versions. The GP-141 is a blued revolver with a 102 mm (4 in) barrel and a continuous ejector

Stainless steel
Security-Six

Ruger GP-161 with
extended ejector shroud
under barrel

Stainless steel KGP-141
and KGP-160

Ruger KGP-160

shroud. The model KGP-141 is the same weapon, but in stainless steel. The blued GP-160 revolver has a 152 mm (6 in) barrel with a short ejector shroud. The stainless steel version has the model number KGP-160. The third type is the GP-161 with a 152 mm (6 in) barrel and a continuous ejector shroud. The same model in stainless steel is the KGP-161.

In 1989, Ruger introduced a number of new versions of the GP-100. The Model GPF-330 is a blued revolver with a caliber of .357 Magnum with a 76 mm (3 in) barrel, a short ejector shroud and a fixed rear sight. The same weapon in stainless steel has the model number KGPF-330. This weapon with a continuous ejector shroud in the blued version was given the model number GPF-331 and in stainless steel the KGPF-331. The same number system applies to the version with a 102 mm (4 in) barrel and a fixed rear sight. The blued version with a short ejector shroud is known as the GPF-340 and in stainless steel it has the model name KGPF-340. This type, blued and with continuous ejector shroud and a 102 mm (4 in) barrel is known as the GPF-341 and in stainless steel the KGPF-341.

In 1993 Ruger brought two new stainless steel versions onto the market. The model KGPF-840 in .38 Special caliber has a 102 mm (4 in) barrel and a short ejector shroud. The second new model is the KGPF-841 with a continuous ejector shroud. The weights of these models are 1049 and 1077 g (37 and 38 oz) respectively. In the same year Ruger also introduced a variety of grips. The original rubber grip with inlaid wood was retained, and has been known since then as the Mansanto Santoprene grip. In addition, Ruger also supplied a totally wooden grip and a rubber combat grip with horizontal grooves. In 1995, Ruger decided to start producing GP-100 revolvers in polished stainless steel: the so-called High-Gloss finish. A letter G preceding the model number indicated these models. These models were then the GKGP-141, the GKGPF-331 and the GKGPF-341. The High-Gloss versions were scrapped from the range in 1997. In the same year, the models KGPF-841 with a caliber of .38 Special and a continuous ejector shroud and the blued GPF-330 with the short housing were also discontinued.

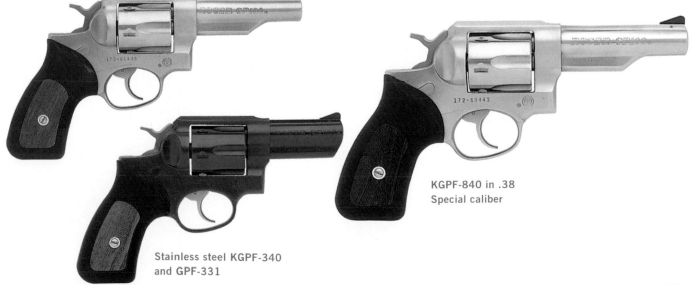

Stainless steel KGPF-340
and GPF-331

KGPF-840 in .38
Special caliber

Old Redhawk
of 1980

RUGER REDHAWK

In 1979 Ruger announced the launch of a new double-action revolver. This was the 6-shot Redhawk in .44 Magnum caliber. This weapon strongly resembles an overgrown Security Six and also has the distinctive removable trigger group. Circumstances dictated that Ruger was unable to present the first prototype until the American Shot Show in 1980 Mass production did not reallz gain momentum until mid 1980. The Redhawk cylinder locking was completely enclosed within the cylinder arm. This system was also later applied to the GP-100 series. The first Redhawk model has a 191 m (7½ in) barrel and a total length of (13 in). This is a heavy revolver with a weight of 1474 g (52 oz). This weapon has an adjustable rear sight with a sight radius of 241 mm (9½ in). They were then only manufactured in stainless steel. In 1984 Ruger decided to give the Redhawk a barrel length of 140 mm (5½ in). The total length of this type is 279 mm (11 in) and it weighs 1417 g (50 oz). In 1985 Ruger introduced the Redhawk in two other caliber versions. The Redhawk with the caliber of .357 Magnum and .41 Magnum with a 140 and 191 mm (5½ and 7½ in) barrel. In addition, Ruger presented the Redhawk KRH-44R with a caliber of .44 Magnum with a built-in telescopic sight mounting system and a barrel length of 191 mm (7½ in). Furthermore, all Redhawks have a front sight that is easily replaced with front sights of different colors. Ruger scrapped the Redhawk with the caliber of .357 Magnum in 1986, as the consumer showed little enthusiasm for this weapon. A blued version of the

Redhawk in both barrel lengths and in both calibers also came onto the market in 1986. This was followed in the same year by a comprehensive series of Ruger Redhawks with the caliber of .41 Magnum and .44 Magnum, the blued Redhawk is available with a 140 and 191 mm (5½ and 7½ in) barrel and as model RH-41R and RH-44R with a built-in telescopic sight mounting. Ruger also manufactured exactly the same series in stainless steel. In 1990, Ruger changed the model identification. The blued Redhawk with a caliber of .41 Magnum with a 140 mm (5½ in) barrel was given the model number RH-415. The same weapon with a caliber of .44 Magnum had the model number RH-445. Ruger applied the same system to the stainless steel versions but with the letter K preceding the identification. The Alloy Steel Redhawk was launched in 1991. It was at that time that Ruger was feverishly trying to lower production costs with the development of cast steel. The milled steel Redhawk was then also still available. The weight of both models remained the same at 1474 g (52 oz). In 1993, the Redhawk versions in the caliber .41 Magnum were abolished, and were survived only by the .44 Magnum revolver in the barrel lengths 140 and 191 mm (5½ and 7½ in). The 191 mm (7½ in) version with the telescopic sight mounting was retained in blued and stainless steel. In 1996, Ruger also brought the Redhawk High-Gloss versions onto the market, in line with the other revolver models. This applied to the stainless steel models GKRH-445 with a 140 mm (5½ in) barrel and the GKRH-44 with a 191 mm (7½ in) barrel. Furthermore the upper bridge over the cylinder was reinforced on all Redhawk versions, increasing the weight from 1474–1531 g (52–54 oz). A year later the Glossy version was withdrawn. In 1997, Ruger also introduced a stainless steel Redhawk in the caliber .45 Long Colt in three versions. The KRH-455 with a 140 mm (5½ in) barrel, the KRH-45 with a 191 mm (7½ in) barrel and the KRH-45R with a built-in telescopic sight mounting.

New Redhawk on .45 Long
Colt caliber

Stainless steel Redhawk
in two different versions

Special Mag-na-port version of Super Redhawk

RUGER SUPER REDHAWK

The arrival of the 6-shot double-action Ruger Super Redhawk revolver with a caliber of .44 Magnum was announced at the start of 1986, although only on as a prototype. This weapon was eventually launched in 1987. The Super Redhawk has the largest and heaviest frame that Ruger ever designed. This revolver has the same cylinder locking as the GP-100. The solid frame has an extra thick upper bridge over the cylinder. The front of the frame is extended in to a thick shroud, in which the barrel is screwed. There are mountings on the upper bridge and on the shroud for a telescopic sight. The grips are the same type as that of the GP-100, a rubber grip with wooden Goncalo Alves inlay. The Super Redhawk is also provided with the transfer bar safety. The Super Redhawk was manufactured exclusively in stainless steel. The first series was manufactured with a 171 mm (7½ in) barrel, but was followed a year later by a version with a 241 mm (9½ in) barrel. The total lengths are 330 and 381 mm (13 and 15 in) respectively and the weights are 1503 and 1644 g (53 and 58 oz). Both versions have an adjustable rear sight with a sight radius of 241 and 286 mm (9½ and 11¼ in). In 1995 Ruger introduced a High-Gloss version of both models, that in fact were once again withdrawn by the end of 1996. In 1997, the Ruger Super Redhawk in the caliber .454 Casull came on the market, a weapon specially intended for silhouette shooters. This stainless steel weapon has a mat gray finish to prevent the reflection of light. This revolver was also capable of firing .45 Long Colt cartridges. The Super Redhawk Casull with the model number KRSH-7454 was only available with a 191 mm (7½ in) barrel and weighed 1503 g (53 oz). This version of the .454 Casull suddenly disappeared in 1998 for no apparent reason. This may have been due to this weapon being the subject of a conflict with respect to the patent rights of this caliber. Evidently, an agreement must have been the result of this conflict, because the Super Redhawk resurfaced in 2000. In 2001, Ruger manufactured the Super Redhawk in the calibers of .44 Magnum, .454 Casull and in the new caliber .480 Ruger. The barrel lengths have remained the same over the years at 191 and 241 mm (7½ and 9½ in). The Super Redhawk in the new caliber .480 Ruger has the model number KSRH-7480 and KSRH-9480 for both barrel lengths.

Mighty Super Redhawk with 241 mm (9¹/₂ in)

Super Redhawk model KSRH-7454 in .454 Casull caliber in Target Gray version

S

SAFARI ARMS

Safari trade mark

The single-action Matchmaster from the Safari Arms company of Phoenix, Arizona is equipped with a number of special features, which means that Combat or concourse shooters do not have to invest extra money on all manner of accessories. This pistol has amongst other things a Smith & Wesson pistol sight (the 'K' sight), a red inlaid front sight, a combat hammer, an ambidextrous safety catch, a square trigger guard, an enlarged ejector port and special magazines. The 6-shot pistol in .45 ACP caliber has a 127 mm (5 in) barrel. The total length of this weapon is 220 mm (8 ¾ in). The height is 126 mm (5 in)

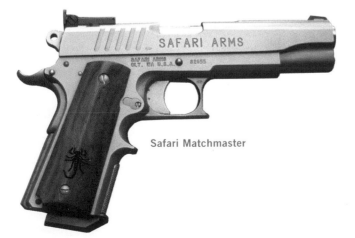

Safari Matchmaster

and this pistol weighs 1135 g (40 oz). The Matchmaster is available in different versions, including one with a waterproof Teflon coating, chromed, in stainless steel, with an alloy frame (Armaloy) or blued. A two-tone version in a combination of blued steel and stainless steel is also in the stores. The Safari Arms pistols can be immediately recognized by the following features: The ergonomically shaped grip with a finger hole indent for the middle finger, with the current model also having a second groove for the ring finger under the trigger guard. In 1983, Safari Arms brought the Phoenix Centennial onto the market in .45 ACP caliber. This is a limited edition jubilee issue of exactly 101 weapons numbered from 1881 up until 1981. This pistol was issued to commemorate the Centennial of the city of Phoenix, Arizona. Another interesting feature of this weapon is the frame, which is manufactured from berylium.

SAKO

Sako logo

The Sako weapons factory of Finland has been manufacturing excellent small caliber sport pistols for decades. However the history of this weapons factory goes back much farther. Immediately after the First World War, the Finnish weapons factory Sako was founded as a work shop for the repair and modification of contemporary military rifles. Many of these weapons were adapted for hunting purposes. The Sako factory is based in Riihimski in southern Finland. In the Second World War, the company almost failed, and in 1946 had to be built up again from scratch. At that time they were also involved in the conversion of military rifles for hunting- and sport weapons. Half way through the previous century, Sako developed their own series of hunting and precision rifles in the entire popular caliber range from .223 Remington up to and including .416 Remington.

In 1986, Sako designed the TRG sniper's rifle. This rifle is also available in a hunting version. In addition, Sako manufactures military rifles, derived from the AK-47, such as the Sako RK-95 in the caliber .223 Rem. or 7.62x39 mm. The Sako concern also has an ammunition factory, where cartridges are produced from .22 Hornet up to and including .375 H&H Magnum. This ammunition has specially developed bullets with fascinating names, such as Hammerhead, Powerhead and Speedhead. In

Sako Tri-Ace match pistol

addition, Sako also manufacture ammunition for handguns, including a special police cartridge: the 9 mm Para KPO.

The 5-shot single-action Sako Tri-Ace sport pistol is one of high quality. Adapter sets for this weapon were available in the calibers .22 LR, .22 Short and .32 Smith & Wesson-Long. This weapon has a total length of 283 mm (11¹/₄ in) and a barrel length of 150 mm (6 in) The height of this pistol is 140 mm (5¹/₂ in) and it weighs 1320 g (46¹/₂ oz) in the caliber .22 LR. In .22 Short this pistol weighs 1255 g (44¹/₄ oz) and in the caliber .32 S&W-Long it weighs 1370 g (48¹/₄ oz). The Tri-Ace has an adjustable micrometer sight with a sight radius of 225 mm (9 in) in .22 Short and 210 mm (8¹/₄ in) in both other calibers. The safety catch is located on the left-hand side of the frame. The magazine release is built in to the grip. In addition, the walnut match stock has an adjustable hand palm support. The Sako Tri-Ace has not been manufactured since 1998.

SARSILMAZ

Trade mark of Sarsilimaz of Turkey

The Turkish company Sarsilmaz was founded in 1880 by the Abdyllatif family. Since then the company leadership has been handed from father to son. Each generation has made a contribution to the continued existence of the company. This weapons factory is based in Dyzce, at the foot of the Pontic mountains. The factory occupies 35,000 square meters and has been extended considerably in the last ten years. The company manufactures a large number of different shotguns for hunting and for police forces. The pistols are derived from the Czech CZ-75 and in addition, Sarsilmaz manufactures a number of pistol models under license from the Italian companies Bernardelli and Tanfoglio. Sarsilmaz has a modern factory with Cad-Cam design systems and computerized CNC production machines. Striking, is the number of colored weapons produced by Sarsilmaz, which are exported mainly to the Middle East, Asia and South-America. All firearms are tested by the Turkish proof house before delivery.

SARSILMAZ GUNE 2000

The Gune 2000 pistol is manufactured under license, based on the Tanfoglio Force 99. The double-action pistol has a composite polymer frame and a steel slide. Extra pressure grooves have been applied to both sides of the slide. The safety catch is on the left-hand side. In addition, the Gune 2000 has automatic firing pin safety. Sarsilmaz only manufactures this weapon in 9 mm Para with a magazine capacity of 16 rounds. The total length of this pistol is 210 mm (8¹/₄ in). The barrel length is 113 mm (4¹/₂ in), and this weapon weighs 850 g (30 oz).

Double-action Gune 2000

SARSILMAZ HANCER

The double-action Hancer pistol of 1999 is a compact version of the Kilinc 2000. The model is derived from the Czech CZ-75 pistol. The slide has guide rails over the whole length. This weapon is in the caliber 9 mm Para and has a magazine capacity of 13 rounds. The safety catch located on the left-hand side of the frame blocks the

Double-action
Sarsilimaz Hancer

results of the German police testing were very interesting. Prior to the testing, various readings were taken, including the distance between the grooves and lands of the barrel on the test weapon. The barrel diameter between the lands was 8.79 mm (.34606 in) and between the grooves this was 9.01 mm (.35472 in). After firing tests of a total of 10,000 rounds the barrel was measured again. The barrel diameter at both measuring points had only increased by 0.01 mm (.00039 in) respectively 8.80 and 9.02 mm (.34646 and .35511 in). The average muzzle velocity of the bullet was also found to have increased slightly to 353 to 355 m/s (1158 to 1165 fps). The average diameter of the 8-shot hit grouping over 25 meters was 95 mm (3³/₄ in) at the start of the test and after 10,000 rounds this diameter had been reduced to 85 mm (3¹/₄ in).

P226 Sport II with 139 mm (5¹/₂ in) barrel

SIG-SAUER P226

The P226 pistol originates from 1980 and was specially manufactured to the technical specifications of the US Army. The Pentagon was searching for a replacement for the old Colt 1911-A1 pistol. They wanted a 9 mm Para pistol with a large magazine capacity. The US Army finally close the Beretta 92F for their service weapon, to the tremendous disappointment of the Swiss. The P226 is derived from the P220 pistol, but the magazine can hold 15 rounds in the caliber 9 mm Para. The locking, the uncocking lever and the firing pin safety are the same as that of the previous models P220 and P225. The total length of the P226 is 196 mm (7³/₄ in). The barrel has a length of 112 mm (4¹/₂ in) and a right-hand twist of 250 mm (9³/₄ in). The height is 139 mm (5¹/₂ in) and when using extra thin grips, the width is 37 mm (1¹/₂ in). This weapon has a fixed rear sight with a sight radius of 160 mm (6¹/₄ in). The empty weight is 845 g (29³/₄ oz) and with a full magazine this pistol weighs 1035 g (36¹/₂ oz). The trigger pressure in double- and single-action is same as that of the P225. In 1997, the P226 pistol was released in a number of sporting versions in 9 mm Para caliber and with an adjustable micrometer sights. The P226 Sport II has an alloy frame and a stainless steel slide. The barrel length of this type is 112 or 139 mm (4¹/₂ or 5¹/₂ in). A second sport model is the P226 Sport II SL with a stainless steel frame and slide. In addition, extra barrel weight can be fitted to this weapon. In this version this pistol weighs 1351 g (47¹/₂ oz). The standard model P226 has been available for some years now in the caliber .40 S&W (12 rounds) and .357 Sig (12 rounds). In 2001 Sig-Sauer brought

Sig-Sauer P226

P226 Sport II LS with added barrel weight

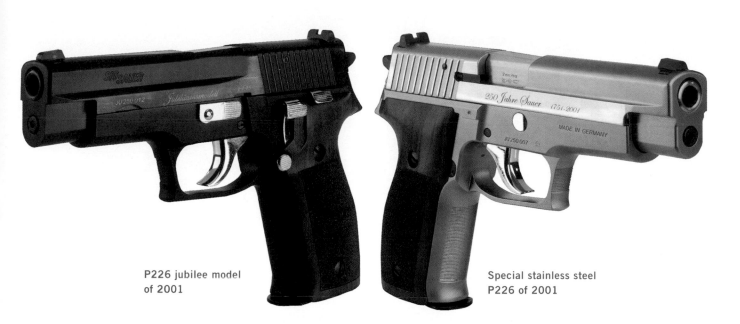

P226 jubilee model
of 2001

Special stainless steel
P226 of 2001

out two special jubilee models to celebrate their 250th anniversary. Only twentyfive of the stainless steel P226-2001 were made. A second commemorative version was the blued version with beautifully gilded controls. This version was limited to sewentyfive weapons.

SIG-SAUER P228

The Sig-Sauer P228 was introduced in 1988 and fitted in well with the existing model series. This is a compact double-action pistol with a large magazine capacity of 13 rounds in the caliber 9 mm Para. The larger magazine of the P220 can also be used in this weapon. Sig-Sauer developed this pistol especially for police and army units to wear inconspicuously. In 1991, a contract was made with the British government to supply a large

number of P226 and P228 pistols. In addition, Sig-Sauer supplied the P228 to a variety of US official bodies, such as the Drugs Enforcement Administration (DEA) and the FBI. The total length of the P228 is 180 mm (7 in). The barrel has a length of 98 mm ($3^3/4$ in) and 6 grooves and lands with a rifling twist of 250 mm ($9^3/4$ in). The height of this weapon is 136 mm ($5^1/2$ in) and the total width is 37 mm ($1^1/2$ in). This pistol has a fixed rear sight with a sight radius of 145 mm ($5^3/4$ in). The empty weight is 740 g (26 oz). The double-action trigger pressure is 4500 g (9.9 lb). In single-action this is 2000 g (4.4 lb). The uncocking lever, the magazine release, the takedown lever and the firing pin safety are the same as that of the other models. An interesting fact is that this weapon is also available with an adapted trigger for women with extra small hands, a so-called Ladies Escort.

Sig-Sauer P228

Jubilee model P228
of 2001

Standard Sig-Sauer P229
with duo-tone P229
version beneath

Sig-Sauer P230
pistol

P230SL with stainless
steel slide

Sig-Sauer P229

In 1991 Sig-Sauer brought the double-action P229
pistol to the market. This weapon was designed as
a service weapon for army and police forces.
A feature of the P229 is the slide, which is
manufactured from stainless steel. This weapon is
available with a blank, blued or mat black K-Kote
slide. The black frame is made of light metal.
The uncocking lever, the takedown lever and
the magazine release are all on the left-hand
side of the frame of this pistol. The firing pin
safety and the locking are made on the same
principal as that of the other Sig-Sauer pistols.
The P229 is available in .40 S&W and .357 Sig caliber
with a capacity of 12 rounds and in 9 mm Para caliber
a capacity of 13 rounds. The fixed rear sight is
interchangeable with five different sight heights and
the front sight with four different heights. This pistol
is also available with the SigLite aspect marking sight.
The total length is 180 mm (7 in) the height is 136 mm
(5¹/₂ in) and the width is 37 mm (1¹/₂ in). The barrel
has a length of 98 mm (3³/₄ in). The rifling twist of the
grooves and lands in .40 S&W caliber is 380 mm
(15 in). In .357 Sig caliber the rifling twist is 406 mm
(16 in) and in 9 mm Para this is 250 mm (9³/₄ in). This
weapon weighs 820 g (29 oz) in .40 S&W and 780 g
(27¹/₂ oz) in the other calibers.

Sig-Sauer P230/P232

The double-action P230 pistol was launched in 1977.
This weapon was originally designed as police pistol,
but only a very few police corps purchased this weapon.
To look at, the P230 is very similar to the Walther
PP and PPK. Originally it was available in 7.65 mm

(.32 ACP) caliber with a capacity of 8 rounds and in
9 mm Short (.380 ACP) or 9 x 18 mm (9 mm Police)
for 7 rounds. A special training model was also available
in .22 LR caliber (10 shot). In 1995 Sig-Sauer
discontinued the 7.65 mm (.32 ACP) caliber version,
this was followed by the 9 x 18 mm version in 1996.
The P230 has the distinctive Sig-Sauer uncocking lever
on the left-hand side of the frame. The takedown lever
is also on the left-hand side of the frame, above the front
of the trigger guard. The magazine release is in the grip
heel. The P230 does not have safety catch, but does
have automatic firing pin safety. This pistol has a recoil
and the barrel is fixed to the alloy frame. The slide is
made of blued steel, however the model P230SL is also
available with a stainless steel slide. The total length of
the P230 is 165 mm (6¹/₂ in), the barrel length is 89 mm
(3¹/₂ in) and the height is 120 mm (4³/₄ in). This pistol
has a fixed rear sight with a sight radius of 112 mm
(4¹/₂ in). The weight is 468 g (16¹/₂ oz).

In 1997 Sig-Sauer launched the model P232 as
successor to the P230. The P232 is a 7-shot double-

P232SL jubilee
pistol of 2001

P239 pistol in 2001
jubilee version

action pistol in 9 mm Short (.380 ACP) caliber. This weapon is also available with a single-action or double-action-only trigger. The total length of the P232 is 168 mm (6½ in) and the barrel length is 92 mm (3½ in). The height is 119 mm (4¾ in) and the width is only 31 mm (1¼ in). This pistol has a fixed rear sight with a sight radius of 120 mm (4¾ in). The empty weight is 465 g (16½ oz). The versions available are: blued, a blued frame and a blank stainless steel slide or totally stainless steel. To celebrate their 250th anniversary in 2001, Sig-Sauer released a special jubilee version of the P232SL in stainless steel in a limited edition of 50 weapons.

Sig-Sauer P239

The compact P239 police pistol originates from 1996 and has a double-action or double-action-only trigger. This weapon is available in 9 mm Para caliber (8 rounds), .40 S&W (7 rounds) or .357 Sig (7 rounds). The P239 is derived from the older P220 model and has the same qualities and safeties. The total length is 172 mm (6¾ in), the height is

130 mm (5¼ in) and the width is 32 mm (1¼ in). The barrel has a length of 92 mm (3½ in). The rifling twist of the 6 grooves and lands in 9 mm Para caliber is 250 mm (9¾ in), in .40 S&W 380 mm (15 in) and in 406 mm (16 in) caliber .357 Sig. This weapon has a fixed rear sight with a sight radius of 132 mm (5¼ in). The empty weight is 720 g (25½ oz) in 9 mm Para and 760 g (26¾ oz) in the other caliber. The frame is made of alloy and the slide is blued steel or, as with the model P239SL, stainless steel. In 2001, Sig-Sauer released the P239SL pistol in a jubilee version as a limited edition of only 25 weapons.

Sig Pro 2009/Pro 2340

In 1999 Sig-Sauer came with a new pistol concept. This weapon has a composite polymer frame with a mounting rail in front of the trigger guard for laser or sight lighting equipment. One distinguishing feature is the interchangeable wrap-around grip, which enables the size of the grip to be adapted. This pistol has a uncocking lever on the left-hand side of the

Sig-Sauer P239
pistol

Sig Pro 2009 pistol
for 9 mm Para

Sig Pro 2340

First Smith & Wesson
weapon produced: the
Volcanic of 1854

frame, with the slide catch just above. The magazine release is on the left-hand side, behind the trigger guard, but is easily transferred to the right hand side. In addition, both the Pro 2009 and the Pro 2340 have an automatic firing pin safety. The removable double-action trigger group can be replaced with a single-action or double-action-only. The Pro 2009 is available in 9 mm Para caliber. This type has a magazine capacity of 15 rounds and it weighs 715 g (25¼ oz). In .40 S&W and .357 Sig calibers this pistol is known as the Pro 2340. It has a capacity of 12 rounds and it weighs 790 g (28 oz). The total length in all calibers is 187 mm (7¼ in) and the height is 144 mm (5¾ in). The barrel has a length of 98 mm (3¾ in). The rifling twist of the 6 grooves and lands in the various calibers are the same as that of the other Sig-Sauer pistols. Both versions have a fixed rear sight with a sight radius of 150 mm (6 in). Both the rear and front sights are interchangeable. The trigger pressure in single-action is 2000 g (4.4 lb), in double-action 1500 g (9.9 lb) and in double-action-only 2700 g (5.95 lb).

SMITH & WESSON

Logo of Smith & Wesson

The original Smith & Wesson company was founded in 1852 by Horace Smith and Daniel B. Wesson. The company was based in Norwich, Connecticut. Their intention was to produce a lever-action pistol with a built-in tubular magazine. This weapon was capable of shooting a self-contained cartridge, which in those days was considered to be a technical achievement. This pistol was capable of firing just as fast as the repeater lever could be operated. In 1854 this weapon was nicknamed the Volcano, following an article in the Scientific American magazine which compared its rapid firing sequence to that of an erupting volcano. In the same year they were awarded a gold medal for this design at the Baltimore Exposition.

In 1854 Smith and Wesson got into financial difficulties, but were saved by the industrialist Oliver Winchester. The company was moved to New Haven in Connecticut, where Winchester had a number of other factories. Smith and Wesson sold their shares in the business to Winchester in 1855. The company name was changed to the Volcanic Repeating Arms Company. This new company continued to benefit from Smith and Wesson's patent rights, and manufactured the Volcanic pistol until 1866. In the same year the company was renamed the Winchester Repeating Arms Company. Smith and Wesson then moved back to Springfield, Massachusetts, the birthplace of Horace Smith.

In 1856 they founded a new company in Market Street for the production of a small pocket revolver, which had been developed by Wesson. Just as they were ready to start production, Wesson discovered that a patent registered by Rollin White already covered a number of parts in the new revolver. This concerned a rear-loading cylinder that had been totally counter-bored. White was approached in order to avoid legal problems, and an agreement was reached whereby White would receive 25 cents for every weapon produced as reward for allowing his patent to be used by Smith and Wesson. The new revolver was given the name Model 1 and fired a small .22 rimfire cartridge. This cartridge was based on the Flobert cartridge of 1849. This revolver was such a success that in 1859 the

Smith & Wesson Model 1
revolver

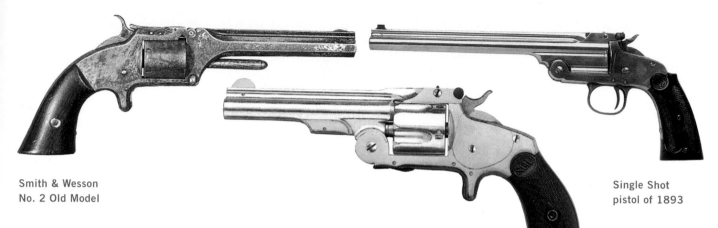

Smith & Wesson
No. 2 Old Model

Pocket Baby Russian

Single Shot
pistol of 1893

company had to move to new factory premises in Stockbridge Street in the center of Springfield. The patent rights of Smith & Wesson & White were infringed on countless occasions, resulting in at least twentyfive law suits against just as many offenders.

In 1861 Smith & Wesson came up with a new model revolver that was appropriately named the Model 2. This revolver had the .32 rimfire caliber. In the same year as the outbreak of the Civil War, there was suddenly a great demand for firearms, one with which the company could hardly keep pace. Sales dropped dramatically after the war and so in 1867 Smith and Wesson decided to restructure. Henry W. Hallot was appointed to sales, with the task of establishing new markets in Europe. Hallot set up sales offices in Germany, the UK and France. Smith & Wesson revolvers attracted a lot of attention at an international trade exhibition in Paris. One of the visitors to this exhibition was the Russian Grand Duke Alexis. He was so impressed by the Smith & Wesson that he placed an order for a large quantity of revolvers on the spot. In 1969 Smith & Wesson bought the W.C. Dodge patent in order to improve the cylinder bridge and swing system of their revolvers. A second patent purchase was for the casing ejection mechanism developed by Charles A. King. Thanks to good turnover in Europe, the company was able to bring a new caliber pistol onto the market in 1869, the .44 rimfire. This was given the name Model 3. The Russian General Gorloff, the military attaché who was stationed at the Russian Embassy in Washington, purchased a Model 3 and sent it to Russia for evaluation. The Russian army hierarchy was so impressed, that in 1871 they placed an order with Smith and Wesson for 20,000 weapons.

In 1870 Smith & Wesson suffered a huge setback. It had been usual for patent rights to be valid for a period of fifteen years, after which they could be freely used by the entire industry. At the time, it was generally considered that fifteen years was enough time to cover development costs. Furthermore, it was felt that a period longer than fifteen years could result in the stifling of development within the industry. In 1869 the American congress decided to change legislation in favor of extending the patent period. In 1870 Rollin White was refused an extension to his patent period by the President Ulysses S. Grant. Various theories exist as to the refusal of this extension. The first theory was that during the Civil War General Grant was not satisfied with the manner in which Smith & Wesson fulfilled their obligations to supply. He even suspected the company of sabotage. A second theory was that America would have to pay higher patent royalties to Smith & Wesson. The army actually wanted to convert a quantity of percussion revolvers into cartridge revolvers in accordance with the White concept. In 1876, the US government decided that they wanted to replace all of percussion revolvers that had been converted to cartridge fire. Smith & Wesson took part in weapon testing. The story goes that the Congress, after pressure from Colt and Remington, decided in favor of the Colt Peacemaker. Ironically, Smith & Wesson were awarded a gold medal in 1876 at the International Centennial Exposition in Philadelphia for the best army revolver design. Due to the absence of a good pocket revolver in the Smith & Wesson range, they decided to develop the 5-shot .38 revolver, which they launched in the same year. This weapon was nicknamed the Baby Russian because of its similarity to its larger brother.

In 1880 the company introduced a series of double-action revolvers in the caliber .32 Smith & Wesson. These included the so-called Lemon Squeezers with a grip safety in the back of the grip. The new gadgetry in these weapons resulted in them being known as the New Departure revolver models. The famous model .38 Military & Police followed in 1899. This predecessor of the current model 10 also fired a new cartridge, the .38 Smith & Wesson Special. In 1908 Smith & Wesson introduced their first revolver with the large N-frame in a new caliber, the .44 Smith & Wesson Special. Smaller versions were available in the calibers .38 Special and .32 Smith & Wesson Long. The official names for this weapon were the Model Hand Ejector Triple Lock or the New Century models. Another type of weapon that arose from the New Century series was the small Model M Ladysmith, a 7-shot Hand Ejector revolver. Hand Ejector in fact implied that the cartridge cases were ejected by means of a hand operated ejector. At the outbreak of the First World in 1914, the company received an order for 75,000 N-frame revolvers in the British caliber .455 Mark II. Another famous Smith & Wesson revolver from that time was the Model 1917. At that time, Colt was manufacturing a similar sort of army revolver. Both weapons fired cartridges in .45 ACP caliber using specially designed 3 round clips, also known as half-moon clips. In 1931, Smith & Wesson developed the famous K-22 Outdoorsman revolver in .22 LR caliber. This weapon is the forefather of all small caliber revolvers that the company were to manufacture. Another famous model followed the .357 Magnum Factory Registered in 1935. This N-frame revolver was only manufactured to order until 1938, after which it went into mass production. The first .357 Magnum was presented to the director or the FBI, J. Edgar Hoover. After the attack by the Japanese on Pearl Harbor in 1941, the USA became involved in the Second World War. Due to the war effort, the company was restructured, and the production of civilian weapons was halted. In that period, Smith & Wesson manufactured more than 1,1 million .38 Military & Police revolvers. In 1945 the company had to switch once again to the production of civilian weapons. In 1946, C.R. Hellstrom was promoted to the position of president of the company. In 1949, he relocated the factory to larger premises in Springfield. In 1948, US Army leaders organized weapon testing for the replacement of the Colt 1911-A1 .45 ACP pistol. Smith & Wesson developed a prototype of a semi-automatic single-action pistol for these tests. This pistol was tested together with other weapons from a variety of companies at the Springfield Armory, which was at that time the state arsenal. Shortly after, the tests were abandoned and the Department of Defense decided to keep the old Colt after all. In 1953, they once again decided to look out for another new army pistol. Smith & Wesson had a new double-action pistol ready and waiting. This weapon had been designed by Joseph Norman, an engineer at the company. The double-action concept was identical to that of the German Walther P38 system. Colt had not been standing still either, and threw the Colt Commander into the fray. In 1954, when the US government abandoned their research once again, Smith & Wesson decided to try their luck with their pistol on the civilian market. The first double-action pistol from Smith & Wesson came on the market in

1955 as the Model 39. The same pistol, but then in a single-action, was introduced as the Model 44. The famous Model 29 followed a year later in .44 Remington Magnum caliber. In 1964, the Wesson family sold the company to the Bangor Punta concern. Director W.G. Gunn, who succeeded Hellstrom in 1963 was given a freehand to take over other companies. Bangor Punta wanted to greatly increase the Smith & Wesson range with the addition of accessories and police equipment. Smith & Wesson handcuffs, Identi-Kit equipment, night binoculars, breathalyzer equipment and leather wear all originated in that period. In addition, Smith & Wesson continued to work tirelessly in the development of new pistol and revolver models.

An enormous breakthrough for Smith & Wesson came in 1967. The Illinois State Police Department introduced the Model 39 as their service weapon. That was the starting signal for many other American police corps to replace their service revolvers with the automatic in 9 mm Para caliber. In 1971, after pressure from the police and other parties, Smith & Wesson introduced the 14-shot pistol model 59 as the larger brother to the Model 39. In 1978, a number of different weapon manufacturers were invited for a third time by the Pentagon to take part in new army trials. They had decided to replace the Colt 1911-A1 after all. This led to Smith & Wesson totally revising their complete large caliber pistol range.

Throughout the army trials, Smith & Wesson had to compete against the eventual winner: Beretta. In 1981, the production of the models 39 and 59 was stopped, and production was switched to the new model types 439, 539, 459 and 559. The number 4 before the old model number indicate that this pistol has an alloy frame. The number 5 means that this pistol has a steel frame. In addition, the feed ramp between the magazine and barrel chamber is slightly longer and not so steep. This allowed the trouble free use of all manner of cartridges with a variety of bullets. This resulted in the total length of this pistols increasing by 5 mm ($^1/_4$ in). The new models were also equipped with automatic firing pin safety and an improved type of cartridge extractor was fitted. In 1982, Smith & Wesson also announced that all new models would be available in stainless steel. The firearms industry had been asking for this for some time. In accordance with tradition, these models were to be known as the Model 639 and 659. In 1984, Bangor Punta, including Smith & Wesson, were taken over by Lear Siegler Corporation of Santa Monica in California. Lear Siegler specialized in the automobile and aircraft industry. Under the management of the new parent company, the range was once again confined to handguns and police equipment. In 1986, the Lear Siegler Corporation was taken over by Forstmann Little & Company. This concern was not interested in Smith & Wesson and sold them in 1987

to the British industrial group Tomkins of
London. Tomkins appointed Bob Muddimer
as interim manager. Under his leadership,
the Autoloader Improvement Project (AIP)
was launched in 1988. This led as the so-
called third generation of Smith & Wesson pistols
with a new trigger mechanism and a cosmetic
metamorphosis. The differences between the old and
new include:

– a wrap-around grip of Delrin or Xenoy composite;
– an ergonomic grip styling, including a finger
  groove under the trigger guard in front of the
  frame;
– an enlarged trigger guard;
– magazines with numbered holes that act as
  a cartridge indicator.
– magazines with rubber bases;
– a flush and widened magazine well;
– new sights with a white triple dot aspect marking;
– an ambidextrous safety catch;
– a new type of automatic firing pin safety;
– a modified trigger action, with a modified trigger
  bar, trigger spring and a modified connection
  between the trigger bar and hammer, resulting in
  a far more supple trigger action.
– a barrel that is made thicker at the muzzle resulting
  in a better seating in the slide.

At the start of 1990, Smith & Wesson introduced
two new versions, for which they reverted to the old
name Lady Smith, for the compact pistol series 3913
LS and 3914 LS. These models have a slightly
modified grip angle in relation to the frame, making
the Lady Smith slightly more suitable as a holster
weapon. In 1990, Smith & Wesson introduced a series
of double-action-only pistols based on the existing
models. In 1992, Ed Schultz became a new director
and he invested heavily in new production line
techniques. His management resulted in the
launching of the Sigma series in 1994. Since then,
Smith & Wesson have brought new pistol and
revolver models onto the market almost every year.
Below are a large number of Smith & Wesson models
according to frame size and type with a sub-division
according to model number. The variations are
described in the basic model description.

SMITH & WESSON MODEL 41

By 1947, two prototypes of this weapon in .22
LR caliber had already been developed and
tested by the then S&W match. However it was
not until 1957 that this pistol went into production.
Manufacture began on a modest scale with only 680
weapons, with a 187 mm (7½ in) barrel, which
included a muzzle brake. Smith & Wesson were
greatly surprised by the enormous demand for this
model. In 1958, the production was increased to
almost 10,000 weapons, but even that was not

Smith & Wesson Model
41 Match pistol

enough to satisfy consumer demand. In 1959, a second
lightweight model was launched with a 127 mm (5 in)
barrel. Smith & Wesson also introduced a less luxury
version in the same year, the Model 46, that was
specially manufactured for US Air Force shooting
matches. This model had a 127 or 178 mm (5 or 7 in)
barrel, without a muzzle brake and was provided with
composite grips. Until 1968, only 4,000 of these
weapons were produced. In 1960, S&W brought out
the Model 41-1, a .22 Short version with an aluminum
slide, but this model did not prove a success and was
only manufactured until 1973.

In 1963, a version with a heavy thick 140 mm (5½
in) barrel was launched with an excellent front sight
with a longer sight radius. The fully adjustable rear
sight was also changed. The same micrometer sight as
on the match pistol, the Model 52, was also adapted
for the new Model 41. One of the factors that had
contributed to the success of this pistol was the
interchangeable barrel concept. Using the trigger
guard, the barrel can be detached from the frame for
the quick replacement of another barrel type. In
addition, the rear sight of this pistol is not fixed on the
slide, but on the extended barrel rib. The slide is
retracted under the rib during repetitive fire. As of
1987 there are three different models on offer,: a
version with a 178 mm (7 in) barrel without
a compensator, a pistol with a heavy 127 mm (5 in)

Right side
of Model 41

barrel and a 'field' version for the hunting of varmint and game.

In 1990, Smith & Wesson only included the versions with a 140 and 178 mm (5¹/₂ and 7 in) barrel in their production program. In 1991, the company also introduced a model with a 152 mm (6 in) barrel, however this model was to be withdrawn from their range within the year. In 1993, they even totally scrapped the Model 41 from their collection. Smith & Wesson received so much adverse reaction from their customers that the Model 41 (New Model) was brought back into production in 1994. The new model was given slightly modified hardwood grips and a Millet micrometer sight. In addition, holes were drilled and tapped in the top of the slide for a telescopic sight mounting. The new M41 is available with a 140 or 178 mm (5¹/₂ or 7 in) barrel. The total length of these versions is 267 and 305 mm (10¹/₂ or 12 in) respectively This weapon with the 140 mm (5¹/₂ in) barrel weighs 1162 g (41 oz). The longer version weighs 1247 g (44 oz).

SMITH & WESSON MODEL 61, 422, 622, 2206 AND SUBSEQUENT MODELS:

MODEL 61 POCKET ESCORT: After the introduction of the famous Model 41 in 1957, Smith & Wesson did little in the field of small caliber pistols until 1970. This was to change in 1970, when they launched the Model 61 Pocket Escort in .22 LR caliber. This is a small 5-shot pistol with a 54 mm (2 in) barrel. Both the frame and the slide are made of steel and this weapon was available in a blued or nickel-plated version. It also has black or white composite grips and a fixed rear sight. The safety catch is located on the left-hand side of the frame, behind the trigger guard. This model was produced from 1970 up to and including 1973.

MODEL 422: Things then went quiet for a while until Smith & Wesson introduced the new Model 422 in 1987. This model was also a compact pistol with a capacity for 10 rounds in .22 LR caliber. This blued weapon has an alloy frame and a steel slide, and was available in two different types. Firstly, the 422 Field

Smith & Wesson
Model 622 with
102 mm (4 in) barrel

with a fixed sight and black composite grips, together with the 422 Target version with an adjustable sight and walnut grips. Both versions were available with an 114 (4¹/₂ in) or 152 mm (6 in) barrel. The total length is 191 and 229 mm (7¹/₂ and 9 in) respectively Both versions weigh 624 or 652 g (22 or 23 oz). In 1992, the magazine capacity was increased to 12 rounds. The model 422 was manufactured from 1987 up to and including 1996.

MODEL 622: In 1989, Smith & Wesson introduced the Model 622. This 10-shot pistol in .22 LR has an alloy frame in 'stainless look' and a stainless steel slide. This weapon was available with an 114 (4¹/₂ in) or 152 mm (6 in) barrel. The total length is 191 or 229 mm (7¹/₂ or 9 in) and it weighs 624 or 652 g (22 or 23 oz). As with the previous model this pistol has two versions: the model 622-Field with a fixed rear sight and black composite grips and the Target model with an adjustable sight and walnut grips. From 1992 up until 1995 this pistol was supplied with a 12-shot magazine, which was later to revert to the 10-shot. Smith & Wesson produced this model from 1989 up to and including 1996.

MODEL 622 VR: In 1996, Smith & Wesson launched the successor of the Model 622. This was the model 622 VR. The letters 'VR' stand for 'Ventilated Rib'.

Smith & Wesson
Model 422

S&W Model 622 with
152 mm (6 in) barrel

Model 622-VR with
ventilated rib

Model 2206 Target

S&W 2206
Target Match

This model has a special barrel rib with machined cooling slots, above the slide, and over the length of the barrel, giving this weapon a slightly more robust appearance, but apart from making this weapon lighter, this is purely cosmetic. This pistol has an alloy frame, a stainless steel slide and a 152 mm (6 in) barrel. The total length of the 622 VR is 229 mm (9 in) and this weapon weighs 652 g (23 oz). The magazine holds 10 rounds in the caliber .22 LR. The rear sight is totally adjustable. In addition, this weapon has black composite grips, but a small series were produced with walnut grips. This pistol was only manufactured in 1996.

MODEL 2206: This is a totally stainless steel version of the model 622, but because of the new third generation numbering this Smith & Wesson was given a four figure model number. This pistol was introduced 1990. This 10-shot weapon was initially available in .22 LR with an 114 mm (4¹/₂ in) or 152 mm (6 in) barrel. As of 1994, this weapon was only manufactured with a 152 mm (6 in) barrel. The total length is 229 mm (9 in) and it weighs 1106 g (39 oz). The standard model has a fixed rear sight and the target model a totally adjustable micrometer sight. Almost all versions of the 2206 have black composite grips.

The model 2206 Target Match has an ergonomic match stock with an adjustable hand palm support. In 1993, production of the 114 mm (4¹/₂ in) versions was stopped. In 1994, Smith & Wesson brought a special target version onto the market with a Millet micrometer sight, walnut grips, and tapped holes in the slide for a telescopic sight mounting. Smith & Wesson stopped manufacturing all 2206 versions in 1996.

MODEL 2213 SPORTSMAN STAINLESS: Smith & Wesson model returned to the old design of the 61 Escort for this 2213. The 8-shot Model 2213 in .22 LR caliber appeared in 1991 and has a stainless steel frame and slide. This pistol has a 76 mm (3 in) barrel,

Entirely stainless
steel Model 2206

Smith & Wesson Model
2213 pocket pistol

Blued S&W
2214

Model 22A Sport with
Hi-Viz bead of 2001

and has a fixed rear sight and black composite grips. The total length is 155 mm (6 in) and this weapon weighs 510 g (18 oz). This weapon was manufactured until 1997.

Model 2214 Sportsman: This version also came onto the market in 1991. This is a blued version of the model 2213 in the same caliber. It has an alloy frame and a steel slide. The total length of the 2214 is 152 mm (6 in). This pistol is slightly lighter due to its alloy frame at 397 g (14 oz). The 2214 also has a magazine capacity of 8 rounds, a fixed sight and black grips. As with the 2213 production of the 2214 was stopped in 1997.

Model 22A Sport: The Smith & Wesson 22A Sport is the successor of the model 2214 and came on the market in 1997. This 10-shot pistol in .22 LR caliber is available with a 102 (4 in), 140 (5¹/₂ in) or a 178 mm (7 in) barrel. The total length is 203, 241 or 279 mm (8, 9¹/₂ or 11 in) respectively. The weights according to the barrel lengths are 794, 907 or 936 g (28, 32 or 33 oz) respectively. This totally blued weapon has an alloy frame and a blued stainless steel slide. The safety catch is located on the left-hand side of the frame, above the grip. In addition, it has an adjustable rear sight and a two-part polymer grip. Around the same time, the Target version was introduced with a heavier, so-called bull barrel of 140 mm (5¹/₂ in). The total length of the Target is 241 mm (9¹/₂ in) and it weighs 1106 g (39 oz). The grip of this target model has a wood laminate or composite grip with a rib for a thumb support. The model 22A Sport is still manufactured. In 2001, Smith & Wesson introduced a new version of the 22A Sport Target. This type is almost identical to the older Target, but has a Hi-Viz front sight, with a special green composite light sensitive sighting bar.

Model 22S Sport: This new type also appeared in 1997 as a stainless steel model of the 22A, except that only the slide is made of blank stainless steel. The alloy frame has a stainless look. The 22S Sport is only available with a 140 (5¹/₂ in) or 178 mm (7 in) barrel. The total length is 241 and 279 mm (9¹/₂ or 11 in) respectively and it weighs 1162 or 1191 g (41 or 42 oz). The magazine capacity is 10 rounds. The rear sight is fully adjustable. In addition, this weapon has a black polymer grip. This model also has a target version with a heavier barrel of 140 mm

New 22A Sport match pistol

Stainless steel
22S Sport

($5^1/_2$ in). The total length is 241 mm ($9^1/_2$ in). The Target weighs 1361 g (48 oz). This pistol has a wood laminate or composite grip with a thumb support. This model is still in production. Smith & Wesson also brought a Hi-Viz version of the 22S Sport onto the market in 2001, but only in the Target version with the heavy 140 mm ($5^1/_2$ in) barrel.

SMITH & WESSON MODEL **39** AND SUBSEQUENT MODELS

In 1953, the US Army decided to look for a new army pistol. Smith & Wesson already had a new double-action pistol ready, designed by Joseph Norman, a company engineer. This double-action concept was identical to the German Walther P38 system. When, in 1954, the US government decided to abandon their research once again, Smith & Wesson introduced this pistol to the civilian market. Smith & Wesson's first double-action pistol was launched in 1955 as the Model 39 in 9 mm Para caliber. They also introduced the same pistol, but with a single-action, as the Model 44. Smith

& Wesson had a huge breakthrough in 1967, when the Illinois State Police Department purchased the model 39 pistol for their service weapon. That was the starting signal for many other American police corps to replace their old service revolvers with the new automatics in 9 mm Para caliber. Due to the demand from various sources, including the police force, Smith & Wesson introduced the 14-shot pistol model 59 as a larger brother of the Model 39 in 1971. In 1981, the production of the models 39 and 59 was stopped and production was concentrated on the new types 439, 539, 459 and 559. The number 4 preceding the old model number indicated that this pistol had an alloy frame. The number 5 indicated that this pistol had a steel frame. In addition, the feed ramp between the magazine and barrel chamber was slightly longer and less steep, which enabled the trouble free use of cartridges with all manner of bullets. The total length of these pistols were consequently increased by 5 mm ($^1/_4$ in). The new models were also equipped with automatic firing pin safety and had an improved type of cartridge extractor. In 1982, Smith & Wesson announced that the new models were also to be available in stainless steel. These models, in keeping with tradition, became known as the Model 639 and 659. In 1988, the Autoloader Improvement Project (AIP) was launched. This led to the so-called third generation of the Smith & Wesson pistols with a new trigger mechanism and a cosmetic metamorphosis. From 1954, Smith & Wesson have manufactured a large number of different models based on the original model 39. These models are:

MODEL 39: The original model 39 was manufactured from 1954 up until 1966. The 8-shot double-action pistol has a blued steel frame and slide. The barrel is 102 mm (4 in) and the rear sight is adjustable. The total length of this weapon is 189 mm ($7^1/_2$ in) and the empty weight is 751 g ($26^1/_2$ oz). The civilian version

Model 22S Hi-Viz,
introduced in 2001

Model 539: In 1980, a totally steel version was launched, also in 9 mm Para caliber, and given the model name '539'. This weapon had the number 5 added to its model name because of its steel.

Model 639: In 1984, Smith & Wesson finally launched a civilian version in stainless steel. Strictly in accordance with tradition this type was given the extra identification of the number '6'. This model was also available with either a single or ambidextrous safety catch mounted on the slide. The early models had a rounded trigger guard, later to be replaced in 1985 with a square one. The model 639 was manufactured until 1988.

Model 3904: In 1988, influenced by the Autoloader Improvement Project (AIP), the model 539 was radically revised. This pistol then became known as the '3904'. The most obvious changes were the ambidextrous safety catch, an enlarged magazine well and a wrap-around Delrin grip. This pistol has a 102 mm (4 in) barrel, a total length of 194 mm (7¹/₂ in) and it weighs 850 g (30 oz). In addition, this weapon was available with either a fixed or adjustable sight. The model 3904 remained in production up until 1990.

Model 3906: This model was also introduced in the same year as the successor to the 639. This pistol was given the model name 3906. This weapon is in the caliber 9 mm Para and has a stainless steel frame and slide. The dimensions are the same as that of the

The old work-horse S&W 39

has walnut grips. The military version is known as the Model 41 and has black composite grips. The same pistol was manufactured between 1958 and 1959 also in a single-action version as the Model 44.

Model 39-1: In 1966 the model 39-1 was introduced as the successor to the old model. This pistol is almost the same as the first model, but has an alloy frame and a steel slide. This weapon was manufactured up until 1971.

Model 39-2: Then came the model 39-2. The only difference with the 39-1 was the modified cartridge extractor. Model 39-2 was manufactured until 1982. In 1968, Smith & Wesson manufactured their first stainless steel pistol. At the time this was a top secret pistol project, and was given the name Model M39-WOX-13A. This weapon was intended for the US Marines. A small number of this series were equipped with a silencer for use by the Navy Seals and was given the name 'hush-puppy'.

Model 439: In 1979, the naming of these pistol models was revised. The model 39-2 was subsequently known as the 439. This weapon had an alloy frame, which was indicated by the number 4. This weapon was available with a single or an ambidextrous safety catch mounted on the slide. The early models have a rounded trigger guard. Since 1980 the model 439 has been manufactured with a square trigger guard.

Model 3906 of the third generation of Smith & Wesson pistols

Compact model
3913

model 3904. Since 1989, it has been supplied with a Novak Lo-Mount rear sight. The production of this weapon was stopped in 1990.

MODEL 3913: This 8-shot model in 9 mm Para caliber was introduced in 1989. This is a slightly more compact version with an 89 mm (3½ in) barrel, and an alloy frame with a stainless steel slide. This pistol has a Novak rear sight and a wrap-around Xenoy grip. An ambidextrous safety catch is located on the slide. In 1998, the name of this weapon was changed to Model 3913 TSW (Tactical Smith & Wesson). This type is still in production. Pistols of the Tactical series have a sight with a tritium aspect marking and do not have a hammer spur. In addition, the Tacticals have a mounting rail under the frame and in front of the trigger guard, intended for special accessories, such as lighting or laser equipment. The total length of the

3913 TSW is 172 mm (6¾ in). The barrel length is 89 mm (3½ in) and the empty weapon weighs 703 g (24¾ oz).

MODEL 3913LS (LADY SMITH): In 1990, the elegant pistol model Lady Smith made its debut. This weapon has an 89 mm (3½ in) barrel. The total length is 172 mm (6¾ in) and it weighs the same as the 3913 TSW, 703 g (24¾ oz). A laser has been used to make the inscription 'Lady Smith' on the frame. This pistol has a Novak rear sight and a gray wrap-around Delrin grip. The frame is made

Blued 3914

of alloy and the slide of stainless steel. The single safety catch is located on the left-hand side of the slide. The 3913LS has a magazine capacity of 8 rounds in 9 mm Para caliber.

MODEL 3914: In 1990, Smith & Wesson also introduced a blued version of the model 3913LS. This weapon does not have the Lady Smith inscription, but does have slightly more rounded corners. This pistol has an alloy frame and a blued steel slide. This type was manufactured until 1996.

MODEL 3914LS (LADY SMITH): Later in 1990, Smith & Wesson brought yet another version onto the market. This model 3914LS has the same inscription as the model 3913LS, but apart from that was identical to the 3914. The model 3914LS was manufactured until 1995.

MODEL 3953: In 1991, the model 3913 was introduced as a double-action-only version. This pistol has an alloy frame, a stainless steel slide and a Novak rear sight. This model is still in production, however it was renamed

Elegant 3913
Lady Smith

Double-action only
Model 3953 of
1991

the Model 3953 TSW (Tactical Smith & Wesson) in 1998. Pistols of the Tactical series have a sight with a tritium aspect marking and do not have a hammer spur. In addition, the Tacticals have a mounting rail under the frame and in front of the trigger guard, intended for special accessories, such as lighting or laser equipment. This 8-shot model in 9 mm Para caliber has a total length of 172 mm (6¾ in), a barrel length of 89 mm (3½ in) and it weighs 703 g (24¾ oz).

MODEL 3954: A double-action-only version of the model 3914 with a blued alloy frame and a blued steel slide. This pistol was produced from 1991 up to and including 1992.

SMITH & WESSON MODEL 52

The 5-shot Smith & Wesson Model 52 Master pistol was designed in 1961 as a match weapon and is derived

from Model 39. The caliber is .38 S&W Wadcutter. This has a bullet type that consists of a cylindrical lead slug with a flat tip, and is among one of the most accurate cartridges. The original Model 52 has the steel frame and the trigger mechanism of the Model 39, but with the double-action trigger disconnected. The Model 52-1 was introduced in 1963. This pistol, with a separately developed single-action trigger system, was manufactured until 1970, and was succeeded by the Model 52-2. This type differs from its predecessor with a modified cartridge extractor. The slide of the M52 has guide rail over the whole length of both sides. In addition, this weapon a special barrel guide bush that can be screwed into the front of the frame to tighten the barrel. The trigger has a trigger stop that can be set from the inside, after first removing the magazine and grips. This weapon has also an accurate adjustable micrometer sight. The safety catch is located on the left-hand side of the slide. In the 'safe' position the firing pin is blocked by a small steel bar that moves in to its path. In this position, the pistol can also be used for dry training because the trigger continues to function. A second safety system is the magazine safety. This weapon cannot be fired until its magazine has been inserted. The total length of this pistol is 226 mm (8 in) and the barrel length is 127 mm (5 in). This weapon weighs empty 1148 g (40¾ oz). The Smith & Wesson Model 52 remained in production until 1994.

SMITH & WESSON MODEL 59, 69 AND SUBSEQUENT MODELS

In about 1970, a large number of American police corps wanted to change from a revolver to a semi-automatic double-action pistol. They generally found that the magazine capacity of the 8-shot Model 39 was too small. Due in part to pressure from police forces,

Model 52 match pistol
in .38 S&W Special
Wadcutter caliber

in 1971 Smith & Wesson introduced the 14-shot pistol model 59 as a larger brother to the Model 39. In 1978, after deciding to replace the Colt 1911-A1, the Department of Defense, at the Pentagon invited a number of weapon manufacturers to take part in army testing,. Smith & Wesson decided to totally re-organized their large caliber pistol series. Smith & Wesson were outshone in the army testing by the eventual winner: Beretta. In 1981, the production of the models 39 and 59 was stopped, and production was switched to the new types 439 and 539 and the new models 459 and 559. The number 4 before the old model number indicate that this pistol has an alloy frame. The number 5 means that this pistol has a steel frame. In addition, the feed ramp between the magazine and barrel chamber is slightly longer and not so steep. This allowed the trouble free use of all manner of cartridges with a variety of tips. This resulted in the total length of this pistols increasing by 5 mm ($^3/_{16}$ in). The new models were also equipped with an automatic firing pin safety and an improved type of cartridge extractor was fitted. In 1982 Smith & Wesson also announced that all new models would be available in stainless steel. These models were to be known as the Model 639 and 659, as model numbers starting with a 6 meant that it was stainless steel. The Autoloader Improvement Project (AIP) was launched in 1988. This led to the so-called third generation of Smith & Wesson pistols with a new trigger mechanism and a cosmetic metamorphosis. The differences between the old and new include:

– a wrap-around grip of Delrin or Xenoy composite;
– an ergonomic grip styling;
– a finger groove under the trigger guard in front of the frame;
– an enlarged trigger guard;
– magazines with numbered holes which act as a cartridge indicator.
– magazines with rubber bases;
– a flush and widened magazine well;
– new sights with a white triple dot aspect marking;
– an ambidextrous safety catch;
– a new type of automatic firing pin safety;
– a modified trigger action, with the trigger bar, the trigger spring and the connection between the trigger bar and hammer was changed, resulting in a far more supple trigger action.
– a barrel that is thicker at the muzzle resulting in a better seating in the slide.

A few versions of the model 59:

MODEL 59: This is an enlarged version of the model 39. The model 59 is a 14-shot semi-automatic double-action pistol in the 9 mm Para, with a 102 mm (4 in) barrel. The total length is 189 mm (7$^1/_2$ in) and the empty weight is 780 g (27$^1/_2$ oz). This

Old Smith & Wesson 59 in 9 mm Para caliber of 1971

pistol has a blued finish, but as of 1972 was also available in a nickel-plated version. This weapon has an alloy frame, a steel slide and black composite grips. The original model was manufactured from 1971 to and including July 1982.

MODEL 459: In 1979, Smith & Wesson brought an altered model onto the market with the model number: 459. The number 4 signified an alloy frame. The blued pistol had black nylon grips. In addition, a choice could be made between a fixed and an adjustable sight. Furthermore, the client was given the option of a single or ambidextrous safety catch mounted on the slide. Until around 1984, the model 459 had a rounded trigger guard. The models from 1984 had a square trigger guard. The dimensions of this weapon are the same as that of the old Model 59, however it is slightly heavier, in spite of the alloy frame at 794 g (28 oz). A small part of the total production was dedicated to the nickel-plated version. The model 459 was manufactured up until and including 1987.

MODEL 559: In 1980, a totally steel version went on the market and was therefore called the Model 559. This pistol has a steel frame and slide, and was available with a fixed or an adjustable rear sight. A total of 3,750 of these pistols were manufactured until production was stopped in 1983.

MODEL 659: The stainless steel version of the 559 was launched in 1982 as the Model 659. This pistol has a stainless steel frame and slide, and was available with either a fixed or adjustable sight. There was also the option of a single or an ambidextrous safety catch mounted on the slide. Until the end of 1984 this model had a rounded trigger guard which was later replaced by a square one. This weapon has a barrel

Model 5903 in
'stainless look'

Smith & Wesson
Model 5904

length of 102 mm (4 in), a total length of 194 mm (7^1/$_2$ in) and it weighs 850 g (30 oz). Model 659 was produced up until 1989.

MODEL 5903: This model was introduced in 1990. This pistol has an alloy frame in 'stainless look' and a stainless steel slide. This weapon was manufactured with either a fixed or adjustable sight. As of 1993, this weapon was fitted with a Novak Lo-Mount rear sight, a wrap-around Xenoy grip and an ambidextrous safety catch mounted on the slide. The model 5903 was manufactured until 1998. There was also a special compact version manufactured in 1990 with the model name 5903-SSV. This pistol has an 89 mm (3^1/$_2$ in) barrel, a Novak rear sight and a wrap-around Delrin grip. The frame is made of alloy in stainless look and the steel slide is blued. There were only 1,500 these weapons manufactured in 1990.

MODEL 5903 TSW: In the year 2000, Smith & Wesson brought their model 5903 Tactical Smith & Wesson onto the market. As with the previous model 5903, this double-action model has an alloy frame and a stainless steel slide. This pistol has a Novak sight with a tritium aspect marking and does not have a hammer spur. In addition, the Tacticals have a mounting rail under the frame and in front of the trigger guard, intended for special accessories, such as lighting or laser equipment. The magazine capacity in 9 mm Para caliber is 15 rounds. This weapon has a total length of 191 mm (7^1/$_2$ in) and the barrel length is 102 mm (4 in). The empty weight is 819 g (28^3/$_4$ oz).

MODEL 5904: In 1988, Smith & Wesson introduced the successor of the older model 459, the new model 5904. The number 4 indicates an alloy frame and has now been added to the end of the model number. This pistol was manufactured in a blued or nickel-plated version with a steel slide. In addition, there is the option of either a fixed or an adjustable sight. The Novak Lo-Mount rear sight became standard from 1983. The magazine capacity of the new series with the four-figure model number was increased to 15 rounds. A small part of the production of the 9 x 21 mm caliber was intended solely for the Italian market. The model 5904 was produced until mid 1999.

MODEL 5905: In 1991 Smith & Wesson manufactured a special series with a steel frame and a steel slide. The totally blued model had a fixed Novak Lo-Mount rear sight and was only manufactured in 1991, and then only in limited numbers.

MODEL 5906: In 1989, Smith & Wesson brought a version onto the market with a stainless steel frame and slide. This model had the number 6 added at the end of the model number to indicate that this weapon was made of stainless steel. This pistol was available with either a fixed or an adjustable sight. As of 1983, a Novak Lo-Mount rear sight was fitted. A small part of the production of 9 x 21 mm caliber went to the Italian civilian market. The model 5906 is still manufactured.

Stainless steel
S&W 5906

S&W 5906-M Military
of 2000

MODEL 5906-M (MILITARY): This typical military version was introduced 2000. This pistol has a stainless steel frame and slide. This weapon is mat black due to a Melonite composite coating. An ambidextrous uncocking lever is located on the slide. This weapon has a Novak triple dot aspect sight. In addition, this weapon has a wrap-around black Xenoy grip complete with a lanyard ring. The 15-shot double-action 5906-M has a total length of 191 mm (7½ in) and a barrel length of 102 mm (4 in). Empty this weapon weighs 1063 g (37½ oz).

MODEL 5906 TSW: In 2000, Smith & Wesson also introduced the Model 5906 in a TSW (Tactical Smith & Wesson) version. This pistol has a Novak Lo-Mount rear sight with a tritium aspect marking. The 15-shot pistol has a double-action trigger action. In addition, there is a mounting rail under the frame in front of the trigger guard, intended for special accessories, such as lighting or laser equipment. The dimensions are identical to that of the other 5906 versions, but is slightly heavier at 1086 g (38½ oz).

MODEL 5924: This is a blued version of the Model 5903 with an alloy frame and a steel slide. In addition, this weapon has a Novak Lo-Mount rear sight. This

pistol was introduced in 1990, but was withdrawn from the range within the year.

MODEL 5926: Like the 5906, a totally stainless steel model, but with a uncocking lever on the left-hand side of the slide. This weapon has a wrap-around Xenoy grip, a Novak sight and was in production from 1990 up to 1993.

MODEL 5943: This type was only manufactured in 1991. This is a double-action-only version of the model 5903. It has a stainless steel slide, an alloy frame and a Novak Lo-Mount rear sight. In the same year Smith & Wesson also launched their special compact version with the model name 5943-SSV. This pistol has an 89 mm (3½ in) barrel and a Novak sight with tritium aspect marking. This type was also only manufactured in 1991.

MODEL 5943 TSW: Introduced in 2000 as the successor to the old model 5943 of 1991. The 15-shot double-action-only model has an alloy frame and a stainless steel slide. The Novak sight has a tritium aspect marking. The hammer does not have a hammer spur. In addition, there is a mounting rail under the frame in front of the trigger guard that is intended for special accessories, such as lighting or laser equipment. The only difference with other 5,900 versions is the weight at 819 g (29 oz).

MODEL 5944: This model was produced from 1991 up to 1992, and is a double-action-only version of the model 5904. This pistol has an alloy frame, a steel slide and a Novak rear sight.

MODEL 5946: Introduced by Smith & Wesson in 1991 as a double-action-only version of the model 5906. This pistol has a stainless steel frame and slide, a Novak Lo-Mount rear sight and a wrap-around Xenoy grip. The barrel length and the total length are the same as that of the other versions. The weight is 1063 g (37½ oz). This model is still in production, but since 2000 as the 5946 TSW.

MODEL 5946 TSW: In the year 2000 Smith & Wesson launched the model 5946 Tactical Smith & Wesson.

Model 5906 TSW:
Tactical Smith & Wesson

Model 5946
double-action only version

This double-action-only model has a Novak sight with a tritium aspect marking. The hammer does not have a hammer spur. In addition, there is a mounting rail under the frame in front of the trigger guard that is intended for special accessories, such as lighting or laser equipment. The weight of this TSW type is 1086 g (38¼ oz).

MODEL 669: In 1986 Smith & Wesson brought a compact version of the Model 659 onto the market. This is a 12-shot double-action pistol with an 89 mm (3½ in) barrel. The total length is 173 mm (6¾ in) and this weapon weighs 737 g (26 oz) with an alloy frame and a stainless steel slide. The rear sight is only adjustable laterally. In addition, this pistol has a wrap-around Delrin grip. This type was manufactured up until 1988.

MODEL 6904: In 1988 the successor of the model 669 came onto the market. The 12-shot blued double-

Model 6904

action pistol in 9 mm Para caliber also has an alloy frame and a steel slide, with a fixed rear sight and a wrap-around Xenoy grip. The total length of the 6904 is 174 mm (6 in). The barrel length is 89 mm (3½ in) and the empty weight is 751 g (26½ oz). This weapon was produced up to and including 1997.

MODEL 6906: In the same year Smith & Wesson introduced this model in 'stainless look'. It has an alloy frame and a stainless steel slide, with a Novak Lo-Mount rear sight. A Novak sight with a tritium aspect marking can be supplied to order. This type also has a wrap-around Xenoy grip. The dimensions are the same as that of the 6904. The model 6906 was manufactured until 2000.

MODEL 6924: This is a version of the model 6904 with a uncocking lever on the left-hand side of the slide. This weapon came as standard with a Novak

Model 6906 with light alloy casing and stainless steel slide

sight with tritium aspect marking and a wrap-around Xenoy grip. This pistol was only produced in 1992.

MODEL 6926: This is a special version of the model 6906 with a uncocking lever on the left-hand side of the slide, a Novak rear sight with tritium aspect marking and a wrap-around Xenoy grip. This pistol was only manufactured in 1991.

MODEL 6944: A double-action-only version of the model 6904. This pistol was provided with a Novak rear sight and a wrap-around Xenoy grip. This weapon was only manufactured in 1991.

MODEL 6946: This 12-shot model is a double-action-only version of the model 6906. It has an alloy frame in 'stainless look' and a stainless steel slide. This pistol has a Novak Lo-Mount rear sight and a wrap-around Xenoy grip. This model was produced until 2000.

MODEL 908: In 1997, this compact model appeared on the market. This is a shortened version of the model 909, as was its successor. This double-action pistol is in the caliber 9 mm Para and has a magazine

Model 6946
double-action only

capacity of 8 rounds. The barrel length is 89 mm
(3¹/₂ in) and the total length is 173 mm (6³/₄ in This
pistol weighs 680 g (24 oz). The hammer does not
have a hammer spur. The safety catch is located on
the left-hand side of the slide. This weapon is mat
blued with an alloy frame and a steel slide. Smith &
Wesson still manufacture this type.

MODEL 909: In 1995 Smith & Wesson introduced
a new model derived from the model 5904. This
pistol has a 102 mm (4 in) barrel and a single row
magazine for 9 rounds. The total length of this
weapon is 187 mm (7³/₄ in) and it weighs 794 g
(28 oz). This totally blued weapon has a frame made
of alloy and a steel slide. It has a fixed sight and
a wrap-around Xenoy grip. The single safety catch is
located on the left-hand side of the slide. This type
was manufactured until 1997.

MODEL 910: This model also came on the market
in 1995. It has the same specifications as the model
909, with the exception of its magazine capacity.
This pistol has a thicker grip, allowing the use of
a 10 round standard magazine. Furthermore, it can

Model 910
service pistol

also take a double rowed
magazine with 15 rounds.
This model is still being
produced.

MODEL 915: This is the forerunner of the model 910.
This weapon was produced from 1992 until 1995.
This 15 shot pistol has a 102 mm (4 in) barrel. The
alloy frame and the steel slide have a mat blued
finish. It has a fixed rear sight and a black wrap-
around Xenoy grip. This was intended as a cheaper
version of the more expensive Smith & Wesson third
generation models, but the idea never really caught
on.

MODEL SUPER 9: This model originates from the
millennium year 2000 and is a bit of an oddball.
Based on the model 5906, Smith & Wesson
developed this pistol for sport shooting. This is a 15-
shot single-action weapon with a 127 mm (5 in)

Smith & Wesson
Super 9 of 2000

barrel. The total length is 216 mm (8¹/₂ in) and it
weighs 1106 g (39 oz). In addition, this weapon has
a totally adjustable micrometer sight. A second
feature worthy of note is the multi-caliber. This pistol
was available with three barrels in 9 mm Para, 9 x
21 mm and the new caliber .356 TSW (Team Smith
& Wesson). The Smith & Wesson Performance
Center developed this new caliber. This weapon has
a stainless steel frame, a stainless steel slide, and
a wrap-around Xenoy grip.

SMITH & WESSON MODEL SERIES 1000 AND 4000

When the 10 mm auto-cartridge was introduced for
the Bren-Ten pistol in 1984, Smith & Wesson spent
a short time developing a pistol in this caliber, but
abandoned the project for more urgent issues. In 1988,
this project was resumed at the request of the FBI
(Federal Bureau or Investigation). The FBI wanted
a pistol in the new caliber to replace their existing
firearms. This consisted largely of the Smith &
Wesson Model 13 M&P (Military & Police) revolvers
in .357 Magnum caliber. A new weapon was designed
for this new 10 mm auto-cartridge but it was based on
the 4506 .45 ACP pistol. This was more complicated
than it appeared. It was not just a case of fitting
a replacement barrel to the 4506 pistol. The gas
pressure of a 10 mm auto-cartridge is higher than that
of the .45 ACP. As comparison, the 10 mm auto-
cartridge reaches a gas pressure of 40,000 psi, the .357
Magnum cartridge 37,600 psi and the .45 ACP
cartridge 'only' 19,500 psi. The FBI asked the Federal
ammunition factory to develop a slightly tamer 10 mm
auto-cartridge. This was a 180 grain JHP (Jacketed
Hollow Point) with a muzzle velocity (V0) of around
350 m/s. Computer and prototype studies showed that
the slide of the 4506 was strong enough to withstand
the faster reloading action (with the higher gas
pressure) of the 10 mm auto-cartridge. In order to
reduce the recoil a heavier recoil spring was fitted. The
FBI-version was given the name the Model 1076-FBI

and was never sold to civilians. This pistol has a special trigger group and 11- and 15-shot magazines. The FBI originally ordered 10,000 weapons, but the first series was rejected. Eventually, the FBI took delivery of 2,400 weapons in 1993. The exterior dimensions of the M1006 are identical to that of the M4506.

The new features of the M4506 pistol were also applied to the M1006 such as:
- ambidextrous safety catch;
- special barrel connection in the slide;
- revamped trigger system (third generation);
- enlarged trigger guard;
- improved grip;
- beveled magazine well;
- triple dot aspect sight;
- rubber protection on the magazines;
- transferable magazine release;
- separate uncocking lever on the left-hand side of the frame (government versions only).

Model 410 in .40 S&W caliber

The mass production of the 1006 started in 1990. This pistol has an ambidextrous safety catch mounted on the slide. In 1990, Smith & Wesson also launched the model 1026. This pistol only has a uncocking lever on the left-hand side of the frame. The production or this model was stopped in 1991. Model 1046, was another member of the 1000-series of which only 148 were manufactured in 1992. This weapon has a 127 mm (5 in) barrel and a double-action-only trigger mechanism. A special feature of this weapon is in spite of being blued it is manufactured in stainless steel.

Other models in the 1000-series are:
- The Model 1066 is a totally stainless steel pistol and has a 108 mm (4¹/₄ in) barrel, an ambidextrous safety catch mounted on the slide, a wrap-around Xenoy grip and a fixed sight. This pistol was produced from 1990 until 1992;
- Model 1076 resembles the previous model, but has a uncocking lever on the left-hand side of the frame. This weapon was produced from 1990 until 1993;
- The Model 1086 is derived from the model 1066, but is a double-action-only version. This pistol was manufactured from 1991 until the end of 1992.

In 1992 Smith & Wesson abandoned the caliber 10 mm auto-cartridge and concentrated on the new pistol caliber .40 Smith & Wesson. They found that the 10 mm cartridge was not only slightly too long, but more importantly the bullet velocity developed was too high. Smith & Wesson introduced a shorter cartridge that fitted a double rowed magazine perfectly. The muzzle velocity and energy is lower than that of the 10 mm Auto-cartridge. Sceptics originally named this cartridge the .40 Short & Weak, however ballistic research demonstrated that it is not only the ideal police cartridge, but is also an excellent sporting caliber for the American civilian market. US weapon legislation had banned the use of magazines that can hold more than 10 rounds, which also meant the end of the 9 mm Para pistols with their large magazine capacity. The advantage afforded by high magazine capacity had been lost, resulting in American shooters prefering the .45 ACP or .40 S&W pistol.

Model 410: This is a straightforward standard pistol version in .40 S&W caliber. This weapon was launched as a police weapon in 1995 and was the successor of the model 411. This 11-shot blued weapon has an alloy frame and a steel slide, with a 102 mm (4 in) barrel, a fixed rear sight and a wrap-around Xenoy grip. The total length of this pistol is 191 mm (7¹/₂ in) and it weighs 808 g (28¹/₂ oz). On the left-hand side of the slide is an uncocking lever. Smith & Wesson still produce this semi-compact service pistol.

Model 411: This was the forerunner of the model 410 reviewed above, and was manufactured from 1992 until the end of 1995. This weapon is also a blued 11-shot pistol in the caliber .40 S&W with an alloy frame, a steel slide and a 102 mm (4 in) barrel. It also has a fixed sight, a Xenoy grip. and as with the model 410 has only a uncocking lever on the left-hand side of the slide.

Model 4003: This weapon was manufactured from 1991 up to 1992 and had a magazine for 11 rounds. This double-action pistol has a 102 mm (4 in) barrel,

Model 411, predecessor
of the Model 410

(28½ oz). In addition, it is equipped with an ambidextrous safety catch mounted on the slide and an 11-shot magazine. This weapon is available with a fixed sight, an adjustable sight or an aspect sight with tritium aspect marking.

MODEL 4013: This is a compact version with an 89 mm (3½ in) barrel, a total length of 171.5 mm (6¾ in) and it weighs 760 g (26¾ oz). This weapon has a stainless steel slide and an alloy frame. This double-action pistol also has an ambidextrous safety catch mounted on the slide and a wrap-around Xenoy grip. This model was introduced in 1991 and is still manufactured. This weapon was originally an 8 shot pistol. Smith & Wesson revamped this model in 1997 and introduced it as the Model 4013 TSW. TSW stands for Tactical Smith & Wesson. The 4013 TSW model has a magazine capacity of 9 rounds in the caliber .40 S&W. The frame is made of alloy and it has a stainless steel slide. It also has a Novak Lo-Mount rear sight with tritium aspect marking. As a double-action weapon this pistol is known as the Model 4013 TSW and as a double-action-only, the Model 4053 TSW.

Novak rear sight and a black wrap-around Xenoy grip. The frame is made of light metal, with a stainless steel slide.

MODEL 4004: Smith & Wesson manufactured this model 4004 in the same period. This is a blued version of the model 4003.

MODEL 4006: This model proved to be a stayer. This double-action weapon was in introduced in 1990. In 1997 it had a facelift with the TSW package and has since been known as the 4006 TSW. The most obvious feature of the TSW is the black mounting rail under the frame, in front of the trigger guard. This can be used to attach all manner of shooting aids such as sight lighting or a laser. This pistol has a stainless steel frame and slide, a 102 mm (4 in) barrel and a wrap-around Delrin grip. The total length of the 4006 TSW is 191 mm (7½ in) and this weapon weighs 808 g

MODEL 4014: This is a blued version of the model 4013. This weapon was manufactured from 1991 up to 1993.

MODEL 4026: This model has a stainless steel slide and an alloy frame. This double-action pistol has

Compact
Model 4013

Model 4006 of 1990
is still in production

Model 4013 TSW

pistol has a fixed Novak Lo-Mount rear sight and a wrap-around Xenoy grip. This weapon does not have an uncocking lever. The only safety feature is the firing pin safety. This pistol is still manufactured in the TSW version as Model 4046 TSW. Both the frame and the slide are made of stainless steel. The dimensions are the same as that of the Model 4043 TSW, however the weight is different at 1072 g (37³/₄ oz).

Model 4043 double-action
only version of Model 4013

only a uncocking lever on the left-hand side of the frame, but is otherwise identical to the model 4013. This pistol was manufactured from 1991 until 1993.

Model 4043 double-
action only

MODEL 4043: This is a double-action-only version of the model 4026, but with a 102 mm (4 in) barrel. This model came on the market 1991 and only has firing pin safety. The same weapon in a blued version was given the model name 4044. This pistol has an alloy frame, a stainless steel slide and a wrap-around Xenoy grip. This model also had a Tactical Smith & Wesson conversion in 1997 when it became known as the Model 4043 TSW. The magazine capacity is 11 rounds in .40 S&W caliber. The total length is 191 mm (7¹/₂ in) and it weighs 808 g (28¹/₂ oz).

MODEL 4046: This is a double-action-only version of the model 4006 , also introduced in 1991. This

MODEL 4053: This is an 8-shot double-action-only version of Model 4013. This pistol dates from 1991, has a Novak Lo-Mount rear sight and is still manufactured. Smith & Wesson revamped this type in 1997 and renamed it the Model 4053 TSW. TSW stands for Tactical Smith & Wesson. Apart from the TSW package, the magazine capacity was also increased to 9 rounds. The frame is made of alloy and the slide is stainless steel. This pistol also has a Novak Lo-Mount rear sight with tritium aspect marking. The double-action-only is known as the Model 4053 TSW. The same pistol with a traditional double-action trigger was given the name Model 4013 TSW.

In 1992 Smith & Wesson introduced a pistol type that was based on the 1000-models in to the 4000-series. This first pistol model in the new caliber had the unusual Smith & Wesson model name of Shorty Forty, but was also known as the Model 4001. This weapon was the result of a large order from the American trading company Lew Horton and was manufactured by the Performance Center of Smith & Wesson. This pistol has a 3.5 ins. Bar-Sto barrel, a Novak Lo-Mount rear sight and a 9-shot magazine capacity. The frame is made of light metal, and the slide is stainless steel.

Model variations are the Tactical Forty with a 127 mm (5 in) barrel and the Compensated Forty, equipped with a compensator.

SMITH & WESSON CHIEFS SPECIAL

In 1999, Smith & Wesson launched a small mini-pistol series which goes by the name of Chiefs Special, available in the calibers 9 mm Para, .40 S&W or .45 ACP. The trigger mechanism is available as double-action or double-action-only. This type of weapon is used in the USA as a service weapon, back-up weapon or for civilian self-protection. All versions have an alloy frame and a steel or stainless steel slide. The versions with a steel slide are totally blued. The pistols with a stainless steel slide are in blank metal. All models have a wrap-around rubber Hogue grip.

Stainless steel Chief's Special in .40 S&W caliber

The CS40 is a double action, the CS40D is a double-action-only pistol. The CS40 and CS40D are available in the same versions as the CS9, in blued or blank metal.

MODEL CHIEFS SPECIAL CS45/CS45D: This is a 6-shot double-action pistol in .45 ACP caliber. This weapon has a barrel length of 83 mm (3¼ in) a total length of 165 mm (6½ in), and it weighs 678 g (24 oz). This type is also available in blued and blank metal versions. This weapon also has a Novak Lo-Mount rear sight, with an ambidextrous safety catch mounted on the slide. The same type is available as the model CS45D in double-action-only and therefore without a safety catch. Both models were introduced In the year 2000 and are still being manufactured.

Blued version of Chief's Special in 9 mm Para

SMITH & WESSON SIGMA SERIES

The development of the Sigma series with their polymer frames, was Smith & Wesson's answer to the ever-increasing competition of the Austrian Glock pistol series. The Sigmas do not have any external safety devices and are double-action-only. The automatic firing pin safety is a built-in internal safety feature. In addition, the trigger consists of two parts, the lower half of which is connected to the top half with a hinge. The lower part must be partially depressed before the trigger can be pulled. The grip fits well in the hand thanks to its ergonomic styling. When they were introduced in 1994, the larger models had an 114 mm (4½ in) barrel. The compact versions had a 102 mm (4 in) or even an 82.5 mm (3¼ in) barrel. The model categories were signified by the letters F, C or M. As of 1999, the SW380 was given a 76 mm (3 in) barrel and the other models a 102 mm (4 in) barrel.

MODEL CHIEFS SPECIAL CS9/ CS9D:
This 7-shot model in 9 mm Para caliber has a 76 mm (3 in) barrel and a fixed triple dot aspect sight. This is a double-action weapon with a total length of 159 mm (6¼ in) and an empty weight of only 590 g (20¾ oz). This weapon is available in a blued version with an alloy frame and a steel slide or with a blank stainless steel slide. The model CS9D is available in the same versions, but with a double-action-only trigger action.

MODEL CHIEFS SPECIAL CS40/CS40D:
This is also a 7-shot pistol in .40 S&W caliber. The barrel has a length of 83 mm (3¼ in). The total length is 165 mm (6½ in) with a weight of 686 g (24¾ oz).

Small Sigma
SW380

Sigma SW40E with
mounting rail in front
of trigger guard

SIGMA SW380: This model was introduced in 1995 as a mini-pistol in .380 ACP or 9 mm Short caliber. As with all Sigmas, this weapon has a polymer frame and a sight tunnel on top of the steel slide and so does not have a separate rear sight or front sight. This pistol has a double-action-only trigger mechanism. A hinged trigger and built-in automatic firing pin safety provide the safety systems. This weapon has a 76 mm (3 in) barrel, a total length of 147 mm (5³/₄ in) and weighs only 397 g (14 oz). The slide is coated with a new type of composite material known as Melonite. The magazine release is a button located at the bottom of the grip. The Sigma SW380 was produced until 2001.

SIGMA SW9C/SW40C: This double-action-only pistol originates from 1995. The letter C stands for Compact. This weapon was manufactured in the 9 mm Para (SW9) and .40 S&W (SW40) calibers. Both types have a 102 mm (4 in) stainless steel barrel, a steel slide and a polymer frame. The magazine release is located on the left-hand side of the frame behind the trigger guard and can be switched for left-handed shooters. The model SW9C is 16-shot, the SW40C has a capacity of 14 rounds. The total length is 175 mm (7 in) for both caliber versions. The weights are 692 g and 700 g (24¹/₂ and 24³/₄ oz) respectively. Both versions were manufactured until 2000.

Sigma SW40C
in .40 S&W caliber

SIGMA SW9E/SW40E: This model has a mounting rail fitted to the front of the frame and in front of the trigger guard for attaching optical or lighting equipment. All Sigmas manufactured from 2000 onwards are provided with these rails. This pistol in 9 mm Para or .40 S&W calibers has a black polymer frame, a steel slide, and a black composite Melonite coating.

Sigma SW40F
pistol

SIGMA SW9F/SW40F: This pistol was introduced in 1994. The model name indicates the caliber and format. The SW9F is a large (wrap-around size) 16-shot 9 mm Para pistol. The same large weapon in .40 S&W caliber is known as the SW40F and can hold 14 rounds. Originally the F-type had an 114 mm (4¹/₂ in) barrel, which was reduced to one of 102 mm (4 in) in 1999. Both models have a fixed triple dot aspect sight, but are also available with a tritium aspect sight. The total length is 197 mm (7¹/₂ in) and it weighs 737 g (26 oz).

SIGMA SW9G/SW40G: Smith & Wesson introduced these two pistol versions with a green 'NATO-look' in 2001. This was aimed at increasing the military sales. The advantage of this type of finish was that it

Sigma SW9V with
stainless steel slide

Sigma SW9G and Sigma
SW40G in NATO green
of 2001

reflects absolutely no light. The stainless steel slide
has a mat black Melonite coating and the polymer
frame is NATO-green. Under the frame, in front of
the trigger guard, is the now familiar mounting rail
for attaching accessories. Both types have a 102 mm
(4 in) stainless steel barrel and a magazine capacity of
10 rounds. The total length is 184 mm (7¼ in) and it
weighs 700 g (24¾ oz) in both calibers. The front
sight has a tritium aspect sight punt and the rear sight
has a double aspect marking.

SIGMA SW9P/SW40P Also new in 2001, were the
Sigma SW9P in 9 mm Para caliber and the
SW40P in .40 S&W with a built-in compensator.
This was indicated with the letter P. The front of the
barrel and the slide have been equipped with a port

which allows the gas pressure developed by the
cartridge to be released just before the bullet leaves
the barrel. The sides of the stainless steel slide are
polished, but the top is mat. Both caliber versions
have a magazine capacity of 10 rounds. The
dimensions are the same as that of the other Sigma
types.

SIGMA SW9V/SW40V: In 1998, Smith & Wesson
decided to bring two Sigma models to the market
with a stainless steel slide and a light gray or black
polymer frame in calibers 9 mm Para and .40 S&W.
These are double-action-only pistols with a magazine
capacity of 16 rounds (SW9V) or 14 rounds
(SW40V). Both have a 102 mm (4 in) barrel. The
letter V in the model name was used from 2000
onwards to indicate the versions with a black polymer
frame and a blank stainless steel slide.

SIGMA SW9VE/SW40VE: From 2000 onwards, all
large Sigma's were provided with a mounting rail
under the frame and in front of the trigger guard. The
'VE' indicates that the pistol has a black composite
frame and a blank stainless steel slide. All types have
a 102 mm (4 in) barrel with the option of a fixed

Sigma SW9P and Sigma
SW40P with integrated
compensator of 2001

Sigma SW40V with black
polymer casing and
stainless steel slide

Compact Model
4516

Semi-compact
4566

Model 4516: This is a compact double-action version of the model 4506 with a 95 mm (3³/₄ in) barrel. The total length is 184 mm (7¹/₄ in) and it weighs 964 g (34 oz). The magazine capacity is 7-shot in .45 ACP caliber. The frame and the slide are made of stainless steel. This weapon also has a Novak Lo-Mount rear sight, and a wrap-around Xenoy grip. This pistol came onto the market in 1991 and was produced until 1999. The trigger guard of this model was modified in 1992, and it became known as the model 4516-1.

Model 4526: This type is almost the same as the model 4506, but only has a uncocking lever on the left-hand side of the frame. The frame and slide are made of stainless steel. This pistol also has a 127 mm (5 in) barrel, a Novak Lo-Mount rear sight and a wrap-around Xenoy grip. The model 4526 was only manufactured in 1991.

Model 4536: Is a compact double-action version of Model 4506 with a 95 mm (3³/₄ in) barrel. It has a uncocking lever on the left-hand side of the frame, and was manufactured from stainless steel. It has a Novak Lo-Mount rear sight and a wrap-around Xenoy grip. This weapon was only produced in 1991.

Model 4546: This is a double-action-only version of the model 4506. This pistol only has firing pin safety and was only manufactured in 1991.

Model 4553 TSW: This is a compact double-action-only pistol from the 4500-series Tactical Smith & Wesson. This weapon is based on the model 4513 TSW. This is a 7-shot weapon with a 95 mm (3³/₄ in) barrel, a total length of 197 mm (7³/₄ in) and an empty weight of 811 g (28¹/₂ oz). The frame is made of light metal, it has a stainless steel slide and a wrap-around Xenoy grip. This pistol has

a double aspect Novak Lo-Mount rear sight. In addition, the 4553 has a mounting rail under the frame, in front of the trigger guard, for attaching special accessories, such as sight lighting or laser equipment. This pistol was introduced in 1999 and is still in production.

Model 4556: This is a double-action-only version of the compact model 4516, with a 95 mm (3³/₄ in) barrel. This weapon was only manufactured in 1991.

Model 4563 TSW: This is a semi-compact double-action pistol with a 108 mm (4¹/₄ in) barrel, an alloy frame and a stainless steel slide. The total length of this weapon is 200 mm (7 in) and it weighs 868 g (30¹/₂ oz). The magazine capacity is 8 rounds in .45 ACP caliber. It has an ambidextrous safety catch mounted on the slide, the familiar Novak Lo-Mount rear sight and a wrap-around Xenoy grip. The 4563 TSW has a mounting rail under the frame, in front of the trigger guard, for attaching special accessories, such as sight lighting or laser equipment. The model 4563 TSW was introduced In the year 2000 and is still in production.

Model 4566: This is a somewhat compact version of the model 4506 with a 108 mm (4¹/₄ in) barrel. This is a totally stainless steel pistol with a Novak rear sight, and an ambidextrous safety catch mounted on the slide. The model 4566 was introduced in 1991 and is still in production. As of 2000 this pistol was renamed the Model 4566 TSW (Tactical Smith & Wesson). The dimensions are the same as that of the Model 4563 TSW, though this weapon only weighs 1108 g (39 oz).

Model 4567: This is a version of the model 4566 with a blued slide. Only 2500 of these weapons were manufactured in 1991.

MODEL 4576: This is a version of the model 4566 with a uncocking lever on the left-hand side of the frame, a Novak Lo-Mount rear sight. The frame and the slide are both made of stainless steel. This model was manufactured from 1991 to 1992.

MODEL 4583 TSW: This is a double-action-only pistol from the 2000-series Tactical Smith & Wesson. This weapon has a 108 mm (4¼ in) barrel and can hold 8 rounds. The dimensions and weight are identical to that of the Model 4566 TSW. This weapon has a double aspect Novak rear sight, the frame is made of light metal, the slide of stainless steel, and it has a wrap-around Xenoy grip. It also has a mounting rail under the frame, in front of the trigger guard, for attaching special accessories, such as sight lighting or laser equipment. This weapon was introduced in 2000 and is still in production.

MODEL 4586: This pistol is a double-action-only version of the model 4566. It has a Novak rear sight,

PC 945 match pistol from the Performance Center of Smith & Wesson

MODEL 945 PC: This is a special match version that was developed and manufactured by the Performance Center of Smith & Wesson for the German company Akah. This pistol has a traditional Colt safety catch on the left-hand side of the frame. This is a totally stainless steel weapon with a Bo-Mar micrometer sight. This 8-shot pistol has a 127 mm (5 in) barrel and was only manufactured in 1999.

MODEL MICRO 945 PC: In 2001, Smith & Wesson manufactured a number of special models for a variety of large American trading companies. They manufactured the Micro 945 for Camfour Distributors with an 82.5 mm (3¼ in) barrel, a total length of 180 mm (7 in) and it weighs 695 g (24½ oz). This compact single-action pistol has a magazine capacity of 6 rounds in .45 ACP caliber. This pistol has an alloy frame and a stainless steel slide. The barrel bushing has a titanium coating. The single sided safety catch is on the left-hand side of the frame. This weapon has a Novak Lo-Mount rear sight and Hogue wood laminated grips. The grip safety is developed in to an extended beavertail.

Model 4586 double-action only in .45 ACP caliber

a stainless steel frame and slide, and a wrap-around Xenoy grip. This weapon was launched in 1991 and is still in production. This pistol has been known as the Model 4586 TSW (Tactical Smith & Wesson) since 2000.

MODEL 457: This compact double-action pistol has a 95 mm (3¼ in) barrel, a total length of 184 mm (7¼ in) and an empty weight of 822 g (29 oz). It has a blued alloy frame and a steel slide. This pistol has a safety catch on the left-hand side of the slide and a 7 round magazine. Production of this weapon started in 1996 and it is still being manufactured.

New 945S-PC pistol of 2001

chambers. The barrel lengths available were 51 mm (2¹/₄ in) or 89 mm (3¹/₂ in). A small series was also manufactured in .22 WMR caliber. The 6-shot revolver was available in a blued or nickel-plated version. In addition, this weapon has a micrometer rear sight and was produced from 1954 to 1974.

MODEL 51 .22/32 KIT GUN MAGNUM RIMFIRE: Smith & Wesson brought this weapon onto the market in 1960. This 6-shot revolver in .22 WMR caliber is manufactured from an adapted light J-Target frame. This weapon has an 89 mm (3¹/₂ in) barrel, sunken cylinder chambers and an adjustable micrometer sight. This revolver could have been purchased in a blued or nickel-plated version, with both versions having a walnut grip. A replacement cylinder in .22 LR caliber was an optional extra. This model remained in production until 1974.

MODEL 60 .38 CHIEFS SPECIAL STAINLESS: This model is the stainless steel version of the model 37 and came on the market in 1965. This weapon was the first revolver that Smith & Wesson produced in a precious metal, and originally was only manufactured with a 51 mm (2¹/₄ in) barrel. In 1972, a version was introduced with a 76 mm (3 in) barrel. In 1990 the 76 mm (3 in) barrel version was given a continuous ejector shroud through to the muzzle. The Model 60 was supplied with walnut grips until 1994, these were then replaced by soft rubber. In 1996, the barrel lengths were somewhat modified to 54 mm (2¹/₄ in) and 76 mm (3 in). This latter version has a continuous ejector shroud through to the muzzle. The total length of both versions is 167 and 191 mm (6¹/₂ and 7¹/₂ in). The weight is 638 or 695 g (23 or 24¹/₂ oz). Interestingly, in the same year the caliber of this revolver was changed from a .38 Special to the .357 Magnum. Anyone familiar with weapons will know that a .357 Magnum revolver can also fire .38 Special cartridges but this will not work vice versa. From 1999 up to the present day, both versions have a 'solid barrel'.

S&W 60LS LadySmith

MODEL 60LS .38 LADYSMITH STAINLESS: This model was developed in 1989. This is a 5-shot revolver, totally in stainless steel and with a 51 mm (2 in) standard barrel or a heavy 76 mm (3 in) barrel. Until 1992, this weapon was supplied with wooden combat grips, which were later followed by soft rubber grips. In 1996, the caliber was modified from .38 Special to .357 Magnum and this weapon was once again given a wooden grip. This model in .357 Magnum caliber is still available, but only with a 54 mm (2¹/₄ in) barrel. The total length is 166 mm (6¹/₂ in) and it weighs 610 g (21¹/₂ oz).

MODEL 63 .22/32 KIT GUN STAINLESS: This is a totally stainless steel revolver with a J-Target frame. The 6-shot weapon in .22 LR caliber has a 102 mm (4 in) barrel, an adjustable rear sight and a walnut grip. In 1992 a version was launched with a 51 mm (2 in) barrel as a standard model. The total length of both types is 159 and 221 mm (6¹/₄ and 8¹¹/₁₆ in) and it weighs 624 or 695 g (22 or 24¹/₂ oz). This revolver is manufactured in different versions:

1982: Model 63-1, barrel retaining pin abolished;
1989: Model 63-2, a special series with a 51 mm (2 in) barrel and a Hogue grip for the trading company Lew Horton;
1989: Model 63-3, modification of the cylinder arm;
1994: Model 63-4, modification of the ejector star; use of an Uncle Mike walnut grip. Model 63 was introduced in 1977 and remained in production until 1999. The same weapon is manufactured in .22 WMR caliber as Model 651 Service Kit Gun Stainless. This revolver has a 102 mm (4 in) barrel and was available with a replacement cylinder in .22 LR. Smith & Wesson produced this weapon from 1983 until 1988. In 1991 the company decided to once again include it in their range until 1999.

New Model 60 Chief's Special Stainless in .357 Magnum caliber

Model 63 .22/32 Kit
Gun Stainless

MODEL 317 AIRLITE: This new 8-shot type in the .22 LR caliber was introduced in 1997. This revolver has an alloy frame in 'stainless look' and a stainless steel cylinder and barrel. This weapon is still in production in different versions:

- Model 317 Airlite Chief has a 48 mm (2 in) barrel, a fixed sight and a black rubber Uncle Mike Boot grip;
- Model 317 Airlite Lady Smith with 48 mm (2 in) barrel, a fixed sight and a laminated grip from Dymondwood. This model has a total length of 157 mm (6¹/₄ in) and it weighs 298 g (10¹/₂ oz) and 281 g (10 oz) for the Ladysmith;
- Model 317 Airlite Kit Gun has a 76 mm (3 in) barrel, an adjustable rear sight and a black rubber Uncle Mike Combat grip. The total length of this weapon is 183 mm (7¹/₄ in) and it weighs 337 g (12 oz). In 2001, Smith & Wesson introduced a new version with a special green composite light sensitive horizontal front sight. This model is known as the 317 Airlite Kit Gun Hi-Viz. This revolver was specially intended for rambling and fishing trips.

MODEL 337 CHIEFS SPECIAL AIRLITE TITANIUM: Smith & Wesson introduced this revolver to their year 2000 program as the lightest central fire revolver in the world. The smallest version is the model 337 Chiefs Special Airlite Titanium Personal Defense. Quite a mouthful for a small revolver weighing only 303 g (10³/₄ oz). In addition, 38 Special P cartridges can be used in this weapon. This ammunition develops a higher gas pressure, with in turn a higher bullet velocity, resulting in a higher bullet energy. Shooting such powerful ammunition from such a light weapon, with such a short barrel and without a compensator can hardly be described as enjoyable. This new revolver model with a Hogue Bantam grip is available with a barrel length of 48 mm (2 in). The total length is 160 mm (6¹/₄ in). The frame, the cylinder arm and the barrel shroud are made of alloy and the cylinder is manufactured from titanium. This revolver is mat black with a gray cylinder. In addition, Smith & Wesson manufactured a version in the year 2000 with an 81 mm (3¹/₄ in) barrel with Ruby Combat, Uncle Mike Boot or Uncle Mike Combat grips. This type has a 'stainless look' with a gray titanium cylinder. In 2001, a new version was launched with a horizontal orange colored composite front sight. This is the Model 337 Kit Gun Airlite Titanium Hi-viz.

MODEL 340 AIRLITE SCANDIUM: Smith & Wesson caused a real sensation in the field of revolvers in 2001 with the introduction of the Scandium revolver range. This metal was discovered in 1879 by the Swedish chemist Lars Nilson. He found a way of isolating the scandium from the mineral euxenite. This mineral was most prevalent in Scandinavia, hence the name Scandium. This is an extremely scarce metal, for 100 tons of euxenite is required to produce just 500 g of scandium. The market price of scandium is currently around $ 1600 per 100 g In 1971, a large supply of scandium was found in the Ukraine. Russian scientists discovered that aluminum became much stronger if a small amount of

Model 317 AirLite and
317 Kit Gun AirLite of
2001 with special Hi-Viz
bead

Model 337 Chief's Special
AirLite Titanium of 2000

340 AirLite Scandium
revolver of 2001

Model 340 AirLite Scandium
Personal Defense of 2001

scandium was added. Alloys containing scandium are far more durable, and have a very high resistance to pressure. The Russians have incorporated this new material in their new Mig fighter planes and in space travel. After the fall of the Iron Curtain, this material became available in the west. In 1999, Smith & Wesson introduced a number of Airlite Titanium revolver models. When the designers became aware of this new scandium, the company introduced a totally new Scandium revolver series in 2001. The first revolver of this new type was the double-action Model 340 Airlite Scandium. This 5-shot weapon in the caliber .357 Magnum has a J-frame and a barrel length of 48 mm (2 in). The total length is 160 mm (6¼ in) and this small revolver weighs 340 g (12 oz). The frame, the cylinder arm and the barrel shroud are made of light metal, strengthened with scandium. The cylinder is manufactured of titanium. The frame has a 'stainless look' and the cylinder is gray in color. In addition, this weapon has a concealed hammer and a Hogue Bantam grip.

MODEL 340 AIRLITE SCANDIUM PERSONAL DEFENSE 2001: The dimensions and the caliber of this revolver are identical to that of the previous scandium Model 340. The only difference is the appearance This weapon has a mat black frame and a dark gray cylinder.

MODEL 360 AIRLITE SCANDIUM 2001: This new model also originates from 2001. The dimensions are the same as that of Model 340, but this weapon has a normal hammer spur. The frame is made of alloy with scandium and has a stainless finish. The titanium cylinder is gray in color. The 5-shot .357 Magnum double-action weapon also has a J-frame and a rubber Hogue Bantam grip.

360 AirLite Scandium in
.357 Magnum, introduced
in 2001

MODEL 360 KIT GUN AIRLITE SCANDIUM HI-VIZ 2001: Smith & Wesson also introduced this model in 2001. This 5-shot revolver in .357 Magnum caliber also has a J-frame and is made of alloy with scandium in a 'stainless look'. The cylinder is manufactured from titanium and is gray in color. This weapon has a 79 mm (3⅛ in) barrel and a total length of 191 mm (7½ in). The weight is 411 g (14½ oz). In addition, this revolver has a horizontal orange colored composite Hi-Viz front sight.

MODEL 442 CENTENNIAL AIRWEIGHT: A 5-shot blued revolver, introduced in 1993 with a 51 mm (2 in) barrel and in .38 Special caliber. In 2000, Smith & Wesson changed the barrel length to 48 mm (2 in) and the caliber to .38 Special P. The total length is 160 mm (6¼ in) and it weighs 425 g (15 oz). This revolver has an alloy frame, with a steel cylinder and barrel. This frame time is known as the JC (C or 'concealed') because the hammer is hidden in the high frame back. The 442 Centennial Airweight is a double-action-only revolver, because the hammer

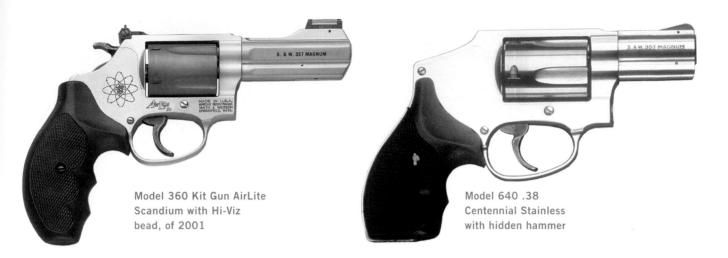

Model 360 Kit Gun AirLite
Scandium with Hi-Viz
bead, of 2001

Model 640 .38
Centennial Stainless
with hidden hammer

cannot be cocked by hand. In 1993 the name 'Airweight' was inscribed on the barrel, this was later changed to a laser engraving located on the right-hand side of the frame. This model is still in production. The version with an alloy frame and a stainless steel cylinder has the model name 642 Centennial Airweight. This revolver in 'stainless look' has the same dimensions and weight as Model 442. In addition, there is also the Model 642 Centennial Airweight Lady Smith with an Uncle Mike's Dymondwood grip.

MODEL 640 .38 CENTENNIAL STAINLESS: This

5-shot model in .38 Special caliber was brought onto the market in 1990 and was then available in two barrel lengths: 51 mm (2 in) or 76 mm (3 in). In 1993 the model with the 76 mm (3 in) barrel was discontinued. In the same year the model 940 was introduced, which was the same revolver, but in 9 mm Para caliber. This type was once again withdrawn in 1999. In 1996 Smith & Wesson changed the caliber to .357 Magnum and the barrel

length to 54 mm (2¹/₈ in). The total length is 166 mm (6⁹/₁₆ in) and it weighs 652 g (23 oz). This weapon has a stainless steel frame and cylinder. This type is also a double-action-only because of the concealed hammer. This revolver is still in production.

MODEL 649 .38 BODYGUARD STAINLESS: This is

a 5-shot stainless steel, double-action-only revolver that came onto the market in 1985. Since 1988 this revolver was named the Model 649-1 due to the modification of the cylinder arm. The model 649-2 was introduced in 1990. The steel hardening process was especially modified for this model. This weapon was also given a wider sight opening. In 1997 Smith & Wesson changed the caliber of the .38 Special to the .357 Magnum and changed the barrel length from 51 mm (2 in) to 54 mm (2¹/₂ in). This weapon has a total length of 166 mm (6⁹/₁₆ in) and it weighs 652 g (23 oz). Both types are shown in the illustration. This revolver is still being produced in .357 Magnum caliber.

Model 442 Centennial
Airweight

The same model decorated
by the Smith & Wesson
Performance Center

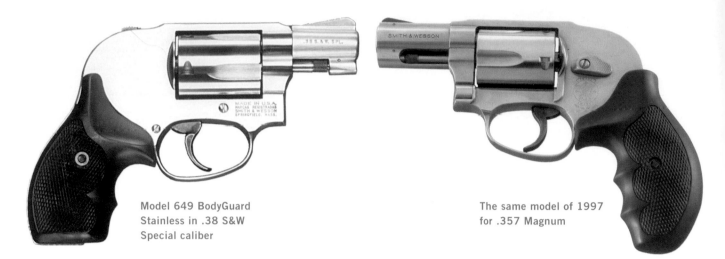

Model 649 BodyGuard
Stainless in .38 S&W
Special caliber

The same model of 1997
for .357 Magnum

MODEL 650 SERVICE KIT GUN STAINLESS: This model
was manufactured from 1983 to 1988 in .22 WMR
caliber. This 6-shot stainless steel double-action
revolver has the small J-frame and a heavy 76 mm
(3 in) barrel. It has a fixed sight and a special wide
combat trigger. A 6-shot replacement cylinder in the
caliber .22 LR was also available. From 1987 this
weapon was given the model name 650-1 due to its
modified cylinder arm.

MODEL 651 TARGET KIT GUN STAINLESS: This model
was produced from 1983 to 1988 in .22 WMR caliber
and with an optional replacement cylinder in .22 LR
caliber. The 6-shot stainless steel double-action

Model 651 Target Kit Gun
Stainless in .22 WMR
caliber

revolver has a Target version of the J-frame with an
adjustable rear sight. This weapon was only
manufactured with a 104 mm (4 in) barrel. The total
length is 219 mm (8¹/₂ in) and it weighs 695 g (24¹/₂
oz). In addition, it has an extra wide combat trigger
and had a walnut grip until 1994 when it was replaced
with a soft rubber combat grip. In 1988, another model
variation was launched, the 651-1 so-called due to the
modified cylinder arm. In 1991, Smith & Wesson

manufactured a small series of 2,500 weapons with
a barrel length of 76 mm (3 in) and a total length
of 178 mm (7 in) and reintroduced this type into
their range, however the production was stopped again
in 1999.

SMITH & WESSON K-FRAME REVOLVERS

The forerunner of all Smith & Wesson small
caliber double-action revolvers is the 6-shot K-22
Outdoorsman from 1931. This blued revolver with
a medium-sized K-frame was manufactured until and
including 1940. In 1941 Smith & Wesson had to
increase the production capacity due to the Second
World War requirements. In 1946
this model was reintroduced to the
S&W range as the Model K-22
Masterpiece. This model and subsequent
models are reviewed below:

**MODEL .38 MILITARY & POLICE/MODEL 10 MILITARY
& POLICE:** This revolver was introduced in
September 1945 as the successor to the .38 Military
& Police Victory Model of the Second World War.
The weapon number of the Victory model was
preceded by the letter V. The series numbers of the
post-war models started with the letter S. After 1948
Smith & Wesson changed this to a letter C, and in
1967 to the letter D.

This 6-shot weapon in the caliber .38 Special was
then manufactured with a 51 mm (2 in), 102 mm
(4 in), 127 mm (5 in) or 152 mm (6 in) barrel in
a blued or nickel-plated version, with fixed sight and
walnut grips. In 1957 this revolver's name was
changed to the Model 10 Military & Police, when it
was given a new type of hammer blocking bar. The
model 10 was available with the same barrel lengths
and in the same versions as the old model. In the
course of 55 years, Smith & Wesson have produced
a large number of different versions for a great variety
of police- and army corps. Some examples are the FBI

Smith & Wesson .38
Military & Police revolver
of 1945

The blued Model 10 with a heavy 102 mm (4 in) barrel is still in production in the stainless steel version and is known as the Model 64.

MODEL 14 K-38 TARGET MASTERPIECE: this 6-shot target revolver in the caliber .38 Special was originally known as the K-38 Target Masterpiece. This weapon originates from 1947 and was manufactured by Smith & Wesson until 1982. In 1957 the name was

Model 10 with a heavy 63.5 mm (2¹/₂ in) barrel, the Model 10 Hong Kong Police from 1983 with a 102 mm (4 in) barrel and Model 10 Brazilian from 1995 with a 76 mm (3 in) barrel and continuous ejector shroud. During its long term of service the Model 10 has undergone a large number of modifications.
After important changes the model number was also changed:
1959: Model 10-1, introduction of the heavier 102 mm (4 in) barrel;
1961: Model 10-2, modification of the ejector bar;

Model 14 K-38 Target
Masterpiece

changed to the Model 14 Target Masterpiece. This weapon was available with a 152 mm (6 in) barrel. This was followed by a version in 1959 with a barrel length of 213 mm (8¹/₂ in). This weapon is blued, however a small number were nickel-plated. This revolver has an adjustable rear sight, walnut grips, and a so-called K-Target frame, that is to say that a provision was made at the top of the K frame bridge for an adjustable rear sight. There are a number of different versions of the Model 14:
1959: Model 14-1, modification of the ejector bar;
1961: Model 14-2, changes to the cylinder stop and the trigger guard;
1967: Model 14-3, modification of the adjusting screw on the rear sight;
1977: Model 14-4, modification of the cylinder arm;
1991: Model 14-5, in 1991 a special version of this model was introduced also named the 14-5 but with a heavier barrel 152 mm (6 in), with an ejector shroud that ran through to the muzzle;

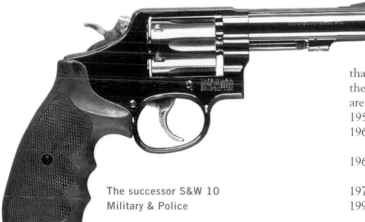

The successor S&W 10
Military & Police

1961: Model 10-3, modification of the ejector bar of Model 10-1;
1962: Model 10-4, changes to the trigger guard;
1962: Model 10-5, changes to the front sight width and the standard barrel;
1962: Model 10-6, modification of the trigger guard of the heavy barrel model;
1977: Model 10-7, modification of the cylinder arm of the standard barrel model;
1977: Model 10-8, the same changes to the heavy barrel model;
1988: Model 10-9, modification of the cylinder arm for the standard barrel model;
1988: Model 10-10, the same changes to the heavy barrel model;

1994: Model 14-6, modification of the ejector star, changes to the adjustable rear sight and introduction of a synthetic grip. This model was manufactured until 2000. From 1961 until 1982 Smith & Wesson also manufactured a Model 14 in a single-action with the omission of the double-action parts of the trigger mechanism.

MODEL 15 K-38 COMBAT MASTERPIECE: This is blued 6-shot double-action revolver that was introduced in 1949 in .38 Special caliber. In 1957, Smith & Wesson changed this weapon's name to the Model 15 Combat Masterpiece. It has a K-target frame and was only originally manufactured with

Model 15 K-38 Combat
Masterpiece

a 102 mm (4 in) barrel. This was followed in 1964 by a version with a heavier 51 mm (2 in) barrel. In 1986, this Model 15 was brought onto the market with a 152 mm (6 in) and a 213 mm (8¹/₂ in) barrel. Both the 51 mm (2 in) and the 213 mm (8¹/₂ in) barrel versions were withdrawn again in 1988. In 1992 production of the model with the 152 mm (6 in) barrel was stopped, leaving only the 102 mm (4 in) barrel version. The total length of this weapon is 237 mm (9¹/₄ in) and it weighs 907 g (32 oz). The model 15 was manufactured until 2000 in the following versions:

1959: Model 15-1, modification of the ejector bar;
1961: Model 15-2, changes to the trigger guard and the cylinder stop;
1967: Model 15-3, changes to the adjusting screw of the rear sight;
1977: Model 15-4, modification of the cylinder arm;
1982: Model 15-5, changes to the trigger mechanism;
1988: Model 15-6, improved cylinder arm catch;
1994: Model 15-7, introduction of synthetic grips, changes to the rear sight and the ejector star. The model 67 is a stainless steel version of this weapon.

Model K-22 Masterpiece/Model 17: Smith & Wesson launched the Model K-22 Masterpiece in 1946. This is a 6-shot revolver with a 152 mm (6 in) barrel in .22 LR caliber. A small production series were manufactured with a 127 mm (5 in) barrel. This revolver has an adjustable micrometer sight and a walnut grip. In 1959, it was renamed the Model 17 K-22 Masterpiece. This steel revolver has counter-bored cylinder chambers, allowing a deeper seating for the .22 LR cartridges. As of 1960, this version was also available with a 213 mm (8¹/₂ in) barrel. In 1986, a version with a heavier 102 mm (4 in) barrel was added. In 1990, Smith & Wesson introduced a new model 17 Masterpiece. This type has a continuous ejector shroud running through to the muzzle. The new model had barrel lengths of 102 mm (4 in), 152 mm (6 in) and 204 mm (8¹/₂ in). The barrel has a raised barrel rib. This new model also has deepened cylinder chambers, an adjustable micrometer sight and a walnut grip. In 1993, the production of this revolver

with the 213 mm (8¹/₂ in) barrel was stopped. In the course of time, a number of different modifications have been made both to the old and new Model 17:

1959: Model 17-1, modification of the ejector bar;
1961: Model 17-2, changes to the trigger guard and the cylinder stop;
1967: Model 17-3, modification of the adjusting screw on the rear sight;
1977: Model 17-4, modification of the cylinder arm catch;
1988: Model 17-5, modification of the cylinder arm;
1990: Model 17-6, a continuous ejector shroud;
1994: Model 17-7, modification of the rear sight and the ejector star.

The last change was made in 1996, when the Model 17 became available with a 10-shot cylinder. The production of this model was stopped in 1999. The successor of this revolver was the Model 617.

Model K-22 Combat Masterpiece/Model 18: This model, in .22 LR caliber was introduced in 1949. This blued 6-shot revolver has a 102 mm (4 in) barrel and an adjustable rear sight in combat style. As with the model 17, the cylinder chambers are counter-bored. This weapon has a walnut grip. In 1957, this model was renamed the Model 18. The following are

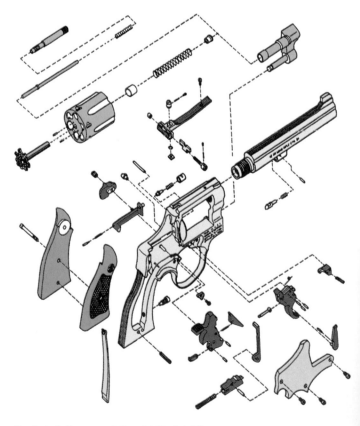

Exploded diagram of the old Model 17

Model 18 K-22 Combat
Masterpiece

the different model numbers together with their modifications:

1959: Model 18-1, changes to the ejector bar;
1961: Model 18-2, modifications to the trigger guard and cylinder stop;
1967: Model 18-3, modification of the adjusting screw on the rear sight;
1977: Model 18-4, changes to the cylinder arm. This weapon was taken out of production in 1985.

MODEL 19 COMBAT MAGNUM: This is one of the most famous Smith & Wesson revolvers. This blued weapon in .357 Magnum caliber was introduced in 1955. Sadly, Smith & Wesson stopped its production in 2000. Only Model 66, the stainless steel version, is still being manufactured. This revolver has a K-Target frame with an adjustable rear sight. Originally, this weapon was only manufactured with a 102 mm (4 in) barrel. In 1963, a version followed

with a 152 mm (6 in) barrel. A third variation was introduced in 1966 with a 63.5 mm (2½ in) barrel. It is quite possible to come across the Model 19 in other configurations, as over the years numerous different versions have been manufactured for police forces and a variety of other clients. One example is the 1995 Special for the American trading company Lew Horton, a type that was also sold in Europe by the German company Akah. Other important special orders were the California Highway Patrol Commemorative model of 1978, the West Virginia State Police Commemorative of 1979 and the Oregon State Police Commemorative of 1981.

Throughout the period of manufacture, a number of different modifications have been made together with changes of the model number:

1959: Model 19-1, changes to the ejector bar;
1961: Model 19-2, modification of the cylinder stop and the trigger guard;

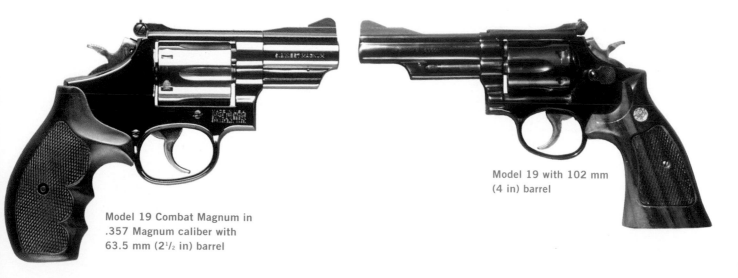

Model 19 Combat Magnum in
.357 Magnum caliber with
63.5 mm (2½ in) barrel

Model 19 with 102 mm
(4 in) barrel

The match version of
Model 19 with 152 mm
(6 in) barrel

1967: Model 19-3, modification of the adjusting screw
on the rear sight;
1077: Model 19-4, modification of the cylinder arm;
1982: Model 19-5, discontinuing of the counter-bored
cylinder chambers;
1988: Model 19-6, changes to the cylinder arm catch;
1994: Model 19-7, the use of synthetic grips, changes
to the ejector star and the rear sight.

MODEL 48 K-22 MASTERPIECE MAGNUM RIMFIRE: This
6-shot model in .22 WMR caliber was introduced in
1959 and has a medium-sized K-frame also used by
Smith & Wesson for more powerful calibers. This
revolver was only available in a blued version and
in the barrel lengths 102 mm (4 in), 152 mm (6 in)
and 222 mm (8³/₄ in). It has a micrometer sight,
counter-bored cylinder chambers and a walnut grip.
A replacement cylinder in .22 LR caliber was
available as an optional extra. This revolver was
produced up to 1986 in the following variations:

1960: Model 48-1, modification of the ejector bar;
1962: Model 48-2, changes to the trigger guard;
1968: Model 48-3, changes to the micrometer sight;
1977: Model 48-4, modification of the cylinder arm.

Model 64 Military & Police
Stainless in .38 S&W
Special caliber

MODEL 64 MILITARY & POLICE STAINLESS: This is the
1970 stainless steel version of the blued model 10,
and is also in .38 Special caliber. This weapon was
available in three different barrel lengths: a 51 mm
(2 in) standard barrel, a heavy 76 mm (3 in) barrel
and a heavy 102 mm (4 in) barrel. It has a fixed rear
sight and a standard K-frame, and was originally
supplied with a walnut grip, however this was
changed to a synthetic grip in 1994. An unspecified
number of these revolvers were manufactured in
.357 Magnum caliber for the Oklahoma Highway
Patrol. Two years later, Smith & Wesson brought
this type onto the market as the Model 65. The
following are known versions of the Model 64 M&P:
1972: Model 64-1, introduction of the heavy 102 mm
(4 in) barrel;
1977: Model 64-2, introduction of the 51 mm (2 in)
barrel; modification of the cylinder arm;
1977: Model 64-3, modification of the barrel
connection cone;
1988: Model 64-4, modified of the cylinder arm catch;
1988: Model 64-5, the same modifications to the
heavier 76 mm (3 in) and 102 mm (4 in)
versions;
This specific 6-shot police revolver is still produced by
Smith & Wesson. Since 2001, Smith & Wesson only
manufactures the Model 64 with the heavy 51 or
104 mm (2¹/₄ or 4 in) barrels. The total lengths are 174
and 225 mm (7 and 8 in) respectively. This weapon
weighs 865 or 1021 g (30¹/₂ or 36 oz).

MODEL 65 MILITARY & POLICE STAINLESS: This is the
stainless steel version of the blued Model 13, but is
also the .357 Magnum version of the Model 64. This
double-action police revolver has a fixed rear sight and
was brought onto the market in 1972. This weapon is
still available with a heavy barrel of 76 mm (3 in) or
102 mm (4 in). This 6-shot revolver with a K-frame
had counter-bored cylinder chambers up to and
including 1982. Until 1994, this weapon was supplied
with a walnut grip, followed later by a synthetic rubber
grip. In 1993, Smith & Wesson manufactured
a special series for Lew Horton with a heavy
76 mm (3 in) barrel, a continuous ejector
shroud and a compensator. This version
was also sold in Europe by the German
company Akah. Since 1972, a number of
different modifications have been made
to this weapon:
1972: Model 65-1, from the start of its
production in 1972, Smith &
Wesson gave this weapon its own
name, the Model 65-1, because
a number of .357 Magnum had
already been manufactured
as the Model 64.

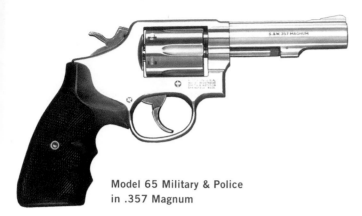

Model 65 Military & Police
in .357 Magnum

Model 66, the stainless steel
version of Model 19

1977: Model 65-2, modification of the barrel connection cone;

1982: Model 65-3, discontinuing of the counter-bored cylinder chambers and barrel retaining pin;

1988: Model 65-4, changes to the cylinder arm catch;

1988: Model 65-5, a second modification of the cylinder arm. The Model 65 and Lady Smith versions are both still in production.

MODEL 65LS .357 LADY SMITH: This type in .357 Magnum caliber came onto the market in 1992 and is still in production at Smith & Wesson. This 6-shot stainless steel revolver is available with a 76 mm (3 in) barrel and a beautiful palisander combat grip. This weapon has a K-frame and a fixed rear sight. The model numbering of the 'old' model 65 of the Lady Smith continued to run consecutively, and so in 1994 the model 65-5 Lady Smith was reintroduced with a modification of the ejector star. The model 65 Lady Smith has a total length of 199 mm (7 in) and it weighs 907 g (32 oz).

MODEL 66 COMBAT MASTERPIECE STAINLESS: This is the stainless steel version of the legendary Model 19, and is also in .357 Magnum caliber. This model was launched in 1970, at first only in the barrel length 102 mm (4 in).

In 1974, Smith & Wesson introduced a version with a 63.5 mm (2¹/₂ in) barrel, followed in 1978 by a version with a 152 mm (6 in) barrel. The total length is 191, 243 or 294 mm (7¹/₂, 9 ¹/₂ or 11¹/ in). This weapon weighs 907, 1049 or 1106 g (32, 37 or 39 oz) respectively. This 6-shot double-action revolver has a K-Target frame with an adjustable rear sight. In 1982, this model's counter-bored cylinder chambers were discontinued. Over the years, Smith & Wesson have manufactured a large number of versions for a variety of clients. A few examples are the Model 66 ISP (Indiana State Police) of 1975 with a 102 mm (4 in) barrel, the Iowa Highway Patrol of 1982 and the Naval Investigative Service of 1988. In the course of time, the following modifications have been carried out:

1977: Model 66-1, changes to the barrel connection cone;

1982: Model 66-2, discontinuing of the counter-bored cylinder chambers and barrel retaining pin;

1986: Model 66-3, new cylinder arm catch;

1994: Model 66-4, changes to the rear sight, the ejector star and the adoption of the Hogue grip.

The model 66 is still being produced in the three original barrel lengths. In 2001, Smith & Wesson introduced a special version with an 81 mm (3¹/₄ in) barrel. This type has a total length of 203 mm (8 in), weighs 1049 g (37 oz), and has a green composite Hi-Viz front sight.

MODEL 67 .38 COMBAT MASTERPIECE: This is the stainless steel version of Model 15. This 6-shot revolver in the caliber .38 Special came onto the market in 1972 with a 102 mm (4 in) barrel and is still in production at Smith & Wesson. It has a K-Target frame, an adjustable rear sight and had a walnut grip until 1994 when it was replaced with a rubber Hogue grip. The ejector bar does not have enclosing shroud, giving this weapon an old fashioned look. The following modifications have been made:

1977: Model 67-1, changes to the barrel connection cone;

Model 65LS Lady Smith

The 617 Target Champion

Model 67 .38 Combat
Masterpiece Stainless

1988: a new cylinder arm catch;
1994: Model 67-3, changes to the ejector star, the rear
sight and the adoption of the Hogue grip.
The total length of this weapon is 225 mm (8 in) and
it weighs 1021 g (36 oz).

MODEL 617 MASTERPIECE STAINLESS: This model
was introduced in 1990 and is still in production.
The .22 LR revolver is a totally stainless steel
version of the old model 17. This weapon has
a modern K-Target frame and is available with a
102 mm (4 in), a 152 mm (6 in) and a 213 mm
(8½ in) barrel. The total lengths are 232, 283 or
343 mm (9, 11 or 13½ in) respectively. This weapon
weighs, depending on the barrel length, 1162, 1276
or 1488 g (41, 45 or 52½ oz). The first series up to
1991 were supplied with and without a continuous
ejector shroud. From 1991, this shroud ran through
to the muzzle, and also served as a barrel weight.
This weapon originally had a walnut grip, but was
replaced in 1994 with a soft rubber combat grip. In
1994, the model 617-1 was released with a modified
rear sight and ejector star, followed in 1996 by a 10-
shot cylinder version. A number of embellished
versions of the Model 617 were launched as special
series models, one example being the 617 Target
Champion.

SMITH & WESSON L-FRAME REVOLVERS

The K-frame made an excellent police revolver,
however sport shooters found this type of frame not to
be up to a staple diet of .357 Magnum cartridges.
Shooters actually wanted a reasonably sized frame with
the strength of the large N-frame. As a compromise,
Smith & Wesson developed the L-frame in 1981. The
majority of revolvers of this type have a continuous
ejector shroud running through to the muzzle. This extra
weight serves to absorb the heavy recoil of the .357
Magnum cartridge. The most well known revolvers with
an L-frame are the models 586 and 686.

MODEL 386 MOUNTAIN LITE AIRLITE SCANDIUM 2001:
Smith & Wesson introduced the Model 386 in to the
new Scandium series in 2001. This 6-shot double-
action revolver in the caliber .357 Magnum has an L-
frame, with a cylinder manufactured from titanium.
The frame, the barrel shroud and the cylinder arm are
all made of alloy with scandium. The barrel bushing is
stainless steel. This weapon is only available with an
80 mm (3¼ in) barrel and has a total length of 206 mm
(8¼ in). The weight is 525 g (18½ oz). The frame has
a 'stainless look' and the cylinder is titanium gray. In
addition, this revolver has a green composite Hi-Viz
front sight.

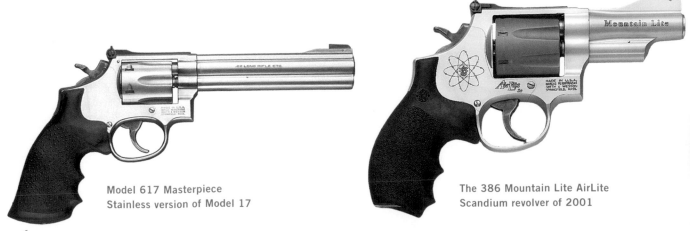

Model 617 Masterpiece
Stainless version of Model 17

The 386 Mountain Lite AirLite
Scandium revolver of 2001

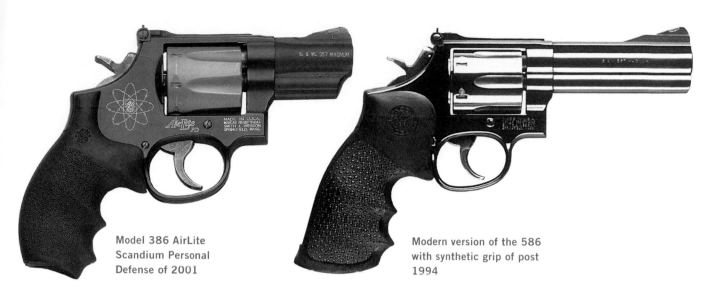

Model 386 AirLite
Scandium Personal
Defense of 2001

Modern version of the 586
with synthetic grip of post
1994

MODEL 386 AIRLITE SCANDIUM PERSONAL DEFENSE 2001: Smith & Wesson also brought out this compact double-action revolver with an L-frame in 2001. As with the previous model, this model is also manufactured from scandium alloy with a titanium cylinder, a mat black frame and a titanium gray cylinder. The barrel length is 63.5 mm (2¹/₂ in) and the total length is 181 mm (7¹/₄ in). This 6-shot weapon in the caliber .38 Special P weighs 496 g (17¹/₂ oz).

Model 586 with 102 mm
(4 in) barrel and wooden
hand grip of 1981

MODEL 586 .357 DISTINGUISHED COMBAT MAGNUM: Smith & Wesson brought the Model 586 onto the market in 1981 as a 6-shot sporting revolver in .357 Magnum caliber, in either a blued or nickel-plated version. This weapon remained in production until 2000 and was available with a 102 mm (4 in), 152 mm (6 in) or 213 mm (8¹/₂ in) barrel with a continuous ejector shroud running through to the muzzle, and an adjustable rear sight. This revolver had a hardwood Goncalo Alves grip until 1994, when it was replaced with a synthetic rubber grip. The Model 586 was a special version with barrel lengths of 152 mm (6 in) and 213 mm (8¹/₂ in) and an adjustable

front sight, which could be adjusted with a catch to four different shooting distances. The production of the model with the 213 mm (8¹/₂ in) barrel was stopped in 1992. In the same year Smith & Wesson also scrapped the nickel-plated version and the adjustable front sight. This revolver was not only used by sport shooters, but also by a variety of American police corps, examples of which being the Model 686 Massachusetts State Police Commemorative of 1986 and the Missouri Conservation Corps of 1987. Over the years, the Model 586 has undergone a number of changes:

1986: Model 586-1, change to the barrel connection cone;
1987: Model 586-2, modification of the firing pin point on the hammer;
1988: Model 586-3, changes to the cylinder arm catch;
1994: Model 586-4, adoption of the synthetic grip; changes to the rear sight and the ejector star.

The illustrated Model 586 with a heavy bull barrel and compensator is a special match version built by the Smith & Wesson Performance Center.

MODEL 686 .357 DISTINGUISHED COMBAT MAGNUM STAINLESS: This is the stainless steel version of the previously reviewed Model 586, although in actual fact

Model 586 Bull Barrel
Compensator

Smith & Wesson Model 686
with 63.5 (2¹/₂ in) barrel

Model 686 Security
Special

Smith & Wesson introduced this revolver a year earlier in 1980. This weapon was originally available with a 102 mm (4 in), 152 mm (6 in) or a 213 mm (8¹/₂ in) barrel. In 1990, a version with a 63.5 mm (2¹/₂ in) barrel was added to the series. This model was available until 1992 with an adjustable front sight for the 152 mm (6 in) and 213 mm (8¹/₄ in) barrels. The model 686 had a Goncalo Alves hardwood grip until 1994, which was later replaced by a rubber Hogue grip.

This revolver has been manufactured in several different versions, examples of which are:
– Model 686 Classic Hunter from 1988 with a 152 mm (6 in) barrel with a solid round cylinder, with flutes between the cylinder chambers;
– Model 686 Black Stainless from 1988 with a 102 mm (4 in) barrel. This was a stainless steel revolver, but with a black finish;

– Model 686 Security Special from 1992 with a 76 mm (3 in) or 102 mm (4 in) barrel and a rubber grip;
– Model 686 Target Champion from 1992 with a mat finish, a 152 mm (6 in) barrel, an adjustable trigger stop and a beautiful walnut Nill grip;
– Model 686 Power Port from 1994 with a 152 mm (6 in) barrel, and a single chamber compensator between the muzzle and the slightly set back front sight. This type is still in production;
– Model 686 Plus. In 1996, Smith & Wesson introduced this 7-shot model in .357 Magnum caliber as the 686 Plus. This type is available with a 64 mm (2¹/₂ in), 102 mm (4 in) or a 152 mm (6 in) barrel. Both the 6-shot and the 7-shot version are still being manufactured;
– Model 686 International DX Competition from 1998 with a solid cylinder and a 152 mm (6 in) barrel. This version is still in production.

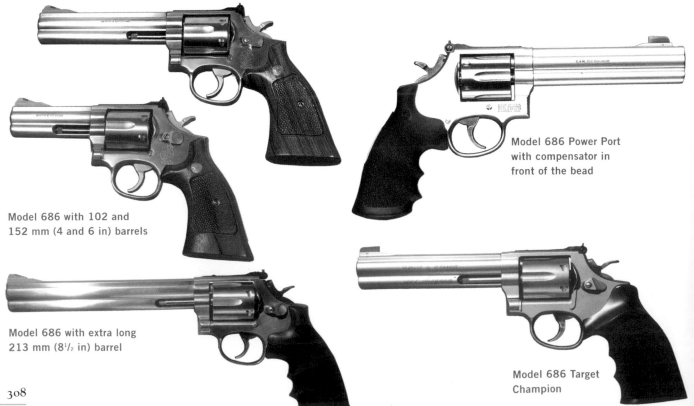

Model 686 with 102 and
152 mm (4 and 6 in) barrels

Model 686 Power Port
with compensator in
front of the bead

Model 686 with extra long
213 mm (8¹/₂ in) barrel

Model 686 Target
Champion

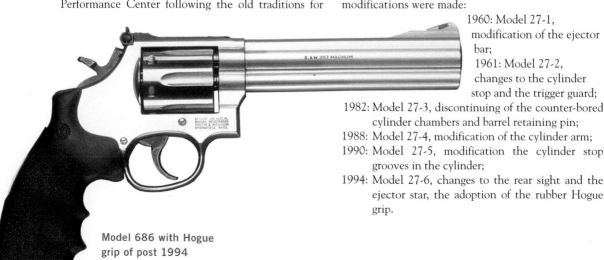

The fine 686 International
DX Competition revolver

As of 1986 this model has undergone a number of modifications including:

1986: Model 686-1, modification of the cylinder transport arm;

1987: Model 686-2, changes to the firing pin point on the hammer;

1988: Model 686-3, adjustment to the cylinder arm;

1994: Model 686-4, changes to the rear sight and the ejector star, the adoption of the rubber Hogue grip.

SMITH & WESSON N-FRAME REVOLVERS

The N-frame of Smith & Wesson is based on the old Hand Ejector New Century Triple Lock models of 1907, 1915 and 1926. These were large heavy revolvers for the calibers .44 S&W, .44-40 Win, and .45 S&W Special together with a range of other ammunition types that are hardly used nowadays, if at all. The authentic N-frame was developed around 1930 for the .38/44 Heavy Duty and the .38/44 Outdoorsman revolvers. The .38/44 was an enhanced .38 Special cartridge, also known as the .38 Super Police. The .38/44 Outdoorsman remained in production until 1966.

MODEL 25 PC HAND EJECTOR 2001: The original Model 25 originates from 1955. This new 2001 revolver was produced by the Smith & Wesson Performance Center following the old traditions for

the trading company, Sports South Inc. This 6-shot double-action weapon in .45 Colt caliber has a barrel length of 152 mm (6 in), a total length of 297 mm (11¾ in) and it weighs 1191 g (42 oz). The finish is the old fashion blued with walnut grips. The short ejector shroud is entirely in keeping with the old style. Hopefully, Smith & Wesson are testing the water with this special series, and will later release a series of weapons in .357 Magnum and .44 Magnum calibers.

MODEL 27 .357 MAGNUM: This beautifully blued 6-shot double-action revolver originates from 1949, when it was manufactured in .357 Magnum caliber with the barrel lengths of 89 mm (3½ in), 127 mm

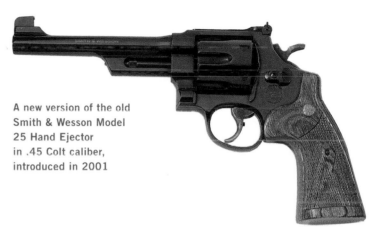

A new version of the old Smith & Wesson Model 25 Hand Ejector in .45 Colt caliber, introduced in 2001

(5 in), 152 mm (6 in), 165 mm (6½ in) or 213 mm (8½ in). This weapon has a micrometer sight, counter-bored cylinder chambers and a walnut grip. From 1949, this weapon number was preceded by the letter S. From 1969, the letter S was replaced with the letter N. In 1957, this model was known simply as the .357 Magnum but was later given the model number 27. In 1975, the models with the 89 mm (3½ in) and 127 mm (5 in) barrels were discontinued, followed in 1992 by the 102 mm (4 in) and 213 mm (8½ in) barrels. The model 27 was manufactured until 1994. Throughout the production period, a large number of modifications were made:

1960: Model 27-1, modification of the ejector bar;

1961: Model 27-2, changes to the cylinder stop and the trigger guard;

1982: Model 27-3, discontinuing of the counter-bored cylinder chambers and barrel retaining pin;

1988: Model 27-4, modification of the cylinder arm;

1990: Model 27-5, modification the cylinder stop grooves in the cylinder;

1994: Model 27-6, changes to the rear sight and the ejector star, the adoption of the rubber Hogue grip.

Model 686 with Hogue
grip of post 1994

Model 27 with heavy
N-frame of 1949

This revolver is sadly no longer manufactured. In the .357 Magnum caliber, together with its 'sister model' 28, it was one of the strongest and most beautiful revolvers ever produced by Smith & Wesson.

MODEL 28 HIGHWAY PATROLMAN: A real practical revolver, just as robust as the Model 27, but with a mat blued finish. This 6-shot double-action revolver was available with a 102 mm (4 in) or a 152 mm (6 in) barrel. This revolver had counter-bored cylinder chambers until 1983. It has an adjustable rear sight and a walnut grip. This weapon was at least as popular with the American police as the Model 19. The Highway Patrolman was brought onto the market in 1954, but from 1957 was known simply as the Model 28. From 1954, the series number began with the letter S, this was later changed to letter N. Smith & Wesson stopped producing these revolvers in 1986. There were only a couple of modifications made to this model during the production period:
1960: Model 28-1, modification of the ejector bar;
1961: Model 28-2, changes to the cylinder stop and the trigger guard;
1982: Model 28-3, discontinuing of the counter-bored cylinder chambers and barrel retaining pin.

MODEL 29 .44 MAGNUM: The Dirty Harry movies have made this the most well known Smith & Wesson

Model 28 Highway
Patrolman

revolver. This weapon, even when shot from the hip, could bring down a sprinting crook from a 100 yards. Normal mortals shoot less accurately, but even so, the Model 29 is a target revolver of the highest order. This 6-shot weapon is manufactured with 102 mm (4 in), 165 mm (6½ in) or 213 mm (8½ in) barrels. As of 1979, a 152 mm (6 in) barrel replaced the 165 mm (6½ in) barrel. This revolver has an adjustable rear sight, counter-bored cylinder chambers and a large walnut grip. This weapon was originally simply called the Model .44 Magnum, but was given the model number 29 in 1957. At its introduction in 1955, this weapon's model number started with the letter S, but was replaced in 1969 by the letter N. Over the years, the Model 29 has been manufactured in a number of special versions for a variety of clients. The most prominent are:

Model 29 in .44 Rem.
Magnum caliber

- Model 29 Silhouette, a special long distance weapon with a 270 mm (10⅝ in) barrel and an adjustable front sight for four different distances. This type was manufactured from 1983 until 1991;
- Model 29 Classic Hunter, manufactured in 1987 with a 6-shot solid round cylinder and a 152 mm (6 in) barrel with continuous ejector shroud. A number of the 5000 weapons had an adjustable front sight;
- Model 29 Magnum Classic, this type was only manufactured in 1990 and had a 191 mm (7½ in) barrel with a continuous ejector shroud;
- Model 29 .44 Classic, manufactured from 1991 up to and including 1994 with a 127 mm (5 in), 165 mm (6½ in) or 213 mm (8½ in) barrel with a continuous ejector shroud.
Over the years a number of modifications have been made:
1960: Model 29-1, changes to the ejector bar;
1961: Model 29-2, modification of the cylinder stop and the trigger guard;
1982: Model 29-3, discontinuing of the counter-bored cylinder chambers and barrel retaining pin;
1988: Model 29-4, changes to the cylinder arm;

Model 29 with 213 mm
(8¹/₂ in) long barrel with
Hogue grip

1990: Model 29-5, enlargement of the cylinder stop grooves in the cylinder;

1994: Model 29-6, changes to the rear sight, the ejector star and the adoption of the rubber Hogue grip.

Model 29 was manufactured by Smith & Wesson up to 2000.

MODEL 610 CLASSIC: this double-action revolver was introduced in 2001. This 6-shot weapon has a N-frame and the caliber 10 mm Auto. Incidentally the cylinder can also take caliber .40 S&W cartridges. The barrel length is 102 mm (4 in) and the total length is 267 mm (10¹/₂ in). The heavier weapon weighs 1418 g (50 oz). Both the frame and the solid cylinder are made of stainless steel. This weapon has an adjustable rear sight and a rubber Hogue combat grip.

MODEL 625-2 .45 STAINLESS: This weapon is officially known as the 'the model of 1989 .45 Stainless' and was launched in 1989 in .45 ACP pistol caliber, the same caliber as the 1988 model. It received the name 'Model

of 1989' in 1989. In December 1989 it was given its current model name: 625-2. This weapon is the stainless steel version of the blued Model 25 in .45 ACP caliber that was produced from 1955 until 1991. Originally, the 625 only had a version with a 127 mm (5 in) barrel with a continuous ejector shroud. However, from 1991 up until the end of 1992 this model was also manufactured with a 76 mm (3 in) or a 102 mm (4 in) barrel. This revolver is still manufactured with a 172 mm (5 in) barrel and over the years has had the following modifications:

1989: Model 625-2, changes to the model name;

1990: Model 625-3, enlarging of the cylinder stop grooves in the cylinder;

1990: Model 625-4, special series for bowling pin shooting and engraved with the name 'Bowling Pin 88';

1991: Model 625-5, special series in the caliber .45 Long Colt;

1994: Model 625-6, changes to the rear sight, the ejector star and the adoption of the rubber Hogue grip.

MODEL 625 MOUNTAIN GUN 2001: In 2001, Smith & Wesson launched this type for official S&W dealers. This 6-shot double-action revolver is in .45 Colt caliber. The N-frame, the cylinder and the barrel are made of stainless steel. The barrel length is 102 mm (4 in) and the total length is 241 mm (9¹/₂ in). This weapon weighs 1120 g (39¹/₂ oz). It has an adjustable rear sight and a rubber Hogue monogrip. A variation on this model was introduced in 2001 in .45 ACP caliber and was given the model name 625 PC-2001. This weapon was built by the Performance Center of Smith & Wesson as a limited edition.

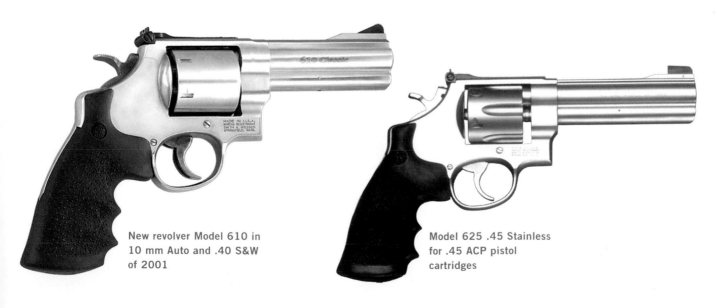

New revolver Model 610 in
10 mm Auto and .40 S&W
of 2001

Model 625 .45 Stainless
for .45 ACP pistol
cartridges

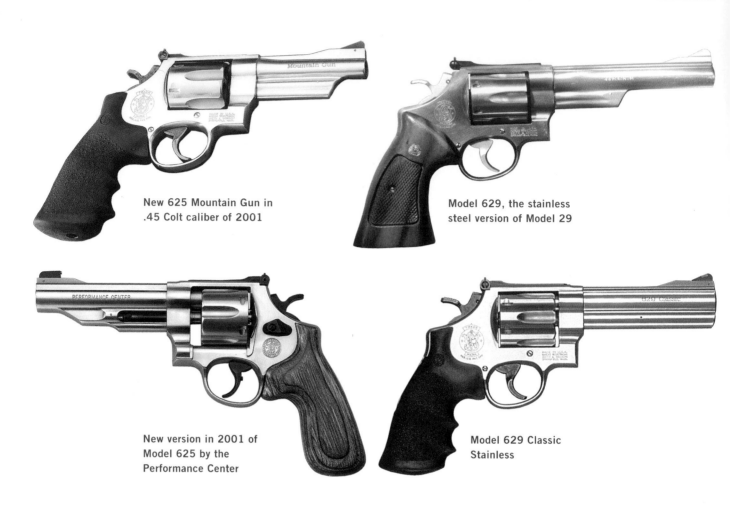

New 625 Mountain Gun in
.45 Colt caliber of 2001

Model 629, the stainless
steel version of Model 29

New version in 2001 of
Model 625 by the
Performance Center

Model 629 Classic
Stainless

MODEL 629 .44 MAGNUM STAINLESS: This is the stainless steel version of Model 29 and was introduced in 1978. The first series 6-shot double-action revolvers had only a 152 mm (6 in) barrel. In 1981, the barrel lengths of 102 mm (4 in) and 213 mm (8½ in) were added. This weapon had counter-bored cylinder chambers until 1982.

A number of different model types of this model have been brought onto the market. The most prominent are:
– Model 629 Classic Stainless with a 127 mm (5 in), 152 mm (6 in) or 213 mm (8½ in) barrel with a continuous ejector shroud. This version has been in production since 1990;
– Model 629 Classic DX Stainless with a 165 mm (6½ in) or 213 mm (8½ in) barrel and continuous ejector shroud. This model originates from 1991 and is still manufactured by Smith & Wesson;
– Model 629 Mountain Gun from 1993 with a 102 mm (4 in) standard barrel. This weapon was developed as a 'backpacker' for travelers who wanted to protect themselves from predators on two or four legs.

– Model 629 has had the following modifications over the years:
1982: Model 629-1, discontinuing of the counter-bored cylinder chambers and barrel retaining pin;
1988: Model 629-2, modification of the trigger mechanism;
1990: Model 629-3, enlarging of the cylinder stop grooves in the cylinder;
1994: Model 629-4, changes to the rear sight, the ejector star and the adoption of the rubber Hogue grip.

MODEL 629 COMPENSATED HUNTER 2001: In 2001, Smith & Wesson introduced this weapon specifically

Model 629 Classic DX

Model 629 Stealth Hunter of 2001 from the Performance Center with green 'Birdsong' coating

Model 629 Compensated Hunter of 2001 from the Performance Center

for hunting. This 6-shot double-action revolver in .44 Magnum caliber was a limited edition built by the Performance Center. The ejector shroud tapers into the muzzle, while on the 191 mm (7¹/₂ in) barrel a special rail is fitted for mounting a telescopic sight. A two-chamber compensator is integrated into the barrel.

MODEL 629 STEALTH HUNTER 2001: This 6-shot double-action revolver in .44 Magnum caliber was also launched in 2001. This weapon has a solid 191 mm (7¹/₂ in) barrel with a Weaver rail for the mounting of a telescopic sight, with all parts being manufactured in stainless steel. As an extra protection against adverse weather conditions, this weapon has been given a special protective coating in NATO-green, known by Smith & Wesson as the 'Black-T Birdsong'. Compensator grooves have been machined into the barrel as in the Mag-Na-Port system. The front of the cylinder chambers are beveled which simplify quick loading. The total length is 325 mm (12³/₄ in) and it weighs 1588 g (56 oz). This revolver is specially manufactured by the Performance Center for the trading company Camfour Distributors.

MODEL 657 .41 MAGNUM STAINLESS:
This 6-shot stainless steel revolver in .41 Magnum caliber originates from 1986 and has a 152 mm (6 in) barrel and is still in production. This weapon has an adjustable rear sight, and was originally manufactured with 102 mm (4 in), 152 mm (6 in) or 213 mm (8¹/₂ in) barrels. In 1988, the version with

the 102 mm (4 in) barrel was discontinued, followed by the 213 mm (8¹/₂ in) barrel in 1993. A special version was released as the Model 657 Magnum Classic Hunter in 1991 with a 165 mm (6¹/₂ in) barrel, a continuous ejector shroud and a solid round cylinder. Modifications made to the Model 657 are:

1988: Model 657-1, modification of the cylinder arm;
1990: Model 657-2, enlarging of the cylinder stop grooves;
1994: Model 657-3, changes to the rear sight, the ejector star and the adoption of the rubber Hogue grip.

In 2001, Smith & Wesson introduced a version with a 191 mm (7¹/₂ in) barrel. This 6-shot stainless steel weapon has a continuous ejector shroud, a solid cylinder and a rubber Hogue combat grip. The total length is 302 mm (11 in) and this weapon weighs 1474 g (52 oz).

Model 657 in .41 Rem. Magnum caliber

SPHINX

Trade mark of Sphinx Systems Ltd

In 1985, this company was still known as ITM, manufacturing the AT84 and AT88S pistols, copies of the Czech CZ-75 pistol. In 1991, this company was renamed Sphinx Systems Ltd and is a weapons factory based in Matn, Switzerland. These pistols are produced using computerized lathes and milling machines. Their largest clients are made up of governments from several countries, that mainly purchase the AT-2000 Police pistol. Generally speaking, only specialist units are equipped with this pistol. Another of their production lines manufacture special match pistols with compensators and telescopic sights, the so-called race-guns.

The Sphinx pistols are made to high standards of quality, which is also reflected in the price. The quality marking 'Swiss Made' is particularly appropriate for these pistols. At the start of 1997 Sphinx were forced to close their factory due to financial reasons. Armin Landolt, the owner of the Action-Sport shooting range complex in Interlaken, purchased Sphinx in June 1997.

SPHINX 2000

The Sphinx 2000 pistol came on the market in 1992. This weapon was available in three different versions. The 2000S pistol has a safety catch on the left-hand side of the frame. On the 2000PS version this catch functions as an uncocking lever. All 2000 versions have automatic firing pin safety. The models 2000P and PS

are the compact versions of the 2000S. These versions are available in 9 mm Para, 9 x 21 mm and .40 S&W calibers. The model 2000S is a 9 mm, and has a magazine capacity of 15 rounds and in the .40 S&W a capacity of 11 rounds. The total length is 204 mm (8 in), the height is 138 mm (5$^{1}/_{2}$ in) and the width is 33 mm (1$^{1}/_{4}$ in). The barrel length is 115 mm (4$^{1}/_{2}$ in) and this weapon weighs 1030 g (36$^{1}/_{4}$ oz). The frame and the slide are made of blued steel, blank stainless steel or in a two-tone-version. This double--action pistol can also be supplied with a double-action--only trigger action. The P and PS models have a total length of 184 mm (7$^{1}/_{4}$ in) and the barrel length is 95 mm (3$^{3}/_{4}$ in). The height of the 2000P is 128 mm (5 in). The magazine capacity of this type is 13 rounds in 9 mm and 10 rounds in .40 S&W. The 2000PS has actually the slide and barrel of the P-model and the frame of the 2000S. The weight of the 2000P is 940 g (33 oz) with the 2000PS weighing 985 g (34$^{3}/_{4}$ oz).

SPHINX COMPETITION/AT3000S

This match version was known as the Sphinx 3000S up until 1995. In 1998, this single-action model was renamed the Competition, with the sub-classifications of Open, Modified and Standard, in accordance with the IPSC shooting classification. All three versions are available in 9 mm Para, 9 x 21 mm and .40 S&W calibers. The Sphinx Open has a magazine capacity of 18 rounds in 9 mm and 14 rounds in .40 S&W. The total length is 275 mm (10$^{7}/_{8}$ in) and the barrel length is 135 mm (5$^{1}/_{4}$ in). The height of this model is 140 mm (5$^{3}/_{4}$ in). The Sphinx Open has a three-chamber compensator on the slide. This pistol does not have sights. This weapon is 33 mm (1$^{1}/_{4}$ in) wide, and it weighs 1100 g (38$^{3}/_{4}$ oz). The Sphinx Modified model has a magazine capacity of 16 rounds in 9 mm and 12 rounds in .40 S&W. This weapon has a two-chamber

Sphinx 2000S pistol in stainless steel and duo-tone

Sphinx AT3000 S

compensator. The total length is 224 mm (8¾ in) and the height is 149 mm (5¾ in). The barrel length is 100 mm (4 in) and it weighs 950 g (33½ oz). The Modified is also supplied without sights. The Sphinx Standard has a barrel length of 120 mm (4¾ in) and a total length of 220 mm (8¾ in). The magazine capacity is the same as that of the Open model. The weight of the standard is 1040 g (36¾ oz).

SPRINGFIELD ARMORY

Trade mark of Springfield Armory

The original Springfield Armory was a US State arsenal that was set up in Massachusetts in 1777. The company has manufactured a large number of weapons for the US Army throughout its history. Well-known rifles of that time are the Springfield Model 1873 'Trapdoor' rifle and Model Springfield M1903. In 1968, the then secretary of defense, Robert S. MacNamarra, shut Springfield down. Three years later, a businessman from Texas purchased the name Springfield along with the patent rights. The new Springfield was no match for the strong opposition and in 1974 it vanished once again. A couple of years later the next buyer appeared, in the persona of Robert Reese, a man with considerable experience in firearms wholesaling. He saw a commercial future for the old company and moved with the company name to Geneso, Illinois, where he set up shop in an old dairy cattle shed. Together with his three sons he produced a series of M1A's, a civilian version of the American M14 army rifle. The current range of Springfield

consists of a series of pistols based on the Colt Government; the M1A National Match .308W (= .308 Winchester) rifle; the M6 Scout Survival carbine: a double barreled carbine in .22 Long Rifle caliber plus .410 shot; the famous M1 Garand rifle .30-06 (also in .308W and .270W calibers); a Beretta BM-59 army rifle in .308W caliber and the SAR-48 manufactured under license, and a copy of the FN-FAL in .308 W caliber. Springfield has also launched a special series of the 1911-A1 pistol, including the Desert Storm and the Gulf Victory, that were associated with the Gulf War. The Springfield range is huge, and includes no less than 21 different pistols based on the Model 1911-A1 pistol. Furthermore, Springfield has a special Custom-shop where a variety of 1911-A1 pistol types are manufactured. Any weapon in the special Custom-series can be ordered in any desired pistol caliber. In November 1992, Springfield Armory was forced to stop trading due to financial problems. In spite of this the company avoided bankruptcy, and resumed trading with a slimmed down company which went by the name of the Springfield Inc. Curiously, this company became a victim of its own success. The company grew too quickly, and unfortunately a number of expensive projects failed. Examples of this are the Linkless 10 mm pistol, that never really got off of the ground. The second disappointment was the Omega project. The Omega pistols, manufactured by Peters Stahl from Germany were launched by Springfield in North America, but were not a success. Thirdly, a loss was made on the SASS pistols. This project involved a single shot conversion set for the Colt 1911 pistol, which enabled the shooter to fire rifle cartridges. To add to this, the company had suffered financially with the IMI project. Springfield had made an agreement with the Israeli company IMI to sell the Uzi machine pistol and the Uzi semi-automatic carbine in North America. With the introduction of the Federal Combat Rifle Ban law, the sale of such weapons were forbidden in the USA. In the meantime, Springfield has risen above this debacle and is flourishing as never before.

SPRINGFIELD 1911-A1

Apart from Colt, Springfield Armory were the first company to manufacture the old Colt 1911 pistol. There are however two differences between the old models: the text on the flanks of the slide is different. On the left-hand side of the frame, behind the trigger guard, is a factory stamp of a flaming grenade. On the right-hand side of the frame, just above the series number, is the old Springfield logo, in the shape of an eagle. In addition, the front sight and the slide are manufactured out of one piece of steel. The single-

Bicentennial model of the
Springfield 1911-A1

Springfield 1911-A1
Mil-Specs

action Springfield 1911-A1 also resembles many of the Colt models, however Springfield did make a couple of improvements to the original model. Firstly, the feed ramp of the barrel chamber was widened, vastly improving the loading, especially of cartridges with the modern variety of bullets and lead slugs. The ejector port in the slide was also enlarged, improving the functioning of the weapon. Springfield themselves, have not manufactured the M1911-A1 .45 ACP pistol for some time now, but has placed production in the hands of the Brazilian weapons factory Imbel of Itajuba, where the SAR-48 rifle is also manufactured for Springfield. Springfield does however still produce variations of the 'old' Colt 1911 concept, with built-in or attached compensators, as special match models or as concourse pistols.

SPRINGFIELD **1911-A1** BICENTENNIAL
In 1977, Springfield brought out a special jubilee model in .45 ACP caliber. The original arsenal was founded in 1777, so in 1977 Springfield celebrated their bicentennial. This pistol is deep blue in color, with a gold livery. A rampant horse, the Colt logo, has been applied to the back slide flanks in gold. The grips are made of walnut. The total length of this pistol is 219 mm (8$^1/_2$ in) and the barrel has a length of 127 mm (5 in).

SPRINGFIELD MIL-SPECS **1911-A1**
In 1995, Springfield introduced the 1911-A1 Mil--Specs pistol in .45 ACP caliber and .38 Super with

a magazine capacity of 7 and 9 rounds respectively. This weapon is based on the original GI model with an anodized finish. This weapon has the original black composite grips and the military hammer. Springfield has fitted a triple dot aspect sight on the slide with a sight radius of 159 mm (6$^1/_4$ in). The total length is 219 mm (8$^1/_2$ in). The barrel has a length of 127 mm (5 in) with a left-hand rifling twist of 406 mm (16 in) for both calibers. This weapon weighs 1009 g (35$^1/_2$ oz). Unlike the original model, the ejector port in the slide is larger and lower. In addition, the magazine well is beveled to improve the speed of magazine replacement.

SPRINGFIELD **1911-A1** STAINLESS/COMPACT STAINLESS
The Springfield 1911-A1 Stainless originates from 1990, when this model had a military style hammer. In 1995 Springfield brought out a new version with a round hammer in combat style. This weapon is available in .45 ACP (8 rounds) and 9 mm Para (9 rounds), and has a stainless steel frame and slide. Front sight and rear sight have a triple dot aspect sight marking. The total length of the large stainless is 219 mm (8$^1/_2$ in) with a barrel length of 127 mm (5 in), and it weighs 1111 g (39$^1/_4$ oz). In addition, Springfield introduced the Stainless Compact in .45 ACP caliber with a magazine capacity of 7 rounds. This type has a total length of 197 mm (7$^3/_4$ in) and a barrel length of 102 mm (4 in). The Stainless Compact weighs 947 g (33$^1/_2$ oz).

Springfield 1911-A1 in
stainless steel

Springfield 1911-A1
Compact Stainless

Tactical Response Pistol
(TRP) of Springfield

Springfield Bureau Model,
civil version of the FBI
special units service pistol

SPRINGFIELD 1911 TRP-TACTICAL RESPONSE PISTOL

Springfield introduced the TRP Series in 1998. TRP stands for Tactical Response Pistol. The 8-shot single-action weapon in the caliber .454 ACP was designed for self-protection and has its fair share of special technical gadgetry. The front and back of the grip is ribbed. This pistol has a low Novak combat sight, with a tuned and polished cartridge extractor, and a special match barrel and bushing. This weapon also has a special speed trigger and an extended beavertail on the grip safety. The first series has an extended safety catch on the left-hand side of the frame, which was changed to an ambidextrous safety catch on the TRP in 1999. At the back of the side flanks of the slide is the inscription 'TRP', with the newer models having the whole word 'Tactical' engraved on the slide. This pistol is available in a blued, stainless steel and a mat black version. The dimensions are the same as that of the Springfield's standard 1911-A1.

SPRINGFIELD 1911-A1 BUREAU

In April 1998, Springfield signed a contract with the FBI to supply 5,000 special 1911-A1 pistols in .45 ACP caliber. The battle for this prestigious order was intense. Springfield had developed a special model for the test program, in accordance with the technical demands of the FBI, who wanted a special single-action pistol for their SWAT teams (Special Weapons and Tactics) and HRT units (Hostage Rescue Team).

David Williams was responsible for this project being Head Master Gunsmith and manager of the Springfield Custom Shop. Springfield decided to launch a new model specifically for the civilian market, the Bureau Model, based on the authentic FBI-model. This pistol has a hand-made adapted slide on a national match frame. It has a match barrel and bushing, with a polished feed ramp to the cartridge chamber. In addition, this pistol has a special speed trigger that is tuned to a trigger pressure of 2000 g (4½ lb). This weapon also has a special match hammer, tumbler, and a tuned and polished cartridge extractor. The grip safety is ambidextrous and is extended into an extra long beavertail. The combat rear sight is from Novak with a tritium triple dot aspect marking. The magazine has been enlarged and beveled. The front and back of the Cocobolo wooden grips are ribbed. This pistol has a so-called Black-T finish and the series number of this weapon start with the letters FBI. Its dimensions are the same as that of the standard 1911-A1.

Champion Tactical with Novak
notched sights of 1999

Springfield Champion Tactical

Springfield produced the compact 1911-A1 Champion in .45 ACP caliber as far back as 1989. In 1999, they introduced the Champion Tactical. This pistol has a large number of technical features incorporated in the FBI Bureau Model. These include the Novak combat rear sight with a triple dot aspect marking, the ribbed grip, the extended beavertail and the combat hammer. The speed trigger has an adjustable trigger stop. The ejector port in the slide is lowered and enlarged, and the magazine well is beveled. The total length of this pistol is 197 mm ($7^3/_4$ in) the barrel length is 102 mm (4 in) and it weighs 947 g ($33^1/_2$ oz).

Springfield Bullseye Wadcutter

The Bullseye Wadcutter dates from 1995 and was manufactured by the Springfield Custom Shop. The standard version of this weapon is in .45 ACP caliber, but other calibers are available on application. A high rib is fitted on the top of the steel slide, which incorporates the adjustable micrometer sight. This weapon has a match hammer, a speed trigger with a trigger pressure of 1588 g ($3^1/_2$ lb) and an adjustable trigger stop. The front and back of the grip is ribbed and the grip safety is extended in to a beavertail. The entire action of this pistol is polished. The match barrel has a length of 127 mm (5 in). The grips are made of walnut. Each weapon is test fired from 50 yards by the Custom Shop personnel and the test target is supplied with the weapon.

Springfield 1911-A1 Hi-Cap Factory Comp

The Springfield Custom Shop has manufactured the High Capacity Factory Compensator race pistol since 1993. This weapon is available in the calibers .45 ACP, 9 x 25 Dillon and .38 Super as standard. The magazine capacities are 15, 17 and 18 rounds respectively. This pistol has a Bo-Mar micrometer sight and the front and back of the side flanks are provided with pressure grooves. The grip is ribbed front and back. The grip safety has an extra long beavertail. The Hi-Cap has the option of a two or three chamber compensators. This type is available in a blued version, a two-tone version or in stainless steel.

Hi-Cap Factory
Compensator
1911-A1 pistol

Springfield Bullseye
Wadcutter match pistol

Hi-Cap Full Race
of Springfield

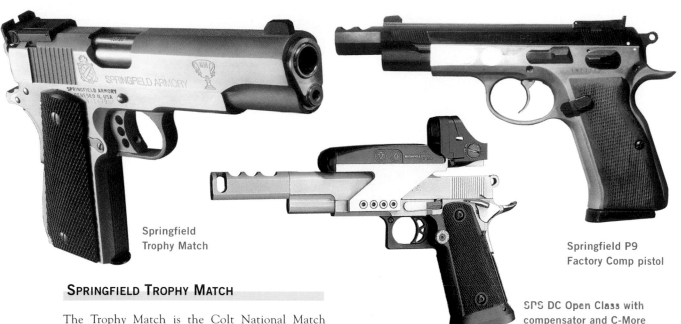

Springfield
Trophy Match

Springfield P9
Factory Comp pistol

SPS DC Open Class with
compensator and C-More
light point sights

SPRINGFIELD TROPHY MATCH

The Trophy Match is the Colt National Match counterpart. This 7-shot single-action Springfield pistol in .45 ACP caliber has a micrometer sight with a sight radius of 172 mm (6³/₄ in). The slide has an enlarged and lowered ejector port. The special match barrel has a length of 127 mm (5 in). The total length is 219 mm (8¹/₂ in) and this weapon weighs 1110 g (35¹/₂ oz), and is available in a blued or stainless steel version.

SPRINGFIELD P9 FACTORY COMP

The P9 Factory Comp pistol is a somewhat older version from 1993. Springfield stopped production of this model in 1995. The P9 is derived from the Czech CZ-75 pistol. This double-action weapon was then available in the calibers 9 mm Para (15-shot), .40 S&W (11-shot) or .45 ACP (10-shot). This pistol has a two-chamber compensator and a micrometer sight with a sight radius of 172 mm (6³/₄ in). The total length of the P9 is 245 mm (9¹/₂ in), including the compensator. The barrel length is 140 mm (5¹/₂ in) and it weighs 961 g (34 oz).

SPS DC CUSTOM

Logo of SPS DC Custom

The Spanish company, SPS DC Custom was founded by two sport shooter friends. They had built their own match pistols, and decided to start doing it on a commercial basis in 1997. SPS is the abbreviation for Special Practical Shooting. The DC comes from the first names of the owners, Diego Cruz and Ceferino Masip. The word Custom speaks for itself. These pistols are especially interesting from a technical aspect. The frame for example is not a frame, but more like an sub-frame made up of a U-shaped piece of steel with a variety of fixing holes, and one large hole allowing the loading of the magazine. A variety of loose components are fixed to this sub-frame with pins and spindles, a separate composite grip is clicked onto the frame, followed by the slide and the pistol is complete. In principal, the SPS DC pistols are built for a 127 or 152 mm barrel (5 or 6 in). The slide is extended for the IPSC Open Class with a multiple chamber compensator. These pistols can be supplied in the calibers 9 mm Para, 9 x 21 mm, 9 x 23 mm, .38 Super, 10 mm Auto, .40 S&W, .45 ACP and also in .22 LR to order.

SPS DC IPSC OPEN CLASS PISTOL

SPS DC manufactures this pistol in accordance with the Open Class rules of the IPSC. This weapon is supplied as standard in caliber 9 mm Para, 9 x 21 mm, 9 x 23 mm or .38 Super with a magazine capacity of 21 or 26 rounds. Other calibers are also available. The total length of this weapon is 278 mm (11 in), due to the long three chamber compensator with a muzzle brake. The barrel length is 127 mm (5 in) and the height is 220 mm (8³/₄ in). This pistol can be supplied without sights or with a C-More red dot sight. The weight of these versions is 1295 g (45³/₄ oz).

SPS DC Precision
Target

SPS DC World
Custom

SPS DC Precision Target Pistol

The qualities of the Standard Plus have also been incorporated in this pistol type. The Precision Target was supplied as standard with a 127 mm (5 in) barrel with a total length of 212 mm (8½ in). The Precision model has a conventional slide, but with an extended slide catch. The second model is the World Custom with extra pressure grooves in the front of the slide. Both have a Bo-Mar micrometer sight. This pistol can be quickly converted into a Modified or an Open Class weapon using the extra SPS DC accessories, two different compensators and a hybrid barrel with a built-in compensator.

Standard Plus
Pistol

SPS DC Standard Plus Pistol

This modular pistol, introduced in 1997, is available in 9 mm Para, .38 Super, .40 S&W, .45 ACP and in other calibers on application. This weapon has a large magazine capacity of 12 rounds in .45 ACP and 15, 17, 21 or 26 rounds in .45 ACP. The total length of this weapon is 212 mm (8½ in) and the height, depending on the choice of magazine, varies from 153 up to 220 mm (6 up to 8¾ in). The weight is approximately 1135 g (40 oz). This pistol is provided with or

a Bo-Mar micrometer sight as standard. The grip is polymer composite and is available in a variety of colors. The steel slide is hard chromed and has pressure grooves on the front and back of the side flanks. The openwork composite trigger has an adjustable trigger stop as standard. There is an extended safety catch on both sides of the sub-frame. The grip safety is extended into a beavertail.

Star

Star's trade mark

The company Echeverria, the manufacturer of the Star pistol, was founded in Eibar in Northern Spain in 1906. Star has since produced a large number of pistol models, such as small caliber pistols, pocket pistols in the calibers 6.35 mm, 7.65 mm and 9 mm Short and army and police pistols in the calibers 9 mm Short, 9 mm Para, 9 mm Largo and .45 ACP. In the period between 1906 until 1919, Echeverria manufactured several waistcoat pocket pistols with such names as Izarra and Protector. Eibar in the Basque territory of Spain was, like Guernica, a well-known region in the field of weapons trading and production, both before and after the Second World War. Well-known names of that era have long since been forgotten, but the products still exist. Some of these weapon types have become real collector's items that now fetch hundreds of times more than their original purchase price. The brand name 'Star' first became official in 1919, although models bearing that name had already been sold. The name

Model 1919, the first
Star pistol

Star Model
F-Sport

Star FR with slide
lock catch

Star has remained in existence for a large range of mainly single-action pistols, almost all based on the Browning-Colt locking system. One of the first pistols that resembled the Colt 1911 and 1911-A1 was the Star Model A of 1921. Star had a name for its swift introduction of new models, especially in the early days.

STAR MODEL 1919 (MODEL 1)

Star introduced this model in 1919, and because it was the first weapon to bear the name of Star, it was named the Star Model 1. This is a curious model. The frame resembles that of an early Colt 1911 and the half-open slide resembles that of a Beretta. This pistol was manufactured until 1929 in the calibers 6.35 mm (.25 ACP), 7.65 mm (.32 ACP) and in 9 mm Short (.380 ACP). The catch for the 8-shot magazine is located on the left-hand side of the frame, above the trigger. The safety catch is at the top of the slide next to the rear sight. When the safety catch is activated, a bar is moved into the path of the hammer preventing it from reaching the firing pin. The takedown lever is in front of the trigger guard, which when pushed up releases the slide from the frame. The total length of this weapon is 178 mm (7 in), the barrel length is 102 mm (4 in) and it weighs 680 g (24 oz). The Model Militar is the army version in 9 mm Largo caliber that was manufactured from 1920 until 1929. This pistol has a length of 200 mm (8 in), the barrel length is 122 mm (4³/₄ in) and it weighs 1100 g (38³/₄ oz).

STAR MODEL F SPORT/MODEL FR

The predecessor of the F Sport is the Model FTB of 1932. This 10-shot single-action pistol in .22 LR caliber has an open slide with a 190 mm (7¹/₂ in) barrel and fixed sights. The frame is the Colt 1911 model. This weapon has a safety catch on the left-hand side of the frame, with the magazine release on the left-hand side behind the trigger guard. This pistol does not have a slide catch. After the Second

World War, Star launched the Model F, as successor to the pre-war pistol. The standard pistol introduced in 1946 has a barrel length of 108 mm (4¹/₄ in). The Model F Target was released in 1947. In principal this is the same weapon with a barrel length of 180 mm (7 in). This was followed a year later by the Model F Sport with a barrel length of 150 mm (6 in). Model FR is a modified Model F Sport and has a slide catch at the top of the left-hand side of the grip, just in front of the safety catch. Star produced these small caliber models up until 1972.

STAR MODEL B/MB

The 9-shot single-action Star Model B in 9 mm Para caliber was introduced in 1928. In the Second World War, the Germans purchased this pistol for there army units, to make up for their temporary shortfall in weapons. In addition, a variety of this series were manufactured with a hollowed out wooden combat

Star Model MB
of 1928

Star BM of 1975

stock, which was also used as a holster. These models were known as the Model MB. Model B served as a Spanish army pistol until 1985, when it was replaced by the Star Model 28 and 30. Model B has a total length of 215 mm (8¹/₂ in), a barrel length of 122 mm (4³/₄ in) and weighs 1085 g (38¹/₄ oz). At first glance, this weapon looks like a Colt 1911-A1, but it does not have a grip safety.

Star Model BM

The single-action Star BM pistol in 9 mm Para caliber is a compact version of Star Model B. The BM has a magazine capacity of 8 rounds and was manufactured by Star in blued and chromed versions between 1975 and 1992. The total length is 177 mm (7 in), the barrel length is 99 mm (4 in) and it weighs 980 g (34¹/₂ oz). This model also strongly resembles the Colt, but does not have grip safety. The safeties, slide catch and magazine release are all on the left-hand side of the frame.

Star Model PD

Model PD pistol in .45 ACP caliber was introduced in 1975 and was produced by Star until 1992. This is a single-action weapon with a magazine capacity of 6 rounds, and is based on the Colt 1911-A1. Model

Star PD pistol in .45 ACP caliber

PD has an alloy frame and a steel slide. The total length of the Star PD is 178 mm (7 in), the barrel length is 95 mm (3³/₄ in) and this weapon weighs 709 g (25 oz).

Star Model 28/Model 30M

Star Model 28 was developed in 1976 for the US Army trials for a new service pistol, however Star was not selected. In 1985, the double-action Star 28 was issued to the Spanish army and to the Guardia Civil, the Spanish police. At the request of the army, Star modified this pistol, after which it became known as the Model 30M (Militar). Two other versions produced for the police were given the model names 30P and 30PK. Model 30M is a double-action pistol in 9 mm Para caliber with a magazine capacity of 15 rounds. The total length of the 30M is 203 mm (8 in) and the barrel has a length of 111 mm (4¹/₂ in). Because the frame and the slide are manufactured in steel, this weapon is heavy at 1134 g (40 oz). The 30M has a laterally adjustable rear sight, a combined ambidextrous safety/uncocking lever on the slide. The magazine release, is a large slide catch on the left-hand side of the frame, behind the trigger guard. The black grips are made of a composite material.

Star 30M 15-shot in 9 mm Para caliber

Star Ten

The Star Ten is a double-action pistol that Star brought out in 1990. This weapon has a steel slide and a steel frame with a built-in trigger guard. The ambidextrous safety catch mounted on the slide also uncocks the hammer. The magazine release was of the type to be used a couple of years later for the Star M205. The nice thing about the Star Ten is the high magazine capacity: 14 rounds in 10 mm Auto caliber. A second special feature is that the standard barrel of 117 mm (4¹/₂ in) can be replaced by a sports barrel of 140 mm (5¹/₂ in)

The special Star Ten

Star 1911 PL with
plastic casing

with compensator ports. An attachment can be fitted at the front of the slide with corresponding compensator grooves. The standard length of this pistol is 212 mm (8¼ in) and the height is 142 mm (5½ in). The width of the grip is only 33.5 mm (1¼ in) due to the use of extra thin grip plates. The Star Ten has a sloping combat sight that resembles the Novak. The sight radius is 175 mm (7 in). The standard version has an empty weight of 1225 g (43¼ oz).

STAR MODEL M205

The Star M205 pistol in 9 mm Para caliber came on the market in 1994. This weapon has a polymer composite frame, which although nothing special nowadays, was at the time. At first sight, this double-action pistol looks quite ordinary, but there are a couple of nice technical gadgets built in. The cartridge extractor for example, is ultra-short, and is therefore not easily broken off. At the back of the slide is a laterally adjustable rear sight. The sight block is fixed with an Allen screw, and can be removed quickly and easily replaced with a higher or lower sighting. The sight radius is 135 mm (5¼ in). The ambidextrous

safety catch at the back of the slide also serves as a uncocking lever. In addition, this pistol also has automatic firing pin safety. Immediately under the safety catch, is the slide catch that is easily reached with the thumb of the shooting hand. The large magazine release is slightly sunken in to the very narrow composite frame, namely 30 mm (1¼ in). The disadvantage with this weapon is that the magazine is single row, with a low magazine capacity of 9 rounds. The trigger is sited in the casing with a rectangular firing lever through which the cartridge holder is inserted. The rest of the action, including hammer and hammer spring, can be removed from the frame in one unit. The total length of the M205 is 175 mm (7 in) and the height is 125 mm (5 in). The barrel has a length of 84 mm (3¼ in) and 6 grooves and lands with a rifling twist of 271 mm (10¾ in). This weapon weighs 775 g (27½ oz). The locking is the Sig-Petter type.

STAR MODEL 1911 PL/PLC

Star Model 1911 PL originates from 1999 and is a single-action pistol in .45 ACP caliber with a magazine capacity of 14 rounds. This pistol has a composite polymer frame with a built-in trigger guard. This frame was manufactured by Star under a license from STI. The total length of this weapon is 219 mm (8½ in) and the barrel length is 122 mm (4¾ in). The width of the frame is 33 mm (1¼ in), and the 1911 PL weighs 1000 g (35¼ oz). Star also manufactures a compact version known as 1911 PLC. The total length of this type is 175 mm (7 in) and the barrel length is 102 mm (4 in). The magazine capacity of the compact version in .45 ACP is 10 rounds and it weighs 800 g (28¼ oz). Both models have a single safety catch on the left-hand side of the frame and automatic firing pin safety.

Star M205 pistol with
plastic casing of 1994

Star Max 8800
pistol

STAR MAX 8800

Star introduced this double-action pistol Max 8800 in the caliber 9 mm Para with a magazine capacity of 13 rounds in 2000. This compact weapon has been designed for self-protection purposes. It has an alloy frame, a steel slide and weighs 775 g (27¼ oz). The combined ambidextrous safety/uncocking lever is located on the slide. This pistol also has automatic firing pin safety and a half-cock safety on the hammer. The rear sight is laterally adjustable using the adjusting screw. The total length is 175 mm (7 in), the barrel length is 89 mm (3½ in) and the width is 33 mm (1¼ in). The Max 8800 is available in a blued or hard chromed version and a half wrap-around rubber grip.

STEYR

Mannlicher

Trade mark of Steyr

The history or the Steyr concern began in 1831, when Josef Werndl was born in the Austrian town of Steyr. His father, Leopold Werndl, was the owner of a weapons factory that manufactured rifle parts for the weapon industry in Vienna. After a period of work placement in Vienna and Prague, Josef joined his father's company, however he could not agree with the conservative production techniques and went quite literally on the wander. In 1849, Josef joined the army, and because of his work experience he was put to work in the state rifle factory in Vienna, where he was introduced to the modern American machines used for mass production. In 1852 Josef went to the industrial region of Thuringia, in Germany where he worked in a variety of weapons factories, until he left for America where he worked for both Remington and Colt in Hartford. At the end of 1853 he returned to Austria bursting with ideas, and set up a firearms workshop in the town of Wehrgraben. In 1864, Josef together with his brother Franz set up the company Josef und Franz Werndl & Comp. in Steyr. In 1866, he tried to convince the Minister of War to equip the army with the Werndl-Holub breech-loading rifle. After comprehensive army trials Werndl was awarded a contract to supply 100,000 rifles of the type Geweermodel 1867. Steyr expanded and even founded a subsidiary in Budapest. These new expansions drained the company's capital and so Werndl decided to consolidate the company by issuing shares in his company, under the new name Oosterreichische Waffenfabriks Gesellschaft based in Vienna. In 1873, Werndl was awarded a contract by the Royal Prussian army to supply no less than 500,000 Mauser rifles Model 1871. Werndl was then showered with government contracts from Chile, China, France, Greece, Iran and Rumania. In 1882 came a massive about-turn. The demand by the European armies for the breech loading rifles had been satisfied, resulting in the lack of large orders. In order to alleviate this crisis situation, Werndl decided to use their production capacity for the manufacturing of other products. Examples of the day were dynamos, electric motors and light bulbs In 1884, Steyr became the first European town with electric street lighting. In 1885, production started on a new breech-loading rifle following the Mannlicher system with a magazine for five cartridges, which resulted in an immediate order for 87,000 weapons. Josef Werndl died in 1899 of pneumonia. The company was continued by a four-man committee up until 1896, when Otto Schänauer took the helm. In the meantime, the company had grown into an enormous concern with several factories and 10,000 employees. Around the turn of the century the company was manufacturing several different products, including bicycles in 1919, followed soon after by cars and trucks. After the Second World War in 1950, Steyr was given permission by the allied forces to resume production of firearms. The company went on to manufacture mainly hunting rifles that were known as the Mannlicher-Schänauer. The company name was changed to Steyr-Daimler-Puch AG in 1987, and the firearms production was placed in a separate subsidiary: Steyr-Mannlicher AG. The modern Steyr concern produces not only hunting- and sports rifles, such as the Steyr-Mannlichers, but also military weapons, such as sniper rifles and the futuristic Steyr AUG (Armee Universal Gewehr) rifle. This company is currently developing the ACR (Advanced Combat Rifle) for trials in the USA. One of the 1974 designs was the GB pistol with striking firearms technology. Unfortunately this weapon never achieved the popularity of some other models, and Steyr stopped production in 1988. In 1994, Steyr introduced a completely new pistol concept: the Steyr SPP (Special Police Pistol). In 2000, Steyr launched yet another new pistol type with a composite frame. This large service pistol has the model name M and a compact version is known as the Model S.

STEYR MODEL GB

The double-action Steyr GB pistol in 9 mm Para caliber was developed in 1974. This weapon utilizes the recoil energy of a fired cartridge and has gas induced retarding. Two gas outlet ports are located half way along the barrel. After firing, the bullet is forced through the barrel. The gas created escapes through the ports and is channeled into a special cylinder between the barrel and the slide. The accumulation of this gas pressure reduces the recoil. After the bullet has left the barrel, the gas pressure is allowed to escape, and the slide returns to its normal position. Steyr can also supply a compensator as an optional extra that fits onto the front of the barrel. The safety catch located on the left-hand side of the slide also serves as a uncocking lever for the hammer. This pistol also has automatic firing pin safety. The total length of the GB is 216 mm (8¹/₂ in), the height is 143 mm (5¹/₂ in) and the width is 37 mm

Steyr SPP (Special Police Pistol)

(1¹/₂ in). This pistol has a magazine capacity of 18 rounds. The barrel has a length of 136 mm (5¹/₂ in). This weapon has a fixed rear sight with white dots on both sides of the rear sight, with a white aiming point on the front sight. The sight radius is 162 mm (6¹/₂ in). The GB pistol weighs empty 845 g (29³/₄ oz) and with a full magazine 1185 g (41³/₄ oz). Steyr had hoped that the Austrian army would adopt the GB as their army pistol, however in 1985 they opted for the Glock 17 pistol. A few years ago, Steyr issued a North American production license to the American company LES from Morton Grove, Illinois, but this was later terminated due to a dispute over quality. The Austrian production of the Steyr GB pistol was stopped in 1988.

STEYR MODEL SPP

The single-action Steyr SPP was brought onto the market in 1994. The abbreviation SPP stands for Special Police Pistol. This weapon is in 9 mm Para caliber and has a standard magazine capacity of 15 rounds. A special magazine for 30 cartridges is also available. The frame of this weapon has a mounting rail for attaching special sighting equipment, and is made of a special unbreakable composite, known as IXEF-1313. This pistol resembles a machine pistol. The barrel of the SPP is provided with threaded muzzle for attaching a special suppresser or a silencer. The SPP pistol has a rotary bolt action, a push button safety catch at the top of the grip above the trigger, and automatic firing pin safety. The total length is 322 mm (12³/₄ in) and the height, including magazine, is 168 mm (6¹/₂ in). The barrel length is 150 mm (6 in). The rear sight is laterally adjustable and the front sight has a height-adjustment. This weapon weighs 1190 g (42 oz).

Steyr GB pistol

The new Steyr M
pistol

STEYR MODEL M/MODEL S

In 2000, Steyr introduced a new pistol type in two versions with a composite frame and a steel slide. A mounting rail for a laser or sight lighting is fitted to both sides of the pistol at the front of the frame, in front of the trigger guard. The trigger action has been described by Steyr as the Reset Action System. When loading, the cocked firing pin is always blocked. There is a safety flap incorporated in the trigger to release the blocking. The second safety is the push button safety catch, at the front of the frame above the trigger guard. The third safety is on the right-hand side of the frame, above the trigger. This is a type of lock that sets the safety using a key supplied with the weapon. A fourth safety is at the back of the slide, a cartridge indicator in the form of a signal pin.

The ambidextrous magazine release is located behind the trigger guard, with the slide catch on the left-hand side of the frame. The trigger pressure is 2500 g (5¹/₂ lb) and the trigger pull is only 4 mm (¹/₄ in). The rear sight has beveled corners and has white sight marks on either side. The front sight has a white triangular sight point.

MODEL M has a total length of 180 mm (7 in), a height of 125 mm (5 in) and a width or 30 mm (1¹/₄ in). The barrel length is 102 mm (4 in). In 2000, this pistol

became available in 9 mm Para (14-shot) and .40 S&W (12-shot). This was followed in 2001 by .357 SIG caliber with a capacity of 12 rounds.

MODEL S is the compact version. This pistol is available in 9 mm Para and .40 S&W, both with a magazine capacity of 10 rounds. The total length of the Model S is 166 mm (6¹/₂ in) and the height is 117 mm (4¹/₂ in). The width is the same as that of the Model M at 30 mm (1¹/₄ in). The barrel has a length of 91 mm (3¹/₂ in) and it weighs 645 g (22¹/₂ oz).

STOEGER

Logo of Stoeger Industries

The American company Stoeger Industries of South Hackensack, New Jersey, is part of Stoeger Canada Ltd of Whitby, Ontario. Another part of the concern is the Stoeger Publishing Company of Wayne, New Jersey, which has published books since 1925, including books on firearms. Stoeger has a fine reputation in the field of firearms, and has produced the American Eagle since 1994 This is a stainless steel pistol based on the famous Luger P08 with its knee joint locking. In 1995, Stoeger introduced the Pro Series 95. These are small caliber weapons, based on the well-known High Standard pistols.

STOEGER AMERICAN EAGLE LUGER

Stoeger has produced the totally stainless steel American Eagle Luger pistol since 1994. This weapon is available in 9 mm Para caliber and has a magazine capacity of 7 rounds and is manufactured in the P08 and Navy versions. Both weapons have the traditional safety catch on the left-hand side of the

The new compact
Steyr S shown
in .40 S&W caliber

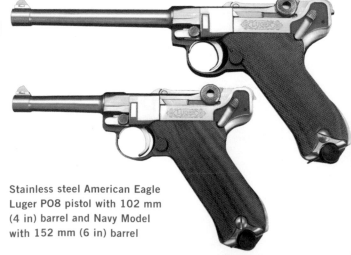

Stainless steel American Eagle
Luger P08 pistol with 102 mm
(4 in) barrel and Navy Model
with 152 mm (6 in) barrel

Pro Series 95 of Stoeger with
Bull Barrel, the 184 mm
(7¹/₄ in) long barrel, and Vented
Barrel model in stainless steel

frame, which when activated displays a signal pin next to the cocking lever on the left-hand side of this pistol. In addition, the cartridge extractor also serves as a cartridge indicator. The large magazine release is at the left-hand side, behind the trigger guard. The model American Eagle Luger P08 has a total length of 193 mm (7¹/₂ in) and a barrel length of 102 mm (4 in). This weapon weighs 851 g (30 oz). The Navy Model has a barrel length of 152 mm (6 in), a total length of 244 mm (9¹/₂ in) and it weighs 907 g (32 oz). Both weapons have walnut grips and are wonderfully finished and polished. Stoeger has also produced both versions in mat black since 2000.

STOEGER PRO SERIES 95

Stoeger introduced their Pro Series 95 in 1995. This series consists of a 10-shot single-action match pistol in three different versions, based on the High Standard pistol. The Stoeger Pro Series 95 in .22 LR caliber are totally stainless steel and the finish is exceptionally beautiful. The trigger, safety catch, magazine release and slide catch located on the right-hand side of the frame are all gilded. These pistols have a handsome black wrap-around Pachmayr rubber grip. A button for changing the barrel is located at the front of the frame. The barrels of the three Pro Series 95 models can all be interchanged.

PRO SERIES 95 BULL BARREL: This model has the distinctive sight bridge with a micrometer sight above the slide. This weapon has a heavy thick barrel

with a length of 140 mm (5¹/₂ in). The total length is 244 mm (9³/₄ in), the sight radius is 222 mm (8³/₄ in) and this weapon weighs 1361 g (48 oz).

PRO SERIES 95 FLUTED BARREL: This version has a fluted barrel with a length of 184 mm (7¹/₄ in) and total length of 286 mm (11¹/₄ in). This weapon also has a sight bridge with a micrometer sight over the slide. The sight radius is 267 mm (10¹/₂ in) and this weapon weighs 1418 g (50 oz).

PRO SERIES 95 VENTED BARREL: This model is based on the High Standard Victor. It has an attractive black, ventilated barrel rib that is extended over the slide. This rib incorporates the micrometer sight with a sight radius of 222 mm (8³/₄ in). This model has a total length of 244 mm (9¹/₂ in), a barrel length of 140 mm (5¹/₂ in) and it weighs 1361 g (48 oz).

STRAYER-VOIGT

Trade mark of
Strayer-Voigt

Founded in 1992, Strayer-Voigt is a relatively young company. The company is based in Grand Prairie, Texas, and has become well known for its special Infinity pistols, that are based on the Colt 1911-A1.

The Infinity pistol and the related models are made to a high quality and have a lot of special technical gadgetry. The frames for this weapon are available in a choice of 4140 steel, 416 stainless steel, 7075-T6 light metal, Ti64 titanium or composite. Strayer-Voigt uses a sort of sub-frame with a built-in grip for the composite Infinity. All models have a beveled magazine well and most have a so-called jet funnel, providing an extra large magazine well. All Strayer-Voigt weapons have an ITS trigger system with an adjustable trigger stop. ITS stands for Interchangeable Trigger System, where a choice is available from nine different replacement triggers in four different colors. These pistols are both highly polished inside and out. All models also have an interchangeable gun lock head. In the slide is a detachable cartridge case claw for conversion to another caliber. This has created an adapter set consisting only of a barrel, a magazine and the claw. The website of Strayer-Voigt is totally unique as it includes a special 'gun builder'. By making selections from a countless number of components, the client can assemble and order their specific dream pistol online. Strayer-Voigt manufacture slides in six different basic shapes with three, five, or seven sloping edges. All slides have a lowered and beveled ejector port. A visit to Strayer-Voigt on the Internet is certainly recommended. (www.sviguns.com).

Infinity pistol in duo-tone finish

STRAYER-VOIGT INFINITY

The Infinity basic model is available in all conceivable calibers. The standard calibers are 9 mm Para, 9 x 25 mm, .38 Super, .357 Sig, 10 mm Auto, .40 S&W, .400 Corbon and .45 ACP. In 9 mm Para caliber the magazine capacity is 17 rounds and in .45 ACP 12 rounds. The total length of the standard model is 220 mm (8¾ in). The height is 148 mm (5¾ in) and the width is 40 mm (1½ in). The barrel length is 127 mm (5 in). The standard weapon in steel or stainless steel weighs 1120 g (39½ oz). This pistol has a Bo-Mar micrometer sight or a Novak combat sight. For the front sight a choice can be made from the standard model, a horizontal fiber-optic sight or a night sight with an illuminous isotope. The grip safety is extra long. The Infinity has the ITS replacement trigger system. The extended safety catch is available in both single and ambidextrous versions, and there is also a choice of six different types of magazine release.

Strayer-Voigt Infinity pistol in stainless and blued steel

Strayer-Voigt Infinity Concealed Carry Compensator/Combat

The Infinity Concealed Carry Compensator is a compact weapon with a composite grip. The bottom of the grip has a jet funnel. The hybrid barrel has four compensator ports and a length of 107 mm (4¼ in). The total length of this weapon is 201 mm (8 in), the height is 140 mm (5½ in) and the width is 40 mm (1½ in). The weight is 990 g (35 oz). This pistol offers a choice of a Bo-Mar micrometer sight or a Novak combat sight. The extended safety catch located on the frame is ambidextrous, and the grip safety has an extra long beavertail. This pistol has .45 ACP as the standard caliber, but other calibers are available. The magazine capacity is 10 rounds. This weapon can also be supplied without the hybrid barrel as the Short Combat, however the technical specifications remain the same.

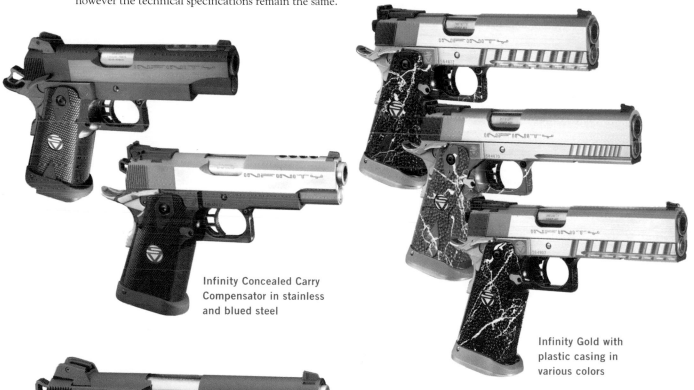

Infinity Gold pistol

Infinity Concealed Carry Compensator in stainless and blued steel

Infinity Gold with plastic casing in various colors

Infinity Short Combat

Strayer-Voigt Infinity Gold

The Infinity Gold pistol has all of the technical distinguishing features of the previous models, except that the 127 mm (5 in) barrel has a gold colored titanium coating. This weapon is available with a Bo-Mar micrometer sight or a Novak combat sight. The Infinity Gold Special has a composite frame that is available in a variety of colors. The extended sub-frame or 'dust cover' has a mounting rail for attaching different sights.

Infinity Match: in stainless
steel with plastic casing and
with stainless steel casing

Infinity Race gun with
Aimpoint telescopic sights

Infinity Race gun
with Bushnell light
point sights

STRAYER-VOIGT INFINITY MATCH

The Infinity Match is available with a blued, stainless
steel, alloy or composite frame. This match model
has a Bo-Mar micrometer sight. The grip safety
has an extra long beavertail. This weapon also has
an interchangeable trigger system, an extended
ambidextrous safety catch, and is available in a large
number of different calibers. In .45 ACP caliber it has
a magazine capacity of 12 rounds. The total length is
244 mm (9^1/$_2$ in), the height is 160 mm (6^1/$_4$ in) and
the width is 39 mm (1^1/$_2$ in). The barrel has a length
of 127 mm (5 in). In alloy or composite this weapon
weighs approximately 1000 g (35^1/$_4$ oz), and in steel
or stainless steel, 1100 g (38^3/$_4$ oz).

STRAYER-VOIGT INFINITY RACEGUN

The Infinity Raceguns really are a class apart and are
available with a variety of sights. In .38 Super or 9 mm
Para caliber this pistol has a magazine capacity of
17 rounds and as many as 27 rounds with an extended
magazine. In .45 ACP the capacity is 12 rounds. This
weapon has a composite frame, an extended
ambidextrous safety catch, an interchangeable trigger,
an extended beavertail and a jet funnel. At the front of

the slide is a four-chamber compensator with a muzzle
brake, which can be combined with a hybrid barrel
with four compensator ports. The total length is
approximately 277 mm (11 in). The height is 189 mm
(7^3/$_4$ in), excluding the sights. The width is
approximately 55 up to 59 mm (2^1/$_4$ up to 2^1/$_2$ in) and it
weighs 1410 g (49^3/$_4$ oz), once again excluding the
sights.

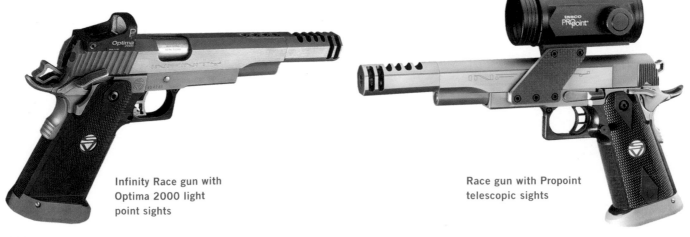

Infinity Race gun with
Optima 2000 light
point sights

Race gun with Propoint
telescopic sights

Infinity Vision and Sceptor

Infinity Crown

STRAYER-VOIGT INFINITY SPECIAL

The Infinity Specials have been given handsome names, such as the Vision, Scepter and Crown. These are the classic models, but they do have an extended ambidextrous safety catch and a Bo-Mar micrometer sight. The front flanks of the slide have extra pressure grooves. This pistol also has an interchangeable trigger system, and both the front and the back of the frame are ribbed. In .45 ACP caliber this weapon has a magazine capacity of 10 rounds. In .40 S&W this is 14 rounds. The total length is 219 or 244 mm (8½ or 9½ in), the height is 151 mm (6 in) and the width is 38 mm (1½ in). The barrel length is 127 or 140 mm (5 or 5½ in).

STRAYER-VOIGT INFINITY STOCK/MODIFIED

The Infinity Stock has a composite frame. In .45 ACP caliber the magazine capacity is 10 rounds and in .40 S&W this is 14 rounds. The total length is 219 mm (8¾ in), the height is 151 mm (6 in) and the width is 38 mm (1½ in). The barrel length is 127 mm (5 in). The heavy Scheumann barrel can be supplied with a hybrid system with four or six compensator ports as optional. This pistol weighs 1145 g and has the ITS trigger system. The extended safety catch is available as single or ambidextrous.

STRAYER-VOIGT INFINITY TARGET MASTER

The Target Master has the standard magazine capacity of the other Infinity models: 10-shot in .45 ACP and 14-shot in .40 S&W. The total length is 219 mm (8½ in), the height is 151 mm (6 in) and the width is 38 mm (1½ in). The barrel has a length of 127 mm (5 in). In addition, this pistol is provided with the ITS system and has a Bo-Mar micrometer sight.

Infinity Target Master

Infinity Stock

Infinity Stock
Modified pistol

OKO Modified Masterpiece
pistol from both sides

STRAYER-VOIGT OKO MODIFIED MASTERPIECE

This Infinity has a hybrid barrel with a length of 127 mm (5 in) and a continuous sloping slide. This weapon is equipped with a carbon fiber mounting system fitted with the OKO sights system. This Czech sight projects a red dot onto the viewing window. This pistol also has a Scheumann hybrid barrel with three compensator ports and a larger compensator slot at the muzzle.

STRAYER-VOIGT TIKI-T

The name Tiki comes from the Polynesian god of creation. The addition of the 'T' stands for titanium, the material from which this gun is made. The Tiki-T has a very special sight system, with a sighting groove along the entire length of the barrel. For night use the slide has four tritium sighting points. This pistol is available in every conceivable caliber and also has a detachable casing claw in the gun head. In addition, this weapon has an ambidextrous and extended safety catch, an extended beavertail grip safety and the ITS trigger system.

The unusual Tiki-T

T

Tanfoglio

![Tanfoglio logo]

Tanfoglio logo

The Italian Tanfoglio company of Gardone has been in existence since 1949. This company was originally known as Tanfoglio & Sabotti, but in 1958, Giuseppe Tanfoglio decided to continue alone, and changed the company name to Fabbrica d'Armi Giuseppe Tanfoglio. The company has been known since 1980 as Fratelli Tanfoglio and is lead by the son Massimo Tanfoglio. Originally, Fratelli Tanfoglio only produced small pocket pistols such as the Sata and the Titan in .22 LR and 6.35 mm (.25 ACP) calibers. However, from 1965 until 1975 they also manufactured a single-action revolver in .22 LR and .22 WMR calibers with the model Buffalo Scout. Since 1980, Tanfoglio has specialized in the manufacture of special pistols for various forms of sports shooting. Tanfoglio mainly manufactures pistol models that are already fitted with a compensator. In addition, the company has a comprehensive series of special custom-components, which would more than satisfy the requirements of any handy DIY enthusiast or gunsmith. Tanfoglio offers for example, seven barrel types, five types of slides, three different hammers, six different compensators, four types of trigger, etc., etc. Many of the models are derived from the CZ-75 pistol model. The custom-department of the company builds every type of pistol to the specifications of the client. Tanfoglio pistols have a polygonal barrel with a conical ring connection that fits tightly into the slide. Tanfoglio pistols were launched in North America by the European American Armory (EAA) Corp. Sharpes, Florida

in1991 with the model name Witness. In 2000 Tanfoglio introduced a prototype of the T-95 pistol with the FAR system. FAR stands for Fast Accurate Reliable. This weapon in 9 mm FAR or 10 mm FAR caliber has a normal recoil. After the weapon is fired , the slide movement is retarded by the extra thick and heavy brass cartridge case in the barrel chamber. This invention was patented by the Italian architect Antonio Cudazzo.

Tanfoglio Buzz

In 1994, Tanfoglio introduced the Stock model with a three gas outlet compensator built into the barrel. This system was also known as the hybrid barrel. This double-action pistol is available in 9 mm Para or 9 x 21 mm caliber with a magazine capacity of 16 rounds, in .45 ACP caliber for 10 rounds and in 10 mm Auto for 11 rounds. In 1995, these were followed by the .38 Super version with a capacity of 17 rounds. In 1999, Tanfoglio launched the Buzz P40F in .40 S&W caliber. The first series was manufactured with a magazine capacity of 15 rounds, but reduced later that year to 12 rounds. The total length of the Buzz is 210 mm (8¼ in). The length of the hybrid polygonal barrel is 113 mm (4½ in) and this weapon weighs 1150 g (40½ oz). The muzzle has a conical ring, that fits tightly in to the slide. The slide and the frame are both made of steel with a mat chromed finish. The safety catch is on the left-hand side of the frame. The enlarged magazine release on the left-hand side behind the trigger guard can be transferred to the right-hand side. The back of the frame runs in to an extended beavertail.

Tanfoglio Buzz with hybrid barrel

Force pistol of 1997
with plastic casing

Force Compact
of 1998

TANFOGLIO FORCE/FORCE COMPACT

The double-action Force originates from 1997 and is available in a large number of calibers. At its introduction, this weapon was available in 9 mm Para or 9 x 21 mm with a capacity of 16 rounds and in .45 ACP with 10 rounds. These were later followed by calibers .38 Super (17-shot), .40 S&W (14-shot), 10 mm Auto (10-shot) and since 2001 the 9 mm FAR (16-shot) and 10 mm FAR (11-shot). This pistol has a black composite frame and a mat black steel slide. The safety catch is located on the left-hand side of the frame. The magazine release on the left-hand side behind the trigger guard can be transferred to the right. The total length of the Force is 210 mm (8¼ in), the barrel length is 113 mm (4½ in) and it weighs 850 g (30 oz).

FORCE COMPACT: Tanfoglio introduced this compact version in 1998. This double-action pistol has a shorter slide and frame and is not available in the FAR-caliber. In 9 mm Para or 9 x 21 mm calibers the magazine capacity is, 13 rounds in .38 Super, 8 rounds in 10 mm Auto, 12 rounds in .40 S&W, and 8 rounds in .45 ACP. The total length is 195 mm (7¾ in). The polygonal barrel has a length of 93 mm (3¾ in) and this weapon weighs 750 g (26½ oz).

LADY FORCE: This weapon came onto the market in 1999. It has the same technical specifications as the Force Compact, but it has been obviously adapted for women. This pistol has a steel slide and the composite frame is available in a variety of colors, such as white, gray, dark gray, pink, green, blue and dark brown.

TANFOGLIO FORCE '99

The Force '99 pistol introduced in 1999 is an improved version of the previous Force model. The composite frame of this double-action pistol has ergonomic styling. In addition, the Force '99 has automatic firing pin safety. This weapon was designed as a service pistol and is available in 9 mm Para or 9 x 21 mm (16-shot) and .40 S&W (12-shot) calibers. The total length is 210 mm (8¼ in) and the length of the polygonal barrel is 113 mm (4½ in). It has an empty weight of 850 g (30 oz).

FORCE '99-22: This pistol in .22 LR caliber was designed as training weapon for the large Force '99. This 10-shot single-action weapon has a total length of 220 mm (8¾ in) a barrel length of 135 mm (5¼ in) and it weighs 600 g (21¼ oz). It also has a composite

Attractively colored
Lady Force

Modified Force
'99 pistol

Force '99-22 in
.22 LR caliber

Special-construction
Gold Custom

frame and an alloy slide. The magazine release on the left-hand side behind the trigger guard can also be transferred to the right-hand side. This weapon has a micrometer sight.

TANFOGLIO GOLD CUSTOM

Tanfoglio launched the Gold Custom pistol at the German IWA firearms trades exhibition in 1992. This is a single-action pistol that was designed for the IPSC Open Class. This weapon has a polygonal barrel and is available with a variety of optional compensators. The steel frame and slide are mat chromed. Both the front and the back of the frame are ribbed. There are tapped holes at the front of the frame for a telescopic sight mounting and this pistol does not have sights. The flanks of the slide have pressure grooves at the front and back. This weapon has an extended safety catch and magazine release on

Old Tanfoglio GT-380
pistol in 9 mm Short
(.380 ACP)

the left-hand side of the frame. The Gold Custom has a total length of 256 mm (10 in), a barrel length of 133 mm (5¾ in) and it weighs 1250 g (44 oz). This weapon can be supplied in 9 mm Para or 9 x 21 mm (16-shot), .38 Super (17-shot), .40 S&W (12-shot), 10 mm Auto (11-shot) or .45 ACP (10-shot) calibers.

TANFOGLIO GT 380

The single-action GT-380 pistol is an old model dating from 1970. This weapon in 9 mm Short (.380 ACP) caliber has a magazine capacity of 7 rounds. The Model GT-32 is in 7.65 mm (.32 ACP) caliber. The total length of both versions is 160 mm (6¼ in). The barrel has a length of 83 mm (3¼ in), and it has conventional grooves and lands. The empty weight is 700 g (24¾ oz). This pistol has a safety catch mounted on the slide that blocks both the trigger and the firing action. In addition,

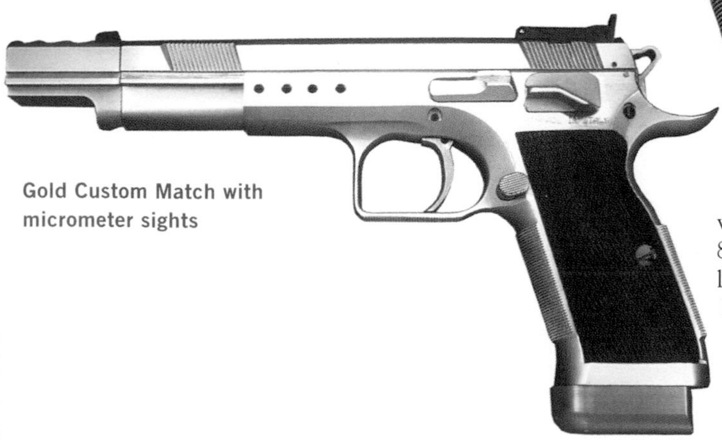

Gold Custom Hi-Capacity
with three chamber
compensator

Gold Custom Match with
micrometer sights

Tanfoglio Limited

Tanfoglio Match in
duo-tone finish

this pistol has magazine safety. The magazine release
is in the heel of the grip.

TANFOGLIO LIMITED

Tanfoglio sold this pistol as the Match until 1996.
Modified in 1997, this weapon was given tapped holes
in the front of the frame for a telescopic sight
mounting, together with a square trigger guard. This
pistol was known as the P19 in 9 mm Para (16-shot),
the P38 in .38 Super (16-shot) and as the P45 in .45
ACP (10 rounds). Tanfoglio introduced the Limited
P40-HC, in 1999, a 15-shot version in .40 S&W
caliber. This pistol has also been available since 2001
in special 9 mm FAR (17-shot) and 10 mm FAR
(11-shot) caliber. The total length is 225 mm (8³/₄ in).
The length of the polygonal barrel is 121 mm (4³/₄ in)
and it weighs 1200 g (42¹/₄ oz). The height of this
weapon is 150 mm (6 in) and the width is 41.5 mm
(1¹/₂ in). The safety catch is located on the left-hand
side of the frame. In addition, the Limited has firing
pin safety, a mat chromed steel slide and frame and
a single-action trigger.

TANFOGLIO MATCH

The single-action Match was manufactured
by Tanfoglio as far back as 1985 and had the
model name TA-90. A new version followed
in 1990, the TA-90 Ultra IPSC approved in
.41 AE caliber. In 1996, Tanfoglio produced the 15-
shot Ultra Match in 9 mm Para caliber for the German
gunsmiths Wischo. This pistol has since been available
in 9 mm Para or 9 x 21 mm (16-shot), .38 Super (17-
shot), .40 S&W (12-shot), 10 mm Auto (11-shot) and
.45 ACP (10-shot) calibers. The total length of the
Match is 220 mm (8³/₄ in) and the polygonal barrel has
a length of 121 mm (4³/₄ in). The height of this
weapon is 142 mm (5¹/₂ in) and the width is 34 mm
(1¹/₄ in). The weight is 1180 g (41¹/₂ oz). The steel
frame is mat chromed and the slide is blued steel. In

addition, this pistol has an extended beavertail, an
extended magazine release and a micrometer sight.

TANFOGLIO STOCK/ EAA WITNESS

The American trading company EAA (European
American Armory) brought this double-action pistol
in .45 ACP caliber to the North American market in
1995 under the name of the Witness. In Europe,
Tanfoglio was selling the same weapon as the Stock
model. This pistol is available in 9 mm Para or
9 x 21 mm, .38 Super, .40 S&W, 10 mm Auto and .45
ACP calibers. The magazine capacities are 16 (9 mm),
17, 12, 11 and 10 rounds respectively. The total length
is 210 mm (8¹/₄ in) and the polygonal barrel has
a length of 113 mm (4¹/₂ in). The height of this model
is 143 mm (5¹/₂ in) and the width is 34 mm (1¹/₄ in).
The empty weight is 1150 g (40¹/₂ oz).

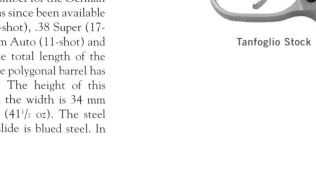

Tanfoglio Stock

TANFOGLIO T-94-F COMPACT

The older version of this model is known as the TZ-75 and is based on the Czech CZ-75 pistol. In 1988, Tanfoglio brought a special version to the market with a square trigger guard. This type was given the model name Pitt Bull and was available in 9 mm Para, 9 x 21 mm and .41 AE calibers. In North America this weapon was sold as the Witness and as of 1992, the model TA-45 in .45 ACP caliber. Until 2000, Tanfoglio produced a number different versions or this type: the T-94-F Compact, the T-95-F Combat, the T-94-R Compact Standard and the T-95-R Standard. The double-action pistols have a safety catch on the frame as well as automatic firing pin safety. These models were available in 9 mm Para and 9 x 21 mm calibers, both 16 shot or 13 shot in the compact version, as well as in .38 Super (17 shot or 13 shot), .40 S&W (12 or 10 shot), 10 mm Auto (14 or 10 shot) and .45 ACP (10 or 8 shot). These pistols were available in mat black, mat chromed or a two-tone finish. The large models have a total length of 210 mm (8¼ in), a barrel length of 113 mm (4½ in) and it weighs 1150 g (40½ oz). The compact versions have a total length of 195 mm (7¾ in), a barrel length of 93 mm (3¾ in) and it weighs 1000 g (35.3 oz). The models T-94-R and T-95-R have a combined safety/uncocking lever on the slide. The two other versions are provided with a safety catch on the frame.

T-94-F
Compact pistol

TAURUS

Trade mark of Taurus

Brazil is usually associated with tropical rain forests, tarantulas, and boa constrictors. The official language of Portuguese dates from the time of the Portuguese colonial empire. Brazil became an independent nation in 1821 when his father, John VI of Portugal, appointed Don Pedro regent of the country. Don Pedro was later crowned Emperor of Brazil. Brazil remained a monarchy until 1889, when a coup d'etat resulted in the federal republic that it is today. As well as rain forests, Brazil has built up a modern and comprehensive industry, mainly in the firearms sector, in which this country plays a leading role in Latin-America. The German immigrant Joao Kluwe founded the Brazilian Taurus factory, known as Forjas Taurus S.A. in 1939. The name is derived from Forjas (forge) and Taurus (bull). The intention was to import the required machines from Germany, however this plan had to be scrapped due to the Second World War. This forced Taurus to design and manufacture its own machines. This meant that production was delayed until the fall of 1942. The first Taurus revolvers looked like exact replicas of Smith & Wesson pistols, but they were not just simply copies. The action was made up of a combination of Colt and Spanish revolver systems. In those days, all Taurus products were sold to the home market. In 1956, the company moved to a new factory, enabling Taurus to increase its production for export. In 1964, the Brazilian firearms industry was dealt an enormous blow. The Brazilian government introduced restrictive firearm legislation. Civilians were no longer allowed to own more than two firearms. In 1968, Taurus started exporting weapons to the USA. The company not only sold weapons under their own brand name, but also produced weapons under the names of a variety of trading companies. Since 1971, Taurus has only sold firearms under its own brand name. Well-known revolver models from that period are the Boxer and the Pocket in .38 Special and the Fox in .22 LR. Taurus also manufactured the Trainer in .38 Special, a copy of the old Military & Police revolver of Smith & Wesson. In 1970, financial and management problems led to Taurus falling into the hands of the Bangor-Punta concern, who also owned Smith & Wesson. This resulted in the exchange of technical know-how between the two factories. In 1977, Taurus was bought back by the directors, Luis Estima and Carlos

Integrated safety lock of Taurus pistols

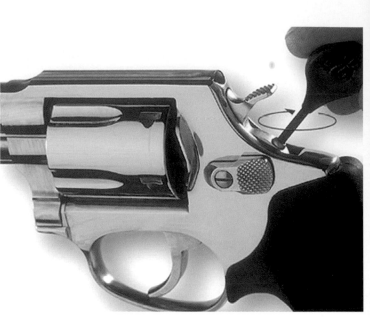

The same safety system for revolvers

Murgel, who devised a new strategy. The options were either to continue producing large numbers of cheap revolvers, or to place the accent on quality. They chose for the latter, and the company was adapted accordingly.

The Taurus concern has four factories in Brazil. The company produces the Taurus revolvers, leather holsters and belts in Porto Alegre. The second factory in Porto Alegre manufactures crash helmets, bulletproof vests and other police equipment. The Sao Paulo unit manufactures Taurus autoloaders and machine pistols. In addition, Taurus together with the Spanish company Gamo, manufactures airguns for the South-American market. Taurus also manufactures armored cars and tanks for the Brazilian army and the South-American market, one example being the 41 ton Osorio combat tank.

Taurus formerly used two types of frames for their revolvers. The small frame for calibers up to and including .38 Special and a larger frame for .22 LR up to and including .357 Magnum. The small type had a firing pin with a transfer bar safety. The larger type was provided with a fixed firing pin point on the hammer and had a blocking bar safety. Since 1989, Taurus has also had a subsidiary in Miami, Florida, where they manufacture small pocket pistols in .22 LR and 6.35 mm (.25 ACP) calibers. In 1998, Taurus announced a new concept for the safety system of all of their handguns. All models since 1998 have a built-in safety lock. The hammer of the Taurus revolvers or pistols can be locked by a key. This prevents the weapon being fired by unauthorized users. Taurus supplies a trigger lock for the older weapons free of charge, except for the postal charges.

Taurus also has a Custom Shop where standard weapons can be adapted, and where a number of small series handguns are manufactured to special specifications. Until 1998, Taurus produced a variety of large caliber series revolvers provided with the Hydraport system, where a number of ports are bored along the barrel. These ports act as gas outlets, and reduce the recoil and upswing of the weapon. Nowadays, almost all of the Taurus revolver barrels are provided with compensator ports.

Taurus Model PT-22/Model PT-25

Taurus has been manufacturing small pocket pistols in .22 LR and 6.35 mm (.25 ACP) calibers since 1980. Originally, these models were the PT-55 in .22 LR and the PT-51 in .25 ACP caliber. These weapons were almost the same as the current models. The biggest difference was the location of the magazine

The small Taurus
with folding barrel

Taurus PT-22 in
.22 LR caliber

Taurus PT-25 in 6.35 mm
(.25 ACP) caliber

release. On the old PT-55 and PT-51 it was on the left-hand side of the grip, however the current versions have this catch on the left-hand side of the frame, behind the trigger guard. These pistols have a swing barrel for maintenance. The catch above the trigger guard is not the safety catch, but is the lock for the swing barrel. The safety catch is at back of the frame on the left-hand side. The new double-action-only model PT-22 was introduced in 1992. This pistol is in .22 LR caliber with a magazine capacity of 8 rounds. The swing barrel has a length of 70 mm (2³/₄ in), the total length is 133 mm (5¹/₄ in) and it weighs 349 g (12¹/₄ oz). This weapon has a fixed rear sight, and is available as blued, nickel-plated or two-tone-version with palisander grips. In addition, the Taurus luxury versions have gilded catches and mother of pearl grips. The new model PT-25 is in 6.35 mm (.25 ACP) caliber with a magazine capacity of 9 rounds. The dimensions and the available versions are the same as that of the PT-22.

TAURUS MODEL PT-52

In the 1995 Shot Show in Las Vegas, Taurus exhibited a completely new pistol type in .22 LR caliber in two different versions. The Taurus PT-52S has a 114 mm (4¹/₂ in) barrel and a total length of 216 mm (8¹/₂ in). This is a single-action pistol with a magazine capacity of 10 rounds. The frame is made from black unbreakable Zytel composite. The

blued weapon has fixed sights and it weighs 765 g (27 oz). The safety slide catch and catch are on the left-hand side of the frame. This weapon also has automatic firing pin safety. Taurus also manufactures the PT-52T with a 152 mm (6 in) barrel and a micrometer sight. The total length of this type is 254 mm (10 in) and it weighs 851 g (30 oz). This pistol has been designed for the novice shooter and is reasonably priced. The PT-52S is for recreational purposes, so-called plinking. The PT-52T is an authentic target version. In 1996, the PT-52 disappeared from the Taurus range. The probable cause was a patent conflict between Taurus and another weapon manufacturer, resulting in the production being stopped.

TAURUS MODEL PT-92

In 1980, Taurus started manufacturing autoloaders. They took over the Beretta factory in Sao Paulo, complete with the production line of the Beretta

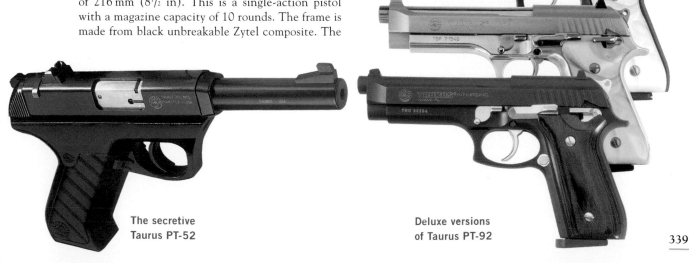

The secretive
Taurus PT-52

Deluxe versions
of Taurus PT-92

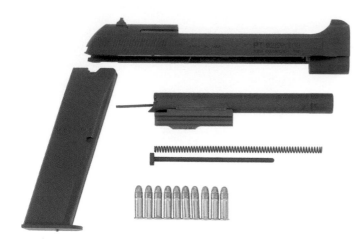

Conversion set in .22 LR caliber
for Taurus PT-92 and PT-99

Blued Taurus PT-99 AF
and PT-99 AF in stainless
steel

Model 92 pistols. Beretta had set up a factory for the South-American market, where they manufactured amongst other things, the Beretta Model 92 pistol for the Brazilian army. After the takeover, Taurus started manufacturing the Model PT-92, a modified version of the Beretta 92. A match version followed in 1981 with the model name PT-99. The PT-92 and related models are provided with the falling block locking, the same system used in the Beretta 92, followed shortly after by automatic firing pin safety. These types were identified by the addition of 'AF' to the model name. The Model PT-92 has a total length of 216 mm (8¹/₂ in), a barrel length of 127 mm (5 in) and it weighs 864 g (34 oz). This is a double-action pistol with a capacity of 15 rounds. This weapon has an ambidextrous safety catch on the frame. This catch has three positions. The first position is the safety position, in which both the trigger and the hammer are blocked. In the second position, this weapon can be safely carried with a cocked hammer and a cartridge in the chamber. This is the 'cocked & locked'-position. The third position serves as a uncocking lever for the hammer. The cartridge extractor also functions as a cartridge indicator. When a cartridge is in the chamber, the cartridge extractor is slightly proud, exposing a red dot. The slide catch is on the left-hand side of the frame, just behind the takedown lever, which is located above the front of the trigger guard. This pistol has a fixed rear sight. The front sight and both sides of the rear sight have a triple dot aspect marking. The standard version has rubber grips. The luxury versions have gilded catches and walnut or mother of pearl grips. This pistol is available in a blued or stainless steel version. In 1991, Taurus introduced the compact Model PT-92 AFC in 9 mm Para with a magazine capacity of 13 rounds. This pistol has a total length of 191 mm (7¹/₂ in), a barrel length of 108 mm (4¹/₄ in) and it weighs 879 g (31 oz). This weapon is available in

a blued, a nickel-plated and a stainless steel version. After the development of a variety of compact models, the production of the PT-92 AFC was stopped in 1998. In 1995, Taurus launched a 10-shot adapter set in .22 LR caliber. As of 1988, the PT-92 models have been provided with a built-in Taurus safety lock.

TAURUS MODEL PT-99

The double-action Taurus PT-99 pistol originates from 1981. This weapon is actually a PT-92 with a micrometer sight. A modification was made in 1983, with the introduction of automatic firing pin safety. This model was known for several years as the PT-99AF. The letters AF stand for Automatic Firing pin (safety). However, this extra identification was dropped in 1990. In addition, the PT-99 has a cartridge extractor that also acts as a cartridge indicator. As with the PT-92, the PT-99 is in the caliber 9 mm Para with a magazine capacity of 15 rounds. The total length is 216 mm (8¹/₂ in) and the barrel length is 127 mm (5 in). The weight of this weapon is 864 g (34 oz). The PT-99 is available in a blued or stainless steel version. Taurus PT-92 models produced after 1997, have the built-in Taurus safety lock.

TAURUS MODEL PT-100

In 1991, Taurus decided to anticipate the demand for the new .40 S&W caliber, and so they introduced the model PT-100 with a fixed sight and the PT-101 with an adjustable micrometer sight. These models were clearly derived from the PT-92 with an ambidextrous safety/uncocking lever on the back of the frame. In addition, the PT-100 and the PT-101 has automatic firing pin safety and a cartridge extractor with a red cartridge indicator dot. Both types are available in a blued or stainless steel version. This double-action

Taurus PT-100
and PT-92 in .40
S&W caliber

Ultra-compact Taurus PT-
111 with titanium slide
and tritium sights

pistol has a magazine capacity of 10 rounds. The total length is also 216 mm (8½ in) and the barrel length is 127 mm (5 in). This weapon weighs 864 g (34 oz). Taurus stopped production of both types in 1997.

TAURUS MODEL PT-111

In 1997, Taurus brought the PT-111 pistol with a composite frame to the market. This is a compact DAO (double-action-only) weapon in 9 mm Para caliber with a magazine capacity of 10 rounds. The total length is 155 mm (6¼ in), the barrel length is 82.6 mm (3¼ in) and this pistol weighs 530 g (18.7 oz). The PT-111 has a fixed combat sight with three white sighting points. In 1997, this pistol was only available in a blue black version, but since 1999 with a stainless steel slide. This 10-shot pistol was designed as back-up weapon. It has a safety catch on the left-hand side of the frame and automatic firing pin safety. The PT-111 is also provided with the Taurus safety lock.

In 1999, Taurus introduced the PT-111 Millennium at the IWA, the German firearms trade exhibition in Nuremberg. This pistol has a dark blue composite frame and a titanium slide, and has the same dimensions as the standard PT-111, but weighs

only 455 g (16 oz). The combat sight has tritium aspect marking. Taurus introduced the same weapon in 9 mm Short (.380 ACP) caliber in 1999. This model is known as the PT-138 and is available in the same versions as the PT-111. The compact PT-111 has also been available in .40 S&W and 45 ACP calibers since the year 2000. This weapon has the model name PT-140 in .40 S&W caliber and as the PT-145 in .45 ACP caliber.

TAURUS MODEL PT-138

Taurus introduced the PT-138 pistol in 1999. This 10-shot weapon in 9 mm Short (.380 ACP) caliber has a double-action-only trigger action. It is the same model as the PT-111 and has a total length of 155 mm (6¼ in). The barrel length is 82.6 mm (3¼ in) and it weighs 530 g (18¾ oz). This weapon also has a safety catch on the left-hand side of the frame, automatic

Taurus PT-111
in 9 mm Para

Taurus PT-138 in 9 mm
Short (.380 ACP) and in
Millennium edition with
stainless steel slide of
2000

Taurus PT-145 in .45 ACP
caliber of 2000

Taurus PT-157 in .357
Sig caliber of 2001

firing pin safety and includes the built-in Taurus safety lock system. In 2000, the PT-138 was renamed the PT-138 Millennium model. This pistol is available in blued steel or with a blank stainless steel slide and a black composite frame.

TAURUS MODEL PT-145

At the end of 1999, Taurus announced that the PT-111 pistol would also be available from 2000 in .45 ACP caliber with the model name PT-145, qualified with the word 'Millennium'. This pistol has a double-action-only trigger action. The magazine capacity is 10 rounds. The safety catch is located on the left-hand side of the frame. This weapon also has automatic firing pin safety and the built-in Taurus safety lock. The total length of the PT-145 is even slightly shorter than the PT-111 and PT-138, at 152 mm (6 in). The barrel length is 83 mm (3¼ in) and it weighs 652 g (23 oz). It has a triple dot combat sight and is available with a mat blued or stainless steel slide and a black composite frame. The same weapon in .40 S&W caliber has the model name PT-140.

TAURUS MODEL PT-157

Taurus introduced this compact pistol in .357 Sig caliber in 2001. This weapon has the model name PT-157 and has a magazine capacity of 10 rounds. It has a double-action-only trigger and is available with a mat blued steel slide or a blank slide in stainless steel. The frame is composite, and this type has also the safety catch on the left-hand side of the frame. In addition, the PT-157 has automatic firing pin safety and built-in Taurus safety lock. The total length is 152 mm (6 in), the barrel length is 83 mm (3¼ in) and it weighs 539 g (19 oz).

TAURUS MODEL PT-911

Taurus launched this compact 9 mm Para pistol in 1993, together with the 8-shot Model PT-908 in stainless steel. The slightly larger 10-shot PT-910 was released in 1995 in a blued or stainless steel version. This pistol has a Browning bolt-action, unlike its big brother, the PT-92. This double-action weapon has a combined safety/uncocking lever on the left-hand side of the frame. In 1997, both types were combined to create a new model, the 10-shot PT-911 in a blued or stainless steel version, with black rubber or palisander grips. Taurus also manufactures two special luxury versions with a blued or mat finish and gilded operating controls. A special titanium version with a tritium aspect sight appeared at the end of 1999. The double-action PT-911 has an ambidextrous safety/uncocking lever on the back of the frame. This safety catch has three positions. The first is the normal safety position. The second position is

Compact Taurus
PT-911 in 9 mm Para

the 'cocked & locked' position, allowing the weapon to be safely carried with a cocked hammer and a cartridge in the barrel chamber. The third position uncocks the hammer. This pistol also has automatic firing pin safety, and the cartridge extractor that also serves as a cartridge indicator. In addition, PT-911 has the built-in Taurus safety lock. The total length of this weapon is 178 mm (7 in), the barrel length is 102 mm (4 in) and it weighs 800 g (28¼ oz). This pistol has a triple dot combat sight.

TAURUS MODEL PT-938

The double-action PT-938 pistol was launched in 1997. This is a 10-shot weapon in 9 mm Short (.380

Taurus PT-938 In 9 mm
Short (.380 ACP)

ACP) caliber. The PT-938 is available in a mat blued version or in stainless steel as the PT-938SS. This weapon is actually the same type as the PT-911, with an ambidextrous safety/uncocking lever with three positions. In addition, this weapon has an automatic firing pin safety and a cartridge extractor that also serves as a cartridge indicator. Since 1998, this pistol was also equipped with the built-in Taurus safety lock. The total length is 165 mm (6½ in) and the barrel length is 95 mm (3¾ in). The weight is 757 g (26¼ oz). The grips are made of black rubber.

TAURUS MODEL PT-940

In 1996, Taurus brought the 900-version in .40 S&W caliber to the market. The Model PT-940 had a magazine capacity of 9 rounds, however in 1999 Taurus made a number of changes to this weapon. These included automatic firing pin safety, increasing the magazine capacity to 10 rounds and the inclusion of the Taurus safety lock. This pistol also has the ambidextrous safety/uncocking lever with three positions and the cartridge extractor that doubles as

Three different versions of
Taurus PT-940 pistol in .40
S&W caliber

a cartridge indicator, as with the other 900-models. The PT-940 is available in a blued or stainless steel version. In addition, Taurus manufactures a couple of luxury versions with gilded controls and walnut or mother of pearl grips. The older model PT-940 from the period 1996 until 1999 has a total length of 190 mm (7³/₄ in), a barrel length of 108 mm (4¼ in) and it weighs 851 g (30 oz). The new type introduced at the start of 1999 has a total length of 178 mm (7 in), a barrel length of 98 mm (3 in) and it weighs 800 g (28¼ oz).

TAURUS MODEL PT-945

In 1995, Taurus introduced the compact 8-shot PT-945 pistol in .45 ACP caliber at the Shot Show in Las Vegas. This double-action pistol has a bolt action that resembles that of the Browning-Sig system. It has a fixed locking lug under the chamber block, while the top of the chamber block fits exactly into the ejector port on the slide. This weapon has an ambidextrous safety/uncocking lever on the frame with the three familiar positions: the safety position, the 'cocked & locked' position and the uncocked position. In addition, this pistol has automatic firing pin safety and the now familiar cartridge indicator. All versions are provided with a triple dot combat sight. This compact pistol is available in blued, or stainless steel and in a number of luxury versions. The blued model PT-945-B4C and the stainless steel

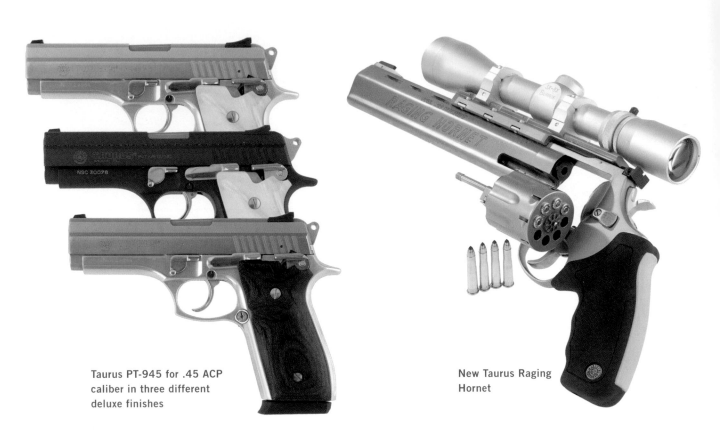

Taurus PT-945 for .45 ACP
caliber in three different
deluxe finishes

New Taurus Raging
Hornet

model PT-945-SS4C has a built-in compensator in the barrel and slide. This pistol has a total length of 191 mm (7¹/₂ in), a barrel length of 108 mm (4¹/₄ in) and it weighs 836 g (29¹/₂ oz).

TAURUS MODEL PT-957

One of the more recent types in the 900-series is the double-action PT-957 pistol in the caliber .357 Sig of 1999. This weapon has a magazine capacity of 10 rounds. The PT-957 has the ambidextrous safety/uncocking lever of the other 900-models. This pistol has the automatic firing pin safety, the cartridge indicator dot on the cartridge extractor, and is available in blued and stainless steel versions with black rubber grips. Taurus has also brought out luxury

editions of this model with gilded controls and palisander grips. The Model PT-957BC of 2000 has a built-in compensator system in the barrel and slide, essential for the compact model because of the high gas pressure and the considerable recoil produced by the .357 Sig cartridge. The total length of the PT-957 is 178 mm (7 in), the barrel length is 92 mm (3³/₄ in) and it weighs 794 g (28 oz).

TAURUS MODEL RAGING HORNET 22H

In 1999, Taurus introduced the 8-shot Raging Hornet revolver in .22 Hornet caliber. This is a .22 rifle cartridge with a centerfire primer. The muzzle velocity is 820 m/s and the bullet energy (E0) is 975 Joules. This large double-action revolver is mainly intended for the hunting of small game or varmint. The long 254 mm (10 in) barrel has a high ventilated barrel rib. The total length is 419 mm (16¹/₂ in) and this weapon weighs 1418 g (50 oz). The cylinder

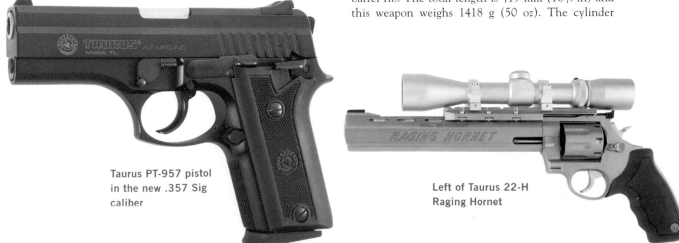

Taurus PT-957 pistol
in the new .357 Sig
caliber

Left of Taurus 22-H
Raging Hornet

The large Taurus 44 in .44
Magnum caliber

Taurus 66 revolver in blued
finish with 102 mm (4 in)
barrel

Taurus 66 in stainless steel
with 152 mm (6 in) barrel

locks in to the cylinder arm at the back of the recoil
shield. This revolver is equipped with a transfer bar
safety, and is manufactured from stainless steel,
with a rubber grip. The Raging Hornet 22-H has
a micrometer sight, but is supplied with a rail for
mounting a telescopic sight.

TAURUS MODEL 44

Taurus Model 44 is a 6-shot double-action revolver in
.44 Magnum caliber. Taurus introduced this revolver
in 1994. The cylinder locking of this older model is at
to the front next to the ejector bar and at the recoil
shield at the back. This weapon is available with
barrel lengths of 102, 165 and 213 mm (4, 6½ and 8½
in). The total lengths are 238, 295 and 349 mm (9½,
11⅝ and 13¾ in) respectively This weapon weighs
1247, 1446 or 1588 g (44, 51 or 56 oz). The model
with the 102 mm (4 in) barrel has a heavy solid barrel
rib. The versions with the longer barrels have
a ventilated barrel rib. All versions have a continuous
ejector shroud and are provided with a micrometer
sight and a rubber grip. Model 44 has a transfer bar
safety. As of 1997, all versions have a built-in
compensator in the barrel with four gas outlets on all
sides of the front sight.

TAURUS MODEL 66

Taurus has been manufacturing the Model 66 in .357
Magnum caliber since 1978, when it was a 6-shot
revolver with a micrometer sight. It was available in
the barrel lengths 76, 102 and 152 mm (3, 4 and 6
in). This double-action revolver has blued and mat
nickel-plated versions. The cylinder locks at the tip
of the ejector bar and at the recoil shield at the back.
The total lengths of the old model are 213, 238 and
289 mm (8½, 9½ and 11½ in) respectively. This
weapon weighs 950, 990 or 1090 g (33½, 35 or 38½
oz). In 1993, Taurus also introduced the Model 66
with a barrel length of 64 mm (2½ in). This revolver
is very similar to the Smith & Wesson Model 19, but
for the fact that the S&W has a fixed firing pin point
and a blocking bar safety. The Taurus 66 has

a separate spring-loaded firing pin in the frame and
transfer bar safety. In the same period, Taurus
produced the same model with a fixed sight groove in
the top bridge above the cylinder. This model is
known as Model 65, and is still in production. In
1997, Taurus introduced a new model 66. This model
has a 7-shot cylinder and is available with a 102 or
152 mm (4 or 6 in) barrel. The total length is 267 or
311 mm (10½ or 12¼ in) and it weighs 1077 or
1134 g (38 or 40 oz). Taurus manufactures this new
type in a blued, a stainless steel or a polished stainless
steel version.

TAURUS MODEL 85

The double-action model 85 originates from 1980.
This is a 5-shot revolver in .38 Special caliber. Taurus
then supplied this weapon with a 51 or 76 mm (2 or 3
in) barrel. In 1993, a stainless steel version was added
to the range. The model 85 has a fixed rear sight. The
cylinder locking is at the tip of the ejector bar and at
the recoil shield at the back. This weapon also has
transfer bar safety. The total length of this older
model is 161.5 mm (6½ in) and it weighs 567 g
(20 oz).

This revolver originally had a rubber grip, but
since 1996, Taurus has given this weapon an Uncle
Mike's Boot grip. Taurus launched the model 85UL
Ultra Light in 1997. This new type has an alloy

Two versions
of Taurus 85

The latest Taurus 85
Police Ultra-Lite
Titanium of 2000

Taurus Model 941
in .22 WMR caliber

frame, a steel barrel and a blued steel or blank stainless steel barrel shroud. The weight of the 85UL is 482 g (17 oz). This is 85 g lighter then the steel version. Since 1999, Taurus has also manufactured the Model 85 revolver in a titanium version. This Total Titanium version has a titanium frame, cylinder and barrel. This weapon is available in a variety of colors, such as blue gloss, mat blue, mat gold, light- and dark gray. The barrels have a built-in compensator with three gas outlets on both sides of the front sight. The weight of the titanium model is 437 g (15^1/$_2$ oz), and this weapon is suitable for .38 Special P ammunition. In 1999, Taurus also released their blued and stainless steel versions in double-action-only. In the year 2000, they introduced yet a new version, the 85 Police Ultra Light Titanium. This revolver also has a double-action-only trigger action and a barrel with a built-in compensator. This weapon has a titanium barrel and cylinder, and only weighs 369 g (13 oz), but is still suitable for P cartridges in .38 Special caliber.

Taurus Model 94/Model 941

Taurus brought this 6-shot Model 94 double-action revolver in .22 LR caliber to the market in 1973. This weapon was then only available with a 152 mm (6 in) barrel and had a micrometer sight. The total length of this old model is 284 mm (11^1/$_4$ in) and it weighs 1106 g (39 oz). It was then available in a blued or nickel-plated version. In 1989, Taurus introduced a new Model 94. This weapon has a 9-shot cylinder, and has barrel lengths of 51, 102 or 127 mm (2, 4 or 5 in). The total length is 162, 222 and 248 mm (6^1/$_4$,

8^3/$_4$ and 9^3/$_4$ in). The weights are 680, 709 or 751 g (24, 25 or 26^1/$_2$ oz) respectively. This revolver has a micrometer sight and a black rubber grip. Taurus also released the Model 94 in stainless steel in 1993. In 1992, Taurus introduced this weapon in .22 WMR caliber with an 8-shot cylinder at the international firearms trades exhibition (IWA) in Nuremberg, German and gave it the name Model 941. Until 1996, this type was available with a 51 or 102 mm (2 or 3 in) barrel, followed in the same year by a version with a 125 mm (5 in) barrel. This revolver has a blued and a stainless steel version, with both the old and the new versions having the cylinder locking at the front of the

Taurus 405 revolver in .40
S&W caliber of 2001

ejector bar and at the recoil shield. In addition, these
models have transfer bar safety.

TAURUS MODEL 405

In 2001, Taurus introduced a new revolver based on the
model 415. This is a 5-shot double-action weapon in
.40 S&W pistol caliber. The 405 has a heavy 51 mm
(2 in) barrel with a built-in compensator with three gas
outlets on both sides of the front sight. The total length
is 168 mm (6½ in) and it weighs 595 g (21 oz). This
weapon has a stainless steel frame and barrel with
a titanium cylinder. The cylinder does not lock at the
front of the ejector bar, but in the cylinder arm. In
addition, this model has transfer bar safety and a Taurus
safety lock on the hammer. The grip is made of rubber.

TAURUS MODEL 415

Model 415 in .41 Magnum caliber came on the
market in 1999. This double-action revolver has
a 5-shot cylinder and a heavy barrel with a length
of 64 mm (2½ in). The barrel has a built-in
compensator with three gas outlets on both sides of
the front sight. The total length is 181 mm (7¼ in)
and it weighs 851 g (30 oz). This revolver has a fixed
sight. The cylinder locks at the front via the cylinder
arm and at the back at the recoil shield. In the year

Taurus 425 Stainless in .41
Magnum and 425 Total
Titanium of 2001

2000, Taurus also introduced this weapon in a Total
Titanium version in the colors, blue gloss, mat blue,
light gray and dark gray. This titanium model weighs
593 g (21 oz) and is suitable for P ammunition.

TAURUS MODEL 425/MODEL 427

This 5-shot double-action model 425 in .41 Magnum
caliber came on to the market in 2000, and Taurus gave it
the name of Tracker. This beautifully finished revolver has
a heavy 102 mm (4 in) barrel with a built-in compensator
with four deeply sunken gas outlets at all edges of the front
sight. The ejector shroud runs through to the muzzle. This
weapon is available in mat stainless steel. In 2001, Taurus
also introduced the Total Titanium version in light and
dark gray. This weapon has a micrometer sight and
a rubber grip. The total length is 238 mm (9½ in). The
normal stainless steel version weighs 1077 g (38 oz) and
the titanium version weighs 822 g (29 oz). In 2002, Taurus
introduced the model 427 in .41 Magnum caliber. This
weapon looks identical to the Model 425, but has
a ventilated barrel and a 6-shot cylinder.

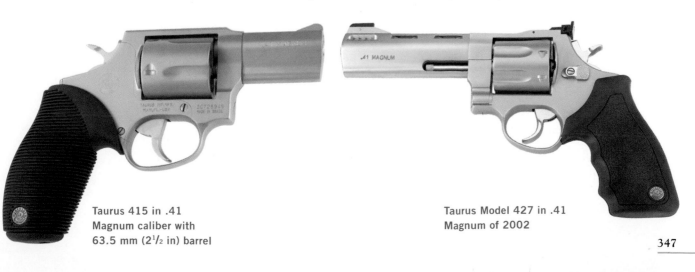

Taurus 415 in .41
Magnum caliber with
63.5 mm (2½ in) barrel

Taurus Model 427 in .41
Magnum of 2002

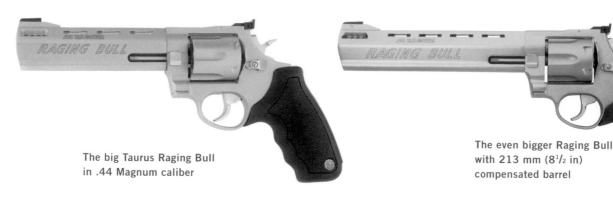

The big Taurus Raging Bull
in .44 Magnum caliber

The even bigger Raging Bull
with 213 mm (8¹/₂ in)
compensated barrel

Taurus Model 444 Raging Bull

Taurus Model 444 Raging Bull dates from 1997. This is a 6-shot double-action revolver in .44 Magnum caliber. It was also manufactured in .45 Long Colt as the Model 45. The Raging Bull 444 is available with a heavy ventilated barrel or 165 or 213 mm (6¹/₂ or 8¹/₂ in). The barrel has a built-in compensator with four sunken gas outlets on both sides of the front sight. The total length is 305 or 356 mm (12 or 14 in) and this weapon weighs 1503 or 1786 g (53 or 63 oz). This revolver has a transfer bar safety and a built-in Taurus safety lock on the hammer. The cylinder of this revolver is locked into the frame via the cylinder arm. Taurus also manufactured the same Raging Bull type in .454 Casull caliber, and gave it the model name .454 Raging Bull.

Taurus Model 445

In 1992, Taurus also launched a new revolver type in .44 Special caliber. This was Model 441 with a micrometer sight and as the Model 431 with a fixed sight. In 1999, this was replaced by the Model 445, in blued, stainless steel and titanium versions. The 5-shot double-action weapon has a 51 mm (2 in) barrel,

a total length of 168 mm (6¹/₂ in) and it weighs 799 g (28¹/₄ oz). This weapon is available in a blued or stainless steel version and with a rubber grip. In addition, this weapon has a fixed sight. The cylinder locks at the front of the ejector bar . Model 445 is also available with a built-in compensator with three gas outlets on both sides of the front sight. As of 1998, the Model 445 has a built-in safety lock. In 1999, Taurus introduced a double-action-only version in blued and stainless steel. In 2000 the Ultra Light version followed with an alloy frame. The weight of Model 445UL is 576 g (20¹/₄ oz). The Model 445 Total Titanium was released in 2001. This revolver is manufactured totally from titanium, weighs 561 g (19³/₄ oz) and is suitable for .44 Special P ammunition. This weapon is available in the colors blue gloss, mat blue, dark and light gray.

Taurus Model 450

The Taurus Model 450 originates from 1999. This is a small 5-shot double-action pocket revolver in .45 Long Colt caliber. This stainless steel weapon has a heavy 51 mm (2 in) barrel with a built-in compensator with three gas outlets on both sides of the front sight. The total length is 168 mm (6¹/₂ in)

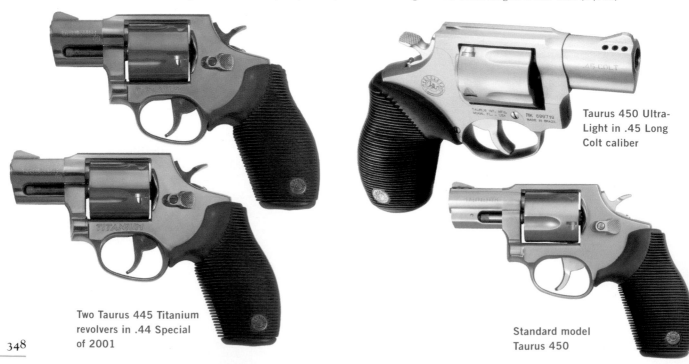

Two Taurus 445 Titanium
revolvers in .44 Special
of 2001

Taurus 450 Ultra-
Light in .45 Long
Colt caliber

Standard model
Taurus 450

Raging Bull in
heaviest Taurus
caliber: .454
Casull

and it weighs 794 g (28 oz). Towards the end of 1999, Taurus also introduced an Ultra Light version, the Model 445UL with an alloy frame. This revolver has the same dimensions as the standard 450, but only weighs 576 g (20½ oz). In 2000, Taurus released the Model 450 Total Titanium. This titanium revolver is suitable for .45 Long Colt cartridges and is available in the colors blue gloss, mat blue, dark and light gray. This revolver type weighs 561 g (19¾ oz). All versions have transfer bar safety, the Taurus safety lock and a black rubber grip.

TAURUS MODEL 454

In 1997, Taurus brought the large Raging Bull revolver in .454 Casull caliber to the market, as this caliber had become popular in North America with hunters and silhouette shooters. This revolver is available both in blued and stainless steel versions. The .454 Casull caliber originated in 1956 and was developed by the American, Dick Casull. He wanted a caliber similar to the .44 Magnum but with much more power, he achieved this by extending the .45 Long Colt casing by 25 mm (1 in). Freedom Arms built the first revolver for this caliber in 1983. A 300 grains bullet fired from a Raging Bull with the 213 mm (8½ in) barrel, achieves a muzzle velocity of 440 m/s (1444 fps), with the gas pressure measuring a respectable 3700 bar. The kinetic muzzle energy of the bullet is 1882 Joules. In comparison, the .44 Magnum with a 275 grains bullet leaves the barrel traveling at 376 m/s (1234 fps) and develops energy of E0 1260 Joules. The 5-shot double-action 454 Raging Bull has ventilated barrels of 127, 165 or 213 mm (5, 6½ or 8½ in). The heavy barrel has a continuous ejector shroud and a built-in compensator with four ports on both sides of the front sight. The total lengths are 292, 305 or 356 mm (11½, 12 or 14 in) respectively, and this weapon weighs 1446, 1503 or 1786 g (51, 53 or 63 oz). This weapon has transfer bar safety and the Taurus built-in safety lock. The cylinder locks into the cylinder arm.

TAURUS MODEL 605

In 1995, Taurus introduced a small pocket revolver in .357 Magnum caliber. This weapon has a 5-shot cylinder and is available in a blued or stainless steel version. As an introduction stunt, Taurus displayed a test weapon at the American Shot Show of that year, that had fired 11,000 powerful .357 Magnum cartridges trouble free, and without demonstrating signs of wear to the weapon. In 1998, this model was also made available in the DAO (double-action-only) version as Model 605CH. The added 'CH' stands for Concealed Hammer. The total length of the Model 605 is 171 mm (6¾ in), the barrel has

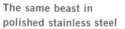

The same beast in
polished stainless steel

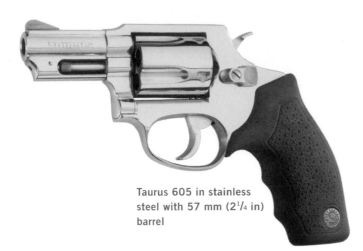

Taurus 605 in stainless
steel with 57 mm (2¹/₄ in)
barrel

Taurus Model 617 in
stainless steel

a length of 57 mm (2¹/₄ in) and weighs 680 g (24 oz). This revolver has a transfer bar and since 1998 it also has a built-in safety lock. The grip is made of rubber.

TAURUS MODEL 608

At the German IWA firearms trades exhibition in 1992, Taurus introduced a new type of revolver in .44 Magnum caliber. This was the model 44CP, in barrel lengths 102 mm (4 in), 165 mm (6¹/₂ in) and 213 mm (8¹/₂ in) and in a blued or stainless steel version. The addition of 'CP' means that this revolver is provided with compensator ports on both sides of the front sight. Since 1995, this weapon has been available in .357 Magnum caliber with the model name 608B for the blued and 608SS for the stainless steel version. These 8-shot versions do not have a built-in compensator. The 102 mm (4 in) barrel has a solid high barrel rib, however in the longer barrel lengths this rib is provided with ventilator ports. The total length of the Model 608 is 238, 295 or 349 mm (9¹/₄,

11¹/₂ or 13³/₄ in). This weapon weighs 1247, 1446 or 1588 g (44, 51 or 56 oz). The Model 608 also has a transfer bar safety and since 1998 a built-in safety lock. The cylinder locks at the tip of the ejector bar. This weapon also has a micrometer sight and a black rubber grip.

TAURUS MODEL 617/MODEL 817

In 1998, Taurus introduced a new type of pocket revolver in .357 Magnum caliber, model 617 with a cylinder capacity of 7 rounds. This double-action revolver is available with or without a built-in compensator and as double-action-only. The total length is 168 mm (6¹/₂ in), the barrel length is 51 mm (2 in) and it weighs 802 g (28¹/₄ oz). This revolver has a blued and a stainless steel version. In 1999 and 2000 new versions came on the market, the gray 617 Titanium Stealth, the 617 Titanium Blue and the mat gold Spectrum Gold. The titanium version weighs 564 g (20 oz). This revolver has a transfer bar system and a Taurus safety lock in the hammer. The same revolver in .38 Special caliber has the model name 817. This 7-shot double-action weapon also has a barrel length of 51 mm (2 in) and a total length of 165 mm (6¹/₂ in). This weapon weighs 595 g (21 oz).

Taurus 608 8-shot in
.357 Magnum caliber

New 617 of 2000
in titanium

Taurus 627 Titanium
Shadow Gray in .357
Magnum caliber

THOMPSON CENTER CONTENDER

Trade mark of Thompson Center

TAURUS MODEL 627

In 2000, Taurus introduced the Model 627 Tracker. This 7-shot double-action revolver is in .357 Magnum caliber. This is roughly the same weapon as the 425 in .41 Magnum. The versions available are made of mat stainless steel or dark gray titanium. (the Stealth) or in light gray (the Shadow). This revolver has a heavy solid 102 mm (4 in) barrel with a built-in compensator. On both sides of the front sight are four sunken gas outlets. This weapon has a micrometer sight and a rubber grip. The total length is 238 mm (9¹/₂ in). The stainless steel version weighs 1077 g (38 oz) and the titanium version weighs 822 g (29 oz). This revolver has a transfer bar safety and a Taurus safety lock. The cylinder locks with the aid of a built-in lug at the front of the cylinder arm. This locking lug is operated with the cylinder axis that runs through the ejector bar.

The American weapons factory Thompson Center Arms is based in Rochester, New Hampshire. Thompson has manufactured the single shot Center Contender pistol since 1966. When the company started they used the slogan 'The most versatile handgun available'. The fact that Thompson issues a life-long guarantee with their Contender pistols is an indication of their quality. The replacement barrels are available in more then twenty calibers, and any desired caliber can be manufactured to order. In 1978, the Super Contender was introduced with a standard barrel of 356 mm (14 in). This weapon not only has a longer barrel, but also a larger rear sight and a longer hand grip. In 1980, the Contender underwent a facelift. Thompson changed the hand grip and started using another sort of wood.

The Contender has four different barrel types, all of which are interchangeable. The tapered 254 mm (10 in) barrel, the 254 and 356 mm (10 and 14 in) thick match barrel (bull barrel) and the 254 mm (10 in) ventilated barrel, with an optional screw-on shot choke for .357 Hot Shot and .44 Hot Shot caliber. These are .357 Magnum and .44 Magnum cartridges with an extra long composite case for lead shot. The barrel of the Contender is the break-open type, that is to say that it swings open in a similar manner to a shotgun. The barrel is released by pushing the trigger guard forwards. This weapon has a firing pin system worthy of note, as it can be simply altered from centerfire to rimfire with a screw on the hammer.

The Contender is a long range weapon. Hunting with handguns is allowed in North America, as in most states, and the Contender was actually designed with this in mind. Since 1980, silhouette shooting has become increasingly popular. This involves shooting at metal targets from distances up to 400 meters. The Contender is available in blued and stainless steel versions.

.357 MAGNUM

Taurus Model 617 in
stainless steel and
Titanium Stealth Gray

Stainless steel Super
Contender with 356 mm
(14 in) barrel

Thompson Center Contender/ Super Contender/Contender G2

The single shot Thompson Contender pistol was introduced in 1967, when it was only available in the calibers .22 Short, .22 Long, .22 LR, .22 WMR, .22 Remington Jet, .22 Hornet and .38 Special. There was a choice of tapered octagonal barrels at 222 or 254 mm (8³/₄ or 10 in). This pistol cost then $ 135. In 1980, this weapon was modernized with amongst other things, a safety catch at the top of the hammer. This not only enables the isolation of the firing pin point, but the catch also serves to change from centerfire to rimfire. In the same year, a large number of barrels in new calibers were added to the range. The Contender was then available in .22 LR, .22 WMR, .22 Hornet, .221 Fireball, .222 Rem., .223 Rem., .256 Win. Magnum, 7 mm TCU (Thompson Center Ugalde), .30 Herrett, .30-30 Win., .35 Rem., .357 Magnum, .357 Magnum Hot-Shot (lead shot bullet), .357 Herrett, .41 Magnum, .44 Magnum, .44 Magnum Hot-Shot (lead shot bullet), .45 Long Colt and .45 Win. Magnum. In the meantime the number of calibers in which the Contender and the Super Contender are manufactured, have been considerably reduced. In

2001, the Contenders were available in the calibers .22 LR Match, .22 Hornet, .223 Rem., 7-30 Waters, .30-30 Win., .357 Magnum, .44 Magnum, .45 Long Colt and .45-70 Gov't. However the number of barrels available in blued or stainless steel versions has been increased. Thompson now supplies barrels in the lengths 254, 356, 413 and 533 mm (10, 14, 16¹/₄ and 21 in) with a micrometer sight or with a raised and ventilated barrel rib. The grip and the hand grip are optional in walnut or rubber. The weapon illustrated is a stainless steel Super Contender with a 356 mm (14 in) long barrel. In 2001, Thompson Center released a modified Contender version, the Contender G2. This new type is equipped with the Encore automatic hammer blocking system.

Thompson Center Encore

Thompson Center brought the single shot Encore pistol to the market in 1997. This weapon's automatic hammer blocking is activated on opening. The Encore used to be available with the barrel lengths of 254 and 381 mm (10 and 15 in). They have now been changed to 305 and 381 mm (12 and 15 in). In 1997, the Encore was available for the calibers .22-250 Rem., .223 Rem., .243 Win., .270 Win., 7 mm BR Rem., 7 mm-08 Rem., 7,62 x 39 mm Russian, .308 Win., .44 Magnum and .444 Marlin. This caliber list changed regularly until 2001. Since 2002, the Encore is available in the calibers .22 Hornet, .22-250 Rem., .223 Rem., .243 Win., .25-06 Rem., .270 Win., 7 mm-08 Rem., .308 Win., .30-06 Springfield, .44

Thompson Center Encore
with standard barrel and
a ventilated barrel
of 305 mm (12 in)

Encore Hunter

Stainless steel Encore with
381 mm (15 in) barrel

Magnum, .45 Long Colt and .45-70 Gov't. The total
length of the Encore is 419 or 495 mm (16¹/₂ from
19¹/₂ in). The weight is 1928 or 2041 g (68 or 72 oz),
depending on the barrel length.

TRUVELO ARMORY

Trade mark of Truvelo Armory of South Africa

The South African company, Truvelo Manufacturers
Ltd was founded in 1966 by the Frenchman Josef
Gebert. The company is based in Midrand and is run
by Franz Josef and his two sons. They originally
manufactured electronic equipment for the traffic
police on the African continent. In 1970, Truvelo
decided to also start building firearms. Since
1994, Truvelo have also been producing
rifle and canon barrels up to and including
20 mm caliber. Well-known products
include the Truvelo sniper rifles in caliber
.50 BMG, .338 Lapua, .300 Win. Magnum
and .308 Win. These sniper rifles have
the guaranteed accuracy of a 1/2 MOA at
500 meters. Truvelo also manufactures a number
of rifles for hunting and sports shooting based on
the Mauser K98 system. In 1990, Alex Du Plesis
developed the ADP pistol, which stands for
Advanced Design Pistol. Du Plesis is weapon
designer and sports shooter, and was born in
Zimbabwe.

TRUVELO ADP

The single-action ADP pistol in 9 mm Para caliber was
developed in 1990 by the South African weapon
designer Alex Du Plesis. This weapon first went into
production in 1994, and was manufactured by the
South African company Aserma in New Germany.
This pistol has a composite frame and roughly the
same gas retarded recoil as the Heckler & Koch P7.
Part of the gas pressure, channeled from immediately
behind the cartridge chamber passes via a gas outlet
port into a pressure cylinder under the barrel. After
firing, a piston delays the return of the slide. The barrel
is fixed to the frame. The ADP pistol also has
automatic firing pin safety. An indicator located at the
back of the slide shows when the firing pin is cocked.
The ADP Mark II followed the first model, the Mark I,
in 1995. The improvements on the Mark I, are an
ambidextrous safety catch and a frame with finger
grooves. In addition, the magazine release of the Mark
II can be transferred to the right hand side. The 10-
shot Aserma ADP Mark II in 9 mm Para caliber
has a total length of 158 mm (6¹/₄ in), a height of
120.5 mm (4³/₄ in) and a width or 29 mm (1¹/₄ in). The
polygonal barrel has a length of 94 mm (3³/₄ in) and
this weapon weighs 525 g (18¹/₂ oz). There is
a takedown lever on both sides of the frame. In 1997,

Truvelo ADP-9 pistol
for 9 mm Para

Aserma was restructured and became Reutech Defense Industries (RDI), and went on to introduce an ADP in .40 S&W caliber. This type is slightly longer at 166 mm (6¼ in), weighs 527 g (18½ oz), and the length of the polygonal barrel is 100 mm (4 in) with a rifling twist of 400 mm (15¾ in). In 1998, Truvelo took over the manufacture of the ADP Mark II. At the international IWA weapon trade exhibition Nuremberg, German, Truvelo introduced two new versions: an ADP in 9 mm Short (.380 ACP) and one in the new .45 ADP caliber. This cartridge deviates slightly from the standard .45 ACP having a 2 mm (¹/₁₆ in) shorter case. Truvelo manufactures the ADP pistol in the following versions:

TRUVELO ADP-380

This 10-shot single-action pistol in 9 mm Short (.380 ACP) caliber has a composite frame. The total length is 151 mm (6 in). The barrel length is 82 mm (3¼ in), the height of this weapon is 114 mm (4½ in) and the width is 28 mm (1¼ in). The weight is 510 g (18 oz). This pistol has a fixed rear sight. The safety catch is ambidextrous and the magazine release can be transferred to the right hand side. The ADP-380 also has automatic firing pin safety.

TRUVELO ADP-9

A 10-shot single-action pistol in 9 mm Para caliber. The total length is 160 mm (6¼ in) and the polygonal barrel has a length of 91 mm (3½ in). The height of this weapon is 116 mm (4½ in) and the width is 28 mm (1¼ in). This weapon has an empty weight of 572 g (20 oz). It has a fixed rear sight. The ADP-9 has an ambidextrous safety catch and automatic firing pin safety. The magazine

release can also be transferred to the right hand side for left-hand handed shooters.

TRUVELO ADP-40

This model has a magazine capacity of 8 rounds in .40 S&W caliber. The total length is 160 mm (6¼ in) and the length of the polygonal barrel is 91 mm (3½ in). The height is 116 mm (4½ in), the width of this weapon is 28 mm (1¼ in) and it weighs 585 g (20½ oz). This pistol has otherwise the same specifications as the other models.

TRUVELO ADP-45

The ADP-45 pistol has a magazine capacity of 6 rounds in .45 ADP special caliber, the cases of these cartridges being 2 mm (¹/₁₆ in) shorter than that of .45 ACP. This weapon has the same dimensions as the ADP-40, but has a different weight at 590 g (20¾ oz).

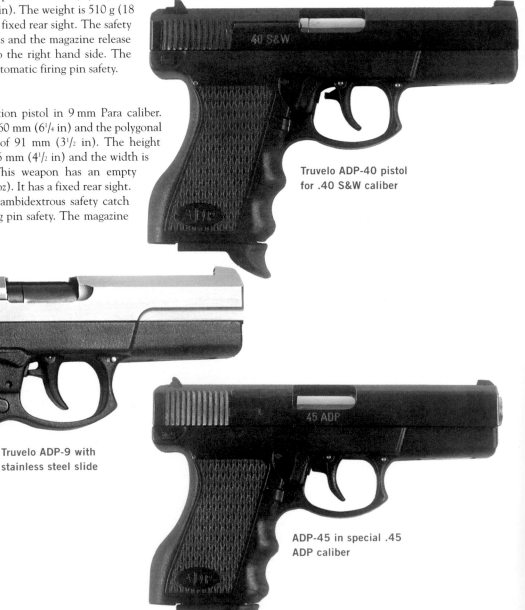

Truvelo ADP-40 pistol
for .40 S&W caliber

Truvelo ADP-9 with
stainless steel slide

ADP-45 in special .45
ADP caliber

U

UNIQUE

Trade mark of Manufacture d'Armes de Pyrénées Françaises (MAPF) of France

The French Manufacture d'Armes des Pyrénées Françaises (MAPF) was founded in 1923. The company is based in Hendaye at the foot of the Pyrenees on the Gulf of Biscay. Up until 1939, MAPF manufactured a large number of pistols under a variety of brand names. These names were often taken from the trading companies that had placed the orders for these pistol models. One example is the Audax pistol that MAPF manufactured from 1931 up until 1939. This small pocket pistol in the caliber 6.35 mm (.25 ACP) was based on the Baby Browning and was sold exclusively by the Cartoucherie Française in Paris. Another pistol from that time was the J.C. Higgins Model 85 in the caliber .22 LR, manufactured for Sears, Roebuck in Chicago. Other model names include the Auto-Stand, Burgham Superior, César, Chantecler, Demon, Elite, Gallia, Mars, Mikros, Perfect, Rapid-Maxima, Saint Hubert, Le Sanspareil, Selecta, Vindex, Western Field and many more. During the German occupation of France in the Second World War, MAPF was forced to manufacture weapons for the German army, and they produced the Kriegsmodel pistol based on their pre-war Model 17 of 1923. This is a 9-shot single-action pistol in 7.65 mm (.32 ACP) caliber. The right-hand side of the slide displayed the German model name '7.65 m/m 9 Schuss'. MAPF also manufacturer the Unique DES-69 sports

pistol and the IS (International Silhouette) pistol, together with a number of rifles and carbines. The TGC Varmint-Match rifle is used extensively by French police units as a sniper's rifle. MAPF also produces the Unique F-11, a small caliber (.22 LR) version of the famous French FAMAS army rifle, a weapon used by the French army and the French Foreign Legion. The company has a long history in the production of police pistols for the French government.

UNIQUE MODEL BCF-66 POLICE

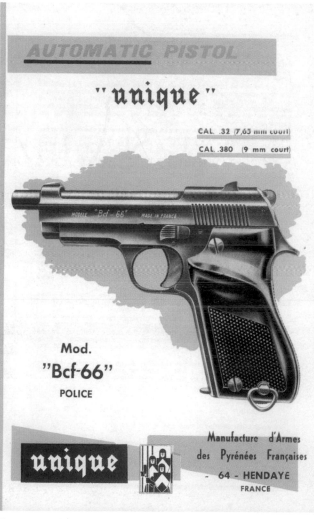

Front page of the instruction manual of 1954 for the Bcf-66 Police model

The Model Bcf-66 Police was introduced in 1954. This single-action pistol was manufactured in 7.65 mm (.32 ACP) caliber with a magazine capacity of 9 rounds and in 9 mm Short (.380 ACP) caliber for 8 rounds. This weapon bears similarities with a number of Beretta pistols. The safety catch is located on the left-hand side of the frame. This weapon also has a magazine safety, as it can not be fired until a magazine has been inserted. As a third safety system, the Bcf-66 has a half-cock lever on the hammer spur. The magazine release is in the grip heel. This pistol has a fixed rear sight and a lanyard ring on the left-hand side of the grip. After the last shot is fired, the slide remains in the rear position, however this pistol does not have a slide catch. The French police have used the Bcf-66 in both calibers. The total length of this weapon is 168 mm (6^1/$_2$ in), the barrel length is 102 mm (4 in) and it weighs 709 g (25 oz). The height is 124 mm (4^7/$_8$ in) and the width is 38.9 mm (1^1/$_2$ in). MAPF stopped production of this model in 1980. The following page shows an old instruction book from 1954.

Unique
Model D6

UNIQUE MODEL D/MODEL E

The model D also originates from 1954 and is still produced by MAPF. This is a 10-shot single-action pistol in .22 LR caliber. This weapon has a safety catch on the left-hand side of the frame, and a magazine safety. The model D is manufactured in a number of different versions.

MODEL D2 has a total length of 184 mm (7^1/$_4$ in), a barrel length of 108 mm (4^1/$_4$ in) and it weighs 680 g (24 oz). The height of the D2 is 127 mm (5 in) and the width is 38 mm (1^1/$_2$ in). This pistol has an interchangeable front sight and a laterally adjustable rear sight with a sight radius of 127 mm (5 in). This model is still being produced.

MODEL D4 is a target version and has a barrel length of 216 mm (8^1/$_2$ in). The total length is 299 mm (11^3/$_4$ in), including muzzle brake, and the height is 127 mm (5 in). This weapon has a width of 38 mm (1^1/$_2$ in) and it weighs 794 g (28 oz). A balance weight of 425 g (15 oz) can be attached to the barrel. This type also has an interchangeable front sight and a laterally adjustable rear sight. The sight radius is 235 mm (9^1/$_4$ in). The model D4 was manufactured until 1974.

MODEL D6 has a barrel length of 152 mm (6 in) and a total length of 229 mm (9 in). The height and width are the same as that of the other D-versions. The sight radius is 172 mm (6^3/$_4$ in) and it weighs 715 g (25^1/$_4$ oz). This model is still being manufactured by MAPF.

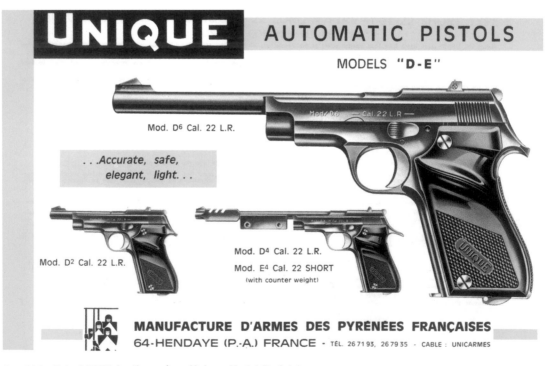

An old leaflet of 1954 for the various Unique Model D pistols

MODEL E4 is a 6-shot rapid fire in .22 Short caliber and has a barrel length of 216 mm (8¹/₂ in), including a muzzle brake. The total length is 299 mm (11³/₄ in) and it weighs 737 g (26 oz). MAPF manufactured this type up until 1975.

UNIQUE MODEL DES 32

MAPF introduced the Model DES 32-U in 1987 for the Center Fire FROM shooting discipline. This single-action pistol in the caliber .32 S&W-Long Wadcutter has a magazine capacity of 5 rounds or 6 rounds in the Military Rapid Fire version. This weapon has adjustments for the trigger pressure, the trigger pull and the trigger stop. The trigger can also be retracted horizontally. This pistol also has a special dry firing system, which allows the shooter to practice without damaging the firing pin. The standard trigger pressure is 1360 g (3 lb). The ergonomic stock has an adjustable hand palm support. The safety catch is located on the right-hand side of the frame, above the trigger guard. The slide catch is at the same height, but on the left-hand side of the frame. The magazine release is built-in to the left-hand grip plate. The total length of this weapon is 285 mm (11³/₄ in) and the barrel length is 150 mm (6 in). The height is 140 mm (5¹/₂ in), the width is 50 mm (2 in) and the weight of this weapon is 1140 g (40¹/₄ oz), excluding balance weights, which are optionally available and weigh 90, 120 or 220 g (3¹/₄, 4¹/₄ or 7³/₄ oz). This pistol has a micrometer sight at the back of the tail piece with a sight radius of 220 mm (8³/₄ in).

Old model DES 69 of 1969

UNIQUE MODEL DES 69/ MODEL DES/VO

The Unique DES 69 came on the market in 1969. This is a single-action pistol in .22 LR caliber and has a magazine capacity of 5 rounds. MAPF still

Newer version of DES 69 pistol

manufactures this weapon and in its time the barrel has hardly changed. The version up until 1985 had a round balance weight that fitted over the barrel. The later version has an angular barrel weight which fits around the circumference of the barrel. The slide flanks of the first model are smooth, with the slides of the later models having vertical pressure grooves. The trigger pressure, the trigger pull and the trigger stop can be set separately, and the trigger is horizontally retractable. The trigger system also has the dry firing feature. This weapon has a micrometer sight with a sight radius of 220 mm (8³/₄ in). The total length of the DES 69 is 285 mm (11¹/₄ in) and the barrel length is 150 mm (6 in). This weapon has a height of 140 mm (5¹/₂ in) and a width or 50 mm (2 in). The weight is 1140 g (40¹/₄ oz). The balance weights have weights of 90, 120 or 220 g (3¹/₄, 4¹/₄ or 7³/₄ oz). This pistol has an ergonomic walnut grip with an adjustable hand palm support. The safety catch is on the left-hand side of the

Unique DES 32 match pistol in .32 S&W Long Wadcutter caliber

First model of DES/VO
pistol for .22 Short caliber

frame. The slide catch is on the right hand side, and
the magazine release is built-in to the bottom of the
right hand grip plate. One variation on this pistol is
the 5-shot DES/VO in .22 Short caliber.

UNIQUE MODEL DES 2000

MAPF introduced the Model DES 2000 pistol in
1987. This 5-shot single-action weapon is in .22
Short caliber and is the successor of the model
DES/VO. This pistol has a large angular barrel with
five compensator ports along the top. The DES 2000
does not have safety catch, but a slide catch on the
right hand side above the grip. The trigger pressure,
the trigger pull, the trigger stop and the trigger
position are adjustable. This weapon also has a dry
firing system. The total length is 290 mm (11^1/$_2$ in),
the height is 135 mm (5^1/$_4$ in) and the width is

50 mm (2 in). The barrel has a length of 150 mm
(6 in). The DES 2000 is equipped with a micrometer
sight with a sight radius of 220 mm (8^3/$_4$ in). The
weight is 1230 g (43^1/$_2$ oz). The walnut grip has an
adjustable hand palm support.

UNIQUE MODEL IS

The Model International Silhouette (IS) is a single
shot break-open pistol, that has been especially
designed for Metallic Silhouette Shooting. MAPF
launched this model in 1985 in calibers .22 LR, .22
Magnum. 7 x 45 GIAT (7 mm TCU), .30-20 Win.,
.357 Magnum and .44 Magnum. A nice feature of this
weapon is that the barrel is screwed into the composite
barrel shroud separately, enabling this weapon to be
easily provided with another barrel in a different
caliber. The outer shroud has a micrometer sight and

Snap-shooting pistol DES
2000 in .22 Short caliber

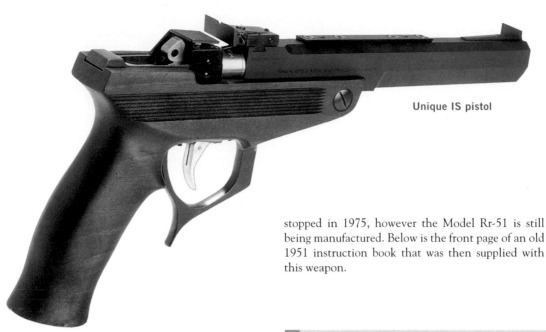

Unique IS pistol

stopped in 1975, however the Model Rr-51 is still being manufactured. Below is the front page of an old 1951 instruction book that was then supplied with this weapon.

a Weaver rail for telescopic sight mounting. This pistol can be broken (opened) by pulling the trigger guard downwards. After loading, the barrel has to be closed by hand, in the same way as a shotgun. This pistol has an automatic safety that can only be operated if the weapon is closed correctly. The trigger pull and the trigger stop are adjustable. The trigger pressure can be set to any desired pressure from 300 up to 1200 g (10½ - 2 lb 10 oz). The total length is 370 mm (14½ in) and the barrel length is 250 mm (9¾ in). The height of this pistol is 165 mm (6½ in) and the width is 40 mm (2 in). The sight radius is 230 mm (9 in) with the standard micrometer sight. This weapon as the Sport Model is available in calibers .22 LR and .22 WMR, has an alloy frame and it weighs 1350 g (47½ oz). The IS Model is intended for the more powerful center fire calibers, having a steel frame and weighing 1750 g (61¾ oz).

UNIQUE MODEL RR-51 POLICE/ FR-51 POLICE

The single-action models Rr-51 and Fr-51 Police were introduced in 1951. Both weapons look the same, but the calibers and magazine capacities are different. The Fr-51 Police has a magazine capacity of 8 rounds in 9 mm Short (.380 AC) caliber. The Model Rr-51 Police is in 7.65 mm (.32 ACP) caliber and can hold 9 rounds. Both versions have magazine safeties and a safety catch on the left-hand hand side of the frame. The magazine release is in the heel of the grip. The total length is 145 mm (5¾ in) and the height is 120 mm (4¾ in). The barrel length in both calibers is 81 mm (3¼ in) and it weighs 750 g (6½ oz). The production of the Model Fr-51 was

FIREARMS

Unique

Automatic Pistols

Models
"Rr-51 POLICE"
"Fr-51 POLICE"

Calibers 7,65 mm. court **(.32)** — **9** mm. court **(.380)**

MANUFACTURE D'ARMES DES PYRENÉES FRANÇAISES

64700 HENDAYE (P.-A.) FRANCE   Tél. (59) 20-71-93   Télex UNICARM 540280 F   Télégr. UNICARMES

Front page of instruction manual of 1951 for the Rr-51 and Fr-51 Police pistol

Valtro 1998 A1 pistol for
.45 ACP caliber

V

VALTRO

Trade mark of Valtro

The company name Valtro is taken from the industrial region of Valtrompia in Northern Italy. In 1988, a number of employees from a variety of firearms factories, decided to go into business for themselves, and founded the company Valtro Span. Their first project was the development of a series of alarm pistols based on the Beretta Cougar, the Beretta 92, the Beretta 85 and the Walther PPK. Valtro also manufactures a series of single barreled shotguns with the pump-action repeater system. The model RO5 has a tubular magazine for 7 rounds in 12 gange. The model PM5 has a large removable magazine for 7 rounds in the same shot gange. In 1998, Valtro brought a .45 ACP pistol on to the market, based on the Colt 1911-A1. The Resolver model followed in 2001 in 9 mm Short (.380 ACP) caliber. The Resolver was already a known model after being launched at the 1993 IWA by the Italian company Sites from Turin. Valtro purchased the rights in 2000. Valtro is equipped with modern Cad-Cam design systems and CNC-computerized production machines. Valtro is determined to position itself at the high end of the sport weapons sector, and will undoubtedly feature strongly in this field in the future.

VALTRO 1998 A1

This autoloader strongly resembles an adapted Custom Colt 1911-A1. This pistol has been manufactured since 1998 in .45 ACP caliber and is of exceptional quality. This single-action pistol has a steel frame and slide based on the Colt 1911-A1 National Match and has a special match barrel of 127 mm (5 in). The total length is 222 mm (8³/₄ in) and this weapon weighs 1134 g (40 oz). The total height is also 127 mm (5 in) and the width is 32.8 mm (1¹/₄ in). The magazine capacity is 8 rounds. The grip safety is in the back of the frame and is developed in to a beavertail. This weapon has a special speed trigger with an adjustable trigger stop and a so-called combat hammer. The ambidextrous safety catch is on the frame. The slide flanks are provided with pressure grooves at the front and back. In addition, this weapon has an enlarged magazine well and a lowered and beveled ejector port. The barrel bushing, the cartridge extractor, the ejector and the trigger mechanism are all hand tuned. The firing accuracy is guaranteed by Valtro to within less than 76 mm (3 in) over a distance of 50 meters. This pistol has an adjustable micrometer sight as standard, but can also be supplied with a tritium aspect marking. As optional extra, Valtro will give this weapon a hard chrome finish or a Black T Bird song coating.

VALTRO RESOLVER

The Resolver was introduced by the Italian company Sites from Turin at the International Waffen Ausstellung (IWA) in 1993. This pistol evidently failed to sell in any numbers, as things were quiet for a while. Valtro launched another weapon at the IWA in 2001, this autoloader is in 9 mm Short (.380 ACP) caliber and has a magazine capacity of 7 rounds. This weapon uses the recoil energy of the fired cartridge and has a recoil. This pistol has a double-action-only trigger and a concealed hammer. The catch behind the trigger is the takedown lever and has nothing to do with the actual trigger action. When this lever is pressed, the slide can be removed from the frame. The magazine release is at left-hand side of the frame,

Valtro Resolver in 9 mm
Short (.380 ACP)

African market. This weapon was issued to the army as the R-4. The shorter version is the R-5, and both have .223 Rem caliber. Following the United Nations weapon embargo in 1977, LIW developed the SS-77 machine gun in .308 Win caliber. In 1981 LIW designed the 22- and 32- shot BXP machine pistol in 9 mm Para caliber. LIW also manufactures armored cars and artillery ordnance. At the time, LIW mainly manufactured firearms for the home market, and to equip the police and the army of the South African republic. In 1991, LIW became part of the Denel industrial group. Denel assigned the Vektor company with the manufacture of light weapons. Other Denel subsidiaries include the companies Musgrave (hunting rifles), Swartklip (ammunition) and PMP (ammunition). Since then, the company has concentrated on the development and manufacture of high quality products at the cutting edge of the military and international market. In those days, Aserma and Reutech Defense Industries, who are also part of LIW, manufactured the Vektor pistol. Since the political about-turn of the South African republic, the rest of the world has shown greater interest in this country's products, with for example, large quantities of Swartklip ammunition being introduced into the European market. South African manufacturers also produce a number of interesting rifles and carbines.

behind the trigger guard, and the safety catch is located on the slide just under the fixed rear sight. This weapon is made totally of stainless steel. The total length is 155 mm (6$\frac{1}{4}$ in). The barrel has a polygonal profile and a length of 86 mm (3$\frac{1}{2}$ in). The height of this weapon is 108 mm (4$\frac{1}{4}$ in) and the width is 30.2 mm (1$\frac{1}{4}$ in). This is due mainly to the use of thick composite grips. When Sites manufactured this pistol, the total width was only 17 mm ($\frac{3}{4}$ in).

VEKTOR/LIW

Trade mark of Vektor

The South African company LIW (Lyttelton Ingenieurs Werk) was founded in 1953 as part of Armscor, a state concern responsible for the development and manufacture of military goods. In 1966, the South African army took the R-1 rifle into service, a FN-FAL L1A1 manufactured under license by the LIW, for which the UK also had a license from Belgian Fabrique National. In addition, they manufactured the UZI machine pistol under license from the Israel Military Industries (IMI). In 1973, IMI also issued a license for the manufacture of their Galil army rifle for the South

VEKTOR CP-1

In 1994, Vektor introduced the CP 1 pistol. The abbreviation CP stands for Compact Pistol. This 13-shot single-action weapon has a composite frame and a steel slide. This weapon looks extremely futuristic with its rounded and ergonomic styling. It has a gas retarded recoil, such as that of the Heckler & Koch P7,

Compact Vektor CP-1

where part of the gas pressure is tapped off from just behind the barrel chamber and sent to a cylinder under the barrel. This cylinder houses a piston. When a shot is fired, the slide's backward thrust is impeded by the piston in the cylinder. As soon as the bullet has left the barrel, the gas pressure is released from the cylinder and the slide returns to its normal position. This system works well, but has the disadvantage of not allowing the use of lead ammunition, as this would clog the gas ports.

One other special feature of the CP-1 is the safety catch, located in front of the trigger guard. When the safety is applied, a red dot is clearly visible. A second safety is the double trigger, perhaps partially derived from the Glock system. The 'small inner trigger' is responsible for the release of the automatic firing pin safety. The magazine release resembles an ambidextrous one, but in fact can only be operated from the left-hand side of the frame. The total length of this pistol is 177 mm (7 in). The polygonal barrel has a length of 100 mm (4 in) and a rifling twist of 254 mm (10 in). The height is 140 mm (5¹/₂ in) with a 13-shot magazine, with an extra finger groove on the rubber base. The height is 128 mm (5 in). with a 12-shot compact magazine. The width of the CP-1 is 28 mm (1¹/₄ in). This pistol has a fixed rear sight with a sight radius of 136 mm (5¹/₂ in), and it weighs 720 g (25¹/₂ oz).

VEKTOR SP-1

The apartheid policies of South Africa forced them into isolation. The United Nations had placed a weapons embargo on the country, and so South Africa had to supply their own weapons. In 1985, LIW started developing a copy of the Beretta Model 92 pistol and the prototype was ready in 1986. In 1988, this weapon went for test inspection, and was subsequently issued to the South African army as their service weapon. This pistol was given the model name Z88. The Z is the first letter or the surname of the then LIW director Theodoor Dirk Zeederberg and the '88' is the year of the army approval. At the time, a number of South African initiatives were being undertaken in the firearms sector. In 1988, Clarbex, a company from Wynberg introduced the Varan PMX 90 pistol in 9 mm Para, however this venture only lasted a couple of years. In 1991, LIW introduced a pistol that was based on the Z88, the 15-shot SP-1 pistol in the caliber 9 mm Para. The letters SP stand for Service Pistol. This weapon has the same falling block locking as the Z88. This locking system is derived from the Beretta Model 92. Beretta had actually copied this system from the Walther P38. The SP-1 pistol does however have a number of other special distinguishing features. The frame is made of alloy and the slide is of blued steel or blank stainless steel. This double-action weapon has an ambidextrous safety catch on the frame, an automatic firing pin safety and a half-cock lever on the hammer. The magazine release is on the left-hand side of the frame behind the trigger guard, but can be changed to the right. The slide catch and the takedown lever are on the left-hand side. The standard SP-1 has a total length of 210 mm (8¹/₄ in). The cold-forged polygonal barrel has a length of 118 mm (4³/₄ in) and a rifling

Vektor SP-1 Target
pistol

Vektor SP-2 for .40
S&W caliber

twist of 254 mm (10 in). The height is 145 mm (5³/₄ in) and the width is 40.5 mm (1¹/₂ in). This pistol has a fixed rear sight, a sight radius of 156 mm (6¹/₄ in), and it weighs 995 g (35 oz). In 1994, LIW announced a sport version that was made available a year later. This SP-1 Target pistol in 9 mm Para caliber has a longer barrel and slide, with an adjustable LPA micrometer sight with a sight radius of 207 mm (8¹/₄ in). The total length of the sport versions is 244 mm (9¹/₂ in) and the barrel length is 150 mm (6 in). The height is 147 mm (5³/₄ in) and the width is 44 mm (1³/₄ in). This weapon weighs 1155 g (40³/₄ oz). The magazine capacity is the same as that of the standard pistol: 15 rounds. In addition, LIW developed the SP-1 sport pistol with a compensator. The total length of this type is 240 mm (9¹/₂ in), the barrel length is 125 mm (5 in) and it weighs 1080 g (38 oz). The SP-1 General's Model is again a compact version of the standard weapon and has a total length of 190 mm (7¹/₂ in).

VEKTOR SP-2

In 1993, LIW introduced an adapter set in the caliber .40 S&W for the SP-1 pistol. This adapter set was given the model name SP-2. In 1995 it was introduced as a separate weapon in .40 S&W caliber. The magazine capacity is 11 rounds. The double-action SP-2 pistol is technically the same as the SP-1. The total length of the SP-2 is 210 mm (8¹/₄ in). The length of the polygonal barrel is 118 mm (4³/₄ in) and the rifling twist is 254 mm (10 in). The height is 145 mm (5³/₄ in) and the width is 40.5 mm (1¹/₂ in). The standard SP-2 has a fixed rear sight with a sight radius of 156 mm (6¹/₄ in), and it weighs 955 g (33³/₄ oz). Since 1999, Vektor has been supplying an adapter set in 9 mm Para for the SP-2.

This pistol was also manufactured as a General's Model compact. The total length is then 190 mm (7¹/₂ in), the barrel length is 103 mm (4 in) and it weighs 890 g (31¹/₂ oz).

Vektor has manufactured the SP-Ultra Sport since 1999. This weapon has a longer barrel of 148 mm (5³/₄ in) with a three-chamber compensator on the slide. The total length is 280 mm (11 in), the height is 154 mm (6 in) and it weighs 1180 g (41¹/₂ oz). The magazine capacity of the SP-2 Ultra Sport is 14 rounds.

The fourth version of the SP-2 is the Competition Model. This pistol has a length of 222 mm (8³/₄ in), a height of 154 mm (6 in), a barrel length of 148 mm (5³/₄ in) and it weighs 1190 g (42 oz).

W

WALTHER

Walther logo

Carl Wilhelm Freund Walther was born in 1858. In the fall of 1886 he opened a firearms workshop in Zella-Mehlis and together with an apprentice, built hunting and skeet rifles. Walther's wife was the daughter of revolver manufacturer Christian Friedrich Pickert. She had five sons, Fritz August, Georg Carl, Willy Alfred, Hans Erich and Carl Lothar. The first three followed an apprenticeship with their father. Hans Erich went into commerce, and Carl Lothar became a toolmaker. The company manufactured hunting- and sporting rifles until 1900, at first primarily with the Martini system and later also with the Aydt system. In 1903, the company moved to larger premises.

The father, Carl Walther was mainly interested in the building of autoloaders, a novelty in those days. In 1908, Walther launched his first pistol in 6.35 mm (.25 ACP) caliber simply called the Model 1. Model 2 to Model 5 followed in the years up to 1915.

The First World War resulted in a lot of activity within the company. The number of employees rose quickly to more then five hundred. Unfortunately, Father Walther did not live to witness this as he died in 1915. The three sons who had been trained by their father, took over the running of the company. After the war, Walther switched to the manufacture of shotguns and small caliber rifles. Around 1924, Fritz August Walther started producing calculating and sorting machines.

In the period between the World Wars, as well as manufacturing excellent sporting weapons, the Walther concern also manufactured military equipment, one example being the Bergmann MP34/1 machine pistol.

Theodoor Bergmann was a gunsmith, and did much work together with the well-known weapon designer Hugo Schmeisser, who had already developed a number of machine pistols for Bergmann, such as the Bergmann MP18/I and the MP28/II. Schmeisser left-hand to work with Haenel, another German weapons factory, and so the MP34/I was developed by one of Bergmann's brothers. In 1932, Schultz & Larsen manufactured a number of prototypes in Denmark. Walther then went on to manufacture these weapons under license in Zella Mehlis. The German army showed no interest in this weapon, and only a few thousand of these machine pistols were produced for the German police, with a small export order being sent to Bolivia. In 1935, Bergmann modified this weapon and gave it the name the Bergmann MP35/I. A few thousand of these were sold to Denmark, Sweden and Ethiopia. In 1940, the rifle 41(W)was developed for the German army, the W standing for Walther. This semi-automatic weapon works using gas pressure. This gas

Several old Walther pistols from before World War

was collected from a curious looking cowl at the muzzle. Thousands of these weapons were produced for use at the Eastern front in the period up to 1943. This weapon was succeeded in 1943 by the G43 rifle, manufactured both by Walther and a number of other factories, such as the Gustloff Werke and the Berliner-Lübecker Maschinenfabrik. The G.(ewehr) 43 had a more customary mechanism in the barrel for the gas collection, very similar to that used today. It also had a removable magazine. This weapon was regularly used as a sniper rifle. During the Second World War, Walther was called on to help with in war effort. The surrender of the German army in 1945 meant the end of the Walther factory. The Walther family fled from the Russian sector, and restarted in Heidenheim near the Schwabian Alps. The firearms ban that had been enforced by the allied forces, led to Walther concentrating on the production of calculating machines and airguns. After the ban was lifted in 1951, the company resumed the manufacturing of weapons in old horse stables in the neighboring Ulm. Sales were so good that Walther had a large factory complex built in 1953. Georg Carl Walther died in 1954. His son Karl-Heinz took over the company, and continued with its expansion until he died in 1983. Economic problems forced the family to sell the company to the Umarex concern in 1993. The origins of Umarex are in fact intertwined with the history or Walther. In 1937, Walther Riem, one of the Walther works managers initially developed the Perfecta alarm pistol, this led to the formation of Mayer & Riem in Arnsberg in 1953. In 1972 this company was turned into the Umarex concern.

Walther GSP in 25th anniversary edition with Walther GSP Atlanta

WALTHER MODEL GSP-22

The Walther GSP originates from 1968 and is a single-action match pistol in .22 LR or .32 S&W-Long Wadcutter caliber. The letters GSP stand for Gebrauchs- und Standard Pistole. This weapon is derived from OSP rapid fire pistol developed in 1962. The GSP pistol has a recoil and has changed somewhat over the years. It was not until after 1977 that adapter sets in .22 LR and .32 S&W-Long WC were available to fit the same frame. The modern GSP does not have safety catch. Older versions from before 1977 did however have a safety catch on the left-hand side of the frame, behind the trigger. This weapon was also given an interchangeable trigger group. There are the options of 1360 g (3 lb) and a 1000 g (2 lb 3oz) trigger unit. The user can set the trigger for half-cocking, as well as the trigger pressure, the trigger pull,

Walther GSP pistol

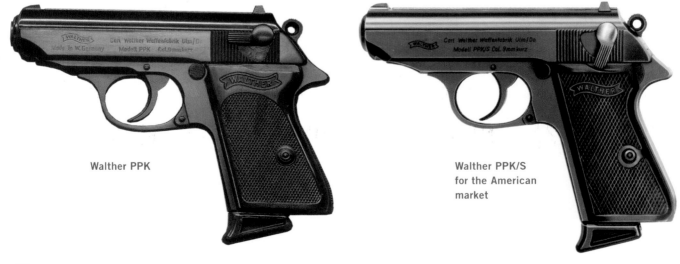

Walther PP

assembled using parts manufactured by Manurhin. In June 1986, Walther resumed the manufacturing of the Model PP themselves. The post-war model is available in calibers 7.65 mm (.32 ACP) and 9 mm Short (.380 ACP). The magazine capacity is 8 and 7 rounds respectively. Occasionally, Walther has also manufactured small series in .22 LR caliber. This weapon has a recoil and the barrel is fixed into the steel frame. The total length of the PP is 170 mm (6¾ in), the barrel length is 98 mm (3¾ in) and the width is 30 mm (1¼ in). The empty weight is 660 g (23¼ oz). The PP has a combined safety/uncocking lever and automatic firing pin safety. At the end of 1999 Walther announced the end of the Model PP production. The last series of 500 weapons were provided with the gold inscription 'Last Edition 1929-1999'.

WALTHER MODEL PPK/MODEL PPK/S/MODEL PPK/E

The double-action Walther Model PPK came on the market in 1931 as a compact version of the larger Walther PP. The fame of the PPK pistol was due in part to the many James Bond films, in which Sean Connery, as secret agent 007, tackled his adversaries. The model name PPK stands for Polizei Pistole Kurz. This weapon was sometimes known as the Polizei Pistole Kriminal, as it was extensively used by criminal special branches in the second half of the last century. The Walther PPK was mainly successful in the USA and was sold there in large numbers. The PPK has a skeleton grip with a wrap-around composite stock. This weapon is manufactured in calibers .22 LR, 7.65 mm (.32 ACP) and 9 mm Short (.380 ACP). The total length of the PPK is 155 mm (6 in), the height is 100 mm (4 in) and the barrel length is 84 mm (3¼ in). The width is 25 mm (1 in) and it weighs 590 g (20¾ oz).

The American Gun Control Act of 1968 signaled the end. The model did not meet the required minimum height of 102 mm (4 in). Curiously, this requirement only applied to imported weapons. In 1969, Walther designed a new version that did meet the requirements, and it was given the name PPK/S. This model has the frame of the Walther PP and the barrel and slide of the PPK. The extra letter 'S' stands for Special. Furthermore, Walther issued a production license to an American representative, Interarms. This meant that because the PPK was being manufactured in American the height stipulations of the Gun Control Act no longer applied. The model PPK/S has a total length of 156 mm (6¼ in) and the barrel length is 83 mm (3¼ in). The height is the same as that of the PP, 109 mm (4¼ in). The width is 30 mm (1¼ in) and it weighs 645 g (22¾ oz). Both the PPK as the PPK/S has a safety catch on the left-hand side of the slide. This catch also serves as a uncocking lever for the hammer. When applied, the safety catch rotates a safety block into the path of the firing pin, allowing the safe release of the hammer. The PPK/S is manufactured in 7.65 mm (.32 ACP) caliber with a magazine capacity of 8 rounds and in 9 mm Short (.380 ACP) caliber for 7 rounds. The model PPK/S is

Walther PPK

Walther PPK/S for the American market

Walther PPK/E of 2000

Jubilee edition of the P5 in 1986

also available in stainless steel. In the year 2000 Walther introduced a new version of the PPK. This model was given the model name PPK/E. This weapon is in fact the same pistol as the PPK/S, but in a polished blued version. The PPK/E is available in calibers .22 LR, 7.65 mm (.32 ACP) and 9 mm Short (.380 ACP). The magazine capacity is 8 rounds in the first calibers and 7 rounds in 9 mm Short (.380 ACP). The total length is 165 mm (6½ in), the barrel length is 86 mm (3½ in) and the height is 113 mm (4½ in). The width is 28 mm (1¼ in) and this weapon weighs 670 up to 720 g (21 up to 23 oz) depending on the caliber.

WALTHER MODEL P5/MODEL P5 COMPACT

In 1978, the Walther P5-Model was introduced in 9 mm Para caliber, and was specially designed for use as a police pistol. This double-action weapon does not have a safety catch, it only has a uncocking lever that also serves as a slide catch. The Walther P5 has in addition, a number of different built-in safeties. The

firing pin is always blocked until the trigger is pulled. Firstly, the hammer cannot reach the tip of the firing pin. The hammer has an opening in the corresponding place. The automatic firing pin safety also provides extra security against being knocked or dropped. As the shooter pulls the trigger, the hammer is cocked and the firing pin is pushed upwards. The hammer can then reach the percussion point of the firing pin, and the automatic firing pin safety is released. The hammer also has a safety lug in the hammer spur, so that the hammer springs back slightly after every shot. Finally, this pistol also has a close safety, which means that it cannot be fired unless the slide is closed correctly. This feature is now included in almost all pistols. This weapon has the same system as the P38, the Walther falling block locking. The ejector port is in the top of the slide. This pistol ejects the empty cases to the left-hand, unlike the other Walther pistol models. A number of complaints came in from the police that this pistol could go off accidentally after falling from a police holster. This led to Walther introducing a conversion set in 1991, which increased the strength

Walther P5
police pistol

Walther P5
Compact

of the automatic firing pin safety spring. The Walther P5 pistol has a total length of 180 mm (7 in), a barrel length of 90 mm (3¹/₂ in) and the height is 129 mm (5 in). The width is 32 mm (1¹/₄ in) and this weapon weighs 795 g (28 oz). The rear sight is laterally adjustable and the sight radius is 134 mm (5¹/₄ in). The trigger pressure in single-action is 2000 g (4.4 lb) and in double-action 4500 g (9.9 lb). The magazine capacity is 8 rounds. The frame of the P5 is made of alloy and it has a steel slide. The finish is in mat black. In 1986 Walther brought out a special jubilee version of the P5 to celebrate the company's centennial. This weapon has a gold inscription on the left-hand side of the slide: '1886-1986' and '100 Jahre Walther'.

Walther introduced the P5-Long pistol at the 1987 IWA, the German firearms trade exhibition. As well as increasing the barrel length of this pistol from 90 to 135 mm (3¹/₂ to 5¹/₄ in), Walther also changed the rifling twist from 250 mm to 475 mm (9³/₄ to 18³/₄ in). The front sight that is fitted on the slide of the standard P5 has here been attached with a band at the front near the muzzle, as is the case with the P38. The sight of the P5-Long has a triple dot aspect marking. In 1987 Walther also launched a compact version of the standard P5 pistol as the Model P5-Compact. This type has a total length of 170 mm (6³/₄ in), a barrel length of 79 mm (3¹/₄ in) and it weighs 750 g (29¹/₂ oz).

WALTHER MODEL P22/MODEL P22-TARGET

At the 2001 American Shot Show in New Orleans Walther introduced the new P22 pistol in .22 LR caliber. This 10-shot double-action weapon was identical to the larger P99 pistol. This weapon can be adapted to the individual shooter by using the interchangeable grip backs, as with the larger P99. All controls including the safeties, slide catches and

Walther P222 Target
pistol of 2001

magazine release are ambidextrous. In addition, the P22 has a cartridge indicator on the cartridge extractor, a magazine safety, a safety lever on the hammer and a falling block safety. The rear sight is laterally adjustable and the front sight is interchangeable. This pistol has locking, a composite frame and a steel slide. The total length of the standard weapon is 159 mm (6¹/₄ in), the height is 114 mm (¹/₂ in) and the width is 29 mm (1¹/₄ in). The fixed barrel has a length of 87 mm (3¹/₂ in). The trigger pressure is 1200 g in single-action and 4600 g (2lb 10 oz and 10lb 2 oz) in double-action. The weight is 555 g (19¹/₂ oz). At the same time, Walther also introduced a special Target version as the P22-Target, a weapon that is technically identical to the P22. The total length of the Target version is 199 mm (7³/₄ in). The height and width are the same as that of the P22. The barrel length is 127 mm (5 in) and it weighs 675 g (23³/₄ oz).

WALTHER P38

In 1937, Walther developed a large double-action pistol in 9 mm Para caliber. This weapon was especially designed with German army large-scale offensives in mind, and so the P38 was scarcely seen on the civilian market. Although the name implies that the P38 was introduced in 1938, the German army never used this weapon officially until April 1940. The P38 has the well-known Walther falling block locking, a system later adopted by several manufacturers including Beretta for the Model 92 pistol. Walther was only one of a number of companies that manufactured this pistol during the Second World War. This was indicated on

Walther P22 pistol of
2001, a .22 LR version
of the big P99

An old model
Walther P38

A more modern P38

the weapon with a special coding. The German army leaders wanted to keep the location of manufacturers confidential for fear of sabotage and bombing raids. The code for Walther was originally indicated by the number '480'. This was later changed to the letters 'ac', supplemented with the last two numbers of the year of manufacture. Walther manufactured approximately 583,000 P38 pistols during the war. In 1942, Mauser had to switch production from the Mauser P08 pistol to the P38. The factory code of Mauser was 'byf', followed by the last two numbers of the production year. In total Mauser manufactured 340,000 P38 pistols until 1945. The code 'cyq' and later 'cvq' was used for the Spree-Werke in Berlin, who produced 285,000 P38 from the end of 1942 up to April 1945. Incidentally, it has often been claimed that the code 'cvq' was the result of a worn stamp where the tail of the letter 'y' had been worn away. After the Second World War, the allied forces banned all German manufacturers from producing firearms. In 1957 Walther resumed the production of the P38, which was taken into service by the new German army as the P1. There are a number of variations of the P38 pistol, including the P38K and the P4. These versions have a shorter barrel and a uncocking lever. The P38K also has automatic firing pin safety. The Walther P4 was originally also known as the P38-IV. Both versions should be seen as part of the evolution in the development of the P38 to the P5. The P4 is no longer provided with automatic firing pin safety, it has an automatic falling block safety, just as

the P5. After the Second World War the P38 pistol was also manufactured by the French company Manurhin. The French armed forces carried off part of the Walther production machinery to France in 1945, together with a large supply of weapon parts. This resulted in a number of P38 pistols being later assembled, bearing both the Mauser codes SVW 45 and SVW 46, combined with the French proof house marks. Manurhin later manufactured the P38 pistol themselves under the name of Pistolet P1. Walther manufactured the P38 pistol until 1997 in .22 LR, 7.65 mm Para and 9 mm Para caliber, with a magazine capacity of 8 rounds. The total length of the P38 is 216 mm (8^1/$_2$ in). The barrel length is 125 mm (5 in). The height of this weapon is 137 mm (5^1/$_2$ in) and the width is 37 mm (1^1/$_2$ in). This pistol has a fixed rear sight with a sight radius of 180 mm (7 in). The weight of this weapon with an alloy frame is 800 g (28^1/$_4$ oz). The version with a steel frame weighs 945 g (33^1/$_4$ oz). The version P4 has a total length of 200 mm (8 in), a barrel length of 110 mm (4^1/$_4$ in), a height of 139 mm (5^1/$_2$ in) and it weighs 800 g (28^1/$_4$ oz). The P38K has a total length of 160 mm (6^1/$_4$ in), a barrel length of 70 mm (2^3/$_4$ in) and it weighs 770 g (27^1/$_4$ oz).

WALTHER MODEL P88

In order to figure in government contracts for new army or police pistols Walther brought the P88 onto the market in 1987. Strangely enough, Walther decided to abandon the trusted falling block locking system for this model and switched to a variation of the Browning bolt-action. A locking lug is attached to the bottom of the barrel chamber that locks the chamber

Walther P88 Champion

Walther P88 Competition

block into the ejector port in the slide. The first series had an ambidextrous combined uncocking lever/slide catch on the frame. As of 1990 this pistol has been manufactured with an ambidextrous combined uncock/safety catch mounted on the slide and an ambidextrous magazine release. The separate slide catch is on the left-hand side of the frame. Using the P88, Walther took part in the US Army trials. It must have left an extremely sour taste in Walther's mouth when the Beretta 92 F was finally chosen, for this pistol has the tried and tested Walther falling block locking. The standard version of the double-action Walther P88 has a total length of 195 mm (7³/₄ in) and a barrel length of 106 mm (4¹/₄ in). The height is 140 mm (5¹/₂ in) and the width is 35 mm (1¹/₂ in). The weight is 800 g (28¹/₄ oz) and the magazine capacity in 9 mm Para caliber is 14 rounds. The automatic safeties of the P88 are the same as that or Model P5.

MODEL P88-COMPACT a shortened version with a total length of 181 mm (7 in), a height of 134 mm (5¹/₄ in) and a width or 33 mm (1¹/₄ in). The barrel length is 100 mm (4 in) and it weighs 822 g (29 oz).

MODEL PC-POLICE is a special police-version of the P88. This type only has an ambidextrous uncocking lever on the slide and the automatic safeties of the P88. The dimensions of the PC Police are the same as that of the P88-Compact.

MODEL P88 COMPETITION has four different versions. The first type has a total length of 181 mm (7 in), a height of 135 mm (5¹/₄ in) and a width or

39 mm (1¹/₂ in). The barrel has a length of 100 mm (4 in) and this weapon weighs 800 g (28¹/₄ oz). The second version is the P88 Competition-5. The total length of this weapon is 206 mm (8 in), the barrel length is 125 mm (5 in) and it weighs 885 g (31¹/₄ oz). The third version is known as the P88 Competition Compensator. This model has a total length of 216 mm (8¹/₂ in) and a barrel length of 125 mm (5 in), excluding the compensator on the slide. The weight is 935 g (33 oz).

MODEL P88 CHAMPION has an adjustable micrometer sight. This type is available with a barrel length of 100, 125 or 150 mm (4, 5 or 6 in). The total lengths are 188, 211 or 232 mm (7¹/₂, 8¹/₄ or 9¹/₄ in) respectively. At the front of the barrel is a hideous looking block, which acts as a barrel weight.

Walther P99, the
new police pistol

The hunting version
of the P99

Various engraved
versions of the P99

WALTHER P99

The double-action Walther P99 pistol originates from
1996. This weapon is available in 9 mm Para (16
rounds) and .40 S&W (12 rounds) caliber. The P99
has a number of special distinguishing features. A large
button is located at the back of the slide to uncock the
cocked firing pin after loading. The cartridge extractor
is on the right-hand side of the slide. When a cartridge
is in the chamber, the cartridge extractor stands
slightly proud, displaying a red dot. When the firing
pin is cocked, a pin carrying a red dot protrudes from
the back of the slide. Finally the back of the grip on the
composite frame can be altered using interchangeable
adapter pieces of different sizes. The ambidextrous
magazine release is at in the back of the trigger guard.
The takedown lever and slide catch are on the left-
hand side of the frame. Rails for mounting special
accessories are fitted at the front and on both sides of
the composite frame. This pistol has an improved
Browning-Petter locking, with a locking lug under the
barrel chamber block. The chamber block locks into
the ejection port in the slide. The standard P99 has
a mat black finish and has been designed as a police
pistol. The P99 in 9 mm Para caliber has a total length
of 180 mm (7 in). The height of this weapon is
135 mm (5^1/$_4$ in) and the width is 29 mm (1^1/$_4$ in). The
barrel length is 102 mm (4 in) and this weapon weighs
630 g (22^1/$_4$ oz). The trigger pressure is 4000 g (8^3/$_4$ lb)
in double-action and 2000 g (4^1/$_2$ lb) in single-action.
The same weapon in .40 S&W caliber has slightly
different dimensions. The total length is 184 mm
(7^1/$_4$ in) and the barrel length is 106 mm (4^1/$_4$ in). The
weight is 655 g (23 oz).

P99 police version with
laser and aiming beam and
(bottom) the P99 Military

Walther P99 QA for special units

Jubilee model P99 for 2000

MODEL P990 is a double-action-only version of the P99. This pistol has a constant trigger pressure of 3500 g (7³/₄ lb) and a trigger pull of 14 mm (¹/₂ in).

Smith & Wesson manufacture approximately the same weapon as a joint venture with Walther. This weapon is known as the SW-99.

WALTHER MODEL R99 LA CHASSE

The American company Smith & Wesson manufactures the R 99 La Chasse revolver for Walther in .357 Magnum caliber. Walther introduced the R 99 as a self-protection weapon. This revolver is available in a mat blued and in a mat stainless steel version. A variety of adapter pieces can be incorporated in the back of the grip on the composite stock, thereby adapting the weapon for the larger hand. The 6-shot double-action revolver has a total length of 215 mm (8¹/₂ in). The barrel length is 76 mm (3 in) and it weighs 980 g. The inscription 'Walther La Chasse' can be found on the frame on the left-hand side of the weapon, with on the barrel, the inscription 'Walther R99'. On the right-hand side of the frame above the

Double-action only P990

MODEL P99 QA has a Quick Action trigger action. Walther developed this weapon for special units. The firing pin is in the half-cocked position as standard. When the trigger is pulled the firing pin is moved a further 3 mm (¹/₄ in) until the pistol is fully cocked, and the shot is fired. The total trigger pull is only 6 mm (¹/₄ in) and the trigger pressure is constant at 3200 g (7 lb 2oz). The uncocking lever of the P99 QA located in the slide has been reduced in size in order to prevent the pistol being uncocked by accident.

MODEL P99 MILITARY differs only from the P99 with its mat green composite frame.

MODEL P99 DUDER/P99 La Chasse is a version for hunting inspectors. This pistol has a composite front sight and a colored composite dot on both sides of the rear sight. The interchangeable adapter piece in the back of the grip is made of walnut.

R99 La Chasse revolver made for Walther by Smith & Wesson

R99 in stainless steel

Stainless steel
Walther TPH

trigger guard there is also the text 'Made in USA by Smith & Wesson Springfield, Mass. for Carl Walther/Ulm'. On the right-hand side of the barrel is the caliber identification '.357 MAGNUM'.

WALTHER MODEL TPH

The TPH is a small pocket pistol that Walther brought on to the market in 1969 in .22 LR and 6,35 mm (.25 ACP) caliber. Walther had intended this weapon mainly for the American market, however this intention was blocked by the Gun Control Act of the same year. This pistol has a height of 93 mm (3³/₄ in) and the minimal height for import weapons was then 102 mm (4 in). Walther found a creative solution to this problem in the form of issuing a manufacturing license to the American company Interarms. This meant that the THP was 'American made' and was therefore no longer subject to import restrictions. The total length of the TPH is 135 mm (5¹/₄ in) and the

width is 23 mm (1 in). In .22 LR caliber it has the barrel length of 71 mm (2³/₄ in) and in 6.35 mm (.25 ACP) this is 73 mm (3 in). The weight is 325 g (11¹/₂ oz). The frame is made of alloy and the slide is blued steel or blank stainless steel. In 1994 Walther produced a limited edition as a jubilee model with the inscription '25 Jahre TPH 1969-1994'. This pistol has recoil locking with a fixed barrel.

WILDEY

Wildey trade mark

The single-action Wildey pistol was developed in 1975 by Wildey J. Moore. This weapon is derived from a 1970 design by the Swedish weapons factory Carl Gustaf. Wildey was plagued with problems from the very start. The supply of this weapon to the weapon trade proved difficult to get off of the ground because Wildey was dependent on suppliers for all manner or parts. Since 1978, Wildey has disappeared from the market place a number of times. This pistol is used for hunting in North- and South America, and is a popular weapon in silhouette shooting. The Wildey pistol was mainly popularized by the film Death Wish III, in which Charles Bronson 'blew away the bad guys'. The Wildey is a so-called gas pressure loader. This principal is mainly applied in rifles. Immediately behind the

Walther TPH pistol in
jubilee edition

Wildey pistol

cartridge chamber, part of the gas pressure is tapped off via a series of ports in the barrel. This gas pressure drives the bolt-action and repeater system. This cycle works as follows: after the pistol is loaded, a cartridge is located in the chamber. The hammer is cocked by pulling the slide backwards. By pulling the trigger, the cartridge in the cartridge chamber is fired. In the short time that the bullet is forced through the barrel, a small part of the created gas pressure is channeled through six gas outlet ports into a cylinder. In the cylinder is a piston and piston rod, which is activated by the gas pressure. The slide is restrained until the bullet leaves the barrel. A locking lug releases the gun lock in the slide, which in turn releases the slide. The slide can then return to its normal position. The cartridge extractor in the slide pulls the empty case from the cartridge chamber, this case is then ejected. As the slide recoils two recoil springs are depressed, and the hammer is once again cocked. When the slide has returned to its normal position, the recoil springs ensure that it is once again thrust forward. As the slide moves forward, it takes a new cartridge from the magazine and pushes it into the barrel chamber. Finally, locking lug rotates the gunlock until the system is once again locked. The pistol is then ready for the next shot. Another feature of the Wildey is the gas regulation. A regulating ring between the frame and the barrel can be rotated in order to close one or more gas outlet ports. This influences the gas pressure supply to the cylinder, this is of special importance for reloaders, where different powder charges are used in the cartridges. The safety catch is located on the left-hand side of the frame. This catch can only be used when the hammer is cocked. In the first position a safety block is rotated between the hammer and the firing pin. The safety catch can also be pushed down further to the second position, this pushes the hammer slightly forwards and blocks it into a sort of halfcocked position. If the weapon is to be fired, the hammer must be first fully cocked by hand. A distinguishing feature

of the Wildey is the interchangeable barrel, making it a simple matter to replace the barrel with a longer one. There are Wildey pistols in a large number of model variations, all of which have more or less the same technical specifications as that of the standard model. This weapon is available (was) in different versions and with barrel lengths of 127, 152, 178, 203 and 254 mm (5, 6, 7, 8 and 10 in). Over the years, the Wildey pistol has been manufactured in different calibers, including .45 Win, Magnum, the 9 mm Winchester Magnum and .475 Wildey-Magnum in the Survivor-model of 1989. There were also a few small series manufactured in the 'wildcat' caliber .357 Peterbilt, developed by the Moores designer Peter Hylenski.

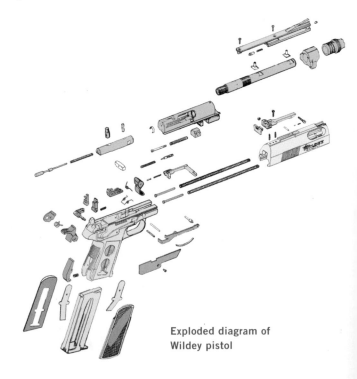

Exploded diagram of Wildey pistol

A comprehensive explanatory glossary

3

ACP:

The usual abbreviation for 'Automatic Colt Pistol' for particular calibers of ammunition. Examples of this are .25 ACP (6.35 mm), .32 ACP (7.65 mm), .380 ATP (9 mm Short) and .45 ACP.

ACP is short for Automatic Colt Pistol

Action of the new Beretta 9000 pistol

ACTION:

The mechanism in a repeating firearm, in other words, for loading and unloading. This term is also used to describe the firing mechanism, such as single-action (abbreviated as SA), double-action (abbreviated as DA) or double-action-only (abbreviated as DAO).

ACTION EXPRESS/AE:

The term for a particular type of cartridge. The .41 Action Express (abbreviated as AE) was developed in 1986 by Evan Whildin, the director of the American company, Action Arms. The Israeli company, Samson, part of IMI (Israel Military Industries), was the first company to produce this cartridge. The cartridge case has a reduced foot with the same diameter as the 9 mm Para (9 x 19 mm) cartridge. Therefore a 9 mm Para pistol can be easily and quickly converted for the .41 AE caliber; only the barrel has to be changed.

Cartridge .41 AE (Action Express)

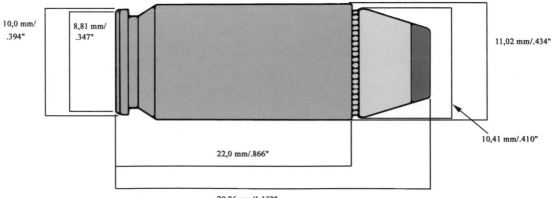

10,0 mm/ .394"

8,81 mm/ .347"

11,02 mm/.434"

10,41 mm/.410"

22,0 mm/.866"

29,26 mm/1.152"

TABLE CALIBER: .41 AE (ACTION EXPRESS)

MAKE	BULLET TIP			VO	EQ
	WEIGHT GRAINS-GRAMS		TYPE	M/S	JOULES
SAMSON	170	11,0	JHP	370	753
SAMSON	200	13,0	FMJ	329	704

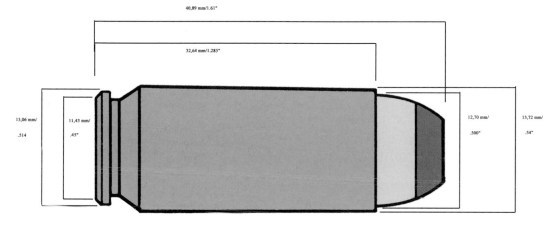

40,89 mm/1.61"

32,64 mm/1.285"

13,06 mm/ .514   11,43 mm/ .45"   12,70 mm/ .500"   13,72 mm/ .54"

The .50 Action Express

The .50 Action Express was designed by Whildin in 1988. The reduced cartridge foot of this .50 AE is the same as that of .44 Magnum cartridge. This means that to change the caliber of a Desert Eagle pistol to .44 Magnum, only the barrel has to be changed.

TABLE CALIBER: .50 AE (ACTION EXPRESS)

MAKE	BULLET TIP			VO	EQ
	WEIGHT GRAINS-GRAMS		TYPE	M/S	JOULES
SAMSON	300	19,4	JSP	421	1.719

ADJUSTABLE SIGHT:

A good adjustable sight can be adjusted both horizontally and vertically. The micrometer sight is a variation on this which can be adjusted extremely accurately. This is important for target practice or with the use of cartridges of different types of ammunition.

Example of an adjustable notched sight on the Browning Buck Mark

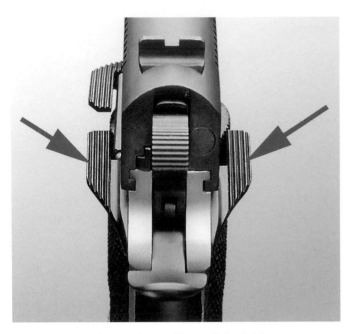

Left/right hand safety-catch on a Charles Daly pistol

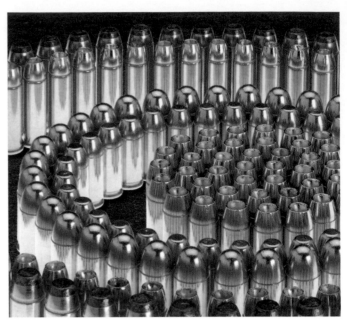

Ranks of Magtech ammunition

AMBIDEXTROUS:

Some of the more expensive models of pistols have different operating elements on either side of the pistol. This is important for some shooting disciplines when it is sometimes necessary to shoot with the 'wrong' or 'weak' hand. It is also useful for left-handed shooters.

AMMUNITION:

Cartridges of every conceivable caliber. The most common classification is for rimfire and centerfire,

depending on the principle of firing. This glossary also contains the cartridges arranged alphabetically by the first letter of the first number: therefore a '.40 S&W cartridge' (pronounced 'forty') appears on page 402 after 'Flint lock'.

AUTOLOADER:

An autoloader is sometimes incorrectly referred to as an 'automatic'. An autoloader is first loaded manually with the first cartridge. At the same time, the firing mechanism is cocked. After firing the pistol, the extractor extracts the empty cartridge case from the

Semi-automatic pistol: the military version of the Walther P99

barrel chamber and ejects it from the firearm. At the same time, the firing mechanism is cocked again. Then a new cartridge is taken from the magazine and placed in the barrel chamber. Finally, the firearm is locked, and a second shot can be fired.

BACKSTRAP:

The back strap is at the back of the grip. In some cases, the back strap is ribbed or serrated for a firmer grip. This is also known as 'checkering'. In Colt pistols and models based on this, the grip safety is often placed on the back strap. This must be firmly pressed before firing or the trigger and/or hammer remain blocked.

BALLISTICS:

This is the science which studies the behavior of projectiles. Internal ballistics concerns the characteristics of a bullet from the moment of firing up to the point that it leaves the muzzle. External ballistics concerns the trajectory of the bullet until it reaches the target. A third type of ballistics concerns the ballistics of injuries. This studies the effect of hitting the target, the distortion of the bullet and the energy produced by striking the target.

Fine trumpet-form barrel of a Charles Daly pistol

BARREL:

The barrel consists of a hollow tube with grooves on the inside known as grooves & lands. These ensure that the bullet rotates around its own axis, (as it passes through the barrel. The extent of this rotation is also affected by the sharpness of the rotating grooves and lands. The length of rotation is also referred to as twist. For example: a twist of 250 mm (9¼ in) means that the grooves and lands rotate completely (360°) over a length of 250 mm (9¼ in). Therefore the external size of the bullet is slightly larger than the internal diameter between the lands (upright edges) in the barrel. Therefore the bullet is pressed through them. This rotation is necessary to give the bullet greater stability in its trajectory. Otherwise, the bullet would start to waver or deviate from its trajectory.

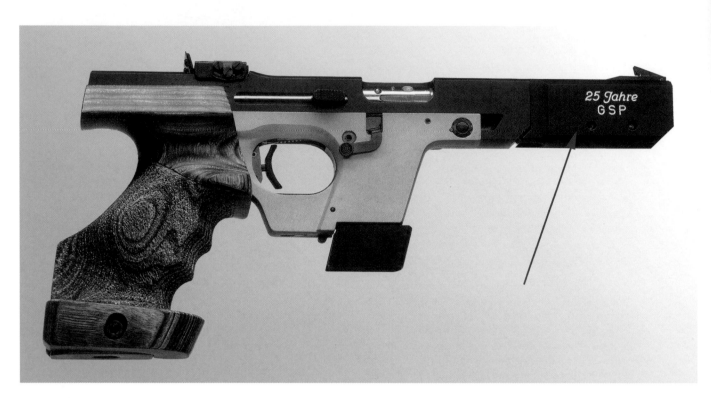

Barrel weight of a Walther GSP

BARREL WEIGHT:

Some match pistols have a separate barrel weight on or around the barrel. This can improve the balance of the firearm for individual shooters. It is also used to reduce the recoil of the firearm. In some firearms, this sort of barrel weight can even be moved along the barrel.

BEAVERTAIL:

The term beavertail refers to an enlarged and often extended back strap. This beavertail fits better in the web (between the thumb and the index finger) of the shooting hand, so that the pistol is more firmly held in the hand. Many large caliber match pistols have a beavertail.

BERDAN PRIMER:

In 1865, A.C. Hobbs of the Union Metallic Company and the American Colonel, H.W. Berdan, designed the so-called Berdan primer. The hole for the primer is at the base of the cartridge. In the middle, there is also a fixed anvil where the firing powder of the primer is struck by the firing pin. The flash of the primer

Example of a beavertail on a Charles Daly pistol

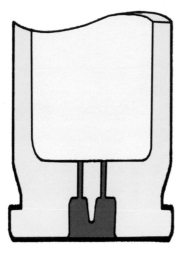

Cross-section diagram of the Berdan ignition

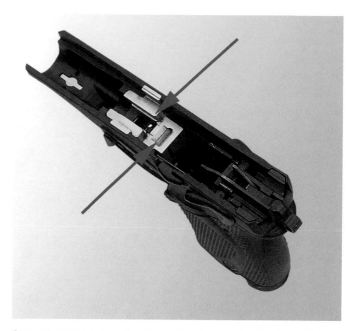

Strengthened recesses for the locking lugs of the Beretta 9000

enters the charge in the cartridge through two or more primer or flash holes. Although this type of primer was an American development, it was used particularly in Europe. Also see Primer, page 425.

BERETTA-9000 LOCKING SYSTEM:

The Beretta 9000 locking system works with two lugs on either side of the chamber block and a fixed locking cam on the bottom of the chamber block. The locking lugs engage the slide directly. After firing, the barrel and the slide move back together. The barrel then moves down through the diagonal locking cam under the chamber block and the lock is removed.

Locking system of the Beretta 9000

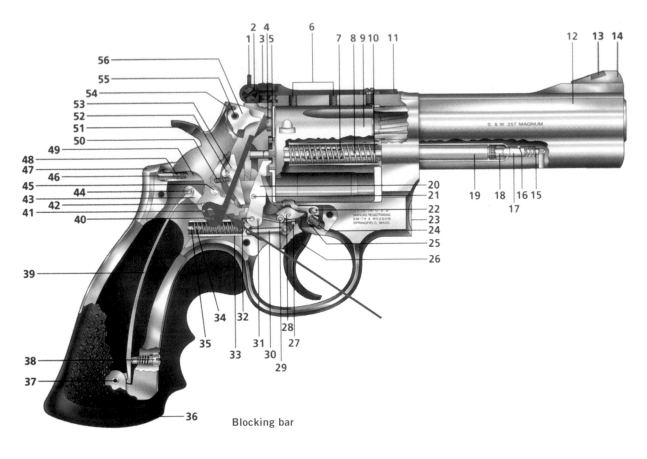

Blocking bar

BLOCKING BAR:

This is usually used for revolvers with a fixed firing pin point on the top of the hammer, as in a Smith & Wesson. Normally the top of the hammer is recessed into a small part of the frame so that the firing pin point does not stick out through the frame. Therefore it cannot reach the primer of the cartridge in the chamber. When the trigger is pulled, the blocking bar moves down slightly. The hammer is no longer held back, so that its firing pin point can strike the primer.

BLOWBACK:

This locking system is used in pistols of a relatively light caliber. The weight of the steel slide means that the locking system is delayed. The bullet has already left the barrel before the slide goes into operation as a result of the reaction of firing. In the illustration, the steel slide is shown in red.

Recoil/blowback locking

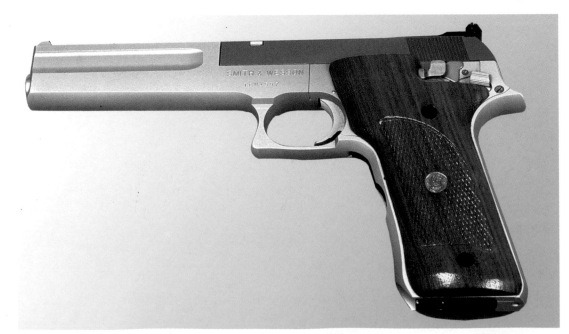

Blued revolver

BLUED:

This term indicates a chemical process in which the surface of the metal is artificially oxidized by particular minerals. This means that the polished metal acquires a dark blue protective layer, which prevents it from becoming rusty.

BOLT-ACTION:

This is a locking system which is used in pistols for long distance shooting. This pistol is actually an extremely short bolt-action rifle. Depending on the system that is used, the hand-operated bolt has a number of locking lugs on the front and/or back. When it is locked, these engage in recesses in the receiver of the pistol so that the bolt and the receiver are one unit. A good example of this sort of mechanism is the Remington XP-100. It is a robust and reliable locking system, resistant to very high gas pressures. These sorts of pistols often use heavy rifle cartridges.

Bolt-action of the Remington XP-100

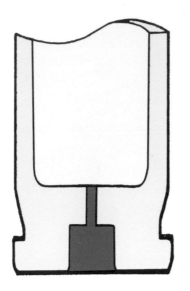

Cross-section diagram of Boxer ignition

Tip-up break open revolver

BOXER PRIMER:

This firing principle was designed in 1867 by the British Colonel E.M. Boxer. There is one central firing hole in the bottom of the cartridge. The primer has a built-in anvil so that the fulminate can be ignited by striking the firing pin. Curiously, this system is also known as the 'American Primer', because it was used particularly in the USA. Nowadays, this is the most usual principle in commercial ammunition because the cartridge case can be easily reloaded. Also see Primer, page 425.

BREAK-OPEN REVOLVER:

This is a system in which the barrel and the frame are connected by a hinge. In order to open the firearm to load or unload it, the barrel is folded up or down. This means that the back of the cylinder become accessible.

BROWNING:

John Moses Browning (1855-1926) was one of the leading designers of firearms in history. He worked for the American company Winchester and the Belgian FN factory, amongst other companies. His name is linked to many pistols and guns.

Pivot of a break open revolver

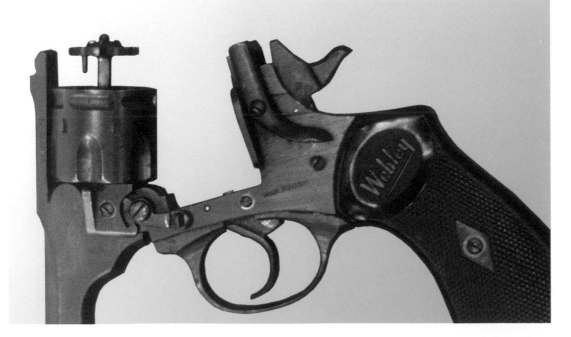

BROWNING-COLT LOCKING SYSTEM:

This system works with one or two hinge points under the barrel. Above the barrel there are one to three cams or lugs. When the pistol is locked, these engage in the corresponding recesses on the inside of the slide.

After the shot, the slide and the barrel move back a few millimeters as a result of the effect of the gas pressure. Then the barrel drops with the help of the hinge point. As a result, the cams disengage from the recesses on the inside of the slide. In this way, the slide and the barrel are disconnected and the slide moves back on its own.

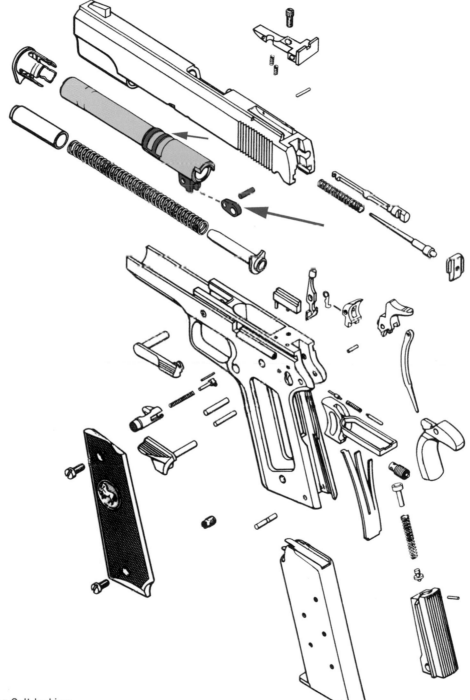

Browning-Colt locking

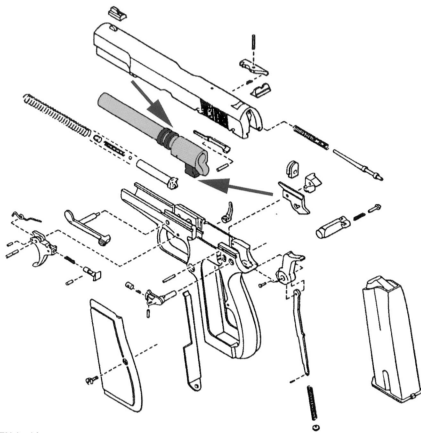

Browning-FN locking

BROWNING-FN LOCKING SYSTEM:

There is one fixed barrel shank under the barrel, instead of a hinge. On the top of the barrel there are two cams or lugs. After the shot, the slide and the barrel both move back a few millimeters. Because of the shape of the barrel shank, the barrel is forced down so that the cams on top of the barrel disengage from the recesses on the inside of the slide. The barrel then remains in place while the slide goes back by itself.

BROWNING-PETTER (SIG) LOCKING SYSTEM:

This system works in almost the same way as the Browning-FN system, but there are no lugs or cams on the top of the barrel. The jacket of the barrel chamber has a particular shape. This solid block in its entirety works as a lock-up. In fact, it fits exactly into the recess of the ejection port in the slide. This is how the pistol is locked.

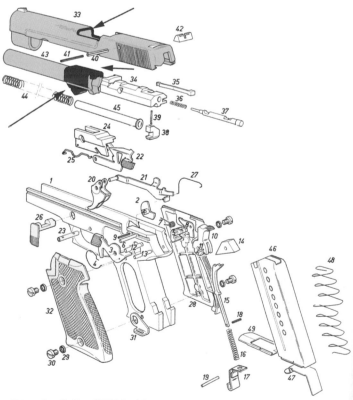

Browning-Petter (SIG) locking

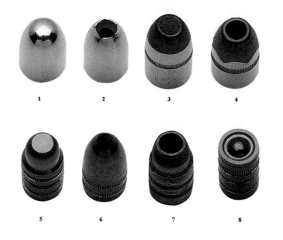

Various types of bullet

BULLET:

The bullet is the projectile which is pressed into the front of the cartridge case. The bullet can have different shapes. It can be pointed, conical, flat or it can have a hollow point. The choice of the specific shape is not arbitrary, but is related to the use of the pistol. For example, the flat-nosed Wadcutter is a real match bullet for a revolver, and for some models of pistols: it is a very stable bullet which produces sharp round holes in the target. A bullet with a hollow point has great stopping force because of the distortion caused after it reaches the target. The bullets shown here are: 1. full mantle jacket; 2. jacketed hollow-point; 3. half-jacket; 4. half-jacket hollow-point; 5. semi- wadcutter; 6. lead round nose bullet; 7. semi-wadcutter hollow-point; 8. wadcutter. The type of bullet is often abbreviated in lists of the manufacturers of ammunition. The most usual abbreviations are:

- FMJ: full mantle jacket
- FP: flat point
- HP: hollow-point
- HV: high velocity
- JHP: jacket(ed) hollow-point
- JSP: jacketed soft point
- LRN: lead round nose
- LSWC: lead semi-wadcutter
- RN: round nose
- SP: soft point
- SWC: semi-wadcutter
- SXT: a special hollow-point from Winchester
- TC: truncated cone (flat or blunt nose)
- WC: wadcutter
- XTP: a special hollow-point made by Hornady

BULLET WEIGHT (GRAINS/GRAMS):

The weight of the bullet is important for reloaders. A special charge is used for each bullet weight in a particular caliber. This is always specifically indicated in the reloading tables of manufacturers of charge and bullets. Internationally the weight of the bullet is always indicated in grains: 1 grain is 0.0648 g. For example, a bullet weight of 158 grains weighs 10.2 g.

CALIBER:

This is the diameter of a rifled barrel, i.e., with grooves and lands, usually measured from land to land. In American and English cartridges this size is given in tenths of inches; in Europe it is usually given in millimeters. The indication of the caliber sometimes gives rise to confusion. In the past, this was not always described very accurately. The 9 x 19 mm caliber is simple and straightforward: a bullet with a diameter of 9 mm in a cartridge case with a length of

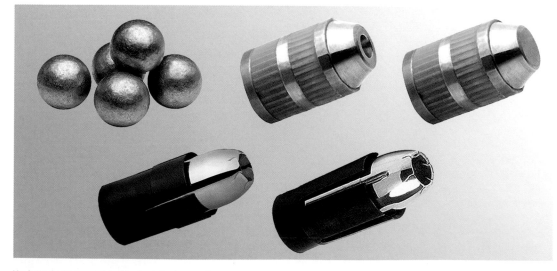

Various bullets and balls for black powder weapons

19 mm (0.75 in). However, is a .357 Magnum cartridge thinner than a .38 Special? If you work it out, it would appear to be, but it isn't. According to the calculation, a .357 in is 9.07 mm, while a .38 in is 9.65 mm. A .357 Magnum cartridge has a bullet with a diameter of .357 in, but a .38 Special cartridge uses the same bullet. The bullet for a .45 ACP cartridge has a diameter of .451 in. A bullet with a caliber of .25 ACP does not measure .25 in, but .257 in, i.e., 6.35 mm, so that the European description of this cartridge is correct. Rifle cartridges are sometimes described in an even more complicated way. Thus the .30-06 Springfield cartridge has a bullet of .30 in, and the figure '06' refers to the year, 1906.

Cut-away diagram of a cartridge

CARTRIDGE:

Almost all rifle, carbine, pistol and revolver cartridges consist of four different parts: the cartridge case, the primer, the powder and the bullet. In general, firing a cartridge takes place as follows: the cartridge is fired because the firing pin strikes the primer of the cartridge. The charge is in the primer. This is a chemical mixture which ignites when it is struck lightly. The small charge ignites in milliseconds, and the flash passes to the charge in the cartridge case. This is how the powder is ignited. The powder in the cartridge produces an enormous quantity of gas during combustion. In a fraction of a second, the pressure in the cartridge case increases so much that the bullet is forcefully pressed out of the cartridge case. The cartridge case itself is tightly sealed on two sides: against the wall of the chamber all round, and against the bolthead at the back. In a cannon, this is known as the breechblock, in a rifle as the bolt, in a pistol it is a slide, and in a revolver it is the recoil plate, which is part of the revolver frame. The cartridge case is usually made of brass. This is a soft, elastic material. When the powder is ignited, the cartridge case expands against the wall of the chamber of the barrel. This results in a good gas seal. This is important,

because the pressure of the gas must be used as much as possible to propel the bullet. The bullet accelerates because of the expanding gas. The gas released by igniting the powder develops enormous pressure: in a 9 mm Para cartridge, up to 2500 atmosphere (at.), in a rifle cartridge up to 4000 at., or more. From the point of view of ballistics, the conversion of powder into energy is fairly inefficient. In fact, of the total energy content of the powder, 25% is transferred to the firearm in the form of heat. Of the remaining 75%, only 35% is transferred to the bullet after the muzzle, while 40% of the total energy leaves the muzzle without being used.

CARTRIDGE CASE:

The cartridge case is like the packaging for the components of the cartridge. The bullet is jammed into the front of the cartridge case. The charge is inside the cartridge case, and the primer is in the bottom of the cartridge case. The most usual material for the cartridge cases of pistol and revolver cartridges is brass, an alloy of copper and zinc. Sometimes brass cartridge cases are also coated in nickel or chrome. The cartridge cases of old ammunition from the war can be made of iron. It is not advisable to use this sort of ammunition in expensive modern firearms.

Examples of cartridge tube materials. Left, brass tube; right, nickel-coated brass – both by Remington

CARTRIDGE INDICATOR:

The cartridge indicator is used by a number of pistol manufacturers as a safety system. It indicates that there is a cartridge in the chamber. For example, this can be seen from a pin which protrudes from the back or top of the slide. Sometimes the extractor itself

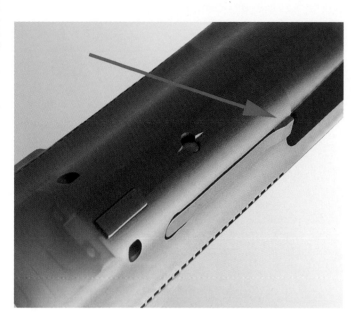

Cartridge indicator on the cartridge extractor of a Beretta pistol

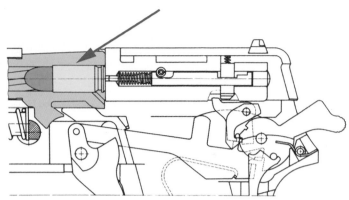

The chamber of the barrel

case. The Berdan system has two or more. When the fulminate ignites in the primer, a flash passes to the charge in the cartridge case. (Also see Berdan and Boxer.)

CHAMBER:

The chamber is the first part of the barrel where the cartridge to be shot is pushing in by the slide or bolt. This part is thicker than the barrel itself. This is necessary because high pressures and a high temperature develop when the cartridge is fired. If the wall of the cartridge chamber were not thick enough, it would explode and the shooter could be struck by the fragments. The firing of a .45 ACP cartridge produces a gas pressure of approximately 1400 bar in the chamber of the barrel; a 9 mm Para cartridge actually produces about 2700 bar. In a revolver, the cylinder has several chambers, depending on the magazine capacity, e.g., 5 rounds, 6 rounds, or even more.

COLT:

Samuel P. Colt lived from 1814 to 1862. He became famous for his revolver designs, and his place in the history of firearms is just as important as that of John Moses Browning. In 1849, Colt was made an honorary colonel of the militia of the American state of Connecticut. After his death, his company marketed one of the best-known firearms, the Colt Single Action Army 1873, or Peacemaker revolver.

COMPENSATOR:

This system is used to counteract the recoil or kickback when a firearm is fired. There are various different systems.

1. Just in front of the muzzle, there are a number of lengthwise holes or slits in the top of the barrel. Just

serves as an indicator. This sticks out slightly when there is a cartridge in the chamber. In Beretta and Taurus pistols, a red dot then appears on the end of the extractor.

CENTERFIRE:

In a centerfire cartridge, the primer is in the middle of the foot of the cartridge case. The Boxer system has a single central flash channel in the foot of the cartridge

Drawing of the centerfire system

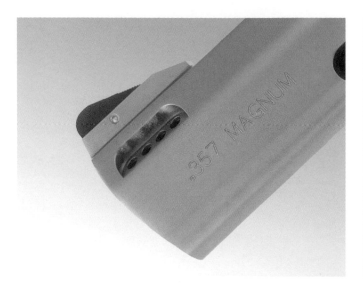

Integral compensator of a Taurus revolver barrel

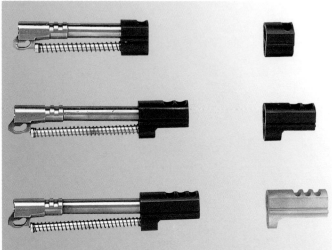

Pistol compensators with single, twin, and triple chambers

before the bullet leaves the barrel, there is an extremely high pressure of gas in the barrel. Some of this escapes via the holes or slits. This produces the effect of a rocket exhaust, so that barrel is forced down. As the barrel wants to lift up at the same time because of the force of the reaction of firing, these forces partly cancel each other out. Mag-Na-Port was the first to use this system.

2. A compensator system can also consist of a sort of end piece attached to the muzzle. In a way, the muzzle is lengthened. The compensator holes or slits are then made in this end piece. If the hole for the pressure of the gas is large, it is described as a single chamber compensator. If there are several of these holes, it can be described as a two, three or four-chamber compensator. In many cases, this sort of compensator also has a cosmetic character so that the firearm looks 'cool'.

CYLINDER:

This is a round piece of steel with a number of cartridge chambers bored through it in a circle. For every shot, the cylinder rotates to the next position, so that a new cartridge chamber is in front of the barrel every time.

Integral compensator in a Taurus pistol barrel and slide

Revolver cylinder of a Kora revolver

Revolver cylinder of a Taurus revolver

CYLINDER AXLE (CYLINDER PIN):

The cylinder rotates around a central axis, which is usually also connected to the ejector rod and the extractor star. When it is unloaded, the ejector rod is manually pushed back if there is a swing-out cylinder. This means that the empty cartridge cases are removed from the cylinder chambers by the extractor star. That is why this rod is known as the ejector rod. In the exploded diagram shown below, the cylinder pin is indicated with a red arrow.

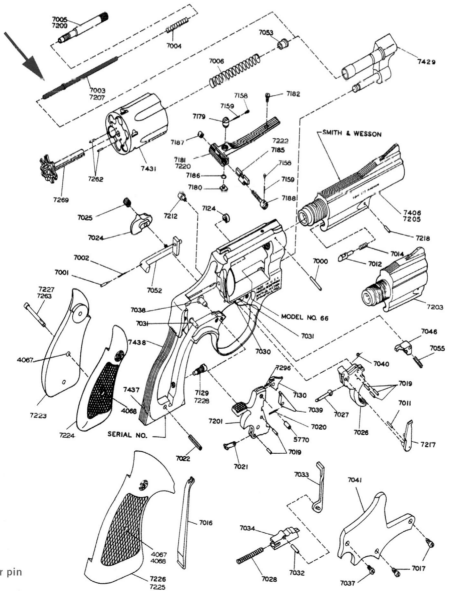

Cylinder pin

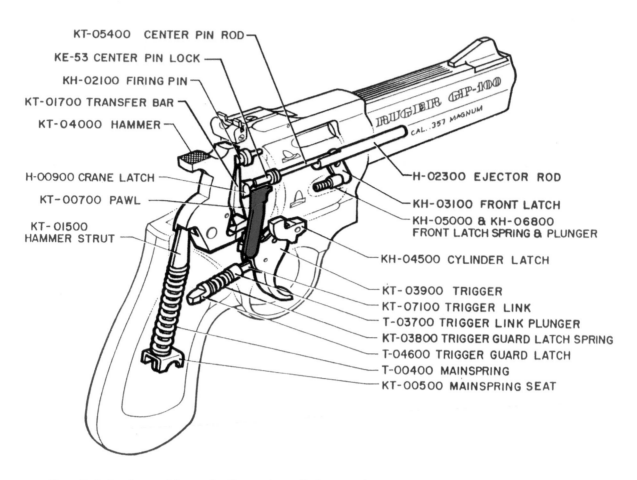

KT-05400 CENTER PIN ROD
KE-53 CENTER PIN LOCK
KH-02100 FIRING PIN
KT-01700 TRANSFER BAR
KT-04000 HAMMER

H-00900 CRANE LATCH
KT-00700 PAWL
KT-01500 HAMMER STRUT

H-02300 EJECTOR ROD
KH-03100 FRONT LATCH
KH-05000 & KH-06800 FRONT LATCH SPRING & PLUNGER
KH-04500 CYLINDER LATCH
KT-03900 TRIGGER
KT-07100 TRIGGER LINK
T-03700 TRIGGER LINK PLUNGER
KT-03800 TRIGGER GUARD LATCH SPRING
T-04600 TRIGGER GUARD LATCH
T-00400 MAINSPRING
KT-00500 MAINSPRING SEAT

The cylinderhand or pawl for moving the revolver cylinder around

CYLINDER HAND/PAWL:

The cylinder hand is usually linked to the trigger mechanism. As soon as the trigger of a double-action revolver is pulled, the cylinder hand presses against the cylinder lug on the back of the extractor star. In this way, the cylinder rotates to the next position. In a single-action revolver the same thing happens when the hammer is cocked.

CYLINDER LATCH:

This is a latch which is usually on the left of the frame, behind the cylinder. It is used to pull back a spring bolt catch. The cylinder can then be folded out of the revolver frame.

Cylinder latch for swinging the cylinder out

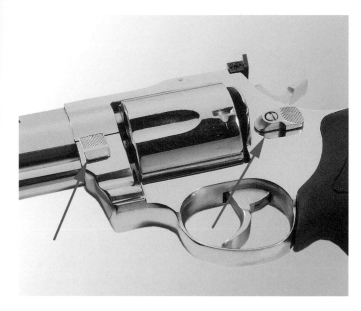

Cylinder lock-up/locking: note the red arrows

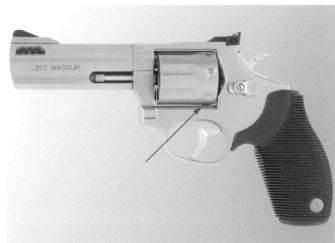

Cylinderstop

CYLINDER LOCK/UP:

This system ensures that the cylinder is safely and firmly locked in the revolver frame. There are a number of locking points.

1. A spring on the cylinder latch fits into a recess at the back of the ejector star. Sometimes this can also be a spring steel bullet.
2. The cylinder hand locks into the revolver frame with a spring cam or steel bearing.
3. The end of the ejector rod locks into a spring pin in the ejector shroud.

In many cases, several systems are combined.

CYLINDER STOP:

This is a small spring cam connected to the trigger group of the revolver. Usually this cam is in the frame below the cylinder. As soon as the cylinder has been rotated once for a new shot, this cam fits into a recess in the cylinder. The cylinder is then blocked. The firearm can be safely fired. Every cylinder chamber has such a recess. In some models of revolvers this cam is built in, in the bridge above the cylinder, but this is unusual. In many revolvers, the recess for the cylinder stop is exactly on the cylinder chambers. However, some models have this recess between the cylinder chambers.

UNCOCKING LEVER:

A mechanism which is usually found on double-action pistols. The system ensures that a cocked hammer can

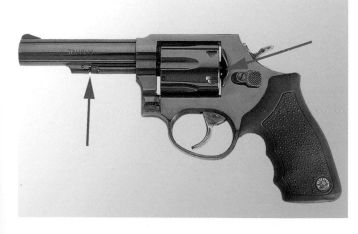

Cylinder lock-up/locking: note the red arrows

Decocking/uncocking lever of Sig P220 pistol

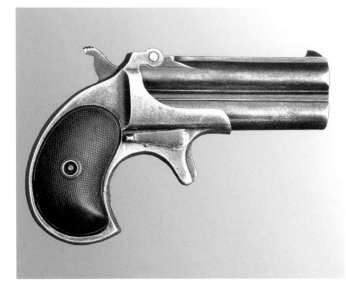

Derringer double-barrel pistol

Double-action pistol

be safely uncocked. This requires some explanation. When a pistol is loaded, a cartridge is also placed into the chamber from the magazine. The hammer remains pulled back and cocked. A uncocking lever ensures that the hammer clicks forwards, though no shot is fired. Usually this is done with the help of a firing pin safety. Sometimes, the firing pin is also pressed back out of reach of the hammer.

DERRINGER:

This is a small pocket pistol, based on an original design by Henry Derringer. The firearm usually has two barrels and no magazine. Therefore it is actually a two-shot pistol. Henry Derringer made these pocket pistols in his Derringer Revolver & Pistol Company in Philadelphia, Pennsylvania. The double 'r' appeared in the name of the pistol in the past, because Henry prohibited other manufacturers from making this type of firearm using his name. The Derringer is still produced today.

DOUBLE-ACTION (DA):

Double-action means that in this type of pistol the hammer is cocked mechanically, during the first stage when the trigger is pulled. In the second stage of the trigger crawl, the hammer is released, moves forwards and the cartridge is fired. In pistols, repeat shots are always fired in the single-action mode. During the

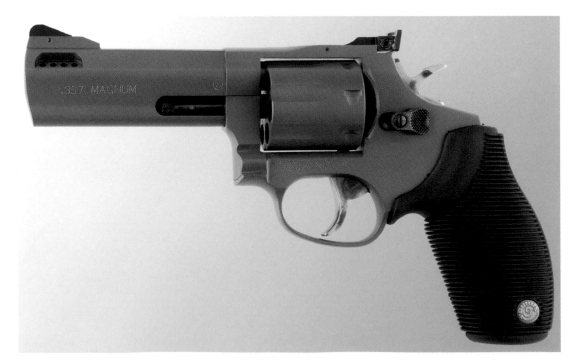

Double-action revolver

Double-action pistol

Ejection port in the slide of a Beretta Cougar

repeat action, the hammer is actually cocked automatically when the slide moves back. In double-action revolvers, the cylinder is rotated when the trigger is pulled. The hammer is cocked at the same time.

DOUBLE-ACTION ONLY (DAO):

Double-action-only is a double-action system which is usually used in pistols and revolvers without an external hammer. Every shot is fired in double-action mode.

A DAO pistol sometimes only has a firing pin safety. This sort of firearm is always carried with a cartridge in the chamber and can therefore be fired extremely quickly. A DAO revolver always has a blocking or transfer bar.

EJECTOR PORT:

This is usually a recess in the slide of the pistol through which the empty cartridge can be ejected from the firearm. At the same time, it serves to check whether the firearm is unloaded. In some pistols, the ejection port can also be part of the locking system. In this case, the solid chamber block of the barrel fits into the ejection port. Also see the Browning-Petter locking system.

EJECTOR:

This part serves to eject the cartridge case which has been used in the shot, through a hole from the side of the slide. Sometimes the firing pin serves as the ejector in combination with the extractor. The Colt 1911 and models based on this contain an ejector in the frame.

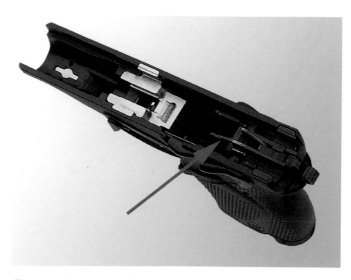

Ejector of the Beretta 9000

Double-action only revolver

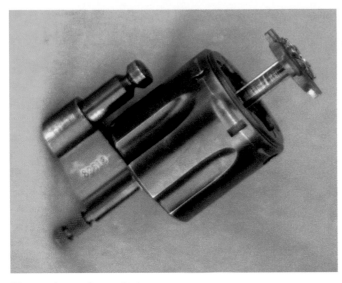

Ejector of a revolver cylinder

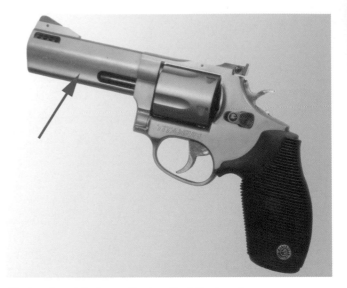

Ejector shroud that runs the length of the barrel

Revolvers could also be said to have an ejector, viz., the extractor star. This is connected to the ejector rod, which has to be operated manually.

EJECTOR ROD:

The cylinder rotates around a central axis connected to the ejector rod and the extractor star. In the case of a swing-out cylinder, the ejector rod is manually pushed back when the firearm is unloaded. The empty cartridge cases are ejected from the cylinder chambers by the extractor star. For this reason, this bar is also known as the ejector bar.

EJECTOR SHROUD:

In a large number of models of revolvers, the ejector bar is encased in a shroud under the barrel. Sometimes this shroud continues right up to the muzzle, and at the same time, serves as a barrel weight. However, an ejector bar can also be locked in a simple lug under the

Ejector shroud runs half the length of barrel

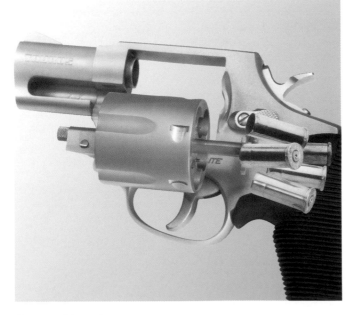

Ejector rod in action

Short ejector shroud

Cartridge extractor

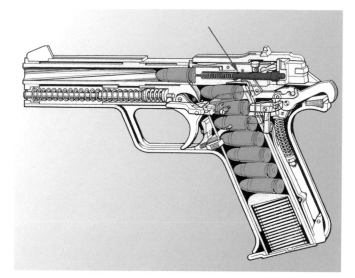

Firing pin with firing pin spring of a Benelli pistol

barrel. In many types of revolver, the ejector shroud forms part of the locking system. In this case, the end of the ejector rod fits into a spring catch in the ejector shroud.

EXTRACTOR:

This is a small hook-shaped component which hooks behind the edge of the cartridge case as soon as it is pressed through the slide of the pistol into the barrel chamber. After the cartridge has been fired, the slide moves back when it has been unlocked so that the extractor extracts the empty cartridge case from the chamber.

Examples of falling-block locking

FALLING BLOCK LOCKING:

This locking system is used by Walther in various models of pistols. In addition, the system is also used in various different Beretta and Taurus models.
The falling block locking works as follows. There is a steel lug under the barrel chamber. In this there is a hinged steel block that connects the barrel and the slide. When a shot is fired, the barrel and the slide first slide back together about 8 mm (.315 in). Then an operating pin of the locking block strikes a lug in the frame. This pin presses the locking block down, so that the locking system between the barrel and the slide is removed. The slide now moves back on its own, ejects the empty cartridge case and possibly replaces a new cartridge. In the illustration, you can see that the upper barrel is locked, while the lower barrel is unlocked.

FIRING PIN:

The firing pin is usually a thin pin. The front is more or less pointed so that it is better able to strike the primer in the bottom of the cartridge case. The firing pin is broader at the back so that it can absorb the strike of the hammer. There is a coiled firing pin spring around the firing pin. When the hammer has struck, the firing pin springs back into its starting position.
In some revolver models the point of the firing pin is by the nose of the hammer. This point strikes through a slit in the frame when the pistol is fired, so that it can touch the primer.

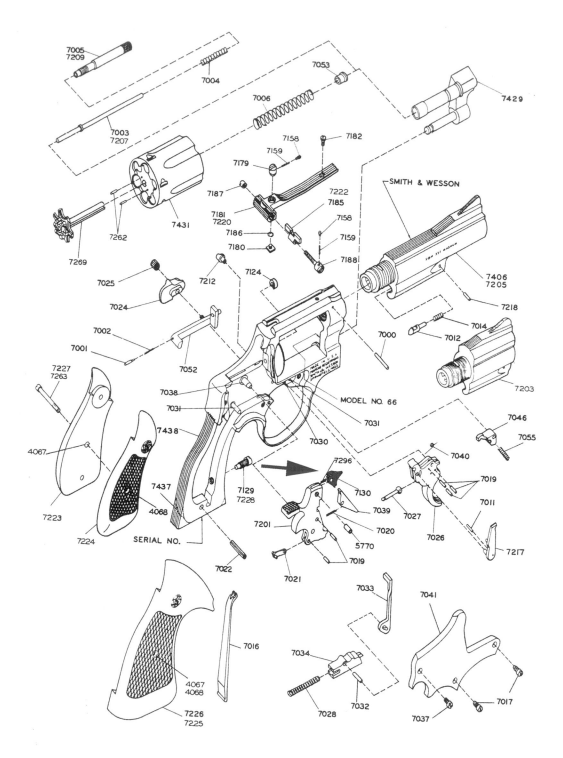

The fixed firing pin point on the hammer of a revolver

FIRING PIN SAFETY:

This blocks the movement of the firing pin lengthwise. There are different systems for this. One of these is the Walther system, in which the firing pin remains in the starting position and cannot be struck by the hammer. In addition, the firing pin is blocked by a firing pin safety peg. By pulling the trigger, this peg is pushed up or down. Depending on the system, this is done by the trigger bar or by a guide bar connected to this. In another system, the firing pin itself is pushed up so that the hammer can strike it.

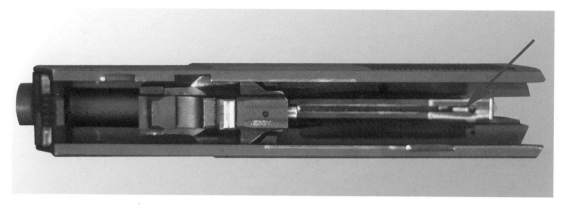

Bottom of the slide of a Walther P5: the firing pin safety peg is indicated by a red arrow

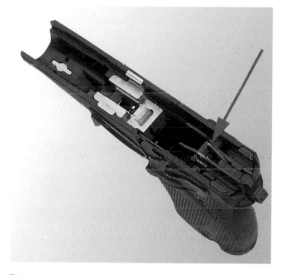

The locating lever for the firing pin safety
of a Beretta 9000

FN 5.7 mm cartridge for the Five-Seven pistol and
FN-P90 machine-pistol

The first illustration shows the bottom of the slide of a Walther P5. The red arrow shows the bottom of the firing pin safety peg. The second illustration shows the top of the frame of a Berretta 9000. The guide bar which pushes the firing pin safety up is indicated with a red arrow. The bar next to this is the ejector. Revolvers often also have a safety system: see the blocking bar (page 384), and the transfer bar (page 442).

5.7 X 28 MM-SS190 CARTRIDGE:

The Belgian arms company Fabrique Nationale (FN) developed this caliber in about 1985. The cartridge is used for their new machine-gun, the P90, and the related army pistol, the Five Seven. FN hopes that this cartridge will replace the 9 mm Para as standard NATO ammunition. The cartridge is most like a rifle

cartridge, but functions perfectly in a pistol. The bullet has an effective range of 200 m, and is able to penetrate the 48-layer bulletproof Kevlar vest.

TABLE CALIBER: 5,7 X 28 MM-SS190				
MAKE	BULLET TIP		VO	EQ
	WEIGHT GRAINS/GRAMS	TYPE	M/S	JOULES
5,7 x 28 MM	93 6	VARIOUS	715	1534

FIXED SIGHTS:

This is a fixed rear sight leaf on the back of the bridge (revolver) or slide (pistol). This type of sight is often used in service arms.

Fixed sights

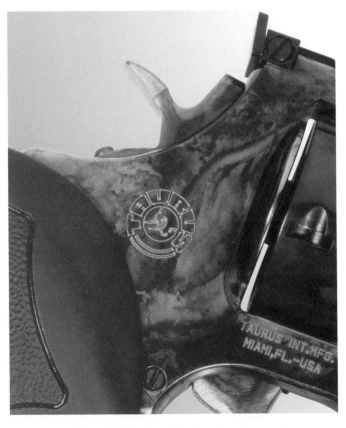

Example of a flame-hardened revolver casing

FLAME-HARDENED:

This term is used for a good method of surface treatment, the flame-hardened surface, which was used particularly during the time of the Wild West. The steel of the revolver frame is first fired up, and then quickly cooled in oil or water.

FLINT LOCK:

This term refers to the use of a piece of flint in the claw of the hammer. When the trigger is pulled, this flint strikes an iron plate known as the steel, creating a spark which falls into a powder pan. From the powder pan there is a small hole into the barrel. In this way, the flash reaches the charge.

.40 SMITH & WESSON CARTRIDGE:

This cartridge was developed jointly by Winchester and Smith & Wesson in 1989. At the time the FBI used the Smith & Wesson model 1076 as a service pistol with a 10 mm Auto cartridge with a lighter charge. The factory engineers thought that the ballistic properties of this cartridge could also be achieved with a shorter cartridge case. This led to narrower grips and also benefited the precision of the shot. Most .40 S&W factory cartridges achieve

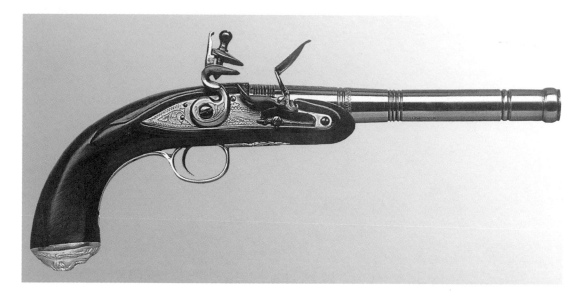

Example of a flintlock pistol by Pietta

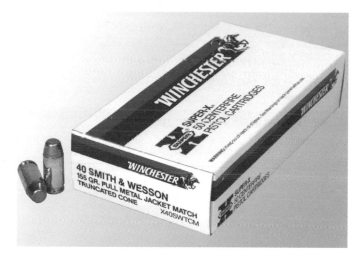

The .40 Smith & Wesson cartridge by Winchester

MAKE	BULLET TIP			VO	EO
	WEIGHT GRAINS/GRAMS		TYPE	M/S	JOULES
WINCHESTER	140	9.1	SUPERCLEAN JSP	352	564
FIOCCHI	145	9.4	FMJ-HP	370	643
REMINGTON	145	9.4	DISINTEGRATOR	331	515
FEDERAL	155	10.0	HYDRA-SHOK JHP	348	606
REMINGTON	155	10.0	JHP	367	678
WINCHESTER	155	10.0	SILVERTIP-HP	367	678
MAGTECH	160	10.4	LSWC	355	653
FEDERAL	165	10.7	HYDRA-SHOK JHP	297	472
REMINGTON	165	10.7	JHP	351	659
WINCHESTER	165	10.7	SXT	344	635
FIOCCHI	170	11.0	FMJ-TC	365	734
FEDERAL	180	11.7	HYDRA-SHOK JHP	300	527
REMINGTON	180	11.7	JHP	309	559
WINCHESTER	180	11.7	SXT	308	553

TABLE CALIBER: .40 SMITH & WESSON

a bullet energy of about 650 Joules in average pistols. This relatively high energy is achieved with high gas pressure. In pistols with a short barrel (up to 89 mm / 3½ in), this produces a large flash at the muzzle, and quite a lot of extra noise. The .40 S&W cartridge is extremely popular. It has now largely replaced both the 10 mm Auto and the .41 AE.

.45 ACP CARTRIDGE:

The .45 ACP cartridge was developed by John Moses Browning. He developed this caliber in 1905. In 1911, Colt marketed the famous Model 1911. In fact, this pistol was also designed by Browning. The .45 ACP was

one of the most powerful military pistol cartridges. Many manufacturers include .45 ACP pistols in their range.

During the Second World War a number of different machine-guns were also used in this caliber, such as the Thompson and the Grease Gun. The Colt 1911 and the modified Model 1911-A1 were manufactured in enormous numbers and copied in many countries. In 1985, the .45 ACP army pistol was replaced in the USA by the Berretta 92F, referred to as the 'Pistol 9 mm M9'. In the past, the .45 ACP proved itself as a first-class army caliber with excellent stopping powers. In addition, it is also popular in the sport of shooting. Encouraged by the demand for more

The .45 ACP (Automatic Colt Pistol) cartridge

power in sports circles, a number of ammunition manufacturers developed .45 ACP+P ammunition. The gas pressure of this is higher than that of the standard .45 ACP. The .45 ACP+P with a bullet of 200 grains (13 g) achieves a muzzle velocity of approximately 305m/s (1000fps). In some countries the civilian use of so-called government calibers is prohibited. This also applies to the .45 ACP cartridge. To get round this prohibition, sports shooters in these countries use .45 HP or .45 Automatic Short. The cartridge case of this cartridge is only 1 mm (.039 in) shorter. The ballistic properties are the same as those of .45 ACP cartridge. The abbreviation 'HP' stands for the manufacturer Hirtenberger Patronen from Austria.

.45 COLT CARTRIDGE:

In 1973, Colt marketed his famous Peacemaker revolver, in combination with this cartridge. In 1875, the American army chose this firearm with the related cartridge as the official weapon for the army. It was used up to 1892 when this revolver was replaced by the Colt New Army and the New Navy in .38 Long Colt caliber.

The .45 Colt played an important role in the Wild West. Originally, it was loaded with 40 grains (2.6 g) of black powder and had a 255 grains (16.5 g) lead bullet. The cartridge is fairly popular with sports

MAKE	BULLET TIP			VO	EQ
	WEIGHT GRAINS-GRAMS		TYPE	M/S	JOULES
WINCHESTER	170	11.0	SUPERCLEAN-JSP	320	564
REMINGTON	175	11.3	DISINTEGRATOR	311	547
FEDERAL	185	12.0	FMJ-SWC-MATCH	236	334
HORNADY	185	12.0	JHP-XTP	290	505
REMINGTON	185	12.0	JSP	305	558
REMINGTON	185	12.0	JHP+P	348	727
WINCHESTER	185	12.0	SILVERTIP-HP	305	558
HORNADY	200	13.0	FMJ	305	605
MAGTECH	200	13.0	LSWC	290	545
FIOCCHI	226	14.6	LRN-TEFLON	230	387
FEDERAL	230	14.9	HYDRA-SHOK-JHP	259	500
GECO/RWS	230	14.9	FMJ	270	550
REMINGTON	230	14.9	JHP	267	531
SELL-BELLOT	230	14.9	FMJ	260	504
WINCHESTER	230	14.9	SXT	268	537

TABLE CALIBER: .45 ACP

shooters and hunters because of its great accuracy. With regard to stopping power, it is only really superseded by the .44 Rem. Magnum, with the exception of less common exotic calibers.

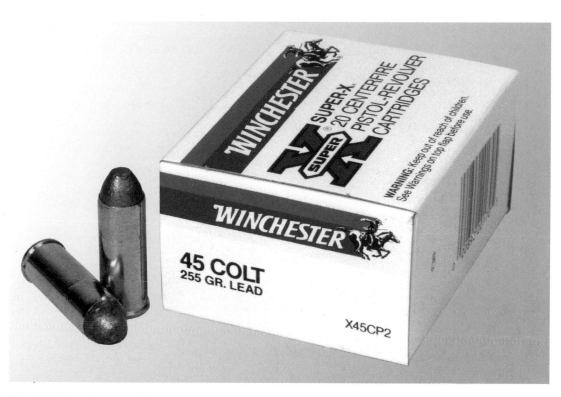

The .45 Colt revolver cartridge

TABLE CALIBER: .45 COLT

MAKE	WEIGHT GRAINS-GRAMS		BULLET TIP TYPE	VO M/S	EQ JOULES
FEDERAL	225	14.6	SWC-HP	274	548
REMINGTON	225	14.6	SWC (KEITH)	293	627
WINCHESTER	225	14.6	SILVERTIP-HP	280	574
REMINGTON	250	16.2	LRN	262	556
WINCHESTER	255	16.5	LRN	262	566

.45 WIN. MAGNUM CARTRIDGE:

The .45 Win. Magnum cartridge was developed by Winchester in 1977 and marketed in 1979. Originally this caliber was intended for use with the well- known Wildey pistol. Later, more manufacturers started making firearms for this cartridge. One example of this is the Grizzly, based on the well-known Colt-1911 A1. Unfortunately the Grizzly is no longer made. Another example is the single shot Thompson Center Contender pistol. The reason for the development of the .45 Win. Magnum was the demand for a pepped-up .45 ACP cartridge from silhouette shooters. Later it also became quite popular with North American hunters. The starting speed of the bullet is almost 70% higher than that of the .45 ACP. The bullet energy is even 200% higher. This means that the .45 Win. Magnum is in the same category as the .45 Rem Magnum.

TABLE CALIBER: .45 WINCHESTER MAGNUM

MAKE	WEIGHT GRAINS-GRAMS		BULLET TIP TYPE	VO M/S	EQ JOULES
WINCHESTER	260	16.8	PARTITION GOLD	366	1128

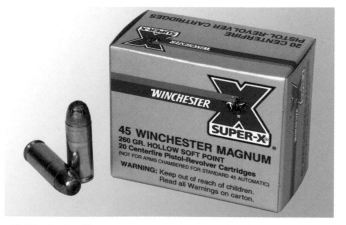

.45 Winchester Magnum

Winchester .44 Remington Magnum cartridge

TABLE CALIBER: .44 REMINGTON MAGNUM

MAKE	BULLET	TIP		VO	EQ
	WEIGHT GRAINS-GRAMS		TYPE	M/S	JOULES
FEDERAL	180	11.7	HI-SHOK JHP	491	1410
HORNADY	180	11.7	JHP-XTP	491	1410
REMINGTON	180	11.7	SEMI-JHP	491	1410
HORNADY	200	13.0	JHP-XTP	457	1358
WINCHESTER	210	13.6	SILVERTIP-HP	381	989
FEDERAL	240	15.6	HYDRA-SHOK-JHP	360	1010
HORNADY	240	15.6	JHP-XTP	412	1324
MAGTECH	240	15.6	SEMI-JSP	360	1010
REMINGTON	240	15.6	SEMI-JHP	360	1010
FEDERAL	250	16.2	FMJ PROF. MATCH	360	1050
WINCHESTER	250	16.2	PARTITION GOLD	375	1139
REMINGTON	275	17.8	JHP CORE-LOKT	376	1258

.44 REMINGTON MAGNUM CARTRIDGE:

The .44 Remington Magnum cartridge was developed jointly by Smith & Wesson and Remington. It was marketed in 1955 in combination with the heavy S&W Model 29 revolver. Many other manufacturers have also made revolvers in this caliber since that time. The development of this cartridge is largely due to a small group of fanatical shooters, including the well-known Elmer Keith. They were looking for the ideal combination of a long shooting distance, precision and bullet energy. For a long time, the .44 Rem Magnum was the most powerful cartridge for handguns. This caliber was not used much for police purposes, except in the film Dirty Harry. As a hunting cartridge, the .44 Rem Magnum is popular with experienced shooters in North and South America. The recoil and the muzzle flash are impressive. The caliber is suitable for medium to heavy game. For example, in Alaska the .44 Magnum is successfully used for hunting deer, moose and bear.

.41 REMINGTON MAGNUM CARTRIDGE:

The .41 Remington Magnum cartridge was marketed in 1964, in combination with the Smith & Wesson Model 57 revolver. This revolver has a so-called N-frame. This is the heaviest Smith & Wesson frame which was originally designed for the .44 Rem. Magnum cartridge. The well-known American writer and hunter, Elmer Keith was one of the designers of this caliber. At that time there was a great deal of debate on the need for a police cartridge with a greater stopping force than the usual .357 Magnum cartridge. In the end, the .41 Rem. Magnum was not used by the

Winchester .41 Remington Magnum cartridge

police on a large scale after all. This cartridge is not used very much by sports shooters either. The .41 Rem Magnum is an excellent cartridge for hunting small to medium game and is regularly used in North America.

TABLE CALIBER: .41 REMINGTON MAGNUM

MAKE	BULLET	TIP		VO	EQ
	WEIGHT GRAINS-GRAMS		TYPE	M/S	JOULES
WINCHESTER	175	11.3	SILVERTIP-HP	381	823
FEDERAL	210	13.6	JHP HI-SHOK	396	1066
REMINGTON	210	13.6	SP	396	1066

Plastic pistol casing of the new Beretta 9000

Light alloy casing of a Smith & Wesson small caliber pistol

FRAME:

The frame of a pistol or revolver is actually the housing for all the vital components, such as the trigger, the locking system, and usually the various safety systems. At the same time, it also includes the grips. Light metal or synthetic frames are used for pistols and revolvers to save weight. A large steel pistol or revolver can easily weigh 1200 to 1500 g (42.3 to 53 oz). It is quite something to carry this pistol about in a holster all day long. Therefore these pistols were provided with a light metal frame from the beginning of the last century. This was usually an aluminum alloy.

In about 1980, Glock was the first manufacturer to use a synthetic frame on a large scale. Subsequently most other arms manufacturers followed this example.

FRONT SIGHT:

This raised area is usually close to the muzzle and consists of a vertical plate or pin. As soon as the bead falls exactly into the recess of the rear sight leaf, the firearm is accurately aimed at the target (see illustration).

Revolver frame

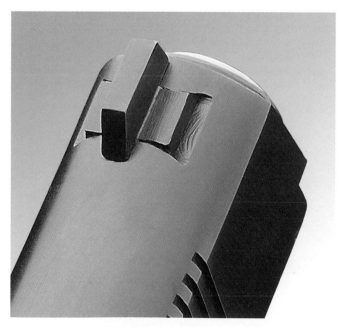

The bead of a Charles Daly pistol slide

GAS PRESSURE:

This pressure is the result of the powder burning in the cartridge case so that the bullet is pressed out of the cartridge case and through the barrel. The gas pressure also ensures that the bullet is shot at its target with formidable speed. The speed is sometimes underestimated, particularly in popular TV series when the hero easily manages to duck to miss a bullet whizzing towards him. The speed is as follows: from the moment that the shooter wants to fire, it is approximately 0.2 seconds before the trigger finger follows the command from the brain. The firing pin strikes the primer in the cartridge approximately 0.005 seconds later, so that the flash reaches the powder via the ignition channel in the foot of the cartridge case. The powder then ignites in the cartridge case in 0.0004 seconds. Altogether it therefore takes 0.2054 seconds. The gas pressure results from the ignition of the powder. After approximately 0.004 seconds, the bullet is released from the cartridge case and starts its trajectory through the barrel. The bullet leaves the barrel at a speed of approximately 300 m/s (average for handguns), after it has been pressed through the barrel, which takes approximately .0012 seconds. The chemical reaction of the powder being turned into gas pressure continues even after the bullet has left the barrel. Depending on the rate of twist and a number of other factors, a bullet which has left the barrel has a rotating speed of approximately 1000 revolutions per second. For example, if the target is 25 meters away, the bullet reaches it in 0.1125 seconds. Therefore, altogether, firing a cartridge takes only 0.323 seconds before the bullet reaches its target. It is interesting that the shooter only feels the recoil 0.2 seconds after the bullet has left the barrel. The gas pressure is indicated in bar or in psi (pounds per square inch; bar x 14.5 = psi). Some examples of gas pressure are shown in the table below.

Gas pressure locking, Steyr GB pistol system

GAS-RETARDED LOCKING:

This system, which is suitable for the heaviest cartridges, could also be described as a recoil action. For this type of construction, there are two different systems.

1. A number of holes are drilled in the barrel. The gas pressure can partly escape through these holes. This gas pressure is trapped in a space between the barrel and the slide. This inhibits the recoil off the slide. One example of this system is the Steyr GB 9 mm Para pistol. One of the holes for the gas to escape through is shown with a red arrow.

2. The system in which the recoil spring, or sometimes

TABLE OF GAS PRESSURE PER CALIBER:

CALIBER	BULLET WEIGHT GRAINS/ GRAMS		MAXIMUM GAS PRESSURE IN BAR
6,35 MM/.25 ACP	50	3,2	1300
7,65 MM/.32 ACP	71	4,6	1800
9 MM KORT/.380 ACP	96	6,2	1600
9 MM PARA/LUGER	125	8,1	2600
.38 SPECIAL	110	7,1	1600
.38 SPECIAL	148	9,6	1200
.38 SPECIAL	158	10,2	1500
.357 MAGNUM	110	7,1	2200
.357 MAGNUM	158	10,2	3100
.357 MAGNUM	180	11,7	2900
.44 REM. MAGNUM	240	15,6	2800
.45 ACP	230	14,9	1400

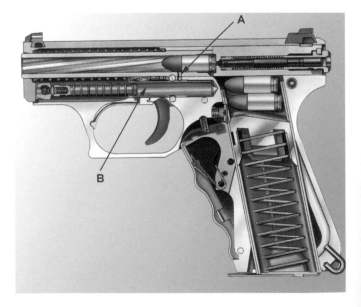

Gas pressure locking , Heckler & Koch P7 system

a separate piston/piston bar with a spring, is fitted in a cylinder. When the shot is fired, part of the gas pressure flows into the underlying cylinder area through a small hole in the barrel, usually just behind the chamber. This means that pressure builds up in the cylinder against a piston head, resulting in a sort of buffer effect. The unlocking is therefore retarded. As soon as the bullet has left the barrel and the barrel is therefore 'open', the gas pressure escapes through the muzzle. Only then can the slide move back, disconnected. One example of this system can be found in Heckler & Koch pistols, for example, the P7 models (P7-M8 and P7-M13). Both gas-retarded locking systems are ingenious systems, with only one disadvantage. Only jacketed bullets can be used because the shavings of lead bullets stop up the hole through which the gas escapes. The illustration on page 408 shows the hole through which the gas escapes (A) and the cylinder area (B).

GRIPS:

Handguns have grips or stocks. The grip plates consist of two loose plates attached to either side of the frame. A stock usually consists of one piece of wood, rubber or synthetic material and encloses the grips of the frame.

Enclosed grip of a Kora revolver

GRIP SAFETY:

Some models of pistols have a grip safety. This is a spring-operated part of the grip. It has to be firmly pressed in with the shooting hand because it is not possible to fire otherwise. The grip safety blocks the trigger, the sear or the hammer. The Colt 1911, 1911-A1, Government and many other makes and models based on these incorporate a grip safety system.

Grip of a Kora revolver

Mother of pearl grip plates of a Taurus pistol

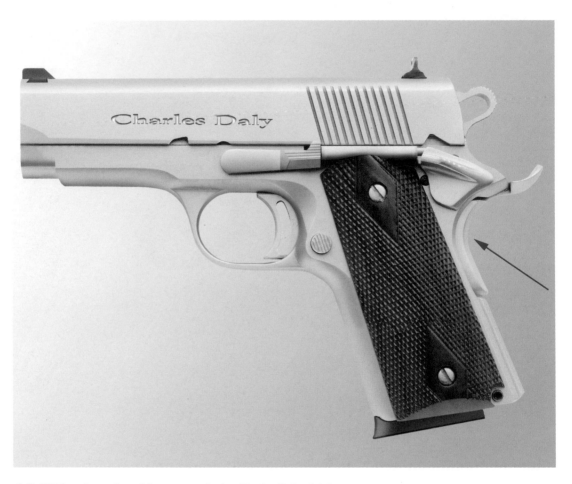

Colt 1911 system grip safety on an exclusive Charles Daly pistol

Heckler & Koch system grip safety of a Greek Ebro P7

A similar sort of system is found in the P7 pistol models of Heckler & Koch. In this case, the grip safety is in front of the grips. By pressing it, the trigger is disconnected and the firing mechanism is cocked.

GROOVES & LANDS/RIFLED:

These are lengthwise grooves on the inside of the barrel. They serve to give the bullet a rotating movement around its axis. This rotation is necessary for the bullet to have greater stability during its trajectory. Otherwise, the bullet could start to waver, which would result in deviations in the trajectory. The extent or speed of this rotation is influenced by the length or sharpness of the rotating grooves and lands. This length of rotation is also known as the twist. For example, a twist of 250mm (9^1/$_4$ in) means that the grooves and lands have rotated through 360° over a length of 250 mm. Therefore the external size of the bullet is also slightly larger than the internal diameter between the upright edges (the lands) in the barrel. In addition, the groove and lands have a great influence on ballistics. Also see Polygonal barrel, page 423. The illustration above shows the lands with a letter A. The deeper grooves are indicated with the letter B.

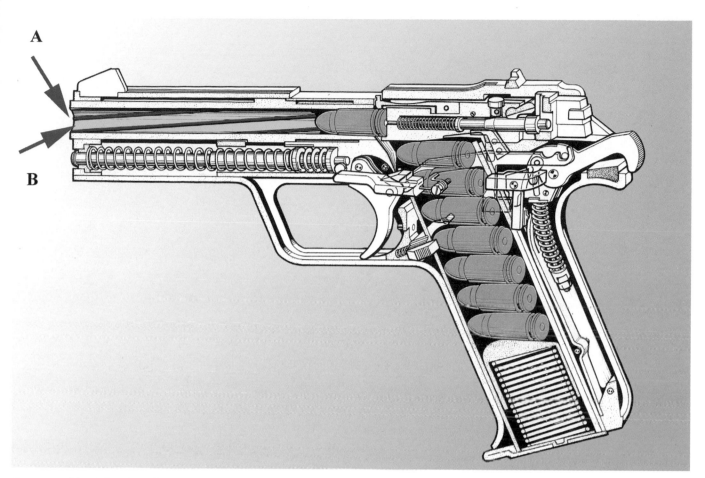

Grooves and lands in a barrel

HALF-COCK SAFETY:

This safety system is sometimes used in pistols or revolvers with an external hammer. When the hammer is pulled back by the thumb, the sear falls halfway down into a safety recess in the foot of the hammer. This safety position cannot be released with the trigger. First, the hammer must be entirely cocked completely with the thumb to the single-action position. In the illustration, the half-cock safety at the foot of the hammer is indicated with number 2. The firing distance is indicated with number 1.

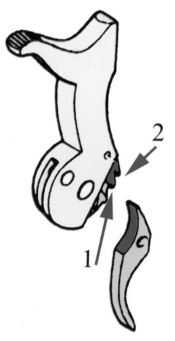

Drawing of half-cock safety system

The hammer of a pistol

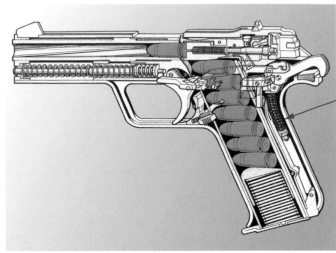

Hammer spring of a pistol

HAMMER:

Many pistols and revolvers have a hammer. This operates in a way that is comparable to a real hammer. As soon as the shooter pulls the trigger, the hammer moves forwards. It strikes the end of the firing pin or directly strikes the primer. Some pistols do not have a

hammer. The firing pin is launched as soon as the trigger rod has made the sear ascend. In this way the firing pin is released, and moves forwards under the pressure of the firing pin spring.

HAMMER SPRING:

The hammer spring produces the pressure of the spring on the hammer. As soon as the trigger is pulled, the hammer moves forwards under the pressure of the hammer or main spring and strikes the firing pin or

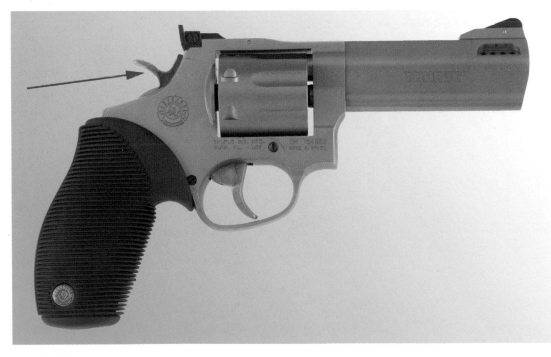

A revolver hammer

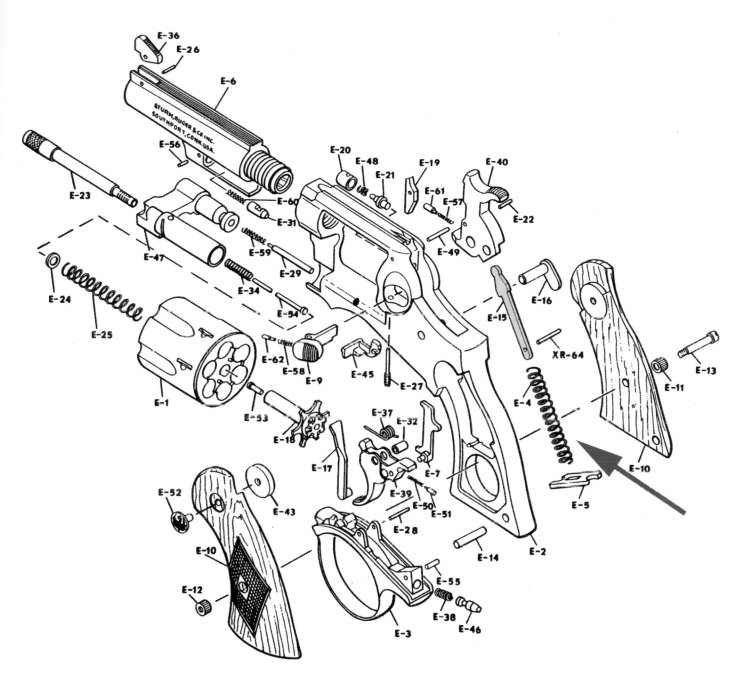

Hammer spring of a revolver

primer. If a coiled spring is used, this is usually coiled around a hammer spring guide. Certain types of revolvers do not have a coiled spring, but a large leaf spring. In both illustrations, the hammer spring is shown in red and the hammer spring guide in yellow.

INCH:

This is the English measurement of length, written as 1 in or 1″, which is 2.54 cm or 25.4 mm.

LANYARD RING:

Revolvers and pistols sometimes have an eye or ring at the bottom of the grip. A lanyard can be passed through this. This is the so-called lanyard ring. If the firearm falls out of the holster, the lanyard ring ensures that it remains close to the shooter. The lanyard ring is usually used for service pistols.

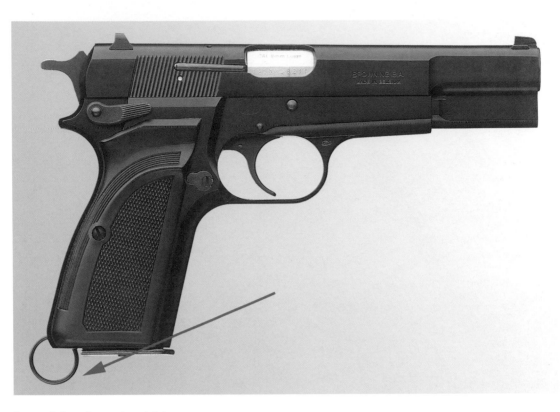

Lanyard ring of a service pistol

LASER SIGHT:

Specialist service pistols as well as sports pistols can be equipped with a laser sight. This is usually in or below the weapon. The mechanism sends a bright, thin, red ray, which hits the target. The laser can be adjusted in the same way as a normal sight.

LOADING GATE SAFETY:

Many revolvers of the single-action type are loaded by means of a loading gate in the recoil plate of the frame. As soon as this opens, the cylinder stop is raised and

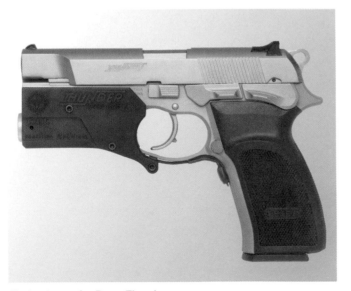

Aiming laser of a Bersa Thunderer

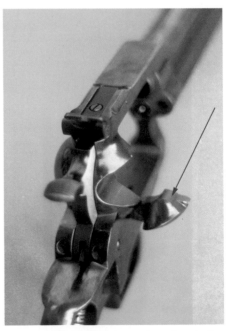

Provided the loading port safety of a single-action revolver is open the hammer is blocked

sometimes the hammer or trigger are also blocked. The cylinder can then be freely rotated by hand, and each chamber can be loaded individually. The empty cartridge cases are ejected one by one from the cylinder chambers in the same way.

LOCKING SYSTEM:

When a pistol is locked, there is a system for locking the barrel and slide. When the pistol is fired, the gas pressure is so great that the system must remain closed until the bullet has left the barrel. There are different sorts of locking systems, such as:
- Berretta-9000 locking system
- Browning-Colt locking system
- Browning-FN locking system
- Browning-Petter (-Sig) locking system
- gas-retarded locking system
- bolt-action locking system
- toggle locking system
- recoil locking system
- roller locking system
- rotation locking
- falling block locking

Cartridge hold/magazine

LOCKUP SAFETY:

Almost all pistols and revolvers have a lockup safety. This prevents a cartridge from being fired if the slide

or cylinder is not entirely closed. In most pistols this works as follows: a lug on the trigger bar engages in a recess on the bottom of the inside of the slide. If the slide is not entirely closed, the trigger bar cannot reach the sear or hammer. For revolvers, the cylinder latch cannot move forwards if the cylinder is not locked in the frame. The trigger remains blocked.

MAGAZINE/CARTRIDGE HOLDER:

This is a loose container for the cartridges. The magazine is placed in the magazine well of a pistol. The magazine of a pistol is very important. Everything depends on good feeding of the cartridges. A magazine spring which is incorrectly mounted can cause problems. Some older models of pistols have an internal magazine.
The magazine usually consists of the following components:
- magazine housing;
- the follower, or the plate which pushes the cartridges up into the magazine at a particular angle. This usually activates the slide catch after the last cartridge has been fired. This means that the slide remains in the last position;
- magazine spring;
- sometimes a floor plate or butt plate.

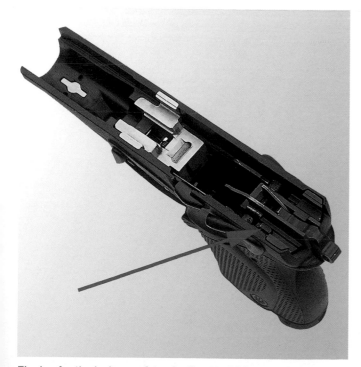

The lug for the lock-up safety of a Beretta 9000 is indicated by a red arrow

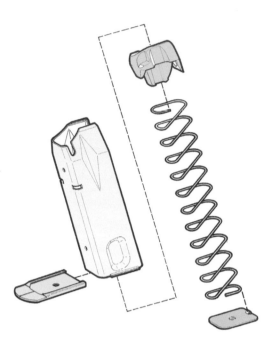

Drawing of a cartridge holder and parts

Double row magazine

Depending on the type, model, make and caliber of the weapon, standard magazines can hold from 5 to more than 30 cartridges. In magazines with a small capacity, the cartridges are piled on top of each other. In magazines with double rows, the cartridges are half on top of each other. This means that more cartridges fit into the magazine. One of the disadvantages is that these magazines must be much thicker. The grip of the pistol is therefore also broader.

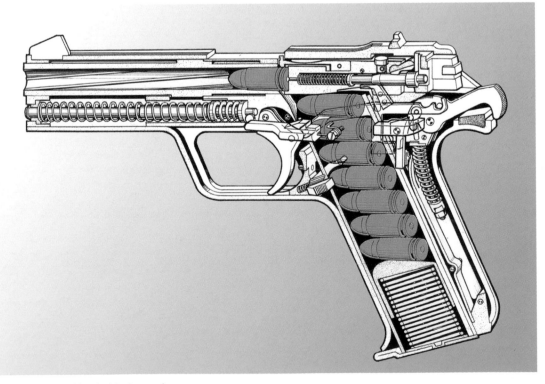

Single row cartridge holder/magazine

Magazine catch behind the trigger guard

MAGAZINE CATCH:

This is the handle, catch or switch with which the magazine can be clipped out of the frame of the pistol. The usual place of this magazine catch is in, next to or behind the trigger guard. In some pistols, this catch is on the bottom, also known as the heel of the grip. This catch is also referred to as the magazine catch.

MAGAZINE SAFETY:

Some pistols have a magazine safety. The system is based on having to take the magazine out of the pistol before it is unloaded or cleaned. This activates the safety device. In most systems, the sear is blocked so

Magazine catch beneath the grip

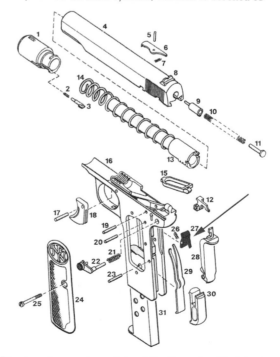

Drawing of magazine safety of the Browning Model 10/22 pistol

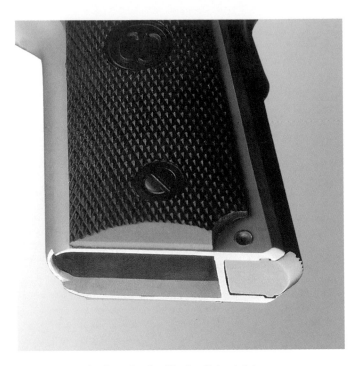

Magazine port in the grip of a Charles Daly pistol

Position of the magazine in a Hämmerli SP-20

that it is not possible to fire. In other models, the trigger bar, the connection between the trigger and the sear, is disconnected. Page 417 has an illustration of a Browning pistol Model 10/22 as an example. The magazine safety is indicated in red.

MAGAZINE WELL:

In most cases, the magazine well is at the bottom of the grip of the frame of the pistol. In modern match pistols, the well is beveled and/or enlarged. In some of the literature on weapons, an enlarged magazine well is known as a 'beveled magazine'.

MATCH LOCK:

Old fifteenth century firearms were fired with the help of a glowing fuse. This was secured in a serpentine. The marksmen would press the glowing fuse into the powder pan by hand. The finely ground powder, known as the pan powder or propellant, would ignite so that the main charge in the barrel was fired. As it was difficult to hold the weapon at the same time as aim and operate the serpentine, the mechanism was developed in about 1450. A firing rod was attached to the serpentine and connected in turn with a long hook. This hook was parallel to the stock so that it was actually a sort of primitive trigger.

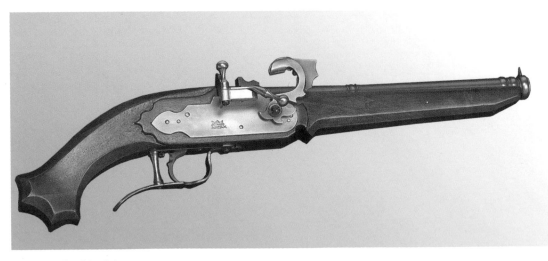

Fuselock pistol by Artax

Example of micrometer sights of a Beretta

MICROMETER SIGHTS:

Sporting pistols and revolvers often have accurately adjustable micrometer sights. This is used to adjust the weapon for a particular shooting distance or a particular type of cartridge.

MUZZLE:

As described under the heading 'barrel', this consists of a hollow tube. The barrel chamber is at one end and the muzzle, where the bullet exits from the firearm, is on the other end. In ballistics, the term muzzle is also used to indicate the speed of the bullet over

Muzzle of a Kora revolver

a particular distance. The speed V0 is the velocity measured at zero meters, i.e., immediately after exiting from the barrel. The indication 'E0' indicates the calculated energy of the bullet at zero meters, immediately after the bullet has left the barrel at the muzzle.

MUZZLE ENERGY:

This is the energy of the bullet measured from the muzzle. In a formula, this is expressed in E0 (energy at zero meters). For handguns, the energy is sometimes also calculated at 25 or 50 meters. For rifles, the energy values are usually indicated as E0, E100 (for 100 meters, etc.). In Europe, this muzzle energy is indicated in Joules; in North America in foot pounds. This indicates the energy of the bullet. The formula is: the muzzle velocity of the bullet (V0) squared, times the weight of the bullet in kilograms, divided by 2 (the force of gravity of the earth). It is easier to calculate the weight of the bullet in grams and multiply the quotient by 1000. An example for a 9 mm Para cartridge:

bullet weight 124 grains = 8.0 grams;
bullet velocity (V0) 360 second/second;
E0=360 x 360 x 8.0 which means
2000 – 518 Joules
To calculate the energy in foot pounds
(ft lb): 518 x 0.738 = 383 ft lb.

MUZZLE VELOCITY (V0):

This is the speed of the bullet measured just after the muzzle. This value is expressed in m/s. A bullet has enormous velocity. Based on the example which was given for muzzle energy for the 9mm Para cartridge with a V0 of 360 m/s, it is 1,296 km per hour (805 mph). As the distance which the bullet travels increases, the velocity decreases significantly. This is because of air resistance and the force of gravity of the earth. The last factor causes the curve of the trajectory. The 9mm Para cartridge is again given as an example:
V0=360 m/s; V25=329 m/s (91.3%);
V50=301 m/s (83.6%)
The curve of the trajectory is as follows: when the sights are adjusted to 25m, i.e., aimed at a target at 25m, the bullet goes 12.5m 40 mm (1.57 in) above the target. At 25m, it is a precise hit, but at 50m the bullet is 37 mm (1.46 in) below the target.

Remington 9 mm Para Disintegrator cartridge

9 MM LUGER CARTRIDGE:

The 9 mm Para cartridge has several different names, such as the 9 mm Luger or the 9 x 19 mm. The caliber was developed in 1902 for the famous German Luger pistol. In 1904, the German navy started to use this weapon and cartridge. The German army followed in 1908. This explains the popular name of the Luger P08, the Pistole (19)08. Since that time, this cartridge has been used in almost every country for government weapons. It was only in 1985 that the USA changed from the Colt 1911-A1 in .45 ACP to the Beretta 92F (M9) in 9 mm Para. The popularity of the 9 mm Para only really started in North America in 1954, when Smith &Wesson marketed the Model 39 pistol. The 9 mm Para cartridge was also widely used in machine-guns. It is the most common pistol cartridge in the world. The 9 mm Para cartridge is also an extremely popular cartridge in sport, but the International Practical Shooting Confederation (IPSC) uses a caliber classification based on bullet energy. The minimum caliber is 9 mm and the minimum bullet energy, the power factor, is 125, and is known as a 'minor caliber'. This power factor is calculated by multiplying the weight of the bullet in grains by the bullet velocity in feet per second. The product has to be divided by 100. Almost all 9 mm Para cartridges achieve the lower limit of 125. For the classification of major caliber, the IPSC adopts a power factor of 175. Therefore, many IPSC shooters use the pepped-up .38 Super Auto cartridge, because this does achieve the major classification. The advantage of a 9 mm Para or a .38 Super Auto pistol is the large magazine capacity. However, in some countries, including the USA, an autoloader may not contain more than 10 cartridges.

Hollow-point 9 mm Para Gold Sabre of Remington

TABLE CALIBER: 9 MM PARA/LUGER

| MAKE | BULLET TIP | | | VO | EQ |
| | WEIGHT | | TYPE | M/S | JOULES |
	GRAINS-GRAMS				
HORNADY	90	5.8	JHP-XTP	415	500
MAGTECH	95	6.2	JSP-FP	410	517
HORNADY	100	6.5	FMJ	372	450
REMINGTON	105	6.8	DISINTEGRATOR	335	382
WINCHESTER	105	6.8	SUPERCLEAN	366	456
FIOCCHI	115	7.5	FMJ-HP	410	626
HORNADY	115	7.5	JHP-XTP	352	465
REMINGTON	115	7.5	JHP+P	381	544
WINCHESTER	115	7.5	SILVERTIP-HP	373	519
FIOCCHI	123	8.0	FMJ-TC-Combat	390	606
FEDERAL	124	8.0	HYDRA-SHOK JHP	341	465
REMINGTON	124	8.0	JHP	343	471
REMINGTON	124	8.0	JHP+P	360	518
FEDERAL	147	9.5	HYDRA-SHOK JHP	305	442
HORNADY	147	9.5	JHP-XTP	320	486
REMINGTON	147	9.5	FMJ-Match	302	434
WINCHESTER	147	9.5	SILVERTIP-HP	308	452

9 x 21 MM CARTRIDGE:

In several European countries and Mexico, amongst others, the civilian use of military calibers is not permitted. Nevertheless, there is a great demand for this sort of cartridge in shooting sports. Therefore the 9 x 21 mm cartridge was developed in 1980. This is also known as the 9 x 21 mm IMI (Israel Military Industries) cartridge. It actually has a 9 mm Para cartridge case extended by 2 mm (¹/₄ in). The ballistic properties are the same as those of the 9 mm Para. Compared to the 9 mm Para, the bullet is usually flatter and pressed deeper into the cartridge case. This means that the total cartridge length is the same as that of the 9 mm Para. For pistols, it is then only necessary to adjust the length of the barrel chamber

because the grip, magazine and feeding ramp retain the 9 mm Para measurements. As soon as the legislation on arms of the different countries in Europe are adapted to conform, this caliber will eventually disappear. A recent development is the 9 x 23 mm pistol cartridge by Winchester, which does have a higher bullet velocity, and therefore power factor.

TABLE CALIBER: 9 x 21 MM

| MAKE | BULLET TIP | | | VO | EQ |
| | WEIGHT | | TYPE | M/S | JOULES |
	GRAINS-GRAMS				
SELL-BELLOT	115	7.5	FMJ	368	508
SAMSON	124	8.0	FMJ	351	493

TABLE CALIBER: 9 x 23 MM

| MAKE | BULLET TIP | | | VO | EQ |
| | WEIGHT | | TYPE | M/S | JOULES |
	GRAINS-GRAMS				
WINCHESTER	125	7.5	SILVERTIP-HP	442	791
WINCHESTER	124	8.0	JSP	445	796

9 x 25 MM DILLON CARTRIDGE:

The well-known IPSC competition marksman, Rob Latham, first used this caliber in 1991 and made it fairly popular. The cartridge had been developed in 1988 by Randy Shelly, in cooperation with Arnd Myne of the American reloading press manufacturer Dillon. The aim was to improve the ballistic properties of the 9 mm cartridge. In addition, they wished to achieve the power factor for the major caliber of IPSC. The power factor of the 9 x 25 mm Dillon is 177, i.e., above the minimum of 175. The caliber is based on a 10 mm Auto cartridge case into which a shoulder is pressed. This means that the diameter of the mouth of the cartridge case is reduced to 9 mm. Meanwhile Shelly has designed a new caliber, the 9 x 30 mm.

TABLE CALIBER: 9 x 25 MM DILLON

| MAKE | BULLET TIP | | | VO | EQ |
| | WEIGHT | | TYPE | M/S | JOULES |
	GRAINS-GRAMS				
DILLON	115	7.5	FMJ	470	828

The 9 x 21 mm cartridge

Example of a phosphate coating

ANODIZING:

This is a method for treating the surface of steel with phosphates. This produces a dull layer which prevents rusting. This type of finish is often used on service weapons as these may not be shiny.

PERCUSSION LOCK:

This system, dating from 1822, was used for a long time up to the introduction of the cartridge. A sort of primer, the percussion primer is slid over a tapering chimney. This is a brass cup filled with lightly

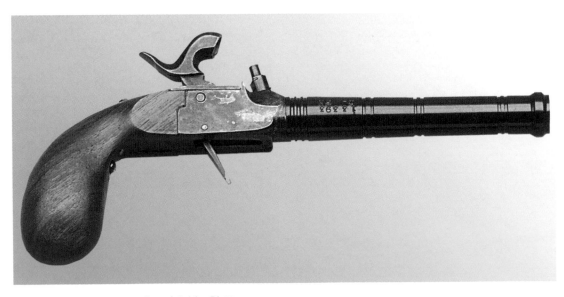

Single shot pocket percussion pistol by Pietta

Replica Remington percussion revolver by Pietta

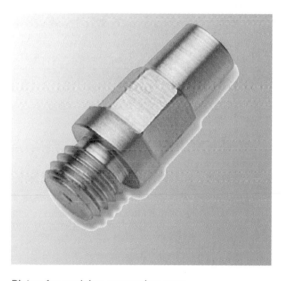

Piston for applying percussion caps

Separate cartridge percussion caps

inflammable fulminate. When the trigger is pulled, it is firmly struck by the hammer. As a result, the fulminate ignites with a bright flash. This passes through the hollow channel of the chimney and ignites the charge in the chamber.

PISTOL:

This is a weapon which does not have a set description. According to the encyclopedia, the pistol is a (short) handgun. Sometimes a pistol is a single shot firearm and sometimes it is an autoloader. The last system is based on the principle that a number of cartridges are placed in the magazine. Because of the recoil of the shot, the empty cartridge case is automatically ejected and a new cartridge is introduced. A pistol is composed of a number of groups of components, the so-called main groups:

a. the slide group
b. the barrel with built-in chamber, and the recoil spring(s) and recoil spring guide
c. the frame group, including the grip;
d. the magazine group

There are single-shot pistols and pistols with several barrels.

POLYGONAL BARREL:

This is a system to add rotation to the bullets without using grooves and lands. This principle is used for example by the firm Heckler & Koch. The inside of the barrel is not completely round, but actually

Main groups (or parts) of a pistol

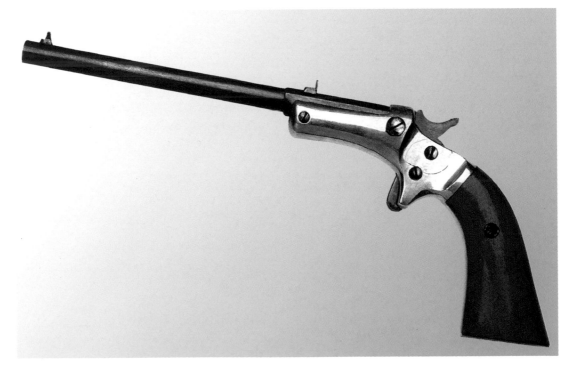

Nineteenth century single shot pistol

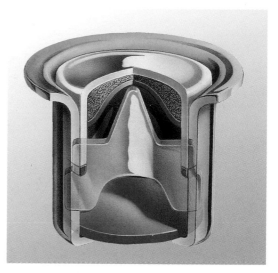

Cut-away drawing of a Remington primer cap

Powder flask by Pietta

polygonal – hence the name. These polygonal planes provide a particular twist, just as in a barrel with grooves.

POWDER/PROPELLANT:

There are several theories about the discovery of gunpowder in Europe. One of these is that the famous Venetian merchant, Marco Polo, brought back the chemical formula for gunpowder from China. He was part of a trading mission which managed to reach the imperial city of Peking after traveling straight through Europe and Asia from 1271 to 1292. Other stories mention the names of Roger Bacon and Berthold Schwarz, a monk from the German city of Freiburg. The German word for gunpowder (Schwarzpulver) is named after this last inventor. It consists of 75% saltpeter, 15% sulfur and 10% charcoal. Modern gunpowders are chemical compounds based on nitrocellulose. It ignites more reliably than blackpowder and can be affected by all sorts of additions. Some of the high gas pressure can be used for the repeat action of a firearm.

PRIMER:

The primer is held in the middle of the foot at the bottom of the cartridge case. It is a brass cup containing a sensitive chemical compound known as the fulminate. This ignites with a flash when the firing pin is struck. The flash passes through the channel into the bottom of the cartridge and ignites the charge in the cartridge case. This channel is shown with a red arrow in the illustration below. The rate of ignition of the primer is approximately between 0.001 and 0.002 seconds. The fulminate is an invention dating from the beginning of the nineteenth century. At that time it still consisted of a mixture of mercury, sulfur antimony and potassium chlorate. Later, 2,4,6 tri-nitro toluene (TNT) was added to this. When it is ignited, chlorine is released which eventually destroys the steel of the barrel. Modern rust-free fulminate consists of a mixture of TNT, lead oxide, barium nitrate, calcium silicide and sulfur antimony.

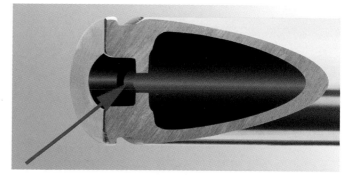

Cross-section of a cartridge base. The flash channel is indicated by the red arrow

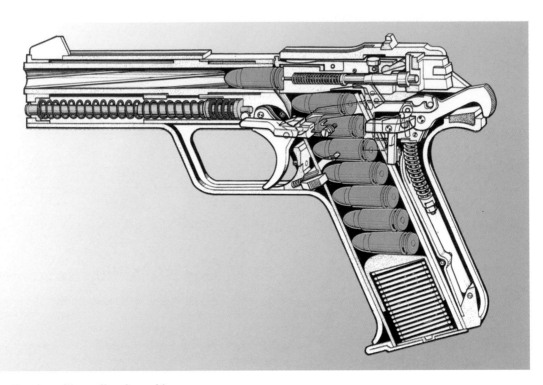

Recoil spring with recoil spring guide

RECOIL SPRING:

When a cartridge has been fired, the slide of the pistol moves back as a result of the reactive force of the gas pressure. During this repeat action a coiled spring is pressed in. As soon as the backward movement of the slide is stopped, this spring recoils again. As a result, the slide moves forwards again. Sometimes this recoil spring is fitted around the barrel. In most cases, the recoil spring is under the barrel around the recoil

spring guide. In the illustration above, the recoil spring is shown in red and the recoil spring guide is shown in yellow.

REVOLVER:

A revolver is a light handgun with a relatively short barrel and a rotating magazine which can contain 5 to 10 cartridges. The group of revolvers can be subdivided into:
– Single-action revolvers in which the hammer must be cocked by hand before the shot is fired. These are usually older models of revolvers in which the cylinder cannot be hinged out of the frame. Loading and unloading is done through a loading gate at the back of the cylinder.
– Double-action revolvers, in which the hammer is cocked mechanically by pulling the trigger. Usually revolvers of this type have a swing-out cylinder to facilitate loading. In a double-action revolver, the hammer can also be cocked by hand in single-action mode. Basically, a revolver consists of the components: frame, barrel and cylinder.

RIMFIRE:

The fulminate is pressed into the thin-walled inside of the bottom of the cartridge. It is ignited when struck by the firing pin. There is certainly not very much fulminate. In the case of .22 LR RWS cartridge there

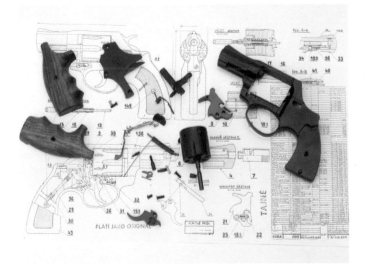

Parts of a revolver

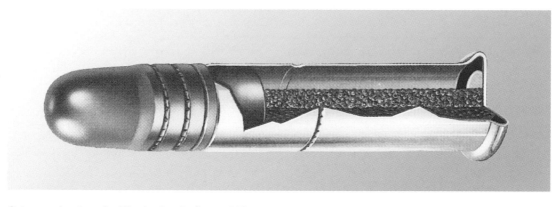

Cut-away drawing of a Winchester rimfire cartridge

is only 0.035 g (0.54 grains) of the erosion-free compound, Sinoxid. Rimfire cartridges of the caliber .22 include the .22 Magnum cartridge (.22 WMR: Winchester Magnum Rimfire). This is often used as a small caliber hunting cartridge. Another rimfire cartridge is the .22 Short for the Olympic rapid fire pistol shooting discipline.

ROLLER-LOCKING:

This system was made famous by the German fire Heckler & Koch, although it was not invented by that firm. The system was successfully used by many large caliber pistols, machine-guns, rifles and carbines of H&K. It works as follows: there are two semi-circular

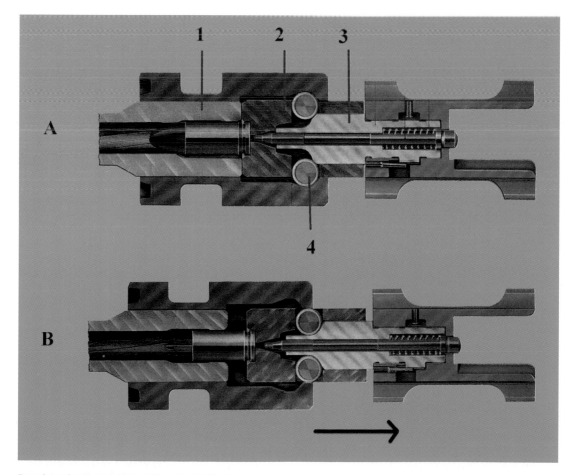

Drawing of roller locking of Heckler & Koch

recesses in the lateral extensions of the barrel. Two steel rollers attached to an extension engage in these. When the pistol is locked, the two steel rollers engage in the recesses on the side of the barrel. After the shot, the slide is forced back by the gas pressure; the two rollers swing in, and when the disconnection is complete, the slide moves back on its own. This is followed by the cycle of ejecting and reloading, just as in other pistols. This system has two advantages: in the first place, the locking system is very stable. Secondly, the recoil is delayed because the two rollers have to swing in first. This is an advantage for shooters, particularly with heavy calibers. One of the disadvantages is the high production cost, because this type of locking system requires great precision in production. Page 427 shows a diagram of this locking system. In A the locking system is shut, in B, the firearm is unlocked. The figures show:

1. barrel with chamber;
2. bolt head;
3. bolt block;
4. locking system rollers.

ROTATION LOCKING:

In several types of autoloaders, there is a rotation locking system which is based on that of rifles, as regards the technology used. The bolt for the firearm, which is fitted in the slide, has a number of bolt-locking lugs at the front. These engage in recesses at the end of the barrel when the system is locked up. As a result of the recoil energy of the firearm, or the gas

pressure of the cartridge that has been fired, the bolt rotates through a few degrees after the shot. As a result, the bolt-locking lugs on the bolt disengage from the recess. In this sort of system, the barrel is sometimes fixed to the frame. Only the bolt and the slide can then be moved. The system is actually comparable to that of a bolt-action rifle, but in this case, the mechanism is operated (semi) automatically. Good examples of this system include the Colt 2000, the Desert Eagle of IMI (Israel Military Industries) and the Berretta Cougar series.

SAFETY CATCH:

A safety catch is operated by hand. The catch which is in the shape of a handle or a rotating or press switch is mounted on the frame of the pistol or on the slide. Depending on the type and model of the pistol, it blocks the hammer and/or the sear and/or the trigger or the trigger bar, and sometimes also the slide itself.

Safety catch on the casing, which usually blocks the slide and trigger

Rotation locking of a Beretta Cougar

Safety catch of a Beretta 9000

Another form of safety catch

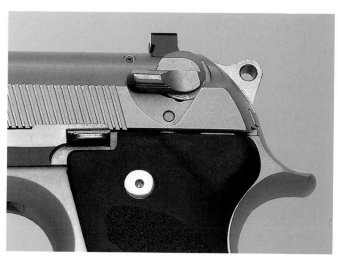

Safety catch on slide. This blocks the firing pin and also acts as uncocking/decocking lever on some pistols

In many models of pistols, the safety catch is mounted on the left of the frame or slide. Modern and often more expensive pistols have an ambidextrous safety catch. Sometimes this catch can be combined with a mechanism which is used to safely uncock the hammer. Also see Uncocking lever.

SEAR:

This mechanism provides the link between the trigger and the hammer. As soon as the trigger is pulled, the sear is tipped so that the blocking of the hammer ceases. The hammer then moves forwards and strikes the firing pin. The illustration below (number 1) shows the sear. The components operate in the following order: the trigger (4) is pulled. This pulls the trigger bar (3) forwards. If the slide is safety shut,

the lockup safety (2) on the trigger bar is pressed down. This means that the trigger bar hooks into the firing lug of the sear (1). The sear turns and releases the hammer.

SECURITY LOCK:

Several makes of weapons have a built in security lock. One of the first in this field was the Brazilian firm Taurus. In 2000, Smith & Wesson announced that they were also considering a security lock system. This resulted in a big row with competing American manufacturers who were not very keen on a system which would incur additional costs.

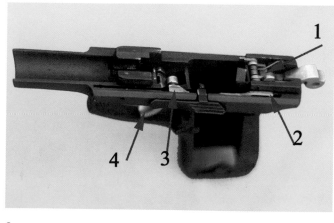

Sear

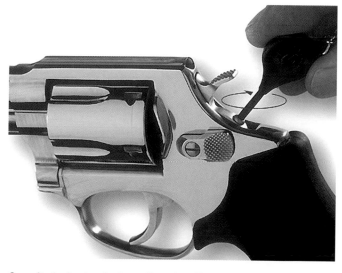

Security lock, standard on all modern Taurus revolvers

Security lock for modern Taurus pistols

SIDEPLATE:

Some makes of revolvers have a removable plate on the left or right of the frame. This is an inspection window to reveal the internal mechanism. It is only opened for repairs or maintenance. The illustration shows the removable grip plate in red.

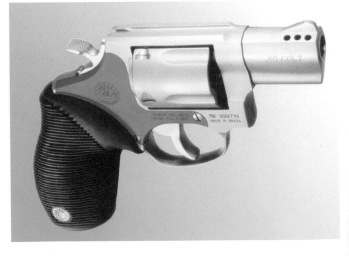

Removable side plate is indicated in red

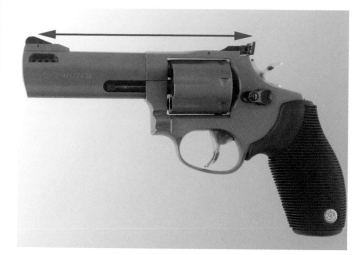

The sighting line is indicated with a red line

SIGHT RADIUS:

This is the total distance from the rear sight leaf to the front sight. For target shooting and long distance shooting a long sight radius is important to aim the weapon accurately.

SIGHTS:

This is the general collective noun for the so-called open sights, i.e. the combination of the rear sight and front sight.

SINGLE-ACTION (SA):

Single-action means that the hammer has to be cocked in advance before every shot. This is done by the repeat action of the pistol. The hammer is automatically cocked by the slide. In a revolver the

Example of sights with notch on the rear of the slide and bead above the muzzle

hammer must be cocked by hand for every shot. The cylinder rotates through one turn so that a new chamber is in front of the barrel.

SLIDE:

The slide of a pistol takes care of the locking system and the repeat action. The slide has the following parts:
— the slide with the breech bock, usually one component;

Colt 1911-A1 single-action pistol

Colt Peacemaker single-action revolver

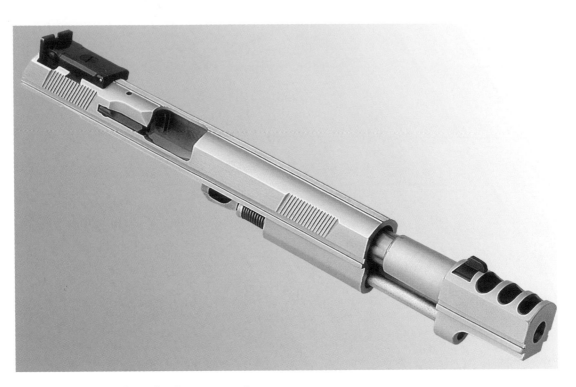

Slide with barrel and three chamber compensator

— the firing pin with the firing pin spring;
— the magazine with a spring, to extract the empty cartridge from the chamber after the shot;
— in some cases, an ejector so that the cartridge which has been shot can be ejected from the side of the slide through the hole in the cartridge case during the reloading action.

SLIDE CATCH:

After the last shot, when the magazine is empty, the slide remains in the last position. The shooter can see that his pistol is 'empty'. He can immediately place a full magazine in the pistol. If the slide catch is pressed down, the slide will move forwards. This also means that a new cartridge is introduced in the chamber.

STOCK:

The term stock is usually used for rifles. If a pistol or a revolver has a grip consisting of one unit, it is sometimes referred to as a stock.

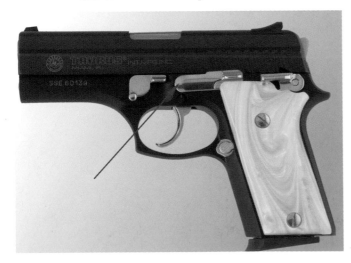

Slide catch

An enclosed stock of a revolver

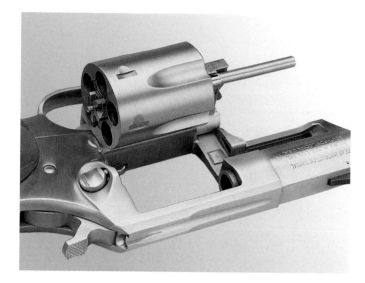

Swing-out cylinder

Take-down lever of a Beretta 9000 pistol

SWING-OUT CYLINDER:

This is a cylinder on a yoke which can be turned from the side of a revolver frame to load or unload the firearm.

TAKEDOWN LEVER:

Many pistols have a rotating or removable catch on the left of the frame, in front of the trigger guard. If this catch is removed or rotated, the slide can be slid off the frame.

Take-down lever of a Taurus pistol

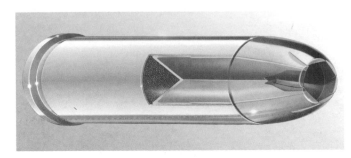

Drawing of the Remington .38 Special HP cartridge

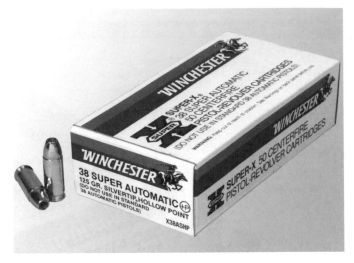

Winchester .38 Super Automatic cartridge

police caliber for revolver cartridges for decades. In this respect it has now been largely replaced by the 9 mm Para cartridge. The .38 Special +P cartridge has been marketed for defense purposes for some time. This is a pepped-up cartridge, usually with a hollow-point bullet to increase the stopping force.

TABLE CALIBER: .38 SPECIAL

MAKE	BULLET TIP			VO	EQ
	WEIGHT		TYPE	M/S	JOULES
	GRAINS-GRAMS				
FIOCCHI	110	7.1	FMJ-FP	360	426
REMINGTON	110	7.1	SEMI-JHP+P	303	326
WINCHESTER	110	7.1	SUPERCLEAN-JSP	297	301
FEDERAL	125	8.1	NYCLAD HP+P	288	336
HORNADY	125	8.1	JHP-XTP	290	341
REMINGTON	125	8.1	JHP+P	297	357
WINCHESTER	125	8.1	SILVERTIP-HP+P	288	336
FEDERAL	129	8.35	HYDRA-SHOK JHP	288	346
WINCHESTER	130	8.4	SXT+P	282	335
HORNADY	140	9.1	JHP-XTP	274	342
REMINGTON	148	9.6	WC-TARGETMASTER	216	225
SELL-BELLOT	148	9.6	WC	213	218
WINCHESTER	148	9.6	WC-SUPERMATCH	216	225
FIOCCHI	158	10.2	FMJ	325	540
GECO/RWS	158	10.2	FMJ OF SP	330	590
HORNADY	158	10.2	JHP-XTP	244	304
MAGTECH	158	10.2	SEMI-JSP	246	310
REMINGTON	158	10.2	SWC	271	376
SELL-BELLOT	158	10.2	FMJ OF SP	271	376

.38 SUPER AUTOMATIC CARTRIDGE:

Colt developed this caliber in 1929 to succeed the .38 ACP cartridge dating from 1900. It is considered to be a good cartridge, amongst other things for steel plates and bowling pins. In the USA, the .38 Super Auto has always been popular, in contrast with Europe. In some European countries, this caliber is widely used because state calibers are not permitted to be used by the civilian market. The .38 Super Auto is more powerful than the 9 mm Para cartridge. It is a good sports cartridge with a flat trajectory.

TABLE CALIBER: .38 SUPER AUTOMATIC

MAKE	BULLET TIP			VO	EQ
	WEIGHT		TYPE	M/S	JOULES
	GRAINS-GRAMS				
WINCHESTER	125	8.1	SILVERTIP-HP	378	579
FIOCCHI	129	8.4	FMJ	360	541
FEDERAL	130	8.4	FMJ	366	563
WINCHESTER	130	8.4	FMJ	370	578
FEDERAL	147	9.5	FMJ	335	533

.357 MAGNUM CARTRIDGE:

Smith & Wesson introduced this caliber in 1985. The cartridge was intended for the new S&W 357 Hand Ejector revolver. This pistol was a reinforced model of the .38-44 Hand Ejector Outdoorsman revolver, dating from 1931. The .357 Magnum is based on the .38 Special, the cartridge case of which was extended by 2.5 mm (1 in). This prevented the new .357 Magnum from being loaded in .38 Special revolvers. These were not able to cope with the much higher gas pressure. Therefore .38 Special cartridges always fit in the cylinder of the .357 Magnum revolver. Conversely, it hardly ever fits. The .357 Magnum was the most powerful revolver cartridge up to the introduction of the .44 Remington Magnum in 1955. Almost all manufactures of handguns make revolvers and/or

Remington .357 Magnum cartridge

.357 SIG CARTRIDGE:

Sig .357 cartridge

This cartridge dates from 1999 and was developed by the Swiss SIG arms factory. The caliber is based on a .40 S&W cartridge case, with a pressed in shoulder for a 9 mm bullet.

In addition to Sig-Sauer, the Austrian arms factory Glock has three models of pistols in this caliber, models 31, 32 and the small model 33. More models and types will certainly follow.

pistols in this caliber. It is an extremely popular caliber. In comparison with the .38 special, the cartridge has approximately twice the muzzle velocity and a muzzle energy which is three times as high.

TABLE CALIBER: .357 MAGNUM

MAKE	WEIGHT GRAINS-GRAMS		BULLET TIP TYPE	V0 M/S	EQ JOULES
WINCHESTER	105	6.8	SUPERCLEAN JHP	503	860
FIOCCHI	110	7.1	FMJ-FP	535	1020
REMINGTON	110	7.1	SEMI-JHP	395	554
FIOCCHI	125	8.1	SEMI-JSP	540	1180
REMINGTON	125	8.1	SEMI-JHP	442	791
FEDERAL	140	9.1	JHP-HI-SHOK	419	799
GECO/RWS	140	9.1	FMJ-SWC	450	990
FIOCCHI	142	9.2	FMJ-TC	460	973
WINCHESTER	145	9.4	SILVERTIP-HP	393	726
FIOCCHI	148	9.6	SEMI-JHP	435	907
FEDERAL	158	10.2	HYDRA-SHOK JHP	376	721
FIOCCHI	158	10.2	SEMI-JSP	450	1036
GECO/RWS	158	10.2	SP	445	1010
MAGTECH	158	10.2	LEAD SWC	376	724
REMINGTON	158	10.2	SWC	376	721
SELL-BELLOT	158	10.2	FMJ OF SP	425	926
WINCHESTER	158	10.2	JHP OF JSP	376	726
REMINGTON	165	10.7	JHP-CORE-LOKT	393	826
REMINGTON	180	11.7	SEMI-JHP	349	713
WINCHESTER	180	11.7	PARTITION GOLD	360	755

TABLE CALIBER: .357 SIG

MAKE	WEIGHT GRAINS-GRAMS		BULLET TIP TYPE	V0 M/S	EQ JOULES
WINCHESTER	105	6.8	JSP	480	783
FEDERAL	125	8.1	FMJ	412	688
REMINGTON	125	8.1	JHP	412	688
WINCHESTER	125	8.1	FMJ-FP	411	686
SELL-BELLOT	140	9.1	FMJ	412	764

.356 TSW CARTRIDGE:

The performance center of Smith & Wesson not only produces special pistols and revolvers, but also develops calibers. One example of this is the .40 S&W cartridge, designed by Paul Liebenberg. He recently designed a cartridge with a cartridge case length of 21.5 mm (¹/₄ in) based on the 9 x 21 mm caliber. This still has to fit into a standard 9 mm Para magazine. He called this new caliber the .356 TSW: Team Smith & Wesson. It is used by the Smith & Wesson factory team in IPSC matches. Because of the high gas pressure of about 45,000 psi, a 147 grain fully jacketed bullet can achieve a muzzle velocity of 372 meters per second (1220 feet per second). This means that the power factor is 179, making the .356 TSW a 'major caliber', according to the IPSC regulations.

TABLE CALIBER: .356 TSW					
MAKE	BULLET WEIGHT GRAINS-GRAMS		TIP TYPE	VO M/S	EQ JOULES
FEDERAL	147	9.5	FMJ-SWC	372	657

TITANIUM FINISH:

In recent years, the use of titanium as a protective layer for firearms has become extremely popular. This takes the place of blued, nickel-plated, chrome or anodized finishes. In addition, the later of titanium can have a color ranging from dull gray to bright blue. Taurus has a number of pistol and revolver models in which the steel components are made entirely from titanium. Titanium was originally used in the aircraft industry. It is an extremely light and strong material.

TOGGLE-LOCKING:

This was one of the first locking systems for an autoloader with a powerful cartridge. It was first used on the Borchardt pistol, and later in an improved form on the famous Luger P08 pistol. From the technical point of view, this system is extremely sophisticated and has never really become 'standard' as was the case for Browning. In fact, it has a number of

Three-dot sights

disadvantages. First, it is relatively complicated and requires great technical skill in production. The tolerance between the various components has to be very low to achieve a good and reliable operation. This also results in high production costs. Secondly, the pistol was originally made for the army. During the

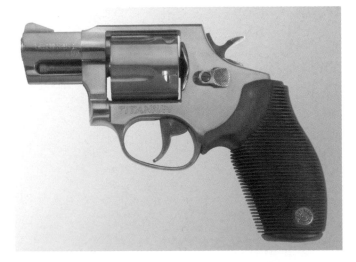

Taurus Titanium revolver

Three-dot sights with twilight markings

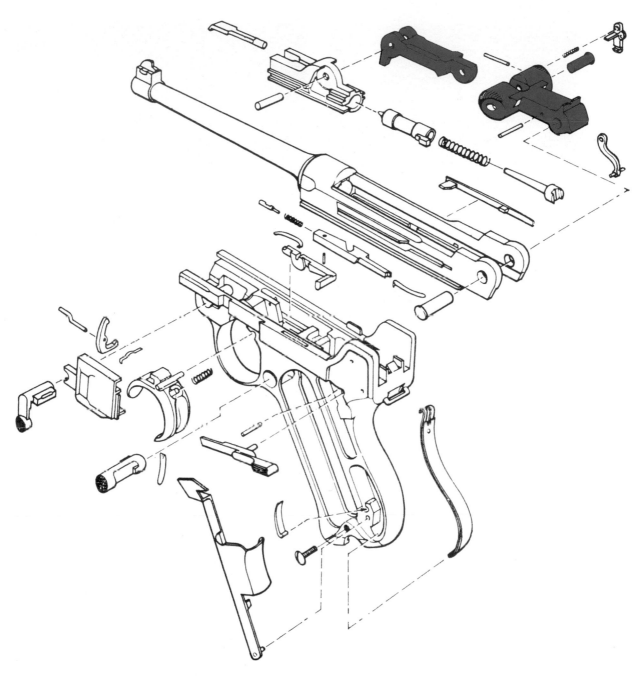

Toggle-locking of the Luger PO8

trench warfare of 1914-1918, it soon became apparent that the weapon was vulnerable to sand and dirt, as well as deviating ammunition.

The fact that the PO8 is still a popular weapon nowadays is probably for nostalgic reasons. The attractive finish and, above all, the characteristic appearance, also help in this respect. The locking system means that the middle rotation point of the toggle locking system is slightly lower in the firing position than the middle line. It is only when the bolt is pushed back by the gas pressure that the rotation

point is above the middle line. This means that the locking-up system is removed.

TRANSFER BAR:

The transfer bar is used in revolvers with a 'floating' spring firing pin enclosed in the frame. Normally the hammer cannot reach the firing pin unless a sort of bar is placed between them. This passes the strike of the hammer onto the firing pin. The bar is only activated at the end of the trigger crawl. The best-known

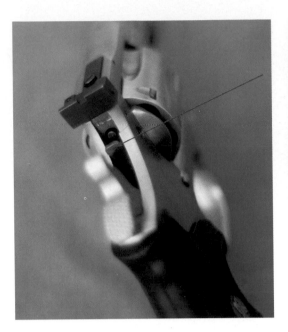

Transfer bar safety

The trigger

revolvers with this system are those made by Ruger. The transfer bar also serves as a falling locking

TRIGGER:

The trigger is part of the firing mechanism. It is the starting point of firing. In general the cycle takes place as follows: the shooter pulls the trigger. There is (usually) a trigger bar on the trigger. The trigger bar is connected to the sear. A lug on the sear hooks into a recess in the foot of the hammer. When the trigger moves the sear tips so that the hammer is released. Under pressure of the hammer spring, it moves forwards and strikes the firing pin or the primer directly, depending on the system. In early firearms the trigger and the hammer were directly connected. With links, such as the trigger bar and the sear, less force is needed to fire the weapon. This is because of the result of lever principles which reinforce each other.

TRIGGER GUARD:

This is a metal or synthetic guard which is fitted around the trigger. The guard protects the trigger so that it cannot easily hook around something. In addition, the trigger guard also serves as an extra grip when firing with two hands.

TRIGGER FORCE/PRESSURE:

This is the force needed to pull the trigger. The trigger force is indicated for each weapon, sometimes separately for single and double-action. Sports weapons often have a light trigger pressure. In service

arms this pressure is higher. For different shooting disciplines a minimum trigger pressure has been set at an international level. Under the category 'standard pistol' the minimum trigger pressure is 1000 g (35$^{1}/_{4}$ oz), for 'sports pistol heavy caliber' and 'military pistol' it is a minimum of 1360 g (48 oz) and for some sports weapons the trigger pressure is adjustable.

Trigger guard

TRIGGER STOP:

This is mainly applied for sports pistols and revolvers. To fire this sort of weapon accurately, the firing moment of the trigger has to be adjusted very precisely. The trigger should not be able to travel any further after this firing moment. It is also known as 'over-travel'.

TRIPLE ASPECT (THREE-DOT) SIGHTS:

Modern handguns often have a colored or white dot in either side of the rear sight leaf. There is also a colored dot on the front sight. As soon as the three dots are horizontally aligned, the weapon is accurately aimed at the target. Sometimes these telescopic sights use a luminous material such as tritium. In this case, it can also be a triple aspect night sight.

.22 LONG RIFLE CARTRIDGE

The history of the .22 rimfire cartridge goes back to 1857. In this year, Smith & Wesson introduced their First Model revolver in the caliber that is now known as the .22 Short. Originally, the cartridge was loaded with 4 grains (0.26 g) of fine powder and had a lead bullet of 29 grains (1.9 g). From 1987, it was loaded with smokeless nitro powder. In 1930, Remington developed the first high velocity cartridge in .22 Short. Since that time, the .22 Short has been popular with sports shooters. There is even an Olympic competition discipline with the .22 Short rapid fire

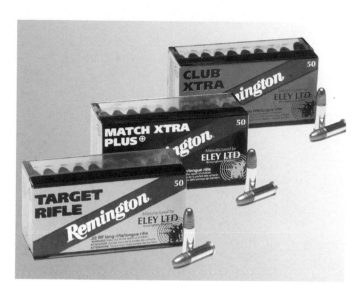

Remington Eley small caliber cartridges

pistol. The .22 Long cartridge dates from 1871. It was made for the seven shot Standard revolver of the American firm, Great Western Gun Works. Since 1874, Remington and Stevens have also used it as a rifle cartridge.

Originally, the .22 Long was loaded with 5 grains (0.32 g) of blackpowder and a 29 grain (1.9 g) lead bullet. Up to about the Second World War, the .22 Long was moderately popular, particularly for hunting small game. This cartridge was actually replaced by the .22 Long Rifle (LR) which was first marketed in 1887. The Peters Cartridge Company was the first to

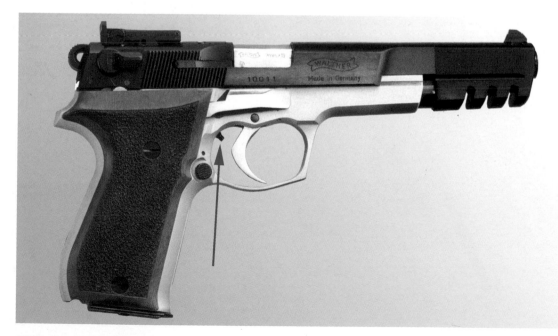

Triggerstop to prevent overtravel

Examples of .22 cartridges

produce this cartridge, commissioned by the Stevens Arms & Tool Company. At the time, the .22 LR had a charge of 5 grains (0.32 g) of blackpowder and a 40 grain (2.6 g) lead bullet. In 1930, Remington made the first high velocity cartridge and introduced it as a hunting caliber. The .22 LR cartridge is the most popular caliber of all time and is still used as a sports cartridge. The high velocity versions are mainly intended for hunting small game at shooting distances up to 75 meters. Many people consider the .22 LR as a 'toy caliber', which is entirely unjustified. The Smith & Wesson First Model revolver introduced in 1857 was actually developed as a weapon for defense. In addition, specialist commando units used a High Standard pistol during the Second World War for their work behind enemy lines. Because of the integrated silencer, this pistol was also known as 'Hush Puppy'.

.22 WINCHESTER MAGNUM RIMFIRE CARTRIDGE:

This cartridge was marketed by Winchester in 1959. The .22WMR was made for their Model 61 rifle for hunting purposes. Ruger and Smith & Wesson also saw the advantages of this caliber and marketed various different models of revolvers. Ruger used the Single-Six revolver for this. It was later succeeded by the Single-Six convertible in .22 LR with an interchangeable cylinder in .22WMR. As a caliber for sports shooting, the .22WMR is almost insignificant. It is used mainly as a hunting cartridge for small game up to 100m.

Remington .22 Short cartridge

TABLE CALIBER: .22 SHORT

MAKE	BULLET TIP			VO	EQ
	WEIGHT		TYPE	M/S	JOULES
	GRAINS-GRAMS				
GECO/RWS	28	1.8	R-25 MATCH	170	26
SELL-BELLOT	28	1.8	SHORT	295	80
ELEY	29	1.9	RAPID MATCH	229	50
REMINGTON	29	1.9	HV-GOLD BULLET	334	106
WINCHESTER	29	1.9	T-22S	315	94

TABLE CALIBER: .22 LR

MAKE	BULLET TIP			VO	EQ
	WEIGHT		TYPE	M/S	JOULES
	GRAINS-GRAMS				
WINCHESTER	33	2.1	YELLOW JACKET	457	219
SELL-BELLOT	38	2.5	HV-HP	390	185
WINCHESTER	38	2.5	LASER	417	217
ELEY	40	2.6	PISTOL MATCH	305	123
ELEY	40	2.6	TENEX	331	145
FEDERAL	40	2.6	TARGET	351	160
FEDERAL	40	2.6	HV	383	191
GECO/RWS	40	2.6	HV-HP	400	206
GECO/RWS	40	2.6	PISTOL MATCH	270	95
REMINGTON	40	2.6	TARGET 22	351	160
SELL-BELLOT	40	2.6	CLUB	330	140
WINCHESTER	40	2.6	X-PERT MATCH	330	140
WINCHESTER	40	2.6	T-22	330	140
WINCHESTER	40	2.6	SUPREME PISTOL	350	159

VENTILATED/VENTED BARREL:

Some models of pistols and revolvers have a raised barrel rib. Long slits may be cut in this barrel rib. This provides extra ventilation for the barrel. The barrel heats up when a shot is fired, creating spirals of hot air in the sight line. A ventilated barrel means that the

TABLE CALIBER: .22 WMR

MAKE	BULLET TIP			VO	EQ
	WEIGHT		TYPE	M/S	JOULES
	GRAINS-GRAMS				
FEDERAL	40	2.6	FMJ	582	440
GECO/RWS	40	2.6	SP	615	491
WINCHESTER	40	2.6	JHP	582	440
FEDERAL	50	3.2	JHP	503	405

.22 Winchester Magnum Rimfire (WMR) cartridge

Wheel-lock system combined here with a fuselock

target is more clearly visible to the shooter. However, the ventilated barrel is also used for cosmetic reasons, as it is attractive.

WHEEL LOCK:

In approximately 1550, firearms already had a hammer in which a flint could be placed between two claws. A wheel which rotated under the pressure of a spring was placed in the lock. Before every shot, a coil spring first had to be wound up with a key. When the marksman then pulled the trigger, the hammer moved forwards. At the same time, the spring was released, and the wheel spun around. The teeth of the wheel scraped the flint in the claw of the hammer, creating a shower of sparks. If all went well, these sparks dropped into the powder pan below. This system is comparable to a modern cigarette lighter.

YOKE/CRANE

In a modern revolver, the swing-out cylinder is connected to a yoke. This serves as a sort of hinge. It fits exactly into a recess in the frame of the revolver.

Cilinderarm

Depending on the make and type of the revolver, the yoke and cylinder are locked into the frame in one or more ways: sometimes at the front of the ejector rod, but usually also by means of a spring which fits in the back of the extractor star. In Dan Wesson revolvers, the yoke itself is locked in the frame with a lug and a bolt.

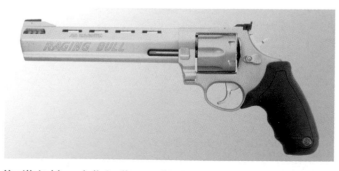

Ventilated barrel rib to disperse heat

Yoke locking of the Dan Wesson revolver

Ackowledgments

This book is dedicated to Gerda Leegsma. She was the director of Textcase Book productions until she unfortunately fell ill in November 2000. She was a great support and strength to me.

I would like to give special thanks to my wife, Annelies Hartink, who performed extremely valuable work, editing all the texts, and for her patience with me and her dedication to the family, allowing me to write undisturbed. In addition, I would like to thank my youngest daughter Judith for the time she saved me by expertly digitizing and processing many photographs.

I would like to thank Mr. Verschoor from the Verschoor arms shop in 's-Gravendeel for his valuable expertise and for making his collection of weapons available for my photographs, as well as my friend J.A.F. Verdick from Zwijndrecht, who was my right-hand man during all the photography.

In addition, I would like to thank the following people in alphabetical order. Without them I could not have produced this book, or it certainly would not have been as complete:

- AKAH: Albrecht Kind GmbH & Co. (Germany)
- Arms Moravia Ltd. (CZ)
- Artax (Italy)
- Astra Sport (Spain)
- Auto-Ordnance Corporation (USA)
- Baikal (Izhevsky Mekhanichesky Zavod (Russia)
- Benelli Armi SA (Italy)
- Beretta (Italy)
- Bernardelli (Italy)
- Bersa SA (Argentina)
- Bold-Action Zwijndrecht BV (NL)
- Briley (USA)
- Browning S.A. (Belgium)
  Bul Transmark Ltd (Israel)
- Caspian Arms Ltd. (USA)
- Casull/Freedom Arms (USA)
- CZ/Ceska Zbrojovka A.s. (CZ)
- Colt's Manufacturing Company Inc. (USA)
- Daewoo Arms Company (Korea)
- Dan Wesson Firearms (USA)
- Domino Armi (Italy)
- Drulov (CZ)
- Erma Sportwaffen (Germany)
- European American Armory (USA)
- Feinwerkbau Westinger & Altenburger GmbH (Germany)
- Fegarmy (Hungary)
- Freedom Arms (USA)
- Galena/AMT (USA)
- Gamba-Renato (Italy)
- Gaucher Armes (France)
- Glock GmbH (Austria)
- Grizzly/L.A.R. Manufacturing Inc. (USA)
- Hämmerli Ltd (CH)
- Harrington & Richardson/New England Firearms (USA)
- Heckler & Koch (Germany)
- High Standard Manufacturing Co. Inc. (USA)
- IAI-Israel Arms International (USA)
- IMI/TAAS-ISRAEL Industries Ltd, (Israel Military Industries)
- Janz/JTL Labortechnik (Germany)
- Kahr Arms (USA)
- KBI/Charles Daly (USA)
- Kel-Tec CNC Industries Inc. (USA)
- Kimber (USA)
- Korriphila-Intertex (Germany)
- Korth Feuerwaffen GmbH (Germany)
- Kroko/Kora Arms (CZ)
- Les Baer Custom Inc. (USA)
- Llama/Fabrinor (Spain)
- Mag-Na-Port International Inc. (USA)
- Manurhin, Manufacture de Machines du Haut-Rhin SA (F)
- Mauser (Mauser/SIG) (Germany/CH)
- Moravia Arms (CZ)
- Navy Arms (USA)
- Norinco (China)
- North American Arms (USA)
- Para-Ordnance Manufacturing Co. Inc. (CND)
- Pardini Armi (Italy)
- Pedersoli-Davide (Italy)
- Peters Stahl GmbH (Germany)
- Pietta (Italy)
- Remington Arms Company (USA)
- Robar Company (USA)
- Rossi-Armas Amadeo SA (Brazil)
- Safari Arms (USA)
- Sarsilmaz Arms Ltd.(Turkey)
- SIG Schweizerische Industrie Gesellschaft (CH)
- Smith & Wesson (USA)
- Sphinx Engineering SA, (CH)
- Springfield Armory (USA)
  SPS/DC Custom Arms (Spain)
- Star (Spain)
- Steyr-Daimler-Puch AG (Austria)
- Stoeger Industries (USA)
- Strayer-Voigt (USA)
- Sturm, Ruger & Company Inc. (USA)
- Tanfoglio SpA (I)
- Taurus International (USA)
- Thompson/Center Arms (USA)
- Truvelo Armory Division (South Africa)
- Tugra Gravur Ltd (Turkey)
- Umarex Sportwaffen GmbH (Germany)
- Unique/Manufacture d'Armes des Pyrénées Francaises (F)
- Valtro (Italy)
- Vektor Arms (South Africa)
- Walther GmbH Sportwaffenfabrik (Germany)
- Weihrauch KG /Arminius (Germany)
- Wildey Inc. (USA)
- Winchester (USA)
- Wischo Jagd- und Sportwaffen (Germany)

and others which have mistakenly not been included.

Interesting internet adresses

- Accu-Tek: www.accu-tekfirearms.com
- Amazon internetboekhandel: www.amazon.com
- Amt/Galena: www.galenaindustries.com
- Auto-Ordnance: www.auto-ordnance.com
- Baikal-Russische wapens: www.mehzavod.ru
- Benelli hagelgeweren:
  www.benelli.it/www.benelliusa.com
- Beretta: www.beretta.com/www.berettausa.com
- Bersa: www.bersa-sa.com.ar
- Briley: www.briley.com
- Browning Arms Company: www.browning.com
- Bul Transmark: www.bultransmark.com
- Caspian Arms: www.caspianarmsltd.com
- Casull: www.casullarms.com
- Charles Daly/KBI: www.charlesdaly.com
- Charter Arms: www.charterfirearms.com
- Colt Firearms: www.colt.com
- CZ/Ceska Zbrojovka: www.czub.cz/www.cz-usa.com
- Dan Wesson: www.dan-wesson.com
- Euopean American Armory: www.eaacorp.com
- Freedom Arms: www.freedomarms.com
  Gamba: www.renatogamba.it
- Glock: www.glockworks.com
- Gunhoo links: www.gunhoo.com
- Gunindex links: www.gunindex.com
- Gunshop: www.gunshop.com
- Hammerli: www.hammerli.com
- Heckler & Koch: www.hecklerkoch-usa.com
- High Standard: www.highstandard.com
- Israel Amrs Int.: www.israelarms.com
- Janz/JTL: www.jtl.de
- Kahr: www.kahr.com
- Kel-Tec: www.kel-tec.com
- Kimber: www.kimberamerica.com
- Lar/Grizzly: www.largrizzly.com
- Les Baer: www.lesbaer.com
- Mauser: www.mauser-werke.de
- Moravia Arms: www.arms-moravia.cz
- Navy Arms: www.navyarms.com
- Nowlin: www.nowlinguns.com
- Para-Ordnance: www.paraord.com
- Pardini: www.pardini.it
- Pedersoli: www.davide-pedersoli.com
- Peters Stahl: www.peters-stahl.com
- Rebo Publishers: www.rebo-publishers.com
- Remington Arms: www.remington.com
- Rossi: www.rossiusa.com
- Ruger (Sturm & Ruger): www.ruger-firearms.com
- Sarsilmaz: www.sarsilmaz.com
- Sig-Sauer: www.sigarms.com
- Smith & Wesson: www.smith-wesson.com
- Sphinx: www.sphinx-systems.ch
- Springfield Armory: www.springfield-armory.com
- SPS-DC: www.sps-dc.com
- Steyer: www.steyr-mannlicher.com
- STI: www.sti-guns.com
- Strayer-Voigt: www.sviguns.com
- Tanfoglio: www.tanfoglio.it
- Taurus: www.taurususa.com
- Thompson Center Arms: www.tcarms.com
- Vektor: www.vektor-denel.za
- Walther: www.carl-walther.de
- Wildey: www.wildeyguns.com
- Winchester/U.S. Repeating Arms:
  www.winchester.com

For questions or comments, contact a.hartink@tip.nl

Index